ENFORCEMENT OF INTELLECTUAL PROPERTY IN EUROPEAN AND INTERNATIONAL LAW

AUSTRALIA
LBC Information Services
Sydney

CANADA
Carswell
Toronto

NEW ZEALAND
Brooker's
Auckland

SINGAPORE AND MALAYSIA
Thomson Information (S.E. Asia)
Singapore

ENFORCEMENT OF INTELLECTUAL PROPERTY IN EUROPEAN AND INTERNATIONAL LAW

The New Private International Law of Intellectual Property
in the United Kingdom and the European Community

BY

CHRISTOPHER WADLOW

SOLICITOR
SIMMONS & SIMMONS
LONDON

LONDON
SWEET & MAXWELL
1998

Published in 1998 by
Sweet & Maxwell Ltd of
100 Avenue Road, Swiss Cottage, London NW3 3PF
(http://www.smlawpub.co.uk)
Computerset by LBJ Typesetting Ltd
of Kingsclere
Printed and bound in Great Britain by
MPG Books Ltd, Bodmin, Cornwall.

No natural forests were destroyed to make this product;
only farmed timber was used and replanted.

A C.I.P. Catalogue
record for this book
is available from
the British Library

ISBN 0421 501 60X

PREFACE

The underlying reason for this book is the increasing dissatisfaction of all sides of industry with the fact that intellectual property rights have to be litigated on a country-by-country basis across Europe under very different national laws and procedures, at great expense, and with the near certainty of inconsistent results. The Brussels Convention on Jurisdiction and the Enforcement of Judgments and the Community Patent Convention long ago held out the prospect of enforcement of intellectual property rights on a pan-European scale, but for various reasons this early promise came to nothing. Now there is a renewed effort to implement the Community patent, but even if that is once again unsuccessful the Community trade mark will undoubtedly provide examples—probably before the end of the decade—of Community intellectual property rights being enforced on a European scale in one single action in one national court.

As for intellectual property litigation under the Brussels Convention, the current situation is accurately summed up by Laddie J. in *Fort Dodge v. Akzo Nobel*:

"Intellectual property litigation in general and patent litigation in particular in Europe is in a state of some disarray. At the moment there appears to be, at least in some quarters, an unedifying competition to secure jurisdiction over proceedings to enforce these commercially important rights."

Where edifying or not, there is no denying the existence of cross-border competition for this jurisdiction; and those who are caught up in it, in whatever capacity, need to know the rules by which such competition—and the litigation it gives rise to—is lawfully conducted. One purpose of this work is to provide such a guide. Another is to contribute to the debate which will eventually resolve today's unavoidable state of disarray.

The shock waves from the collision of the Brussels Convention with the common law of intellectual property may have taken 10 years to be felt; but when they began to register, their effect was little short of seismic. A few years ago practitioners began to notice that the Dutch courts were assuming the right under the Convention to grant injunctions against infringement anywhere in Europe. The three principal English cases decided to date allow the existence of cross-border jurisdiction in respect of unregistered intellectual property rights, but effectively deny it for patents and trade marks. However, if the Dutch

v

view of the law should turn out to be right, then the English courts must already enjoy precisely the same international jurisdiction in Brussels Convention cases, including jurisdiction over pan-European patent infringement actions. Some may think that in striking a balance "between speed and thoroughness," the thoroughness for which the English courts are traditionally renowned becomes even more important, as well as easier to justify, when one is dealing with a market which consists of an entire Continent, rather than a single country.

Thoroughness, rather than speed, has been my own *credo*. More than 12 years ago, I promised to readers of the *European Law Review* the imminent publication of a monograph which would have been the very distant ancestor of the present work. In the intervening period it has grown enormously, but some traces of the monograph format remain. In particular, my treatment of several issues has not attempted to avoid controversy, to an extent not normally to be expected in a practitioners' text. It remains my own opinion that the Brussels Convention does create an unprecedented degree of extraterritorial jurisdiction in infringement actions for registered and unregistered intellectual property rights alike; even to the extent that invalidity of foreign registered rights may be raised as an *inter partes* defence.

Once again, my thanks go to Simmons and Simmons, and particularly to Kevin Mooney, for their continuing support for a project which has been even more protracted than *The Law of Passing-Off*. Until March 1997 the present work proceeded on the slowest of slow tracks and I could legitimately claim that unlike its predecessor, it had not detracted from time spent on my fee-earning practice. Then came the need to deal with *Pearce* and *Coin Controls* and the cases they spawned, and without a generous allowance of time from Simmons and Simmons I would not have been able to complete and publish this book as promptly as has happened.

I am no less grateful to Simmons and Simmons and to various clients for the opportunities I have had to gain experience, in actual cases, of some of the problems discussed in the text, and to follow cases abroad (and especially in the Netherlands) either as first hand or through colleagues here. I should also like to offer my thanks to Maitre Pierre Véron and Dr Joachim Feldges (and to their firms and colleagues) for their help with French and German material.

I have endeavoured to state the law at January 31, 1998, including *Fort Dodge v. Akzo Nobel* in the Court of Appeal. In so far as the corresponding Dutch case, *Akzo Nobel v. Webster* is concerned, I have been able to include a paragraph on the first instance judgment in Chapter 1 but not to take account of its implications elsewhere in the work.

Christopher Wadlow

21 Wilson Street,
London
EC2M 2TX

ACKNOWLEDGMENTS

Grateful acknowledgment is made to the following authors and publishers for their permission to quote from their works:

BERTRAMS: "Cross-Border Prohibitory Injunction in Dutch Law" (1995) 26 *International Review of Industrial Property and Copyright Law* 618.
Reprinted by kind permission of Wiley-VCH.

BRINKHOF: "Transborder Injunctions and the Kort Geding" presented at the Herschel Smith Seminar on Intellectual Property and Private International Law, Cambridge, February 24, 1996.
Reprinted by kind permission of Judge Brinkhof.

CARTER: "Decisions of British Courts during 1990 Involving Questions of Public or Private International Law" [1990] B.Y.B.I.L. 377.
Reprinted by kind permission of Cambridge University Press and Peter Carter.

KOUMANTOS: "Copyright and PIL in the Face of the International Diffusion of Works" *WIPO Symposium on the Future of Copyright and Neighbouring Rights.*
Reprinted by kind permission of the International Bureau of the World Intellectual Property Organisation (WIPO).

LAGARDE: "Application de la Convention d'Execution aux Actions en Contrefacon de Brevets Nationaux" *Droit International et Actions en Contrefacon de Brevet dans la CEE* (Nice, 1974).
Reprinted by kind permission of the Centre du Droit de l'Entreprise.

MANGINI: "The Legal Framework for Infringement and Revocation Proceedings in Patent Matters in the Contracting States of the European Patent Convention" (1993) 14 *International Review of Industrial Property and Copyright Law* 776.
Reprinted by kind permission of Wiley-VCH.

NORTH & FAWCETT: *Cheshire and North's Private International Law* (12th ed., 1992).
Reprinted by kind permission of Butterworth & Co. (Publishers) Ltd.

ULMER: *Intellectual Property and the Conflict of Laws* (1978).
Reprinted by kind permission of Kluwer Law International.

ACKNOWLEDGMENTS

The following publishers and firms have also given us permission to reproduce translations or extracts from case reports for which we are very grateful:

Butterworth & Co. (Publishers) Ltd
Gleiss Lutz Hootz Hirsch
LBC Information Services
New Zealand Council of Law Reporting
The Incorporated Council of Law Reporting for England and Wales

While every care has been taken to establish and acknowledge copyright, and contact the copyright owners, the publishers tender their apologies for any accidental infringement. They would be pleased to come to a suitable arrangement with the rightful owners in each case.

CONTENTS

TABLE OF CASES

TABLE OF CONVENTIONS AND TREATIES

TABLE OF E.C. DIRECTIVES AND REGULATIONS

TABLE OF LEGISLATION

TABLE OF STATUTORY INSTRUMENTS
AND RULES

INTRODUCTION: THE PRESENT AND FUTURE OF INTERNATIONAL INTELLECTUAL PROPERTY LITIGATION

A. THE STATE OF THE ART

Why this book?

The subject matter of this book is the new private international law of **1–01** intellectual property in the United Kingdom and the European Community. Most of the legislation dealt with is new in the sense that it has only been in force in the United Kingdom for a relatively short time: 10 years in the case of the Brussels Convention on Jurisdiction and the Enforcement of Judgments in Civil and Commercial Matters, but much less for the Private International Law (Miscellaneous Provisions) Act 1995, the Rome Convention on the Law Applicable to Contractual Obligations and the Community Trade Mark Regulation. The Community Patent Convention was last revised in 1989 and is not yet in force at all, but at long last there are active proposals to implement the Community patent, this time by Regulation. Even under the Brussels Convention, however, the actual court decisions of crucial interest are less than a year old in the case of England,[1] and scarcely much older for other contracting states. It is equally novel for intellectual property practitioners to need to have any interest in private international law at all; but recent developments on the Continent and in this country alike make it clear that neither litigants nor their advisers can any longer assume that that an infringement action in England will raise no international issues more difficult than that of service of the writ out of the jurisdiction.

1–02 The private international law of intellectual property is not confined to issues of choice of law in intellectual property disputes. The applicable law in an infringement action ought simply to be the *lex loci delicti commissi*, and it is issues of jurisdiction, justiciability and enforcement which actually loom much larger to the litigant contemplating cross-border infringement proceedings. Similar issues arise, and have their own regimes, under the various Community instruments creating E.C.-wide intellectual property rights which will soon have to be enforced by litigation in national courts. Indeed, much of the law covered in this work is dictated by Community treaties or legislation: in particular the Brussels Convention; the Rome Contracts Convention; the Community Patent Convention and the Community Trade Mark Regulation. These sources cannot be understood without reference to the case law of the European Court of Justice. Other aspects of law covered are wholly defined by domestic legislation, as with the Private International Law (Miscellaneous Provisions) Act 1995, or require reference to other common law jurisdictions.

Plan of the book

1–03 After the Introduction provided by the present chapter, Chapters 2 and 3 deal respectively with the application of the jurisdictional provisions of Title II of the Brussels Convention on Jurisdiction and the Enforcement of Judgments to intellectual property from an international and a domestic perspective.[2] Chapter 2 is principally written around sources of law which are of general relevance for the whole Community,

---

[1] *Pearce v. Ove Arup* [1997] F.S.R. 641 (Lloyd J.); *Coin Controls v. Suzo* [1997] F.S.R. 660 (Laddie J.) and *Fort Dodge v. Akzo Nobel* [1998] F.S.R. 222, CA.
[2] Except that Arts 21 and 22 (*lis alibi pendens* and related actions) are dealt with in Chap. 8.

in particular the Convention itself, the Official Reports prepared by the draftsmen, and decisions of the European Court of Justice. After the introduction provided by Section A of Chapter 2, Section B explains the principles which apply to the interpretation of the Convention. Section C describes the general rules under which jurisdiction is allocated by the Brussels Convention and Section D summarises the relevant "special jurisdictions" of Articles 5 and 6. Other jurisdictional provisions of relevance, other than the exclusive jurisdictions of Article 16, are dealt with in Section E. Section F deals in more detail with one of the special jurisdictions, which is jurisdiction based on the place of tort. A topic of particular importance in intellectual property is that of exclusive jurisdiction over proceedings concerned with the registration or validity of registered intellectual property rights under Article 16(4). Section G addresses this, and since there is only one decision of the European Court of Justice directly in point it also examines the wider context provided by decisions of the Court on the other exclusive jurisdictions of Article 16. Finally, Section H describes the special regime for resolving entitlement disputes over pending European patent applications and examines the argument that enforcement of European patents is outside the regime of the Brussels Convention altogether.

Whilst the sources of law described in Chapter 2 are of undoubted **1–04** authority and general relevance, it cannot possibly be said that their application to typical intellectual property infringement actions is clear or uncontroversial. Chapter 3 concentrates on United Kingdom decisions applying the Brussels Convention to intellectual property infringement actions and the still unresolved issues arising from them. Section A provides an historical overview of the process by which the importance of the Convention to intellectual property has belatedly come to be appreciated in this country. Section B deals with the domestic body of cases on Article 24, dealing with "provisional measures." Section C describes the application of the Convention to specific intellectual property rights to date and Section D explains, and criticises, the English interpretation of the exclusive jurisdiction provision of Article 16(4) adopted by Laddie J. in *Coin Controls v. Suzo*[3] and the Court of Appeal in *Fort Dodge v. Akzo Nobel*.[4] Since the correctness of these two decisions is admittedly not beyond controversy, Section E examines other possible interpretations of Article 16(4) and concludes that one corresponding more closely to the Dutch view is likely to be preferred in the European Court of Justice.

Chapters 4 and 5 deal with enforcement of the new Community **1–05** intellectual property rights; specifically Community patents, trade marks, plant variety rights and designs. These all are, or will be, unitary and autonomous Community-wide intellectual property rights each of which will be subject to a pan-European regime for grant, enforcement and invalidation which will incorporate much of the Brussels Convention into schemes with many shared features and some significant differences.

---

[3] [1997] F.S.R. 660 (Laddie J.).
[4] [1998] F.S.R. 222, CA.

Chapter 4 deals principally with the institutions responsible for litigation relating to the proposed Community intellectual property rights. After an historical introduction in Section A, Section B describes the institutions proposed for the Community patent and Section C those existing or proposed for the Community trade mark, plant variety right and design. Section D examines the institutional differences, although many of these may be expected to disappear if the Community Patent Convention is actually superceded by a Community Patent Regulation.

1–06   Chapter 5 describes procedure in the action for infringement of these Community intellectual property rights, which is very similar whichever nominate right one is dealing with. After the introduction of Section A, Section B describes the roles of the various systems of law which interact and govern different issues. Section C describes how the Brussels Convention is incorporated, modified or excluded in its application. Section D deals with the jurisdiction-allocating provisions of the Community Patent Convention and the Regulations for the other Community intellectual property rights and Section E with the types of action which are permitted and with *locus standi* to sue. The complicated provisions dealing with co-pending proceedings as between court and court, or court and office, are dealt with in Section F and other modifications to national first instance procedure in Section G. Section H describes the Community law of remedies for infringement and the territorial scope of any relief, and Section I re-examines whether the legislators' stated aim of preventing forum shopping is likely to be achieved, or was ever desirable in the first place.

1–07   Chapter 6 reverts almost entirely to pure domestic United Kingdom law, as influenced more by the other common law jurisdictions than by Continental Europe. Infringement actions on foreign intellectual property rights are all but unknown in the common law, and Section A provides an introduction to the various possible reasons for this. However, it is now all but certain that the Brussels Convention will require the English courts to assume jurisdiction in at least some cases, and to ascertain the law applicable to foreign infringements the courts will now have to apply the Private International Law (Miscellaneous Provisions) Act 1995, the application of which to intellectual property is summarised in Section B. Sections C, D and E examine from various perspectives why it is that actions for infringement of foreign intellectual property rights were previously unknown or unsuccessful. Section C describes the prevailing line of authority in terms of the application to intellectual property of the *Mocambique* rule[5] favoured by Vinelott J. in *Tyburn v. Conan Doyle*[6] and by a number of English judges subsequently. An alternative, if now obsolete, theory in terms of the double actionability rule of *Phillips v. Eyre*,[7] is described and criticised in section D. Section E returns to the *Mocambique* rule and the sources invoked by Vinelott J. to conclude that the rule, though still valid at least to some

---

[5] The rule in *British South Africa Co v. Companhia do Mocambique* [1893] A.C. 602, HL.
[6] [1990] R.P.C. 185 (Vinelott J.).
[7] (1870) L.R. 6 Q.B. 1.

extent, is more flexible than *Tyburn v. Conan Doyle* allowed and has a different underlying rationale. Finally, Section F says what little can be said in the present state of the law about the action for breach of confidence in an international context.

Chapter 7 deals principally with another source of Community law, in the form of the Rome Convention on the Law Applicable to Contractual Obligations and its application to intellectual property contracts. After the introduction of Section A, Section B describes the Convention, its incorporation into domestic law, and its probable impact. Since much of the Rome Convention, unlike the Brussels Convention, is not radically dissimilar to the common law, Section C deals with the old common law cases on the private international law of intellectual property contracts which may still be relevant. One area where the Rome Convention is fundamentally different to the common law is in its treatment of "mandatory rules," which are those rules the parties cannot contract out of. Section D describes how the Convention deals with mandatory rules and Section E gives existing examples of mandatory rules in English law. **1–08**

Finally, Chapter 8 returns to the law of the Brussels Convention, in the context of the recognition and enforcement of foreign judgments under Title III and the implications of pending foreign proceedings. Section A explains why the topic is an important one. With a pan-European regime for the automatic enforcement of almost all *inter partes* judgments—injunctive or monetary, final or interlocutory—no business with assets anywhere in Europe can afford to turn its back on litigation, no matter what objections it may have to the jurisdiction of the court in question. Section B deals with the situation when identical or related causes of action are pending in two courts, and with the obligation or discretion of the court second seised to decline jurisdiction. This body of law may perhaps be turned to advantage by the prospective defendant, as described in Section C on pre-emptive negative declarations. A topic of particular concern at the moment as a result of *Fort Dodge v. Akzo Nobel*[8] is whether the English courts can ever restrain infringement proceedings in foreign courts by anti-suit injunction, and this is examined at length in Section D. Finally, Section E deals with the provisions for recognition and enforcement for foreign judgments, and the perhaps surprisingly limited circumstances in which the merits of the case or the jurisdiction of the foreign court may be re-examined. **1–09**

Ulmer's *Intellectual Property Rights and the Conflict of Laws*

The only existing work in English dealing with the subject matter of this work, in the broad sense, is *Intellectual Property Rights and the Conflict of Laws* by the late Professor Eugen Ulmer, which was originally written in German and completed in 1970. An updated translation into English was published in 1978. Ulmer's underlying objective was to propose a draft set of rules in relation to intellectual property rights for **1–10**

[8] [1998] F.S.R. 222, CA.

inclusion in a proposed E.C. convention on private international law. To that end, Ulmer's study concentrates on giving a comparative account of the conflict of laws applying to intellectual property in the then E.C. member states (but including the United Kingdom), principally in the sense of ascertaining the applicable law for infringements and for contracts relating to intellectual property. Within its field of inquiry Ulmer's work is definitive and the present work does not attempt to cover the same ground.

1–11   Apart from the passage of 20 years since Ulmer's work was written, there are a number of reasons why the time is ripe for a work on the private international law of intellectual property, written from the point of view of an English practitioner mainly interested in the prospect of enforcing intellectual property rights on a European or wider scale. The perspective from which this book is written is the first distinction: it is descriptive of the law more than prescriptive; addressed to practitioners rather than academics or governments; and—to my regret—it cannot claim to be a comprehensive exercise in comparative law. Conversely, it covers English law in more detail than Ulmer.

1–12   Secondly, the past few years have seen an explosion of intellectual property litigation on a pan-European scale, principally in the courts of the Netherlands. The jurisdiction of the Dutch courts is most often based on the 1968 Brussels Convention on Jurisdiction and the Enforcement of Judgments in Civil and Commercial Matters to which the United Kingdom is a party. If the Dutch assertion of extraterritorial jurisdiction is sound, then England, as one of the natural centres for European patent litigation, should equally benefit. Ulmer hardly touches on the implications of the Brussels Convention, which had only just started to have effect when he wrote, but its application to intellectual property continues to be fraught with uncertainty.

1–13   Thirdly, Ulmer scarcely deals with enforcement of unitary intellectual property rights existing on a Community-wide scale as a result of E.C. legislation or special treaties. Again, this is hardly surprising since only the Community patent was in prospect when Ulmer was writing, and that originally in the form of a draft which has since undergone many revisions. Regulations for Community trade marks and plant variety rights are now already in force, and a Community Design Regulation will shortly follow. Even the long-moribund Community patent may yet be revived by way of a Community Patent Regulation.

1–14   Finally, the private international law of intellectual property contracts can now be addressed on the basis of a definitive Convention rather than the preliminary draft available to Ulmer, and again the present work concentrates on the effect of the Rome Contracts Convention on the law of the United Kingdom.

B. THE TERRITORIALITY PRINCIPLE

Introduction

By way of an introduction to Chapters 2 and 3, the section which **1–15** follows the present one summarises the extent to which national courts in several Brussels Convention contracting states are already willing or likely to enforce patents on an extraterritorial or pan-European basis. What is true for patents may for present purposes also be taken as applying *mutatis mutandis* to the other registered intellectual property rights and perhaps *a fortiori* to copyright, although it is in international patent litigation that the attractions of multinational enforcement are greatest and the underlying policy issues most acute.

It is the Dutch courts that have led the way in granting pan-European **1–16** injunctive relief, so that the District Court of the Hague has come to be regarded, according to one's viewpoint, as either the Mecca[9] or the Reno of international patent litigation. Dutch internal law does differ from that in most other contracting states in the willingness to grant interlocutory injunctions against alleged patent infringement and the availability of a special expedited procedure known as *kort geding*. However, the international jurisdiction of the Dutch courts in Brussels Convention cases does not depend more than slightly on peculiarities of domestic law, and if the Dutch cases are rightly decided then the same international jurisdiction is enjoyed by the courts of every contracting state, even if they do not yet appreciate the fact.

Laddie J. summarised these developments in *Fort Dodge v. Akzo* **1–17** *Nobel*[10] as follows:

"Until comparatively recently, intellectual property rights such as patents, trade marks and copyrights were viewed as entirely national in scope and effect. This was particularly so in the case of patents which in the United Kingdom were a grant from the Crown. The monopolies or quasi-monopolies created were effective only within the jurisdiction. Therefore only a court here could determine the validity of a British patent and rule on its infringement. A United Kingdom patent, copyright or trade mark could only be infringed by activities carried out within the jurisdiction of United Kingdom courts. Further, the courts here could not and would not attempt to determine issues of validity and infringement of foreign intellectual property rights. The proprietor of an intellectual property right here would, in most cases, own equivalent rights under the national legislation of other countries. For very many years there have been international conventions which facilitate the creation of parallel national intellectual property rights. For example, an inventor might

[9] de Wit, "The Dutch Court—Injunctive Hell for Cross-Border Infringers" [1993] October *Patent World*, 19.
[10] [1998] F.S.R. 222, CA.

well protect his invention in the United Kingdom, France and Germany by separate national patents in those countries. If a competitor made in Germany a product which allegedly used the invention and then exported it for sale in France and England, the patentee could sue in each country for the activities within the jurisdiction of each national court which were alleged to infringe the national patents. He could, of course, decide to sue in some but not all of the countries in which infringements were thought to have been committed. Thus he might decide to sue only in Germany so as to cut off the infringements at source. However, save in this limited respect, he could not choose in which forum he could litigate. He could not ask the English courts to determine whether or not, say, a German patent, even if equivalent to the United Kingdom patent, was infringed. Numerous cases both in this country and in other common law countries gave effect to these principles. I understand that the same general approach has been followed by all of our neighbours. German courts would only determine whether acts in Germany infringe a German patent and Dutch courts would only determine whether acts in Holland infringe a Dutch patent. This approach had a lot to commend it. Not only were intellectual property rights national in character but, in the absence of a properly thought out and organised federal system, the domestic court would normally be the most convenient for determining the interrelated issues of validity and infringement.

Recently this parochial approach to intellectual property litigation has been shaken, and in significant respects destroyed. About seven years ago the Dutch courts started to express a willingness to grant cross-border injunctions prohibiting, for example, a litigant before the Dutch courts from infringing a United Kingdom patent in this country. Not only could a Dutch national or resident be restrained from infringing, say, a British or French patent but, it appears, a British national who may have done nothing within the jurisdiction of the Dutch courts, if brought into the proceedings there could be ordered not to infringe the French and British patents. As a result of provisions of the 1968 Brussels Convention on Jurisdiction and Enforcement of Judgments in Civil and Commercial Matters ('the Convention'), it appears that any such order would have to be enforced by the domestic courts here and in France. Following on from this development, lawyers in this country and elsewhere started to look at whether their national courts had the power to entertain such trans-national applications. In particular, and perhaps belatedly, in this country attention turned to the Convention which is made part of our law by virtue of S. 2(1) of the Civil Jurisdiction and Judgments Act, 1982."

8

The principle(s) of territoriality

What one has observed in the events summarised in the foregoing **1–18** passage is a major departure from one aspect of the principle of territoriality as it was previously understood.[11] Since "territoriality" is a term which recurs throughout the present work it would seem helpful to attempt to define it. In fact, this proves to be impossible. Cornish[12] conveniently identifies four separate and independent aspects of the principle of territoriality in the context of intellectual property. They may be freely summarised as: (1) the effects of the intellectual property right in each country are determined by the law of that country; (2) the intellectual property right only affects activities in the territory for which it is granted; (3) the right may be asserted only by nationals of the country for which it is granted, and others given similar status by law; and (4) the right may be asserted or challenged[13] only in the courts of the country for which it is granted.

Aspects (1) and (2) are both statements of the principle that intellec- **1–19** tual property rights have no extra-territorial effect. It follows from (1) that an intellectual property dispute is governed wholly by the law of the state in which the infringement occurs and that there is no scope for the application of any law other than the law of the protecting state as the *lex loci delicti commissi*. This is the sense in which Ulmer[14] describes the principle:

> "The so-called principle of territoriality is put forward as the theoretical basis of the link with the law of the protecting country, above all in Dutch, German, Italian and Scandinavian legal theory and in the case-law of the United Kingdom. In patent law the principle may be traced back to the concept that the right is a monopoly right which is conferred by the state through the granting of a patent and that this measure of conferment is effective only within the borders of the state. In other fields of law, particularly copyright, such a special measure of conferment is no doubt lacking: in the place of the privilege granted at the beginning of the copyright protection to the author, or printer, which by its very nature was territorially limited in its effect, there has evolved the principle that the copyright arises directly *ex lege* with the creation of the work. However, the concept has been retained that the effect of the statutory regulation of the copyright is limited to the national territory in which the statute has been promulgated. To complete the picture it is customary to refer to the law of tort: an infringe- ment of the copyright or the industrial, property right appears as a

[11] In fact, most major Continental jurisdictions can provide at least isolated examples of foreign intellectual property rights being litigated, even prior to the Brussels Convention. See Ulmer, *op cit.*, and literature cited for individual jurisdictions below.

[12] Cornish *Intellectual Property* (3rd ed., 1996), para. 1–29.

[13] "Or challenged" is a gloss.

[14] Ulmer, *Intellectual Property Rights and the Conflict of Laws* (1978), para. 15.

tortious act which is to be judged according to the law of the place in which it was committed."

1–20   The necessary converse to (1) is that intellectual property legislation is not extraterritorial. Each state defines its own laws for its own territory. In English law this is normally no more than an application of the presumption against statutes having extraterritorial effect, though more recent statutes may in terms specify the territorial scope of what constitutes an infringement. The third aspect is outside the scope of the present work. Entitlement to the enjoyment and exercise of intellectual property rights is now governed almost wholly by the major international conventions.

1–21   It is the fourth aspect of territoriality with which the present work is principally concerned. It may be restated in terms of the issues of infringement and validity of intellectual property rights being justiciable only in the courts of the protecting state. This principle was formerly as widely recognised as the others, but it does not necessarily follow from either (1) or (2). There has been widespread confusion between the proposition that intellectual property laws are not extraterritorial, and the quite separate proposition that they are not justiciable in foreign courts. Very few statutes or laws (other than relating to personal status) are actually extraterritorial in fact or in intent; but that does not stop foreign courts routinely applying them consistently with the rules of private international law. What is remarkable about intellectual property is that to all intents and purposes it has simply been assumed to have been outside the scope of private international law altogether: the courts of the United Kingdom have consistently refused to adjudicate on infringements of intellectual property rights occurring abroad, and by and large the courts of other countries have done the same.

1–22   Even these four heads are not necessarily comprehensive, because territoriality, like intellectual property itself, is not so much a single well-defined entity as a family of concepts with certain unifying features. Thirty years ago any article with "territoriality" in the title could be assumed to deal with the doctrine of international exhaustion of rights, and in all probability concluded that territoriality and international exhaustion were incompatible. We now have international exhaustion of intellectual property rights within the European Community, and no one seems to think that territoriality has been dealt a mortal blow. Again, there was once a school of thought that one aspect of the territoriality principle operated to make contracts relating to intellectual property rights subject to the law of the protecting state, but few would now disagree that the normal rules of the private international law of contracts apply. Territoriality has such a wide range of meanings that it may fairly be criticised for being a term without a concept, and in some of its ramifications without much justification:

> "Several conceptions of territoriality are possible, ranging from refusal of protection for foreign works or refusal of protection against infringements abroad to application of the *lex fori* or, sometimes, of the *lex loci protectionis*.

This multiplicity of interpretations rendered the territoriality concept either unusable or arbitrary. In trying to be a passkey able to open several doors, it finally opened only the one that each performer wanted to have it open. It was also arbitrary from another point of view: it was lacking—it is still lacking—a legal basis. There exists no legal text, whether national or international, that establishes and defines the territoriality concept as such, although there are several texts imposing one or other of the possible interpretations."[15]

There is a central core to the principle of territoriality which is that **1–23** each sovereign state sets its own laws within its own territory. Territoriality may therefore be consistent with a state attaching legal consequences to acts taking place abroad, if they have sufficiently serious effects at home, as is already accepted in the closely related field of competition law. Conversely, territoriality in the narrow sense need not be inconsistent with foreign courts enforcing intellectual property rights existing in other states, to the extent that specific conventions or international usage allow them to assert jurisdiction. When the dust has settled, it will probably be realised that territoriality and the multinational enforcement of intellectual property rights in one set of proceedings are perfectly compatible with one another in principle. What makes the two incompatible in practice—apart from major differences in civil procedure and remedies—is the comparative law of intellectual property, under which laws which look very similar in theory may be very different in application.

Territoriality and the major international conventions.

The major international conventions[16] might be thought to have some **1–24** bearing on what is meant by territoriality, and on the application of the principle in the internal law of the various contracting states. In fact, as Ulmer explains, the conventions are of very limited relevance in private international law[17]:

[15] Koumantos, "Copyright and PIL in the Face of the International Diffusion of Works," in *WIPO Symposium on the Future of Copyright and Neighbouring Rights* (1994), p. 233.
[16] Principally the Paris Convention for the Protection of Industrial Property (1883) and the Berne Convention for the Protection of Literary and Artistic Works (1886). See Bodenhausen, *Guide to the Application of the Paris Convention for the Protection of Intellectual Property* (1968); Ladas, *Patents, Trademarks and Related Rights: National and International Protection* (1975); Ricketson, *The Berne Convention for the Protection of Literary and Artistic Works: 1886–1986* (1987); Stewart, *International Copyright and Neighbouring Rights* (2nd ed., 1989). See also Boytha, "Some Private International Law Aspects of the Protection of Authors' Rights" [1988] *Copyright* 39; Koumantos, "Private International Law and the Berne Convention" [1988] *Copyright* 415; Cornish, "The International Relations of Intellectual Property" (1993) 52 C.L.J. 46; Evans, "The Principle of National Treatment and the International Protection of Intellectual Property" [1996] E.I.P.R. 149; Howell, "Intellectual Property, Private International Law and Issues of Territoriality" (1997) 13 *Canadian Intellectual Property Review* 209.
[17] Ulmer, *Intellectual Property Rights and the Conflict of Laws* (1978), para. 16. Internal references omitted.

"The main support for the theory of the link with the law of the protecting country is provided by the international conventions. All the major international conventions, the Paris Convention, the RBC[18] and UCC,[19] are based on the principle of national treatment. In the Paris Convention it is stated that the nationals of any country of the Union shall, as regards the protection of industrial property, enjoy in all other member countries the advantages that their respective laws now grant, or may thereafter grant, to nationals (. . .); and in a similar manner the copyright conventions provide that the authors of works protected thereby may claim in all Contracting States basically the rights which the laws of such states grant to authors who are their own nationals (. . .). The principle of national treatment, it is true, is subject to extensions and limitations, as already mentioned (. . .), but in principle it is one of the main buttresses of the law of the conventions."

1–25   The principle of national treatment is consistent with that of territoriality in the narrow sense. After all, if an author or inventor from a contracting state carried his own personal law around with him wherever he went,[20] there would be no need for him to invoke the principle of national treatment on a state-by-state basis. It implies that it is for each contracting state to define the availability and effects of intellectual property rights within its own territory—subject to whatever minimum standards may be set by the relevant convention—and to afford equal protection to its own nationals and the nationals of other contracting states. It is interesting that the principle of territoriality was actually strengthened when the major conventions substituted the almost unqualified principle of independent national treatment[21] for that of dependent[22] or reciprocal[23] treatment, since the latter two would frequently invite an enquiry into the substantive law of a foreign state and even into its application to the facts of a particular case. Under the developed principle of national treatment, a court never had to apply or investigate any law but its own in order to do justice within its own territory.[24]

[18] Revised Berne Convention.

[19] Universal Copyright Convention.

[20] As was once contemplated in academic writing, under the theory of the "uniform link" described by Ulmer, *op. cit.* para. 14.

[21] For patents, Paris Convention, Art. 4*bis*, introduced at the 1900 Brussels Conference; for copyright Art. 5(2) of the Berne Convention introduced at the Berlin Conference in 1908. As to the latter, see Ricketson, *The Berne Convention for the Protection of Literary and Artistic Works: 1886–1986* (1987), paras 5.63 and 5.86.

[22] Where the rights enjoyed in state A are defined by reference to those enjoyed by the same party in state B.

[23] Where the rights enjoyed by nationals of state B in state A, are defined by reference to those enjoyed by nationals of state A in state B.

[24] Had dependent protection lived on into the 20th century, the familiarity of this exercise in comparative law might have led to foreign intellectual property rights being enforced far earlier than actually occurred. As it happens, at least one case where foreign protection was investigated so as to define the scope of protection under English law has been mistaken for a case where a foreign intellectual property right was enforced in England. See para. 6–143.

The memorandum of Professor Cornish produced for the House of **1-26** Lords during the passage of the Private International Law (Miscellaneous Provisions) Act 1995 is to the same effect[25]:

"Throughout the world the main IP rights (patents, copyright, registered designs, registered trade marks, etc) are accepted to be territorial in character. Thus UK law alone applies to alleged infringements in the UK and cannot apply to acts outside the UK: see eg Patents Act 1977, section 60, 132(2)–(4); Copyright, Designs and Patents Act 1988, section 16; Trade Marks Act 1994, section 9(1). At an early stage, there was some consideration (particularly in countries with a strong inheritance of natural law thought) of IP being considered universal, rather than territorial.

One consequence would have been that an individual's IP was determined around the world by that of his nationality or domicile (*lex origins*, rather than *lex loci delicti*). This would have meant that an author with a long term of copyright at home could insist upon it in a country which only gave a shorter time to its nationals; an inventor from a country which allowed patents on pharmaceutical substances could demand such a patent in a country where it would not otherwise be available. This was so plainly unacceptable that it was abandoned as an approach. Hence the clear rule that for acts done within the UK only UK law can apply.

Another consequence of territoriality can be that a country grants an IP right only to its own citizens. This prospect led to the basic international conventions in the field, the first principle of which is that each member state undertakes to accord its national IP to nationals of the other member states. (eg Paris Convention on Industrial Property Art. 2(1), Berne Convention on Literary and Artistic Works, Art. 5). The principle of territoriality is plainly acknowledged in these Convention rules, since they apply the 'principle of national treatment': foreigners with Convention rights get the same protection in a country as is given to its own nationals. Accordingly in international law any conflict between *lex origins* and *lex loci delicti* is eliminated: it is the latter which is applied."

However, neither national treatment nor any other doctrine of the **1-27** conventions addressed the wider questions of jurisdiction or the conflict of laws. The passage from Ulmer continues:

"The rule of conflict of laws contained in the principle of national treatment is admittedly not a complete rule of conflict. The conventions provide that persons protected may claim the protection of national laws in every contracting state. The RBC speaks of the laws of the country 'where protection is claimed'. The wording is

[25] In *Proceedings of the Special Public Bill Committee* HL Paper 36 (1995), evidence, p. 64.

ambiguous. Logically it does not imply a reference to the *lex fori*. If, for example, a German impresario performs a protected work in Denmark, the author bringing an action in Germany cannot claim the protection of German copyright law. The protection which may be claimed under the RBC may be granted according to German law only if the act of infringement is committed in Germany. It is true that in legal practice the action is usually brought in the country in which the infringement is committed. When this is the case, then in practice the *lex fori* coincides with the law of the country for whose territory the protection is claimed.

However, the question remains open whether, in the event of infringements abroad, when, according to the general rules of procedural law, a venue is established within the country, legal protection may be claimed before the national court on the basis of the foreign copyright or industrial property right. For instance, in the above-mentioned example, can the action brought in Germany against the German impresario be based upon the infringement of Danish copyright law? This question is not settled in the conventions. From the point of view of private international law it certainly seems consistent to expand the rule which may be derived from the conventions into a complete rule of conflict of laws whereby protection of intellectual property rights, irrespective of the country in which the action is brought, is to be governed by the law of the country in whose territory the act of infringement took place. The question is, however, whether for the jurisdiction of the courts the general rules of procedural law are determinative, or whether, in the case of intellectual property rights, a limitation of international jurisdiction must be accepted in the sense that legal protection may be claimed only before national courts on the basis of the national copyright or industrial property right. Such a limitation of international jurisdiction has been accepted in the past, usually with reference to the principle of territoriality. More recent legal developments, however, make this limitation appear outdated. In particular this is true of the Member States of the EEC on the basis of the Convention on Jurisdiction and the Enforcement of Judgments in Civil and Commercial Matters of 27 September 1968."

C. PATENT LITIGATION ON A PAN-EUROPEAN SCALE

Pan-European litigation in the Netherlands and the *kort geding*

1–28   In his evidence to the House of Lords Select Committee on the European Communities in 1986, Judge van der Veen of the Dutch Supreme Court described Dutch patent litigation practice and advised their Lordships[26]: "Since an injunction can only be based on a patent

---

[26] Report of the House of Lords Select Committee on the European Communities: *A European Community Patent* (1986), evidence, p. 174. For early Dutch cases, see Bodenhausen, "Du Droit International Privé Néerlandais dans le Domaine de la Propriété Industrielle" [1947] *Propriété Industrielle* 118.

having effect within the Netherlands only, an injunction can have no extraterritorial effect." However, within three years the Dutch Supreme Court itself was to give a decision in the field of trade marks which called this into question; and within a decade the grant of extraterritorial injunctions by the Hague District Court in all types of intellectual property cases would become a matter almost of routine, if not to foreign litigants, then at least to their Dutch advisers.

Pan-European or wider injunctive relief from the Dutch courts has **1–29** almost invariably been sought in proceedings under a unique procedure known as *kort geding*. Contrary to widespread belief, little or nothing within the scope of the present work turns on the special nature of this procedure, which is equally applicable in a purely domestic Dutch context. Although extraterritorial injunctions are a development of the past decade, the *kort geding* procedure as such has existed since at least the nineteenth century. None the less, an outline of *kort geding* procedure helps in understanding the cases and writings referred to below.[27]

The term *kort geding* literally means "short procedure" but any **1–30** attempt at translation into English risks being misleading and the Dutch term[28] is now widely recognised, if not always perfectly understood.[29] In patent actions, *kort geding* proceedings can only be brought before the court of the President of the District Court of the Hague, and actual conduct of the proceedings is delegated to one of a small number of vice-presidents so as to ensure consistency and specialist expertise. The relief sought in *kort geding* proceedings is typically a prohibitory injunction (*verbod*) on either a domestic, or extraterritorial basis, but other relief is possible, including mandatory injunctions, recall of infringing products, identification of customers or suppliers,[30] publication of the judgment, and interim damages.

---

[27] For *kort geding* proceedings in general see Brinkhof, "Summary Proceedings and Other Provisional Measures in Connection with Patent Infringement" (1993) 24 I.I.C. 762. Jan Brinkhof was formerly a first instance judge in the Hague District Court, and is now a judge of the Hague Court of Appeal. For the international application of the procedure see Brinkhof, "Could the President of the District Court of the Hague Take Measures Concerning the Infringement of Foreign Patents" [1994] E.I.P.R. 360; Bertrams, "Cross-Border Prohibitory Injunctions in Dutch Law" (1995) 26 I.I.C. 618; de Wit, "Die Anwendungspraxis des EuGVÜ und des LugÜ in Patent- und Markensachen mit internationalen Bezug durch die Gerichte in den Nederlanden" [1996] *Mitteilungen der deutschen Patentanwälte* 225; Brinkhof, "Between Speed and Thoroughness: The Dutch 'Kort Geding' Procedure in Patent Cases" [1996] E.I.P.R. 499; Brinkhof, "Geht das Grenzüberschreitende Verletzungsverbot im niederländishen einsweiligen Verfügungsverfahren zu weit?" [1997] GRUR Int. 489.

[28] "Geding" is pronounced ge-ding with a short "e" and the stress on the second syllable. Further nuances of pronunciation, as of meaning, are likely to baffle any but a Dutch lawyer.

[29] "Attempts to translate the content of *kort geding* invariably lead to misunderstandings . . . it is sufficient to state that the literal translation of *kort geding* is 'short procedure' and that the procedure is, for many litigants, an attractive combination of speed, simplicity and low legal costs." *Per* Brinkhof "Transborder Injunctions and the *Kort Geding*" (paper presented at Herschel Smith Seminar or Intellectual Property and Private International Law, Cambridge, February 24, 1996).

[30] Both rare, and the latter only in cases of piracy.

1–31   *Kort geding* procedure is commenced by a written summons stating the plaintiffs' complaint. There is now routinely provision for exchange of written arguments and evidence leading to an oral hearing of about half a day, which typically takes place within about two to three months of the summons. A reasoned written decision is then issued within about two weeks. The *kort geding* judgment can be appealed to the Hague Court of Appeal and thence by appeal *en cassation* to the Dutch Supreme Court but any order at first instance is normally effective immediately, notwithstanding any appeal. Alternatively, the unsuccessful party can commence ordinary proceedings since the *kort geding* is a procedure in its own right and does not finally determine the rights of the parties. In ordinary proceedings the issues of infringement and validity are considered *de novo* and the previous *kort geding* judgment has no weight. In practice, however, ordinary proceedings are rare although appeals from the *kort geding* decision are common.

1–32   The issues which may be litigated in *kort geding* are extremely wide-ranging. The plaintiff must, in principle, demonstrate urgency although as a practical matter this has typically been assumed in his favour. Again, factors which in England would go to the balance of convenience have tended to be assumed in favour of the plaintiff. There is a presumption that damages are hardly ever adequate compensation for patent infringement, although recent decisions show greater appreciation of the unquantifiable damage which may be caused to the defendant if the injunction turns out to have been unjustified. As well as contesting these issues and challenging jurisdiction, the defendants[31] may deny infringement and challenge validity. All these issues are likely to be addressed in evidence and in the *kort geding* judgment, although any decision is essentially interlocutory and a finding of probable invalidity, especially, does not purport to have any effect *in rem*.

1–33   If extraterritorial relief is claimed then individual issues may need to be addressed on a country-by-country basis, possibly with evidence from foreign lawyers. Dutch conflicts of law rules apply the *lex loci delicti commissi* to issues of substantive law, although where there is harmonising legislation such as the European Patent Convention the burden of proof of the relevant foreign law is effectively reversed.[32] Procedural issues are always governed by Dutch law, and the availability or appropriateness of summary or interlocutory relief is treated entirely as a matter for Dutch law rather than the *lex loci*. The latter is crucial to the attractiveness of *kort geding* to plaintiffs, since the majority of European

---

[31] There are almost always multiple defendants.

[32] Brinkhof, "The Desirability, Necessity and Feasibility of Co-operation between Courts in the Field of European Patent Law" [1997] E.I.P.R. 226, reprinted from *The Law and Practice of the Enlarged Boards of Appeal of the EPO during its First Ten Years* (1996) explains that the Dutch view is that Art. 69 EPC creates a true European standard of infringement, so that the Dutch courts would be wrong to apply *Catnic* in England and *Formstein* in Germany. Although the pragmatic English view is that a "European patent" is no more and no less than a bundle of national patents, support can be found for the opposite (somewhat Platonic) view: Singer, *The European Patent Convention* (Revised English Edition, ed. Lunzer, 1995), para. 2.02.

jurisdictions outside the Netherlands are extremely reluctant to grant interlocutory relief in patent infringement cases.[33]

The status of *kort geding* injunctions under the Brussels Convention

There appears to be a widespread misunderstanding of the relation- **1–34** ship of *kort geding* proceedings to the Brussels Convention. Contrary to what is often said, the Dutch courts do not purport to derive international jurisdiction directly from Article 24 of the latter.[34] The only relevance of Article 24 is to permit *kort geding* proceedings to go ahead, notwithstanding the possible existence of earlier proceedings of some sort elsewhere. The Dutch courts consider their practice to be consistent with Article 16(4),[35] since the court seised of the *kort geding* proceedings does not purport to revoke or uphold foreign registered intellectual property rights: it simply forms a view as to whether they are presumptively strong enough to justify the grant of an injunction, in a manner reminiscent of pre-*Cyanamid* practice in England. Judge Brinkhof of the Hague Court of Appeal has explained the Dutch understanding of the Article[36]:

"The question sometimes arises, with reference to Article 16(4), whether Dutch courts in fact have jurisdiction over disputes concerning infringements of foreign patents where the defendants claim that an injunction may not be imposed because either Opposition Proceedings have commenced at the European Patent Office in Munich, or nullity proceedings have started. The Dutch courts certainly consider that they have jurisdiction in *kort geding* proceedings to assess the chances of success of either the revocation proceedings before national courts or the opposition proceedings in the European Patent Office in order to grant an injunction or to refuse to award an injunction. Nevertheless, neither the Dutch Supreme Court nor the ECJ have provided an answer to this question.

Finally, it is necessary to make brief mention of Article 24 (. . .)[37] As far as I know, Dutch courts in *kort geding* proceedings have never

[33] Dutch theory is that once a patent has been granted, the proprietor is prima facie entitled to an injunction against any infringement and it requires strong reasons to withhold provisional relief. One assumes that Dutch practice became settled in the days when the Netherlands had the strictest examination by any patent office in Europe, so that it was generally safe to assume that a granted Dutch patent was valid. Registration countries, and even those with less strict examination systems, understandably take a different view.

[34] Permitting the grant of provisional and protective measures by a court which does not have substantive jurisdiction over the action as such. See paras 2–74 and 3–23 *et seq.*

[35] Assigning exclusive jurisdiction in proceedings relating to the registration or validity of registered intellectual property rights. See para. 2–101.

[36] Brinkhof, "Transborder Injunctions and the *Kort Geding*" (paper presented at Herschel Smith Seminar on Intellectual Property and Private International Law, Cambridge, February 24, 1996).

[37] Text of Art. 24 omitted.

regarded themselves, in recent years, as having jurisdiction over disputes where foreign patents are being infringed by defendants who are domiciled in Contracting States except where the court can base its jurisdiction on Articles 2, 5(3) or 6(1) of the Brussels Convention."

1–35   Actual practice in *kort geding* is generally to found jurisdiction on a combination of Articles 2 and 6(1), although Article 5(3) may have some residual importance. So in *Hoffmann-La Roche v. Organon Teknika*,[38] for instance, there were 10 defendants, all in the same group, with two domiciled in the Netherlands and one each in Belgium, Austria, France, Germany, Italy, England, Sweden and Switzerland. It has not escaped the notice of Dutch industry that despite attempts to portray *kort geding* as a weapon against international counterfeiters, it actually bears most heavily on Dutch research-based industrial companies and especially benefits those of their competitors who are domiciled outside the Brussels and Lugano contracting states and have no assets in Europe.

Examples of Dutch practice in patent cases

1–36   As is the case for several Continental jurisdictions, there are isolated examples of foreign intellectual property rights being litigated in the Netherlands well before the Brussels Convention. However, the current practice of the Dutch courts can be traced back directly to the decision of the Dutch Supreme Court in a trade mark case, *Interlas v. Lincoln*, in which the Supreme Court held[39]:

> "Unless resulting otherwise from the law, the type of obligation or a contract, any person who is obliged to another person to deliver something or to perform or desist from an action can be ordered to do so by a judge on application by the party entitled. In general there is no reason for assuming that there are no grounds for such an order if the legal obligation must be performed outside the Netherlands, and possibly under foreign law.
>
> There is no support in the law for a restrictive interpretation, which would, in an age of increasing cross-border contacts, lead to the undesirable result in practice that a Dutch plaintiff whose rights have been infringed by unlawful actions of a cross-border nature, such as the infringement of intellectual property rights, acts of unfair competition in more than one country, or cross-border environmental pollution, would be obliged to bring an action before the courts of each of the countries in question."

1–37   The extraterritorial assertion of jurisdiction in that case was quite modest, since it involved only the other two Benelux territories, all three

---

[38] Hague Court of Appeals, September 12, 1996.
[39] Supreme Court of the Netherlands, November 24, 1989. This translation is taken from Bertrams, *op. cit.*

of which share a common trade mark law. Moreover, there was and is a Benelux Court of Justice which could determine the consistency of this exercise of jurisdiction with the Benelux Trade Mark Agreement. However, the principle stated in the second paragraph was soon taken out of its original context and extended to the other intellectual property rights, on a pan-European and occasionally-worldwide basis.[40] Examples are now so numerous that only a few important ones can be given.[41]

The two cases from which the Dutch practice might be said to have become widely known are *Applied Research Systems v. Organon International*[42] and *Chiron v. Akzo Pharma-Organon Technika*.[43] In the *Applied Research Systems* case, the plaintiffs were granted an injunction against a total of nine defendants for all 10 EPC contracting states. The effect of the injunction was to terminate clinical trials on the defendants' human follicle-stimulating hormone, despite which the Hague Court of Appeals expressly disregarded the fact that preliminary measures would not have been available in the majority of those states.[44] In *Chiron v. Akzo Pharma-Organon Technika* Chiron was the owner of a European patent for Hepatitis C diagnosis and vaccination.[45] An American company, UBI, had granted Akzo and several companies in its group worldwide rights to sell a competing diagnostic kit which allegedly infringed the Chiron patent. Relying on the *Lincoln v. Interlas* decision, the Hague District Court and the Court of Appeals held that once jurisdiction over the foreign defendants was established or conceded,[46] the court had a *duty* to grant extraterritorial relief if the patent appeared to be valid and infringed.

The latest development in the higher courts of the Netherlands appears to be increasing recognition that the *kort geding* procedure is inherently unsuitable for complicated multinational cases, and that too little weight had previously been given to the legitimate interests of the defendants and to factors which in England would be considered on the balance of convenience.[47] These reservations were initially expressed by

1–38

1–39

---

[40] It is of interest that the early cases do not seem to have been based on any analysis of the Brussels Convention; on the contrary, what one finds is that the Dutch courts initially granted extraterritorial injunctions as a matter of policy and in reliance on domestic law, and only subsequently turned to the Brussels Convention to find justification for an existing practice.

[41] As well as the articles cited above n. 27, I have referred to see Vles and Oosting, "Choosing a National Forum for Transborder IP Relief" (Paper presented at UIA Congress, Madrid, September, 3–7, 1996) which summarises a great many more cases.

[42] Hague Court of Appeals, February 3, 1994; see Gielen and Ebbink, "First Europe-wide Biotech Patent Injunction" [1994] E.I.P.R. 243.

[43] Hague Court of Appeals, December 1, 1994.

[44] To which one may now add the fact that clinical trials are not considered to infringe under German law: *Klinische Versuche I* (Case X ZR 99/92) [1997] R.P.C. 623 (Bundesgerichtshof) applying Community Patent Convention, Art. 31(b).

[45] The same underlying invention as was involved in the U.K. *Chiron v. Organon Teknika; Chiron v. Murex* litigation; although the Chiron patent litigated in the U.K. had been obtained by the national, rather than the European, route.

[46] The foreign defendants were deemed to have submitted pursuant to Art. 18 by not contesting the jurisdiction with sufficient vehemence.

[47] *Hoffmann-La Roche v. Organon Teknika*, below.

Judge Brinkhof of the Hague Court of Appeals in an article,[48] and were soon given effect. So in the patent case of *Hoffmann-La Roche v. Organon Teknika*[49] the Court of Appeals held[50]:

"The case is also certainly complicated, both as far as concerns the technical and the legal issues. Apart from the Dutch defendants, eight defendants were summoned to appear before the Court from eight different jurisdictions. This makes it inevitable to answer questions of private international law, as well as to examine the infringement under the law of eight different countries. Considerable efforts are expected from the defendants to prepare and coordinate their defence, since they were given two months to do so. Also taking into account the considerable financial interest of the case—in first instance Organon mentioned a loss of over 200 million guilders—and the effects on employment upon allowance of the claims, the Court believes that the present case was not suitable to be examined in preliminary proceedings, notwithstanding the opportunity given to the parties after the Writ of Summons to put their position on paper before the hearing. There is too big a risk that the interests of the defendants will not be sufficiently safeguarded. And so in the view of this Court the President should have dismissed the claims of HLR, because within the framework of preliminary proceedings he could neither have acquired the understanding required for a justified decision, nor sufficiently oversee the consequences of the decision."

However, there has been no detectable weakening of the Dutch view that jurisdiction over foreign infringements may be asserted on the combined basis of Articles 2 and 6(1) of the Brussels Convention, and that extraterritorial preliminary injunctions are consistent with Article 16.[51]

---

[48] Brinkhof, "Gaat het grensoververschrijdend verbod in kort geding over de schreef?" [1996] *Bijblad Industriele Eignedom* 258; Brinkhof, "Geht das Grenzüberschreitende Verletzungsverbot im niederländishen einsweiligen Verfügungsverfahren zu weit?" [1997] GRUR Int. 489 corresponds. Even in the original Dutch text, one notes that the judgments of Aldous J. in *Plastus v. 3M* and *Chiron v. Organon Teknika (No. 10)* are quoted from.

[49] (Hague Court of Appeals, September 12, 1995, Brinkhof, Fasseur-van Santen and Grootoonk JJ.).

[50] I regret I do not know the source of this translation; there is a lively *samizdat* trade in Dutch judgments.

[51] The Dutch approach to the Convention has been re-affirmed, specifically with reference to *Coin Controls v. Suzo*, in *Palmaz v. Cordis* (Hague District Court, October 29, 1997) and *Cordis v. Boston Scientific* (Hague District Court, December 2, 1997), with the latter also taking notice of the English Court of Appeal decision in *Fort Dodge v. Akzo Nobel*. The Dutch view is that the interpretation of Art. 16(4) in *Coin Controls v. Suzo* is tenable, but that pending the reference in *Fort Dodge v. Akzo Nobel* they will continue to follow their previous practice as being more consistent with the policy of the Convention, since it enables "related actions" to be consolidated and reduces litigation costs and the risk of inconsistent decisions. For the judgment in *Akzo Nobel v. Webster* itself—the Dutch counterpart to *Fort Dodge v. Akzo Nobel*—see para. 1–54, below.

Germany[51a]

The Netherlands apart, it is in Germany that extraterritorial jurisdiction in intellectual property cases has received the most consideration in the courts and by commentators.[52] By way of introduction, German patent litigation procedure has a number of characteristic features which need to be noted. Issues of infringement and validity are strictly separated—with validity being for the Federal Patent Court (*Bundespatentgericht*) in Munich and infringement for 10 regional trial courts (*Landgerichte*), although in practice patent litigation is concentrated in only three of these: Dusseldorf, Munich and Mannheim. Because of this separation of jurisdiction, infringement actions may have to be stayed pending the determination of validity. Summary proceedings for interlocutory injunctions are known in German law but are relatively little used in patent cases in comparison to the Dutch *kort geding* procedure[53]; probably because ordinary proceedings are quite fast,[54] or because the requirement of urgency is strictly applied[55] or because the plaintiff has to show a strong case on infringement and validity has to be virtually beyond doubt. Like *kort geding* the summary proceedings are free-standing, although the defendant in the summary proceedings can require full proceedings to be commenced. Both the cases which follow are examples of full proceedings and there does not appear to be any case to date of an extraterritorial injunction being granted in summary proceedings.

1–40

[51a] I am grateful to Dr Joachim Feldges of Pünder, Volhard, Weber & Axster, Munich, for help with this paragraph.

[52] See the pioneering article by Stauder, "Die Anwendung des EWG-Gerichtssands- und Vollstreckungsübereinkommens auf Klagen im gewerblichen Rechtsschutz und Urheberrecht" [1976] GRUR Int 465 and 510. See also Neuhaus "Das EuGVÜ und das LugÜ soweit heirvon Streitigkeiten des gewerblichen Reschttsschutzes betroffen werden" [1996] *Mitteilungen der deutschen Patentanwälte* 257; König, "Materiellrechtliche Probleme der Anwendung von Fremdrecht bei Patentverletzungsklagen und -Verfügungsverfaren anch der Zuständigkeitsordnung des EuGVÜ [1996] *Mitteilungen der deutschen Patentanwälte* 296; Reimann, "Foreign Infringements of IP; Interrelated Questions of Validity of Rights—German View" (paper presented at Herschel Smith Seminar on Intellectual Property and Private International Law, Cambridge, February 24, 1996); Feldges, "Report on Germany" (paper presented at the BIICL Workshop on the Enforcement of European Patents in Domestic Courts, March 25, 1997); von Meibom and Pitz, "Cross Border Injunctions in International Patent Infringement Proceedings" [1997] E.I.P.R. 469 (translated from "Grenzüberschreitende Verfügungen im internationalen Patentverletzungsverfahren" [1996] *Mitteilungen der deutschen Patentanwälte* 181); Stauder, von Rospatt and von Rospatt, "Grenzüberschreitender Rechtsschutz fur europäische Patente" [1997] GRUR Int. 859.

[53] According to Feldges, *op. cit.* the Dusseldorf District Court deals with about 250 patent and utility model cases per year, of which only 20 are summary proceedings.

[54] A figure of nine months is quoted as typical, although this is subject to the infringement action not being stayed for nullity proceedings in the Federal Patent Court, and does not allow for any appeal.

[55] Feldges, *op. cit.*, says that Munich applies a strict rule that summary proceedings must be commenced within one month after knowledge of infringement and Dusseldorf applies a more flexible period of six weeks. These periods correspond to English practice. Compare Dutch practice (paper by de Ranitz, *loc. cit.*) where the period for commencing *kort geding* proceedings is nominally six months but in practice is indefinite.

1–41   There are isolated examples of extraterritorial assertions of jurisdiction in German intellectual property law prior to the Brussels Convention.[56] However, the cases of present interest may be said to begin in 1994.[57] In *MCC Nederland v. Rexnord Kette*[58] the German defendants were restrained from infringing a United Kingdom patent.[59] They had exhibited an allegedly infringing machine at a trade fair in Birmingham. On the question of jurisdiction, the court held[60]:

> "Die Klage ist zulässig; insbesondere die internationale Zuständigkeit des angerufenen Landgerichts Düsseldorf ist gegeben. Sie ergibt sich aus Artikel 2 Satz 1 des EWG Übereinkommens über die gerichtliche Zuständigkeit und die Vollstreckung gerichtlicher Entscheidungen in Zivil- und Handelssachen vom 27. September 1968[61] (GVÜ), das seit dem 1. Januar 1987—mithin vor Klageerhebung (. . .)—im Verhältnis zum Vereinigten Königriech in Kraft getreten ist (. . .). Personen, die ihren Wohnsitz oder Sitz in dem Hoheitsgebiet eines Vertragsstaates haben, sind danach ohne Rücksicht auf ihre Staatsangehorigkeit vor den Gerichten dieses Staates zu verklagen. Da Artikel 16 Nr. 4 GVÜ eine Ausnahme—im Sinne einer ausschließlichen Zuständigkeit der Gerichte des Vertragsstaates, in dem die Erteilung des Patents erfolgt ist—nur für Nichtigkeitsklagen gegen Patente vorsieht, gilt Artikel 2 Abs. 1 GVO auch für Verletzungsklagen aus einem ausländischen Patent, und zwar auch insoweit, als die Klage—wie hier—darauf gerichtet ist, der beklagten Partei die Vornahme bestimmter Handlungen in dem betreffenden ausländischen Staat zu untersagen (. . .)."[62]

1–42   On the merits, the Dusseldorf court held that the question of infringement by the defendants' conveyor was to be determined according to British law. Referring to sections 125(1) and 130(7) of the Patents Act 1977, Article 69 of the European Patent Convention and the decision of Hoffmann J. in *Improver v. Remington*[63] it held that the

---

[56] See Ulmer, *op. cit.*, and Stauder, *op. cit.*
[57] At the time of writing, both the cases which follow were under appeal.
[58] Dusseldorf District Court, February 1, 1994.
[59] GB Patent 2 037 690, not a European patent (U.K.). The invention was for conveyor belts (*e.g.* for bottles) using magnets to keep the belt in position round corners.
[60] Citations omitted.
[61] *sc.* the Brussels Convention.
[62] In free translation by the author: "The claim is admissible, and in particular the international jurisdiction of the Dusseldorf District Court is established. It results from Article 2, paragraph 1 of the Brussels Convention, which entered into force in relation to the UK on 01 January 1987 (. . .). Persons who are resident or have their seat in the territory of a contracting state, must be sued, regardless of their nationality, before the courts of that state. Although Article 16, paragraph 4 of the Convention constitutes an exception by giving exclusive jurisdiction of the courts of the contracting state in which the patent was granted, this only applies to claims for invalidation of a patent; and Article 2, paragraph 1 of the Convention equally applies to infringements of the foreign patent insofar as the claim—as was the case here—is aimed at preventing the Defendant from doing such things in that foreign state."
[63] [1990] F.S.R. 181; [1993] GRUR Int. 245 *sub nom* Epilady IX. The Court also referred to an article by Sir Douglas Falconer at [1989] GRUR Int. 471.

patent was infringed, despite a feature allegedly taking the defendants' product outside the literal wording of the claims. The defendants also pleaded that the patent was invalid as a result of certain pieces of prior art and prior user and for extension of disclosure and scope of protection on amendment. Under German domestic practice, the District Court would not have investigated validity at all but the court held that the various allegations of invalidity failed on the facts, and in reaching its decision it applied the United Kingdom Patents Act 1977, ss. 1(1), 2(2), 72(1)(a), (d) and (e) and 74(1)(a) as well as law under the European Patent Convention. In the result, an injunction was granted against infringement but the plaintiffs were held to be disentitled to damages or profits by virtue of section 68 of the 1977 Act, since the assignment of the patent to them had not been registered until after the only proven act of infringement.

The other German case to date is of almost equal interest. In *Kaiser v.* **1–43** *Chemax*[64] the first defendant was an English company (in liquidation) which had previously acted as exclusive distributor for the plaintiff's cleaning chemicals, but which started selling products which the plaintiff claimed were infringements of its European patent.[65] One of the former directors of the English company was domiciled in Germany, and was joined as a co-defendant.[66] The court held that it had jurisdiction over all defendants, in respect of infringement of the United Kingdom patent:

"Die internationale und ortliche Zuständigkeit des Landgerichts Düsseldorf ergibt sich aus Art. 6 Nr. 1 des Übereinkommens der Europäischen Gemeinschaft über die gerichtliche Zuständigkeit und die Vollstreckung gerichtlicher Entscheidungen in Zivil- und Handelssachen (EuGVÜ) vom 27. September 1968 (. . .) i.V.m. der auf die Geltendmachung ausländischer Patentrechte entsprechend anwendbaren Vorschrift des §143 Abs. 2 patg. und der Verordnung der Landesregierung Nordrhein-Westfalen uber die Zuweisung von Patentstreitsachen, Sortenschutzstreitsachen, Gebrauchsmusterstreitsachen und Topographieschutzsachen an das Landgericht Düsseldorf vom 28. Juni 1988 (. . .). Gemäß Art. 6 Nr. 1 EuGVÜ kann eine Person, die ihren Wohnsitz in dem Hoheitsgebiet eines Vertragsstaats hat, wenn mehrere Personenen zusammen verklagt werden, auch vor dem Gericht verklagt werden, in dessen Bezirk (nur) einer der Beklagten seinen Wohnsitz hat, so daß auf dem Wohnsitz eines Streitgenossen auch die internationale Zuständigkeit für die Klagen gegen die anderen Streitgenossen basiert. Die hierfür erforderliche Konnexität der Klagen (. . .) ist gemäß Art. 22 Abs. 3 EuGVÜ bereits dann gegeben, wenn zwischen den Klagen

---

[64] Dusseldorf District Court, January 16, 1996.
[65] EP 0 329 959. The patent was in force in both Germany and the U.K.
[66] The joinder of five individual defendants did not depend solely on their legal status as directors. The court referred to evidence that there has been a conspiracy, involving the German-domiciled director, to "flood the market" with an infringing cleaning fluid in place of that of the plaintiffs.

eine so enge Beziehung besteht, daß eine gemeinsame Verhandlung und Entscheidung geboten erscheint. Da ein solcher sachlicher Zusammenhang aufgrund des gegen alle Beklagten gerichteten Klagevorwurfes der gemeinschaftlichen Patentverletzung gegeben ist, können auch die in England ansässigen Beklagten zu 1, 3, 4 und 6 vor dem Landgericht Düsseldorf verklagt werden, da der Beklagten zu 5 seinen Wohnsitz in Nordrhein-Westfalen und damit im Zuständigkeitsbereich des Landgerichtes Düsseldorf hat, dem Patentstreitsachen für das Land Nordrhein-Westfalen durch die genannte Verordnung zugewiesen sind."[67]

1–44   The court went on to hold that the defendants had supplied a cleaning product which infringed the patent and which had not been obtained from licensed sources. The defendants again alleged that the patent was invalid.[68] However the defendants' only citations of prior art had already been dismissed by the Federal Patent Court in proceedings against the German patent from which the European and United Kingdom patents took priority, and the Dusseldorf court did not investigate validity any further.

France (1): Introduction[69]

1–45   To date, there is only one directly relevant court decision in France and that concerns the enforcement of a Dutch extraterritorial injunction, rather than any assertion of extraterritorial jurisdiction in patent cases by the French courts themselves. This is the case of *Eurosensory v. Tiemann*[69a] in which the Hague District Court had granted a *kort geding*

---

[67] In free translation: "The international and local competence of the Landgericht Dusseldorf results from Art. 6(1) of the 1968 Convention, as well as Paragraph 143(2) of the Patent Law and the Regulation of the Regional Government of Nordrhein-Westfalen and the delegation of such competence in patent, utility model (etc) matters to the Landgericht Dusseldorf, dated 28 June, 1988. Under Art. 6(1) of the Brussels Convention, a person domiciled in the territory of a contracting state, if sued with other persons, can also be sued in the territory of the domicile of another co-defendant; so that the domicile of one co-defendant can found international jurisdiction over other co-defendants. The necessary connection (. . .) under Art. 22(3) of the Convention is established if there is a close connection between the actions, so that joined proceedings are appropriate. As such a factual connection has been established against all the defendants for alleged complicity in patent infringement, the defendants (1, 3, 4 and 6) who are domiciled in England can be brought before the Dusseldorf District Court, through the domicile of the fifth defendant in Nordrhein-Westfalen, which is within the jurisdiction of this Court in patent cases according to the said Regulation."

[68] They had applied to the United Kingdom Patent Office for revocation, though only on the day after the German oral proceedings.

[69] I am grateful to Maitre Pierre Véron of Lamy, Véron, Ribeyre & Associés, Lyon, for help with these paragraphs.

[69a] *Cour d'Appel de Paris*, January 28, 1994; see Véron, "Les 'Euro-Injonctions' Devant la Justice Francaise" (1995) 57 *Revue du Droit de la Propriété Intellectulle* 13. A similar result was reached by the *Cour d'Appel de Versailles* in a trade mark case, *Medicale Equipex v. Farmitalia Erba* (January 25, 1989). For further Dutch proceedings in the same case, see *Medicale Equipex v. Farmitalia Carlo Erba* [1995] I.L.Pr. 577 (Amsterdam Court of Appeal).

injunction restraining the defendants Eurosensory from infringing a European patent[69b] in all designated states, including France, under penalty of an *astreinte* for breach of the injunction. The plaintiffs Tiemann registered the Dutch judgment with the *Tribunal de Grande Instance de Paris*, and Eurosensory appealed to the *Cour d'Appel de Paris* pursuant to Article 36 of the Brussels Convention. Eurosensory sought a stay pending an appeal which was pending in the Netherlands, or a decision that recognition was contrary to *ordre public* in France because the French courts would not have granted a provisional injunction in the same circumstances. The *Cour d'Appel de Paris* refused the appeal, holding that the appellants were, in effect, inviting the court to ignore Articles 29 and 34 by re-examining the mertis; and that the public policy exception of Article 27(1) did not allow the recognising court to apply its own *ordre public* to the question of whether the foreign judgment should have been granted. Apart from *Eurosensory v. Tiemann*, the only court decision of relevance appears to be *Banco de Santander v. Kortex*,[69c] in which a French software company successfully sued a Spanish bank before the *Tribunal de Commerce de Paris* for copyright infringements committed in Spain, but jurisdiction appears to have been conceded and the appeal turned on questions of the applicable law.

Apart from *Eurosensory*, the likely response of the French courts to an **1–46** application for a extraterritorial relief in a patent infringement action has to be deduced from academic writing and the general law.[70] Writing in 1974,[71] Professor Lagarde referred to the deliberate absence from the Brussels Convention of any specific provisions relating to infringement actions as such and posed the question[72]:

"Ce qui est le plus intéressant, c'est le cas où le défendeur est domicilié dans la Communauté. Dans ce cas, il faut rechercher—ce

---

[69b] EP 237 090.

[69c] *Cour d'Appel de Paris*, October 18, 1996.

[70] For a recent and comprehensive survey, on which the present paragraph is gratefully based, see Mousseron, Raynard and Véron, "L'Euro-Injonction" [1996] I *Dossiers Brevets*. See also Huet, "L'Incidence de la Territorialité des Marques et Brevets Nationaux sur la Competence des Tribunaux Français en Materière de Contrefaçon" in *Melanges offerts a Jean-Jacques Burst* (1997).

[71] Many of the issues which have subsequently become of practical importance because of the activities of the Dutch courts were addressed by papers in the conference report *Droit International et Actions en Contrefaçon de Brevet dans la CEE* (Nice, 1974) which included contributions by Droz, Lagarde (see below), Mathely, Mousseron and Savignon amongst others.

[72] Lagarde, "Application de la Convention d'Execution aux Actions en Contrefaçon de Brevets Nationaux—Rapport de M. Le Professeur Paul Lagarde" in *Droit International et Actions en Contrefaçon de Brevet dans la CEE* (Nice, 1974). In free tranlsation by the author: "The more interesting situation arises when the defendant is domiciled in the Community. In that case, it is first necessary to establish the court or courts which are competent to entertain the action for infringement; and secondly, to establish whether the competent courts for the infringement action are also competent to entertain incidental or preliminary questions. I say 'preliminary' because I do not want to prejudge the nature of the questions capable or arising on infringement as *préalable* or *préjudiciel*. / For example, preliminary questions of the validity of the patent, interpretation, the claims, etc."

sera le premier point—le ou les tribunaux qui sont compétents pour connaître de l'action en contrefaçon; et le second point sera de rechercher si le ou les tribunaux compétents pour l'action en contrefaçon sont également compétents pour connaître des questions préalables ou préliminaires. Je dis 'préliminaires,' parce que je ne veux pas prendre parti sur le caractère préalable ou préjudiciel des questions qui pourront se poser à l'occasion de la contrefaçon.

Par exemple: questions préliminaires de validité du brevet, interprétation, revendications, etc.''

1–47   After considering relatively simple applications of Articles 2, 5(3) and 6(1) Lagarde went on to the case of parallel infringements by the same defendant in several member states[73].

"Je prends un exemple: je suppose que le même contrefacteur a commis des actes de contrefaçon en France, en Allemagne, et aux Pays-Bas, étant entendu, puisque nous sommes dans le cadre des brevets nationaux, que le breveté a déposé un brevet dans chacun des trois pays. Alors, ici, pourra-t-il y avoir connexité et obligation pour le tribunal second saisi de se dessaisir? Tout va dépendre, vous allez le voir, de l'attitude du breveté, plus précisément du tribunal que le breveté aura saisi en premier lieu.

Dans cette hypothèse de pluralité de contrefaçons, en réalité, il y a contrefaçon de plusieurs brevets de pays différents.

Le breveté peut tout d'abord assigner le contrefacteur devant un tribunal de l'Etat de son domicile. C'est la règle de l'article 2 de la Convention.

Dans ce cas, ce tribunal est compétent pour connaître de tous les actes qui sont reprochés au contrefacteur, quel que soit le pays dans

---

[73] "I shall give an example: suppose that the same infringer has committed acts of infringement in France, Germany and the Netherlands, it being understood, since we are considering national patents, that the patentee has registered a patent in each of these three countries. Will there be a situation of related actions so that the court second seised must decline jurisdiction? That will depend, as will be seen, on the attitude of the patentee and in particular on the court which the patentee caused to be first seised. / On this hypothesis of multiple infringements, there is really infringement of several patents of different countries. / The patentee could first of all sue the infringer before a court of the state of his domicile. That is the rule of article 2 of the Convention. / In that case, the court is competent to entertain all the acts pleaded against the infringer, wherever they may have been committed in and whatever the patent that may have been infringed. Moreover, if after conferring jurisdiction on the court of the defendant's domicile in this way, the patentee wanted to change his mind and sue in the court of one of the places of infringement then there would have to be a renunciation of jurisidiction. / The other possibility which is given to the patentee is not to sue the infringer in the court of his domicile, but in the court of one of the countries where the acts of infringement occurred. / In this case the court first seised, for example the Dutch court for an infringement in the Netherlands, can only take jurisdiction over acts of infringement which have been committed on Dutch territory. But the infringements in Germany and France are not normally within the jurisdiction of the Dutch court, because the Dutch court is only competent in so far as it is the court of the place of the tort, which is to say only in respect of infringement of the Dutch patent."

lequel ils ont été commis, quel que soit le brevet qui a été contrefait. Donc, dans ce cas, si, après avoir saisi le tribunal du domicile du contrefacteur, le breveté veut se raviser et saisir le tribunal d'un des lieux de contrefaçon, Il pourra y avoir lieu à un dessaisissement.

—L'autre possibilité qui est donnée au breveté c'est de commencer a assigner le contrefacteur, non pas devant le tribunal de son domicile mais devant le tribunal de l'un des pays où des actes de contrefaçon ont été commis.

Dans ce cas, ce tribunal premier saisi, par exemple le tribunal hollandais parce qu'il y a eu une contrefaçon aux Pays-Bas, ne peut connaître que des actes de contrefaçon qui ont été commis sur le territoire hollandais. Mais la contrefaçon qui s'est produite en Allemagne et la contrefaçon qui s'est produite en France ne sont pas, normalement, de la compétence des tribunaux hollandais, puisque le tribunal hollandais n'est compétent qu'en tant que tribunal du lieu du délit, donc simplement en tant que tribunal de l'action en contrefaçon du brevet hollandais."

Finally, for present purposes, Professor Lagarde dealt with the issue of preliminary questions, including validity[74]: **1–48**

---

[74] "It is clear that in most cases the defendant in the infringement action will want to raise defences involving preliminary questions such as the interpretation of the claims, the defence of prior personal possession, the invalidity of the patent, etc. / Specialists in intellectual property, in general, believe and assert that because of differences in the legislation concerning these defences which may be raised as preliminary issues, only the courts of the patent could—and should—be competent to answer these questions. And their conclusion—or their assumption—would be that the court seised of the infringement, unless it should happen to be the court of the state which had granted the patent, should stay it own proceedings for the defence to be determined before the courts of the country of registration, before resuming the case on the issue of infringement. / I say quite simply that this view is condemned by the Convention. This is clear for incidental questions which do not concern the validity of the patent, because from the silence of the Convention as to these questions (for example, the interpretation of the claims) it follows that one must admit that the court competent to try the infringement is equally competent to try these when pleaded by way of defence. That is an application of the rule according which the judge seised of the claim is also seised of any defence to it. / The same is true for incidental questions to do with the crucial problem of patent validity. / Admittedly, at first sight article 16 of the Convention appears to lead to the opposite conclusion, since article 16 tells us that [omitted]). / So although one might believe that this exclusive jurisdiction always applies to questions of the validity of a patent, and in particular to invalidity raised as a defence; this exclusive jurisdiction actually only comes into play when the question of the validity of the patent is raised *à titre principal* in the jurisdiction of a contracting state. / In fact, when the question is only raised as an incidental one, the court seised of the infringement action is not bound to decline jurisdiction. / This rule appears in the Convention in Article 19, which is not perhaps of dazzling transparency on a first reading, but whose sense cannot be doubted. / [omitted] / Article 19 does not envisage a case in which the court of a contracting state is only seised *à titre incident* of a question which is subject to one of the exclusive jurisdictions. Consequently, an *a contrario* argument leads one to say that the judge is not obliged to decline jurisdiction. / Recall that we already have examples of cases in domestic law in which there was no hesitation in pronouncing, even before the Convention came into force, on preliminary questions of the validity of a

"Il est évident que, dans la plupart des cas, le défendeur à la contrefaçon va essayer de faire barrage à l'action qui est dirigée contre lui, en soulevant des incidents, des questions préliminaires, telles que l'interprétation des revendications, l'exception de possession personnelle antérieure, la nullité du brevet, etc.

Les spécialistes de propriété industrielle, en général, pensent et affirment qu'en raison des divergences de législation concernant les matières qui font l'objet de ces exceptions préliminaires, seuls les tribunaux de l'Etat du brevet pourraient—devraient—être compétents pour trancher ces questions préliminaires. Et leur conclusion—ou leur souhait—serait que le tribunal saisi de la contrefaçon, si, par extraordinaire, il n'est pas le tribunal de l'Etat qui a délivré le brevet, devrait surseoir à statuer, considérer l'exception comme une exception préjudicielle, et la faire trancher par un tribunal de l'Etat du brevet, avant de reprendre le litige sur les suites de la contrefaçon.

Je dis nettement que cette position est condamnée par la Convention. C'est évident pour les questions préalables qui ne touchent pas à la validité du brevet, car dans le silence de la Convention sur ces questions (par exemple sur l'interprétation des revendications), il faut admettre que le tribunal compétent pour connaître de la contrefaçon est également compétent pour connaître de ces exceptions préliminaires. C'est la règle selon laquelle le juge de l'action est le juge de l'exception.

Ceci est certain aussi pour les questions préalables qui touchent au problème crucial de la validité des brevets.

Certes, une lecture rapide de l'article 16 de la Convention paraît conduire à la solution contraire, puisque l'article 16 nous dit: 'sont seuls compétents, sans considération de domicile . . . en matière d'inscription ou de validité des brevets . . . les juridictions de l'Etat contractant sur le territoire duquelle dépôt . . . a été effectué'.

Alors on pourrait croire qu'il y a une compétence exclusive pour les questions de validité du brevet, et notamment pour les questions préjudicielles, mais cette compétence exclusive ne joue que lorsque la question de validité du brevet est posée à titre principal aux juridictions d'un Etat contractant.

En effet, lorsque la question n'est posée qu'à titre incident, le tribunal saisi de la contrefaçon n'est pas obligé de se dessaisir.

La règle apparaît dans la Convention, dans l'article 19, qui n'est peut-être pas d'une clarté aveuglante à la première lecture, mais dont le sens ne parait pas douteux:

patent. I discovered, in preparing this paper, and old judgment of the Court of Appeal of Liege from 1908 which reads: 'if the Belgian courts do not have the power to revoke patents granted by a foreign power, they are undoubtedly competent to examine, in the context of a case of which they are seised, and subject to conforming to the rules of the legislation by which the patents are governed, the question of the existence or the validity of patents granted in foreign countires.' / So, this is not the first time that this has happened. / The solution, which will certainly shock many of you, calls for certain further observations, and I should like to make two."

'Le juge d'un Etat contractant saisi à titre principal d'un litige pour lequel une juridiction d'un autre Etat contractant est exclusivement compétente en vertu de l'article 16, se déclare d'office incompétent.'

Cet article 19 n'envisage pas le cas où le tribunal d'un Etat contractant n'est saisi qu'à titre incident d'une question qui fait l'objet d'une compétence exclusive. Par conséquent, l'argumentation a contrario conduit à dire que ce juge n'est pas obligé de se dessaisir.

Remarquez que nous avons des exemples, dans notre jurisprudence nationale, de juridictions qui n'ont pas hésité à se prononcer, bien avant l'entrée en vigueur de la Convention, sur des questions préalables de validité de brevet. J'ai retrouvé, en préparant cet exposé, un vieil arrêt de la Cour d'appel de Liège, de 1909, qui nous dit que 'si les tribunaux belges n'ont pas le pouvoir d'annuler des brevets accordés par une puissance étrangère, ils sont incontestablement compétents pour examiner, à l'occasion d'une contestation dont ils sont saisis, et sauf à se conformer aux règles de la législation à laquelle les brevets sont soumis, la question de l'existence ou de la validité des brevets conférés en pays étranger'.

Donc, ce n'est pas la première fois que cela se produit.

Cette solution, qui va choquer beaucoup d'entre vous, appelle quand même un certain nombre d'observations, et je voudrais en faire deux."

France (2): Opinion subsequent to 1974

As in Germany, it appears to have been the activities of the Dutch **1–49** courts from about 1990 onwards that reawakened interest in the possibility of extraterritorial actions for patent infringement. Academic opinion subsequent to Professor Lagarde's 1974 paper is summarised by Mousseron, Raynard and Véron[75]:

[75] "L'Euro-Injonction" [1996] I *Dossiers Brevets*. Citations and notes omittted. In free translation: "The question arises of competition between two judicial authorities. The question is whether, for example, the Dutch or any other judge—having jurisdiction for the claim for infringement of the French patent or for a European patent designating France—or another patent, can or cannot have jurisdiction in respect of a claim for revocation of the patents providing the basis for the action for infringement. Article 14 [*sc.* 19] of the Convention reads [omitted]. / A hasty reading seems to require the judge hearing the infringement claim to declare inadmissible any claim for revocation, which would appear to be reserved to the judge of the state of registration by the previously cited Article 19. A more careful reading of the text leads, however, to important nuances in its scope of application and content. / It is to be noted that the regime imposed by this Article 14 [*sc.* 19] applies only in so far as the action for infringement is concerned '*à titre principal*' and Professor P. Lagarde [above] observes:

'This article 19 does not envisage the situation in which the court of a contracting state is only seized *à titre incident* of a question which is to do with one of the exclusive jurisdictions. Consequently, an *a contrario* argument leads one to say that the judge is not obliged to decline jurisdiction' ".

"La question se pose en cas de compétition entre deux autorités judiciaires. Il s'agit, alors, également de savoir si, par exemple, le Juge—hollandais ou tout autre—compétent sur l'action en contrefaçon du brevet français comme du brevet européen désignant la France—ou de tout autre—peut ou non être compétent sur l'action en annulation des brevets supportant l'action en contrefaçon. L'article 14 de la Convention répond:

'Le juge d'un Etat contractant saisi à titre principal d'un litige pour lequel une juridiction d'un autre Etat contractant est exclusivement compétent en vertu de l'article 16, se déclare d'office incompétent'.

Une lecture rapide paraît imposer au Juge de la contrefaçon de déclarer irrecevable une action en annulation qui paraît bien réservée au Juge de l'Etat de délivrance par l'article 19 de la Convention précitée. Une lecture plus appuyée du texte conduit, toutefois, à d'importantes nuances sur son domaine et son contenu.

Intéressant le domaine de la règle posé par cet article 14 la règle ne joue, en effet, qu'autant que l'action en contrefaçon est formée 'à titre principal' et Le Pr. P. Lagarde observe:

'Cet article 19 n'envisage pas le cas où le tribunal d'un Etat contractant n'est saisi qu'à titre incident d'une question quifait l'objet d'une compétence exclusive. Par conséquent, l'argumentation *a contrario* conduit à dire que ce juge n'est pas obligé de se dessaisir'.

Faut-il encore s'entendre sur le sens à attacher à la formule *'le Juge d'un Etat contractant saisi à titre principal'* et la qualification à cet égard de la réplique d'un défendeur en contrefaçon invoquant la nullité du brevet. Les Prs. J. Foyer et M. Vivant observent[76]:

'Si cette invocation de la nullité du brevet prend le ton d'une demande reconventionnelle, nous pencherions, pour notre part, pour considérer qu'il s'agit là d'une demande principale, simplement faite 'en réponse' à une autre demande pour

---

[76] Translation continues: "Is it also necessary to understand the expression 'the judge of a contracting state seised *à titre principal*' and how one is to characterise the raising of invalidity by defendant in an infringement action. Professors J. Foyer and M. Vivant [*Le Droit des Brevets*, p. 61] observe:

'if the reliance on the invalidity of the patent takes the form of a counterclaim, we would prefer, for our part, to consider that it is in the nature of a principal demand, merely made "in response" to another demand and for which the rule of article 19 cannot be invoked *a contrario*. If it only arises as a defence (so as only to say, for example, that there cannot be any infringement because there is no valid patent) then article 19 interpreted *a contrario* permits it to go ahead. The logic of the rule understood in its context leads us to conclude that the foreign judge can only declare the patent in question to be invalid but cannot revoke it with any effect in law.'

For our part, we consider that the counterclaim is the ordinary mode of obtaining the revocation of a patent and may even be the only procedure, except in the case where the patent in question had already been declared invalid with *erga omnes* effect, which was equivalent, prior to the reform of 1978, to revocation."

laquelle ne pourrait être invoqué le jeu de l'article 19 *a contrario*. S'il ne s'agit que de défense (faire dire seulement, par exemple, qu'il ne peut y avoir contrefaçon parce qu'il n'y a pas de brevet valable), alors l'article 19 interprété *a contrario* trouverait à jouer. La logique de la règle ainsi resituée dans une perspective judiciaire d'ensemble nous pousse à penser que le juge étranger ne pourrait que déclarer tenir pour nul le brevet en discussion mais non l'annuler avec effets de droit'.

Nous pensons, pour notre part, que la demande reconventionnelle est le mode ordinaire d'obtention de l'annulation d'un brevet et même la seule forme procédurale hors le cas où le dit brevet aurait déjà été annulé avec l'effet *erga omnes* qui s'attache, depuis la réforme de 1978, à pareille annulation.

S'agissant du contenu de l'article 14, le Pr. M. Vivant observe[77]:
'On peut envisager au moins trois interprétations.

La première, très certainement excessive, consisterait à dire que le juge devant se déclarer incompétent, lorsqu'il est saisi à titre principal, ne peut à l'inverse le faire quand il n'est saisi qu'incidemment. L'argument serait précieux [*sc.* spécieux.]

Sans tomber dans un tel excès, on peut aussi relever simplement que l'obligation de se dessaisir ne s'impose au juge que lorsqu'il est saisi à titre principal. Si tel n'est pas le cas, l'obligation disparaît—sans que pour autant naisse l'obligation inverse—et il appartient au juge d'apprécier l'opportunité qu'il y aurait à retenir la connaissance d'une question visée à l'article 16. C'est l'interprétation, déjà annoncée par le rapporteur, que fournit M. Droz et qu'adopte le professeur Lagarde.

---

[77] Translation continues: "Concerning the content of Article 14 [*sc.* 19] Professor Vivant [*Juge et Loi du Brevet*, p. 169] observes:

'One can imagine at least three interpretations. / The first, which certainly goes too far, would consist in saying that if the judge would have no jurisdiction when seised *à titre principal*, he would not be permitted to do so (*i.e.* decline jurisdiction) when seised *à titre incident*. The argument is specious. / Without going as far as that, one can propose the simple answer which is that the obligation to decline jurisdiction only arises at all when the judge is seised *à titre principal*. If that is not the case, the obligation disappears—without having given rise to any converse obligation—and it is for the judge to take the opportunity given to him to retain jurisdiction over a question envisaged by Article 16. That is the interpretation, already stated by the *rapporteur*, which was proposed by M. Droz and adopted by Professor Lagarde. / Finally, there is a third reading suggested by M. Tappin which insists less on the fact that the absence of jurisdiction arises from being seised *à titre principal* than on whether, in that case, the lack of jurisdiction must be declared of the court's own motion. Seised *à titre incident*, the judge ought not be able to do this. But he remains obliged to declare his lack of jurisdiction if that is raised by one of the parties. There is thus a sort of shift in the nature of the rule which, though naturally one of '*ordre public communautaire*' becomes a private *inter partes* matter when invoked *à titre incident*. It is by no means certain that this was the intention of the authors of the Convention. / A choice has to be made, of which the second interpretation is, by reason of its flexibility, the one which is best suited to promote European integration.'

In the case where the judge of the action for infringement entertained the action for revocation, he could '*consult*' the judiciary of the state of registration."

Enfin, la troisième lecture suggérée par M. Tuppin insiste moins sur le fait que l'incompétence est liée à une saisine à titre principal que sur celui que cette incompétence est, dans cette hypothèse, proclamée d'office. Saisi à titre incident, le juge n'aurait plus cette faculté. Mais il resterait tenu de constater son incompétence si celle-ci était soulevée par l'une des parties. Il y aurait ainsi une sorte de déplacement de la nature de la règle qui, d'"ordre public communautaire' qu'elle est normalement, deviendrait, évoquée à titre incident, d'intérêt privé. Il n'est pas certain que ce fut la volonté des auteurs de la Convention.

Il appartiendra à la jurisprudence d'opérer un choix, encore que la seconde interprétation soit, par sa souplesse, celle qui aille le mieux dans le sens d'une intégration européenne.'

Au cas où le Juge de la contrefaçon recevrait l'action en annulation, il pourra '*consulter*' le Juge de l'Etat de délivrance."

The United Kingdom

1–50 Although the Brussels Convention has had the force of law in the United Kingdom since 1987, it was previously thought that actions in respect of infringements of foreign intellectual property rights were precluded by a peculiarity of the English private international law of tort, which required any infringement to be actionable under English law as well as the relevant foreign law.[78] That rule was abolished with effect from May 1, 1996.[79] Within a year, two cases had decided that the Brussels Convention does permit relief to be granted in England in respect of copyright,[80] or patent,[81] infringement abroad, although the latter case also held that the raising of a defence of invalidity deprived the English court of substantive jurisdiction over infringement of foreign patents.[82] Neither of these cases was appealed[83] but both judgments have now been approved by the Court of Appeal in *Fort Dodge v. Akzo Nobel*.[84] Subject to any judgment by the European Court of Justice on the reference ordered by the Court of Appeal in the *Fort Dodge* case, *Pearce v. Ove Arup* and *Coin Controls v. Suzo*[85] may be taken as representing English law, at least for the time being. The latter case also asserted, though *obiter*, that the English courts could grant extraterritorial interlocutory injunctions under Article 24 in a similar manner to those in Dutch practice.

[78] See Chap. 6.
[79] The Private International Law (Miscellaneous Provisions) Act 1995, see paras 6–20 *et seq.*
[80] *Pearce v. Ove Arup* [1997] F.S.R. 641 (Lloyd J.).
[81] *Coin Controls v. Suzo* [1997] F.S.R. 660 (Laddie J.).
[82] See generally Chap. 3.
[83] *Coin Controls v. Suzo* settled. *Pearce v. Ove Arup* was decided against the plaintiff on the merits so there could be no appeal by the defendants on the issue of jurisdiction.
[84] [1998] F.S.R. 222, CA.
[85] [1997] F.S.R. 660 (Laddie J.).

D. THE FUTURE

The reference to the European Court of Justice in _Fort Dodge v. Akzo Nobel_

In the present state of the law one can hardly disagree with the observation of Laddie J. in _Fort Dodge v. Akzo Nobel_[86] to the effect that "intellectual property litigation in general and patent litigation in particular in Europe is in a state of some disarray." The different views of the law and their consequences for litigants were summarised by Laddie J. as follows: **1–51**

> "_Coin Controls_ has not met with universal acclaim, not least since it is, apparently, well-known that the Dutch courts have no intention of following the same line of reasoning. They think _Coin Controls_ is wrong. The result of this is that the courts of England and Holland on this critical issue have adopted very different stances. In particular a patentee who sues for infringement of patent in Holland can ask the Dutch courts to restrain infringement in, say, England whereas the converse is not possible when validity is in issue—at least until _Coin Controls_ is overturned by the Court of Appeal or a higher court, or is ignored by other High Court judges. British lawyers and litigants feel that the playing field is not even."

In _Fort Dodge v. Akzo Nobel_ itself five defendants to patent infringement proceedings in the Netherlands sought interlocutory and final anti-suit injunctions in England to restrain the continuation of the Dutch proceedings in so far as they related to infringement of a United Kingdom patent, or the enforcement of any Dutch judgment in respect of the latter.[87] Laddie J. and the Court of Appeal refused the interlocutory injunctions sought, holding that bona fide differences in the interpretation of the relevant Articles existed and that it would be wrong to impose a contentious interpretation of the Convention on the Dutch courts. Although Laddie J. as a first instance judge could not make a preliminary reference to the European Court of Justice under the 1971 Protocol on Interpretation to the Brussels Convention, an appeal by Fort Dodge was expedited and the Court of Appeal decided to do so. **1–52**

After the judgment of the Court of Appeal refusing the interlocutory anti-suit injunction,[87a] a co-pending appeal in another action, _Boston Scientific v. Cordis,_[87b] appears to have been consolidated with that in _Fort Dodge v. Akzo Nobel_ for the purposes of the preliminary reference and **1–53**

---

[86] [1998] F.S.R. 222, CA.
[87] See para. 8–52 below for comments on anti-suit injunctions in these circumstances.
[87a] On October 27, 1997.
[87b] An appeal from a refusal of Jacob J. to grant an anti-suit injunction (October 30, 1997).

the following order was made for questions to be referred to the European Court of Justice[87c]:

"Article 177 gives to the European Court of Justice jurisdiction to give rulings upon interpretation. Questions of interpretation have arisen before us which we consider require answers to the following questions which are necessary to enable us to give judgment. We are indebted to the parties for their assistance in fomulation of these questions.

1. In the case of patents granted pursuant to European applications pursuant to the European Patent Convention, are the provisions of Article 2 and/or 64 of the European Patent Convention provisions which govern jurisdiction in relation to particular matters (ie proceedings for infringement of such patents) within the meaning of Article 57 of the Brussels Convention?

2. If the answer to quesiton 1 is 'yes'; is the effect that, notwithstanding any other provision of the Brussels Convention, proceedings for infringement of a patent granted pursuant to a European application can only be brought in the Courts of the country in which the patent is registered?

3. Where, under the national law of the State in which a patent is registered, the question of infringement of the patent depends upon the validity of the patent (so that, where validity is in issue, the questions of infringement and validity would be tried together in the Courts of the State):
    (i) do the Courts of the State in which the patent is registered have exclusive jurisdiction in respect of both questions pursuant to Articles 16(4) and/or 19 of the Brussels Convention?
    (ii) should the Courts of a State in which the patent is not registered decline jurisdiction pursuant to Article 19?

4. Does Article 24 enable a Court not otherwise having jurisdiction in a matter to grant provisional relief in circumstances where there are no proceedings seeking final relief pending or imminent before any Court having jurisdiction under the Brussels Convention as to the substance of the matter?

5. Does the fact that two patents registered in different Contracting States stem from the same European patent application provide a sufficient connection for jurisdiction to be claimed under Article 6 in respect of a person not domiciled in the State where litigation is pending against a Defendant who is so domiciled where the allegations in that litigation are:
    (i) of infringement of both patents by the domiciled person,

---

[87c] Order of December 17, 1997. The draft questions originally proposed by the Court of Appeal in their judgment of October 27, 1997 are also of interest. The court proposed three questions corresponding, except in details of wording, to questions 3, 4 and 5 as referred. Questions 1, 2 and 6 were new in December. See Karet "Suit, Anti-suit" [1998] E.I.P.R. 76.

> (ii) or infringement only of the patent in the State where litigation is pending by the domiciled person, but the non-domiciled person is alleged to infringe the other patent?
> 6. Are the answers to any of the preceding questions different (and if so, which) if the proceedings are kort geding proceedings in the Netherlands in respect of a European patent and the designated State is other than the Netherlands?"

The Dutch reaction to *Fort Dodge v. Akzo Nobel*

In the absence of any anti-suit injunction in *Fort Dodge v. Akzo Nobel*,[87d] the Dutch litigation went ahead and in December 1997 the Hague District Court rendered an interim judgment in the corresponding Dutch infringement proceedings, *Akzo Nobel v. Webster*.[87e] To summarise, the court repudiated the widespread view that it claimed to derive any extraterritorial jurisdiction from Article 24; held that Article 16(4) did not compel it to decline jurisdiction over foreign infringement claims once validity was put in issue; reasserted the view that Article 6(1) permitted the joinder of foreign defendants alleged to infringe foreign European patents corresponding to that infringed in the Netherlands; but acknowledged that even in the absence of a doctrine of *forum non conveniens* Article 6(1) did not apply where the connection between the claim against the foreign defendants and the forum was so tenuous as to the amount to an abuse of process.

1–54

The plaintiffs were the two Dutch companies, Akzo Nobel and Intervet International, and there were eight defendants of which three were domiciled in the Netherlands and the others in the United Kingdom (four) or Australia (one). The patent alleged to be infringed was a European patent for which 12 countries had been designated.[87f] As regarded jurisdiction over the British defendants, the court held that its previous interpretation of Article 6(1) was correct in principle: there was no doctrine of *forum non conveniens* under the Convention, and foreign defendants could be sued in the Netherlands for alleged infringement of corresponding European patents in other designated contracting states:

1–55

> "Akzo's claims against the Dutch defendants on the one hand and the British defendants on the other concern the same product and are based on the alleged infringement of patents, which, it is true, are subject to territorial limits but have been granted in accordance with the rules of the European Patent Convention (EPC) and, pursuant to Article 69 of said Convention, must all be interpreted in

[87d] [1998] F.S.R. 222, CA.

[87e] District Court of the Hague, December 23, 1997 (Numann, Hensen and Verduyn JJ.). Once again, I regret I do not know the ultimate source of the informal translation which is quoted from below. To conform with English usage I have substituted "Article" for "Section" in the original translation, and "Section" for "Chapter". EEX is the standard Dutch code for the Brussels Convention.

[87f] EP 0 189 958 designating Austria, Belgium, France, Germany, Greece, Italy, Liechtenstein, Luxembourg, the Netherlands, Sweden, Switzerland and the U.K.

the same manner. Although this does not necessarily mean that separate treatment and adjudication of the claims against the various groups of defendants would lead to mutually exclusive legal consequences, it would involve the risk of conflicting decisions, which might lead to the exact situation that the authors of the EEX (and of the EPC) sought to avoid. Accordingly, the court holds the view that the relationship required for applicability of EEX Article 6, subsection 1, exists between the legal claims at issue.

Webster[87g] states that, now that they have been summoned to appear in a Dutch court of law, the British defendants find themselves in a worse legal position than if they had been summoned to appear in a British court of law.

This argument—even if the assertion on which it is based is correct—does not detract from the applicability of EEX Article 6.1. Although the main rule of the EEX regulations governing competence seems to be inspired in part by the idea that it is generally more desirable for a defendant to appear in a court of law in his/her own country, the mere existence of the special competence grounds of EEX Section 2 demonstrates that the authors of the Convention recognized that there may be good reasons for departing from that main rule. EEX does not provide for the possibility of overruling the jurisdiction derived from Article 6.1 in a case where allowing such jurisdiction might worsen the defendant's legal position. After all, a decision in that sense would lead to introduction of the *forum non conveniens* principle into EEX, which was rejected by the Court of Justice.

Not being permitted to apply the *forum non conveniens* principle also involves that, in a case where the economic interests of the proceedings are concentrated in a certain country, the forum of another country is not allowed to decline to exercise jurisdiction as a *forum non conveniens*.

1–56 However, the absence of a doctrine of *forum non conveniens* was not inconsistent with the court being able to decline jurisdiction against foreign defendants when the connection of the dispute with the Netherlands was so tenuous that invocation of Article 6(1) might be considered abusive, as was the case here:

"In the opinion of the court, said forum is permitted to decline to exercise jurisdiction pursuant to EEX Article 6.1 in the event of abuse of authority. The fact that a restriction due to abuse of authority is not directly apparant from EEX Article 6.1—other than stipulated at the end of EEX Article 6.2—may be regarded as an omission. Commonly accepted principles of proper litigation dictate that, if necessary, also in the event that Article 6.1 applies, a court will follow the principle that, under certain circumstances, an appeal to a certain jurisdiction may be regarded as abuse. This is the case,

---

[87g] *sc.* all but one of the defendants.

for example, if the minimum reason required for acceptance of a special authority pursuant to EEX Article 5.3 or Article 6.1 or any of the other competence grounds stipulated in EEX Section 2 has come into being, through the agency of the plaintiff, for example by eliciting infringing activities. However, Webster does not assert that abuse of authority applies in this case.

As the court understands it, Webster considers abuse of authority in this case to be contained in the circumstance that Akzo attempts to derive jurisdiction from an infringing activity on the part of the Dutch defendants which, in absolute terms, is so important that Akzo's claim against the defendants can be allowed by a Dutch court, but which, considered in relation to the infringing activities on the part of the British defendants, is so insignificant that Akzo is not entitled to invoke it.

According to the court, such a circumstance may lead to the view that co-summoning foreign defendants constitutes abuse of authority. Akzo has not challenged the assertion that, economically, 99.6% of the alleged infringement of its patent occurs on UK territory and the remaining 0.4% in the Netherlands. Such a ratio can be deemed to be so disproportionate that Akzo should be denied the right to submit its full claim i.e. including its claims against the Dutch defendants, to a Dutch court of law.

The Court shall therefore assume jurisdiction in the principal action against the Australian defendant as well as the Dutch defendants. It shall declare itself incompetent in relation to the British defendants."

Turning to the application of Articles 16(4) and 19, the court **1–57** reconsidered whether it has jurisdiction, as against the remaining defendants, in respect of infringements of the European patent(s) outside the Netherlands. Here, the court refused to compromise its previous jurisprudence or follow *Coin Controls v. Suzo*[87h]:

"As regards the jurisdiction challenged by Webster on the basis of EEX Article 19 in conjunction with Article 16.4, the court takes the following position.

In principle, EEX does not play a role in establishing the jurisdiction of this court with respect to the Dutch and Australian defendants, as it derives its jurisdiction from the rules of internal and general international procedural law. However, the situation is different in so far as EEX Article 16 applies. Regardless of where the defendants have their registered offices, said provision is to be taken into account in, *inter alia*, situations where the registration or validity of a patent registered in a (EEX) Contracting State is at issue.

This defence is relevant, because this court is also asked to assess, in respect of said defendants, the alleged infringing activities carried out outside the Netherlands.

[87h] [1997] F.S.R. 660 (Laddie J.).

The court therefore asks itself the question of whether, if necessary, it is competent to take measures outside the Netherlands vis-a-vis the Dutch and Australian defendants, including assessment of the question of whether defendants outside the Netherlands infringe the Akzo patent, and if so, the question of whether a remedy in the form of a prohibition or damages should be provided. (. . .)[87i]

The documents submitted by Webster demonstrate the invalidity proceedings have been instituted in the United Kingdom by, among others, defendant no. 7, both as proceedings on the substance of the case and by way of provisional arrangement proceedings.

In this context, the defendants referred to the ruling of the British Patents Court, dated 26 March 1997, in the matter of *Coin Controls Limited/SUZO International (UK) Limited & co*. The court holds the view that great importance must be attached to the decisions of other European courts regarding the application of EEX— especially if it concerns an elaborately reasoned and documented decision as is the case here. Nevertheless, the court is of the opinion that a decision deviating from that handed down by the British court is called for in this case."

1–58   The court went on to postulate two solutions to the problem posed by the ambiguity of Article 19 and the expression "preliminary or incidental matter" in the Jenard Report. The first was the British solution under which the court seised of the infringement action as such had to declare itself incompetent in respect of the foreign part of the claim once validity was put in issue. The second was for the infringement court to retain jurisdiction over the infringement claim *in toto* but to stay its own proceedings if necessary pending the outcome of foreign revocation proceedings. As to the first, the Dutch court doubted if challenging validity could properly be described as a preliminary or incidental matter, but contrasted this with Jenard's express statement that claims for patent infringement were governed by the general law of the Convention. It admitted that the second solution was open to the objection that a stay of the infringement proceedings would create delay and lead to an undesirable multiplicity of proceedings, although the latter objection applied *a fortiori* to the solution of *Coin Controls v. Suzo.*

"This objection also applies (if not even more so) to the first solution referred to in ground number 11.2: there, too, a dispute is first brought before the court of the country where the patent is infringed whereupon—following the defence—the concomitant costs turn out to have been a waste and that new proceedings must be instituted in the countries where the patent has been registered. Another objection to this first solution is that it tempts defendants

---

[87i] A paragraph relating to the application of unmodified Dutch private international law is omitted.

to conduct invalidity defences for the sole purpose of nullifying the jurisdiction of an initially competent court, thus forcing the patentee to incur extra costs as it will often be necessary for the patentee to institute proceedings in more than once country. In this way, the *Coin Controls* principle prevents patent disputes from being tried in the rapid and affordable manner that is commonly deemed to be more expedient.

Another advantage of the second solution is that, in a number of cases, the judgement will be that—even if the patent is valid—there has been no infringement. In such cases, the proceedings can be decided locally without (if invalidity has only been invoked by way of defence) any invalidity proceedings having to be instituted and in any event without having to wait for them. Moreover, it should not be forgotten that, as an exception to the main rule, EEX Article 16.4 should be interpreted in a restrictive rather than an extensive sense. Cf. the ruling of the Court of Justice of 15 November 1983 in the matter of *Duijnstee/Goderbauer* (case number 288/82), Netherlands Case Law 1984, 695, which did not even address the issue of patent validity."

The Dutch court therefore considered that the solution of *Coin* **1–59** *Controls v. Suzo* was undesirable in its practical implications and was only to be adopted if actually compelled by the terms of the Brussels Convention, which was not the case. A comparison with German practice and the practice of the Dutch courts in proceedings for interim injunctions showed that justice could be done by the infringement court assessing the prospect of the invalidity defence succeeding and staying the infringement proceedings if appropriate. The infringement proceedings would therefore be allowed to proceed against the Dutch and Australian defendants, subject to final judgment not being given until the relevant foreign courts had ruled on validity.

Finally, the court denied that it derived any relevant extraterritorial **1–60** jurisdiction from Article 24 of the Brussels Convention. Article 24 applied to provisional remedies against a foreign-domiciled defendant, but not to provisional measures intended to have extraterritorial effect. So far as the Dutch and Australian defendants were concerned, Article 24 was irrelevant. Article 16(4) did not prevent the grant of provisional relief because the Dutch court did not propose to deliver any final judgment on the validity of any foreign patent.

"In so far as the claim has been filed by way of provisional arrangement as referred to in Article 51 of the Netherlands Code of Civil Procedure, it can be regarded as a preliminary measure as referred to in EEX Article 24. The jurisdiction that is exclusively based on Article 24 provides for a jurisdiction that is limited to measures in the Contracting State of the court applied to.

In relation to the Australian and Dutch defendants, the jurisdiction of this court is not based on EEX Article 24, which means that the limitation described in the previous ground can be left out of consideration.

39

If (also) applied to as a court for provisional arrangements, the Dutch court can in principle also derive jurisdiction from EEX Article 24 for the British defendants. However, the provisional measures claimed vis-a-vis these defendants will have to take effect in the United Kingdom, i.e. outside the Netherlands. Accordingly, this court will declare that it has no jurisdiction in respect of the claims filed against the British defendants.

This court has jurisdiction in respect of the remaining defendants. EEX Article 16.4 does not impede this jurisdiction, because a provisional arrangement, by its nature, involves that the court will not give final judgment on the validity of the patent if this quesiton arises as a preliminary question."

On the merits, the court held that there was inadequate evidence of infringement and proposed to refer questions to an independent expert.

The prospects for a resolution by the European Court of Justice

1–61   At first sight, the questions put to the European Court of Justice in *Fort Dodge v. Akzo Nobel; Boston Scientific v. Cordis*[88] ought to answer all of the outstanding issues between the Dutch and English courts on the application of the Brussels Convention to intellectual property infringement actions. Unfortunately there is some reason for caution in hoping that the reference will resolve these issues once and for all, quite apart from the unavoidable possibility of the parties in one or both referred cases settling their differences before the preliminary reference is decided. The actual outcome of the Dutch proceedings in *Akzo Noble v. Webster*[89] now means, subject to any appeal, that the United Kingdom defendants achieved almost as much in the Netherlands as they had hoped for in England.[90]

1–62   The further possibility—at least in relation to *Fort Dodge v. Akzo Nobel*—is that the Court of Appeal may have referred these questions in such circumstances that the European Court of Justice would be entitled to decline to answer them. Though the Court of Appeal has undoubtedly asked questions which urgently need to be answered in the abstract, those questions arguably did not need to be answered by the Court of Justice in order for the application for the anti-suit injunctions as such to be decided on a permanent as well as an interlocutory basis. Whilst the Court of Appeal could not have anticipated what would happen in the Netherlands, two points were always obvious. One was that the competence of the Court of Appeal to make a preliminary reference crucially

[88] [1998] F.S.R. 222, CA.
[89] District Court of the Hague, December 23, 1997 (Numann, Hensen and Verduyn JJ.). See above, para. 1–54.
[90] The case against the four U.K. defendants was struck out; the remaining defendants (three Dutch, one Australian) might still object to the extraterritorial assertion of jurisdiction over their acts (if any) outside the Netherlands but the Dutch court proposed not to deliver any final judgment until validity had been determined in the revocation petition, and no interlocutory relief was ordered.

depended on the claim to a final anti-suit injunction, since it had independently decided not to grant an interlocutory one. The other was that the claim to a final anti-suit injunction would depend not only on the outcome of the preliminary reference, but also on the assumption that when the ruling of the Court came back, there would still be Dutch proceedings to enjoin and a reason for enjoining them. What might be suggested against the course followed by Court of Appeal is that it made the reference not for its own benefit in the instant case, but so that the Dutch courts might be told how to apply the Brussels Convention in cases yet to come.

Alternatively, the Court might hold that anti-suit injunctions are inherently incompatible with the Brussels Convention,[91] and that the application for the injunctions ought to have been dismissed for reasons which do not depend on the validity of the conflicting interpretations given to Articles 6(1), 16(4), 19 and 24; still less on the relevance of Articles 2 and 64 of the European Patent Convention.

It is perhaps too much to hope that an equally wide-ranging preliminary reference as compared to that in *Fort Dodge v. Akzo Nobel* is likely to be made by the Dutch courts themselves in the near future. References have previously been ordered in *kort geding* infringement proceedings by the Dutch Supreme Court, the *Hoge Raad*, but have been abortive because the underlying litigation settled.[92] As for the Hague Court of Appeal,[93] which has a discretion to make a reference, it would not be surprising if it took the view that speed was the essence of *kort geding* proceedings and that it would not be fair to either party to delay its own judgment for the 18 months or more likely to be taken for the European Court of Justice to give a ruling. Of course, since what is in contemplation is a *preliminary* reference, the Hague Court of Appeal could not simply grant or refuse the *kort geding* relief and ask the European Court of Justice to rule subsequently on its consistency with the Brussels Convention. **1–63**

Apart from *Fort Dodge v. Akzo Nobel*, a number of cases now pending before the European Court of Justice may clarify the operation of Article 24 in the general law, and especially how it applies to *kort geding* proceedings. At first sight *Van Uden Africa Line v. Deco Line*[94] on a reference from the *Hoge Raad* is most promising, as raising the question of how Article 24 applies to a provisional award of damages in a contract case against a defendant domiciled in Germany. Unfortunately, the Article 24 issue is complicated by the presence of an arbitration clause in the underlying agreement, and the possibility that the Dutch courts had **1–64**

---

[91] Questions regarding anti-suit injunctions to restrain foreign proceedings brought in breach of an arbitration clause have been referred to the Court in *Alfred C. Toepfer v. Cargill* (November 25, 1997, CA) but the terms of reference are confined to the relevance of Arts 1(4) and 21.

[92] The *Hoge Raad*, as a court of last resort, is obliged to make a preliminary reference unless the law is *acte clair*, and has always been conscientious in doing so.

[93] First instance courts cannot make references for preliminary rulings under the Brussels Convention.

[94] Case C–391/95, pending.

general jurisdiction anyway under Article 5(1).[95] *Hermes v. FHT Marketing*[96] on a reference from the District Court of Amsterdam raises the question of the direct applicability to provisional measures of Article 50 of TRIPs.[97] *Mietz v. Intership Yachting*[98] on a reference from the German Supreme Court is less directly relevant but may provide an opportunity for the Court to reformulate the law under Article 24. None of these cases is relevant to practice under Article 16(4).[99]

The case for an advisory reference under Article 4 of the 1971 Protocol

1–65   Finally, in the context of references to the European Court of Justice, Article 4 of the 1971 Protocol on Interpretation of the Brussels Convention may be mentioned. That Article provides:

1. The competent authority of a Contracting State may request the Court of Justice to give a ruling on a question of interpretation of the Convention or of one of the other instruments referred to in Article 1 if judgments given by courts of that State conflict with the interpretation given either by the Court of Justice or in a judgment of one of the courts of another Contracting State referred to in point 1 or 2 of Article 2. The provisions of this paragraph shall apply only to judgments which have become *res judicata*.
2. The interpretation given by the Court of Justice in response to such a request shall not affect the judgments which gave rise to the request for interpretation.
    [. . .]

1–66   In contrast to Article 177 E.C. and Article 3 of the 1971 Protocol, what Article 4 contemplates is that a reference may be made although the proceedings to which it would be relevant are no longer pending in the national court. On the contrary, it is actually necessary for there to be a judgment which has become *res judicata*, and the opportunity for an Article 4 reference might arise either because no appeal from that judgment was made, or because any appeal settled. Article 4 quite expressly contemplates a reference which is not a preliminary one, but

---

[95] See the report of the reference by the *Hoge Raad* [1996] I.L.Pr. 269.

[96] Case C–53/96, pending. See [1996] O.J. C95/14 for the questions referred by the District Court.

[97] In particular, whether *kort geding* proceedings are within Art. 50(1) of TRIPs and whether Art. 50(6) of TRIPs has direct effect so as to require proceedings on the merits to be commenced within a reasonable period, which hardly ever happens with *kort geding*. See para. 3–37. The provisional view of the Amsterdam District Court (contrary to the prevailing Dutch opinion) was that Art. 50 probably was directly effective. *Contra* Jacob J. (in the context of Art. 32 of TRIPs) in *Lenzing's European Patent* [1997] R.P.C. 245.

[98] Case C–99/96, pending.

[99] At the time of going to press, Opinions had been delivered by the Advocate-General (Léger A.-G. in both cases) on June 10, 1997 in Case 391/95 *Van Uden v. Deco-Line* and on October 8, 1997 in Case 99/96 *Mietz v. Intership Yachting*.

which raises questions which need to be answered by the Court because of their wider importance and the existence of divergent national decisions. The Jenard Report[1] comments:

"Article 4 lays down a new procedure based in part on the *pourvoi dans l'interet de la loi*' and in part on the procedure for giving advisory opinions. All the countries of the Community, with the exception of the Federal Republic of Germany, have a form of appeal for the clarification of a point of law which enables the competent judicial authority, in this instance the Procurators-General of the Courts of Cassation, to appeal against a final decision which misunderstands or misapplies either the letter or the spirit of the law. The purpose of this appeal is to avoid perpetuating an erroneous interpretation of the law where the parties have omitted to appeal against the decision which includes that interpretation . . .

Article 4 is designed to make for a uniform interpretation of the Convention by introducing a procedure complementary to the request for a preliminary ruling provided for in Article 3. The purpose is to ensure a uniform interpretation for the future wherever existing judgments are in conflict.

In the last analysis, this procedure occupies an intermediate position between the *pourvoi dans l'interet de la loi*', from which it differs in that it does not entail the setting aside of a judgment which is ultimately shown to have misinterpreted the Convention, and that of an advisory appeal. The procedure is, however, limited to cases in which a court has already given judgment.

Paragraph 1 defines the cases in which the competent authority of a State may apply to the Court of Justice. It will be for that authority to decide whether it is advisable to refer a matter to the Court, and it will presumably not do so unless the national judgment includes reasons which might lead to an interpretation different from that previously given by the Court of Justice or by a foreign court. If there are no factors involved which make it likely that the principles established in the decided cases would be changed, the national authority could always seek to clarify the point of law by appealing in its own country in accordance with the procedure there in force.

[. . .]

It may be wondered what are the implications of a ruling on interpretation given on the basis of Article 4. The ruling certainly is not binding on the parties. It must be acknowledged that such a ruling has no force in law, and that accordingly nobody is bound by it. But clearly it will have the greatest persuasive authority and will for the future constitute the guideline for all Community courts. In this respect it may be compared with the decision on a *pourvoi dans*

---

[1] The Report on the 1971 Protocol, prior to the accession of the U.K.

l'interet de la loi'. Such a decision is binding on nobody, but constitutes a decision of principle of the greatest importance for the future, and one which judges will generally follow."

1–67   It can hardly be doubted that there is a serious conflict between existing judgments of the English courts on the application of Article 16(4) to intellectual property infringement actions, and the jurisprudence of the Dutch courts; and in particular with several decisions of the Hague Court of Appeals which is a court referred to in Article 2(2) of the Protocol. That conflict is more than likely to be repeated in any future English cases. The procedure under Article 4 of the 1971 Protocol has never yet been applied in practice, but if the litigation in *Fort Dodge v. Akzo Nobel* should settle without the preliminary reference in that case being decided, then invocation of Article 4 would deserve serious consideration as an alternative means of obtaining a binding interpretation of at least Article 16(4).

Reform of the Brussels Convention in prospect

1–68   The other means by which differences in the interpretation of Article 16(4) might be resolved is by amendments to clarify or reform the Brussels Convention itself. An Intergovernmental Conference will begin in 1998 (initially under the British Presidency of the European Union) to decide whether amendments to the Brussels and Lugano Conventions are desirable on the thirtieth anniversary of the former. A Consultation Paper[2] issued by the Lord Chancellor's Department in April 1997 mentioned in passing the uncertainty surrounding the interpretation of Article 16(4),[3] but had the misfortune to have been written shortly before the decisions of Lloyd J. in *Pearce v. Ove Arup*[4] and Laddie J. in *Coin Controls v. Suzo*.[5] For whatever reason, no comments on Article 16(4) were specifically invited and the consultation period expired well before the decisions of Laddie J. and the Court of Appeal in *Fort Dodge v. Akzo Nobel*[6] brought home the differences between the Dutch and English courts in the interpretation of Article 16(4). At the time of writing, it is believed that no proposals to amend Article 16(4) have been tabled by any delegation to the 1998 Conference and that the Conference would be reluctant to discuss proposals while the reference in *Fort Dodge v. Akzo Nobel* was pending, although the situation may change as the Conference progresses.

Other provisions of wider relevance are certain to be addressed by the Conference and may result in the Conventions being amended, though the process is likely to be slow. Those of particular relevance to intellectual property include the application of Articles 5(3), 6(1), 21, 22 and 24.

---

[2] *The Operation of the Brussels and Lugano Conventions.*
[3] Para. 81 of the Consultation Paper.
[4] [1997] F.S.R. 641 (Lloyd J.).
[5] [1997] F.S.R. 660 (Laddie J.).
[6] [1998] F.S.R. 222, CA.

Community intellectual property rights and the Green Paper on patent litigation

At the time of writing, the Community Trade Mark Regulation is in **1–69** force and applications are being lodged at the Office in Alicante at a rate far in excess of what was predicted. The Community Plant Variety Regulation is also in force, and the Community Design Regulation is all but final. Litigation to enforce these Community intellectual property rights is an imminent prospect. However, it is in the field of patents that the first proposals for Community-wide registered intellectual property rights were made and the Community Patent Convention has existed in one form or another since 1975, though without being brought into force.[7] A Green Paper[8] by the E.C. Commission published for consultation in June 1997 makes radical new proposals for implementing the Community patent and for further harmonisation of patent law.

The central feature of the Green Paper is the intention to replace the **1–70** Community Patent Convention with a Regulation which could be enacted as normal Community secondary legislation under Article 235 E.C. and which would not require a separate international treaty.[9] This course is now felt to be justified by the decision of the European Court of Justice in *Spain v. Council (Supplementary Protection Certificates)*[10] and its Opinion on the WTO and TRIPs.[11] It would circumvent many of the problems of ratification and perpetual re-negotiation which have bedevilled the Community Patent Convention as such. Some consequential amendments to the European Patent Convention would be necessary, but might be expected to present fewer problems in comparison.[12] However, the Green Paper acknowledges or assumes that no new Community court could be created by the proposed Regulation.[13] The major institutional innovation of the Regulation approach is therefore that it calls for the abandonment of a central Community patent appeal court in the form of COPAC. The Court of First Instance would take over some of the functions of COPAC in that it would hear appeals from Revocation Boards in the European Patent Office, but the manner in which the Court of First Instance is constituted under Article 168a E.C. means that there could be no provision for appeals or references to it from Community patent courts in member states.

Absent a central second instance court corresponding to COPAC, the **1–71** Green Paper proposes two options.[14] The first would be to revert quite

---

[7] See Chap. 4.

[8] *Green Paper on the Community Patent and the Patent System in Europe*, COM(97) 314 final, dated June 24, 1997.

[9] *ibid.*, para. 3.2.

[10] Case C–350/92 [1995] E.C.R. I–1985.

[11] Opinion 1/94 [1994] E.C.R. I–5267. See para. 4–31.

[12] The European Patent Convention, Pt IX, contemplates arrangements for the grant of unitary patents and was drafted with the Community Patent Convention in mind. However, it may be doubted if a Regulation constitutes an "agreement" for the purposes of EPC, Art. 142.

[13] *ibid.*, para. 3.4.

[14] *ibid.*, para, 3.4.

closely to the scheme of the 1975 Community Patent Convention under which national courts would have no effective jurisdiction over the validity of Community patents, which would always be within the exclusive jurisdiction of new Revocation Divisions to be established in the European Patent Office. National courts would hear infringement actions, actions for declarations of non-infringement and actions for pre-grant compensation, and although a defendant wishing to challenge validity would have to counterclaim in the national court, the ruling on validity would actually be made by the European Patent Office, pending which the infringement action would be stayed if the national court considered that the revocation proceedings raised serious grounds of invalidity. Appeals from the Revocation Divisions would lie to the Court of First Instance (not to the existing Boards of Appeal of the EPO) with a limited further appeal to the European Court of Justice on points of law. Revocation or amendment would have effect in all member states.

1–72   The other proposed solution would be for the courts of member states hearing actions for infringement to have jurisdiction to entertain counterclaims for revocation and rule on invalidity, but only with effect for their own territory.[15] Jurisdiction over invalidity might be extended to the whole of the Community, but only if the national court had pan-European infringement jurisdiction, thereby introducing a degree of symmetry between the relief available to the plaintiff on the claim and the risk of invalidation on the counterclaim. Under this option, there would be the possibility of a Community patent being valid in some member states, but not in others, potentially causing it to lose much of its character as a unitary Community intellectual property right.

1–73   The Green paper also makes suggestions to alleviate the problem of translations into all the Community's official languages, for fees, for links between the European Patent Convention and the Community patent, and for various as yet unharmonised issues of substantive patent law such as rights of prior use or personal possession, the patentability of computer software and the rights of employee-inventors. It does not otherwise propose changes to the substantive law of the Community patent or the procedure for litigation,[16] except in so far as necessitated by the various options for dealing with invalidity.

1–74   Although the Green Paper presents the reversal of the 1985 amendments to the Community Patent Convention as a virtue, increasing legal certainty and removing opportunities for delay, yet one wonders if this is no more than an attempt to put on a brave front in the face of the inevitable. Given the perceived constitutional impossibility of creating

---

[15] The Green Paper wrongly describes this option as corresponding more closely to the architecture of the original 1975 Community Patent Convention. In fact, it corresponds only to Art. 90 of the latter which was a last-minute compromise procured by the U.K. delegation. Art. 90 was applicable only to contracting states entering a reservation, was of restricted effect, and was intended to phase out after a maximum period of 15 years. It is the first of the Green Paper proposals—strict bifurcation of infringement and validity—which corresponds more closely to the architecture of the 1975 Convention.

[16] Although the Green Paper criticises Art. 34 of the Protocol on Litigation, without proposing how it would improve the treatment of co-pending proceedings.

COPAC by Regulation, and the political improbability of bringing the Community Patent Convention as such into force in the foreseeable future, there must be a temptation to present the only remaining options as something better than two variations on Hobson's Choice. It is true that entrusting the validity of a Community patent in its entirety to a national first instance court is distinctly unattractive to patentees,[17] and would be doubly unattractive without COPAC being there to provide redress, but the problem is at least partly due to the previous failure to restrict the number of Community patent courts to those with genuine and acknowledged expertise in patent litigation. The Commission is also seriously out of touch if it considers that the European Patent Office deals quickly or efficiently with oppositions or that its decisions enjoy universal respect.

The Green Paper also noticeably fails to strike a balance between the **1–75** legitimate interests of plaintiffs and defendants: the latter are not invariably pirates or even infringers, and an over-zealous system of patent enforcement (as sometimes in the United States at the present time) is probably as much a source of competitive disadvantage as one which is too weak. The present author's personal view is that the 1985 amendments to the Community Patent Convention were desirable and that any reversion to the scheme of the 1975 Convention would be a retrograde step, to be contemplated only if there is no alternative way of bringing the Community patent into being. Litigation will not be simplified and will certainly not be accelerated if every major patent action involves infringement proceedings as such in at least one national court, which will probably be stayed pending determination of validity elsewhere, national appeals on the issue of infringement, revocation proceedings at the European Patent Office in Munich, and an almost inevitable appeal from the latter to the Court of First Instance in Luxembourg with the final possibility of a further appeal to the European Court of Justice itself.[18] Nor does the Green Paper address the likelihood of radically different approaches to issues of infringement persisting in the 15 different member states, or the potentially significant problem of the national trial court (or national court of appeal) and the European Patent Office or the Court of First Instance giving inconsistent interpretations to the patent in the respective contexts of infringement and invalidity.

In the last resort, the proposed Community Patent Regulation may be **1–76** an example of too little, too late. It has always been a feature of the Community Patent that it has been driven by political considerations, with too little concern for the interests of users. A hearsay summary of the likely effect of the Convention given by one representative of an

---

[17] The present author has compared the odds unfavourably to Russian roulette: Wadlow, "Enforcing Community Patents" [1990/91] December/January *Patent World* 36.

[18] That would not exhaust the opportunities to take points to the European Court of Justice, since the latter would have jurisdiction to hear preliminary references under Art. 177 E.C. even from first instance courts, on any aspect of the law of the Regulation.

unidentified multinational company was recounted by Dr Stephen Stewart in his evidence to the House of Lords in 1986[19]:

> " 'My patent'—they are very possessive—'will be attacked by some infringer in Palermo or Oporto and I will have to go down to Palermo or Oporto to defend it. I will appear before a judge in his 20's, sitting in his shirt sleeves, who, after a hearing of a quarter of an hour, will tell me my patent is invalid in a language I cannot understand.' "

1–77   The Green Paper recognises this and other problems, but national vested interests may not, and in the past it is the national interests which have prevailed. In particular, unless the problem of mandatory translations into every Community language can be resolved it is highly unlikely that Community patent filings will gather the critical mass necessary to make the system viable. The problem is not just one of cost, though that is important, but also of the logistics and practicality of getting complicated specifications in new technologies reliably and promptly translated into the more obscure Community languages when the supply of expert technical translators is necessarily limited. Widespread adoption of the Community patent would itself make these problems worse.[20] As for the advantages of Community-wide enforcement, the present likelihood is that whatever system any Regulation eventually enacts will have to compete with pan-European enforcement of national or European patents in national courts under the Brussels Convention.[21] It is not impossible that the best hope for the Community patent is that patent litigation under the Brussels Convention will either be stifled (if the English view prevails) or will degenerate into such a free-for-all that industry will welcome even a flawed Community Patent Regulation.

Further proposals for patent litigation reform in Europe: a Community Patent Circuit Court

1–78   The Community Green Paper is by no means the only proposal for reform of patent law and litigation in Europe.[22] Suggestions have been made by individuals, professional bodies, interest groups and other European institutions for reform of the operation of the European Patent Convention[23] and even for its incorporation into the Community

---

[19] Report of the House of Lords Select Committee on the European Communities: *A European Community Patent* (1986), evidence, p. 54.

[20] As if this were not enough, five Eastern European states (Poland, the Czech Republic, Hungary, Slovenia and Estonia), each with its own language, are likely to join the E.C. at about the same time as any Community Patent Regulation comes into force.

[21] This assumes that the Dutch courts, rather than the English, are closer to the correct interpretation of Art. 16(4) of the Brussels Convention.

[22] For an overview and further specific proposals see Straus, *The Present State of the Patent System in the European Union* (1997).

[23] Braendli, "The Dynamism of the European Patent System" (1991) 22 I.I.C. 177; The EPO Working Paper *Charting a Course* (1993); Braendli, "The Future of the European Patent System (1995) 26 I.I.C. 818; Jacob, "The Enlarged Board of Appeal of the EPO: A Proposal" [1997] E.I.P.R. 224.

legal order[24]; for better co-operation between national courts in infringement proceedings and for harmonisation of the law of civil procedure[25]; as well as a variety of proposals as to how the Community patent should be taken forward. A very provisional and subjective view of responses to the Green Paper is that there is considerable enthusiasm for the Community patent, if the problem of translation costs can be overcome, but that there is little or no support for bifurcating jurisdiction between infringement and validity or for increasing the jurisdiction of the European Patent Office. That leaves the problem of validity either being entrusted *in toto* to first instance courts with no genuine expertise in patent litigation, or to various solutions which all compromise the unitarty character of the Community patent according to whether, where and in what circumstances its validity may be put in issue.

One proposal which would avoid these problems is for a true   **1–79** Community patent court of first instance which would hear actions for infringement and counterclaims for revocation of Community patents on a pan-European basis:[26]

> "Aimed at securing harmonized interpretation of the EPC and CPC throughtout the EU and throughout all judicial instances, the concept of the 'Community Patent Courts' of first instance under the Protocol on Litigation should be reexamined and efforts undertaken to construe[27] this court as a central 'Community Patent Court' of first instance, having branches in all or some Member States. The composition of said court should be European, i.e. constituted of judges from several Member States.[28] Legal means should also be sought in order to ensure an expeditious procedure through all instances under the Litigation Protocol."

[24] Bossung, "The Return of European Patent Law to the European Union" (1996) 27 I.I.C. 287; Armitage "EU Industrial Property Policy: Priority for Patents" [1996] E.I.P.R. 555; Willems, "The EPC: The Emperor's Phantom Clothes?" (Stephen Stewart Lecture, November 20, 1997, to be published in [1998] I.P.Q. No. 1). The latter's avowed intent was "to bury the EPC, not to praise it." *Contra* van Benthem, "The European Patent System and European Integration" (1993) 24 I.I.C. 435.

[25] Brinkhof, "The Desirability, Necessity and Feasibility of Co-operation between Courts in the Field of European Patent Law" [1997] E.I.P.R. 226, reprinted from *The Law and Practice of the Enlarged Boards of Appeal of the EPO during its First Ten Years* (1996): Ryberg, "Procedural Law for Patent Litigation" (1997) 28 I.I.C. 904.

[26] Straus, *op. cit.* For a related proposal see Brinkhof, *op. cit.*, drawing on a suggestion for an EPC two-tier European Patent Court originally made in Brinkhof, "The Extent of Protection Conferred by European Patents—Problems and Suggestions" (1990) 21 I.I.C. 488. Franzosi, "A European Patent Court?" (letter) [1997] E.I.P.R. 550 questions the compatibility with the Brussels Convention of such a court having jurisdiction over national (including European) patents and proposes an essentially advisory body. The rest of the present paragraph assumes that the jurisdiction of the new court would (initially) be confined to Community patents; but any provision of the Brussels Convention, even Art. 16(4), can be overridden by Community harmonising legislation: Art. 57(3).

[27] *sc.* constitute.

[28] Footnote to the text quoted reads "Under this suggestion 'branches' of the Central 'Community Patent Court' of First Instance, are not to be necessarily understood as permanent institutions but could be conceived as circuit courts, composed always of at least one member whose nationality would be of the state in which the Court would meet, hence, as a rule, the state of the residence of the defendant."

1–80   This proposal would take the reform made by the 1985/9 Protocol on Litigation further by one logical step, providing for a Community court to have jurisdiction at trial as well as at second instance level. Whilst the trial court in contemplation would be a new and independent Community institution, it is expected that it would be staffed by suitably experienced judges from the member states and that it would sit in as many centres as might be needed.[29]

1–81   A further advantage of the proposal is that confidence in the legal and technical ability of its judiciary would make it that much less necessary for any second instance Community court to reconsider in detail every matter of fact and law decided by the first instance court as is contemplated for COPAC.[30] This would not only make second instance procedure faster, simpler and cheaper; but it would also mean that the second instance court could perform its functions without having to consist of full-time specialists in patent law—as is the case already for the English Court of Appeal and every national court of final instance in patent matters. It could also have a predominantly written procedure without undue prejudice to litigants, which would minimise the inconvenience and cost arising if it sat in only one place. These considerations would open the way for suitably qualified chambers of the Court of First Instance to act as the second tier court to the Community Patent Circuit Court.

1–82   Paradoxically perhaps, a true community patent court of first instance might be easier to constitute as a Community institution under Article 235 E.C.[31] than would be the case for COPAC. The problems with creating COPAC by Regulation are, potentially, twofold: there is the underlying question of whether either of Articles 100a or 235 E.C. empowers the Community to create a judicial—as opposed to an administrative—institution with an independent legal personality as part of the Community legal order. That question, to which no certain answer can yet be given, applies equally to a first instance court. However the second and more fundamental objection to establishing COPAC by Regulation lies in the precedent established with the Court of First Instance itself. Not only was that court constituted by amendment to the E.C. Treaty and without independent legal status,[32] but a deliberate

---

[29] The proposed court should not be confused with the "Community patent courts" of first and second instance in the Protocol on Litigation to the Community Patent Convention, since these are existing national courts. Nor should it be confused with the Court of First Instance established under Art. 168a E.C., which in fact if not in name principally serves as a second tier court hearing appeals (called "actions for annulment") from Community institutions.

[30] The Common Appeal Court or Community Patents Appeal Court intended to be established under the Protocol on Litigation to the Community Patent Convention.

[31] Or, more controversially, Art. 100a. There is much to be said for aiming for unanimity. So far as litigation of national and European patents is concerned, Art. K.1 (6) T.E.U. (the Maastricht Treaty) now provides a Community vehicle for "judicial cooperation in civil matters" which improves on Art. 220 E.C.

[32] The Court of First Instance is "attached to the Court of Justice." It was established pursuant to Art. 168a E.C., which was originally inserted into the E.C. Treaty by the Single European Act and subsequently amended by the T.E.U.

decision was taken not to confer on it any power to entertain preliminary references from the courts of member states.[33] Any attempt by the Commission or the Council to create by Regulation a second tier court to which appeals from courts in member states would be referred would probably be regarded by the European Court of Justice as an unacceptable erosion of its own jurisdiction, and the Court would have the last word on the compatibility of any Regulation with the Community legal order. Conversely, if the Community patent were implemented by Regulation rather than separate treaty then national first and second instance courts in their capacity as Community patent courts could not be deprived of the right to make a request for a preliminary ruling to the European Court of Justice on any aspect of the law of the Regulation, with fatal effects on the scheme of the Protocol on Litigation.[34]

These objections apply with much less force to a Community Patent **1–83** Circuit Court of first instance. If an appeal lay of right from the latter to the Court of First Instance, and on points of law from the Court of First Instance to the European Court of Justice, then no existing judicial institution of the Community would have its position in the Community legal order undermined and the best use would be made of existing institutions.[35] The latter consideration, if no other, militates against conferring true first instance jurisdiction on the Court of First Instance since that would have the effect of swamping that court with an excessive volume of highly complex technical litigation, and the Court of Justice with an excessive volume of appeals. In its 1991 Discussion Paper *Reflections on the Future Development of the Community Judicial System*[36] the Court of First Instance proposed the following arrangements which would be quite similar in many respects to those now under consideration if one substituted the Court of First Instance for COPAC:

"It is therefore worth considering, so far as both trade-marks and patents are concerned, whether this technical litigation might not be resolved within the framework of a four-tier structure: an administrative office; national or Community courts of first instance; a Community court of appellate jurisdiction (such as COPAC) acting to the greatest possible extent as a filter; and lastly, review by the Community court confined strictly to the most important questions of law and possibly coupled with machinery for a fresh filtering of

---

[33] Art. 168a E.C. excludes the Court of First Instance from hearing "questions referred for a preliminary ruling under Article 177." This is presumably dictated by Opinion 1/76 [1977] E.C.R. 741. Technically, it might not preclude it from hearing preliminary references in other circumstances, but the latter might be regarded by the Court of Justice as the thin end of an unacceptable wedge.

[34] Case *127/73 BTR–SABAM* [1974] E.C.R. 51; [1974] 2 C.M.L.R. 269.

[35] There ought to be no objection to not conferring on the Community Patent Circuit Court jurisdiction to make preliminary references under Art. 177 E.C., because it would not be a "court or tribunal of a member state" and because the European Court of Justice would exercise ultimate appellate jurisdiction over it so as to remain the final arbiter of Community law.

[36] (1991) 16 E.L. Rev. 175.

actions at this last stage. It does seem to be essential to deflect away from the Court of Justice or the Court of First Instance an excessive volume of business of this type which would fetter the capacity of the non-specialised Community courts to deal with cases."

1–84   Under the proposal for a Community Patent Circuit Court, the Court of First Instance might become an intermediate court of appeal from any and all specialist Community first instance intellectual property court(s), and it would have the opportunity to recruit patent specialists and appoint specialist chambers which in due course might exercise an extended appellate jurisdiction over the European Patent Office as well as over OHIM.[37] The Community Trade Mark Regulation—which received approval from the Court in *Spain v. Council (supplementary protection certificates)*[38] already provides an example of judicial or quasi-judicial institutions—in the form of OHIM's Boards of Appeal[39]—being created by Regulation and made subject to the appellate jurisdiction of the Court of First Instance. There is no problem of principle in the Court of First Instance hearing appeals by way of action for annulment from a Community institution, since—staff cases aside—that is its main day-to-day function. All that would be needed to that effect would be a resolution of the Council pursuant to Article 168a(2) E.C. and suitable amendments to the rules of procedure of the Court of First Instance.

1–85   Whilst the present work is principally concerned with existing law—or at least with existing legal texts—rather than with suggestions for future legislation, this is one proposal which could have major and beneficial implications both to implementation of the Community Patent Convention and eventually for the regime for litigation of national and European patents under the Brussels Convention.

---

[37] The Community Trade Mark and Designs Office, *sub nom.* the "Office for the Harmonisation of the Internal Market."

[38] Case 350/92 [1995] E.C.R. I–1985; [1996] 1 C.M.L.R. 415. If Case T–159/97R *Ferrao v. OHIM* [1997] E.T.M.R. 439 goes beyond the refusal of provisional relief, it may cast further light on the judicial status of the Boards of Appeal of OHIM. Compare the decision of Jacob J. in *Lenzing's European Patent* [1997] R.P.C. 245 holding, in effect, that the Boards of Appeal of the EPO are judicial bodies: Cook "Judicial Review of the EPO and the Direct Effect of TRIPs in the European Community" [1997] E.I.P.R. 367.

[39] Confirmation that the Boards of Appeal of OHIM are judicial institutions may be found in the rearguard action fought by the Government of Luxembourg to have OHIM in its entirety based in Luxembourg, pursuant to the 1965 Merger Treaty (the Decision of the Representatives of the Governments of the Member States on the Provisional Location of Certain Institutions and Departments of the Communities, Art. 3). An abortive compromise proposal was for the Boards of Appeal to be based in Luxembourg, and the rest of OHIM in Spain. See Elzaburu and Baz, "The Registration Procedure" in Franzosi, ed., *European Community Trade Mark* (1997), p. 360.

INTELLECTUAL PROPERTY RIGHTS AND THE BRUSSELS CONVENTION: THE GENERAL LAW

A. INTRODUCTION

Coverage of this chapter

2–01   The Convention on Jurisdiction and the Enforcement of Judgments in Civil and Commercial Matters 1968 (the Brussels Convention) governs questions of jurisdiction in disputes with an international element where there are certain specified connecting factors between the parties to the dispute or its subject matter and one or more of the contracting states to the Convention.[1] Where there are no such connecting factors, domestic law continues to apply.[2]

To give a complete account of the operation of the Convention would require a whole book devoted to the subject.[3] The present chapter is principally concerned with the provisions of the Convention which would be relevant to the conduct of an action for infringement of an intellectual property right in the courts of a contracting state, when the right sought to be enforced is one existing under the laws of one of the other contracting states to the Convention. It deals principally with sources of law which are of general and undisputed application: the Brussels Convention itself, the Jenard and Schlosser reports[4] and decisions of the European Court of Justice. Unfortunately, the application of these sources to intellectual property actions is anything but straightforward or uncontroversial and they are silent or inconclusive precisely where help with interpretation is most needed in practice. For this reason, the provisions of the Convention dealt with here include not only those which are likely to arise directly in the course of such an infringement action; but also some which are necessary to understanding the general scheme of the Convention or which are helpful, perhaps by analogy, in interpreting the provisions directly relevant to intellectual property. For convenience—and because it is an illustration of the action of Article 57(1) of the Brussels Convention—the present chapter also deals with

---

[1] All 15 E.C. states have signed the Brussels Convention, including the United Kingdom. The Convention is amended from time to time by Accession Conventions and this affects the precise text in force. The text of the Convention (as amended by the 1978 Accession Convention) is printed at [1978] O.J. L304/77 and as Sched. 1 to the Civil Jurisdiction and Judgments Act 1982. As amended by the San Sebastian Convention it is printed at [1990] O.J. C189/2. The Convention is also set out in *Butterworths' Jurisdiction, Foreign Judgments and Awards Handbook* (1994) and in most of the specialist works cited below. Updated dates of ratification and entry into force are published monthly in *International Litigation Procedure*. At the time of writing the most recent entrants to the E.C. (Austria, Finland and Sweden) have not yet ratified.

[2] See Chap. 6.

[3] For the general law of the Convention see Collins, *The Civil Jurisdiction and Judgments Act 1982* (1983); Hartley, *Civil Jurisdiction and Judgments* (1984); Kaye, *Civil Jurisdiction and the Enforcement of Judgments* (1987); Lasok and Stone, *Conflict of Laws in the European Community* (1987); Dashwood, Hacon and White, *A Guide to the Civil Jurisdiction and Judgments Convention* (1987); O'Malley and Layton, *European Civil Practice* (1989); Anton and Beaumont, *Civil Jurisdiction in Scotland* (2nd ed., 1995); Briggs and Rees, *Civil Jurisdiction and Judgments* (2nd ed., 1997) as well as Dicey and Morris, *The Conflict of Laws* (12th ed., 1993); Cheshire and North's *Private International Law* (12th ed., 1992) and Tritton, *Intellectual Property in Europe* (1996). Ulmer, *Intellectual Property Rights and the Conflict of Laws* (1978) has surprisingly little to say about the Convention. Stauder, "Die Anwendung des EWG-Gerichtssands- und Vollstreckungs- übereinkommens auf Klagen im gewerblichen Rechtsschutz und Urheberrecht" [1976] GRUR Int. 465 and 510 (though now outdated) is much more comprehensive. See also Wadlow, "Intellectual Property and the Judgments Convention" (1985) 10 E.L. Rev. 305; White, "Civil Jurisdiction and Judgments Act 1982" [1986] CIPA 94; Tritton and Tritton, "The Brussels Convention and Intellectual Property" [1987] E.I.P.R. 349; Burnside and Burnside, "Patent Litigation under the Judgments Convention" [1988] (March) *Patent World* 18. For more recent periodical literature in the context of English law and practice see Chap. 3, n. 1.

[4] See para. 2–18.

the special regime for jurisdiction over disputes relating to the ownership of European patent applications.

2–02   The following chapter, Chapter 3, deals with the recent but developing body of authorities in the United Kingdom which are specifically relevant to intellectual property. That chapter also deals with certain issues for which any commentary in the present state of the law has to be a matter of personal judgment. Enforcement of judgments in intellectual property actions, which has yet to become an issue of more than theoretical importance, is dealt with in Chapter 8, which also covers the doctrine of *lis alibi pendens* under the Convention and two possibilities for pre-emptive forum shopping by prospective defendants. An outline of the developing law of the Convention in other important contracting states has already been given in Chapter 1.

2–03   There are other reasons why intellectual property lawyers need to understand the operation of the Brussels Convention. Plaintiffs in other member states may allege jurisdiction over English defendants, or over infringements of English intellectual property rights.[5] If so, the circumstances in which the courts may assume jurisdiction are governed by the Convention, as are the recognition and enforcement in England of a judgment obtained abroad. The Convention, rather than domestic law, governs the jurisdiction of the English courts over defendants domiciled in other Convention member states, so actions for infringement of British intellectual property rights in the English courts may involve the Convention if relief is sought against defendants domiciled abroad, whether on the basis that they actually infringed in England or that they should be joined as joint tortfeasors.[6] A Modified Convention scheme applies between the three jurisdictions which make up the United Kingdom. Disputes as to contracts, licences or entitlement to intellectual property rights, including ones between employer and employee, are governed by the provisions of the Convention applicable to contracts. Finally, the regimes under the Community Patent Convention, the Community Trade Mark Regulation and the Community Design Regulation for the enforcement of Community patents, trade marks and designs are based on the Brussels Convention with modifications and directly incorporate many of the general provisions of the Brussels Convention.[7]

The Brussels and Lugano Conventions

2–04   Article 220 of the E.C. Treaty committed the member states to a number of objectives which were desirable for the creation of the common market, but which for one reason or another required action outside the institutional structure of the Community after further negotiations between the states themselves. One of these objectives was

---

[5] See Chap. 1.

[6] See Chap. 3. Jurisdiction under Art. 16(4) (revocation proceedings, see para. 2–101) is always governed by the Convention, regardless of domicile.

[7] See Chap. 5.

"the simplification of formalities governing the reciprocal recognition and enforcement of judgments of courts or tribunals and of arbitration awards."[8] A committee of experts was set up in 1960, producing a preliminary draft in 1964 and a further draft which was adopted in 1966. The Brussels Convention was entered into by the original six member states of the European Economic Community in 1968 and came into force in 1973. A Protocol on Interpretation allowing the European Court of Justice to give preliminary rulings on the Convention was signed in 1971 and came into force in 1975.

The accession of the United Kingdom, Ireland and Denmark to the **2–05** European Community in 1973 occasioned substantial revisions to the Brussels Convention which were made by the Accession Convention of 1978. The accession of Greece in 1982 resulted in only formal changes, but more important amendments to the Brussels Convention were made by the San Sebastian Convention of 1989 which provided for the accession of Spain and Portugal. The Accession Convention for Austria, Finland and Sweden was signed in 1996. It makes only technical amendments.

Despite its status as a treaty in its own right in public international **2–06** law, the Brussels Convention is part of the Community legal order and membership by non-E.C. states would be problematical. So as to create as uniform a system for jurisdiction and recognition of judgments as possible throughout the E.C. and EFTA blocs, a separate but very similar convention was concluded in 1988 under the name of the Lugano Convention. With the accession of the majority of the EFTA bloc to the E.C. and the Brussels Convention, the Lugano Convention is of declining importance.[9] The provisions of the Lugano Convention are in terms almost identical to those of the Brussels Convention and it does not receive separate treatment in this work.

The legal effect of the Conventions

In the United Kingdom, the Brussels Convention has the force of law **2–07** by virtue of section 2 of the Civil Jurisdiction and Judgments Act 1982, as amended, as do the 1971 Protocol on Interpretation and the Accession Conventions.[10] English texts of the Conventions are set out in Schedules to the Act "for convenience of reference" but are no more authoritative, even in the United Kingdom, than the other authentic texts. A modified version of the Brussels Convention applies as between the three jurisdictions which make up the United Kingdom.[11] The

[8] Though the Brussels Convention does not, in fact, apply to arbitration awards at all. This aspect of Art. 220 has still to be realised.
[9] In due course, only Iceland, Liechtenstein, Norway and Switzerland can be expected to be members of the Lugano Convention but not the Brussels Convention.
[10] The commencement date for the Brussels Convention was January 1, 1987 and for the Lugano Convention May 1, 1992.
[11] Civil Jurisdiction and Judgments Act 1982, s. 16 and Sched. 4. The Modified Convention is not dealt with separately in this work. For present purposes, the main differences are that Art. 5(3) expressly applies to *quia timet* actions and there is no provision corresponding to Art. 16(4).

Lugano Convention has the force of law by virtue of amendments made to the Civil Jurisdiction and Judgments Act 1982 by the Civil Jurisdiction and Judgments Act 1991.

2–08   Quite apart from the provisions of the Civil Jurisdiction and Judgments Act 1982, the Brussels Convention has the status of a constituent part of the Community legal order. It was concluded under Article 220 E.C. and is closely connected to the E.C. Treaty itself. It is to interpreted according both to its own principles and objectives and to its relationship to the E.C. Treaty.[12] It is directly effective in all member states. As such, it automatically takes precedence over national law even in the absence of specific national implementing measures. So, for example, in the patent case of *Duijnstee v. Goderbauer*[13] the Dutch Supreme Court was both obliged and empowered to refer the question of its own jurisdiction to the European Court of Justice, although as a matter of Dutch domestic law it had no power to take the point of its own motion. As a source of Community law the Convention is paramount, and as with the E.C. Treaty itself the effects of this are only now beginning to be fully appreciated.[14]

2–09   The Brussels Convention expressly does not affect the application of any other conventions, existing then or in the future, to which member states may be parties and which govern jurisdiction or the recognition and enforcement of judgments in relation to particular matters.[15] Rather more surprisingly, perhaps, the Convention also permits derogations to be made by way of provisions governing jurisdiction or the recognition and enforcement of judgments in relation to particular matters which are or which will be contained in Community legislation or national laws implementing Community harmonisation measures.[16] The Community Trade Mark Regulation makes use of this power.[17]

The Convention summarised in an intellectual property context: *Pearce v. Ove Arup*

2–10   A convenient summary of the provisions of the Brussels Convention most likely to be relevant to intellectual property infringement actions was given by Lloyd J. in *Pearce v. Ove Arup*,[18] where an English plaintiff sued English and Dutch defendants for an alleged infringement of copyright involving the construction of a building in Rotterdam. First, Lloyd J. dealt with the general approach to the interpretation of the Convention in the light of the objectives it was intended to achieve, the relevant sources of law and the legislative technique adopted:

[12] Case 12/76 *Tessili v. Dunlop* [1976] E.C.R. 1473; [1977] 1 C.M.L.R. 26.
[13] Case 288/82 [1983] E.C.R. 3663; [1985] 1 C.M.L.R. 220.
[14] See *Pearce v. Ove Arup Partnership* [1997] F.S.R. 641 (Lloyd J.). See also paras 3–47 *et seq.*
[15] Art. 57(1). See also paras 2–130 *et seq.* and Chaps. 4 and 5.
[16] Art. 57(3).
[17] See para. 5–31.
[18] [1997] F.S.R. 641 (Lloyd J.). This was the first case in which infringement of a foreign proprietary intellectual property right was asserted in the English courts under the Brussels Convention. See para. 3–47.

"The Brussels Convention has the force of law in the United Kingdom directly, not as applied by national legislation: see section 2(1) of the 1982 Act. Any question as to its meaning and effect is to be determined in accordance with the principles laid down by, and any relevant decision of, the European Court: section 3(1). Such questions may be referred to the European Court only by an appellate court, so I cannot avoid deciding this difficult and controversial question in that way. I am to take judicial notice of any decision of, or expression of opinion by, the European Court on any such question, I may consider the so-called *Jenard* and *Schlosser* reports in ascertaining the meaning and effect of the Convention and I am to give those reports such weight as is appropriate in the circumstances: section 3(2) and (3). . . .

The first concern of the Brussels Convention is with the enforcement and recognition of judgments within the European Community: cf. Treaty of Rome Article 220 and the preamble to the Convention. The Convention adopts the direct approach, rather than the indirect approach, to that problem, by laying down the circumstances in which the courts of the Contracting States are to have jurisdiction to entertain actions involving an international element within the Community. The alternative indirect approach would not prescribe the circumstances in which an action may be brought in the courts of a Contracting State but only the circumstances in which a judgment of such a court is one which is to be recognised by the courts in other Contracting States. By adopting the direct approach the Convention establishes an autonomous system of international jurisdiction in relations between the member States. The rules are applicable independently of any proceedings for international recognition or enforcement. This approach was seen as allowing increased harmonisation of laws, providing greater legal certainty, avoiding discrimination, and facilitating the ultimate objective of 'free movement' of judgments: see the *Jenard* report, Chapter 2 Section C."

He then confirmed that an action for copyright infringement was **2–11** within the scope of the Convention and referred to the fundamental rule of jurisdiction:

"An action for breach of copyright is plainly within the scope of the civil and commercial matters to which the Convention applies: Article 1. The fundamental rule as to jurisdiction is laid down by Article 2: a person domiciled in a Contracting State shall be sued in the courts of that State. There are exceptions to that principle, some of which provide an alternative forum in particular circumstances, and others which exclude the court of domicile in favour of another forum which is to have sole jurisdiction. All of these exceptions are to be interpreted narrowly, as appears from decisions referred to below. That Article 2 provides the fundamental position is emphasised by Article 3 whose first sentence is as follows:

'Persons domiciled in a Contracting State may be sued in the courts of another Contracting State only by virtue of the rules set out in sections 2–6 of this title [that is to say Articles 5–18].'

Article 4 leaves national law to govern local jurisdiction as regards defendants who are not domiciled in a Contracting State, except where any of the exclusive provisions of Article 16 applies."

2–12 Next, the facts of the case led him to consider two articles which derogate from the general rule by permitting a defendant to be sued in a court which is not that of his domicile. These are Articles 5(3) and 6(1), and they will be pervasively relevant to intellectual property infringement actions:

"Two of the special rules of jurisdiction could be relevant to such a case as the present.

The first is Article 5(3) as follows:

'a person domiciled in a Contracting State may, in another Contracting State, be sued . . . in matters relating to tort, delict or quasi delict, in the courts for the place where the harmful event occurred.'

An action for compensation for infringement of copyright is a matter relating to tort, delict or quasi delict. It would therefore be possible to bring this action, as regards Dutch copyright, in the Netherlands, no doubt in the courts of Rotterdam, as the place where the harmful event occurred.

The second alternative which is relevant is Article 6(1) as follows:

'A person domiciled in a Contracting State may also be sued where he is one of a number of Defendants in the courts for the place where any one of them is domiciled.'

The First Defendant is certainly domiciled in the United Kingdom and it seems that the Second Defendant may be. The Fourth Defendant certainly is not and it seems that the Third Defendant is not, so they are sued in England on the basis of this Article."

2–13 Finally, Lloyd J. considered Article 16, giving exclusive jurisdiction in certain cases regardless of the domicile of the defendant:

"I should also note two of the exclusive jurisdiction provisions, in Article 16(1) and (4) as follows:

'The following courts shall have exclusive jurisdiction, regardless of domicile:

(1) in proceedings which have as their object rights in rem in immovable property or tenancies of immovable property, the courts of the Contracting State in which the property is situated;

(4) in proceedings concerned with the registration or validity of patents, trade marks, designs, or other similar rights required to be deposited or registered, the courts of the

Contracting State in which the deposit or registration has been applied for, has taken place or is under the terms of an international convention deemed to have taken place.'"

All these provisions are considered in more detail in the following sections.

B. THE INTERPRETATION OF THE BRUSSELS CONVENTION

Introduction: common law and civil law

The Brussels Convention is an international treaty originally drafted in **2–14** Continental style by representatives of the original six member states of the European Economic Community, and the United Kingdom was not initially a party. Literal interpretation in the common law tradition would be inappropriate. The correct approach of the English courts has been summarised by Bingham L.J. in *Re Harrods (Buenos Aires) Ltd*[19] as follows:

"In interpreting the 1982 Act our task is, as always, to ascertain the intention of Parliament and give effect to it. But in so far as the Act is intended to give legal effect to the Conventions and to implement the United Kingdom's international obligation to give legal effect to the Conventions, we must assume (in the absence of a clear indication to the contrary, which is not to be found here) that Parliament intended the Conventions to be incorporated into English law so as faithfully to reflect the international consensus embodied in them. The Conventions themselves are in part set out in Schedules to the Act, but it cannot be doubted that in interpreting them we are required first to consider the objectives and scheme of the Conventions and secondly the general principles which stem from the corpus of the national legal systems of the Contracting States. For this purpose we must adopt an international and *communautaire*, not a national and chauvinistic, approach. Although these Conventions do not expressly provide, like Article 18 of the Rome Convention (see the Contracts (Applicable Law) Act 1990 and the schedule thereto), that 'In the interpretation and application of the preceding uniform rules, regard shall be had to their international character and to the desirability of achieving uniformity in their interpretation and application,' it is plain that that is the basis upon which we should act."

To much the same effect is the following quotation from the judgment **2–15** of Steyn L.J. in *Continental Bank v. Aeakos Compania Naviera*[20] in the

[19] [1992] Ch. 72; [1991] 4 All E.R. 334; [1991] 3 W.L.R. 397, CA.
[20] [1994] 1 W.L.R. 588; [1994] 2 All E.R. 540.

context of an application for an injunction restraining litigation in Greece:

> "In construing the Brussels Convention it is important to put aside pre-conceptions based on traditional English rules. The Convention is a radical new regime governing the international legal relationships of the contracting states. It is intended to eliminate obstacles to the functioning of the common market and to further the evolution of a vast single market: Jenard Report (Official Journal 1979 No. C. 59, p. 19). The genesis of the Convention is the jurisprudence of the civil law rather than the common law. Since the original states were all civil law countries, and the United Kingdom played no role in the drafting of the Convention, this is hardly surprising. Traditionally, English courts assert a discretion to enjoin a party by injunction from pursuing foreign legal proceedings in breach of an exclusive jurisdiction clause. The idea that a national court has discretion in the exercise of its jurisdiction does not generally exist in civilian systems: Schlosser Report (Official Journal 1979 No. C. 59, p. 97, para. 76)."

2–16   Despite what was said by Bingham and Steyn L.JJ., it should not be assumed that the courts of civil law jurisdictions possess an infallible insight into the working of the Brussels Convention which is denied to the common lawyer. As the Jenard Report itself makes clear, some of the most fundamental principles of the Convention were adopted despite being strongly at variance with the consensus embodied in existing bilateral treaties to which the original six member states were parties, or with the domestic procedural laws of some or all of the Six.[21] So much so, that the Jenard Committee felt it had to defend itself against the charge that it had gone beyond its terms of reference. In France, for example, the relevant personal connecting factor for jurisdiction was nationality rather than domicile; and there was a widely accepted principle that a person could always sue or be sued in the courts of his country of nationality or domicile. In contrast, the Convention regards nationality as irrelevant and the principle of *actor sequitur forum rei* is paramount.

2–17   Nor are individual decisions of Continental courts necessarily any more reliable than those of courts in the United Kingdom,[22] and there are distinct national variations in quality. The Dutch courts consistently tend to take an expansive view of their jurisdiction,[23] but, unlike some

---

[21] The Brussels Convention "differs fundamentally from treaties and conventions of the same type previously concluded" according to Jenard, giving five heads of differences.

[22] What would one make of a decision purporting to apply the Brussels Convention but holding, in effect, that recognition of a German judgment was automatically contrary to public policy and must be refused regardless of the underlying facts of the case? That is the effect of the decision of the *Cour d'Appel* of Poitiers in *Société de Transports Internationaux Dehbashi v. Gerling Conzem*, [1996] I.L.Pr. 103 holding that to enforce a judgment which did not contain any reasoning was contrary to French public policy, so that the German judgment sought to be enforced was a total nullity.

[23] See para. 1–28 for the Dutch practice in granting pan-European injunctions in intellectual property cases.

others, are conscientious in making references to the European Court of Justice. It is notoriously all but impossible to persuade an Italian court to stay its proceedings on the basis of an exclusive jurisdiction or arbitration clause. The actual result in *Continental Bank v. Aeakos Compania Naviera*[24] implied that the Greek courts were ignoring or misunderstanding the Brussels Convention and needed unsolicited assistance from the English Court of Appeal to apply it properly. Many would agree with this conclusion on the facts, but it is hardly free from the charge of chauvinism.

Jenard, Schlosser, (etc.), guide interpretation of the Convention

Interpretation of the Brussels Convention and related protocols or 2–18 conventions is aided by the official reports prepared by the various committees of experts responsible for them.[25] The first and most important of these is the report by Mr P. Jenard who acted as *rapporteur* for the committee of experts which drafted the 1968 Brussels Convention itself. The Jenard Report takes the form of a detailed commentary on the text of the Convention, with background material on previous bilateral conventions, the domestic laws of the original six member states and the policy choices facing the committee.[26] The other report of importance is that of Dr Peter Schlosser who was *rapporteur* for the committee which prepared the 1978 Accession Convention for the United Kingdom, Ireland and Denmark.[27]

The Jenard and Schlosser reports are important and influential. Both 2–19 are frequently referred to in judgments of the European Court of Justice and the opinions of the Advocates-General. It is rare to find a decision openly at variance with either report. In the United Kingdom, section 3(3) of the Civil Jurisdiction and Judgments Act 1982 provides for them to be considered in ascertaining the meaning and effect of any provision of the Conventions and given such weight as appropriate.

Interpreted by the ECJ on a pseudo-177 procedure

The jurisdiction of the European Court of Justice to interpret the 2–20 Brussels Convention derives from the 1971 Protocol on Interpretation and not from Article 177 E.C. There are some important differences reflecting the fact that a decision on the interpretation of the Brussels Convention is hardly ever likely to determine the substantive rights of the parties, and the undesirability of allowing procedural appeals to

---

[24] [1994] 1 W.L.R. 588, [1994] 2 All E.R. 540.
[25] The Jenard Report is published at [1979] O.J. C59/3 and the Schlosser Report at [1979] O.J. C59/71. Both are more conveniently set out in *Butterworths' Jurisdiction, Foreign Judgments and Awards Handbook* (1994) and several of the specialist texts.
[26] Jenard produced a separate report on the 1971 Protocol on Interpretation.
[27] Other reports of limited relevance for present purposes are the Jenard and Moller Report on the Lugano Convention, and the Cruz, Real and Jenard Report on the San Sebastian Convention. There is also a report by Evrigenis and Kerameus on the Accession Convention for Greece.

delay proceedings unduly or allow judgment debtors to postpone execution.[28]

2–21   Article 1 of the 1971 Protocol (as amended) provides that the Court of Justice of the European Communities is to have jurisdiction to give rulings on the interpretation of the Brussels Convention and Protocol and the various Accession conventions. Article 2 identifies the national courts which may request rulings. In deliberate contrast to Article 177 E.C., rulings may only be sought by appellate courts. Article 3 obliges identified national courts of last resort, including the House of Lords, to make a reference for a ruling when a decision on the interpretation of the Convention is necessary in order to give judgment. Other appellate courts have complete discretion whether or not to make a reference. Article 4, which has no counterpart in Article 177 E.C., allows the public authorities of a contracting state to request the European Court of Justice to give rulings in certain cases where a national court appears to have misinterpreted the Convention, but without *inter partes* effect.[29] Article 5 provides for procedure under Article 177 E.C. to apply *mutatis mutandis* to the 1971 Protocol.

2–22   Section 3(1) of the Civil Jurisdiction and Judgments Act 1982 requires United Kingdom courts to determine any question relating to the meaning or effect of the Convention in accordance with the principles laid down by the European Court and any relevant decision of the Court. The European Court of Justice does not have jurisdiction to interpret the Modified Convention which applies between England, Scotland and Northern Ireland[30]; nor the Lugano Convention.[31]

Familiar terms in the Convention may have an "independent" meaning

2–23   Not surprisingly, the Brussels Convention is full of terms which may have a definite meaning in any given legal system, but which do not necessarily have the same meaning in all, especially after the common law jurisdictions of the United Kingdom and Ireland joined the six original Civil law members.[32] The Convention itself hardly ever defines the terms it uses. In several early cases, this raised the question of where one looked for a definition of a concept that was in dispute: to the *lex fori*, to the *lex causae* or to some independent source?

---

[28] See the commentary in the Jenard Report on the 1971 Protocol on Interpretation.

[29] See the commentary on Art. 4 in the Jenard Report and para. 1–65 above. It appears never to have been applied, but in Case 42/76 *de Wolf v. Cox* [1976] E.C.R. 1759; [1977] 1 C.M.L.R. 12 a corresponding procedure in Dutch domestic law was invoked by the Attorney General of the Hoge Raad and led to a reference by that court to the European Court of Justice. Since the only issue was over the procedure for enforcing an undisputed debt of a few pounds, it is not surprising that neither litigant wanted to fund even a first level appeal.

[30] Case C–346/93 *Kleinwort Benson v. City of Glasgow* [1995] E.C.R. I–615; [1995] All E.R. (E.C.) 514.

[31] Although the Community Plant Variety Rights Regulation E.C. 2100/94 purports to incorporate the Lugano Convention, thereby raising the problem of the latter being interpreted on an Art. 177 E.C. reference. See para. 5–52.

[32] Case 12/76 *Tessili v. Dunlop* [1976] E.C.R. 1473; [1977] 1 C.M.L.R. 26.

The European Court of Justice has consistently held that the majority   **2–24** of the legal terms of art in the Brussels Convention have an independent or autonomous meaning to be defined as a matter of Community law, so that the meaning the term bears in any particular national legal system is inconclusive. An exercise in comparative law may be useful to help ascertain the single, independent, meaning of a term or concept used in several legal systems; and once that meaning has been defined national law may have a role in relating the facts of the case to the standard set by the Convention. So, for example, under Article 5(1) one looks to the applicable law of the contract to identify the "place of performance of the obligation in question."[33] For Article 5(3), national tort law decides, within limits, whether the event relied on is harmful to a sufficient extent to found jurisdiction.[34] Neither of these exceptions compromises the principle that the jurisdictional provisions of the Convention are to receive an autonomous interpretation, independent of the meaning of words and phrases in national law.

A convenient summary of the earlier cases in a context particularly   **2–25** relevant to intellectual property is to be found in *Duijnstee v. Goderbauer*,[35] where the Court had to answer a question from the Dutch Supreme Court as to whether the expression "proceedings concerned with the registration or validity of patents" in Article 16(4) was to be determined according to national law in the form either of the law of the courts putatively given exclusive jurisdiction or the *lex fori*; or was to be given an independent interpretation:

> "The Court has several times had occasion to consider the criteria to be used for the definition of the concepts appearing in the Convention. Thus, in its judgment of 22 February 1979 in Case 133/78 (*Gourdain v. Nadler* [1979] ECR 743), it stated that 'in order to ensure, as far as possible, that the rights and obligations which derive from [the Convention] for the Contracting States and the persons to whom it applies are equal and uniform', it is necessary that the terms of Article 1 of the Convention should not be interpreted 'as a mere reference to the internal law of one or other of the States concerned,' and 'the concepts used in Article 1 must be regarded as independent concepts which must be interpreted by reference, first, to the objectives and scheme of the Convention and, secondly, to the general principles which stem from the corpus of the national legal systems.' The Court also stressed the need for an independent interpretation in its Judgment of 21 June 1978 in Case 150/77 (*Bertrand v. Ott* [1978] ECR 1432), in relation to the terms used in Article 13 and in the second paragraph of Article 14 of the Convention, and in its judgment of 22 March 1983 in Case 34/82 (*Martin Peters Bauunternehmung v. Zuid Nederlandse Aannemers Vereniging* [1983] ECR 987), in relation to the terms used in Article 5 (1) of the Convention.

[33] *ibid.*
[34] Case C–68/93 *Shevill v. Presse Alliance* [1995] E.C.R. I–415.
[35] Case 288/82 [1983] E.C.R. 3663; [1985] 1 C.M.L.R. 220.

In the present case, both an interpretation according to the law of the Contracting State whose courts have jurisdiction under Article 16 (4) and an interpretation according to the *lex fori* would be liable to produce divergent solutions, which would be prejudicial to the principle that the rights and obligations which the persons concerned derive from the Convention should be equal and uniform.

Thus the term 'proceedings concerned with the registration or validity of patents' contained in Article 16 (4) must be regarded as an independent concept intended to have uniform application in all the Contracting States."

2–26   Most recently, the proposition has been confirmed by the Court in *Rutten v. Cross Medical*,[36] where the context was Article 5(1):

"It is settled law that, in principle, the Court of Justice will interpret the terms of the EC Judgments Convention autonomously so as to ensure that it is fully effective, having regard to the objectives of Article 220 of the EC Treaty, for the implementation of which it was adopted.

That autonomous interpretation alone is capable of ensuring uniform application of the Convention, the objectives of which include unification of the rules on jurisdiction of the Contracting States, so as to avoid as far as possible the multiplication of the bases of jurisdiction in relation to one and the same legal relationship and to reinforce the legal protection available to persons established in the Community by, at the same time, allowing the plaintiff easily to identify the court before which he may bring an action and the defendant reasonably to foresee the Court before which he may be sued."

2–27   Virtually the only concept of importance which does not have an independent meaning is that of domicile, which Article 52 refers to national law. Even this, however, is subject to two qualifications. One is that Article 53 provides for the domicile of a corporation or association to be its seat; the other is that for the United Kingdom the Civil Jurisdiction and Judgments Act 1982, Part V, defines domicile for purposes of the Brussels Convention in a manner corresponding to Continental law. Otherwise, even terms as familiar as "tort" or "contract" do not necessarily have the same meaning in the Brussels Convention as they do in domestic law, so that the characterisation of an action as one or the other for domestic purposes is irrelevant to whether jurisdiction may exist under Article 5(1) or 5(3).[37]

---

[36] Case C–383/95 [1997] E.C.R. I–19 following Case C–125/92 *Mulox IBC v. Geels* [1993] E.C.R. I–4075.

[37] Case C–26/91 *Jacob Handte v. TMCS* [1992] E.C.R. I–3967. A claim which French law anomalously regarded as contractual did not confer jurisdiction under Art. 5(1).

The golden rule: derogations from the fundamental principle to be construed narrowly

The case law of the European Court of Justice on the Brussels **2–28** Convention is not extensive and many important provisions have been considered in only a few decisions, perhaps on facts unlikely to be repeated. In practice, therefore, if the Convention itself is unclear and the Jenard and Schlosser reports do not help then the only remaining source of guidance is likely to be the application of general principles approved by the Court. As noted by Bingham L.J., the basic principle is that the Convention is to be given a purposive or teleological interpretation in the light of the intentions of the contracting states. In practice, however, purposive construction has progressively been reduced by the Court to the single overriding principle that the fundamental rule of the Convention is that of Article 2 and that all derogations from this rule are to be construed strictly.[38]

> "The Convention achieves that objective[39] by laying down a number of jurisdictional rules which determine the cases, exhaustively listed in Sections 2 to 6 of Title II of the Convention, in which a defendant domiciled or established in a Contracting State may, under a rule of special jurisdiction, or must, under a rule of exclusive jurisdiction or prorogation of jurisdiction, be sued before a court of another Contracting State.
>
> The rules on special and exclusive jurisdiction and those relating to prorogation of jurisdiction thus derogate from the general principle, set out in the first paragraph of Article 2 of the Convention, that the courts of the Contracting State in which the defendant is domiciled are to have jurisdiction. That jurisdictional rule is a general principle because it makes it easier, in principle, for a defendant to defend himself. Consequently, the jurisdictional rules which derogate from that general principle must not lead to an interpretation going beyond the situations envisaged by the Convention."

In practice too, the European Court of Justice has been a great deal **2–29** less consistent in the application of this principle of teleological interpretation than it would like to give itself credit for. Two articles of particular interest to intellectual property lawyers are Articles 5(3) and 16(4), the former giving jurisdiction in tort cases to the courts of "the place where the harmful event occurred"; the latter dealing with exclusive jurisdiction in cases concerned with the registration or validity of patents or other registered intellectual property rights. Neither

[38] Case C–26/91 *Jacob Handte v. TMCS* [1992] E.C.R. I–3967. See also Case C–288/92 *Custom Made Commercial v. Stawa* [1994] E.C.R. I–2913, holding that Art. 5(1) should be applied in its strict and literal meaning even when that led to its acknowledged purpose being frustrated.

[39] As stated in the Jenard Report.

provision is unambiguous, and the approach actually taken to each by the Court in the decided cases hardly corresponds to what one would expect from abstract principles.

2–30   One might have expected, for instance, that all of Article 5 would receive a restrictive interpretation as a derogation from the general rule of Article 2 that defendants should be sued in the courts of their domicile, and this is what the Court has confirmed.[40] If so, one might have expected that the various sub-rules of Article 5 would stand or fall together. What one sees in practice is that Article 5(3)—tort—was initially given such a wide interpretation in *Reinwater*[41] and *Kalfelis v. Schroeder*[42] that in *Shevill v. Presse Alliance*[43] the Court was compelled to create a new rule, with no basis in the Convention, to restore some sort of balance; whereas Article 5(5)—liability for a branch, agency or other establishment—has at times been at risk of being interpreted out of existence.[44] Article 5(1)—contract—could hardly avoid falling between these extremes, but even before its text was modified by the San Sebastian Convention it had received an interpretation generous to employee plaintiffs when the contract was one of employment, and a comparatively restrictive one for ordinary commercial contracts.

2–31   The cases on Article 16, dealing with the exclusive jurisdictions, do not always show the Court in any better light. In *Rosler v. Rottwinkel*[45] it interpreted Article 16(1) to hold that the Italian courts had exclusive jurisdiction over a dispute between two Germans about a three-week letting of a holiday flat in Italy; notwithstanding German applicable law, an express contractual submission to the jurisdiction of a German court and the absence of any compelling Italian governmental interest in Herr Rottwinkel's spoilt holiday and unpaid electricity bill.[46] The decision was widely condemned and resulted in the Brussels Convention being amended. A new Article 16(1)(b) gave concurrent jurisdiction over tenancies for temporary private use to the courts of the defendant's domicile, but only if they were for a maximum period of six consecutive months, both parties were natural persons, and they were both domiciled

---

[40] For example, Case 32/88 *Six Constructions v. Humbert* [1989] E.C.R. 341.

[41] Case 21/76 *Bier v. Mines de Potasse d'Alsace* [1976] E.C.R. 1753; [1977] 1 C.M.L.R. 284. The judgment immediately preceded the earliest statement by the Court of the principle of restrictive interpretation in the context of the Brussels Convention, which is Case 24/76 *Salotti v. RUWA* [1976] E.C.R. 1831; [1977] 1 C.M.L.R. 345 interpreting Art. 17 strictly as being a derogation both from Art. 2 and Arts 5 and 6. In *Reinwater* itself, Capotorti A.-G. refused to treat Art. 5 as a derogation from Art. 2.

[42] Case 189/87 [1988] E.C.R. 5565. *Kalfelis* interprets "tort" in Art. 5(3) as including all sources of liability other than contract, which is covered by Art. 5(1). Such an interpretation may well be purposive in the true sense, but could hardly be less restrictive.

[43] Case C–68/93 [1995] E.C.R. I–415.

[44] See paras. 2–53 and 2–54.

[45] Case 241/83 [1985] E.C.R. 99; [1985] 1 C.M.L.R. 806.

[46] Criticism of this aspect of the decision is reasonable in the light of the Jernard and Schlosser reports, but once the Court had decided that *any* aspect of such a case fell within the exclusive jurisdiction, it was obviously expedient to try to have all the claims resolved in the same court.

in the same contracting state.[47] All the same, the Court itself has continued to hold out *Rosler v. Rottwinkel* as a decision which gave Article 16(1) an interpretation at once purposive and restrictive.

Yet the real lesson to learn from *Rosler v. Rottwinkel* is that there is **2–32** inherently a tension between a simplistic rule of interpretation which asserts that all the special and exclusive jurisdictions are to be interpreted strictly, and a more sophisticated one which recognises the many diverse and conflicting policies and interests underlying the Convention and is capable of leading to the opposite result.[48] The decision in *Rosler v. Rottwinkel* may have been inconvenient, absurd and even unjust, but as the Opinion of Slynn A.-G. in that case demonstrated, it was an injustice which the member states were quite prepared to contemplate. The very limited qualification to Article 16(1) made by the San Sebastian Convention shows just how little ground the member states were subsequently prepared to concede, even on such a trivial aspect of national sovereignty.[49] In the one case to date on Article 16(4) the Court has purported to give a purposive construction to the requirement that proceedings concerned with the registration or validity of patents, etc., should be brought in the courts of the country of registration.[50] In reality, it ignored the undoubted and well-documented reasons for this provision in favour of some reasons of its own invention, which on closer inspection do even begin to justify the special provisions for registered intellectual property rights.[51]

The impact of the Convention on national substantive and procedural law

As a general rule, the Brussels Convention does not affect the **2–33** substantive law applicable to a cause of action. Its effects on national law are confined to realising its objectives of allocating jurisdiction, governing certain aspects of procedure such as *lis alibi pendens* and related actions, and creating a uniform regime for the recognition and enforcement of judgments.[52] The general principle was stated by the European

---

[47] The corresponding Art. 16(1)(b) of the Lugano Convention is rather more sensible: only the tenant need be a natural person and although neither party can be domiciled in the country where the property is situated, they need not both be domiciled in the same contracting state. However the Lugano Convention, unlike the Brussels Convention, permits reservations even to this modest reform.

[48] No legitimate process of purposive construction could have resulted in a solution corresponding to Art. 16(1)(b), and the result in a future case would be equally absurd if a German rented his Italian holiday home to an Austrian friend, or if the home was owned by a company for tax reasons.

[49] See the Jenard and Moller Report on the Lugano Convention, paras 49 *et seq*, and the Cruz, Real and Jenard Report on the San Sebastian Convention, para. 25. The most controversial aspect of *Rosler v. Rottwinkel*—the application of Art. 16(1) to rent—was left untouched.

[50] Case 288/82 *Duijnstee v. Goderbauer* [1993] E.C.R. 3663; [1985] 1 C.M.L.R. 220. See para. 2–115.

[51] See para. 2–117, below.

[52] For recognition and enforcement, see Chap. 8.

Court of Justice in *Sanicentral v. Collin*[53] where a choice-of-court clause was held valid under the Convention, although it would have been void under national law at the date of the contract:

> "It is appropriate to answer this point by stating, on the one hand, that the Convention does not affect rules of substantive law and, on the other hand, that, as the Convention seeks to determine the jurisdiction of the courts of the contracting States in the intra-Community legal order in regard to matters of civil jurisdiction, the national procedural laws applicable to the cases concerned are set aside in the matters governed by the Convention in favour of the provisions thereof."

2–34   All the same, whenever there is a conflict between the Brussels Convention and national law, the former must prevail, regardless of whether the rule of national law in conflict with the Convention is characterised as one of substantive law, private international law or procedure. The national court may continue to apply its own law, but only provided that the effectiveness of the Convention in that regard is not thereby impaired[54]:

> "It should be emphasised that it is not the object of the Convention to unify procedural rules, but to allocate authority to courts to take cognizance of civil and commercial matters in intra-Community relations and to facilitate the enforcement of judicial decisions. Therefore a clear distinction should be drawn between jurisdiction and the conditions for admissibility of an action.
>
>   . . .
>
> It should, however, be added that the application of national rules of procedure should not interfere with the practical effect of the Convention. As the Court held in Case 288/82, *Duijnstee v. Goderbauer*, the court should not apply conditions of admissibility laid down by national law which would have the effect of limiting the application of the jurisdiction rules set out by the Convention."

2–35   To the same effect, *Shevill v. Presse Alliance*[55] concerned a libel published on an arguably *de minimis* scale in the United Kingdom, where the plaintiff had sued. One of the questions referred by the House of Lords to the European Court of Justice concerned whether it was national law or the Convention which governed the issue of whether sufficient harm had occurred in England to found jurisdiction under Article 5(8):

> "In the area of non-contractual liability, the context in which the questions referred have arisen, the sole object of the Convention is

[53] Case 25/79 [1979] E.C.R. 3423; [1980] 2 C.M.L.R. 164.
[54] Case 365/88 *Kongress Agentur Hagen v. Zeehage* [1990] E.C.R. I–1845.
[55] Case C–68/93 [1995] E.C.R. I–415.

to determine which court or courts have jurisdiction to hear the dispute by reference to the place or places where an event considered harmful occurred.

It does not, however, specify the circumstances in which the event giving rise to the harm may be considered to be harmful to the victim, or the evidence which the plaintiff must adduce before the court seised to enable it to rule on the merits of the case.

Those questions must therefore be settled solely by the national court seised, applying the substantive law determined by its national conflict of laws rules, provided that the effectiveness of the Convention is not thereby impaired."

C. JURISDICTION: GENERAL PRINCIPLES

Scope of the Convention: "civil and commercial matters"

Article 1 of the Brussels Convention states that the Convention shall **2–36** apply in "civil and commercial matters whatever the nature of the court or tribunal." The Convention does not apply to criminal matters except when a criminal court has jurisdiction to grant civil relief by way of damages or restitution[56] in what are principally criminal proceedings.[57] The distinction between civil and commercial matters on the one hand, and administrative ones on the other, is familiar in many Continental legal systems and corresponds to the civil law distinction between private and public law. A passage introduced by the 1978 Accession Convention, with the common law systems of the United Kingdom and Ireland in mind, clarifies the distinction by expressly excluding revenue, customs[58] or administrative matters. Other matters excluded from the scope of the Convention for various reasons are listed in Article 1. They are briefly: personal status and capacity, property rights arising from marriage, wills and succession; bankruptcy and corporate insolvency; social security; and arbitration.

There is no doubt that the Convention applies to intellectual property, **2–37** even though the workings of national patent and trade mark offices are to some extent a matter of administrative law. This is clear, at the very

---

[56] So Copyright, Designs and Patents Act 1988 s. 108 probably does not fall within Art. 5(4) since the only civil relief which can be ordered is delivery up.

[57] A situation covered by Art. 5(4). Criminal prosecution for patent infringement is now all but unknown, but prosecution of copyright and trade mark counterfeiters is important. Local law will determine whether civil relief can be awarded in the criminal proceedings. If not, then a criminal conviction or acquittal will be outside the scope of the Convention, and so not entitled to recognition. Foreign criminal convictions cannot be pleaded either at common law or under the Civil Evidence Act 1968, s. 11: *Union Carbide v. Naturin* [1987] F.S.R. 538, CA.

[58] It probably follows that litigation arising from the seizure of counterfeit goods by customs authorities, *e.g.* under Copyright, Designs and Patents Act 1988, s. 111 or Trade Marks Act 1994, s. 89, is outside the scope of the Convention.

least, from Article 16(4) giving exclusive jurisdiction in proceedings concerned with the registration or validity of patents, trade marks, designs, etc., to the courts of the contracting state of the registration. A number of United Kingdom cases have proceeded on the basis that the Convention applies to ordinary infringement actions and the like.[59] However, matters concerning the registered intellectual property rights might be regarded as being close to the boundary with the excluded subject of administrative law, and just such a consideration was alluded to by Darmon A.-G. in the libel case of *Shevill v. Presse Alliance*[60] as a reason for adhering more closely to the principle of territoriality than might otherwise be appropriate.

2–38   The European Court of Justice has held that actions by or against a public authority acting in exercise of its powers as such are outside the scope of the Convention,[61] though the concept may be a difficult one to apply in practice, and especially for common lawyers unused to any fixed distinction between public and private law. It is suggested that proceedings relating to Crown use would be an example of patent-related proceedings that probably fell outside the scope of the Convention altogether, as being a matter of public or administrative law rather than private law. The position of other quasi-administrative proceedings such as applications for compulsory patent licences is unclear, although there is probably little practical difference between saying that these are altogether excluded from the scope of the Convention, and saying that they fall within the exclusive jurisdiction of Article 16(4).[62]

Jurisdiction based on the defendant's domicile in a contracting state

2–39   The basic jurisdictional rules of the Brussels Convention are set out in Articles 2 and 3:

> Article 2
>
> Subject to the provisions of this Convention, persons domiciled in a Contracting State shall, whatever their nationality, be sued in the courts of that State.
>
> Persons who are not nationals of the State in which they are domiciled shall be governed by the rules of jurisdiction applicable to nationals of that State.
>
> Article 3
>
> Persons domiciled in a Contracting State may be sued in the courts of another Contracting State only by virtue of the rules set out in Sections 2 to 6 of this Title. (. . .)[63]

---

[59] See Chap. 3.

[60] Case C–68/93 [1995] E.C.R. I–415.

[61] Case 29/76 *Eurocontrol I* [1976] E.C.R. 1541; [1977] 1 C.M.L.R. 88 and Joined Cases 9–10/77 *Eurocontrol II* [1977] E.C.R. 1517; [1980] 1 C.M.L.R. 566; Case 814/79 *Netherlands v. Ruffer* [1980] E.C.R. 3807; [1981] 3 C.M.L.R. 293.

[62] The 1975 Luxembourg Diplomatic Conference which adopted the Community Patent Convention considered adding a new Art. 16(6) to the Brussels Convention to deal with compulsory licences of Community patents: see para. 5–62.

[63] A country-by-country list of specific exorbitant grounds of jurisdiction, no longer available against Convention-domiciled defendants, is omitted.

Article 2 is the basic rule of the Convention. If a defendant is **2–40** domiciled in a contracting state, then he is prima facie entitled to be sued there. Those responsible for drafting the Convention explicitly rejected any general rule which would have allowed the plaintiff to sue in the courts of the state of his own nationality or domicile. Various national rules of exorbitant jurisdiction are enumerated in Article 3 and are prohibited from being relied on against defendants domiciled in a contracting state. For England, the only exorbitant rule excluded is that allowing jurisdiction to be based on service of the writ on the defendant during his temporary presence in the jurisdiction.[64] For several Continental states, the rules excluded correspond to Articles 14 and 15 of the French Civil Code, providing that a French national can always sue or be sued in the French courts.[65] As the European Court of Justice explained in *Dumez v. Hessische Landesbank*[66]:

"On this point the Convention, in laying down the system for conferring jurisdiction in Title II, sets out the general rule in Article 2 that the courts of the State of the defendant's domicile shall have jurisdiction. In addition the Convention shows that it is not in favour of the courts of the plaintiff's domicile having jurisdiction by stating, in Article 3(2), that national provisions to that effect shall not apply as against defendants domiciled in the territory of a contracting State.

Only by way of exception to the general rule that the courts of the State of the defendant's domicile have jurisdiction does Section 2 of Title II provide for a number of special jurisdictions, which include that of Art 5(3). As the Court has already held these special jurisdictions, which can be chosen at the plaintiff's option, are based on the existence of a particularly close connection between the dispute and courts other than those of the defendant's domicile, which justifies conferring jurisdiction on those courts on grounds of the efficient administration of justice and proper organisation of the action.

To achieve this object, which is of fundamental importance in a convention which should promote the recognition and enforcement of judgments outside the State in which they are made, it is essential to avoid the multiplication of competent courts, which increases the risk of irreconcilable judgments, which is a ground for refusing recognition or enforcement pursuant to Article 27(3) of the Convention.

Furthermore this object precludes any interpretation of the Convention which, apart from the cases expressly provided for, could lead to recognising the jurisdiction of the courts of the plaintiff's domicile and which would thus enable the plaintiff to determine the competent court by choosing his own domicile."

[64] The other two rules identified for the U.K. apply only in Scotland.
[65] See the Jenard Report, commentary on Art. 3.
[66] Case 220/88 [1990] E.C.R. 49 (translation from [1990] I.L.Pr. 299).

Jurisdiction over persons not domiciled in a contracting state: Article 4

2–41   The position of defendants not domiciled in a contracting state is that subject to Article 16, dealing with exclusive jurisdiction, and the proviso to Article 4, national law continues to apply. In the case of the United Kingdom, that means that jurisdiction continues to be determined according to RSC, Ord. 11, r. 1(1).

> Article 4
>
> If a person is not domiciled in a Contracting State, the jurisdiction of the courts of each Contracting State shall, subject to the provisions of Article 16, be determined by the law of that State.
>
> As against such a defendant, any person domiciled in a Contracting State may, whatever his nationality, avail himself in that State of the rules of jurisdiction there in force, and in particular those specified in the second paragraph of Article 3, in the same way as nationals of that state.

2–42   The effect of the second paragraph is that as against a defendant not domiciled in a contracting state, a plaintiff domiciled in any contracting state may avail himself of any rule of exorbitant jurisdiction which in terms is only for the benefit of nationals. This has no effect in the United Kingdom, since no English or Scottish rule of exorbitant jurisdiction depends on nationality, but United Kingdom domiciled plaintiffs may invoke the rule in actions in other contracting states, such as France, against defendants not domiciled in any contracting state.

The domicile of companies and individuals

2–43   The Brussels Convention does not contain any general definition of domicile, providing only:

> Article 52
>
> In order to determine whether a party is domiciled in the Contracting state whose courts are seized of a matter, the court shall apply its internal law.
>
> If a party is not domiciled in the State whose courts are seized of the matter, then in order to determine whether the party is domiciled in another Contracting State, the court shall apply the law of that State.[67]

2–44   For individuals, the Brussels Convention is completely silent as to how to determine domicile and the matter is left entirely to the internal law of each member state. For legal persons such as companies and other associations, and for trusts, there is a modicum of harmonisation:

---

[67] A further paragraph dealing with domicile of dependence was removed by the San Sebastian Convention.

Article 53

For the purposes of this Convention, the seat of a company or other legal person or association of natural or legal persons shall be treated as its domicile. However, in order to determine that seat, the court shall apply its rules of private international law.

In order to determine whether a trust is domiciled in the Contracting State whose courts are seized of the matter, the court shall apply its rules of private international law.

Although the Brussels Convention refers the question of domicile to national law, for the purposes of the Convention the courts of the United Kingdom apply a definition of domicile which is completely different to that at common law. The Civil Jurisdiction and Judgments Act 1982 contains detailed provisions for determining the domicile of individuals,[68] corporations and associations,[69] persons deemed to be domiciled in the United Kingdom for certain purposes;[70] trusts[71] and the Crown.[72] In contrast to common law domicile, Convention domicile attaches a person not to a legal system but to a particular place: an individual is typically domiciled where he is resident; a company is domiciled at the place where it has its registered office or where its central management or control is exercised. It follows that a company may easily have two domiciles, and may be domiciled in two different countries if it is incorporated in one but managed and controlled in another. **2–45**

Matters of no or limited relevance to jurisdiction under the Convention

In view of the unfamiliarity of much of the Brussels Convention scheme, it may be worth listing some matters which are of little or no relevance under the Convention, although in pre-existing national law they may have been of considerable importance. **2–46**

First, the domicile or nationality of the plaintiff is almost always irrelevant. If the defendant is domiciled in a contracting state, then jurisdiction against him is determined exclusively by the terms of the Brussels Convention regardless of whether the plaintiff is domiciled in a contracting state or not. A plaintiff from the United States or Japan is, with one exception, in exactly the same position as one from France or Germany. Secondly, nationality, as opposed to domicile, is hardly ever a relevant connecting factor for either plaintiffs or defendants. The only exception to either of these principles is that of Article 4, providing that plaintiffs domiciled in any contracting state may invoke the rules of exorbitant jurisdiction of a contracting state, against a defendant not

---

[68] s. 41.
[69] s. 42 and 43.
[70] s. 44.
[71] s. 45.
[72] s. 46.

domiciled in a contracting state, in exactly the same way as nationals of that state.

2–47   Thirdly, many of the traditional common law bases for exorbitant jurisdiction are not available under the Convention. This is most obvious for the rule allowing jurisdiction to be based on the service of originating process on the defendant during his temporary presence in England. This is expressly precluded, in the case of defendants domiciled in a contracting state, by Article 3. However, other familiar rules have no counterpart in the Convention, such as that of RSC, Ord. 11, r. 1(1)(d) giving jurisdiction in contract cases if the contract was made in England or was governed by English law. Neither of these is of the slightest relevance under the Brussels Convention; and one looks instead to any written exclusive jurisdiction clause, to the "place of performance of the obligation in question," or to the domicile of the prospective defendant. This illustrates a more general rule, which is that the Brussels Convention attaches little or no importance, except perhaps in the case of the exclusive jurisdictions of Article 16, to assigning jurisdiction to a court familiar with the workings of the *lex causae*, no matter how arcane. It is taken for granted that a French or German court can perfectly well enforce a contract governed by Danish law, or an English court determine liability for a tort committed by an English defendant in Spain or Italy.

2–48   Fourthly, the various common law bases for declining or refusing jurisdiction are generally inapplicable under the Convention. The general character of the Brussels Convention is that its provisions on jurisdiction are mandatory. The court validity first seised of an action typically has no discretion to decline jurisdiction on grounds such as *forum non conveniens*, international comity, public policy or discretionary factors in general. The theory is that legal certainty prevails and that the underlying policy considerations have already been taken care of in the Convention itself. As the Jenard Report puts it: "the rules of jurisdiction codified in Title II determine which State's courts are most appropriate to assume jurisdiction, taking into account all relevant matters . . ." As will be seen, English courts have sometimes found it very difficult to accept that the Convention completely sweeps away most, if not all, of the common law grounds on which they have previously refused to entertain actions for infringement of foreign intellectual property rights.

2–49   The Schlosser Report comments on the pre-existing situation in the United Kingdom and how it would change under the Convention[73]:

> "The idea that a national court has discretion in the exercise of its jurisdiction either territorially or as regards the subject matter of a dispute does not generally exist in Continental legal systems. Even where, in the rules relating to jurisdiction, tests of an exceptionally

---

[73] Schlosser Report, paras 76, 78. Schlosser concludes that "the United Kingdom and Irish delegations did not press for a formal adjustment of the 1968 Convention on this point."

flexible nature are laid down, no room is left for the exercise of any discretionary latitude. It is true that Continental legal systems recognize the power of a court to transfer proceedings from one court to another. Even then the court has no discretion in determining whether or not this power should be exercised. In contrast, the law in the United Kingdom and in Ireland has evolved judicial discretionary powers in certain fields. In some cases, these correspond in practice to legal provisions regarding jurisdiction which are more detailed in the Continental States, while in others they have no counterpart on the Continent. It is therefore difficult to evaluate such powers within the context of the 1968 Convention . . .

According to the views of the delegations from the Continental Member States of the Community such possibilities are not open to the courts of those States when, under the 1968 Convention, they have jurisdiction and are asked to adjudicate.

Article 21 expressly prohibits a court from disregarding the fact that proceedings are already pending abroad. For the rest the view was expressed that under the 1968 Convention the Contracting States are not only entitled to exercise jurisdiction in accordance with the provisions laid down in Title 2; they are also obliged to do so. A plaintiff must be sure which court has jurisdiction. He should not have to waste his time and money risking that the court concerned may consider itself less competent than another. In particular, in accordance with the general spirit of the 1968 Convention, the fact that foreign law has to be applied, either generally or in a particular case, should not constitute a sufficient reason for a court to decline jurisdiction. Where the courts of several States have jurisdiction, the plaintiff has deliberately been given a right of choice, which should not be weakened by application of the doctrine of *forum conveniens*."

2–50 Finally, the Convention is very different in the scope it provides for refusing to recognise or enforce foreign judgments. Judgments, once given, should circulate freely. The principle is that of full faith and credit, even if that expression is not actually used. In particular, a foreign judgment can never be reviewed on its merits and there are only very limited opportunities for challenging the jurisdiction of the foreign court. Once a court in a contracting state has entered judgment against a defendant who has been properly served, then the opportunities for re-opening the case when enforcement is sought in another contracting state are virtually non-existent.

D. THE SPECIAL JURISDICTIONS

Jurisdiction for contracts: place of performance of obligation in question

2–51 By way of exception to Article 2, Article 5 provides for a number of instances in which courts other than those of the defendant's domicile have concurrent jurisdiction under the Convention, against defendants domiciled in a contracting state. Article 5(1) gives jurisdiction "in matters relating to contract" to "the courts for the place of performance of the obligation in question." The remainder of the Article (which was modified by the San Sebastian Convention) further explains this concept in the case of contracts of employment. The expression "matters relating to contract" has an independent meaning,[74] so that the characterisation of a claim as contractual or not under English law (or the applicable law) is not conclusive. The "obligation in question" also has an independent meaning. Outside employment law, it means the principal obligation actually sued on,[75] rather than some underlying "characteristic performance" in the sense of the Rome Contracts Convention.[76] National law as the applicable law of the contract may have to be consulted to identify the place of performance of this obligation.

Jurisdiction based on place of tort

2–52   Article 5(3), conferring jurisdiction over defendants domiciled in a contracting state in matters relating to tort on "the courts for the place where the harmful event occurred" is considered in detail at paragraphs 2–77 *et seq.* below.

Branches and agencies

2–53   Article 5(5) gives jurisdiction "as regards a dispute arising out of the operations of a branch, agency or other establishment" to the courts of the place where the branch, etc., is situated. As with all the Article 5 jurisdictions, it applies only to persons domiciled in a contracting state. The Article has been given a restricted interpretation by the European Court of Justice and is principally invoked in contract disputes where the contract was concluded with the branch and it is desired to sue the foreign principal. The Court has, however, held that the Article also applies to non-contractual obligations arising from the activities of the branch in the country in which it is situated;[77] and it would not seem to be relevant whether the tort in question was ordered or authorised by the head office or was committed by the branch inadvertently or on its own initiative.

2–54   The possibility of basing jurisdiction on Article 5(5) should be borne in mind if a branch has committed or threatened an infringement, and it is desired to sue the foreign owner of the branch alone, or join him as a co-defendant. Although jurisdiction under Article 5(5) and substantive liability under internal law are quite different, the case law of the Court suggests that if Article 5(5) applies then there is likely to be a better than arguable case of joint tortfeasorship against the head office. The converse is not true, and many cases of joint tortfeasorship under

---

[74] Case C–26/92 *Jacob Handte v. TMCS* [1992] E.C.R. I–3967.
[75] Case 266/85 *Shenavai v. Kreischer* [1987] E.C.R. 239; [1987] 3 C.M.L.R. 782.
[76] As to which see para. 7–30.
[77] Case 33/78 *Somafer v. Saar-Ferngas* [1978] E.C.R. 2183; [1979] 1 C.M.L.R. 490.

English internal law would not involve a branch in the sense of Article 5(5). In the ordinary case, therefore, it is to be doubted if reliance on Article 5(5) would add anything useful to Articles 2, 5(3) and 6(1) and it would be pointless to assume the burden of proving that the local infringer was a "branch" in the restricted sense of Article 5(5).

One possible exception might be where the branch operated in the country of infringement but was not domiciled there. Since a company is unlikely to be domiciled in every country where it does business, and since the nature of a branch precludes it from having much autonomy, it is quite plausible that its "seat" will be abroad and may correspond to that of its parent. In that case, jurisdiction over the branch under Article 5(3) would not justify joining the parent under Article 6(1), because the latter can be relied on only when jurisdiction over the first defendant is based on domicile. The Article would also be of use where infringement had been committed by a branch, and the branch had ceased to exist. A further advantage of Article 5(5) is that, in comparison to Article 5(3), there is currently no reason to suppose that the jurisdiction a court enjoys under Article 5(5) is ever confined to giving relief only in respect of damage suffered in its own territory.[78]

2–55

Despite an early indication to the contrary, Article 5(5) is not confined to disputes arising out of the operations of the branch within the contracting state within which the branch is established.[79]

The meaning of "branch, agency or other establishment"

From the decided cases, the first element of Article 5(5) is one of control by the foreign parent. In *de Bloos v. Bouyer*[80] the European Court of Justice held that "branch, agency or other establishment" was to be given an independent meaning, rather than one derived from national law, and that the grantee of an exclusive sales concession could not be regarded as within Article 5(5) when he was not under the direction or control of the grantor. The element of control was affirmed in *Blanckaert & Willems v. Trost*[81] where Article 5(5) was held to be inapplicable to an independent commercial agent, free to arrange his own work and possibly representing several competing organisations. Perhaps the best short test is that the "branch, agency or other establishment" should be an "extension" of the parent, a term coined in *Somafer v. Saar-Ferngas*[82] and applied in *SAR Schotte v. Parfums Rothschild*[83] where the French parent company had no "dependent branch, agency or other establishment" as such in Germany, but pursued its activities "through an independent[84] company with the same name and identical management

2–56

---

[78] See para. 2–86.
[79] Case C–439/93 *Lloyd's Register of Shipping v. Campenon Bernard* [1995] E.C.R. I–961; [1995] All E.R. (E.C.) 531 not following Case 33/78 *Somafer v. Saar-Ferngas* [1978] E.C.R. 2183; [1979] 1 C.M.L.R. 490 in this respect..
[80] Case 14/76 [1976] E.C.R. 1497; [1977] 1 C.M.L.R. 60.
[81] Case 139/80 [1981] E.C.R. 819; [1982] 2 C.M.L.R. 1.
[82] Case 33/78 [1978] E.C.R. 2183; [1979] 1 C.M.L.R. 490.
[83] Case 218/86 [1987] E.C.R. 4905.
[84] *i.e.* legally distinct. The Rothschild companies had argued that Rothschild GmbH, as a subsidiary of Parfums Rothschild SARL, could not be a "branch, agency or establishment" of the latter.

which negotiates and conducts business in its name and which it uses as an extension of itself." The French company was therefore subject to German jurisdiction.

2–57   The other element of Article 5(5), and one conflicting to some degree with that of dependency, is that the branch, agency or other establishment must apparently be a substantial one with at least some of the attributes of a separate existence. The two elements are found together in *Somafer v. Saar-Ferngas*[85] where the European Court of Justice held that the concept of a branch, agency or other establishment implied

> "a place of business which has the appearance of permanency, such as an extension of the parent body, has a management and is materially equipped to negotiate business with third parties so that the latter, although knowing that there will if necessary be a legal link with the parent body, the head office of which is abroad, do not have to deal directly with the parent body but may transact business at the place of business constituting the extension."

2–58   Again, in *Blanckaert & Willems v. Trost*[86] merely transmitting orders to the parent, without being involved in either negotiating their terms or arranging their execution, fell short of acting as a "branch, agency or other establishment." However, in *SAR Schotte v. Parfums Rothschild*[87] the Court contemplated that the management of the "extension" and the management of the parent might be one and the same, and gave altogether more emphasis than *Somafer* to the legitimate interests of parties dealing with what may in fact be a shell company, but which is held out as something more.

Trusts

2–59   Article 5(6) provides that where a trust is created by operation of a statute or a written instrument, or is created orally and evidenced in writing, then a settlor, trustee or beneficiary may be sued in his capacity as such in the courts of the contracting state where the trust is domiciled; as an alternative to the courts of the defendant's domicile. By section 45(3) of the Civil Jurisdiction and Judgments Act 1982 a trust is domiciled in a part of the United Kingdom if and only if the system of law of that part of the United Kingdom is the system of law with which the trust has its closest and most real connection: in other words, a trust is domiciled in England if English law is the proper law of the trust Jurisdiction under Article 5(6) is apparently not excluded by Article 16(1) though the trust is one of land or other real property[88]; and *a*

---

[85] Case 33/78 [1978] E.C.R. 2183; [1979] 1 C.M.L.R. 490.
[86] Case 139/80 [1981] E.C.R. 819; [1982] 2 C.M.L.R. 1.
[87] Case 218/86 [1987] E.C.R. 4905.
[88] In Case C–294/92 *Webb v. Webb* [1994] E.C.R. I–1717 the European Court of Justice held that Art. 16(1) did not prevent the English Courts having jurisdiction under Art. 2 over a dispute about the existence of a constructive or resulting trust of an apartment in France. Art. 5(6) was neither relevant nor necessary, since the trust was not in writing and the defendant was domiciled in England, but in a conflict with Art. 16, Arts 2 and 5 would stand or fall together.

fortiori a written trust of one or more patents would fall under Article 5(6) notwithstanding the exclusive jurisdiction Article 16(4) confers on the courts of the country of registration in matters concerned with the registration or validity of patents and other registered intellectual property rights.[89]

Trusts are of interest in intellectual property litigation in two main contexts. One is where one person holds the bare legal title to an intellectual property right and another the beneficial interest. This typically arises when there is an agreement or other source of obligation to assign, an assignment which is defective in form, or an unregistered assignment of a right for which dealings are required to be registered. Even if the requirement of writing were met in this case, Article 5(6) would not create jurisdiction against third parties such as infringers. Its only relevance would be to allow an equitable owner to add the bare legal owner as a defendant (as is common practice if he will not assign his legal title or allow his name to be used as plaintiff) without needing to rely on Article 2 or Article 6(1). The other is where a constructive trust is imposed by law as restitution for wrongdoing, for instance in the law of breach of confidence, or where an agent registers a trade mark in his own name when it properly belongs to his principal. In the latter case, there is no written instrument at all and Article 5(6) cannot apply.

2–60

Joinder of multiple defendants: Article 6(1)

Article 6(1) allows several defendants to be sued in the courts of the place where any one of them is domiciled. It reads:

2–61

> A person domiciled in a Contracting State may also be sued—
> Where he is one of a number of defendants, in the courts for the place where any one of them is domiciled.

For there to be jurisdiction under Article 6(1), then there must already be at least one defendant over whom jurisdiction exists by reason of domicile. If jurisdiction over the other defendant(s) can only be based on one of the other provisions of the Convention, such as Article 5(3), then Article 6(1) cannot apply.

In contrast to Article 6(2), Article 6(1) contains no express qualification to prevent forum shopping. However, the potential the Article has for misuse has been recognised in the Jenard Report, by the European Court of Justice, and in English law. The Jenard Report comments:

2–62

> "It follows from the text of the Convention that, where there are several defendants domiciled in different Contracting States, the plaintiff can at his option sue them all in the courts for the place where any one of them is domiciled.

---

[89] This would be consistent with Case 288/82 *Duijnstee v. Goderbauer* [1983] E.C.R. 3663; [1985] 1 C.M.L.R. 220. Compare Case C–294/92 *Webb v. Webb* [1994] E.C.R. I–1717 to *Kakkar v. Szelke* [1989] 1 F.S.R. 225 CA, decided under the Protocol to the European Patent Convention. The latter may be too *communautaire* in its reasoning.

In order for this rule to be applicable there must be a connection between the claims made against each of the defendants, as for example in the case of joint debtors. It follows that action cannot be brought solely with the object of ousting the jurisdiction of the courts of the State in which the defendant is domiciled.

Jurisdiction derived from the domicile of one of the defendants was adopted by the Committee because it makes it possible to obviate the handing down in the Contracting States of judgments which are irreconcilable with one another."

2–63   The Jenard Report was referred to with approval by the European Court of Justice in the first case to consider the application of Article 6(1), *Kalfelis v. Schroeder*[90]:

"The principle laid down in the Convention is that jurisdiction is vested in the courts of the State of the defendant's domicile and that the jurisdiction provided for in Article 6(1) is an exception to that principle. It follows that an exception of that kind must be treated in such a manner that there is no possibility of the very existence of that principle being called in question.

That possibility might arise if a plaintiff were at liberty to make a claim against a number of defendants with the sole object of ousting the jurisdiction of the courts of the State where one of the defendants is domiciled. As is stated in the report prepared by the committee of experts which drafted the Convention (. . .), such a possibility must be excluded. For that purpose, there must be a connection between the claims made against each of the defendants.

In order to ensure, as far as possible, the equality and uniformity of the rights and obligations under the Convention of the Contracting States and of the persons concerned, the nature of that connection must be determined independently.

In that regard, it must be noted that the abovementioned report prepared by the committee of experts referred expressly, in its explanation of Article 6(1), to the concern to avoid the risk in the Contracting States of judgments which are incompatible with each other. Furthermore, account was taken of that preoccupation in the Convention itself, Article 22 of which governs cases of related actions brought before courts in different Contracting States.

The rule laid down in Article 6(1) therefore applies where the actions brought against the various defendants are related when the proceedings are instituted, that is to say where it is expedient to hear and determine them together in order to avoid the risk of irreconcilable judgments resulting from separate proceedings. It is for the national court to verify in each individual case whether that condition is satisfied.

It must therefore be stated in reply to the first question that for Article 6(1) of the Convention to apply there must exist between

[90] Case 189/87 [1989] E.C.R. 5565.

various actions brought by the same plaintiff against different defendants a connection of such a kind that it is expedient to determine those actions together in order to avoid the risk of irreconcilable judgments resulting from separate proceedings."

The principle stated in *Kalfelis* may be more ambiguous than appears at first sight. It is defined in terms of a risk of *irreconcilable* judgments resulting if the additional defendant is not joined. This was a reference to Article 27(3) prohibiting recognition of a judgment, which is irreconcilable with one given in a dispute between the same parties in the state in which recognition is sought. The concept of irreconcilable judgments had an independent meaning which was relatively narrow. As the Court explained in *Hoffman v. Krieg*,[91] "In order to ascertain whether two judgments are irreconcilable within the meaning of Article 27(3), it should be examined whether they entail legal consequences that are mutually exclusive." However in *The Tatry*[92] the Court acknowledged that the expression "irreconcilable judgments" had a wider meaning that this in the context of Article 22: "In order to achieve proper administration of justice, that interpretation must be broad and cover all cases where there is a risk of conflicting decisions, even if the judgments can be separately enforced and their legal consequences are not mutually exclusive." It is uncertain which of these interpretations (or even a third) applies to Article 6(1), though it is unlikely that mere inconsistency in result or reasoning amounts to irreconcilablity in this sense. **2–64**

It is suggested, by analogy with the treatment of Article 6(2) of the Convention by the European Court of Justice in *Kongress Agentur Hagen v. Zeehaghe*,[93] that Article 6(1) is not mandatory and does not oblige a court to allow the joinder of additional defendants where its own procedural rules give it a discretion to refuse, provided that the effectiveness of the Convention is not prejudiced and the discretion is exercised without discrimination on the ground of nationality or foreign domicile.[94] **2–65**

Counterclaims: Article 6(3)

Article 6(3) permits a person domiciled in a contracting state to be sued "on a counter-claim arising from the same contract or facts on which the original claim was based" in the court in which the original claim is pending. In comparison to English practice, the requirement for the counterclaim to be based on the same facts as the original claim is relatively limiting. There is a distinction between a counterclaim for separate relief, which must fall within Article 6(3) if the court is to **2–66**

---

[91] Case 145/86 [1988] E.C.R. 645.

[92] Case C–406/92 [1994] I–E.C.R. 5439.

[93] Case C–365/88 [1990] E.C.R. I–1845.

[94] The suggestion in the text is not uncontroversial. It may depend on how generously Art. 6(1) is interpreted in the light of *Kalfelis*. For Art. 6(1) in English intellectual property law, see paras 3–10 *et seq.*

entertain it in the absence of any other basis for jurisdiction under the Convention; and a defence properly so called, which can always be raised even if the party relying on it would have to go to another court to sue on it as a cause of action in its own right. In *Danvaern v. Otterbeck*[95] the European Court of Justice explained the scope of Article 6(3) in the context of a defence of set-off under Danish law.[96]

"By its first question the national court asks whether Article 6(3) of the Convention applies to the situation where a defendant, who is being sued in a court which has jurisdiction over him, pleads in reply a claim which he allegedly has against the plaintiff.

The national laws of the Contracting States generally distinguish between two situations. One is where the defendant pleads, as a defence, the existence of a claim he allegedly has against the plaintiff, which would have the effect of wholly or partially extinguishing the plaintiff's claim. The other is where the defendant, by a separate claim made in the context of the same proceedings, seeks a judgment or decree ordering the plaintiff to pay him a debt. In the latter case, the separate claim can be made for an amount exceeding that claimed by the plaintiff, and it can be proceeded with even if the plaintiff's claim is dismissed.

Procedurally, a defence is an integral part of the action initiated by the plaintiff and therefore does not involve the plaintiff being 'sued' in the court in which his action is pending, within the meaning of Article 6(3) of the Convention. The defences which may be raised and the conditions under which they may be raised are determined by national law.

Article 6(3) of the Convention is not intended to deal with that situation.

By contrast, a claim by the defendant for a separate judgment or decree against the plaintiff presupposes that the court in which the plaintiff has brought proceedings also has jurisdiction to hear such an application.

Article 6(3) is specifically intended to establish the conditions under which a court has jurisdiction to hear a claim which would involve a separate judgment or decree. (. . .)

The answer to the national court's first question must therefore be that Article 6(3) of the Convention applies only to claims by defendants which seek the pronouncement of a separate judgment or decree. It does not apply to the situation where a defendant raises, as a pure defence, a claim which he allegedly has against the plaintiff. The defences which may be raised and the conditions under which they may be raised are governed by national law."

2–67   The situation in *Danvaern v. Otterbeck* was that the court seized of the action would apparently have lacked Convention jurisdiction over the

---

[95] Case C–341/93 [1995] E.C.R. I–2053.
[96] Danish law did not distinguish in terms between a counterclaim by way of set-off and one with a view to a separate judgment.

counterclaim, though the counterclaim was not within the exclusive jurisdiction of any other court. The Convention is silent as to whether Article 6(3) is subject to Article 16 or overrides it, but the fact that voluntary submission to the jurisdiction cannot override Article 16 strongly suggests that Article 6(3) is subject to Article 16 also.[97] The reason for allowing counterclaims in derogation from the general provisions as to jurisdiction is normally said to be that by commencing proceedings in a particular court the plaintiff has implicitly submitted to its jurisdiction, but submission can never override the exclusive jurisdictions of Article 16. This analysis would not be inconsistent with the reasoning of the Court in *Meeth v. Glacetal*,[98] where a counterclaim by way of set-off was allowed to proceed although at first sight it was contrary to an exclusive choice-of-court agreement. Although the point was not expressly decided in *Lieber v. Göbel*,[99] that case proceeded throughout on the unchallenged assumption that a counterclaim arguably within Article 16(1) was to be treated in exactly the same way as an ordinary claim. Whatever the relationship between Articles 6(3) and 16, however, it is suggested on the authority of *Danvaern v. Otterbeck* that a defendant cannot be deprived of a valid defence simply because he would be unable to rely on the same facts as the basis for a counterclaim. This must be true whether the bar to the counterclaim arises under national law or under the provisions of the Convention.

The possible treatments of counterclaims for revocation in actions for infringement of registered intellectual property rights is dealt with at paragraphs 2–101 *et seq.*

Ancillary causes of action: "accessory jurisdiction"

Legal systems with a federal system of courts may recognise a doctrine **2–68** under which courts seised of a cause of action within their normal designated jurisdiction may also deal with related causes of action which would not otherwise be within their jurisdiction, so as to avoid multiplicity of proceedings. If any such doctrine exists under the Brussels Convention, it has no express textual basis and is confined to disputes which are principally contractual in nature.[1] If the dispute is in tort, then jurisdiction over every cause of action relied on has to be separately justified under Article 5(3) or under one of the other jurisdiction-conferring provisions of the Convention.[2] This was the conclusion reached by the European Court of Justice in *Kalfelis v. Schroeder*,[3] where

---

[97] Tritton, *Intellectual Property in Europe* (1996) reaches this conclusion by analogy with Case 24/76 *Salotti v. RUWA* [1976] E.C.R. 1831; [1977] 1 C.M.L.R. 345 and Case 25/76 *Galeries Segoura v. Rahim Bonakdarian* [1976] E.C.R. 1851; [1977] 1 C.M.L.R. 361, both of which give Art. 17 precedence over Art. 6.

[98] Case 23/78 [1978] E.C.R. 2133; [1979] 1 C.M.L.R. 520.

[99] Case C–292/93 [1994] E.C.R. I–2535.

[1] Case 34/82 *Peters v. ZNAV* [1983] E.C.R. 987; [1984] 2 C.M.L.R. 605 arguably contemplates this, but the scope and even the existence of the doctrine are uncertain.

[2] Art. 22 may be relevant, but presupposes that the court first seised has jurisdiction over both actions.

[3] Case 189/87 [1988] E.C.R. 5565. See also Case 220/84 *AS Autoteile v. Malhe* [1985] E.C.R. 2267; [1986] 3 C.M.L.R. 321.

the final question referred by the *Bundesgerichtshof* was in these terms: "Does Article 5(3) of the EEC Convention confer, in respect of an action based on claims in tort and contract and for unjust enrichment, accessory jurisdiction on account of factual connection even in respect of the claims not based in tort?" The Court answered the question in the negative:

"With respect to the second part of the question, it must be observed, as already indicated above, that the 'special jurisdictions' enumerated in Articles 5 and 6 of the Convention constitute derogations from the principle that jurisdiction is vested in the courts of the State where the defendant is domiciled and as such must be interpreted restrictively. It must therefore be recognized that a court which has jurisdiction under Article 5 (3) over an action in so far as it is based on tort or delict does not have jurisdiction over that action in so far as it is not so based.

Whilst it is true that disadvantages arise from different aspects of the same dispute being adjudicated upon by different courts, it must be pointed out, on the one hand, that a plaintiff is always entitled to bring his action in its entirety before the courts for the domicile of the defendant and, on the other, that Article 22 of the Convention allows the first court seised, in certain circumstances, to hear the case in its entirety provided that there is a connection between the actions brought before the different courts.

In those circumstances, the reply to the second part of the second question must be that a court which has jurisdiction under Article 5(3) over an action in so far as it is based on tort or delict does not have jurisdiction over that action in so far as it is not so based."

2–69   The treatment of accessory causes of action, which are not permitted, should be distinguished from that of preliminary or incidental questions.[4] A court may answer a question over which it would have no jurisdiction in isolation, if it is necessary to do so in order to decide an issue of which it is validly seised.

E. OTHER RELEVANT JURISDICTIONS

Exclusive jurisdictions: Article 16

2–70   Article 16 of the Brussels Convention confers exclusive jurisdiction on the courts of specific member states, regardless of the domicile of any party, in five instances which may be briefly summarised as: land and tenancies, the internal affairs of corporations, public registers, registered intellectual property rights and the enforcement of judgments. Article 4

[4] See para. 3–105.

expressly provides that it is Article 16, rather than national law, which applies even in the case of proceedings against a party not domiciled in a member state. See paragraphs 2–101 *et seq.*

Jurisdiction by agreement: Article 17

Article 17 deals with agreements to confer exclusive jurisdiction on **2–71** particular courts. The general principle is that such agreements are fully binding if at least one party is domiciled in a contracting state, and if no party is so domiciled then the chosen court must still be given a right of first refusal. However, Article 17 is expressly subordinate to Article 16, so the agreement of the parties cannot prevail against the exclusive jurisdictions of the latter. This is important, since it means that jurisdiction over the validity of patents, etc., cannot be conferred by agreement on a court which does not have exclusive jurisdiction already pursuant to Article 16(4).

> Article 17
>
> If the parties, one or more of whom is domiciled in a Contracting State, have agreed that a court or the courts of a Contracting State are to have jurisdiction to settle any disputes which have arisen or which may arise in connection with a particular legal relationship, that court or those courts shall have exclusive jurisdiction. Such an agreement conferring jurisdiction shall be either—
>
> (a) in writing or evidenced in writing or,
>
> (b) in a form which accords with practices which the parties have established between themselves, or
>
> (c) in international trade or commerce, in a form which accords with a usage of which the parties are or ought to have been aware and which in such trade or commerce is widely known to, and regularly observed by, parties to contracts of the type involved in the particular trade or commerce concerned.
>
> [. . .]
>
> Where such an agreement is concluded by parties, none of whom is domiciled in a Contracting State, the courts of other Contracting States shall have no jurisdiction over their disputes unless the court or courts chosen have declined jurisdiction.
>
> [. . .]
>
> Agreements or provisions of a trust instrument conferring jurisdiction shall have no legal force if they are contrary to the provisions of Articles 12 or 15, or if the courts whose jurisdiction they purport to exclude have exclusive jurisdiction by virtue of Article 16.
>
> If an agreement conferring jurisdiction was concluded for the benefit of only one of the parties, that party shall retain the right to bring proceedings in any other court which has jurisdiction by virtue of this Convention [. . .]

Article 17 deals in terms only with exclusive jurisdiction agreements in **2–72** the narrow sense of jurisdiction being conferred on one court alone to the exclusion of all others. The common situation, in English practice, of a choice-of-court clause conferring non-exclusive jurisdiction, possibly on one of several courts at the plaintiff's option, was dealt with on the same basis by Hoffmann J. in *Kurz v. Stellar*,[5] but the reasoning has been criticised and is difficult to reconcile with the actual terms of Article 17.

Voluntary submission and failure to contest jurisdiction in time: Article 18

2–73   Article 18 provides that, apart from the other jurisdiction-conferring provisions of the Convention, a court of a contracting state has jurisdiction over any defendant[6] who enters an appearance, unless the appearance was entered solely to contest the jurisdiction or unless Article 16 would be contravened. It follows that unless the case is within one of the exclusive jurisdictions of Article 16, the service of a defence on the merits always operates to waive any defect in the jurisdiction of the court.[7] Conversely, if the case is within Article 16 the court must decline jurisdiction of its own motion pursuant to Article 19 and not even voluntary submission by the defendant can make any difference.

Provisional and protective measures: Article 24

2–74   The enforcement provisions of the Brussels Convention generally apply only to *inter partes* proceedings in which the defendant has been validly served and has had sufficient time to arrange his defence.[8] *Ex parte* orders such as *Mareva* and *Anton Piller* orders are to this extent outside the normal rules of the Convention, even if granted in connection with main proceedings which fall within it. However, *ex parte* orders may need to be continued on an *inter partes* basis if they are to be effective; and ordinary interlocutory injunctions may be granted either *ex parte* or *inter partes*. In the latter case they are as much subject to the provisions of the Brussels Convention as final injunctions granted after trial.

Article 24 provides:

> Application may be made to the courts of a Contracting State for such provisional, including protective, measures as may be available under the law of that State, even if, under this Convention, the courts of another Contracting State have jurisdiction as to the substance of the matter.

[5] [1992] Ch. 196; [1991] 3 W.L.R. 1046; [1992] 1 All E.R. 630 (Hoffmann J.).
[6] The Article does not require the defendant to be domiciled in a contracting state.
[7] The case law of the European Court of Justice allows a defence on the merits to be filed at the same time as a challenge to jurisdiction, without prejudice to the latter. Cases 150/80 *Elefanten Schuh v. Jacqmain* [1981] E.C.R. 1671; [1982] 3 C.M.L.R. 1 and 27/81 *Rohr v. Ossberger* [1981] E.C.R. 2431; [1982] 3 C.M.L.R. 29.
[8] Art. 27(2); Case 125/79 *Denilauler v. Couchet Freres* [1980] E.C.R. 1553; [1981] 1 C.M.L.R. 62; Case 166/80 *Klomps v. Michel* [1981] E.C.R. 1593; [1982] 2 C.M.L.R. 773; Case 49/48 *Debaecker v. Bouwman* [1985] E.C.R. 1779; [1986] 2 C.M.L.R. 400; Case C–305/88 *Lancray v. Peters* [1990] E.C.R. I–2725.

The Article has been considered by the European Court of Justice in **2–75** relatively few decided cases.[9] In *Denilauler v. Couchet Freres*[10] the Court examined the relationship of Article 24 to the normal rules of the Convention on jurisdiction and enforcement to conclude that although *ex parte* procedures such as *saisie conservatoire* were permitted by the Convention, orders so made fell outside the scheme for automatic enforcement.

> "Article 24 does not preclude provisional or protective measures ordered in the State of origin pursuant to adversary proceedings— even though by default—from being the subject of recognition and an authorization for enforcement on the conditions laid down in Articles 25 to 49 of the Convention. On the other hand the conditions imposed by Title III of the Convention on the recognition and the enforcement of Judicial decisions are not fulfilled in the case of provisional or protective measures which are ordered or authorized by a court without the party against whom they are directed having been summoned to appear and which are intended to be enforced without prior service on that party. It follows that this type of judicial decision is not covered by the simplified enforcement procedure provided for by Title III of the Convention. However, as the Government of the United Kingdom has rightly observed, Article 24 provides a procedure for litigants which to a large extent removes the drawbacks of this situation.
>
> The reply to Questions 1 and 2 should therefore be that judicial decisions authorizing provisional or protective measures, which are delivered without the party against which they are directed having been summoned to appear and which are intended to be enforced without prior service do not come within the system of recognition and enforcement provided for by Title III of the Convention."

Denilauler v. Couchet Freres leaves open the question of how far the **2–76** concept of "provisional, including protective measures" extends beyond *saisie conservatoire* and its English equivalent, the *Mareva* injunction.[11] Some guidance is provided in *Reichert v. Dresdner Bank (No. 2)* where it was argued that a French procedure for avoiding fraudulent preferences, the *action paulienne*, might come within Article 24. The Court denied this and defined the scope of Article 24 in the following terms:

> "Therefore the 'provisional or protective measures' referred to in Article 24 should be understood as meaning measures which, in

---

[9] Other cases on Art. 24 are not particularly informative for present purposes. Case 143/78 *De Cavel v. De Cavel (No. 1)* [1979] E.C.R. 1055; [1979] 2 C.M.L.R. 547; Case 120/79 *De Cavel v. De Cavel (No. 2)* [1980] E.C.R. 731; [1980] 3 C.M.L.R. 1 and Case 25/81 *C.H.W. v. G.J.H.* [1982] E.C.R. 1189; [1983] 2 C.M.L.R. 125 all turned on the application of Art. 24 when the principal proceedings were arguably outside the scope of the Convention altogether, as relating to matrimonial relationships or property. See Collins, "Provisional Measures" in *Essays in International Litigation and the Conflict of Laws* (1994).

[10] Case 125/79 [1980] E.C.R. 1553; [1981] 1 C.M.L.R. 62.

[11] Case C–261/90 [1992] E.C.R. I–2149.

matters coming within the ambit of the Convention, are intended to maintain a legal or factual situation in order to safeguard rights an application for the recognition of which has been made to the court with jurisdiction as to the substance of the matter.

Although an action like the *action paulienne* in French law offers protection for the creditor's charge by preventing a voluntary reduction in the debtor's assets, it does not have the object of maintaining a factual or legal situation pending a judgment by the court with jurisdiction as to the substance of the matter. The purpose of such an action is to alter the legal status of the assets of the debtor and the beneficiary by applying to the court to order the disposition made by the debtor to defraud the creditor of his rights to be set aside as against the creditor. Such an action cannot therefore be classified as a provisional or protective measure within the meaning of Article 24 of the Convention.

It follows from what has been said that the reply to be given to the national court is that an action provided for in national law, such as the *action paulienne* in French law, whereby a creditor seeks to set aside, vis-a-vis himself, a transfer of rights *in rem* in immovable property in a manner which he considers to be a fraud on his rights, is not within the scope of Articles 5(3), 16(5) and 24 of the Convention of 27 September 1968 on Jurisdiction and the Enforcement of Judgments in Civil and Commercial Matters."

F. JURISDICTION BASED ON PLACE OF TORT

Article 5(3): its terms and treatment in the Jenard and Schlosser Reports

2–77   Article 5 of the Brussels Convention lists seven instances where jurisdiction is conferred on the courts of specified contracting states according to the subject matter of the proceedings and the existence of certain connecting factors; but it does not oust the concurrent jurisdiction of the courts of the defendant's domicile under Article 2. In its original 1968 version, the matters covered were contract, maintenance, tort, ancillary civil relief in criminal proceedings and disputes arising from the operations of branches or agencies. The 1978 Accession Convention added trusts and salvage. Article 5 applies only when the defendant is domiciled in a member state of the Convention. The Article is mandatory, and the courts of contracting states must take jurisdiction under it even if their internal law would not otherwise permit them to do so.[12]

2–78   Article 5(3) reads

---

[12] See the passages quoted from the Jenard Report, below. By way of exception, Art. 5(4) expressly gives jurisdiction for civil claims in criminal proceedings only to the extent local law permits such claims to be brought.

A person domiciled in a Contracting State may, in another Contracting State, be sued— . . .

In matters relating to tort, delict or quasi-delict, in the courts of the place where the harmful event occurred.

The Jenard Report contains the following commentary on Article 5 in general, and on Article 5(3) specifically:

"Articles 5 and 6

Articles 5 and 6 list the situations in which a defendant may be sued in a Contracting State other than that of his domicile. The forums provided for in these Articles supplement those which apply under Article 2. In the case of proceedings for which a court is specifically recognized as having jurisdiction under these Articles, the plaintiff may, at his option, bring the proceedings either in that court or in the competent courts of the State in which the defendant is domiciled.

One problem which arose here was whether it should always be possible to sue the defendant in one of the courts provided for in these Articles, or whether this should be allowed only if the jurisdiction of that court was also recognized by the internal law of the State concerned.

In other words, in the first case, jurisdiction would derive directly from the Convention and in the second there would need to be dual jurisdiction: that of the Convention and that of the internal law on local jurisdiction. Thus, for example, where Netherlands law on jurisdiction does not recognize the court for the place of performance of the obligation, can the plaintiff nevertheless sue the defendant before that court in the Netherlands? In addition, would there be any obligation on the Netherlands to adapt its national laws in order to give that court jurisdiction?

By adopting 'special' rules of jurisdiction, that is by directly designating the competent court without referring to the rules of jurisdiction in force in the State where such a court might be situated, the Committee decided that a plaintiff should always be able to sue a defendant in one of the forums provided for without having to take the internal law of the State concerned into consideration. Further, in laying down these rules, the Committee intended to facilitate implementation of the Convention. By ratifying the Convention, the Contracting States will avoid having to take any other measures to adapt their internal legislation to the criteria laid down in Articles 5 and 6.[13] The Convention itself determines which court has jurisdiction.

Adoption of the 'special' rules of jurisdiction is also justified by the fact that there must be a close connecting factor between the

---

[13] In contrast to the position in the U.K., international treaties were self-executing in all six of the original contracting states.

dispute and the court with jurisdiction to resolve it. Thus, to take the example of the forum *delicti commissi*, a person domiciled in a Contracting State other than the Netherlands who has caused an accident in The Hague may, under the Convention, be sued in a court in The Hague. This accident cannot give other Netherlands courts jurisdiction over the defendant. On this point there is thus a distinct difference between Article 2 and Articles 5 and 6, due to the fact that in Article 2 domicile is the connecting factor. (. . .)

Forum *delicti commissi* (Article 5(3))[14]

This jurisdiction is recognized by the national laws of the Member States with the exception of Luxembourg and the Netherlands, where it exists only in respect of collisions of ships and of road accidents. . . .

The fact that this jurisdiction is recognized under most of the legal systems, and incorporated in the majority of the bilateral conventions, was a ground for including it in the Convention, especially in view of the high number of road accidents.

Article 5(3) uses the expression 'the place where the harmful event occurred.' The Committee did not think it should specify whether that place is the place where the event which resulted in damage or injury occurred, or whether it is the place where the damage or injury was sustained. The Committee preferred to keep to a formula which has already been adopted by number of legal systems (Germany, France)."

2–79   The Schlosser Report contains no general commentary on Article 5 as a whole but makes the following observations about Article 5(3)[15]:

"Jurisdiction in matters relating to tort

Article 5(3) deals with the special tort jurisdiction. It presupposes that the wrongful act has already been committed and refers to the place where the harmful event has occurred. The legal systems of some States provide for preventive injunctions in matters relating to tort. This applies, for example, in cases where it is desired to prevent the publication of a libel or the sale of goods which have been manufactured or put on the market in breach of the law on patents or industrial property rights. In particular the laws of the United Kingdom and Germany provide for measures of this nature. No doubt Article 24 is applicable when courts have an application for provisional protective measures before them, even if their decision has, in practice, final effect. There is much to be said for the proposition that the courts specified in Article 5(3) should also have jurisdiction in proceedings whose main object is to prevent the imminent commission of a tort."[16]

---

[14] The commentary on Art. 5(4) is omitted, as are detailed references to the internal laws of the original six contracting states and to existing bilateral conventions.

[15] Schlosser Report, para. 134.2.

[16] For commentary on *quia timet* actions see para. 2–98.

The meaning of "tort" and its application to intellectual property infringement actions

Like most of the expressions used in the Brussels Convention, "tort, **2–80** delict or quasi-delict" has an independent or autonomous meaning and an action can fall within Article 5(3) whether or not it is regarded as tortious under the internal law of any particular state. Conversely, the fact that an action may be characterised as tortious under a state's internal law is not conclusive that it falls within Article 5(3). However, in contrast to most Articles which derogate from the fundamental principle that the defendant should be sued in the courts of his domicile, Article 5(3) has been given a relatively wide interpretation.

The question of whether Article 5(3) should be given an independent **2–81** meaning or should be left to internal law was answered by the European Court of Justice in *Kalfelis v. Schroeder*.[17]

"The second question submitted by the Bundesgerichtshof is intended essentially to ascertain, first, whether the phrase 'matters relating to tort, delict or quasi delict' used in Article 5 (3) of the Convention must be given an independent meaning or be defined in accordance with the applicable national law and, secondly, in the case of an action based concurrently on tortious or delictual liability, breach of contract and unjust enrichment, whether the court having jurisdiction by virtue of Article 5 (3) may adjudicate on the action in so far as it is not based on tort or delict.

With respect to the first part of the question, it must be observed that the concept of 'matters relating to tort, delict or quasi-delict' serves as a criterion for defining the scope of one of the rules concerning the special jurisdictions available to the plaintiff. As the Court held with respect to the expression 'matters relating to a contract' used in Article 5 (1) . . . having regard to the objectives and general scheme of the Convention, it is important that, in order to ensure as far as possible the equality and uniformity of the rights and obligations arising out of the Convention for the Contracting States and the persons concerned, that concept should not be interpreted simply as referring to the national law of one or other of the States concerned.

Accordingly, the concept of matters relating to tort, delict or quasi-delict must be regarded as an autonomous concept which is to be interpreted, for the application of the Convention, principally by reference to the scheme and objectives of the Convention in order to ensure that the latter is given full effect.

In order to ensure uniformity in all the Member States, it must be recognized that the concept of 'matters relating to tort, delict and quasi-delict' covers all actions which seek to establish the liability of a defendant and which are not related to a 'contract' within the meaning of Article 5 (1).

[17] Case 189/87 [1988] E.C.R. 5565.

It must therefore be stated in reply to the first part of the second question that the term 'matters relating to tort, delict or quasi-delict' within the meaning of Article 5 (3) of the Convention must be regarded as an independent concept covering all actions which seek to establish the liability of a defendant and which are not related to a 'contract' within the meaning of Article 5 (1)."

2–82 Although this is a wide definition to give a provision which derogates from Article 2 of the Convention, the correctness of *Kalfelis* has not been called into question in subsequent cases before the European Court of Justice.[18] Applying the *Kalfelis* definition to the nominate intellectual property rights, it seems clear that infringement of any of the statutory intellectual property rights would fall within Article 5(3), as would the common law action for passing-off. The only major problem in English law is caused by the equitable nature of the action for breach of confidence.[19]

2–83 The conclusion that infringement of a patent, copyright, trade mark or design, and passing-off, are "matters relating to tort" within the meaning of Article 5(3) is reinforced by the reference in the Schlosser Report to the Article covering, *inter alia*, injunctions to prevent "the sale of goods which have been manufactured or put on the market in breach of the law on patents or industrial property rights." The Jenard Report states, in relation to the exclusive jurisdictions under Article 16: "Other actions, including those for infringement of patents, are governed by the general rules of the Convention." Admittedly, "general rules" might equally well refer to Article 2 rather than Article 5(3), but the conclusion that Jenard contemplated actions for infringement falling within Article 5(3) is borne out by the thought that if they did not, then his committee could only have intended that infringement actions would always have to be brought in the courts of the defendant's domicile, which might not be the courts of the state under whose laws the intellectual property right in question existed. This interpretation of Article 5(3) is therefore necessary to preserve the universal practice of actions for infringement of intellectual property being within the jurisdiction of the courts of the state where the right in question exists and has been infringed.

2–84 No case before the European Court of Justice to date has had to deal with infringement of intellectual property rights under the Convention, though in *Duijnstee v. Goderbauer*[20] the European Court of Justice cited with approval the passage from the Jenard Report quoted above. The issue was one of entitlement—as between an employee and the liquidator of his employers—to a number of patents in different countries. In

---

[18] *Kalfelis* was applied without criticism in Case C–261/90 *Reichert v. Dresdner Bank (No. 2)* [1992] E.C.R. I–2149. Case C–346/93 *Kleinwort Benson v. City of Glasgow* [1995] E.C.R. I–615; [1995] All E.R. (E.C.) 514 squarely raised the question of causes of action in restitution but failed to define the relationship between Arts 5(1) and (3) because the Court held it had no jurisdiction.

[19] See *Kitechnology BV v. Unicor GmbH Plastmaschinen* [1995] F.S.R. 765, CA, and para. 3–74.

[20] Case 288/82 [1983] E.C.R. 3663; [1985] 1 C.M.L.R. 220.

Shevill v. Presse Alliance[21] Darmon A.-G. drew an analogy with the treatment of jurisdiction over infringement adopted in the Community Patent Convention in deciding how jurisdiction over a claim for libel was to be dealt with under Article 5(3).

The meaning of "the place where the harmful event occurred:" *Reinwater*

Perhaps surprisingly, the meaning of the expression "the place where the harmful event occurred" was considered by the European Court of Justice even before it ruled, in *Kalfelis*,[22] that "tort" was a concept with an independent meaning under the Convention. The facts of the *Reinwater* case, *Bier v. Mines de Potasse d'Alsace*,[23] were that the plaintiff *Bier* had a horticultural business near Rotterdam in the Netherlands which drew water for its crops from the river Rhine. A second plaintiff was the *Stichting Reinwater*, a Dutch foundation which existed to promote improvement in the quality of water in the Rhine basin. The high salinity of the water caused damage to the seedlings cultivated by Bier and it was obliged to take expensive measures to counter it. The defendants were a French mining company domiciled at Mulhouse which discharged more than 10,000 tonnes per day of residual chloride salts into the Rhine from their works in Alsace, and this was considered to be a principal cause of the high salinity of the water of the Rhine even as far downstream as Rotterdam. The European Court of Justice upheld the jurisdiction of the Dutch courts.

> "The form of words 'place where the harmful event occurred', used in all the language versions of the Convention, leaves open the question of whether, in the situation described, it is necessary, in determining jurisdiction, to choose as the connecting factor the place of the event giving rise to the damage, or the place where the damage occurred, or to accept that the plaintiff has an option between the one and the other of those two connecting factors. As regards this, it is well to point out that the place of the event giving rise to the damage no less than the place where the damage occurred can, depending on the case, constitute a significant connecting factor from the point of view of jurisdiction. Liability in tort, delict or quasi-delict can only arise provided that a causal connection can be established between the damage and the event in which that damage originates. Taking into account the close connection between the component parts of every sort of liability, it does not appear appropriate to opt for one of the two connecting factors mentioned to the exclusion of the other, since each of them can, depending on the circumstances, be particularly helpful from the point of view of the evidence and of the conduct of the proceedings. To exclude one option appears all the more undesirable in that, by

2–85

---

[21] Case C–68/93 [1995] E.C.R. I–415.
[22] Case 189/87 [1988] E.C.R. 5565.
[23] Case 21/76 [1976] E.C.R. 1735; [1977] 1 C.M.L.R. 284.

its comprehensive form of words, Article 5(3) of the Convention covers a wide diversity of kinds of liability. Thus the meaning of the expression 'place where the harmful event occurred' in Article 5(3) must be established in such a way as to acknowledge that the plaintiff has an option to commence proceedings either at the place where the damage occurred or the place of the event giving rise to it. . . .

Thus it should be answered that where the place of the happening of the event which may give rise to liability in tort, delict or quasi-delict and the place where that event results in damage are not identical, the expression 'place where the harmful event occurred', in Article 5(3) of the Convention, must be understood as being intended to cover both the place where the damage occurred and the place of the event giving rise to it. The result is that the defendant may be sued, at the option of the plaintiff, either in the courts for the place where the damage occurred or in the courts for the place of the event which gives rise to and is at the origin of that damage."

The European Court of Justice thus implicitly decided that "the place where the harmful event occurred" bore an independent meaning in the Convention and was not to be interpreted according to the *lex loci delicti commissi* or the proper law of the tort.

The treatment of concurrent jurisdiction under Article 5(3): *Shevill v. Presse Alliance*

2–86   One issue left open by *Reinwater*,[24] was the respective extent of the jurisdiction of the Dutch and French courts, in so far as the latter did not derive jurisdiction from the defendant's domicile. The Reinwater Foundation had not tried to claim, in the Rotterdam court, any remedy in respect of damage caused by pollution elsewhere in the Rhine basin. In *Shevill v. Presse Alliance*,[25] the defendants were the French publishers of the newspaper *France-Soir*. They published an article about a raid by French drug squad officers on a *bureau de change* in Paris operated by Chequepoint SARL, in which Chequepoint and a Miss Shevill were mentioned. Miss Shevill was English, but was temporarily working for Chequepoint in Paris. Shevill, Chequepoint SARL and two other companies in the group commenced proceedings for libel in the English courts, alleging that the article implicated them in drug-trafficking and money laundering, and the House of Lords ordered a reference to the European Court of Justice under the Protocol on Interpretation. Only about 230 copies of *France-Soir* circulated in England, the defendants had published an apology, and the plaintiffs expressly limited their claim to damages for harm caused by publication in England.

---

[24] Case 21/76 *Bier v. Mines de Potasse d'Alsace* [1976] E.C.R. 1735; [1997] 1 C.M.L.R. 284.
[25] Case C–68/93 [1995] E.C.R. I–415.

The House of Lords referred a total of seven questions, falling into **2–87** two groups. The first group of questions concerned whether England was a or the "place where the harmful event occurred" within the meaning of Article 5(3) and *Reinwater*. The second group concerned whether the English courts should apply their own normal rules, or a different standard, in deciding whether sufficient damage had occurred as a result of the publication to found jurisdiction. The European Court of Justice took it as settled case law that jurisdiction under Article 5(3) arose equally for the courts of the place where the damage as such occurred, and to those of the place where the event giving rise to the damage took place. Applying that principle to the facts the Court concluded:

"In the case of a libel by a newspaper article distributed in several Contracting States, the place of the event giving rise to the damage, within the meaning of those judgments, can only be the place where the publisher of the newspaper in question is established, since that is the place where the harmful event originated and from which the libel was issued and put into circulation.

The court of the place where the publisher of the defamatory publication is established must therefore have jurisdiction to hear the action for damages for all the harm caused by the unlawful act.

However, that forum will generally coincide with the head of jurisdiction set out in the first paragraph of Article 2 of the Convention.

As the Court held in *Mines de Potasse D'Alsace*, the plaintiff must consequently have the option to bring proceedings also in the place where the damage occurred, since otherwise Article 5(3) of the Convention would be rendered meaningless.

The place where the damage occurred is the place where the event giving rise to the damage, entailing tortious, delictual or quasi-delictual liability, produced its harmful effects upon the victim.

In the case of an international libel through the press, the injury caused by a defamatory publication to the honour, reputation and good name of a natural or legal person occurs in the places where the publication is distributed, when the victim is known in those places.

It follows that the courts of each Contracting State in which the defamatory publication was distributed and in which the victim claims to have suffered injury to his reputation have jurisdiction to rule on the injury caused in that state to the victim's reputation.

In accordance with the requirement of the sound administration of justice, the basis of the rule of special jurisdiction in Article 5(3), the courts of each Contracting State in which the defamatory publication was distributed and in which the victim claims to have suffered injury to his reputation are territorially the best placed to assess the libel committed in that state and to determine the extent of the corresponding damage.

Although there are admittedly disadvantages to having different courts ruling on various aspects of the same dispute, the plaintiff always has the option of bringing his entire claim before the courts either of the defendant's domicile or of the place where the publisher of the defamatory publication is established.

In light of the foregoing, the answer to the first, second, third and sixth questions referred by the House of Lords must be that, on a proper construction of the expression 'place where the harmful event occurred' in Article 5(3) of the Convention, the victim of a libel by a newspaper article distributed in several Contracting States may bring an action for damages against the publisher either before the courts of the Contracting State of the place where the publisher of the defamatory publication is established, which have jurisdiction to award damages for all the harm caused by the defamation, or before the courts of each Contracting State in which the publication was distributed and where the victim claims to have suffered injury to his reputation, which have jurisdiction to rule solely in respect of the harm caused in the state of the court seised."

Application of *Reinwater* and *Shevill* to intellectual property infringement actions

2–88   There is no doubt that the general principle stated in *Reinwater*[26] applies whatever the nature of the tort in question, subject to whatever qualifications are imposed by the decision in *Shevill v. Presse Alliance*.[27] The judgment of the European Court of Justice in *Shevill* itself was expressed in terms applicable to libel actions, corresponding to the scope of the questions referred to the Court by the House of Lords. However, it is suggested that *Shevill* is of as general application as *Reinwater*, and that it applies whenever there is a tort involving a single causative event in one state and actual harm in a number of other states. Since *Reinwater* itself applies to torts of every description, the alternative would be to say that in torts other than defamation a court would have jurisdiction to grant relief in respect of all contracting states if it had jurisdiction by virtue of domicile or under either head of *Reinwater*. The better view is that defamation is by no means the only tort for which some restriction on the broad doctrine of *Reinwater* is desirable.

2–89   Newspapers are not the only goods which circulate throughout the whole Community and libel actions are not the only type of litigation that newspaper publishers face. An action for copyright infringement could equally well be brought, according to the unqualified doctrine of *Reinwater*, in every country where a paper is sold, and the arguments for restricting a national court's power to award damages roughly in proportion to the number of copies involved seem equally cogent. Whenever the subject matter of an infringement action is consumer goods, it may be assumed that at least some infringing sales will be found in virtually every contracting state. To the extent that *Shevill* regards

---

[26] Case 21/76 *Bier v. Mines de Potasse d'Alsace* [1976] E.C.R. 1735; [1997] 1 C.M.L.R. 284.
[27] Case C–68/93 [1995] E.C.R. I–415.

opportunities for forum shopping as undesirable in their own right, its reasoning applies as much to infringement of intellectual property rights as to libel. Even to the extent that the decision in *Shevill* turned on unique features of one country's substantive and procedural law, similar considerations are likely to arise for other causes of action. English courts, for example, might regard the French law of personal privacy with much the same surprise as French courts view English libel law.

Against this, it might be said that the Court in *Shevill* was particularly **2–90** concerned by the problems which would arise in libel actions. That concern was twofold: all national newspapers and many regional ones are likely to circulate at least to some extent in all the member states, so without some qualification of *Reinwater* the plaintiff would have an unlimited choice of jurisdictions in which to sue. To allow the plaintiff an open-ended choice of forum would be serious; but this was compounded by the fact that the standard of liability for defamation is much lower in the United Kingdom than is generally applied on the Continent; and the English courts are widely perceived as being too ready to grant excessive awards of damages. Léger A.G. was quite explicit that one reason for confining the jurisdiction of the English courts to damage occurring in England was the "generosity" of the English courts towards victims of defamation and the risk of markedly divergent solutions arising in different member states as a result of the unharmonised nature of substantive defamation law.

The first consideration applies equally to intellectual property **2–91** infringement actions, though the second is much less worrying where one is dealing with fields where much harmonisation of substantive law has taken place. The opinions of the Advocates General in *Shevill*[28] are not confined to factors relevant only to defamation actions. Léger A.-G. referred to the Community Trade Mark Regulation. Darmon A.-G. concluded his opinion on this point by citing the jurisdictional scheme of the Community Patent Convention as a model to follow, commenting that where one was "on the fringes" of civil matters, it was advisable to adhere, within certain limits, to the principle of territoriality. This factor applies to intellectual property infringement actions with much more force than to actions for defamation.

Infringement actions: the places contemplated in *Shevill*

On the assumption that both *Reinwater*[29] and *Shevill*[30] apply to **2–92** intellectual property infringement actions, it is necessary to distinguish the "the place of the event giving rise to the damage" from "the place where the damage occurred." The latter, it is suggested, always includes the place where the infringement actually took place. Since for England it hardly matters where within the jurisdiction the infringing act occurs,

---

[28] Opinions were delivered by both Darmon A.-G. and Léger A.-G.
[29] Case 21/76 *Bier v. Mines de Potasse d'Alsace* [1976] E.C.R. 1735; [1977] 1 C.M.L.R. 284.
[30] Case C–68/93 [1985] E.C.R. I–415.

the English courts will always have jurisdiction under the second head of *Shevill* in respect of infringements committed in England. Since one is dealing with terms which have an independent meaning under the Convention, it is probably irrelevant that in the majority of the intellectual property torts damage is not the gist of the action under English law.[31]

2–93 The meaning of "the place of the event giving rise to the damage" in relation to infringement is perhaps more difficult. In the case of copyright infringement, at least, a ready analogy may be drawn with defamation. If an article in a newspaper infringes copyright, then the place from which the newspaper is published is the place of the event giving rise to the damage and the courts of that place have jurisdiction under the first head of *Shevill*, irrespective of domicile, in relation to infringement throughout all the member states. In each country in which the newspaper is published and where copyright is infringed, the local courts also have jurisdiction under the second head of *Shevill*, but with their jurisdiction being confined to relief for damage arising in the contracting state in question. The same analysis would apply to an infringing book or other publication, or an infringing broadcast. Likewise, in the case of goods the production of which infringes a patent, the site of the defendant's factory would probably be the place of the event giving rise to the damage. The same analysis would apply even if the manufacture of goods as such did not infringe for some reason, as long as infringement took place in at least some of the member states to which the goods were exported.

2–94 It is inherent in *Reinwater* and *Shevill* that the courts of "the place of the event giving rise to the damage" have jurisdiction whether or not the event constituted a tort under their internal law, or was complete within their territory. Their jurisdiction derives directly from the Convention, as interpreted by the European Court of Justice in those two cases. Even if their internal law would not normally allow them to entertain an action on a tort committed abroad, the mandatory effect of Article 5(3) would prevail.[32] They would apply their private international law to determine liability for the allegedly harmful event(s), wherever those may have occurred. Of course, to the extent that no tort had been committed within their territory because no damage had arisen, no relief would be available, but that would not prevent relief being granted in respect of other member states where damage had occurred.

Indirect economic loss cannot found jurisdiction

2–95 Whatever the scope of *Shevill v. Presse Alliance*[33] and its application to intellectual property infringement actions, one of the broader interpretations which might conceivably be given to *Reinwater*[34] can be rejected

---

[31] Compare Case C–68/93 *Shevill v. Presse Alliance* [1995] E.C.R. I–415 itself, where the formula was applied although damage was presumed, and must have been slight.

[32] See para. 2–77 and the passage there quoted from the Jenard Report. For the contrary view in English law see para. 3–42.

[33] Case C–68/93 [1995] E.C.R. I–415.

[34] Case 21/76 *Bier v. Mines de Potasse d'Alsace* [1976] E.C.R. 1735; [1977] 1 C.M.L.R. 284.

with confidence. From the decisions of the European Court of Justice in *Dumez v. Hessische Landesbank*[35] and *Marinari v. Lloyd's Bank*[36] it follows that indirect financial damage cannot be relied on to found jurisdiction. So that, for example, if infringement occurs only in Germany, an English company cannot give jurisdiction to the English courts by claiming that it suffers economic loss at its head office and place of business in England. According to Warner A.-G. in *Netherlands v. Ruffer*,[37] "it has never been suggested . . . much less held by the Court, that the place where the harmful event occurred could be the place where the plaintiff company has its seat or the place where the amount of damage to its business was quantified." The general rule for torts causing economic loss, is that the existence of indirect parasitic damage suffered outside the actual place of infringement or by more than one person, cannot confer jurisdiction under Article 5(3), even if such damage would be recoverable under national law.

In *Dumez*, the facts were that the German defendant bank had **2–96** allegedly caused the insolvency of German subsidiary companies of the French plaintiffs by withdrawing credit facilities from another company on whom the subsidiaries were dependent. The parent companies commenced actions in the French courts claiming damages against the bank. On a reference from the *Cour de Cassation*, the European Court of Justice held that the French courts had no jurisdiction under Article 5(3).

> "[I]t should be noted, firstly, that *Mines De Potasse* relates to a situation where the damage (in that particular case, damage caused to crops in the Netherlands) occurred at some distance from the place of the causal event (the discharge of saline effluent into the Rhine by an enterprise established in France) but by the direct effect of the causal agent, viz. the saline waste and its physical displacement.
>
> By contrast, in the present main action the damage allegedly caused to Dumez and Oth by the German banks' withdrawal of credits granted to the developer for financing building work had its origin and direct consequences in one and the same member-States, viz. the State where the banks granting the credit, the prime contractor and the subsidiaries of Dumez and Oth which had undertaken to carry out the work were established. The harm claimed by the parent companies Dumez and Oth is only an indirect consequence of the financial losses originally suffered by their subsidiaries by reason of the withdrawal of the credits and the resulting termination of the building work.
>
> It follows that, in a case like the present main action, the alleged injury is only an indirect consequence of the harm originally suffered by other legal persons who were the direct victims of

[35] Case 220/88 [1990] E.C.R. 49.
[36] Case C–364/93 [1995] E.C.R. I–2719; [1986] All E.R. (E.C.) 84.
[37] Case 814/79 [1980] E.C.R. 3807; [1981] 3 C.M.L.R. 293.

damage occurring in a place different from that where the indirect victim suffered harm later.

Therefore it is necessary to decide whether the term 'place where the damage occurred' within the meaning of *Mines De Potasse* can be understood to refer to the place where the indirect victims of the harm discover the harmful consequences to their own property. (. . .)

It follows from what has been said that although, according to the Court's case law, the phrase 'the place where the harmful event occurred' in Article 5(3) of the Convention may refer to the place where the damage occurred, the latter should be taken to mean only the place where the causal event, giving rise to delictual or quasi-delictual liability, directly produced the harmful effects in relation to the person who is the immediate victim.

In addition, the place where the original damage was manifested normally has a close connection with the other elements creating liability, which is generally not the case with regard to the domicile of the indirect victim.

The reply to be given to the question put by the court making the reference should therefore be that the rule of jurisdiction laid down in Article 5(3) of the Convention cannot be construed as permitting a plaintiff pleading damage which he claims to he the consequence of the harm suffered by other persons, who were the immediate victims of the harmful act, to bring proceedings against the perpetrator of that act in the courts of the place in which he himself discovered the damage to his assets."

2–97   While *Dumez* was expressly concerned with harm indirectly arising in one state from damage suffered by a third party in another state, the same principle has been applied where only one party is involved. In *Marinari v. Lloyd's Bank*[38] the plaintiff attempted to sue in the Italian courts, where he was domiciled, for compensation in respect of an act occurring in England. The European Court of Justice ruled that Article 5(3) did not apply to give jurisdiction to the courts of a place where the plaintiff claimed to have suffered financial loss consequential upon initial damage arising and suffered by him in another contracting state.

Threatened or incomplete torts: *quia timet* actions

2–98   The case law of the European Court of Justice on the Brussels Convention is silent as to whether Article 5(3) applies where no "harmful event" has yet occurred, in other words whether it allows *quia timet* actions to be brought in the courts of a contracting state where the commission of a tort is in prospect.[39] The Schlosser Report favoured such jurisdiction: "There is much to be said for the proposition that the

---

[38] Above.

[39] Though Art. 5(3) might not apply in this case, the courts of the defendant's domicile would always have jurisdiction.

courts specified in Article 5(3) should also have jurisdiction in proceedings whose main object is to prevent the imminent commission of a tort" though Schlosser noted that not all member states provided in their internal law for preventive injunctions in matters relating to tort.[40] If on its true interpretation Article 5(3) does extend to *quia timet* actions, then the problem arises that, according to the Jenard Report, Article 5 is of mandatory effect,[41] and except for Article 5(4) obliges the courts of contracting states to assume jurisdiction regardless of whether their internal law would otherwise have permitted it. Schlosser's comments are therefore perhaps more consistent with proposing amendment to Article 5(3) than to guiding its interpretation in the form in which it stands. The Community Patent Convention and the Community Trade Mark Regulation both expressly contemplate *quia timet* actions, but only if they are available under national law.[42] The intra-UK Modified Convention[43] expressly applies Article 5(3) to *quia timet* actions, but in *Kleinwort Benson v. City of Glasgow*[44] the Court gave the difference between Article 5(3) of the Brussels Convention itself and the corresponding provision of the Modified Convention as being one reason why it had no jurisdiction to interpret the latter, and the only difference is that relating to threatened torts.

At first sight these questions may appear to be of considerable **2–99** practical significance. *Quia timet* jurisdiction will most frequently be of importance in connection with applications for urgent interlocutory relief, and the availability and effectiveness of such relief varies enormously from one contracting state to another. However, on more detailed analysis the question of jurisdiction under Article 5(3) may be largely academic. Assuming that *Shevill v. Presse Alliance*[45] applies to injunctive relief as it does to the award of damages, then only the courts of the place where the harmful event *originated* would have jurisdiction under Article 5(3) extending to all other contracting states. The place of origin of the harmful event will frequently correspond to the defendant's domicile, whose courts would already have unlimited jurisdiction under Article 2, so *quia timet* jurisdiction under Article 5(3) on the basis of where a threatened tort would originate once committed would be redundant. The courts of other individual contracting states might have concurrent jurisdiction under *Shevill* by virtue of being the courts of the place where the harmful event *occurred*, or rather was expected to occur, but that jurisdiction would be confined to granting injunctions with effect in their own territory. Since every court may grant "preliminary, including protective, measures" in respect of its own territory, whether or not it has substantive jurisdiction under the Convention, any additional *quia timet* jurisdiction conferred by Article 5(3) would again

---

[40] See the passage from the Schlosser Report quoted at para. 2–77, above.

[41] See para. 2–77 and the passage quoted from the Jenard report.

[42] Community Patent Convention, Protocol on Litigation, Art. 15(1)(a); Community Trade Mark Regulation, Art. 92(a).

[43] Civil Jurisdiction and Judgments Act 1982, Sched. 4.

[44] Case C–346/93 *Kleinwort Benson v. City of Glasgow* [1995] E.C.R. I–615; [1995] All E.R. (E.C.) 514.

[45] Case C–68/93 [1995] E.C.R. I–415.

largely be redundant unless Article 24 is confined to *Mareva*-type relief. That leaves *quia timet* relief under Article 5(3) principally of interest in only two circumstances: where there are good reasons for suing in the place where infringement is expected to originate, and no defendant is domiciled there; and where final relief needs to be sought in a place where the defendant is not domiciled and infringement is threatened but has not occurred. Bearing in mind the fact that in intellectual property infringement actions the plaintiff can often choose between several defendants, and the possibility of adding further defendants under Article 6(1); and any *quia timet* jurisdiction under Article 5(3) becomes of residual importance only.

2–100   The recommendation of the Schlosser Report notwithstanding, there are reasons of policy why the European Court of Justice might not be minded to extend the interpretation of Article 5(3) to threatened torts. In the first place, such an interpretation hardly corresponds to the actual wording of the Article or its treatment in leading cases such as *Reinwater*.[46] Admittedly, the principle that Article 5—as a derogation from a general principle of the Convention—should be interpreted narrowly has not been applied with complete consistency, but it is still influential. Two reasons why a relatively narrow interpretation might be favoured in this instance are the avoidance of forum shopping and the desirability of legal certainty. The Court has been careful to avoid interpretations of Article 5(3) which would in effect automatically allow the plaintiff to sue in the courts of his own domicile; or which, worse still, would give him an unlimited choice of forum. The prospect of damage occurring from a tort not yet committed is inevitably a much more uncertain basis for jurisdiction than damage that has actually occurred, and potentially lends itself to exploitation by unscrupulous plaintiffs or courts with expansionist tendencies. The problem is made worse by the fact that, by analogy with the Court's answer to the second group of questions in *Shevill*, each national court would probably be entitled to apply its own internal law as to what constituted a sufficient threat to infringe, and that once it had granted an injunction no other court in which the injunction was sought to be enforced would be able to re-examine the facts on which jurisdiction had been based, even if they amounted to little more than a legal fiction. For the time being, it is probably best to regard *quia timet* jurisdiction under Article 5(3) as no more than an interesting possibility.

G. INTELLECTUAL PROPERTY AND THE EXCLUSIVE JURISDICTIONS

The exclusive jurisdictions: Article 16

2–101   Article 16 of the Brussels Convention confers exclusive jurisdiction on the courts of specific member states, regardless of the domicile of any party, in five instances which may be briefly summarised as: land and

---

[46] Case 21/76 *Bier v. Mines de Potasse d'Alsace* [1976] E.C.R. 1735; [1977] 1 C.M.L.R. 284.

tenancies, the internal affairs of corporations, public registers, registered intellectual property rights and the enforcement of judgments. The Article provides:

The following courts shall have exclusive jurisdiction, regardless of **2–102** domicile:

(1) in proceedings which have as their object rights *in rem* in, or tenancies of, immovable property, the courts of the Contracting State in which the property is situated[47];

(2) in proceedings which have as their object the validity of the constitution, the nullity or the dissolution of companies or other legal persons or associations of natural or legal persons, or the decisions of their organs, the courts of the Contracting State in which the company, legal person or association has its seat;

(3) in proceedings which have as their object the validity of entries in public registers, the courts of the Contracting State in which the register is kept;

(4) in proceedings concerned with the registration or validity of patents, trade marks, designs, or other similar rights required to be deposited or registered, the courts of the Contracting State in which the deposit or registration has been applied for, has taken place or is under the terms of an international convention deemed to have taken place;

(5) in proceedings concerned with the enforcement of judgments, the courts of the Contracting State in which the judgment has been or is to be enforced.

The mandatory effect of Article 16 is clear from by Articles 4, 17, 18 **2–103** and 19 which provide (so far as relevant) as follows:

Article 4

If a person is not domiciled in a Contracting State, the jurisdiction of the courts of each Contracting State shall, subject to the provisions of Article 16, be determined by the law of that State. . . .

Article 17 (. . .)

Agreements . . . conferring jurisdiction shall have no legal force if . . . the courts whose jurisdiction they purport to exclude have exclusive jurisdiction by virtue of Article 16. . . .

Article 18

Apart from jurisdiction derived from other provisions of this Convention, a court of a Contracting State before whom a defendant enters an appearance shall have jurisdiction. This rule shall not

---

[47] For simplicity, the original text of Art. 16(1) is printed. The San Sebastian Convention added a subpara. (b) (omitted here) to reverse the effect of Case 241/83 *Rosler v. Rottwinkel* [1985] E.C.R. 99; [1985] 1 C.M.L.R. 806 on holiday lettings by creating a special rule for short term private rentals between natural persons with the same domicile. See para. 2–28, above.

apply where appearance was entered solely to contest the jurisdiction, or where another court has exclusive jurisdiction by virtue of Article 16.

Article 19

Where a court of a Contracting State is seised of a claim which is principally concerned with a matter over which the courts of another Contracting State have exclusive jurisdiction by virtue of Article 16, it shall declare of its own motion that it has no jurisdiction.

2–104   Finally, Article 28 provides that a judgment "shall not be recognised" if it conflicts, *inter alia*, with the provisions of Article 16; and Article 34 gives conflict with Article 28 as a reason for refusing to enforce such a judgment.[48] This is an altogether exceptional provision, since the normal rule of the Brussels Convention is that questions of jurisdiction cannot be re-litigated on an application to enforce a judgment.

The effects of Article 16 summarised

2–105   To summarise Article 16, the normal rules of the Convention are wholly superseded in the case of the five exclusive jurisdictions. In each case to which it applies, the Article assigns jurisdiction to the courts of one contracting state alone,[49] determined exclusively by the *situs* of the subject matter of the proceedings. The domicile of the parties, and even whether or not the defendant is domiciled in a contracting state,[50] are quite irrelevant. In these respects, Article 16 both confers jurisdiction on courts which might not otherwise have it, and takes it away from those courts which might otherwise be seised by virtue of the defendant's domicile or otherwise. The stringency of Article 16 is emphasised by the fact that the parties cannot confer jurisdiction on another court by consent or submission, and that any court other than the one specified by Article 16 is obliged under Article 19 to decline jurisdiction of its own motion. A judgment given in breach of Article 16 cannot be recognised or enforced in any other member state, and in Convention terms would appear to be completely ineffective. If, notwithstanding Article 19, a court purports to assume jurisdiction over a case which is within the exclusive jurisdiction of another court then, in contrast to the normal rule of *lis alibi pendens*, the court which enjoys exclusive jurisdiction is not obliged to stay its own proceedings.[51]

2–106   Because each of the five paragraphs of Article 16 confers exclusive jurisdiction on the courts of a contracting state, the Article is inapplicable when the connection by way of subject matter is with a state not a

[48] See paras 8–109 *et seq.*
[49] There is a theoretical possibility of two courts having concurrent exclusive jurisdiction, principally under Art. 16(2) since a corporation can be domiciled in more than one state. Art. 23 obliges all courts other than the one first seised to decline jurisdiction in this case.
[50] Art. 4.
[51] See para. 8–109.

party to the Convention; so that, for instance, a case involving land in South America or the validity of a Japanese patent would not be within the exclusive jurisdictions, and the normal rules of the Convention would apply. This causes problems, because on one interpretation of the interrelationship between Article 2 and Article 16, it would appear that the English courts would be obliged—comity and *forum non conveniens* notwithstanding—to entertain actions against a defendant domiciled in England, in respect of land situated in, or intellectual property rights existing under, the laws of a foreign non-member state.[52]

Article 16 is a derogation from one of the fundamental principles of **2–107** the Convention, and the European Court of Justice has consistently asserted that as such, it should be construed as narrowly as is consistent with giving effect to the presumed intentions of the framers of the Convention.[53]

The commentary on Article 16 in the Jenard Report

The Jenard Report explains and justifies the exclusive jurisdictions in **2–108** the following general terms relating to all of them, and then deals with each of the five heads separately:

"Article 16 lists the circumstances in which the six States recognise that the courts of one of them have exclusive jurisdiction. The matters referred to in this Article will normally be the subject of exclusive jurisdiction only if they constitute the principal subject-matter of the proceedings of which the court is to be seised.

The provisions of Article 16 on jurisdiction may not be departed from either by an agreement purporting to confer jurisdiction on the courts of another Contracting State, or by an implied submission to the jurisdiction (Articles 17 and 18). Any court of a State other than the State whose courts have exclusive jurisdiction must declare of its own motion that it has no jurisdiction (Article 19). Failure to observe these rules constitutes a ground for refusal of recognition or enforcement (Articles 28 and 34).

These rules, which take as their criterion the subject-matter of the action, are applicable regardless of the domicile or nationality of the parties. In view of the reasons for laying down rules of exclusive jurisdiction, it was necessary to provide for their general application, even in respect of defendants domiciled outside the Community. Thus, for example, a Belgian court will not, on the basis of Article 53 of the Law of 1876 or of Article 637 of the draft Judicial Code, which in actions against foreigners recognise the jurisdiction of the courts of the plaintiff, have jurisdiction in proceedings between a Belgian and a person domiciled, for example, in Argentina, if the

---

[52] The problem of *Re Harrods (Buenos Aries) Ltd* [1992] Ch. 72; [1991] 3 W.L.R. 397; [1991] 4 All E.R. 334, CA. Unfortunately, the case settled before a reference from the House of Lords to the European Court of Justice had been decided.

[53] See paras 2–28 and 2–117.

proceedings concern immovable property situated in Germany. Only the German courts will have jurisdiction. . . .

Patents[54]

Article 16(4) applies to proceedings concerned with the registration or validity of patents, trade marks, designs or other similar rights, such as those which protect fruit and vegetable varieties, and which are required to be deposited or registered.

A draft convention has been drawn up by the EEC countries relating to patent law. The draft includes rules of jurisdiction for the Community patent, but it will not apply to national patents, which thus fall within the scope of the Judgments Convention.

Since the grant of a national patent is an exercise of national sovereignty, Article 16(4) of the Judgments Convention provides for exclusive jurisdiction in proceedings concerned with the validity of patents.

Other actions, including those for infringement of patents, are governed by the general rules of the Convention.

The expression 'the deposit or registration has been applied for' takes into account internal laws which, like German law, make the grant of a patent subject to the results of an examination. Thus, for example, German courts will have exclusive jurisdiction in the case of an application to the competent authorities for a patent to be granted where, during the examination of the application, a dispute arises over the rights relating to the grant of that patent.

The phrase 'is under the terms of an international convention deemed to have taken place' refers to the system introduced by the Madrid Agreement . . . and also to the Hague Arrangement . . . for the international registration of designs. Thus where a trade mark is deposited at the International Office at the request of the German authorities, the French courts will have exclusive jurisdiction in disputes relating, for example, to whether the mark should be deemed to have been registered in France."

The commentary on Article 16 in the Schlosser Report was confined to the new Article Vd of the Protocol to the Brussels Convention, and is considered at paragraph 2–130.

Article 16(1) inapplicable to intellectual property

2–109   Some English decisions treat intellectual property rights as a form of immovable property, at least for some purposes, so the question arises as to whether Article 16(1) is capable of applying. In view of the express treatment of registered intellectual property rights in Article 16(4), it is suggested that it would be inconsistent for Article 16(1) to apply to any intellectual property rights, registered or unregistered. Nothing in the

---

[54] The fact that the sub-heading in Jenard reads "patents" rather than "industrial property" or "intellectual property," despite the scope of Art. 16(4), is worth noting in passing.

wording of Article 16(1), the commentary in the Jenard and Schlosser Reports, or the case law of the European Court of Justice suggests that Article 16(1) is concerned with anything other than land and tenancies, and the Court has many times affirmed that Article 16 should be given a restrictive interpretation.

In any event, it would be wrong to attempt to understand Article 16(1) in terms of English decisions as to whether intellectual property rights *qua* property are movable or immovable.[55] Quite apart from the uncertainty of the answer, the terms employed in Article 16 must be given an independent or autonomous interpretation, regardless of their meaning in national law. Finally, even if it might be said that intellectual property was within the meaning of "immovable property" for the purposes of Article 16(1), infringement actions as such would not "have as their object rights *in rem* in . . . immovable property" and would not fall within the exclusive jurisdiction. The consistent case law of the European Court of Justice on Article 16(1) is that it has no application to actions which are *in personam*,[56] and infringement actions as such cannot be said to have effect *erga omnes* as Article 16(1) contemplates.

Cases where Article 16(4) is clearly inapplicable: copyright, unfair competition and breach of confidence

Article 16(4) is in terms confined to the registered intellectual **2–110** property rights. These are listed non-exclusively in the Article as patents, trade marks and (registered) designs, to which the Jenard Report adds registered plant variety rights. This extended listing was complete for the United Kingdom, but other categories of registered intellectual property rights exist in the laws of other member states, such as petty patents and utility models. Supplementary protection certificates might now be added, if they do not already fall within the autonomous meaning of "patents" in Article 16(4), and new categories of registered intellectual property rights may yet be created.

English domestic law has previously shown a tendency to group **2–111** together all categories of intellectual property rights, registered and unregistered, when it comes to deciding whether to entertain actions in respect of infringement abroad. The only exceptions have been actions for passing-off and breach of confidence, which are not self-evidently actions to enforce proprietary rights with a local *situs*. The question of whether English law has been correct to avoid drawing distinctions between the various nominate intellectual property rights is considered elsewhere. For present purposes, what matters is to note that there might have been an instinctive tendency in the common law mind to assume that Article 16(4) applied to intellectual property rights of whatever nature, whether registered or not, and to assert that any such assumption would be wrong.

Although the correct approach to the interpretation of the Brussels **2–112** Convention is purposive, rather than literal, the European Court of

---

[55] As to which see para. 6–55.
[56] Except in relation to tenancies.

Justice has consistently held that Article 16, in common with other articles derogating from the general rules of the Convention, should be given a narrow interpretation. The decision of the Court in *Duijnstee v. Goderbauer*[57] expressly applied this principle of restricted interpretation to Article 16(4). To interpret the Article as applying any more broadly than to those intellectual property rights which are enumerated or which fall within the concept of "rights required to be deposited or registered" would be to contravene this principle as well as the express wording of the Convention.

2–113   Nor would such a wide interpretation be justified by any of the purposes for which Article 16(4) may have been adopted. The Jenard Report gives two reasons for excluding the registration or validity of patents from the general rules of the Convention: the prospect of a specific international regime for Community patents[58] and the fact that the grant of patents is an exercise of national sovereignty. Neither applies to copyrights. No Community regime for copyright enforcement was or is in prospect. Copyrights are not granted by the state and do not involve the exercise of sovereign power: they arise in all member states *ex lege* from general legislation. Because copyright is not the subject of grant or registration, the concept of validity does not apply. Copyright either exists or it does not and the court hearing a copyright action has to decide the question of subsistence on its own and without the benefit of any previous decision of an administrative body or any entry in an official register. If the claim fails because copyright does not exist or is not owned by the plaintiff, then the effect of the judgment is purely *inter partes* and there is no register entry to revoke or rectify. Finally, the Jenard Report states expressly that "other actions, including those for infringement of patents, are governed by the general rules of the Convention." If patent infringement actions were not intended to fall within Article 16(4), then the same should be true a *fortiori* for actions for infringement of copyright or other intellectual property rights, registered or unregistered.

2–114   Compared to the Jenard Report, the European Court of Justice has attributed other intentions to the drafters of Article 16, but the final result is no different. According to the Court in *Duijnstee v. Goderbauer*[59] and consistently with several cases under Article 16(1), the exclusive jurisdictions are justified by a rule of convenience in that "those courts are best placed to adjudicate upon cases in which the dispute concerns the validity of the patent or the existence of the deposit or registration." The reasoning, discussed below, is unconvincing but cannot justify confining jurisdiction over copyright, passing-off, unfair competition or breach of confidence exclusively to the courts of the *situs*.[60]

[57] Case 288/82 [1983] E.C.R. 3663; [1985] 1 C.M.L.R. 220.
[58] This assumes that the second paragraph of the commentary on Art. 16(4) is more than just a sidenote. By way of comparison, bankruptcy was excluded altogether from the scope of the Convention because of the prospect, still unfulfilled, of a separate convention dealing with it.
[59] Case 288/82 [1983] E.C.R. 3663; [1985] 1 C.M.L.R. 220.
[60] It is also noticeable that the supposed rule of convenience has only ever been applied one way, so as to take cases outside Art. 16.

Duijnstee v. Goderbauer

Only one case before the European Court of Justice to date has dealt **2–115** expressly with the meaning of Article 16(4). In *Duijnstee v. Goderbauer*[61] the liquidator of an insolvent Dutch company and a former employee of the company brought proceedings against one another in the Netherlands, each claiming ownership of patents or patent applications in the Netherlands and a total of 22 other countries, five of which were member states of the Convention. At first instance and on appeal, both sets of proceedings failed on the merits and without any reference being made to Article 16(4), but on a final appeal to the Dutch Supreme Court, the *Hoge Raad*, the Court of its own motion questioned the compatibility of the proceedings with the Brussels Convention and ordered a reference to the European Court of Justice of three questions: whether an appellate court was obliged to apply Article 19 of its own motion when its jurisdiction was normally confined to issues raised by the parties; whether the term "proceedings concerned with the registration or validity of patents" had an independent meaning; and, if so, whether the claims before the Dutch courts were within it.

The Court answered the first two questions by stating that the **2–116** provisions of the Convention, including Article 19, over-rode inconsistent national law and that the terms of Article 16(4) had an independent meaning and were not to be determined either according to the *lex fori*, or the law of the state given exclusive jurisdiction under Article 16(4).[62] In answer to the third question, the Court replied:

"In order to reply to the third question, reference must again be made to the objectives and scheme of the Convention.

In that regard, it must be noted that the exclusive jurisdiction in proceedings concerned with the registration or validity of patents conferred upon the courts of the Contracting State in which the deposit or registration has been applied for is justified by the fact that those courts are best placed to adjudicate upon cases in which the dispute itself concerns the validity of the patent or the existence of the deposit or registration.

On the other hand, as is expressly stated in the report on the Convention, 'other actions, including those for infringement of patents, are governed by the general rules of the Convention.' That statement confirms the restrictive nature of the provision contained in Article 16(4).

It follows that proceedings 'concerned with the registration or validity of patents' must be regarded as proceedings in which the conferring of exclusive jurisdiction on the courts of the place in which the patent was granted is justified in the light of the factors

---

[61] Case 288/82 [1983] E.C.R. 3663; [1985] 1 C.M.L.R. 220. This paragraph and that following contain material from Wadlow, "Intellectual Property and the Judgments Convention" (1985) 10 E.L. Rev. 305.

[62] See para. 5–07.

mentioned above, such as proceedings relating to the validity, existence or lapse of a patent or an alleged right of priority by reason of an earlier deposit.

If, on the other hand, the dispute does not itself concern the validity of the patent or the existence of the deposit or registration, there is no special reason to confer exclusive jurisdiction on the courts of the Contracting State in which the patent was applied for or granted and consequently such a dispute is not covered by Article 16(4).

In a case such as the present, neither the validity of the patents nor the legality of their registration in the various countries is disputed by the parties to the main action. The outcome of the case in fact depends exclusively on the question whether M Goderbauer or the insolvent company BV Schroefboutenfabriek is entitled to the patent, which must be determined on the basis of the legal relationship which existed between the parties concerned. Therefore the special jurisdiction rule contained in Article 16(4) should not be applied.

In that regard, it should be pointed out that a very clear distinction between jurisdiction in disputes concerning the right to the patent, especially where the patent concerns the invention of an employee, and jurisdiction in disputes concerning the registration or validity of a patent was made both in the European Patent Convention signed in Munich on 5 October 1973 and in the Community Patent Convention signed in Luxembourg on December 1975, which has not yet entered into force. Although those two Conventions are not applicable in this case, the fact that they expressly accept such a distinction confirms the interpretation given by the Court to the corresponding provisions of the Brussels Convention.

The reply to the third question should therefore be that the term 'proceedings concerned with the registration or validity of patents' does not include a dispute between an employee for whose invention a patent has been applied for or obtained and his employer, where the dispute relates to their respective rights in that patent arising out of the contract of employment."

The real and ostensible policy justifications for Article 16

2–117   The main importance of *Duijnstee v. Goderbauer*[63] lies in the approach the European Court of Justice took to the interpretation of Article 16. In terms of general principles the Court broke no new ground. It confirmed its rule that provisions such as Article 16 which detract from the right of the defendant to be sued in the courts of his own domicile should be interpreted no more widely than is essential for the purpose for which they were included.[64] This approach had already been applied to Article

[63] Case 288/82 [1983] E.C.R. 3663; [1985] 1 C.M.L.R. 220.
[64] See para. 2–28.

16(1) of the Brussels Convention in *Sanders v. van der Putte*.[65] What is more interesting is the purpose attributed by the Court to Article 16(4) itself, as this is likely to be the determining factor in deciding what kinds of proceedings concerned with patents and other registered rights may be brought outside the contracting state in which the right in question is registered.

Article 16 applies to a number of classes of proceedings with little in   **2–118** common. Apart from patents they cover land and tenancies, internal affairs of companies and associations, public registers, and the enforcement of judgments. All these exceptions are additional to the matters excluded from the Convention altogether by Article 1 such as administrative law, revenue, personal status, matrimonial relations and property, bankruptcy and social security. What apparently unifies Article 16 is that all these matters are ones which traditionally have been regarded as outside the proper jurisdiction of foreign courts, as is the case with many of the matters excluded from the Convention altogether by Article 1. The Jenard Report generally justifies the exclusions of Article 16 as being common in the internal laws of member states, and expressly refers to national sovereignty in the case of patents and public policy in the case of land. It is hard not to believe that patents and land, at least, were excluded from the normal rules of jurisdiction precisely because of questions of national sovereignty and the almost universal rule that the courts of one country do not give judgment on property immovably situated in another.

Despite the commentary in the Jenard Report, the Court has   **2–119** explained the exclusive jurisdictions almost entirely in terms of a rule of convenience. The reason for Article 16(1) is said to be that the proceedings contemplated "result frequently in checks, inquiries and expert assessments which must be carried out on the spot."[66] Article 16(4) is purportedly "justified by the fact that those courts [given exclusive jurisdiction] are best placed to adjudicate upon cases in which the dispute itself concerns the validity of the patent or the existence of the deposit or registration."[67]

This explanation of Article 16 as a rule of convenience is totally   **2–120** unconvincing. The mere existence of an entry in a register is hardly ever in dispute, and would be easy to prove even if the register were in a foreign country. If the tailpiece to Article 16(4) applies, it *will* be in a foreign country, and not necessarily one which is a contracting state to the Brussels Convention.[68] Questions of fact regularly met in cases to which the general rule of Article 2 applies are often far more difficult to investigate from abroad. A surveyor may travel from Luxembourg to the furthest corners of Europe to see if a building has

---

[65] Case 73/77 [1977] E.C.R. 2383; [1978] 1 C.M.L.R. 331. See para. 2–125.

[66] *Sanders v. van der Putte, ibid.*

[67] Case 288/82 *Duijnstee v. Goderbauer* [1983] E.C.R. 3663; [1985] 1 C.M.L.R. 220. See para. 1–116.

[68] See the final paragraph of Jenard's commentary on Art. 16(4), quoted above at para. 2–108.

been built to the contractual specification, but *Sanders v. van der Putte* assumes that he cannot so much as cross the border into France or Belgium to see if another building encroaches onto a neighbour's land.[69] Patent validity is normally fought entirely by reference to published documents equally easily available everywhere. If the European Patent Office in Munich can revoke a European patent for all the contracting states to the Brussels Convention, then why is it inconceivable for the *Landgericht München* to do the same? If anything, the *Landgericht* is more experienced in obtaining evidence from abroad and giving its proper weight. An infringement action as such is far more likely than a revocation action to require the sort of experiments and site inspections which are supposedly one of the justifications for Article 16, and in neither case is there any guarantee that they will take place in the forum.[70]

2–121   Alternatively, if the Court in *Duijnstee v. Goderbauer* meant no more than that patent validity raises questions of law which are best decided by a court used to applying that law, then it stated a truism applying equally to every legal question imaginable. The Brussels Convention consistently and quite deliberately gives little or no weight to allocating jurisdiction so that the *lex causae* will correspond to the *lex fori*, and its underlying policy that defendants are to be sued in the courts of their domicile will often have the opposite effect.[71] In fact, patent law has been harmonised to such a considerable extent that this purported justification is much less relevant now for patents than for many other claims outside the scope of Article 16. The law of patent validity has even been harmonised more effectively that that of infringement, to which the normal provisions of the Convention apply.

2–122   It is also ironic that of all the intellectual property rights, it is those for which the law is in the least harmonised state which are most clearly outside the scope of Article 16(4). Harmonisation of patent law was in prospect in 1968 and was well advanced in 1983, when *Duijnstee v. Goderbauer* was decided. The laws of registered trade marks, plant varieties and registered designs are being comprehensively harmonised, but copyright has been subject to only marginal harmonisation and such consistency as is to be found is mainly attributable to the Berne Convention. Unfair competition has never been harmonised and is

[69] Case 158/87 *Scherrens v. Maenhout* [1988] E.C.R. 3791 actually applies this nonsense to a farm consisting of some parcels of land, only seven kilometres apart, which happened to be on opposite sides of the Netherlands–Belgium border. The dispute was not even one about boundaries, but about an alleged oral lease of the whole farm. Case C–292/93 *Lieber v. Göbel* [1994] E.C.R. I–2535 introduces a welcome if belated note of realism.

[70] Inspection might be needed to determine if a machine alleged to be a prior use anticipates, but a prior use anywhere in the world is as invalidating as one at home. Inspection is more likely to be needed on the issue of infringement, to which Art. 16(4) does not apply, and if the goods are imported then any inspection must take place where they are manufactured.

[71] One might have thought, for instance, that the English law of trusts was no less difficult for a civil law court to grasp than our law of real property, but Case C–294/92 *Webb v. Webb* [1994] E.C.R. I–1717 decided that an action to enforce a trust, even one of real property, was governed by Art. 2, and not by Art. 16(1).

barely affected by the Paris Convention or by TRIPs. A comparative survey by Ulmer, carried out for the E.C. Commission in the 1960's, showed just how diverse national laws were.[72]

The most convincing reason for saying that Article 16 was not drafted simply to specify the most convenient court to decide certain matters is the fact that the parties, no matter how much they may want to do so, cannot have those matters decided by a court which happens to be more convenient for them. Unlike every other provision of the Convention conferring jurisdiction Article 16 cannot be excluded by agreement or submission, and under Article 19 a court must decline jurisdiction of its own motion if faced with an action reserved to another court under the Article. Nothing could show more clearly that the contracting states regarded Article 16 as giving effect to a principle of general and overriding public importance, and the fact is recognised in Jenard's commentary on Article 19 describing that provision as "essential since the exclusive jurisdictions are conceived to be matters of public policy."   **2–123**

Despite all these considerations, the Court seems firmly to have adopted the proposition that Articles 16(1) and (4) alike must be interpreted no more widely than is essential to give effect to their presumed intention of ensuring that the matters specified are to be decided by the courts best able to determine the relevant facts and apply the relevant law. This principle will almost certainly become the most important factor in deciding which types of proceedings fall within Article 16(4) itself, and which are governed by the general rules of the Convention.   **2–124**

Case law on the other Article 16 jurisdictions in the ECJ

In the absence of any better authority under Article 16(4), some further guidance may be obtained from the more numerous decisions of the European Court of Justice under the other provisions of Article 16 and in particular Article 16(1).[73] In the first case on Article 16, *Sanders v. van der Putte*,[74] the Court stated the general principle, already referred to above, that the exclusive jurisdictions should be interpreted no more widely than was necessary to give effect to their intention. It also set the tone for what was to come by explaining that intention in terms of the smooth administration of justice by courts familiar with local laws and conditions, rather than anything to do with the preservation of national sovereignty.   **2–125**

> "As regards the matters listed under sub-paragraphs (2), (3), (4) and (5) of that Article it is clear that the courts which are given

---

[72] As for breach of confidence, *Kitechnology BV v. Unicor GmbH Plastmaschinen* [1995] F.S.R. 765, CA, concludes that in England it is not even a tort at all.

[73] Two cases on Art. 16(5) do not add much: Case 220/84 *AS Autoteile v. Malhe* [1985] E.C.R. 2267; [1986] 3 C.M.L.R. 321 and Case C–261/90 *Reichert v. Dresdner Bank (No. 2)* [1992] E.C.R. I–2149. Both are consistent with a restrictive application of Art. 16, purportedly justified by the specialised nature of the law.

[74] Case 73/77 [1977] E.C.R. 2383; [1978] 1 C.M.L.R. 331.

exclusive jurisdiction are those which are the best placed to deal with the disputes in question.

The same applies to the assignment of exclusive jurisdiction to the courts of the contracting state in which the property is situated in matters relating to rights *in rem* in, or tenancies of, immovable property.

In fact, actions concerning rights *in rem* in immovable property are to be judged according to the rules of the state in which the immovable property is situated since the disputes which arise result frequently in checks, enquiries and expert assessments which must be carried out on the spot, with the result that the assignment of exclusive jurisdiction satisfies the need for the proper administration of justice.

Tenancies of immovable property are generally governed by special rules and it is preferable, in the light of their complexity, that they be applied only by the courts of the state in which they are in force. The foregoing considerations explain the assignment of exclusive jurisdiction to the courts of the state in which the immovable property is situated in the case of disputes relating to tenancies of immovable property properly so called, that is to say, in particular, disputes between lessors and tenants as to the existence or interpretation of leases or to compensation for damage caused by the tenant and to giving up possession of the premises."

2–126 This rule has been applied with almost complete consistency, the only exception being the notorious decision in *Rosler v. Rottwinkel*,[75] where, ironically enough, the Opinion of Slynn A.-G. displays a more sincere attempt at purposive construction than does the mainstream of authority.[76] In *Sanders v. van der Putte* itself, Article 16(1) was held not to apply to a sub-lease of a flower shop, premises and business alike, as a going concern. In *Scherrens v. Maenhout*[77] there was no doubt that Article 16(1) applied, but the property in dispute was a farm of which five hectares and the buildings were in Belgium and 12 hectares in the Netherlands. The Court held that each part was subject to the exclusive jurisdiction of the Dutch or Belgian courts, as the case might be. However, the properties were not contiguous and the court acknowledged that:

"It is, however, possible that cases may arise in which immovable property whose component parts are situated in two contracting States but are the subject of a single lease has special characteristics such as will necessitate an exception to the general rule of exclusive jurisdiction described above. This might occur when, for example,

[75] Case 241/83 [1985] E.C.R. 99; [1985] 1 C.M.L.R. 806. The Court interpreted Art. 16(1) to hold that the Italian courts had exclusive jurisdiction over a dispute between two Germans about a three-week letting of a holiday flat in Italy.
[76] See also para. 2–28.
[77] Case 158/87 [1988] E.C.R. 3791.

the immovable property situated in one contracting State is adjacent to the property in another State and the property is situated almost entirely in one of those States. In those circumstances it might be appropriate to regard the property as a single unit and deem it to be entirely situated in one of those States for the purposes of conferring on the courts of that State exclusive jurisdiction over the tenancy of that property."

In *Reichert v. Dresdner Bank (No. 1)*[78] Article 16(1) was held not to apply to a French *action paulienne* whereby the bank sought to set aside an allegedly fraudulent disposition of a property in Antibes.

2–127

"In those circumstances, Article 16(1) must be interpreted as meaning that the exclusive jurisdiction of the Contracting State in which the property is situated does not encompass all actions concerning rights *in rem* in immovable property but only those which both come within the scope of the Brussels Convention and are actions which seek to determine the extent, content, ownership or possession of immovable property or the existence of other rights *in rem* therein and to provide the holders of those rights with the protection of the powers which attach to their interest.

The *action paulienne*, however, is based on the creditor's personal claim against the debtor and seeks to protect whatever security he may have over the debtor's estate. If successful, its effect is to render the transaction whereby the debtor has effected a disposition in fraud of the creditor's rights ineffective as against the creditor alone. The hearing of such an action, moreover, does not involve the assessment of facts or the application of rules and practices of the *locus rei sitae* in such a way as to justify conferring jurisdiction on a court of the State in which the property is situated.

Finally, although in certain Member States the rules governing the public registration of rights in immovable property require public notice to be given of legal actions seeking to have transactions affecting such rights avoided or declared ineffective as against third parties and of judgments given in such actions, that fact alone is not enough to justify conferring exclusive Jurisdiction on the courts of the Contracting State in which the property affected by those rights is situated. Such rules of national law are based on the need to afford legal protection to the interests of third parties, and such protection can be ensured, if need be, by public notice in the form and at the place prescribed by the law of the Contracting State in which the property is situated."

Even before the amendment to Article 16(1) came into force,[79] *Hacker v. Euro-Relais*[80] decided that the Article did not apply to a package

2–128

---

[78] Case C–115/88 [1990] E.C.R. I–27.
[79] The San Sebastian Convention amended Art. 16(1) to reverse the effect of *Rosler v. Rottwinkel*. See para. 2–28, but the amendment applied only when both parties were natural persons.
[80] Case C–280/90 [1992] E.C.R. I–1111.

holiday including the rental of a holiday home. In *Webb v. Webb*[81] the Court held that an equitable claim to ownership of a holiday flat in Antibes was not within Article 16(1), since although the ultimate object was to recover possession the action was one *in personam* rather than one *in rem*. It was a coincidence that the trust property was a flat in France, rather than one in England or even an yacht. Finally, *Lieber v. Göbel*[82] involved yet another holiday property in the South of France, this time in Cannes. The Court held that a counterclaim for compensation for occupation under a void transfer of ownership was not within the exclusive jurisdiction of the French courts.

2–129   What can be deduced from these cases? First, that the Court is determined that the exclusive jurisdictions should be interpreted as narrowly as possible. Even more than in other areas, the Court applies the principle that derogations from the general rule of Article 2 should be construed as strictly as possible, consistently with their assumed purpose. To that end, it is willing to ignore the real reasons for them documented in the Jenard Report in favour of invented reasons of its own, which lead more easily to a restrictive interpretation. Secondly, that only actions *in rem* in the narrow sense are within the Article, and that actions *in personam* fall under the general provisions of the Convention, even if their subject matter is real property.[83] Thirdly, that the Court has recognised the inconvenience to all parties which is bound to result if one of several closely related claims is within the exclusive jurisdictions, and others are outside.[84] Since the Brussels Convention has no doctrine of ancillary jurisdiction, and since the court with exclusive jurisdiction over the claims *in rem* is not particularly likely to have jurisdiction over the claims *in personam*, the only answer is to deny that Article 16 applies at all.[85] Finally, one notices that national sovereignty has no place in the Court's understanding of Article 16. It is even willing to concede, if *obiter*, that in certain circumstances the courts of one state may have *exclusive* jurisdiction over rights *in rem* in respect of land situated in another.[86]

---

[81] Case C–294/92 [1994] E.C.R. I–1717.

[82] Case C–292/93 [1994] E.C.R. I–2535.

[83] Except for actions in relation to tenancies, which are covered by the express words of Art. 16(1).

[84] One of the absurdities of Case 241/83 *Rosler v. Rottwinkel* [1985] E.C.R. 99; [1985] 1 C.M.L.R. 806 was that since the parties had signed an agreement with a German choice-of-court clause, there was no way that the tortious or contractual claims could be brought in the same court as those relating to the tenancy as such, even if the Italian court would otherwise have had jurisdiction under Art. 5.

[85] Subject, now, to Art. 6(4).

[86] Case 158/87 *Scherrens v. Maenhout* [1988] E.C.R. 3791, above.

H. SPECIAL REGIMES FOR COMMUNITY AND EUROPEAN PATENTS

Introduction

With certain exceptions, the Brussels Convention is applied to litiga-   **2–130**
tion concerning Community patents and trade marks by virtue of Article
13 of the Community Patent Convention and Article 90 of the Community Trade Mark Regulation respectively.[87] The Brussels Convention
is always subordinate to international conventions governing jurisdiction
and the enforcement of judgments in relation to specific matters, though
its provisions still apply to the extent that those conventions are silent.[88]
It is, therefore, unnecessary for the Convention expressly to contain
derogations for the European Patent Convention and the Community
Patent Convention, although it does acknowledge their existence in
passing. The principle that the Brussels Convention is subordinate to
Community legislation governing jurisdiction in particular matters
applies to the Community Trade Mark Regulation.[89]

The one issue specifically addressed is the application of Article 16(4)
to European Patents. In the absence of an express provision it might
have been argued that exclusive jurisdiction in relation to the registration or validity of European patents, even once granted, vested in the
courts of Germany by virtue of the European Patent Office in Munich
being the place where the registration had been applied for. Article Vd
of the Protocol to the Brussels Convention added by the 1978 Accession
Convention, therefore provides:

> Without prejudice to the jurisdiction of the European Patent Office
> under the Convention on the grant of European patents, signed at
> Munich on 5th October 1973, the courts of each Contracting State
> shall have exclusive jurisdiction, regardless of domicile, in proceed-
> ings concerned with the registration or validity of any European
> patent granted for that State which is not a Community patent by
> virtue of the provisions of Article 86 of the Convention for the
> European patent for the common market, signed at Luxembourg on
> 15th December 1975.

Article Vd, and the relationship between the Brussels Convention and   **2–131**
the European Patent Convention or Community Patent Convention
were explained in the Schlosser Report.[90]

> "Since the 1968 Convention entered into force, two Conventions on
> patents have been signed which are of the greatest international

---

[87] See Chap. 5. It is noteworthy that Art. 16(4) is not one of those Articles of the
Brussels Convention excluded by either of these Articles.
[88] Art. 57(1), interpreted in Case C–406/92 *The Tatry* [1994] E.C.R. I–5439.
[89] Art. 57(3) of the Brussels Convention.
[90] Schlosser Report, para. 173.

importance. The Munich Convention on the grant of European patents was signed on 5 October 1973 and the Luxembourg Convention for the European patent for the common market was signed on 15 December 1975. The purpose of the Munich Convention is to introduce a common patent application procedure for the Contracting States, though the patent subsequently granted is national in scale. It is valid for one or more States, its substance in each case being basically that of a corresponding patent granted nationally. The aim of the Luxembourg Convention is to institute in addition a patent granted *ab initio* for all States of the Community in a standard manner and with the same substance, based on Community law; such a patent necessarily remains valid or expires uniformly throughout the EEC.

Both instruments contain specific provisions on jurisdiction which take precedence over the 1968 Convention. However, the special jurisdiction provisions relate only to specific matters, such as applications for the revocation of patents pursuant to the Luxembourg Convention. Article 16(4) of the 1968 Convention remains relevant for actions for which no specific provision is made. In the case of European patents under the Munich Convention it is conceivable that this provision might be construed as meaning that actions must be brought in the State in which the patent was applied for and not in the State for which it is valid and in which it is challenged. The new Article Vd of the Protocol annexed to the 1968 Convention is designed to prevent this interpretation and ensure that only the courts of the State in which the patent is valid have jurisdiction, unless the Munich Convention itself lays down special provisions.

Clearly, such a provision cannot cover a Community patent under the Luxembourg Convention, since the governing principle is that the patent is granted, not for a given State, but for all the Member States of the EEC. Hence the exception at the end of the new provision. However, even in the area covered by the Luxembourg Convention patents valid for one or more, but not all, States of the Community are possible. Article 86 of that Convention allows this for a transitional period to which no term has yet been set.[91] Where the applicant for a patent takes up the option available to him under this provision and applies for a patent for one or more, but not all, States of the EEC, the patent is not a Community patent even though it comes under some of the provisions of the Luxembourg Convention but merely a patent granted for one or more States. Accordingly, the courts of that State have exclusive jurisdiction under Article Vd of the Protocol annexed to the 1968 Convention. The same is true for any case in which a national patent is granted in response to an international application, e.g. under the Patent Co-operation Treaty opened for signature at Washington on 19 June 1970.

[91] Art. 81 of the 1989 Community Patent Convention.

It only remains to be made clear that Article 16(4) of the 1968 Convention and the new Article Vd of the Protocol annexed to the Convention also cover actions which national legislation allows to be brought at the patent application stage, so as to reduce the risk of a patent being granted, and the correctness of the grant being subsequently challenged."

The remainder of the present section deals with provisions as to jurisdiction specific to the European Patent Convention, other than the jurisdiction of the Office itself in respect of applications and opposition proceedings. The Community Patent Convention is dealt with in Chapters 4 and 5.

The Protocol to the European Patent Convention

The European Patent Office has no jurisdiction to decide whether or not an applicant or some other party is entitled to the benefit of a pending European patent application or to a European patent once granted. Jurisdiction in respect of applications is governed by the Protocol on Jurisdiction and the Recognition of Decisions in Respect of the Right to the Grant of a European Patent (Protocol on Recognition) which is annexed to the European Patent Convention.[92] The Protocol is given effect in English law by section 82 of the Patents Act 1977 and is implemented in the laws of the other contracting states of the European patent system.   **2–132**

The Protocol on Recognition does not specify what body of law is to be applied by the court hearing the entitlement claim. It is to be assumed that the court would first have to characterise the claim, for instance as one in contract or trust; then apply its normal rules of private international law to identify the system of law governing the claim; and finally apply that body of law to decide the claim on the merits. It is not to be assumed that the substantive issue of entitlement would be governed by the *lex fori* of the court having jurisdiction under the Protocol. As between two American claimants, for instance, the courts of Germany might have jurisdiction and find themselves applying the law of an American state.   **2–133**

The terms of the Protocol on Recognition

Article 1 of the Protocol on Recognition states that courts of the EPC contracting states shall have jurisdiction to decide claims, against the applicant, to the right to the grant of a European patent and contemplates that the claim may be in respect of one or more of the contracting states. The term "courts" includes administrative authorities as appropriate. The detailed rules as to jurisdiction are governed by Articles 2 to 6   **2–134**

---

[92] See Le Tallec, "The Protocol on Jurisdiction and the Recognition of Decisions in Respect of the Right to the Grant of a European Patent" (1985) 16 I.I.C. 318.

inclusive. By Article 2, if the applicant for the European patent has his residence or principal place of business within one of the contracting states of the European Patent Convention, then the proceedings *must* be brought against him in the courts of that contracting state. Article 2 has been interpreted by the English Court of Appeal in *Kakkar v. Szelke*[93] as meaning that the English Courts cannot be given jurisdiction contrary to the Protocol by reformulating the claim, for instance as one for breach of trust.

2–135   By Article 3, if the applicant has his residence or principal place of business outside the contracting states and the party claiming the right to grant of the European patent has his residence or principal place of business within one of the contracting states, then it is the courts of the latter state which have exclusive jurisdiction. Article 4 contains overriding provisions when the dispute is between employer and employee and Article 5 allows exclusive jurisdiction to be conferred on a court of any contracting state by written agreement. If none of the foregoing articles apply, then the courts of the Federal Republic of Germany have exclusive jurisdiction. Courts in any contracting state must decline jurisdiction of their own motion if the claim is brought in breach of the Protocol or if a claim on the same subject matter and between the same parties has previously validly been brought in a court of another contracting state.

2–136   By Rule 13 of the Implementing Regulations to the European Patent Convention the European Patent Office is obliged to stay its own proceedings on being notified that a claim to entitlement has been made, unless the claimant irrevocably consents to their continuing. Article 9 of the Protocol requires the decision of a court in a contracting state to be recognised without invocation of any special procedure in the other contracting states. This would be necessary, for instance, if Rule 13 were waived and the European patent proceeded to grant before the decision was given. If Rule 13 applied, then the decision would be implemented by the European Patent Office itself pursuant to Article 61 of the European Patent Convention. By Article 11(1), the Protocol on Recognition takes precedence over any conflicting provisions of other agreements on jurisdiction or the recognition of judgements, presumably including the Brussels Convention itself.

The Protocol and decisions of courts in non-contracting states

2–137   The Protocol on Recognition itself does not appear to deal with the possibility that a court outside a contracting state could have jurisdiction over a claim to the benefit of a European patent application, perhaps even by prior agreement or submission. Although the decision of such a court might be binding *inter partes*, the Protocol and the European Patent Convention itself are at best extremely cautious in how they treat a decision by a court of a non-contracting state. Since entitlement is

---

[93] [1989] F.S.R. 225, CA.

quite likely to be litigated on a Worldwide scale, and often between parties neither of whom has any connection with Europe, this is a serious omission.

By Article 9 of the Protocol, final decisions as to entitlement by a **2–138** court of a contracting state are made binding, but nothing is said about decisions by courts of non-contracting states. If such a decision has to be enforced after grant of the European patent, then it is relevant that Article 11(2) of the Protocol on Recognition expressly provides that the Protocol does not affect the implementation of agreements between contracting states and other states. Supposing the application is still pending, as it normally will be, then Article 61 of the European Patent Convention governs the rights of the successful claimant who may take over the pending application, file a new one, or request refusal. Article 61 simply refers in terms to a "final decision" that a person other than the applicant is entitled to the benefit of the application and at first sight is not confined to final decisions of courts of contracting states. However, the successful claimant is only entitled to rely on Article 61 "in respect of those contracting states . . . in which the decision has been taken or recognised, or has to be recognised on the basis of the Protocol on Recognition." It seems to follow that the successful claimant can only invoke Article 61 in respect of a decision by a court in a non-contracting state, to the extent that the decision has actually been recognised in the individual contracting states, for instance under bilateral treaties.[94] Even an obligation to recognise, if not arising under the Protocol on Recognition, would not seem to suffice.

Articles 2 and 64 EPC and the reference in *Fort Dodge v. Akzo Nobel*

The final respect in which it might be suggested that the European **2–139** Patent Convention is relevant arises in the context of the preliminary reference to the European Court of Justice made by the Court of Appeal in *Fort Dodge v. Akzo Nobel; Boston Scientific v. Cordis*.[95] The first two questions in that reference ask:

> "1. In the case of patents granted pursuant to European applications pursuant to the European Patent Convention, are the provisions of Article 2 and/or 64 of the European Patent Convention provisions which govern jurisdiction in relation to particular matters (ie proceedings for infringement of such patents) within the meaning of Article 57 of the Brussels Convention?
>
> 2. If the answer to question 1 is 'yes'; is the effect that, notwithstanding any other provision of the Brussels Convention, proceedings for infringement of a patent granted pursuant to a European application can only be brought in the Courts of the country in which the patent is registered?"

---

[94] Note that the Application under Art. 61 must be made within three months of the decision becoming final, which hardly allows much time for registration.
[95] [1998] F.S.R. 222, CA. See para. 1–51, above.

Articles 2 and 64 respectively provide:

Article 2

European patent

(1) Patents granted by virtue of this Convention shall be called European patents.
(2) The European patent shall in each of the Contracting States for which it is granted, have the effect of and be subject to the same conditions as a national patent granted by that State, unless otherwise provided in this Convention.

Article 64

Rights conferred by a European patent

(1) A European patent shall, subject to the provisions of paragraph 2, confer on its proprietor from the date of publication of the mention of its grant, in each Contracting State in respect of which it is granted, the same rights as would be conferred by a national patent granted in that State.
(. . .)
(3) Any infringement of a European patent shall be dealt with by national law.

2–140   The supposed relevance of Articles 2 and 64 derives from Article 57(1) of the Brussels Convention, providing. "This Convention shall not affect any conventions to which the Contracting States are or will be parties and which in relation to particular matters, govern jurisdiction or the recognition or enforcement of judgments." The argument that infringement of European patents (U.K.) is justiciable only in the courts of the United Kingdom (and *mutatis mutandis* for the other EPC contracting states) therefore requires two far from self-evident propositions to be made out: that the relevant provisions of the EPC are ones which can be said to "govern jurisdiction or the recognition or enforcement of judgments" and that the reference to national law means pure domestic law, excluding the Brussels Convention.[96] Neither of these survives further scrutiny.

Do Articles 2 and 64 EPC govern jurisdiction or the recognition and enforcement of judgments?

2–141   The argument based on Articles 2 and 64 of the European Patent Convention was not addressed by Laddie J. in either *Coin Controls v. Suzo*[97] or *Fort Dodge v. Akzo Nobel*,[98] and seems to have come to

---

[96] This assumes that domestic law renders actions on foreign patents non-justiciable, which is not necessarily the case outside the U.K. and which it is certainly not within the competence of the European Court of Justice to determine.
[97] [1997] F.S.R. 660 (Laddie J.).
[98] [1998] F.S.R. 222, CA.

prominence for the first time on the appeal in the latter case,[99] in which the Court of Appeal observed:

"Mr Silverleaf QC who appeared for the Appellants submitted that such a conclusion was contrary to the Paris Convention of 1883 as revised, the Agreement of Trade-Related Aspects of Intellectual Property Rights (commonly referred to as TRIPs), the European Patent Convention and Article 222 of the Treaty of Rome. We do not believe that these Conventions or the Treaty are directly concerned with jurisdiction. No doubt it was contemplated, prior to the Brussels Convention, that intellectual property rights, being national rights, would be litigated in the State where the right was registered. Indeed there are cases in this country which so held. Even so, those Conventions and the Treaty are not inconsistent with the provisions of the Brussels Convention which apply to intellectual property rights just as much as to other rights. That we believe to be *acte claire*."

It is suggested that a number of arguments support the Court of Appeal's conclusion. First, there are the terms of Articles 2 and 64 of the European Patent Convention.[1] On their face, they are principally concerned with substantive patent law and not with issues of jurisdiction as such in infringement actions.[2] It is true that Article 64(3) may implicitly require European patents to be litigated according to the same rules of procedure as national patents, but that is as far as it goes. This distinction is confirmed by the existence of clear and express rules governing jurisdiction and recognition of judgments in the Protocol on Recognition to the EPC.[3] **2–142**

Secondly, nothing in the *travaux préparatoires*[4] to the European Patent Convention or the Minutes of the 1973 Munich Diplomatic Conference **2–143**

---

[99] It is of interest that the three draft questions originally proposed by the Court of Appeal for reference to the European Court of Justice did not mention EPC Arts 2 and 64 at all.

[1] It is to be assumed, from the terms of the reference, that the other conventions and treaties cited by the appellants were not considered to add anything to the argument based on the EPC.

[2] It might be suggested, reversing the plaintiff's argument in *Pearce v. Ove Arup* [1997] F.S.R. 641, that a provision of substantive law may indirectly have consequences in procedural law; but even if that were otherwise to the point it ignores the fact that the European Patent Convention, unlike the Brussels Convention, is not part of the Community legal order and cannot have direct effect.

[3] The Protocol on Jurisdiction and the Recognition of Decisions in respect of the Right to the Grant of a European Patents. See above, para. 2–132. A comparable distinction was noted in Case 288/82 *Duijnstee v. Goderbauer* [1983] E.C.R. 3663; [1985] 1 C.M.L.R. 220.

[4] Art. 64 EPC corresponds to Art. 18 of the First and Second Preliminary Draft Conventions both of which read "A European patent shall confer on its proprietor, from the date of publication of its grant, in each Contracting State in respect of which it is granted, the same rights as would be conferred by a national patent granted in that State. Any infringement of a European patent shall be dealt with under the laws of that State." There is no relevant commentary in the Report on either preliminary draft. In passing, the change from "the laws of that state" to "national law" would be consistent with recognition of multinational infringement actions, though this is no more than speculation.

indicates that Article 64 was intended to have the effect contended for in *Fort Dodge v. Akzo Nobel*.[5] For Article 57 of the Brussels Convention to apply, it is not sufficient for Article 64 to contemplate that pre-Brussels Convention national law should apply to infringement actions. It must actually impose that result so as to *govern* jurisdiction. The view that Article 64 is not concerned with jurisdiction and does not displace the normal rules of Articles 2 and 5(3) of the Brussels Convention is confirmed by Singer, who was one of the founding fathers of the European Patent Convention, attended the Munich Conference on behalf of the German Patent Office, and whose book *The European Patent Convention* expressly contemplates extraterritorial enforcement of European patents pursuant to Articles 2 and 5(3) of the Brussels Convention.[6]

Is the reference to "national law" exclusive of the law of the Brussels Convention?

2–144   Nor is the argument any stronger on its second point, which depends on the body of law in contemplation, as "national law" in Article 54(3) EPC. In so far as the words "dealt with" in Article 64(3) might be taken as referring to jurisdiction as such, rather than the general law of civil procedure and remedies, the question arises as to why the national law in contemplation should exclude the Brussels Convention. Even if it may be said that Articles 2 and 64 of the EPC have some relevance to jurisdiction over infringement actions, they self-evidently do not constitute a complete code. It is clear from the judgment of the European Court of Justice in *The Tatry*[7] that to the extent an Article 57(1) convention is silent, the rules of the Brussels Convention still apply. As the Schlosser Report observed.[8]

> "Both instruments [EPC and CPC] contain specific provisions on jurisdiction which take precedence over the 1968 Convention. However, the special jurisdiction provisions relate only to specific matters, such as applications for the revocation of patents pursuant to the Luxembourg Convention. Article 16(4) of the 1968 Convention remains relevant for actions for which no specific provision is made."

[5] The discussion of what was to become Art. 64(1) and (3) (Art. 62 in the working draft) was derisory: Minutes of the 1973 Munich Diplomatic Conference, Main Committee I, paras 96 and 97 which together consist of five lines of text. The only substantial discussion related to products obtained directly by means of the patented process (Minutes, paras 121 *et seq.*, now corresponding to EPC Art. 64(2)) and reversal of the burden of proof (Minutes, paras 138 *et seq.*, such provisions were left to national law).

[6] Singer, *The European Patent Convention* (Revised English Edition, ed. Lunzer, 1995), para. 64.07. This is consistent with the views expressed by Singer at the time in "The Infringement of Supranational Patent Rights in a Future Europe" [1973] *Industrial Property* 380.

[7] Case C–406/92 [1994] I–E.C.R. 5439.

[8] para. 173.3.

The European Patent Convention was signed in 1973, five years after the Brussels Convention and in the same year as the latter came into force for the original six contracting states. For France, Germany and four others, the relevant national law incorporated and was largely defined by the Brussels Convention, and the three new members of the European Communities in 1973 (including the United Kingdom) were obliged by their Treaty of Accession to the E.C. to adopt the Brussels Convention in due course. It had been stated in the Jenard Report that the Brussels Convention intended actions for infringement of national patents to be "governed by the general rules of the [Brussels] Convention."[9] How then can it be suggested that the very general words of Articles 2 and 64 EPC required any EPC contracting state which was also a party to the Brussels Convention to disregard the latter in relation to actions for infringement of European patents?

The contemporary opinion of Ulmer[10] was that, in the six Brussels **2–145** Convention contracting states, actions for infringement of industrial property rights and copyright could be brought on a pan-European basis in the courts of the defendants domicile or pursuant to Article 5(3):

"In these circumstances it is particularly gratifying that the question has been clarified within the EEC by the Convention on Jurisdiction and the Enforcement of Judgments in Civil and Commercial Matters of 27 September 1968. The Convention, which has already been ratified by the six original member states of the EEC provides basically as follows:

Persons domiciled in a contracting state shall be answerable to the courts of that state, whatever their nationality (Article 2); further, under Article 5(3) in matters relating to tort (delict or quasi-delict), persons may be sued in another contracting state in the courts for the place where the damage or injury has occurred.

Article 16 of the Convention provides for an exception to these rules by conferring exclusive jurisdiction for specified cases. For industrial property rights the rule in Article 16(4) is of importance: in actions relating to the registration or validity of patents, trademarks, designs, or other similar rights required to be depositied or registered, the courts of the contracting state in which the deposit or registration has been applied for, has taken place or is under the terms of an international convention deemed to have taken place, shall have exclusive jurisdiction.

An action for infringement of copyright or of an industrial property right may, therefore, be instituted both in the contracting state in which the defendant is domiciled and in the contracting state in which the damage or injury has occurred. The fact that Articles 2 and 5(3) of the Convention are applicable also to actions based on industrial property rights (and correspondingly on

---

[9] Jernard Report on Art. 16(4).
[10] Ulmer, *Intellectual Property Rights and the Conflict of Laws* (1978), para. 29.

copyright) may be conclusively deduced from the fact that in Article 16 exclusive juridiction is provided only for actions concerning the validity of registration of industrial property rights, whereas in other respects the general rules as to jurisdiction are to suffice.

The exclusive jurisdiction of the courts of the protecting country provided by Article 16(4) for actions concerning the registration or validity of industial property rights is of importance above all for actions of which the object is the revocation or withdrawal of patents or the cancellation in the registers of trademarks or designs."

2–146   The 1978 Accession Convention which amended the Brussels Convention on the accession of the United Kingdom, Ireland and Denmark was drafted after the European Patent Convention had come into force, and with the latter in contemplation.[11] Yet nothing in the Accession Convention itself, or the Schlosser Report on it, suggests that Jenard's commentary was wrong or was intended to be superseded. The only relevant provision of the Accession Convention was Article Vd of the Protocol which was intended to avoid a possible misconstruction of Article 16(4) by preserving the exclusive jurisdiction of national courts in "proceedings concerned with the registration or validity of any European patent granted for that state" against an argument that exclusive jurisdiction would otherwise have vested in the courts of Germany as the courts for the place where the application for the European patent had been made.[12]

2–147   It must finally be admitted that the argument based on the EPC cannot be applicable to national patents not granted by the European route. Assume it to be clear beyond argument that as a matter of long-standing domestic law, infringements of foreign patents are not justiciable in the United Kingdom. That is not a result of any international convention or Community legislation so Article 57 has no application and the normal rules of the Brussels Convention apply. It might be suggested that the problematic Article 6(1) of the Brussels Convention is less obviously applicable where one is dealing with a bundle of patents obtained by the national route, as opposed to a bundle of European patents; but it would still follow that where a single legal person had infringed several national patents, then he could be sued for all his infringements in the courts of his domicile pursuant to Article 2 or in the courts of the place of the tort identified by Article 5(3). It would be illogical, to say the least, if the opposite conclusion were reached if he infringed several European patents. But the argument to that effect is circular. Article 2(2) EPC provides that European patents are to "have the effect of and be subject to the same conditions as a national patent granted by that State." A national patent granted by the state is subject to the ordinary rules of the Brussels Convention, so how can a European patent be treated any differently?

---

[11] As is demonstrated by Art. Vd of the Protocol and the commentary thereon in the Schlosser Report, see above. Schlosser was even a professor at the University of Munich, the home town of the EPO.

[12] See above, para. 2–130.

CHAPTER 3

THE BRUSSELS CONVENTION APPLIED TO INTELLECTUAL PROPERTY IN NATIONAL PRACTICE

A. INTRODUCTION AND OVERVIEW

Historical introduction to the Convention in English law

3–01   The Brussels Convention has had the force of law in the United Kingdom since January 1, 1987, but it has taken a full ten years for the English courts to address expressly the questions of whether, or in what circumstances, actions for infringement of foreign intellectual property rights can be brought here.[1] Even now, there are only three decided

---

[1] For literature on the Brussels Convention, see Chap. 2, n. 3, above. The major intellectual property textbooks have had relatively little to say about the application of the Convention to intellectual property, but see Cornish, *Intellectual Property* (3rd ed., 1996), paras 2–71 *et seq.*; Merkin and Black, *Copyright and Designs Law*, paras 2.14 *et seq.*; Vitoria *et. al.*, *Encyclopaedia of United Kingdom and European Patent Law*, paras 10–501 *et seq.*; White, ed., *CIPA Guide to the Patents Acts* (4th ed., 1995), paras 96.09 and 96.10; *European Patents Handbook* section 30.4. See also Wadlow, "Intellectual Property and the Judgments Convention" (1985) 10 E.L. Rev. 305; Tritton and Tritton, "The Brussels Convention and Intellectual Property" [1987] E.I.P.R. 349; Arnold, "Can One Sue in England for Infringement of Foreign Intellectual Property Rights" [1990] E.I.P.R. 254; Floyd and Purvis, "Can an English Court Restrain Infringement of a Foreign Patent?" [1995] E.I.P.R. 110; Adams, "Choice of Forum in Patent Disputes" [1995] E.I.P.R. 497; Jooris, "Infringement of Foreign Copyright and the Jurisdiction of the English Courts" [1996] E.I.P.R. 127; Kempner and Fricker, "Can the UK Courts face the Dutch Challenge on Cross-Border Injunctions in Intellectual Property Cases? [1996] E.I.P.R. 377; O'Sullivan, "Cross-Border Jurisdiction in Patent Infringement Proceedings in Europe [1996] E.I.P.R. 654; Franzosi and de Sanctis, "The Increasing Worldwide Significance of European Patent Litigation (1997) 25 AIPLA Q.J. 67; Dutson, "The Internet, the Conflict of Laws, International Litigation and Intellectual Property" [1997] J.B.L. 495. For case notes and comments on *Pearce v. Ove Arup* and *Coin Controls v. Suzo* see: Briggs, (1997) 113 L.Q.R. 364; Cohen, [1997] E.I.P.R. 379; Dutson, (1997) 46 I.C.L.Q. 918; Inglis and Gringrass, [1997] E.I.P.R. 396; Tugendhat, (1997) 113 L.Q.R. 360; Wolanski, [1997] Ent. L.R. 143. For a comment on *Fort Dodge v. Akzo Nobel*, see Karet, [1998] E.I.P.R. 76.

cases directly in point.[2] There is a rather larger body of cases in which issues under the Brussels Convention have been canvassed, and opinions expressed *obiter* as to how infringement actions should be dealt with under the Convention.[3] Unfortunately, several of the latter betray an unfamiliarity with the Convention and its underlying policies and techniques, or an unwillingness to accept that the Convention imposes a radically different regime on English judges used to exercising any international jurisdiction in this area with extreme caution, or not at all.

In the present state of the law, it is impossible to reconcile all these **3–02** opinions or to avoid expressing an admittedly personal opinion as to which are right. The thesis of the present chapter is that the view of the Brussels Convention expressed by Lloyd J. in *Pearce v. Ove Arup*[4] and Laddie J. in *Coin Controls v. Suzo*[5] is essentially correct. The Convention *does* permit and may even require actions for infringement of foreign intellectual property rights, registered or unregistered, to be entertained in England as the place of the defendant's domicile, or under one of the other jurisdiction-creating provisions of the Convention.[6] To that extent, the Convention wholly overrides inconsistent national doctrines such as those of *forum non conveniens* or international comity as embodied in the *Mocambique* rule.[7] It is also suggested, however, that each of *Pearce v. Ove Arup* and *Coin Controls v. Suzo* needs reconsideration on one subsidiary point which did not arise in the other case. *Pearce v. Ove Arup* is not necessarily right to say that the former rule of double actionability is abolished by the Brussels Convention in cases to which the latter applies.[8] As for *Coin Controls v. Suzo*, its treatment of Article 16(4) is probably not ideal either in terms of consistency with the law under the Convention or in its practical consequences; though in the absence of better guidance from the European Court of Justice no interpretation of that provision can confidently be said to be right and few can be ruled out altogether.[9]

The paramount nature of the Convention

The reason for the paucity of decided cases hitherto is almost certainly **3–03** to be found in the interaction of the Brussels Convention with purely English doctrines of private international law, and specifically the rules

---

[2] *Pearce v. Ove Arup* [1997] F.S.R. 641 (Lloyd J.), *Coin Controls v. Suzo* [1997] F.S.R. 660 (Laddie J.) and *Fort Dodge v. Akzo Nobel* [1998] F.S.R. 222, CA.

[3] See para. 3–42, below.

[4] [1997] F.S.R. 641 (Lloyd J.).

[5] [1997] F.S.R. 660 (Laddie J.).

[6] This is now affirmed, though in an interlocutory judgment, by the Court of Appeal in *Fort Dodge v. Akzo Nobel* [1998] F.S.R. 222, see below.

[7] The rule in *British South Africa Co v. Companhia do Mocambique* [1893] A.C. 602, HL. See paras 6–48 *et seq.*

[8] This is considered elsewhere at para. 6–104. Lloyd J. is certainly right to say that double actionability as applied to intellectual property infringement in *Def Lepp v. Stuart Brown* [1986] R.P.C. 273 is inconsistent with the Brussels Convention, but it does not necessarily follow that the *lex loci delicti* can simply be substituted.

[9] See paras 3–78 *et seq.*

in *Phillips v. Eyre*[10] and *British South Africa Co v. Companhia do Mocambique*.[11] The consensus was formerly that actions to enforce foreign rights in the English courts would have been bound to fail under the double actionability rule of *Phillips v. Eyre*, or would always have been refused for reasons of international comity. As to the first, the enactment of the Private International Law (Miscellaneous Provisions) Act 1995 means that the former English rules of conflict of laws no longer doom such actions to failure on that ground.[12] In fact, it was even accepted by Lloyd J. in *Pearce v. Ove Arup*[13] that enactment of the Convention should have precedence over the rule in *Phillips v. Eyre*, although the point will soon be of little more than academic interest. So far as comity is concerned, the Brussels Convention has its own mandatory rules which override inconsistent national law. What is now reasonably certain, is that to the extent that traditional notions of comity have not been incorporated into the Convention, and specifically into Article 16, they have simply ceased to have effect in cases to which the Convention applies.[14]

3–04   In both *Pearce v. Ove Arup* and *Coin Controls v. Suzo*[15] the defendants argued unsuccessfully that the *Mocambique* rule continued to apply, notwithstanding the Civil Jurisdiction and Judgments Act 1982 and the incorporation of the Brussels Convention into domestic law. In *Pearce v. Ove Arup* alone, the cause of action (if any) had accrued before commencement of the Private International Law (Miscellaneous Provisions) Act 1995 and the defendants also argued that the double actionability rule prevented the court from entertaining the action. Both these arguments were rejected.

3–05   In *Pearce v. Ove Arup*[16] Lloyd J. concluded:

> "My conclusion on this point is that the Convention does require an English court to accept jurisdiction where an action is brought against an English domiciled defendant (with or without other defendants) for breach of a Dutch copyright, and to hear that action on the merits, and thus overrides, so far as is necessary for that purpose, both Rule 203 and the *Moçambique* rule, even though neither of them is a rule as to jurisdiction. Each of them, to the

[10] (1870) L.R. 6 Q.B. 1, CA. See para. 6–07.
[11] [1893] A.C. 602, HL.
[12] For the Private International Law (Miscellaneous Provisions) Act 1995 see paras 6–19 *et seq.*
[13] [1997] F.S.R. 641 (Lloyd J.).
[14] The concerns of Briggs, *op. cit.*, and Tugendhat, *op. cit.*, (which are not specific to intellectual property) may partly be met by two considerations. First, that double actionability *qua* a rule for choice of law is not necessarily inconsistent with the Convention, it is only the misapplication of the rule as if it were one of justiciability that offends. Secondly, that former English rules of justiciability, of whatever kind, are only superseded in so far as the Convention provides its own complete code in the form of Article 16. Other such rules need not be affected unless the proper operation of the Convention is impaired.
[15] [1997] F.S.R. 660 (Laddie J.).
[16] [1997] F.S.R. 641 (Lloyd J.).

extent that they would preclude the English court from hearing such an action, would in my judgment impair the effectiveness of the Convention by frustrating the operation of the basic rule in Article 2, and must therefore give way in order to allow the jurisdictional rules of the Convention to have their proper effect. The position is quite different from other exclusionary rules, such as Acts of State, because both Rule 203 and the *Moçambique* rule proceed on the clear premise that the English courts are not a suitable forum for such an action whereas the courts of another country are appropriate. It seems to me that, where that other country is another Contracting State, this is a position which subverts the policy and provisions of the Convention. To borrow a phrase from another area of Community law, although they are not rules as to jurisdiction, they are 'measures having an equivalent effect' to rules of jurisdiction, and are inconsistent with the mandatory effect of the Convention and its basic rule as to domicile-based jurisdiction in Article 2."

And in *Coin Controls v. Suzo*[17] Laddie J. followed Lloyd J. in the following terms: **3–06**

"When considering the Convention, it is necessary to have at the forefront of one's mind the profound changes it is designed to effect to the ground rules used for deciding in which courts actions shall be brought. Our judge-made rules are, we hope, based on the common sense principle of deciding which court is the most suited to determine the issues between the parties, in other words what is the *forum conveniens*. The explanation for the *Moçambique* rule given by Lord Herschell and the reluctance expressed by Aldous J. in *Plastus* and *Chiron* are full of reliance on that principle. The trouble is that one man's *forum conveniens* may be another's *forum inconveniens*. If different legal systems have slightly different rules on justiciability, there is a risk of competing litigation in different countries. Most practitioners familiar with disputes with an international flavour will have experienced the somewhat unseemly tussles which sometimes have taken place between courts of different countries trying to assert exclusive jurisdiction over a common dispute.

One of the purposes of the Convention is to replace the differing domestic rules, at least in relation to forum, by a simple set of rigid provisions forcing litigation into the courts of one country and out of the courts of others. As the Schlosser report states:

'. . . in accordance with the general spirit of the 1968 Convention, the fact that foreign law has to be applied, either generally or in a particular case, should not constitute a sufficient reason for a court to decline jurisdiction. Where the

---

[17] [1997] F.S.R. 660 (Laddie J.).

courts of several States have jurisdiction, the Plaintiff has deliberately been given a right of choice, which should not be weakened by application of the doctrine of *forum conveniens*.

During the course of his submissions, Mr. Miller frequently pointed to the inconvenience or worse which would flow from accepting Mr. Silverleaf's argument and allowing the three foreign claims to be litigated here. I accept that inconvenience may be caused if Mr. Silverleaf is right and, of course, I share the sentiments expressed by Aldous J. in *Plastus*. But if the Convention requires the courts to accept the foreign claims, then the same rules apply to other Contracting States and none of us have the power or right to ignore or override it. If the Convention gives jurisdiction to the courts of one country, they cannot reject the gift. They must accept it and act on it."

3–07   Most recently, the Court of Appeal in *Fort Dodge v. Akzo Nobel*[18] agreed with both Lloyd and Laddie JJ. and also dismissed arguments to the contrary based on various international conventions not directly concerned with issues of jurisdiction:

"We believe that Articles 2 and 5(3), subject to the exclusion contained in Article 16, apply to actions in respect of intellectual property rights. Thus an owner of an appropriate right can take proceedings in respect of that right either in the country of domicile of the Defendant or where the infringement takes place. The decision to that effect of Lloyd J. in *Gareth Pearce v Ove Arup Partnership Ltd* (1997) FSR 641 was correct."

The place of the tort: Article 5(3) and *Shevill v. Presse Alliance*

3–08   Relatively little English authority exists to date on the question of how Article 5(3) of the Brussels Convention applies to infringing goods which originate in one jurisdiction and are finally disposed of in another, perhaps after passing through a third. This is not surprising, since the decision of the European Court of Justice most in point is still relatively recent[19] and that case renders previous *dicta* obsolete.[20]

3–09   In *Modus Vivendi v. British Products Sanmex*[21] the question arose of whether the English or Scottish courts had jurisdiction under the Modified Convention[22] over an action for passing-off by the export of

---

[18] [1998] F.S.R. 222, CA. This was on an unsuccessful application for an injunction restraining proceedings in the Netherlands to enforce a U.K. patent. See para. 2–139 above and para. 3–55 below.

[19] Case C–68/93 *Shevill v. Presse Alliance* [1995] E.C.R. I–415.

[20] Such as that of Dillon L.J. in *Molnlycke v. Procter & Gamble (No 4)* [1992] R.P.C. 21 stating that it was not in doubt that the "harmful event" occurred in England where the infringing nappies were sold. Since they were manufactured in, and imported from, Germany, the better analysis is that both England and Germany had jurisdiction under Art. 5(3), subject to whatever qualification arose from Art. 16.

[21] [1996] F.S.R. 790 (Knox J.). See para. 3–68.

[22] Civil Jurisdiction and Judgments Act 1982, s. 16 and Sched. 4.

deceptive goods to China. Knox J. applied *Shevill v. Presse Alliance* to conclude that the place where the harmful event *occurred* was China, and that it had *originated* in Scotland, where the goods had been produced. The Scots courts, therefore, had jurisdiction. The reasoning is equally applicable to other causes of action. The argument that economic loss is felt at the plaintiff's place of business, so as to allow him to sue in the courts of his own domicile was also rejected in *Kitechnology v. Unicor*[23] in the context of an action for breach of confidence.

Article 6(1) in English law: multiple defendants

Another preliminary issue which needs to be mentioned because of its general relevance is joinder of multiple defendants under Article 6(1) of the Brussels Convention, which permits defendants domiciled in any contracting state to be sued in the courts of the contracting state in which any one of them is domiciled. Article 6(1) does not apply when the basis of jurisdiction over the principal defendant is other than domicile. The extraterritorial jurisdiction of the Dutch courts, has in fact, been justified principally in terms of Article 6(1) rather than Article 24. In England, Article 6(1) fell to be interpreted well before the English courts first contemplated granting extraterritorial injunctive relief, because Article 6(1) is equally applicable where the action is solely one for infringement of a United Kingdom intellectual property right and it is sought to join a defendant domiciled in another contracting state as a joint tortfeasor. **3–10**

It has been decided in England that the criterion to apply is that of a "good arguable case" and that if no such case exists both against the English-domiciled defendant(s), and against the proposed foreign defendant(s), then joinder under Article 6(1) is excluded.[24] It is therefore impossible to manufacture jurisdiction over a foreign-domiciled defendant by bringing proceedings against a nominal defendant domiciled in England. If there is no English-domiciled defendant against whom a good arguable cause of action can be asserted; then there is no jurisdiction under Article 6(1) over any foreign defendant, even if the existence of a cause of action against that foreign defendant is clear. If there is a good arguable case against an English defendant, then a foreign defendant can be joined under Article 6(1) only if there is also a good arguable case against that defendant individually. The causes of action against the foreign and English defendants do not have to be identical, but they must be very closely related. **3–11**

Article 6(1) and its relationship with Article 5(3) have been considered in the context of an English patent infringement action by the **3–12**

---

[23] [1995] F.S.R. 765; [1994] I.L.Pr. 568, CA. Citing Case C–220/88 *Dumez v. Hessische Landesbank* [1990] E.C.R. I–49. See also the passing-off case of *Mecklermedia v. DC Congress* [1997] F.S.R. 627 (Jacob J.).

[24] *Molnlycke v. Procter & Gamble (No 4)* [1992] R.P.C. 21. For Art. 6(1) in the general law see Fawcett, "Multi-Party Litigation in Private International Law" (1995) 44 I.C.L.Q. 744.

Court of Appeal in *Molnlycke v. Procter & Gamble (No. 4)*.[25] The facts were that the plaintiffs had sued English and American defendants for infringement of a United Kingdom patent for disposable nappies and wished to add a German company in the same corporate group as a third defendant. It was acknowledged that their only reason for doing so was to obtain discovery from the German company. The Court of Appeal held that the plaintiffs had shown that there was a good arguable case that the German company were joint tortfeasors, so as to allow them to be joined under Article 5(3). That being the case, it did not matter that the purpose of joinder was to obtain discovery. Dillon L.J. would have held, *obiter*, that if jurisdiction could only have been based on Article 6(1) then it would have been improper to have joined the German company solely to obtain discovery.

3–13   In one respect at least the reasoning in *Molnlycke v. Procter & Gamble (No. 4)* is open to criticism.[26] Dillon L.J. in the Court of Appeal relied, in part, on the difficulty of forming a view on the likely outcome of a complicated patent infringement action, and on the consideration that the factual basis on which jurisdiction had been asserted would be re-examined at trial, thereby distinguishing the case from one such as *Attock Cement v. Romanian Bank*[27] where the judge had no alternative but to "grasp the nettle" on the interlocutory application. Unfortunately for this analysis, there are important differences under the Convention between a finding that a defendant is not liable, and a finding that he is not subject to the jurisdiction. It is no part of the Convention scheme for questions of jurisdiction to be postponed to trial or re-opened there. They must be decided once and for all, not least because a defendant cannot defend on the merits without submitting irrevocably to the jurisdiction.

3–14   This leads to the other problem not addressed by the Court of Appeal, which is that the decision by one court to assume or refuse jurisdiction directly affects not just the conduct of the case before it, but the jurisdiction of courts in other member states by virtue of Articles 21 and 22. This was hardly relevant in *Molnlycke v. Procter & Gamble (No. 4)*, but one can imagine other instances where the English courts would assume jurisdiction, and corresponding foreign proceedings would be struck out under Article 21 or stayed under Article 22, only for the English court to conclude at trial that the factual basis for jurisdiction was wanting, and leaving the parties to start again from scratch in the proper forum. Until the European Court of Justice has had the opportunity to clarify what it intended in *Effer v. Kantner*,[28] it cannot be said with certainty that a threshold set at the level of the "good arguable case" is necessarily what was intended by the Convention.

---

[25] *ibid*.
[26] Apart from Dillon L.J.'s implicit treatment of Art. 16, as to which see paras 3–43 and 3–116.
[27] [1989] 1 W.L.R. 1147; [1989] 1 All E.R. 1189, CA.
[28] Case 38/81 [1982] E.C.R. 825; [1984] 2 C.M.L.R. 667.

Article 6(1) applied post *Molnlycke*

In *Chiron v. Evans Medical*[29] the plaintiffs Chiron sought a declaration of non-infringement under the inherent jurisdiction of the Court in respect of a patent of which the defendants Evans were registered proprietors. Two other defendants were Murex, the parent company of Evans, and SmithKline Beecham Biologicals SA ("SKBB"), a Belgian company which was the worldwide exclusive licensee under the patent. SKBB applied for service of the writ on them to be set aside and for them to be struck out as defendants, both on the grounds that there was no cause of action against SKBB for a declaration and for lack of jurisdiction under the Brussels Convention. Distinguishing *Biogen v. Medeva*,[30] and applying *Kalfelis v. Schroeder*,[31] Robert Walker J. held that SKBB were properly joined under Article 6(1) of the Brussels Convention and had properly been served in Belgium without leave.

3–15

More recently, Article 6(1) was held in *Pearce v. Ove Arup*[32] to justify in principle the joinder of three defendants domiciled in the Netherlands, although the claim was struck out as bound to fail on the facts.[33] Article 6(1) also arose in *Coin Controls v. Suzo*,[34] where the plaintiffs sued a total of four defendants in respect of infringement of United Kingdom, German and Spanish patents:

3–16

"Initially the argument based on Article 6(1) appeared strong. When Suzo UK was being sued here for joint liability for the alleged acts of infringement in Germany and Spain, Article 2 allowed the plaintiff to bring the proceedings here in its country of domicile and then Suzo Holland and Suzo Germany could be brought in as co-defendants in relation to those foreign torts. In fact, as explained above, I have come to the conclusion that there is no arguable case against Suzo UK in respect of those foreign torts so this argument does not survive. But that is not an end of the matter. Both Suzo UK and Suzo Holland are being sued here for infringement of the UK patent. Mr. Silverleaf says that this is to all intents and purposes the same cause of action as will be brought under the Spanish and German patents. The allegedly infringing article, the Cube Hopper, is the same, the three patents are identical and the similarities in the actions are cemented by the provisions of the European Patent Convention ('EPC'). That not only creates a single, supranational patent application and grant procedure, but also imposes on all courts the necessity of construing the national patents in the same way in accordance with EPC Article 69. Furthermore what the EPC is creating is a 'European

---

[29] [1996] F.S.R. 863 (Robert Walker J.).
[30] [1993] R.P.C. 475 (Aldous J.).
[31] Case 189/87 [1988] E.C.R. 5565.
[32] [1997] F.S.R. 641 (Lloyd J.).
[33] See para. 3–47, below for the facts, and para. 3–49 for the passage applying Art. 6(1).
[34] [1997] F.S.R. 660 (Laddie J.).

Patent'. Although that patent is then granted in respect of individual countries and, in each, is treated like a national patent (EPC Article 64(1)), nevertheless those national patent rights can be considered as cuttings taken from the European Patent stock and planted in the national soil. That is why Suzo UK's three patents are, at least for the moment, identical.

Since the causes of action in relation to infringement here, in Germany and in Spain are essentially identical, Article 6(1) allows them to be tied together in one court of the plaintiffs choice. The interrelationship between the actions is highlighted if one looks at the position of Suzo Holland. That company is being sued here for infringement of the UK patent (cause of action 5 referred to above). It is, however, also accused of infringing the identical patents in Germany and Spain by exploiting the same allegedly infringing product in those countries. The three causes of action levelled at Suzo Holland are clearly related, but if this is so, then the cause of action against Suzo Germany must be related because cause of action 1 is identical to cause of action 2 set out above."[35]

3–17 However, although Article 6(1) might have allowed all the defendants to be sued together in England in respect of all three patents, Laddie J. held that Article 16(4) precluded him from proceeding with the actions on the German and Spanish patents once the defendants had indicated that they intended to put their validity in issue. In the result, the action proceeded only in respect of the United Kingdom patent, against Suzo UK as primary infringer and Suzo Holland as joint tortfeasor; the former being domiciled in England and the latter in the Netherlands. Finally, Laddie J. alluded to the relationship between Articles 6(1) and 22, which would have led to the conclusion that the German and Spanish defendants could also have been joined under Article 6(1) in respect of the German and Spanish infringements, but for Article 16(4):

"In this judgment I have accepted the argument that, absent an attack on validity, it would be possible in circumstances similar to those existing in this case to bring proceedings here for infringement of foreign patents. That is crucially dependent on the fact that the UK and foreign patents are identical. Proceedings for determining infringement of them can therefore be regarded as related for the purpose of Article 6(1). That may well not be so where the patent claims in the various countries are materially different either because the patents were applied for separately through the national patent offices or because they began life as an EPC application but have been subject to different amendments in different countries after grant."[36]

---

[35] *per* Laddie J., *ibid*. For the designation of the causes of action see para. 3–56.
[36] This analysis depends on there being different infringers in different contracting states, as will often be the case. If the same legal person infringed in all he could be sued in the state of his domicile, whether or not the patents were in the same form around Europe.

Finally, the Court of Appeal has considered Article 6(1) from the **3–18** opposite point of view in *Fort Dodge v. Akzo Nobel*,[37] where the question was whether the Dutch courts had jurisdiction over three English-domiciled companies in respect of the infringement of a United Kingdom patent, when it was not alleged that the English companies had been involved in the alleged acts of infringement of the corresponding Dutch patent.

> "Article 6(1) provides another special jurisdiction in that a Defendant, who is one of a number of Defendants, may be sued in the State where one of them is domiciled. The Article has been interpreted as being an exception to the general rule and is to be treated in such a way as to avoid the principle set out in Articles 1 to 5 being called into question. In *Kalfelis v. Schroeder*, Case 189/87 (1988) ECR 5565 the European Court said that there must be a connection between the claim made against the person not domiciled in the State where the litigation is pending and the claim made against the party domiciled in that State. The connection must be of 'such a kind that it is expedient to determine those actions together in order to avoid the risk of irreconcilable judgments resulting from separate proceedings.'
>
> In the present case there has been no examination of the facts and therefore no concluded view can be reached as to whether there is the necessary connection in respect of some of the Appellants. However, a number of Appellants are only alleged to have infringed the United Kingdom patent and it would appear tenuous to suggest that it was expedient to determine together an action for infringement of a Dutch patent, with which they are not concerned, and a United Kingdom patent with which they are, so as to avoid irreconcilable judgments. They are actions relating to two different national rights. True they stem from the same patent application and similar rules of construction will be applicable, but the rights given by those patents are national rights limited in territory to the State in which they are registered and the ambit of the monopolies will not necessarily be the same as amendment is possible. There is no risk of irreconcilable judgments because a judgment on infringement in the United Kingdom will depend upon a national right having effect only in the United Kingdom. The same applies to a judgment on the Dutch patent."

The case and opportunity for reform

It will be seen in the following sections that the English courts do not, **3–19** in general, welcome whatever extraterritorial jurisdiction is thrust upon them in intellectual property matters by the Brussels Convention. What is worse is that the application of the Convention should be so uncertain

[37] [1998] F.S.R. 222, CA.

and that so little attention should have been paid to its practical implications.[38] In *Coin Controls v. Suzo*,[39] Laddie J. observed:

"In coming to these conclusions, I cannot pretend to be happy that the consequences for intellectual property litigation have been thought through properly in the Convention. The fact that registered and unregistered rights (e.g. passing off and registered trade mark proceedings) may be subject to different regimes could well produce a proliferation of litigation rather than the opposite. Furthermore the conclusions I have come to mean that a defendant can, within limits, forum shop by deciding whether to attack validity. But this perhaps is no worse than the forum shopping available to the plaintiff as a result of *Pearce*. It is not difficult to think of cases where the Convention may produce truly absurd results. For example an English company might be sued in England for unfair competition in Holland or Germany by alleged misuse of an unregistered trade name. The court here will not only have to decide questions of Dutch and German law but also factual issues relating to the pronunciation and meaning of similar words spoken in Dutch or German. The fact that this may be the consequence of the Convention does not alter its meaning. Similarly the fact that what are likely to be essentially the same issues of patent validity may have to be litigated in a number of countries simultaneously is unlikely to impress the user of the EPC patent system, but this appears to be an inevitable consequence of Article 16(4) of the Convention and the fact that the Community Patent Convention has not been brought into operation. There is much to be said from the user's point of view for a system where an international patent application leads to a patent having international effect and which needs only to be litigated in one country. That is not yet the system which we have."

3–20   For patents and other registered rights, including trade marks, it is certainly fair to criticise the Convention in respect of the interaction between infringement and invalidity and the conflict which occurs from subjecting the two to radically different regimes. An opportunity to correct this omission may occur at the 1998 Conference to revise the Brussels Convention on its thirtieth anniversary. It is to be hoped that the Conference will not simply put the question to one side in the hope that an all-embracing answer will be provided by the European Court of Justice on the reference in *Fort Dodge v. Akzo Nobel*.[40] However, the obvious impracticality of the solution of *Coin Controls v. Suzo* is perhaps

---

[38] Although it is more than arguable that the Convention scheme was perfectly workable among the original six member states in 1968; and that it is the accession of new states with different litigation regimes, and reforms in some of the original six, that have given rise to problems. See paras 3–137 *et seq.*

[39] [1997] F.S.R. 660 (Laddie J.).

[40] [1998] F.S.R. 222, CA.

a reason in its own right for seeing if another interpretation of the relevant provisions of the Convention can be reached on existing materials with more acceptable results, and this is attempted below at paragraphs 3–114 onwards.

Before joining Laddie J. in describing the state of affairs for trade **3–21** marks and passing-off as "truly absurd" one ought to note that this is not a unique fault of the Brussels Convention. For well over a century English courts have asserted a jurisdiction to restrain the export of "instruments of deception" on the basis that the disposal of such goods in the foreign market for which they were intended would deceive,[41] and this has involved answering precisely the factual questions contemplated by Laddie J. for markets far more distant and unfamiliar than Continental Europe.[42] Well before the Convention, too, English courts were prepared to grant damages and injunctions in respect of acts of unfair competition abroad which would have been actionable as passing-off in England.[43] The latter procedure required the relevant foreign law to be pleaded and proven[44]; the former was all the more remarkable for applying English law to transactions in a foreign sovereign state.

In this respect, the only effect of the Convention has been to remove **3–22** the discretion that the court formerly had to refuse to entertain actions in the latter category under the doctrine of *forum non conveniens*, but that doctrine never affected actions for passing off by the export of instruments of deception. The absurdity that an action for passing-off abroad might proceed, whereas one on otherwise identical facts for trade mark infringement would be struck out without regard to the merits is precisely that reached at common law.[45] It is the Convention which opens the possibility of the two being heard together, especially if one gives Article 16(4) a more restrictive interpretation than Laddie J. was prepared to do.

B. PROVISIONAL MEASURES AND ARTICLE 24

The problem of "provisional" measures under Article 24

The treatment of jurisdiction over intellectual property infringement **3–23** actions is complicated by the question of whether Article 24 of the Brussels Convention permits interlocutory relief to be granted in cases

---

[41] The *locus classicus* is *Johnson v. Orr Ewing* (1882) 7 App. Cas. 219, HL, where goods were exported to Aden. See Wadlow, *The Law of Passing-off* (2nd ed., 1995), para. 4.49 and supplement. Historically, this jurisdiction has been most often invoked in respect of remote and undeveloped markets where difficulties of proof are compounded, but where local laws of intellectual property or unfair competition might be expected to be non-existent or ineffective.

[42] The exercise will no doubt become more familiar as English courts begin to enforce Community trade marks, though the problems will be similar.

[43] Wadlow, *op. cit.* para. 4.50 and supplement.

[44] Nor can the Brussels Convention be blamed for the fact that in *Harrods plc v. Harrods (Buenos Aires) Ltd* [1997] F.S.R. 420 Neuberger J. was required to decide hypothetical questions of liability for unfair competition under Argentinean Law as understood in the early 20th century; as well as making findings of fact about the shopping habits of wealthy Argentineans in that period.

[45] See paras 6–16 and 6–88.

where there would otherwise be no jurisdiction.[45a] For several years prior to *Coin Controls v. Suzo*,[46] it had been well known that the Dutch courts were regularly granting pan-European injunctions against infringement of patents and other intellectual property rights under the *kort geding* procedure.[47] The latter has no precise counterpart in English law and in form as well as name is all but unique to the Netherlands.[48] In English terms, it combines features of summary judgment and interlocutory relief. Unlike an interlocutory injunction properly so called, an order in *kort geding* proceedings is final unless it is appealed or unless either party commences normal proceedings on the same issues.[49] The *kort geding* proceedings as such come to an end with grant or refusal of an injunction. The procedure also corresponds to summary judgment in so far as validity and infringement are the main live issues and the plaintiff must show a case considerably stronger than under the *Cyanamid* criteria.[50] Conversely, the interlocutory aspects of the *kort geding* procedure are seen in the fact that the plaintiff must demonstrate "urgency," (though in some respects the latter has all but been reduced to a legal fiction,[51] presumed in favour of the plaintiff)[52]; that the balance of convenience can be taken into account[53]; that an order in favour of either party can be superseded by subsequent full proceedings as well as set aside on appeal; and that the plaintiff is routinely required to compensate the defendant if an injunction is wrongly granted. It is, perhaps, best seen as a discretionary and defeasible final order *nisi*

[45a] See Collins, "Provisional Measures" in *Essays in International Litigation and the Conflict of Laws* (1994) for a comprehensive survey of provisional measures in English, European and International Law.

[46] [1997] F.S.R. 660 (Laddie J.).

[47] See para. 1–28 and references there cited.

[48] Although similar free-standing proceedings for an interlocutory injunction are available in Germany. See *Mecklermedia v. DC Congress* [1997] F.S.R. 627 (Jacob J.).

[49] *Queare* whether the practice of allowing *kort geding* proceedings to stand on their own is compatible with Art. 50(6) of TRIPs. See para. 3–36, below. If the latter does not apply, then this simply emphasises again that a *kort geding* injunction is much more than a provisional measure in any sense.

[50] *American Cyanamid v. Ethicon* [1975] A.C. 396, HL.

[51] At first sight the *de facto* rule is that the plaintiff must commence proceedings within about six months, which is not greatly inconsistent with English practice. However, several cases have held that time does not run against the plaintiff while an opposition or appeal is pending in the European Patent Office, so a defendant may find itself subject to *kort geding* proceedings perhaps five years or more after the patent was granted. Prejudice of this type was taken into account on the balance of convenience in *Hoffman La Roche v. Organon Technika*, Hague Court of Appeals, September 12, 1995.

[52] In his evidence to the House of Lords, Judge van der Veen of the Dutch Supreme Court observed that "In practice all infringement cases are deemed to be urgent." *Report of the Select Committee on the European Communities, A European Community Patent* (1986), Evidence, p. 173. At that time, invalidity could not be raised as a defence in *kort geding* proceedings and no extraterritorial jurisdiction was asserted: *ibid.* p. 174.

[53] Though *Hoffman La Roche v. Organon Technika* above consciously marked a radically new change of direction in deciding a case in favour of the defendant primarily on the balance of convenience. Previously, the balance of convenience had been a relatively minor factor, further undermining the claim of *kort geding* to be a provisional procedure.

available on a special accelerated procedure—*kort geding* literally meaning "short delay"—which exists in parallel with normal proceedings.[54] Not surprisingly, the normal and longer procedure has few attractions for the plaintiff unless *kort geding* proceedings have already failed, damages are sought or the accrued delay exceeds even Dutch standards of tolerance.

In *Coin Controls v. Suzo* Laddie J. accepted, though *obiter* and **3–24** apparently without argument, that the Dutch practice of granting pan-European injunctions in *kort geding* proceedings was justified under Article 24 of the Brussels Convention, and was not therefore inconsistent with his own interpretation of Articles 16(4) and 19 of the latter, which had led him to the conclusion that he had no jurisdiction over an action for infringements of German and Spanish patents if their validity was put in issue. It is implicit that had *Coin Controls v. Suzo* been an appropriate case for interlocutory relief, then Laddie J. would have felt able to grant interlocutory injunctions in respect of the Spanish and German patents as well as the English patent, on suitable conditions and presumably taking arguments as to their validity into account to the extent contemplated in his own judgment in *Series 5 Software v. Clarke*.[55]

> "I am aware that interlocutory injunctions effective abroad have been granted in patent matters by the Kort Geding procedure in Holland. Such powers arise out of Article 24 of the Convention which is of very wide scope and apparently is not limited by the provisions of Article 16. It therefore has no direct bearing on the issues I have to raise. Further, in view of the fact that I have decided in any event not to grant interlocutory relief, the questions of whether or not this court has the jurisdiction to grant such relief in respect of infringements abroad and, if so, the considerations which would have to be taken into account in deciding whether to do so and the conditions it might feel obliged to impose on a plaintiff granted any such relief do not arise for consideration in this case."

With respect, it is suggested that this not only misunderstands the **3–25** Dutch jurisprudence but attributes to Article 24 a meaning which is considerably wider than it ought to be allowed to bear. Article 24, it is suggested, does not *confer* international jurisdiction at all; it merely permits national courts to continue to exercise their pre-existing jurisdiction under national law in certain limited circumstances where it is expedient for them to do so in derogation from the normal rules of the Convention.

It is true that many, if not all, of the Dutch cases on pan-European **3–26** injunctions assert or assume that the *kort geding* procedure is within the scope of Article 24. However, no case decided to date seems to have based jurisdiction solely on this ground. In many cases the principal

---

[54] Normal proceedings are themselves now subject to an accelerated procedure, raising the question of whether jurisdiction will be treated any differently compared to *kort geding*.
[55] [1996] F.S.R. 273 (Laddie J.).

defendant is a Dutch company over which the Dutch courts have general jurisdiction under Article 2, and its foreign distributors can then be joined under Article 6(1). If the principal defendant is abroad, then a distributor domiciled in the Netherlands can almost invariably be found and sued; with a rather more strained interpretation of Article 6(1) and *Kalfelis v. Schroeder*[56] leading to the foreign principal and foreign fellow distributors being joined as co-defendants without reliance on Article 24. Finally, Article 5(3) can support extra-territorial jurisdiction in many cases, although after the restriction imposed in *Shevill v. Presse Alliance*[57] extra-territorial jurisdiction under Article 5(3) is unlikely to exist in practice unless the court would already have had jurisdiction by virtue of domicile under Article 2.

3–27   The relationship of Article 24 to Article 16 is not stated in the Convention. Rather than concluding that Article 24 overrides Article 16 when no other provision of Title II is expressed to do so, it would be safer to interpret them both restrictively so that no conflict arises. If one allows that infringement and invalidity can be litigated *inter partes* without infringing Article 16(4), then the courts of the defendant's domicile can always grant pan-European interlocutory relief without relying on Article 24, and there is no need to give a broad interpretation to the latter.

The interpretation of Article 24

3–28   These developments up to *Coin Controls v. Suzo*[58] occurred, it would seem, without either the Dutch courts or anyone else attempting to interpret Article 24 from first principles or seriously questioning their underlying assumptions: that Article 24 encompasses free standing, long-term—if not strictly permanent—pan-European extraterritorial injunctive relief against alleged infringement; and that *kort geding* proceedings fall within Article 24 because as a matter of Dutch law they are not final in legal theory, no matter that they are all but final in practice. As to the latter, the scope and interpretation of Article 24 are matters of autonomous Community law, and the characterisation of *kort geding* proceedings as "provisional" in Dutch domestic law is no more relevant than the similar characterisation of the *action paulienne* under French law in *Reichert v. Dresdner Bank (No. 2)*.[59] The conclusion that any order which is not final in domestic law must be provisional in the sense of Article 24 is an obvious *non sequitur*. As will be seen, a purposive interpretation of Article 24 leads to the conclusion that the relevant question is not whether the order is final in this or any other sense, but whether the order sought is of such a nature that it is most appropriately granted by a court which is not that seised of the main action.[60] The

[56] Case 189/87 [1988] E.C.R. 5565.
[57] Case C–68/93 [1995] E.C.R. I–415.
[58] [1997] F.S.R. 660 (Laddie J.).
[59] Case C–261/90 [1992] E.C.R. I–2149.
[60] See Case 125/79 *Denilauler v. Couchet Freres* [1980] E.C.R. 1553; [1981] 1 C.M.L.R. 62; Case C–261/90 *Reichert v. Dresdner Bank (No. 2)* [1992] E.C.R. I–2149 and para. 2–74.

question depends on the autonomous meaning to be given to Article 24, and in the absence of authority precisely in point has to be approached from first principles.

In contrast to *Coin Controls v. Suzo*, the judgment of the Court of **3–29** Appeal in *Fort Dodge v. Akzo Nobel*[61] expressly proceeded on the basis that nothing turned on any peculiarities of Dutch internal law and Article 24 was interpreted, rightly it is suggested, as applying only when the provisional relief was sought as an aid or adjunct to the claim for final relief elsewhere:

> "Article 24 relates to provisional, including protective, measures. As explained in the Jenard Report application may be made to the Courts of a Contracting State for such provisional measures as may be available under the internal law of that State. However, the measures must be provisional and, in our view, granted in aid of or as an adjunct to some final determination then in contemplation.
>
> Upon the evidence before this Court, provisional relief by way of injunction would not be granted in the United Kingdom to restrain continuance by the Appellants of the acts complained of as infringement because of the delay by the Respondents in taking action. However that delay may or may not be determinative in the eyes of a Dutch Court. But that is the Court in which Akzo seek provisional relief in respect of acts taking place in the United Kingdom, and it is for that Court to determine the effect of the delay.
>
> Mr Silverleaf accepts that a Dutch Court has to apply Dutch law when deciding whether to grant provisional relief pursuant to the jurisdiction conferred by Article 24. He submits that the United Kingdom Patents Courts has by reason of Articles 2, 5 and 16(4) exclusive jurisdiction over the dispute between Akzo and the English domiciled Appellants relating to the United Kingdom patent. It follows, he submits, that provisional relief could only be granted in aid of or as an adjunct to a final determination in the United Kingdom Courts. Akzo have not initiated any proceedings in the United Kingdom and have not stated any intention of doing so. It followed that there was no jurisdiction under Article 24 to grant provisional relief as sought by Akzo.
>
> Mr Prescott QC, who appeared for the Respondents, submits that the Dutch Court can order provisional relief as an adjunct to Akzo's claim for final relief in the Dutch proceedings. That provisional relief would do justice between the parties pending resolution of the question of validity by the United Kingdom Patents Court.
>
> The crucial difference between the submissions of the parties is the effect of Article 16(4). If the United Kingdom Courts have exclusive jurisdiction over the dispute concerning the United Kingdom patent, then there is no justification for the Respondents

---

[61] [1998] F.S.R. 222, CA. Although the main proceedings in the Netherlands were not under the Dutch *kort geding* procedure, see para. 1–54 above, the live issue was whether the Dutch Court would or might grant an interlocutory injunction against patent infringement in the U.K., where a petition for revocation was pending.

attempting to obtain from the Dutch Court even provisional relief as an aid to or an adjunct of the claim for final relief in respect of the United Kingdom patent. It would be vexatious to seek such relief. If our conclusion as to the proper application of Article 16(4) is correct, it follows that Article 24 does not provide jurisdiction to grant provisional relief restraining infringement within the United Kingdom as an adjunct to the claim for full relief pleaded in the Dutch proceedings."

Article 24 in the case law of the European Court of Justice

3–30   Article 24 is pre-eminently a derogation from the general principle of the Brussels Convention that defendants are prima facie entitled to be sued in the state of their domicile. Indeed, on the Dutch approach as understood by Laddie J. in *Coin Controls v. Suzo*,[62] it is an exception to every jurisdiction-allocating provision of Title II including Article 16 itself. As such, one would expect it to receive as restrictive an interpretation as is consistent with its purpose in the scheme of the Convention as a whole. In its rather limited jurisprudence on Article 24 the European Court of Justice has confirmed that Article 24 applies to *inter partes* as well as *ex parte* provisional relief.[63] However, the reasoning of the Court in *Denilauler v. Couchet Freres*[64] hardly supports the conclusion that Article 24 is intended to have any extraterritorial effect at all, still less that it provides a sufficient basis for pan-European injunctive relief:

"An analysis of the function attributed under the general scheme of the Convention to Article 24, which is specifically devoted to provisional and protective measures, leads, moreover, to the conclusion that, where these types of measures are concerned, special rules were contemplated. Whilst it is true that procedures of the type in question authorizing provisional and protective measures may be found in the legal system of all the Contracting States and may be regarded, where certain conditions are fulfilled, as not infringing the rights of the defence, it should however be emphasized that the granting of this type of measure requires particular care on the part of the court and detailed knowledge of the actual circumstances in which the measure is to take effect. Depending on each case and commercial practices in particular the court must be able to place a time-limit on its order or, as regards the nature of the assets or goods subject to the measures contemplated, require bank guarantees or nominate a sequestration and generally make its authorization subject to all conditions guaranteeing the provisional or protective character of the measure ordered.

The courts of the place or, in any event, of the Contracting State, where the assets subject to the measures sought are located, are

[62] [1997] F.S.R. 660 (Laddie J.).
[63] Case 125/79 *Denilauler v. Couchet Freres* [1980] E.C.R. 1553; [1981] 1 C.M.L.R. 62 and see para. 2–74.
[64] Case 125/79 [1980] E.C.R. 1553; [1981] 1 C.M.L.R. 62.

those best able to assess the circumstances which may lead to the grant or refusal of the measures sought or to the laying down of procedures and conditions which the plaintiff must observe in order to guarantee the provisional and protective character of the measures ordered. The Convention has taken account of these requirements by providing in Article 24 that application may be made to the courts of a Contracting State for such provisional, including protective, measures as may be available under the law of that State, even if, under the Convention, the courts of another Contracting State have jurisdiction as to the substance of the matter."

Whilst this is in terms most appropriate to *Mareva*-type orders, the **3–31** practical inconsistency of the Dutch interpretation of Article 24 with the reasoning of *Denilauler v. Couchet Freres* need not be dwelt upon. On the contrary, it leads to the conclusion that the relevant question for the application or not of Article 24 is whether the "provisional" order sought is of such a nature that it is most appropriately granted by a court other than that seised of the main action. This is most obviously true for orders in the nature of *saisie conservatoire*. In *Reichert v. Dresdner Bank (No. 2)*[65] the Court defined "provisional or protective measures" as meaning "measures which . . . are intended to maintain a legal or factual situation in order to safeguard rights an application for the recognition of which has been made to the court with jurisdiction as to the substance of the matter." Whilst this recognises that Article 21 does not prevent the operation of Article 24, it also confirms the very subordinate status of the latter. Article 24 is not free-standing; it presupposes the existence of proceedings on the merits, presumably in another court and probably in another contracting state, and its purpose is to support them, not to pre-empt their result or frustrate their continuation.[66] Of course, in the normal course of events the *kort geding* infringement proceedings stand alone, which begs the very question of whether Article 24 can justify them.

The consistency or not of Dutch practice with the express terms of **3–32** Article 24 turns on the qualification "such provisional . . . measures *as may be available under the law of that state* . . ." The interpretation implicitly given to the Article in Dutch practice is almost entirely permissive: if a remedy of a provisional nature is available in Dutch law then it can be imposed in all contracting states where there is arguably infringement. However, although this interpretation may seem tenable on the language of Article 24, it leads straight to precisely the situation which *Denilauler v. Couchet Freres* is concerned to avoid. Far from allocating jurisdiction to the court best qualified to "to assess the circumstances which may lead to the grant or refusal of the measures sought" it leads to the conclusion that any otherwise incompetent court

[65] Case C–261/90 [1992] E.C.R. I–2149.
[66] Compare *Republic of Haiti v. Duvalier* [1990] 1 Q.B. 202, CA; interpreting Art. 24 as an obligation to make national provisional measures available in aid of litigation in other contracting states.

may grant interlocutory relief in respect of any contracting state or all of them. There is nothing unique about the status of the District Court of the Hague under the Convention; if it can provisionally remove a life-saving drug from Portuguese or Finnish hospitals then the opposite applies *mutatis mutandis*. It is no answer that the issues with which the Dutch court really concerns itself—infringement and validity—can be adjudicated on a Continental scale, because that simply leads to the conclusion that it is not dealing with "provisional" relief in the sense of *Denilauler v. Couchet Freres* at all.[67]

3–33   There is an alternative reading of Article 24 of more restricted effect, which is that the court invoking Article 24 can order provisional and protective relief only to the extent that the plaintiff is entitled to the relief wholly by reference to its own internal law, without needing to invoke its private international law or any foreign body of law. A Dutch patent, trade mark or copyright has no extraterritorial effect. To the extent that a Dutch court grants an injunction in relation to infringement in the United Kingdom or Germany, it is not granting relief which is available under its own law. It is applying its own procedural law cumulatively with the substantive law of a foreign contracting state in a manner which Article 24 does not contemplate. The *reductio ad absurdum* of the Dutch approach is to imagine that the United Kingdom or German patents act was repealed outright. Clearly no injunction could be granted in respect of the United Kingdom or Germany, but why not, if the inquiry under Article 24 begins and ends with the availability of relief as a matter of Dutch law?

3–34   The effect of this interpretation is not to exclude extraterritorial relief altogether from the scope of Article 24. If, for instance, Dutch law permits an order corresponding to a *Mareva* injunction to be granted with extraterritorial effect then well and good. If, however, Dutch law permits only the seizure of assets within the territorial jurisdiction of the Netherlands then the gap cannot be filled by the Dutch courts invoking the English *Mareva* jurisdiction or the jurisdiction of French and Belgian courts to grant orders of *saisie conservatorie*. So much, one might have thought, was obvious from the express terms of Article 24, which aims to put existing national procedures at the disposal of litigants in other contracting states, not to create remedies or jurisdiction where none would otherwise exist. As Gullmann A.-G. put it in *Reichert v. Dresdner Bank (No. 2)*[68]:

> "It [Article 24] has only a limited object, i.e. to retain for each member-State the option of continuing to apply its national rules of jurisdiction with a view to taking provisional measures . . . The measures referred to in Article 24 are only those which seek to give

[67] Nor is it any answer that the Finnish or Portuguese authorities might invoke the *ordre public* exception of Art. 27(1) and refuse to recognise the Dutch injunction, if the only supplier was subject to the personal jurisdiction of the Dutch courts or had assets in the Netherlands that could be attacked.

[68] Case C–261/90 [1992] E.C.R. I–2149.

provisional judicial protection for certain claims and which depend on a later judgment concerning the justification of the claim."

Conversely, in a breach of confidence case, provisional enforcement of a contractual or equitable obligation of confidence arising from and governed by English law, by the English courts, might be within Article 24, even if the English courts did not have substantive jurisdiction and even if the threatened breach was abroad.[69]

Nor would this interpretation create injustice in practice. The courts **3–35** of the defendant's domicile as well as the courts of the place where the infringement originated in the sense of *Shevill*[70] would always have full jurisdiction to grant comprehensive and internationally enforceable *inter partes* extraterritorial relief. Courts with general jurisdiction do not need to rely on Article 24. Article 24 would be of residual benefit in the cases for which it was apparently intended, which are those where some form of *ex parte* or temporary order was justified, but could not usefully be made by the court properly seised of the action as such because the enforcement provisions of the Convention do not apply to *ex parte* orders. In general, this sort of relief would have to be applied for on a state-by-state basis but that is inherent in the fact that *ex parte* orders are not entitled to automatic recognition and enforcement.

Provisional measures in TRIPs and for Community intellectual property rights

A relatively narrow interpretation for Article 24 of the Brussels **3–36** Convention would also have the advantage of consistency with the way the expression "provisional measures" is used in Article 50 of TRIPs. Two points to note are that Article 50 distinguishes in terms between a decision to order provisional measures, and a decision on the merits; and that the power of judicial authorities to grant orders to prevent goods entering circulation by imports or other means (TRIPs being concerned only with international trade) is expressly confined to orders affecting "channels of commerce *in their jurisdiction.*"

(1) The judicial authorities shall have the authority to order prompt and effective provisional measures:
　　(a) to prevent an infringement of any intellectual property right from occurring, and in particular to prevent the entry into the channels of commerce in their jurisdiction of goods, including imported goods immediately after customs clearance;
　　(b) to preserve relevant evidence in regard to the alleged infringement.
(2) The judicial authorities shall have the authority to adopt provisional measures *inaudita altera parte* where appropriate, in

[69] Compare *Kitechnology BV v. Unicor GmbH* [1995] F.S.R. 763; [1994] I.L.Pr. 568, CA.
[70] Case C–68/93 [1995] E.C.R. I–415.

149

> particular where any delay is likely to cause irreparable harm to the right holder, or where there is a demonstrable risk of evidence being destroyed.
>
> . . .
>
> (6) Without prejudice to paragraph 4,[71] provisional measures taken on the basis of paragraphs 1 and 2 shall, upon request by the defendant, be revoked or otherwise cease to have effect, if proceedings leading to a decision on the merits of the case are not initiated within a reasonable period, to be determined by the judicial authority ordering the measures where a Member's law so permits or, in the absence of such a determination, not to exceed 20 working days or 31 calendar days, whichever is the longer.
>
> (7) Where the provisional measures are revoked or where they lapse due to any act or omission by the applicant, or where it is subsequently found that there has been no infringement or threat of infringement of an intellectual property right, the judicial authorities shall have the authority to order the applicant, upon request of the defendant, to provide the defendant appropriate compensation for any injury caused by these measures.

3–37   Mention may also be made of the situation under the Community Patent Convention and Community Trade Mark Regulation. Both provide that a court which has substantive Community-wide jurisdiction—typically by virtue of the defendant's domicile—may grant provisional, including protective measures, in respect of the whole Community; but both expressly provide that no other court has such jurisdiction.[72] In particular, a court which has jurisdiction by virtue of an infringement taking place within its own territory cannot grant either interlocutory or final relief in respect of any other state.

The relationship of Article 24 with Articles 19 and 21

3–38   More recently, another use for Article 24 has been asserted in the Netherlands so that the Dutch courts could continue to grant pan-European injunctions even if the defendant had taken the initiative by commencing proceedings for a pan-European declaration of non-infringement elsewhere.[73] Another court may be seised of the substantive issues, but in the Dutch view Article 24 must be interpreted as overriding Article 21 (and Article 19, if necessary) so that the *kort geding* proceedings may go ahead in parallel to whatever proceedings are pending elsewhere.

The anomaly of the Dutch position is that if it is correct then courts in any and all of the 15 contracting states could entertain proceedings for

---

[71] Dealing with *ex parte* measures.

[72] Community Patent Convention, Protocol on Litigation, Art. 36(2); Community Trade Mark Regulation, Art. 99(2).

[73] For such declaratory actions see para. 8–28.

inter partes provisional relief in all of the other 14, and either consecutively or in parallel. The Dutch courts may be unique in their interpretation of the Brussels Convention, the availability of the *kort geding* procedure and their willingness to grant pan-European relief; but they have no special status under the Convention. If they are right, then the patentee who failed to win round the District Court of the Hague—and that Court is by no means a soft touch for undeserving plaintiffs—could still tack all round Europe in search of relief until funds or patience were exhausted. The better conclusion is that Article 24 can coexist with Articles 19 and 21 precisely because the provisional measures contemplated by the latter are strictly subordinate in effect to whatever litigation on the merits may be in progress elsewhere; and the absence of any provision against multiplicity of proceedings for provisional measures is an indication that each court applying Article 24 will in general grant provisional measures only in respect of its own territorial jurisdiction.

Article 24 and orders for evidence-gathering

The question may arise as to whether the concept of "provisional measures" within Article 24 applies to measures which are essentially intended to gather evidence rather than to preserve the status quo in some sense. Broadly speaking, and subject to what is said above, the options are as follows. (1) That Article 24 implicitly requires national courts to make domestic provisional procedures for gathering evidence available to courts and litigants in other contracting states; this seems to correspond to the view of the draftsman of section 28 of the Civil Jurisdiction and Judgments Act 1982 but it was subjected to important qualifications by the Inner House of the Court of Session in *Union Carbide v. BP Chemicals*.[73a] (2) That the courts of contracting states may now make *inter partes* orders[73b] of this nature intended to be executed in other contracting states, and expect them to be recognised and enforced pursuant to Title III; or (3) that the Convention has no application to orders relating to the conduct of litigation since these are wholly governed by specialist conventions, and in particular the 1970 Hague Convention on the Taking of Evidence Abroad in Civil and Commercial Matters.[73c]

3–39

The question in its wider context was considered in the Schlosser Report in relation to Article 25 of the Brussels Convention. Schlosser posed the question:

[73a] [1995] F.S.R. 449 (SC, IH), see below.

[73b] Orders equivalent to *Anton Piller* orders, since they are always made *ex parte* cannot fall under Tit. III of the Convention on any analysis.

[73c] Given effect in English law by the Evidence (Proceedings in Other Jurisdictions) Act 1975. In *CFEM Facades v. Bovis Construction* [1992] I.L.Pr. 561 (Simon Goldblatt Q.C., deputy judge, QBD) the High Court recognised, but only in part, an interlocutory French order for expert inspection of a building in London and for taking evidence from witnesses. In so far as the order regulated procedure in the French action, it was held to be outside the Brussels Convention. The deputy judge did acknowledge, however, that reliance on Article 24 might co-exist with reliance on the 1975 Act.

"Article 25 emphasizes in terms which could hardly be clearer that every type of judgment given by a court in a Contracting State must be recognized and enforced throughout the rest of the Community. The provision is not limited to a judgment terminating the proceedings before the court, but also applies to provisional court orders. Nor does the wording of the provision indicate that interlocutory court decisions should be excluded from its scope where they do not provisionally regulate the legal relationships between the parties, but are for instance concerned only with the taking of evidence. What is more, the legal systems of the original Member States of the Community describe such interlocutory decisions in a way which corresponds to the terms given by way of example, in Article 25. Thus, in France court decisions which order the taking of evidence are also called 'judgements (d'avant dire droit)'. In Germany they are termed '(Beweis) beschlusse' of the court. Nevertheless, the provisions of the 1968 Convention governing recognition and enforcement are in general designed to cover only court judgments which either determine or regulate the legal relationships of the parties. An answer to the question whether, and if so which, interlocutory decisions intended to be of procedural assistance fall within the scope of the 1968 Convention cannot be given without further consideration."

3–40   And after considering the relevance of the Hague Conventions of 1965 and 1970 Schlosser replied:

"If it were desired that interlocutory decisions by courts on the further conduct of the proceedings, and particularly on the taking of evidence, should be covered by Article 25 of the 1968 Convention, this would also affect decisions with which the parties would be totally unable to comply without the court's cooperation, and the enforcement of which would concern third parties, particularly witnesses. It would therefore be impossible to 'enforce' such decisions under the 1968 Convention. It can only be concluded from the foregoing that interlocutory decisions which are not intended to govern the legal relationships of the parties, but to arrange the further conduct of the proceedings, should be excluded from the scope of Title III of the 1968 Convention."

In *Union Carbide v. BP Chemicals*[73d] the plaintiffs in an English patent infringement action applied to the Court of Session for recovery of documents held at the defendants' plant at Grangemouth in Scotland[73e] to enable them to plead and particularise infringement of the two patents in suit in the English infringement proceedings. The application was made pursuant to the Administration of Justice (Scotland) Act 1972, s.1, as extended by the Civil Jurisdiction and Judgments Act 1982, s.28.

[73d] [1995] F.S.R. 449 (SC, IH).
[73e] There was also initially an application for inspection of the plant, but this was not pursued.

The latter put at the disposal of litigants in England and other Brussels Convention contracting states a Scots procedure for early (or even pre-action) inspection of documents, premises and things which had previously only been available to Scots plaintiffs or prospective plaintiffs.

The Outer House ordered service of a process description containing **3–41** a detailed description of the process alleged to infringe, and an appeal to the Inner House was dismissed. The judgment of the Lord President, Lord Hope, on appeal distinguished between the application of section 28 and Article 24 to parties to the foreign processings on the one hand, and to mere witnesses on the other.

> "I see a clear distinction in this regard between cases where the party against whom the order under section 28 is sought is the same party as that against whom the proceedings in the other jurisdiction have been brought, and cases where the proceedings have not yet been brought or the party is a stranger to those proceedings. The power to make the order is available in all these cases, but there is an important difference between them which will be relevant to the quesiton whether or not the power should be exercised.
>
> Where the party is a stranger to the proceedings in the other jurisdiction, or where proceedings which are likely have not yet been brought there, it may be difficult to obtain an order in the other jurisdiction which can be enforced against him, unless recourse is had to the Scottish court which *ex hypothesi* has jurisdiction to make and enforce the order against him here. It may be thought that Article 24 of the Convention was concerned especially with this difficulty, so that effective measures of a provisional or protective nature could be obtained in the courts of another Contracting State which the court of the Contracting State which has jurisdiction over the subject matter cannot provide or cannot provide effectively. If that is the situation, the power which is available under section 28 of the 1982 Act in regard to the preservation and detention of documents and other property can be exercised to give effect to Article 24 of the Convention. This is unlikely to give rise to the risk of producing injustice, or of doing something which may be regarded as vexatious or oppressive, as between the parties to the proceedings in the other jurisdiction. Nor is the risk of doing this likely to arise when an order for the production and recovery of the documents and other property is made, in the exercise of the wider power available under section 28, in these circumstances.
>
> But where the party against whom the order is sought is already a party to the proceedings in the other jurisdiction, the problem which the court of that jurisdiction might have in making its orders effective should not arise. This is because that court already has jurisdiction over that party in respect of all matters relating to those proceedings in its own court. In my opinion the Scottish court must be especially careful in cases which fall into this latter category—especially when it is the wider power under section 28 which is

sought to be exercised—not to be drawn into a situation where it is persuaded to grant a discretionary remedy which the other court, possessed of a similar power to grant a discretionary remedy, would not provide in the same circumstances. For the Scottish court to do this could be seen to risk creating an injustice in those other proceedings, because it would be subjecting the party to an order which the court in the other jurisdiction would not be willing to grant in the knowledge of its own rules and practices. This, as I have said, is an area of particular difficulty, as the question how the discretion would be exercised by the other court in regard to its own rules is not something which this court can determine."

On the facts and after examination of English authority, the Inner House was satisfied that the order made at first instance was not in excess of what might have been ordered had a corresponding application been made by the plaintiffs to the High Court in England, and that the Lord Ordinary had exercised his discretion reasonably in granting it.

C. INFRINGEMENT OF SPECIFIC INTELLECTUAL PROPERTY RIGHTS

Introduction: early or inconclusive cases

3–42   Prior to *Pearce v. Ove Arup*[74] and *Coin Controls v. Suzo*,[75] both considered below, the Brussels Convention received only marginal or inconclusive consideration from United Kingdom courts in the context of intellectual property infringement actions. The first modern attempt at claiming extraterritorial jurisdiction was *Def Lepp v. Stuart Brown*,[76] decided in April 1986 and therefore prior to commencement of the Civil Jurisdiction and Judgments Act 1982 on January 1, 1987; so the unmodified common law applied to the decision of Browne-Wilkinson V.-C. that no action for infringement of Dutch or Luxembourg copyrights could be brought in England. *Tyburn v. Doyle*[77] was decided after the Act gave the Convention the force of law in the United Kingdom, but the parties were both domiciled in the jurisdiction, the relief sought was a declaration of rights under American copyright and trade mark law, and the case was not treated as one to which the Convention had even marginal relevance. In the Scottish case of *James Burrough Distillers v. Speymalt Whisky Distributors*[78] the Outer House of the Court of Session likewise refused to entertain an action for infringement of Italian trade marks. There is no mention of the Brussels

---

[74] [1997] F.S.R. 641 (Lloyd J.).
[75] [1997] F.S.R. 660 (Laddie J.).
[76] [1986] R.P.C. 273 (Browne-Wilkinson V.-C.).
[77] [1990] R.P.C. 185 (Vinelott J.).
[78] [1991] R.P.C. 130 (SC, OH).

Convention in the judgment, so it is to be assumed either that the petition originating the action narrowly antedated the coming into force of the Civil Jurisdiction and Judgments Act 1982; or that the court regarded the Convention as irrelevant to an action between parties domiciled in Scotland.

In *Molnlycke v. Procter & Gamble (No. 4)*,[79] Articles 5(3) and 6(1) of **3–43** the Brussels Convention were applied to the joinder of a German company as joint tortfeasors in an action for infringement of a United Kingdom patent, in which an English company and its American parent were already defendants. Joinder of the German company was allowed, with Dillon L.J. holding that a patent infringement action was one for tort within Article 5(3), and was not within the exclusive jurisdiction of Article 16(4).

> "It is not in doubt that patent infringement falls within the rubric in Article 5(3), matters relating to tort, delict or quasi-delict. It is also not in doubt that, for the purposes of Article 5(3), the 'harmful event' was the marketing of the allegedly infringing nappies in England; so the 'harmful event' occurred in England.
> Infringement is not within the exclusive jurisdiction provisions of Article 16, subhead (4) of which refers to proceedings concerned with the registration or validity of patents and other similar rights. In these proceedings registration and validity are not in issue."[80]

Rather more controversially, Dillon L.J. went on to assert that for **3–44** reasons apparently extraneous to the Brussels Convention and unconnected with Article 16(4), an action for infringement of a United Kingdom patent could only be brought in the courts of some part of the United Kingdom.

> "But from the nature of a United Kingdom patent, proceedings for infringement of a United Kingdom patent can only be brought in a United Kingdom court, in the present case the English court, and could only be founded on infringement in England. The German court could entertain an action for infringement of the comparable German patent, but could not entertain a claim for infringement of an English patent. Conversely the English court could not entertain a claim for infringement of a German patent. English patent law as embodied in the Patents Act 1977 is founded on international convention,[81] not just European Community convention, but, subject to certain special provisions of the Act, its application by the English court is a matter of English law."

---

[79] [1992] R.P.C. 21, CA.

[80] In fact, validity had already been challenged by the first and second defendants.

[81] This is presumably an allusion to the European Patent Convention, but although Art. 57(1) of the Brussels Convention makes the latter subordinate to conventions governing jurisdiction in particular matters, it cannot be said that the EPC affects jurisdiction except in pre-grant entitlement disputes, where it creates a special regime. See paras 2–130 *et seq.*

Since only infringement of the United Kingdom patent was in issue this was plainly *obiter*, and it is suggested elsewhere that any such rule previously existing under English law has been swept away by the Convention.[82] In *Chiron v. Organon Teknika; Chiron v. Murex (No. 10)*[83] Aldous J. contemplated granting an injunction in respect of Dutch and other foreign patents, but concluded (without reference to the Convention) that it would not be right to do so. This case is discussed in more detail below, as is *Plastus v. 3M*[84] which did not directly involve the Convention, since the defendants were domiciled in America and the action for a declaration of non-infringement in respect of French and German patents was struck out on other grounds.

3–45   In *LA Gear v. Whelan*[85] Mummery J. took the view that the distinction between local and transitory actions precluded an action in Ireland for infringement of a United Kingdom trade mark, but since no such claim had been advanced in Ireland he was surely right to hold that the Irish infringement and passing-off action and an English action for infringement of the United Kingdom mark were not "for the same cause of action" so as to require the latter to be dismissed or stayed pursuant to Article 21 of the Brussels Convention. Jacob J. reached a similar decision in *Mecklermedia v. DC Congress*,[86] holding that an English action for passing-off ought to proceed despite a pending trade mark infringement action in Germany between the defendants and licensees of the plaintiff. The wider question of whether the German court could entertain an action for passing-off in England was deliberately left unanswered.

3–46   Finally, in *Chiron v. Evans Medical*[87] Robert Walker J. observed that an action for a declaration of non-infringement did not fall under the exclusive jurisdiction:

> "I should also perhaps note at this point, before turning to the facts in a little more detail, that Article 16 of the Brussels Conventions provides for exclusive jurisdiction in some cases, regardless of domicile, so as to override the more general rules. Article 16(4) gives jurisdiction in proceedings concerned with the registration or validity of patents to the courts of the contracting state in which the registration has taken place. Article 16(4) does not apply to infringement proceedings. It is reasonably clear that Chiron's petition would fall within Article 16(4) (if anything turned on that) but that this action does not, especially since I am told that Evans is now seeking to amend its counterclaim to plead that Chiron's present clinical trials in the United Kingdom are actual infringements and Evans is seeking to claim an injunction in respect of those alleged infringements."

[82] See paras 3–55 and 6–15 *et seq.*
[83] [1994] F.S.R. 325 (Aldous J.).
[84] [1995] R.P.C. 438 (Aldous J.).
[85] [1991] F.S.R. 670 (Mummery J.).
[86] [1997] F.S.R. 627 (Jacob J.).
[87] [1996] F.S.R. 863 (Robert Walker J.).

In that case Chiron were the applicants for the declaration, Evans (an English company) were the patent proprietors, and a petition by Chiron for revocation of the patent was already pending.

Copyright: *Pearce v. Ove Arup*

The first case in which infringement of a foreign intellectual property right was actually alleged in England, in reliance on the Brussels Convention, was *Pearce v. Ove Arup*.[88] The plaintiff had designed a town hall for London Docklands as a project while he was an architectural student. He claimed that the second and third defendants had obtained access to his drawings and had infringed his English and Dutch copyrights by the design and construction of a building called the Kunsthal in Rotterdam. The first defendants were a firm of civil engineers domiciled in England who had built the Kunsthal, and he claimed that they had infringed his Dutch copyright. The fourth defendants were the owners of the Kunsthal. The defendants applied to strike out the action on the grounds that it was not justiciable in England under the Brussels Convention, and as a separate matter that the absence of sufficient similarities between the town hall and the Kunsthal meant that it was bound to fail. **3–47**

The arguments for the defendants on the former point were summarised by Lloyd J. as follows[89]: **3–48**

"Apart from the effect of the Brussels Convention, an action in England complaining of breach of a foreign copyright would be bound to fail. There are two reasons for this. A claim for breach of a foreign statutory intellectual property right (copyright, patent, trade mark, or registered design) is regarded as local, just as a claim for damages for trespass to foreign land is, and as one which should not be entertained by an English court: see *British South Africa Co v. Companhia de Moçambique* (foreign land); *Def Lepp Music v. Stuart-Brown* (copyright) where there was no allegation of a foreign copyright as such, but it was alleged that a UK copyright had been infringed by acts done outside the jurisdiction which were held not to be actionable. This proposition, which I will call the *Moçambique* rule, was found to be supported by Australian decisions concerning patent infringement including *Norbert Steinhardt & Son Ltd. v. Meth*. The *Def Lepp Music* decision was followed in *Tyburn Productions Ltd v. Conan Doyle*. But for the Brussels Convention, therefore, I would have to strike out the action as regards breach of Dutch copyright as not being justiciable.

Moreover the *Def Lepp Music* case shows that such a claim would also fail because the choice of law rule as regards double actionability, deriving from *Phillips v. Eyre*, and discussed in *Boys v.*

[88] [1997] F.S.R. 641 (Lloyd J.).
[89] Citations omitted.

Chaplin, would not be satisfied. That rule is currently set out as Rule 203 in Dicey and Morris, Conflict of Laws 12th. edn. at page 1487 to 8, and I will refer to it, for short, as Rule 203. The Rule has been abolished by section 10 of the Private International Law (Miscellaneous Provisions) Act 1995 but only with prospective effect as from 1st May 1996. The repeal therefore does not assist the Plaintiff and I do not have to consider its effect.

(. . .)[90]

The Plaintiff says, however, that these rules have to be regarded as abrogated, or modified, insofar as they preclude the court from hearing an action which, in accordance with the Brussels Convention, may or must be brought in the English court. Mr. Speck for the Plaintiff also says that Rule 203 is not so inflexible as to preclude the present action in any event, and relies on *Red Sea Insurance Co Ltd v. Bouygues S.A.* However it seems to me that only the Convention can enable him to overcome the *Moçambique* rule and, if it does so, it would also remove any problem presented by rule 203. I therefore need not consider the ambit of Rule 203."

3–49   Lloyd J. went on to consider whether the continued existence of the *Mocambique* rule and the double actionability rule were consistent with the court's obligations under the Brussels Convention. He first concluded that the combined effect of Articles 2 and 6(1) was that he had Convention jurisdiction over all four defendants in respect of both the English and Dutch infringements, though concurrently with the courts of the Netherlands. Although no defendant argued that the case was within one of the exclusive jurisdictions of Article 16, he considered the point of his own motion and concluded that neither Article 16(1) nor (4) applied. This led to the question of whether the Convention or the *Mocambique* rule prevailed: did the Convention preserve pre-existing rules of justiciability or did it supersede them?

"Thus, applying the articles of the Convention, I would come to the conclusion that the English courts have jurisdiction in relation to an action against the first defendant on the basis of its domicile and against the other defendants together with the first defendant on the basis of Article 6(1), even though the courts of the Netherlands would also have jurisdiction, on the basis of the domicile of the fourth defendant and possibly the third defendant, and in particular the courts of Rotterdam would have jurisdiction as being the place where the harmful event occurred, under Article 5(3).

If the territorial approach of English law were applied so as to exclude an action being brought against a defendant domiciled in the United Kingdom (or, for that matter, any other defendant properly served in accordance with the rules as to jurisdiction) for

---

[90] A passage dealing with the effect of s. 30 of the Civil Jurisdiction and Judgments Act 1982, omitted here, is dealt with at para. 6–68.

INFRINGEMENT OF SPECIFIC INTELLECTUAL PROPERTY RIGHTS

breach of a Dutch copyright, the quixotic position would be reached that the court is required to accept jurisdiction under Article 2 but would immediately strike out the action as non-justiciable. Of course, in every such case there would be an alternative forum under Article 5(3) even if there were not, as here, a yet further alternative forum under Article 6(1). But it is said for the Plaintiff that this approach would impair the effectiveness of the Convention, by eliminating one of the jurisdictions provided for under the Convention—and the basic one at that. It would not be a case in which Article 2 provides the general rule and Article 5 (and 6) provides optional special jurisdictions which the plaintiff may choose: see *Handelskwekerij G.J Bier B.V v. Mines de Potasse d'Alsace S.A.*, Case 21/76, [1978] QB 708, at 729, paragraphs 9–10. In this case, the Plaintiff would only be able to choose the supposedly alternative jurisdictions under Article 5(3) or 6(1). (. . .)[91]

It might therefore be said that to apply the *Moçambique* rule or Rule 203 deprives the fundamental rule of its content and calls into question, in the particular case, the very existence of the principle. The question here is not of the interpretation or effect of the exception, but the effect of the Defendants' submission would be similar to that which the European Court warned against in that case.

Against that, it is said that the Convention only governs rules as to jurisdiction; it does not affect rules of substantive law or choice of law (such as Rule 203) or other rules procedural or otherwise as to the admissibility of proceedings, such as the *Moçambique* rule. The objections raised by the defendants to the claim on this aspect are based on a choice of law rule and a justiciability rule, neither of which has to do with jurisdiction and which, it is said, are therefore not affected by the Convention."

Lloyd J. went on to consider a number of decisions of the European **3–50** Court of Justice on the effect of the Convention on national procedural and substantive law: *Sanicentral v. Collin*,[92] *Kongress Agentur Hagen v. Zeehaghe*[93] and *Shevill v. Presse Alliance*[94]; all of which led to the conclusion that the question was whether the rule of national law impaired the effectiveness of the Convention:

"On the one hand it is said that the national rules relied on are conditions of admissibility which have nothing to do with the designation of the court which is to have jurisdiction and which are therefore left by the Convention to the application of national law, just as the Convention would leave unaffected rules such as about

---

[91] A quotation from *Kalfelis v. Schroeder* is omitted.
[92] Case 25/79 [1979] E.C.R. 3423; [1980] 2 C.M.L.R. 164.
[93] Case 365/88 [1990] E.C.R. 1845.
[94] Case C–68/93 [1995] E.C.R. I–415.

Acts of State. On the other hand it is said that the operation of the rules relied on here (unlike rules as to Acts of State) would impair the effectiveness of the Convention and they must therefore be overridden, although only so far as is necessary to allow Article 2 to have its full effect.

The English rules would have a similar effect to Article 16(4) as regards excluding jurisdiction from English courts, but in a wider range of cases, not being limited to registrable rights. However that point by itself does not necessarily demonstrate that the English rules are incompatible with the Convention. The Convention applies to all Contracting States, and I know not what the local law of other Contracting States may have said on this point. If any of them would otherwise have permitted an action within the scope of Article 16(4) to be brought in a State other than that of the registration of the relevant right, that rule would be automatically overridden by the Article. It is true that this Article derives from the same policy as the English rule of territoriality, as mentioned by the House of Lords in the *Mocambique* case and by Vinelott J. in *Tyburn Productions v. Conan Doyle*, but that does not of itself mean that the Article is the only permissible extent of such an exclusionary rule."

3–51   Citing the Schlosser report, he concluded that:

"My conclusion on this point is that the Convention does require an English court to accept jurisdiction where an action is brought against an English domiciled defendant (with or without other defendants) for breach of a Dutch copyright, and to hear that action on the merits, and thus overrides, so far as is necessary for that purpose, both Rule 203 and the *Moçambique* rule, even though neither of them is a rule as to jurisdiction. Each of them, to the extent that they would preclude the English court from hearing such an action, would in my judgment impair the effectiveness of the Convention by frustrating the operation of the basic rule in Article 2, and must therefore give way in order to allow the jurisdictional rules of the Convention to have their proper effect. The position is quite different from other exclusionary rules, such as Acts of State, because both Rule 203 and the *Moçambique* rule proceed on the clear premise that the English courts are not a suitable forum for such an action whereas the courts of another country are appropriate. It seems to me that, where that other country is another Contracting State, this is a position which subverts the policy and provisions of the Convention. To borrow a phrase from another area of Community law, although they are not rules as to jurisdiction, they are 'measures having an equivalent effect' to rules of jurisdiction, and are inconsistent with the mandatory effect of the Convention and its basic rule as to domicile-based jurisdiction in Article 2."

3–52   This led to the conclusion that the court had Convention jurisdiction over the first defendants under Article 2, as they were domiciled in

England, and over the other defendants under Article 6(1). However on the substantive issue of copyright infringement Lloyd J. concluded that the alleged similarities between the town hall design and the Kunsthal were too tenuous to allow the action to proceed, and struck the whole action out as an abuse of process. The claim in respect of the English copyright was also held to be time-barred.

The public policy aspect of patents: *Chiron v. Murex* and *Plastus v. 3M*

In contrast to the position for copyright, the grant of a patent has **3–53** always been regarded in English law as an exercise of sovereign power with potentially important economic and social consequences. That is one of the two reasons why, at common law, the English and common law courts have refused to entertain actions for infringement of foreign patents.[95] In two decisions in 1994, Aldous J. took the opportunity to reconsider the position in the light of more recent developments, including the Brussels Convention and the practice of the Dutch courts in granting extraterritorial injunctions. In *Chiron v. Organon Teknika; Chiron v. Murex (No. 10)*[96] the principal issue was whether the court should exercise its discretion to limit the scope of permanent injunctions against infringement so as to allow the defendants Murex to continue selling one infringing product (a diagnostic kit to assist doctors in the treatment of hepatitis C patients) and to continue otherwise infringing research and development activities. After refusing to qualify the scope of the injunctions to which Chiron were prima facie entitled, Aldous J. continued:

> "I have already referred to the fact that the Dutch Court granted an injunction restraining infringement of the equivalent Dutch patent in Holland and also granted injunctions in relation to corresponding patents in other European countries. I understand that the Dutch Court concluded that the law of infringement and validity was the same in Holland as in those other countries and therefore its conclusion should be applied to those countries as well as in Holland.
>
> At one time I wondered whether it would be right for this court to do the same as the Dutch Court, but have concluded that it would not be right for this court to grant an injunction which had an effect outside the United Kingdom. Further I believe that the Dutch Court was correct not to grant an injunction preventing trade in the United Kingdom. Even though the basic law as to validity and infringement of patents is the same in Holland as it is in this country, the factual matrix is unlikely to be the same as the procedure for ascertaining the facts and scientific evidence are different. Further this case shows that there are many considerations which have to be taken into account by a United Kingdom

[95] See Chap. 6.
[96] [1994] F.S.R. 325 (Aldous J.).

judge before deciding that injunctive relief is appropriate, which do not appear to be relevant in a Dutch Court. Thus it would be unlikely that a Dutch Court could be sure that an injunction would be appropriate in the United Kingdom upon an application in Holland for interlocutory, preliminary or final relief."

3–54   The second case was *Plastus Kreativ v. 3M*[97] where the issue was whether the High Court could grant a declaration that the plaintiffs did not infringe certain patents of the defendants in force in France and Germany; as well as the United Kingdom for which statutory jurisdiction existed under section 71 of the Patents Act 1977. After striking out the action in respect of the French and German patents on the ground that the claims for declarations were outside both the statutory and the inherent jurisdiction of the court to grant declaratory relief, Aldous J. went on to make the following admittedly *obiter* observations with respect to infringement proceedings as such under the Brussels Convention. The Convention was cited by the plaintiffs only by way of background, because the defendants were not domiciled in a contracting state.

"Mr. Ashton also took me to the provisions of the Brussels Convention contained in Schedule 1 to the Civil Jurisdiction and Judgments Act 1982. He submitted that against the background where the law of patents had been harmonised in the United Kingdom, Germany and France, there could be no reason not to decide infringement of German and French patents in the United Kingdom, although the question of validity may be precluded under Article 16 of the Brussels Convention.

Having regard to the conclusion that I have already reached, there is no need for me to decide those issues of law and I believe it would not be right for me to do so at this time. Clearly the submissions of the defendants have considerable force based, as they are, upon the considered judgment of Vinelott J. and the established law. However, it may be necessary at some time to decide whether that is so plainly right as to prevent persons from arguing the point. Certainly that was the view of Vinelott J. (. . .)[98]

I also believe that it would not normally be right for the courts of this country to decide a dispute on infringement of a foreign patent in respect of acts done outside this country provided there is an adequate remedy in the relevant country. The local court is able to look at the particular acts in the context in which they are carried out. If it happened that there was not an adequate remedy in the other state, then it might be appropriate that action be taken in a state in which there was an appropriate remedy.

[97] [1995] R.P.C. 438 (Aldous J.).
[98] The paragraph omitted is quoted below as part of the judgment of Laddie J. in *Coin Controls v. Suzo* [1997] F.S.R. 660, at para. 3–61.

I have come to the conclusion that this court has no jurisdiction to hear this claim and for that reason I believe that the allegations in respect of the German and French patents must be struck out. My general comments as to the convenience of this court trying issues of infringement of foreign patents have not played any part in the decision that I have arrived at."

Infringement of foreign patents: *Coin Controls v. Suzo* and *Fort Dodge v. Akzo Nobel*

In contrast to the *Chiron*[99] and *Plastus*[1] cases, *Coin Controls v. Suzo*[2] did actually raise the question of whether an action for infringement of foreign patents could be brought in England under the Brussels Convention. The plaintiffs sued for infringement of corresponding United Kingdom, German and Spanish patents. There were four defendants: an English company which was a subsidiary of a Dutch parent ("Suzo Global"), another Dutch company in the same group ("Suzo Holland"), and a German company also in the group ("Suzo Germany"). The plaintiffs had no Dutch patent, but sued in England for infringement of the United Kingdom, German and Spanish patents and alleged that all four defendants were joint tortfeasors in all three countries. Laddie J. first of all decided that as an early date for a full trial was possible, interlocutory relief would be inappropriate and so Article 24 of the Brussels Convention was inapplicable.

3–55

As a matter of English law, Laddie J. then decided that the plaintiffs had pleaded a sufficient case of infringement against the English defendant and its Dutch sister company, but that the Dutch parent company and the German company were not arguably joint tortfeasors in respect of the alleged English infringements. He reached similar conclusions in relation to alleged joint liability for infringement in German and the Netherlands, so that five arguable causes of action remained: (1) infringement of the German patent in Germany committed by Suzo Germany; (2) infringement of the German patent in Germany, as a joint tortfeasor, committed by Suzo Holland; (3) infringement of the Spanish patent in Spain, as a joint tortfeasor, committed by Suzo Holland; (4) infringement of the United Kingdom patent in England committed by Suzo UK and (5) infringement of the United Kingdom patent in England, as a joint tortfeasor, committed by Suzo Holland. He went on to consider whether any of claims (1), (2) and (3), the foreign claims, were justiciable in England.

3–56

An argument based on the double actionability rule as explained in *Def Lepp v. Stuart Brown*[3] was immediately dismissed as inconsistent with section 10 of the Private International Law (Miscellaneous Provisions) Act 1995. Laddie J. went on to consider whether the *Mocambique* rule[4]

3–57

---

[99] *Chiron v. Murex (No 10)* [1994] F.S.R. 325 (Aldous J.).
[1] *Plastus v. 3M* [1995] R.P.C. 438 (Aldous J.).
[2] [1997] F.S.R. 660 (Laddie J.).
[3] [1986] R.P.C. 273 (Browne-Wilkinson V.-C.).
[4] The rule in *British South Africa Co v. Companhia do Mocambique* [1893] A.C. 602, HL. See paras 6–48 and 6–114.

prevented the foreign claims from being entertained. First, he followed Lloyd J. in holding that section 30 of the Civil Jurisdiction and Judgments Act 1982 had not abolished the *Mocambique* rule for intellectual property. Intellectual property was analogous to immovable property properly so called for certain purposes, but was not within the scope of section 30 of the 1982 Act:

> "If the *Moçambique* rule has been destroyed or limited in relation to patent and similar rights, that must be as a result of our adherence to the Brussels Convention, not because of the 1982 and 1995 Acts. It follows that, in the absence of any change in our law brought about by the convention, the three foreign claims are not justiciable here and I would order them to be struck out of the plaintiff's pleadings."

3–58   Turning to the Brussels Convention, Laddie J. rejected a submission by the defendants that the Convention governed only personal jurisdiction, and left subject-matter jurisdiction or "justiciability" for national law. He concluded:

> "I must confess to finding it hard to accept this submission. Article 2 sets out the primary rule of the Convention. It follows that, say, an English domiciled defendant *must* be sued in England unless another Article provides an alternative possible forum. Although Article 5 provides a list of particular types of proceedings which may be brought in other courts, it is not all embracing. There are causes of action which fall outside its scope and the scope of any other Article (save Article 2). It follows that for the latter causes of action, the Convention only provides one forum. If that happens then, pursuant to Article 3, the courts of no other Contracting State can accept jurisdiction. The result will be that the proceedings may be forced into the exclusive grasp of a court which, according to Mr. Miller's argument, may have to decline to hear it because of domestic restrictions on justiciability. I understood Mr. Miller to accept that this was a possibility. In my view this cannot be the meaning and effect of the Convention.
>
> Halfway through the hearing of this application, Lloyd J. gave judgment in the *Pearce* case. He came to the conclusion that this argument, advanced by the defendants in his case, was wrong. Mr. Miller agreed that *Pearce* was not helpful to him. If I may say so, it appears to me that the *Pearce* decision is correct and, prima facie, the Convention can force the courts of a Contracting State to entertain and *determine* foreign infringement proceedings."

3–59   In the result, Laddie J. concluded that he had jurisdiction in principle to entertain the foreign infringement claims. The remaining issue, that of Article 16(4) and exclusive jurisdiction over validity is considered below at paragraph 3–78.

The judgment of Laddie J. in *Coin Controls v. Suzo*[5] was approved in all significant respects by the Court of Appeal in *Fort Dodge v. Akzo Nobel*[6] where the opposite situation arose, in that proceedings to enforce a United Kingdom patent were pending in the Netherlands, and the English petitioners sought an injunction to restrain their continuance.[7]

Chiron and *Plastus* criticised

In reaching the conclusion that the Brussels Convention applied to **3-60** intellectual property infringement actions, neither Lloyd J. nor Laddie J. ignored previous *obiter* opinions which would have led to the contrary result. However, both concluded that they had no discretion to decline jurisdiction. As Lloyd J. put it[8]

> "So far as I know this is the first English case in which the point put to me has been argued. The comments of judges that I have cited and referred to show a reluctance to accept jurisdiction in relation to the infringement of foreign intellectual property rights. There may well be sound policy reasons for that reluctance, including a judge's natural hesitation at having to decide, possibly in the absence of national decisions, what some unclear provision of foreign law means. I note that in the Schlosser report, at paragraph 78, it is remarked that under the Convention the Contracting States are not only entitled to exercise jurisdiction in accordance with the provisions laid down in Title 2; they are also obliged to do so. It is not, therefore, a case in which this court has a discretion, to which such policy considerations are relevant: either the case is not justiciable, because of the *Moçambique* rule and Rule 203, or it must be accepted because Article 2 prevails."

Likewise, in *Coin Controls v. Suzo*[9] Laddie J. quoted with approval **3-61** from the judgment of Aldous J. in *Plastus v. 3M*[10] and sympathised with the continuing application of the *Moçambique* rule to intellectual property, but concluded that the Convention allowed him no discretion.[11]

> "The principles which applied to land in *Moçambique* apply equally well to attempts to litigate foreign intellectual property rights in English courts. Those rights give rise to monopolies or quasi-monopolies which are strictly territorial in nature. In the case of patents, historically their purpose was to encourage and protect local industry. So courts following the common law tradition have

---

[5] [1997] F.S.R. 660 (Laddie J.).
[6] [1998] F.S.R. 222, CA.
[7] See para. 3–81, below.
[8] In *Pearce v. Ove Arup* [1997] F.S.R. 641 (Lloyd J.).
[9] [1997] F.S.R. 660 (Laddie J.).
[10] [1995] R.P.C. 438 (Aldous J.).
[11] Citations omitted.

declined to entertain actions concerned with the enforcement of foreign intellectual property rights; see *Potter v. Broken Hill* and *Tyburn v. Conan Doyle*. In *Plastus Kreativ AB v. Minnesota Mining and Manufacturing Co.*, Aldous J. explained some of the reasons why he was not attracted to the task of adjudicating here on foreign intellectual property, and particularly patent, rights:

'For myself I would not welcome the task of having to decide whether a person had infringed a foreign patent. Although patent actions appear on their face to be disputes between two parties, in reality they also concern the public. A finding of infringement is a finding that a monopoly granted by the state is to be enforced. The result is invariably that the public have to pay higher prices than if the monopoly did not exist. If that be the proper result, then that result should, I believe, come about from a decision of a court situated in the state where the public have to pay the higher prices. One only has to imagine a decision of this court that the German public should pay to a British company substantial sums of money to realise the difficulties that might arise. I believe that, if the local courts are responsible for enforcing and deciding questions of validity and infringement, the conclusions reached are likely to command the respect of the public. Also a conclusion that a patent is infringed or not infringed involves in this country a decision on validity as in this country no man can infringe an invalid patent. In the present case the plaintiffs admit the validity of the patent and therefore there is no dispute upon the matter. However, it will be implicit in the judgment of this court that there has been infringement, and that, between the parties, the patent is valid. Thus, I believe it is at least convenient that infringement, like validity, is decided in the state in which it arises.'"

3–62   One may readily go further than Aldous J. in describing the effects the patent system may have on the public at large. As *Chiron v. Murex (No. 10)*[12] itself shows, the grant of an injunction against infringement may potentially remove a life-saving drug from the market, or inhibit essential research and development by the defendant. Conversely, refusal of an injunction may deprive the patent proprietor of the means and the incentive to conduct its own research. In an extreme case, which is actually exemplified by *Chiron v. Murex*, the losing party might be driven out of business altogether.[13] However, these factors are not unique to patent litigation. A multi-plaintiff product liability suit could easily have comparable effects, and there is no doubt that such an action would fall within the general provisions of the Convention. The possibility of an

[12] [1994] F.S.R. 325 (Aldous J.).
[13] Following an interim award of £6 million damages (*Chiron v. Murex (No. 13)* [1996] F.S.R. 578) Murex went into receivership. The receivers obtained leave to join in the appeal to the House of Lords by the defendants UBI, and the litigation was settled.

English court ordering a German pharmaceutical company to pay compensation in England on a scale which would force it to raise its prices in its home market is a real one. Or again, one can hardly imagine a suggestion more controversial than that the courts of Germany or the Netherlands should be able to rule on whether a French mining company was acting tortiously in discharging 11,000 tonnes of chemical pollutant per day into the Rhine,[14] though the discharge was authorised by the competent French authorities. Yet this was precisely what the European Court of Justice itself allowed two decades previously in the *Reinwater case, Bier v. Mines de Potasse d'Alsace*.[15] No doubt a judgment which might have the effect of closing down an important French industry with the loss of perhaps thousands of jobs would be more likely "to command the respect of the [French] public" if taken by a French court, but for all that the Dutch courts had jurisdiction.

Even in the context of patents, one crucial issue is already the subject **3–63** of extraterritorial jurisdiction under United Kingdom law, in that proprietorship of a European patent application can be decided by a foreign court or patent office under the Protocol on Recognition and Enforcement to the European Patent Convention, and the foreign decision is to be recognised as if it were one made by the High Court or the Comptroller.[16] In the popular imagination, at least, the question of whether a patent for a life-saving drug should be owned by an academic institution, a medical charity, a multinational conglomerate or a scatterbrained inventor might be at least as important as the question of which court should enforce it.[17] Conversely, the United Kingdom Patent Office enjoys extensive jurisdiction under sections 12 and 82 of the Patents Act 1977 to determine ownership of foreign patents in circumstances which foreign states might regard as an intrusion. There is no new principle in this, and the Brussels Convention itself contemplates extraterritorial jurisdiction over patent ownership.[18] Twenty years ago, the House of Lords decided that Bristol-Myers had no licence to sell amoxycillin anywhere in the world outside the United States and Canada,[19] thereby deciding in favour of Beecham what would have been Bristol's first line of defence in any infringement action. The worldwide

---

[14] Unless it be that a Dutch court can order the immediate shutdown of four nuclear reactors at a Belgian power station on the application of Dutch environmental pressure groups: the relief claimed in *De Stichting Natuur en Milieu v. Energiebedrijven van het Scheldeland Ebes* [1990] I.L.Pr. 246, Middleberg District Court. The Dutch court held it had no jurisdiction under Art. 5(3) because no "harmful event" had yet occurred, an interpretation of the Convention by no means free of controversy in its own right.

[15] Case 21/76 [1976] E.C.R. 1735; [1977] 1 C.M.L.R. 284. Capotorti A.-G. expressly denied all relevance to "the danger of the difficulties which it is feared might be encountered in the execution in France of a Dutch judgment incorporating a finding against the respondent."

[16] Patents Act 1977, s. 83.

[17] Compare *Kakar v. Szelke* [1989] 1 F.S.R. 225, CA, holding that the courts of Sweden had exclusive jurisdiction to determine equitable ownership of a U.K. patent.

[18] Case 288/82 *Duijnstee v. Goderbauer* [1983] E.C.R. 3663; [1985] 1 C.M.L.R. 220. See para. 2–115.

[19] *Beecham v. Bristol Laboratories International SA* [1978] R.P.C. 521, HL.

litigation settled, but not before Bristol had argued in several countries that it was for local courts and not the House of Lords to decide the issue.

3–64   Supposing one agrees in principle with Aldous J. that "it would not normally be right for the courts of this country to decide a dispute on infringement of a foreign patent in respect of acts done outside this country," then can effect be given to this statement of policy consistently with the Brussels Convention? The Convention itself allows very little scope for national courts to take account of policy considerations of this kind. Both Lloyd J. and Laddie J. concluded, rightly it is suggested, that the Convention obliged them to assume jurisdiction over foreign infringements.

3–65   The policy considerations stated by Aldous J. are still potentially relevant in four respects. First and most importantly, just such discretionary considerations as were mentioned by Aldous J. in *Chiron v. Murex (No. 10)*[20] have expressly been recognised by the European Court of Justice as relevant to the interpretation of Article 24, dealing with provisional measures.[21] Since there is a widespread, but probably erroneous, belief that Article 24 gives *carte blanche* for the courts of one contracting state to enforce intellectual property rights existing in any or all of the others, this is an important qualification. Secondly, these factors were and are part of the factual background or matrix within which the Convention was drafted, so it is legitimate to refer to them in interpreting it. The Jenard Report itself justifies Article 16(4) expressly on the ground that the grant of patents is an exercise of national sovereignty and describes the compulsory application of Article 19 as "essential since the exclusive jurisdictions are conceived to be matters of public policy." Unfortunately, perhaps, this background has been all but ignored by the European Court of Justice in practice.

3–66   Thirdly, one of the ways by which the European Court of Justice ascertains the meaning of provisions of the Convention which have an autonomous or independent meaning is by seeing if there is a prevailing consensus as to how comparable issues are dealt with in the domestic law of the member states.[22] At the present time, only the courts of the Netherlands clearly favour exercising extraterritorial jurisdiction in patent cases and even that is a development which has taken place after the date the Convention was adopted. Finally, such considerations might at first sight be thought to justify the courts of one state in invoking the public policy exception of Article 27(1) to refuse to recognise or enforce a judgment by a foreign state purportedly enforcing with extraterritorial effect a patent granted by the state in which recognition was sought. On closer analysis, however, there is very little scope for applying this exception.[23]

---

[20] Above.

[21] Case 125/79 *Denilauler v. Couchet Freres* [1980] E.C.R. 1553; [1981] 1 C.M.L.R. 62; Case C–261/90 *Reichert v. Dresdner Bank (No. 2)* [1992] E.C.R. I–2149. See paras 2–14 and 3–30.

[22] Though the Court is not obliged to do so and the exercise has become less popular as the number of member states, and the diversity of their legal systems, has grown.

[23] See paras 8–125 *et seq.*

These considerations aside, the scheme of the Convention does not **3–67** allow the English courts to refuse to entertain an action for infringement of a foreign patent in a contracting state on grounds of comity, public policy or *forum non conveniens*. If jurisdiction exists, and the English court is the Court first seised, then it has no choice but to exercise that jurisdiction, proceed diligently with the action and give judgment on the merits. It would only be if the true interpretation of Article 16(4) were to exclude infringement actions altogether from the normal rules of the Convention that the English courts could decline jurisdiction over an action for infringement of a patent registered in another contracting state and in that case the prohibition would be absolute.[24] Article 16 requires any court to decline jurisdiction, if necessary of its own motion, if the cause of action is one within the exclusive jurisdiction of the courts of another contracting state. There is no scope for any exercise of discretion or any inquiry as to whether or not an adequate remedy would be available there.

Trade marks and passing-off

Although registered trade marks and passing-off are dealt with **3–68** together in the present paragraph, there is an important difference in that the action for passing-off is not concerned with registered rights so Article 16(4) can have no application. In legal analysis the action for trade mark infringement corresponds to that for patent infringement so that the reasoning of *Coin Controls v. Suzo* applies[25]; whereas that for passing-off corresponds to the action for copyright infringement and is subject to much the same analysis as in *Pearce v. Ove Arup*.[26] One difference compared to the latter is that there has never been any conceptual difficulty in entertaining actions for passing-off abroad, subject to the requirement of double actionability being met.[27]

However, causes of action for trade mark infringement and passing-off **3–69** (or for unfair competition, where such a tort exists) are likely to arise on the same facts and this gives rise to difficulties of its own.[28] So in the Scottish case of *James Burrough Distillers v. Speymalt Whisky Distributors*[29] a claim for passing off in Italy was allowed to stand, although one for infringement of Italian trade marks was struck out, though without reference in either case to the Brussels Convention. In *LA Gear v. Whelan*[30] and *Mecklermedia v. DC Congress*,[31] Articles 21 and 22 of the

[24] See para. 3–116, rejecting this interpretation of Art. 16. For an argument based on Art. 57(1) of the Brussels Convention and Arts 2 and 64 of the European Patent Convention see para. 2–139. It is obviously inapplicable to national patents.

[25] [1997] F.S.R. 660. Subject to the criticism of the latter decision at paras 3–93 *et seq.*

[26] [1997] F.S.R. 641 (Lloyd J.).

[27] See para. 6–16 and Wadlow, *The Law of Passing-off* (2nd ed., 1995), para. 4.50 and supplement.

[28] See the criticism advanced by Laddie J. in *Coin Controls v. Suzo* [1997] F.S.R. 660, above. para. 3–19.

[29] [1991] R.P.C. 130 (SC, OH).

[30] [1991] F.S.R. 670 (Mummery J.).

[31] [1997] F.S.R. 627 (Jacob J.).

Convention were held not to apply as between trade mark infringement actions in one jurisdiction and passing-off actions in another.[32]

3–70 In *Modus Vivendi v. British Products Sanmex*[33] the plaintiffs alleged that butane gas refills manufactured by the defendants in Scotland were shipped to China where they were passed off as the plaintiffs' refills so as to make the defendants liable for passing-off by the export of "instruments of deception." However, both the corporate and personal defendants were domiciled in Scotland and the question therefore arose of whether the English or Scottish courts had jurisdiction under the Modified Convention scheme which applies between the parts of the United Kingdom.[34] The plaintiffs' claim was that although the refills had been manufactured in Scotland, England was the "place where the harmful event occurred" in the sense of *Shevill v. Presse Alliance*[35] either because that was where they suffered damage, or because the refills had been shipped from English ports. Knox J. held that such connections as there were with England were insufficient to found jurisdiction and struck the action out.

> "The problem before me is to transpose these principles [of *Shevill*] into a passing off claim where there is a geographical separation between the place of the action of the defendant giving rise to and at the origin of the damage—in the present case somewhere in the United Kingdom, whether Scotland or England is disputed—and the place where the misrepresentation involved in the passing off took effect—in the present case Hong Kong and the People's Republic of China—and the place where economic loss was suffered by the plaintiff, a drop in sales by the plaintiff.
>
> It was pointed out to me that there are two distinct categories of activities by way of passing off. First, there is passing off by the defendant of inferior goods as the goods of the plaintiff. That harms the local goodwill of the plaintiff for fairly obvious reasons. Secondly, there is passing off intrinsically just as good wares of the plaintiffs as the goods of the plaintiff, although they are in fact the defendants. That does the goodwill no intrinsic harm—it may even improve it—but it does harm the plaintiff through the loss of sales which it must be assumed would otherwise have yielded a profit.
>
> Mr Speck submitted that at least in the second category the only place where the harmful event occurred, in the sense of the place where the damage occurred, is the place where the sales are lost. I do not accept that. In my view in both categories mentioned above, that is to say both where there is passing off by the defendant of inferior goods as the plaintiffs and where there is passing off by the defendant of goods of at least as good quality of the plaintiff's goods, the place where the damage occurred is the place where the passing off was effected.

[32] See para. 8–24 for treatment of Arts 21 and 22 in this context.
[33] [1996] F.S.R. 790 (Knox J.).
[34] Civil Jurisdiction and Judgments Act 1982, s. 16 and Schedule 4.
[35] Case C–68/93 [1995] E.C.R. I–415.

I see no good reason for attributing a different place for the two categories which I have mentioned since they both equally constitute the tort of passing off. The place where loss is suffered is, I accept, where sales fall but that is not in my view anything more than where the damage is suffered which, consistently with what is said explicitly by Advocate-General Leger in the *Shevill* case and implicitly by the European Court of Justice in the same case is not of itself enough to constitute the place where the damage occurred. I see no inconsistency in this solution, with the yardstick by which the European Court of Justice has approached these problems, that is to say by seeking to identify the places with a particularly close connecting factor between the dispute and the court other than that of the defendant's domicile in order to justify the attribution of jurisdiction to that other court.

If one supposes that the passing off in the present case was effected in a Convention country, say, for example, France, rather than in distant Hong Kong or the People's Republic of China, there would in my view be seen to be close connecting factors with France where, to put it neutrally, the illicit incursion into the plaintiff's goodwill, whether by way of impairment through the sale of shoddy goods or of misappropriation through the misrepresentation that perfectly adequate goods were those of the plaintiff rather than those of the defendant, occurred.

I have therefore reached the conclusion that England, for all that it was apparently where the plaintiff claims to have suffered loss, is not the place within the meaning of Article 5(3) where the harmful event occurred as the place where the damage occurred."

Turning to the other head of *Shevill*, he concluded that Scotland **3–71** rather than England was the place where the harmful event originated, so that the Scots courts had jurisdiction:

"I can deal more shortly with the question whether England was the place where the event giving rise to and at the origin of the damage occurred. This of course turns upon the geographical location of what the defendant company did. So far as its own manufacturing can filling process is concerned there is no doubt that that occurred in Scotland. The plaintiff relies on the fact, which it claims is at least arguably shown, that the transaction whereby the cans were exported in the plaintiff's livery were set up by a Mr Phelan, an English resident, whom the plaintiffs allege to have acted as the defendants' agent. This is disputed by the first defendant which claims that Mr Phelan was acting for the dishonest Chinese-based buyer.

Secondly, the plaintiff relies on the fact that the offending cans were printed on the first defendant's order by an English resident company and the cans, with the infringing material upon it, were then sent to Scotland where they were filled by the defendant and exported, it is claimed, via England. The point of export is not established firmly probably largely because the first defendant's records have, as the evidence has shown, been damaged by a flood in December 1994. I assume, for present purposes, that the goods did travel through England on their way to Hong Kong. They were sent c.i.f. but that is about all that is known about the terms on which the carriers operated by whom the goods were transported.

Whether one looks at it narrowly or, as I would prefer to do, broadly, it seems to me that the event which gave rise to the damage relied upon should be placed in Scotland. A broad approach is in my view to be preferred because I respectfully agree with what Steyn J. said in *Minster Investments Ltd v. Hyundai Precision and Industry Co. Ltd* [1988] 2 Lloyd's Rep. 621 at 624 after the *Mines de potasse* case which was quoted by him but obviously before the *Dumez, Marinari* and *Shevill* cases which had not yet been decided. He said this at page 624:

> 'In my judgment, common sense and policy considerations require one to ask where in substance the cause of action in tort arises, or what the tort is most closely connected with.' "

3–72 The most recent case in point is *Mecklermedia v. DC Congress*[36] where Jacob J. held that an action for passing-off in England should not be struck out or stayed as a result of the existence of a trade mark infringement action in Germany, in which the positions of the parties were nearly reversed.[37] The facts were that the plaintiffs claimed goodwill in England in relation to various publishing activities and organising trade shows under the name *Internet World*. The defendants DC had also organised shows under the name *Internet World*, in Dusseldorf in 1996 and in Vienna in 1997 and they had promoted their shows in the United Kingdom. Some of the promotional activity had been directed towards exhibitors at, or visitors to, the plaintiffs' shows. Although the defendants' activities actually took place abroad, the plaintiffs' United Kingdom goodwill stood to be damaged by promotion of the shows in the United Kingdom so there was a serious question of passing-off to be tried.

3–73 Jacob J. held that the passing-off action fell within Article 5(3) in that the "place where the harmful event occurred" was England, where the plaintiffs' goodwill and reputation existed. All the elements of the tort—goodwill, misrepresentation and damage—would have to be made out in England. This was not such a case as *Dumez v. Hessische Landesbank*[38] where the harm relied on was only indirect or consequential. Articles 2 and 5(3) applied equally and gave the plaintiffs an option of where to sue. Just such a choice of alternative jurisdictions was expressly contemplated in *Shevill v. Presse Alliance*.

---

[36] [1997] F.S.R. 627 (Jacob J.).
[37] For aspects of the decision arising under Arts 21 and 22, see para. 8–24.
[38] Case 220/88 [1990] E.C.R. 49.

Breach of confidence

The action for breach of confidence presents unique difficulties in **3–74** private international law because of its uncertain and complex legal classification.[39] The analysis is simplest where there is an express contractual obligation of confidence in which case Article 5(1) or 17 of the Brussels Convention is likely to apply; but there may be no contract, or the information may have wrongfully been passed to third parties.[40] The non-contractual obligation of confidence is generally taken to be equitable in nature, but the private international law of equitable obligations is very undeveloped. Needless to say, civil law jurisdictions with no doctrine of equity have to give it a different classification— probably as a branch of the law of unfair competition or employment, depending on the relationship of the parties.[40a] Otherwise, and even in the common law, confidential information is sometimes, and controversially, treated as a form of property; and the action for breach of confidence as quasi-tortious or as providing a restitutionary remedy.

Only one English decision to date has dealt expressly, if inconclusively, **3–75** with the application of the Brussels Convention to the action for breach of confidence.[41] In *Kitechnology v. Unicor*[42] two German-domiciled defendants were given access to the plaintiffs' confidential technology for manufacturing a special type of piping with a view to acquiring rights to manufacture. One company in the defendants' group was given the right to distribute the plaintiffs' piping, but another company also started unauthorised manufacture in Germany allegedly using the plaintiffs' confidential information and assisted by German former employees of the plaintiffs. The plaintiffs commenced proceedings in England to enforce contractual and equitable obligations of confidence and asserted jurisdiction over the German-domiciled defendants based on express contractual submissions to the jurisdiction by two defendants under Article 17, and on Article 5(3) in respect of the non-contractual causes of action and against the other defendants. The plaintiffs were domiciled in various countries, but included two companies manufacturing pipe respectively in England and Germany. None of the defendants were domiciled in England.

At first instance, Millett J. held that Article 5(3) applied to the claims **3–76** against all the defendants and that the scope of the jurisdiction clauses

---

[39] For choice of law in breach of confidence cases see paras 6–163 *et seq.*

[40] In another context, Case C–26/91 *Jacob Handte v. TMCS* [1992] E.C.R. I–3967 confirms that Art. 5(1) requires privity and can only be asserted against parties to the contract relied on. Conversely, Darmon A-G has suggested that a claim founded simultaneously in contract, tort and unjust enrichment should be governed wholly by Art. 5(1): Case C–68/93 *Shevill v. Presse Alliance* [1995] E.C.R. I–415, para. 77 and cases there cited.

[40a] The action for misappropriation of trade secrets in American law is categorised as one in tort or restitution: *Restatement (3d) Unfair Competition* (1995) s.40 comment (a).

[41] Some difficulties are illustrated indirectly by *Berkeley Administration v. McClelland* [1995] I.L.Pr 210, CA, but the issues for which the case is reported are unrepresentative.

[42] [1995] F.S.R. 765; [1994] I.L.Pr. 568, CA.

did not have to be decided.[43] He therefore refused to set aside service of the writ. On appeal, the Court of Appeal held that the non-contractual claims did not fall within Article 5(3) and that the court had jurisdiction only in so far as it was based on the jurisdiction agreements or was for provisional measures under Article 24. As to the former, the Court cited *Kalfelis v. Schroeder*[44] for the proposition that "tort, delict or quasi-delict" should be given an autonomous meaning and went on to hold that it was impossible at that time to say whether the equitable claim for breach of confidence was within the extended meaning of "tort" ambiguously canvassed in *Kalfelis*. The question was indistinguishable in principle from that of whether a claim in restitution fell within Article 5(3), then under consideration in the local authority swaps litigation.[45] It was therefore inconclusive that under English domestic law the action for breach of confidence was not characterised as one in tort. However, on any interpretation of Article 5(3) it could not be said that England was "the place where the harmful event occurred" since the alleged breaches of confidence had taken place in Germany and it was insufficient that the plaintiffs might have suffered indirect or consequential loss in England.

3–77   Two subsidiary points from *Kitechnology v. Unicor* are worth noting for their practical importance. One is that the exclusive jurisdiction clause in the "Look-See Agreement" under which the first defendants had obtained access to the plaintiffs' confidential information was construed quite widely,[46] so as to cover not only contractual claims *strictu sensu* but also closely related claims in tort or equity. The other is that the English courts had jurisdiction to grant provisional measures under Article 24 of the Convention and section 25 of the Civil Jurisdiction and Judgments Act 1982, though it is unclear what interlocutory relief was sought.

D. INVALIDITY AND REVOCATION OF PATENTS: *COIN CONTROLS v. SUZO*

The problem

3–78   For actions for infringement of United Kingdom patents or other registered intellectual property rights brought in the English courts, the Brussels Convention presents few conceptual difficulties. The act of infringement is a tort over which the court has jurisdiction under Article 5(3), since "the place where the harmful event occurred" is bound to include England; and the court will derive jurisdiction over validity

---

[43] [1994] I.L.Pr. 560.

[44] Case 189/87 [1988] E.C.R. 5565.

[45] Then pending in the European Court of Justice *sub nom* Case C–346/93 *Kleinwort Benson v. City of Glasgow* [1995] E.C.R. I–C15; [1995] All E.R. (EC). 514; though in the result the Court held it had no jurisdiction and declined to answer the question.

[46] Applying *Continental Bank v. Aeakos* [1994] 1 W.L.R. 588, CA.

directly from Article 16(4). The only practical problem concerns *quia timet* actions for threatened infringement against defendants not domiciled in England. On one reading of Article 5(3), only the courts of the defendant's domicile would have jurisdiction in these circumstances.[47] As the Maxwell Committee[47a] concluded:

"The exclusive jurisdiction given by Article 16(4) does not extend to actions for infringement of patents. The normal rules of jurisdiction in the Convention, including the jurisdiction based on the place of delict under Article 5(3) will apply. Because of the territorial nature of national patent rights, Article 5(3) will probably have the result in most cases that a court in the State whose courts would have jurisdiction as to validity will have jurisdiction in an infringement action. We think that in almost every case where a United Kingdom court has jurisdiction by reason of Article 16(4) in matters of validity it will also have jurisdiction in proceedings relating to infringement, either under Article 2 or under Article 5(3) or Article 5(5)."

The main problems which arise do so in the opposite respect: **3–79** jurisdiction over infringement under Articles 2 and 6(1) especially, but perhaps also under Articles 5(3) and 5(5), is likely to exist concurrently for courts in other member states which would not be those having exclusive jurisdiction over validity under Article 16(4). To what extent may such courts entertain actions for infringement of a foreign patent at all; and if they may do so, how are they to deal with the possibility that the patent may be invalid? If infringement actions are to be allowed outside the courts of the place of infringement—for instance in the courts of the defendant's domicile—then there are three possible ways to deal with validity. The court seised of the infringement action could refuse to enter into the question of validity at all, requiring the defendant to bring a separate revocation action in the appropriate country to determine that question; it could rule on validity with *inter partes* effect but without entertaining a counterclaim or purporting to revoke the patent; or it could assume full jurisdiction and purport to order the relevant national patent office to revoke the patent if it found it invalid. It must be admitted that each of these approaches has serious problems and one is likely to be preferred over the others as much on considerations of policy and even expediency as on the precise terms of the Convention.[48] Indeed, the problems may be so severe as to lead one to conclude that jurisdiction over infringement as such should be declined, at least if validity is actually or prospectively in issue.[49]

The remainder of the present section deals in detail with the only case **3–80** to date in English law in which a claim to enforce a foreign patent

[47] See para. 2–98.
[47a] Report of the Scottish Committee on Jurisdiction and Enforcement (1980), para. 5.173.
[48] See paras 3–114 *et seq.*, below.
[49] The solution of *Coin Controls v. Suzo* [1997] F.S.R. 660, see below.

actually arose: *Coin Controls v. Suzo.*[50] In the following section, the various options are considered from first principles and a different solution to that advanced in *Coin Controls v. Suzo* is preferred, if only tentatively.[51]

Patent validity and Article 16(4): *Coin Controls v. Suzo* and *Fort Dodge v. Akzo Nobel*

3–81   Only two English decisions to date have addressed these questions. In *Coin Controls v. Suzo*[52] Laddie J. considered the effect of Article 16(4) of the Brussels Convention, conferring exclusive jurisdiction "in proceedings concerned with the registration or validity of patents . . ." on the courts of the contracting state where the patent was registered. Article 16 is buttressed by Article 19, providing that "Where a court of a Contracting State is seised of a claim which is principally concerned with a matter over which the courts of another Contracting State have exclusive jurisdiction by virtue of Article 16, it shall declare of its own motion that it has no jurisdiction."

3–82   In deciding that the Brussels Convention prevailed over the previous national rule that actions for infringement of foreign patents are inherently non-justiciable, Laddie J. had followed the recent decision of Lloyd J. in the copyright case of *Pearce v. Ove Arup.*[53] However, copyright is not a registered intellectual property right within Article 16(4), nor does a copyright infringement action fall within Article 16(1), so the further point did not fall to be decided. In that case, Lloyd J. had held:

> "Copyright is not a right required to be deposited or registered so Article 16(4) has no application to a copyright action. Even in relation to a registered right such as a patent, an action in which registration or validity are not at issue, for example where the only issue is ownership of the patent or (unusually) where only infringement is at issue, is not within Article 16(4) and is governed by the general rules: see *Duijnstee v. Goderbauer*. It was not argued before me that Article 16(1) applied to the present case and, even though Article 19 requires the court to consider such a question of its own motion, I am satisfied that Article 16(1) does not apply. Whether or not an intellectual property right such as a copyright could be regarded as within the category of 'immovable property' for the purposes of this Article, a phrase which no doubt requires a Convention-based uniform interpretation rather than resorting to

---

[50] [1997] F.S.R. 660 (Laddie J.). Laddie J. subsequently followed his own judgment in *Fort Dodge v. Akzo Nobel* and both his judgments were approved in the Court of Appeal in the latter case. Since *Coin Controls v. Suzo* contains the more extensive reasoning, it will be used as the basis of discussion for the rest of the present section.

[51] See paras 3–114 *et seq.*, below.

[52] [1997] F.S.R. 660 (Laddie J.).

[53] [1997] F.S.R. 641 (Lloyd J.).

the interpretations applied by each national law (such as section 90(1) of the Copyright, Designs and Patents Act 1988), the action is not one which has as its object rights *in rem* in copyright."

In *Coin Controls v. Suzo*, the plaintiffs sued in England for infringe- **3–83** ment of British, German and Spanish patents. The defendants had not actually attempted to put the validity of the German and Spanish patents in issue, but they had indicated their intention to do so. That led Laddie J. to consider the relationship between Article 16(4) and the general provisions of the Convention. Article 19 obliged a court of a contracting state to decline jurisdiction of its own motion when seised of a claim which was principally concerned with a matter over which the courts of another contracting state had exclusive jurisdiction. No decision of the European Court of Justice had interpreted what was meant by "principally concerned," but Laddie J. alluded to the commentary in the Jenard Report and the comparison it drew with "preliminary or incidental matters." He then went on to reject an argument for the plaintiffs that Article 19 was concerned only with the claim as such, in favour of the conclusion that the Article was concerned with all the issues between the parties, and that where validity was an important issue Article 19 applied:

> "I cannot accept the argument that Article 19 is only concerned with claims, meaning the assertions made by the party who initiates the proceedings. It must be concerned with what is in issue before the court. In some patent infringement proceedings it is really only validity which is in dispute. The function of Article 19 appears to me to be to ensure that litigation covered by the exclusive jurisdiction provisions of Article 16 are determined in the court having exclusive jurisdiction. If Mr. Silverleaf was right, which court would have jurisdiction would be determined by which party managed to commence proceedings first.
>
> In the absence of binding authority, I also do not accept the second argument as to the meaning of 'principally concerned.' I can see no reason to give the Article a narrow linguistic interpretation. The Jenard report suggests that what is excluded is incidental matter. Something which is a major feature of the litigation is not incidental and is therefore a matter with which the action is principally concerned. The issue which has to be decided then is whether the three foreign claims sought to be raised in the English courts are principally concerned, in this broad sense, with the issue of validity of the foreign patents."

In the result, Laddie J. held that jurisdiction over the foreign **3–84** infringement claims as such necessarily fell away once it was apparent that validity would be in issue. This was so even for the German patent, although in Germany infringement and validity would have been litigated in different courts.

> "The defendants are entitled to plead the invalidity of the patents put against them and the plaintiff cannot avoid the effect of Article

19 by telling them that they can not. However, rather than waste the costs of requiring the defendants to plead invalidity here as a precursor to the claims being struck out, where, as here, it is plain that validity is to be put in issue, the court should take the course of striking out the relevant claims forthwith. The result will be that all claims against Suzo Germany will be struck out and that company should be removed from the proceedings. Although Suzo Holland remains a party in relation to the allegations of infringement of the UK patent, all claims against it in respect of the German and Spanish patents must be deleted."[54]

3–85   The judgment of Laddie J. in *Coin Controls v. Suzo*[55] and his interpretation of Article 16(4) were approved by the Court of Appeal in *Fort Dodge v. Akzo Nobel*[56] where the question arose in the opposite context of whether the Dutch court was interpreting the Brussels Convention correctly in continuing to entertain proceedings for infringement of a United Kingdom patent after the validity of the latter had been put in issue by a petition for revocation in the English Patents Court:

"Article 16 is in Section 5 of the Convention which contains exceptions to the general rule. It is headed 'Exclusive Jurisdiction'. Article 16(4) provides that the Courts of the State in which a patent is registered have exclusive jurisdiction 'in proceedings concerned with the registration or validity' of the patent. There can be no doubt that all proceedings for revocation of a patent have to be decided by the Court of the State where the patent is registered. In this case proceedings for revocation of the United Kingdom patent have to be decided by the English Patents Court. That also applies to proceedings 'concerned with the registration or validity of patents'. What is the ambit of those words?

In the Jenard Report (OJC 59 5.3.79 p36), Article 16(4) is considered. The Report concludes that:

'Since the grant of a national patent is an exercise of national sovereignty, Article 16(4) of the Judgments Convention provides for exclusive jurisdiction in proceedings concerned with the validity of patents. Other actions, including those for infringement of patents, are governed by the general rules of the Convention.'

It follows that Article 16(4) should be construed as differentiating between actions for infringement and proceedings concerned with validity.

In the United Kingdom it is possible to have both an action for infringement by a patentee and the equivalent action for a declaration of non-infringement by a person threatened by a patent. Where

---

[54] *ibid.*
[55] [1997] F.S.R. 660 (Laddie J.).
[56] [1998] F.S.R. 222, CA.

questions of infringement and validity both arise it is invariably not possible to conclude there is infringement without validity being determined. An extreme example, known as a *Gillette* defence, is where the alleged infringer's case is that the patent is invalid if the alleged infringing acts fall within the ambit of the claims. That appears to be part of the Appellants' contentions in this case. It follows that the split contemplated in the Jenard Report between actions for infringement and proceedings concerned with validity cannot always be made.

As Article 64 of the European Patent Convention requires the national law to be determinative of what will and what will not amount to infringement, it follows that when there is a bona fide challenge to the validity of a United Kingdom patent, any proceedings for infringment must in English eyes be 'concerned with' the validity of the patent. Often, perhaps normally, the issue of validity will be the principal element of the dispute. No conclusion as to the chances of a claim of infringement succeeding can be made until a decision has been reached as to the strength of the allegations of invalidity. No concluded view on infringement can be reached until a decison has been reached as to whether any amendment should be made and the attack on the patent has been rejected.

In the present case the Appellants have raised a substantial attack on the validity of the United Kingdom patent and also intend to rely upon a *Gillette* defence. This is a case therefore in which no conclusion on the infringement can be reached without consideration of the validity of the patent. We believe that for the purposes of Article 19 the claim by the Respondents in respect of acts carried out in the United Kingdom are principally concerned with validity of the United Kingdom patent and therefore by reason of that Article and Article 16 the claim falls within the exclusive jurisdiction of the United Kingdom Court."

And the Court went on to approve the passage in *Coin Controls v. Suzo* in which Laddie J. had said: **3–86**

"As I have said, validity is frequently in issue, and sometimes the most important issue, in English patent infringement proceedings. This is now enshrined in section 74(1)(a) of the Patents Act 1977. We have always taken the view that you cannot infringe an invalid patent. This was restated by Aldous J in the passage from *Plastus* quoted above. However the fact that the defendant can challenge validity does not mean that he will. In *Plastus* he did not. Until he does, only infringement is in issue and the approach in *Pearce* applies. The court cannot decline jurisdiction on the basis of mere suspicions as to what defence may be run. But once the defendant raises the validity the court must hand the proceedings over to the courts having exclusive jurisdiction over that issue. Further, since Article 19 obliges the court to decline jurisdiction in relation to claims which are 'principally' concerned with Article 16 issues. it seems to follow that jurisdiction over all of the claim, including that part which is not within Article 16 must be declined. It may well be that if there are multiple discrete issues before a court it will be possible to sever one or more claims from another and to decline to accept jurisdiction only over those covered by Article 16, but I do not believe that that approach applies where infringement and validity of an intellectual property right are concerned. They are so closely interrelated that they should be treated for jurisdiction purposes as one issue or claim."

3–87   However, both Laddie J. and the Court of Appeal agreed in *Fort Dodge v. Akzo Nobel* that the interpretation of Article 16(4) was not *acte clair*, and that contrary opinions were tenable. The Court of Appeal therefore ordered a reference to the European Court of Justice under the 1971 Protocol on Interpretation to the Brussels Convention.[57]

The likely implications of *Coin Controls v. Suzo* in English practice

3–88   In *Coin Controls v. Suzo*[58] Laddie J. held that English proceedings for infringement of German and Spanish patents were (or rather, would be) "principally concerned" with the validity of those patents, so as to lead to the application of Article 19; and in *Fort Dodge v. Akzo Nobel*[59] Laddie J. and the Court of Appeal both considered that the pending Dutch proceedings for infringement of a United Kingdom patent were "principally concerned" with the validity of that patent—at least once the English petition for revocation had been launched—so that the jurisdiction of the Dutch court over any infringement in England was displaced. However, it should not be thought that the principle of *Coin Controls v. Suzo* may be reduced, in practice, to a *de facto* rule against entertaining foreign infringement actions on the ground that validity is more or less bound to be put in issue. That interpretation was expressly rejected by Laddie J. in *Coin Controls v. Suzo* and it is suggested that he was right to do so.[60] However, the inevitable consequence is that jurisdiction can unpredictably be displaced according to whether, when and where validity is put in issue; and possibly according to whether the invalidity attack is perceived as being a principal or incidental issue in the litigation. *Coin Controls v. Suzo* itself seems to assume that if invalidity is raised at all, then it must inevitably be one of the principal issues so that Article 19 can be applied almost automatically[61] and *Fort Dodge v. Akzo Nobel* seems to stand for the same proposition. However, exceptions can be imagined: for instance an attack on the sufficiency of

---

[57] As to which see para. 1–51, above.
[58] [1997] F.S.R. 660 (Laddie J.).
[59] [1998] F.S.R. 222, CA.
[60] See para. 3–116.
[61] It is notable that *Coin Controls v. Suzo* says no more than that validity was being challenged. It is unclear if Laddie J. was even given draft particulars of objections. However, in *Fort Dodge v. Akzo Nobel*, below, the grounds of invalidity would have been apparent from the Petition for Revocation.

the disclosure supporting certain subsidiary claims might leave the validity of the principal independent claims unchallenged.

English courts are conditioned to expect validity always to be put in **3–89** issue in proceedings for infringement of a patent. Even if the arguments for invalidity are not seriously expected to succeed, they may still restrict the scope the plaintiff has for manoeuvre in arguing that the defendant's product or process falls within the patent claims. However, there are infringement actions in which validity is not put in issue. If the defendant is a parallel importer, then exhaustion of rights is likely to be the only live defence. If there is a dispute about the scope or existence of a licence, then the defendant may prefer to rely on the defence that his acts are licensed, which would be inconsistent with an attack on the validity of the licensed patent. If the validity of the patent has previously been upheld, then there are potential penalties in costs in re-litigating its validity in a second action. So although one may expect validity to be challenged, one can never be certain that this will be the case until the defence is actually served. Even then, it is possible for the defence to be amended to add or drop a defence of invalidity. Again, although it is universal practice to counterclaim for revocation of the patent in suit, this is not strictly necessary and invalidity may be raised as a pure defence without any counterclaim.

Except for the exclusive jurisdictions, objections to the jurisdiction of a **3–90** court under the Convention must be raised by the defendant before the filing of a defence on the merits.[62] The filing of a defence, and *a fortiori* a counterclaim, generally operates as an implicit and irrevocable submission to the jurisdiction by virtue of Article 18. The special and overriding nature of Article 19 means that this particular rule does not apply to Article 16, but the conclusion that a court may prima facie have jurisdiction over a claim which may be displaced by the nature of the defendant's defence on the merits is surprising and anomalous compared to the general rule that entry of an appearance automatically waives any original defects in jurisdiction. The conclusion is no less surprising when a mere indication of an intention of the grounds on which the defendant intends to defend has the same effect; or when, apparently, the same analysis leads to the conclusion that the court has a precarious and revocable jurisdiction, effective while only infringement is in issue but displaced as soon as invalidity is pleaded.

One of the problems of *Coin Controls v. Suzo* is that it opens the **3–91** possibility of jurisdiction being destroyed at any time, presumably with retroactive effect, if the defendant is allowed to plead invalidity at a later stage in the action. A related but more serious problem in terms of its implications for the principle of legal certainty is whether challenging validity in the courts of state B, pursuant to Article 16(4), destroys the jurisdiction of the courts of state A which may already be seised of an infringement action in which validity is not in issue. *Fort Dodge v. Akzo*

---

[62] Conversely, if a foreign defendant does not enter an appearance then Art. 20 requires the court to examine its jurisdiction of its own motion before granting a default judgment, another indication that jurisdiction must be ascertainable from the pleaded claim.

Nobel seems to contemplate this, but without considering its implications. *Coin Controls v. Suzo* also begs the question of whether the court may investigate whether a plea of invalidity is raised bona fide, or simply to defeat the jurisdiction; and whether it is ever permissible to investigate the relative importance of the issues of validity and infringement in a particular case. The two are frequently inextricably related, but cases do exist where invalidity is pleaded for tactical reasons but without any real expectation of success.

3-92   It would be wrong though to suppose that defendants will automatically raise invalidity, perhaps on demonstrably spurious grounds, simply in order to thwart the plaintiff's attempt at forum shopping and escape the risk of a pan-European injunction. The Brussels Convention is as much concerned with *recognition* of judgments in favour of either party as with *enforcement* of injunctions and other orders. Under the Convention, a finding of non-infringement for the defendant is as much entitled to recognition throughout the contracting states as one of infringement in favour of the plaintiff. For the defendant with a strong non-infringement defence there are real attractions in having the litigation decided in one court on a Continental scale, even if the price is to concede that the patent is valid. That, after all, is what the plaintiffs in *Plastus v. 3M*[63] attempted to do in reverse by the route of a declaration of non-infringement. The option is even more attractive if the defendant is or can become an opponent in the European Patent Office, since that provides a separate forum for challenging validity with European-wide effect.[64] The problem is that the price may seem worth paying when the infringement action starts; but may appear too dear as the trial approaches, confidence ebbs, and perhaps the opposition is dismissed. Is the defendant then to be allowed to destroy the international jurisdiction of the court by amending to raise invalidity, or is he to be confined to his original case in circumstances where a defendant in purely national proceedings would have been allowed to amend? And if *Fort Dodge v. Akzo Nobel* is right in its wider ramifications, then could the defendant unilaterally destroy the jurisdiction of the court seised of the infringement claim—perhaps even after judgment and pending an appeal[65]—by applying for revocation of the patent in the courts of the country where it was registered? Neither possibility is satisfactory. It is no answer to allow amendment on terms, because where the Article 16 exclusive jurisdictions are concerned the parties' consent cannot override the obligation to decline jurisdiction.

---

[63] [1995] R.P.C. 438 (Aldous J.).

[64] Oppositions can be only filed within nine months after notice of grant (Art. 99(1) EPC) but if an opposition or appeal is already pending then anyone sued for infringement can intervene as an "assumed infringer" within three months (Art. 105).

[65] It is implicit from Case 288/82 *Duijnstee v. Goderbauer* [1983] E.C.R. 3663; [1985] 1 C.M.L.R. 220 that the obligation under Art. 19 for courts to examine claims of their own motion for compliance with Art. 16 applies to appellate courts as well as first instance courts.

Coin Controls v. Suzo criticised for its interpretation of Article 19

The crucial starting point for the decision in *Coin Controls v. Suzo*[66] is **3–93** that Article 19 is concerned with the *issues* which may arise in the course of the litigation, rather than the *claims* asserted by the plaintiff. It has to be acknowledged that the commentary by Jenard does appear to lend itself to the more generous interpretation of Article 19 favoured by Laddie J., and that neither the Jenard Report, nor any of the other official Reports, has more to be said on this point than was quoted by him. The relevant passage in Jenard reads:

> "The words 'principally concerned' have the effect that the court is not obliged to declare of its own motion that it has no jurisdiction if an issue which comes within the exclusive jurisdiction of another court is raised only as a preliminary or incidental matter."

Laddie J. expressly relied on this passage in saying that "the Jenard report suggests that what is excluded is incidental matter" and probably had the same passage from Jenard in mind in concluding that the application of the Article depended on issues rather than claims. However, Jenard's commentary is a gloss on Article 19, not a paraphrase, and Laddie J. perhaps went too far in reading the word *or* in "a preliminary or incidental matter" conjunctively. A preliminary question is not necessarily incidental: it may even be determinative, as the Convention implicitly recognises elsewhere.[67]

On the analysis of Laddie J., therefore, the court may legitimately take **3–94** into account the actual or anticipated raising of a defence of invalidity to conclude that it has no jurisdiction over infringement as such. Whilst it cannot be said that this is plainly wrong, there are a number of reasons why the opposite conclusion is to be preferred. First, there is the wording of Article 19 itself which speaks in terms of "a *claim* which is principally concerned with a matter over which the courts of another Contracting State have exclusive jurisdiction by virtue of Article 16." Even when dealing with the Brussels Convention, an interpretation is not necessarily to be rejected because it corresponds to the literal meaning of the Article. Under the prevailing doctrine of purposive construction in the European Court of Justice, Article 19 is probably to be given a restrictive interpretation, corresponding to that to be given to Article 16 itself.

Where the Convention means "issue." as opposed to "claim," it is **3–95** quite capable of saying so. Article 26, providing for the automatic recogniton of judgments, reads in part: "Any interested party who raises the recognition of a judgment as the principal issue in a dispute, may . . .

---

[66] [1997] F.S.R. 660 (Laddie J.).

[67] Art. 26 third para. even contemplates that an "incidental question" may be determinative. See further paras 3–105 *et seq.* In normal usage one may refer a preliminary question to the European Court of Justice, but no court would bother to refer something that was not a major feature of the litigation.

apply for a decision that the judgment be recognised." One significance of the choice of wording in Article 26 is that recognition of a foreign judgment can benefit either party; it cannot be assumed that only the plaintiff will want to have the foreign judgment recognised. For example, a defendant in subsequent proceedings may wish to rely on a previous foreign judgment as creating an estoppel *per rem judicatam* in his favour.[68] The foreign judgment creating the *res judicata* is no part of the plaintiff's claim, but once its recognition is raised as "the principal issue" the party relying on it can apply for the appropriate decision using the expedited procedure appropriate for enforcement. If recognition of a foreign judgment is only an incidental question, then the final paragraph of the Article applies regardless of the context in which the question arises: "If the outcome of proceedings in a court of a Contracting State depends on the determination of an incidental question of recognition that court shall have jurisdiction over that question."

3–96   One of the uncertainties of *Coin Controls v. Suzo* is whether the relevant analysis is solely in terms of issues rather than claims, or whether both are considered. In other words, what rule applies when a case is prima facie within Article 16 in terms of what is *claimed*, but the defendant concedes the point so that there is no *issue* to decide? The question is pehaps more likely to apply to some of the other Article 16 jurisdictions than to Article 16(4), but one might imagine, for instance, that *Suzo* had petitioned in England to revoke Coin Controls' German and Spanish patents, and Coin Controls had conceded that they were invalid and should be revoked. Would the High Court then have had jurisdiction to order revocation, Articles 16(4) and 19 notwithstanding? Self-evidently not, one would think, but this leads one back to the conclusion that it is the claim, and not the issue, which matters. Similar comments apply to default judgments, consent orders, and revocation proceedings defended solely on some collateral ground, such as a contractual no-challenge clause. At the very least, the claim and issue criteria must be applied cumulatively to produce a sensible result.

The overriding importance of legal certainty

3–97   *Coin Controls v. Suzo*[69] and especially *Fort Dodge v. Akzo Nobel*[70] may also be criticised for the practical implications of the decisions. The general principle of the Convention is one of legal certainty: jurisdiction should be exercised or declined according to precisely ascertainable rules at the earliest possible moment, not least so that courts in other contracting states will know where they stand if they are called upon to apply Article 21 or 22 and dismiss or stay co-pending or related

---

[68] The Jenard Report gives the example of a dispute on a negotiable instrument in Belgium, when the Italian courts had already declared the same instrument to be void for fraud.
[69] [1997] F.S.R. 660 (Laddie J.).
[70] [1998] F.S.R. 222, CA.

proceedings. This is true *a fortiori* under Article 16, which the European Court of Justice has justified as having "the advantage of providing for a clear and certain attribution of jurisdiction covering all circumstances, thus fulfilling the purpose of the Convention, which is to assign jurisdiction in a certain and predictable way."[71]

Consistently with this principle, the existence or not of jurisdiction must be decided once and for all—subject to any appeal—in terms of the plaintiff's claim, and jurisdiction cannot be displaced by whatever defence may be raised on the merits, still less by supervening events occurring months or years later and perhaps even in the courts of another contracting state. That is not to say that all the allegations in the claim must be taken at face value, and a court seised of a claim can investigate the factual basis of those allegations which are necessary to confer jurisdiction, but if those allegations are made out with a sufficient degree of certainty then even the existence of a complete defence on the merits would not deprive the court of jurisdiction. The court must, after all, have jurisdiction to find for either party with binding effect. Nor is the court deprived of jurisdiction by the existence of a counterclaim or set-off which would extinguish the principal liability. In *Lieber v. Göbel*[72] it was unsuccessfully alleged that the French courts had exclusive jurisdiction under Article 16(1) over a counterclaim to an action in Germany. It does not seem to have been contemplated at any stage that German jurisdiction over the action as such would have been prejudiced by lack of jurisdiction over the counterclaim, although the two arose out of the same transaction. **3–98**

As a separate matter, the Convention is generally hostile to any interpretation which leads to allocation of jurisdiction depending on subjective appraisal. On one interpretation of *Coin Controls v. Suzo* it is implicit that the court is permitted, and perhaps required, to undertake an exercise in weighing up the various issues to decide in every case which are likely to be principal and which preliminary, incidental or otherwise subordinate.[73] While some such exercise cannot be avoided altogether on the wording of Article 19, it is again suggested that it is to be confined to the pleaded claim as such and that the Convention does not contemplate a weighing-up of the various issues or their relative importance. **3–99**

A final problem arises at the point at which any judgment in an infringement action comes to be recognised and enforced abroad. Article 28 obliges the recognising court to refuse to recognise a judgment delivered in breach of Article 16. However, the recognising court is bound by the findings of fact on which the originating court based its **3–100**

---

[71] Case 241/83 *Rosler v. Rottwinkel* [1985] E.C.R. 99; [1985] 1 C.M.L.R. 806.
[72] Case C–292/93 [1994] E.C.R. I–338.
[73] The other interpretation, which seems to be more consistent with the actual result in *Coin Controls v. Suzo*, is that validity is conclusively deemed to be a principal issue once it is raised. This avoids the problem of subjectivity, but at the cost of giving Art. 19 an interpretation which is just as mechanical as the one which Laddie J. seeks to avoid and which fails to correspond to its actual terms.

jurisdiction. Is a decision that the Article 16 issue was a "preliminary or incidental matter" a finding of fact and so conclusive? The problem is particularly acute under the analysis of *Coin Controls v. Suzo* in terms of issues rather than claims, since the more the originating court is allowed to delve into the facts of the case before deciding whether or not Article 16 applies, the more the recognising court is fettered in undertaking the independent review of the latter's jurisdiction contemplated by Article 28. One is led back to the conclusion that the integrity of the system is best served by confining the investigation by both the orignating court and the recognising court to the claim stated by the plaintiff. Since the presence or absence of jurisdiction on the face of the pleading is almost a pure matter of law, the recognising court can then apply Article 28 unimpeded the previous decision of the originating court.

A subsidiary point on *Coin Controls v. Suzo* deserves brief mention. There is nothing contrary to the spirit or practice of the Convention in the conclusion that jurisdiction might depend on the outcome of a race by the parties to commence proceedings first. That is what happens already under Article 21, and it is expressly contemplated for the exclusive jurisdictions in Article 23. Once again, the preference for an arbitrary but definite rule is manifest.

The case law of the European Court of Justice on Article 16

3–101   In its case law on Article 16(1), the Court has adopted an approach which does indeed focus on the formal characterisation on the plaintiff's claim as such, rather than on the underlying subject matter of the claim or the relative importance of the issues which the claim indirectly raises.[74] Although there are certain obvious differences in wording and subject matter between Articles 16(1) and (4), it is suggested that the same policy underlies them both. The words *"in rem"* do not appear in Article 16(4), but proceedings concerned with registration and validity are implicitly just as much *in rem* as those under Article 16(1). As to the distinction between the forms of words "have as their object" compared to "concerned with," other authentic texts make it clear that any difference is no more than a quirk of the English translation.[75] In the one case to date on Article 16(4), the European Court of Justice has indeed followed its own jurisprudence on Article 16(1).[76]

3–102   The approach of the Court is perhaps clearest for *Sanders v. van der Putte*[77] where two Dutch parties had concluded an agreement for the sub-lease of the business and premises of a flower shop at Wuppertal in

---

[74] It is unfortunate that *Fort Dodge v. Akzo Nobel* [1998] F.S.R. 222, CA, though concluding that the interpretation of Art. 16(4) is not *acte clair*, does not expressly cite a single one of the decisions of the European Court of Justice on Art. 16; not even Case 288/82 *Duijnstee v. Goderbauer* [1983] E.C.R. 3663; [1985] 1 C.M.L.R. 220.

[75] "Other language versions use the same wording for all five paragraphs and make it clear that it is the subject matter, rather than the purpose, of the proceedings to which reference is made." O'Malley and Layton, *European Civil Practice* (1989), para. 20.04.

[76] Case 288/82 *Duijnstee v. Goderbauer* [1983] E.C.R. 3663; [1985] 1 C.M.L.R. 220.

[77] Case 73/77 [1977] E.C.R. 2383; [1978] 1 C.M.L.R. 331. See para. 2–125.

Germany with goodwill and as a going concern. On a reference from the Dutch Supreme Court, the European Court of Justice held that Article 16(1) did not apply to a dispute where the principal aim of the underlying agreement concerned the operation of a business. There was undoubtedly a dispute about a "tenancy of immovable property" but since that was not the principal subject matter of the claim, Article 16(1) did not apply. The fact that the defendant as tenant disputed the very existence of the lease under which he was sued was held not to make any difference to the Court's conclusion.[78] *Sanders v. van der Putte* is authority for three propositions incompatible with *Coin Controls v. Suzo.*[79] First, that jurisdiction over an otherwise justiciable claim is not destroyed by the defendant raising as a defence an issue squarely within one of the exclusive jurisdictions and going to the very foundation of the plaintiff's claim; secondly, that even the inherent presence of an issue relating to immovable property does not take the case as a whole into the realm of Article 16, provided that the claim as such is not predominantly within the terms of Article 16(1). Thirdly and finally, *Sanders v. van der Putte* is the origin of the doctrine that the Article 16 jurisdictions should be given a restrictive construction. There is even persuasive authority that a mixed claim, partly *in personam* and partly *in rem*, falls outside Article 16(1) if the two claims arise from the same transaction.[80]

The converse situation to *Sanders v. van der Putte* arose in *Rosler v. Rottwinkel.*[81] Here the case was held to fall under Article 16(1) because the plaintiff's claims were expressly based on a tenancy agreement; although the principal claim was for compensation for loss of holiday enjoyment and damage to movable property which could equally well have sounded in tort,[82] and which hardly raised any issues justifying the application of Article 16. There was apparently no dispute over the existence or terms of the tenancy agreement as such. Although *Rosler v. Rottwinkel* has been criticised for its rather mechanical application of Article 16, what one notices again is that it is not the real underlying issues which defined the application or not of Article 16, but the legal characterisation of the plaintiff's claim as one for breach of a tenancy agreement. Conversely in *Hacker v. Euro-Relais,*[83] Article 16(1) was held not to apply, because the plaintiff's claim for another spoilt holiday was

3–103

---

[78] Note that the defendant fought the case on the merits, but only challenged jurisdiction on appeal once he had lost. If Art. 16(1) had applied, then even his actual submission to the jurisdiction of the Dutch courts would have been ineffective to cure their lack of subject matter jurisdiction.

[79] [1997] F.S.R. 660 (Laddie J.).

[80] *per* Darmon A.-G. in Case C–292/93 *Lieber v. Göbel* [1994] E.C.R. I–2535 citing with approval Gothot and Holleaux, *La Convention de Bruxelles du 27 Septembre 1968— Competence Judiciaire et Effects des Jugements dans la CEE* (1985). *Quaere* how this relates to Art. 6(4).

[81] Case 241/83 [1985] E.C.R. 99; [1985] 1 C.M.L.R. 806.

[82] And those for unpaid utilities bills could have been framed in restitution.

[83] Case C–280/90 [1992] E.C.R. I–1111.

essentially contractual but the contract was not characterised as a tenancy.[84]

3–104   Again, in *Webb v. Webb*[85] one finds that a claim in respect of real property in France was allowed to proceed in England notwithstanding Article 16(1), because it was framed as one to enforce a trust and it was coincidental that the trust property was land in France. According to Darmon A.-G.: "The jurisdiction *ratione materiae* of a court must necessarily be assessed in the light of the *subject matter* of the claim, <u>as defined in the originating application</u>, without looking at purpose."[86] The argument that the claim fell under Article 16(1) because the *purpose* of the plaintiff was to own the flat was rejected by Darmon A.-G. and by the Court.[87] *A fortiori*, one would suppose, the jurisdiction of the English court could not have been displaced by the defendant attempting to counterclaim for a declaration that he was the unencumbered owner of the property in law and equity. *Lieber v. Göbel*[88] is particularly interesting in the present context because it actually involved a counterclaim alleged to fall under Article 16(1). The counterclaim was for compensation for wrongful occupation of an apartment in France transferred between the parties 10 years previously under a settlement of legal proceedings which was subsequently set aside. The Court held that the counterclaim was neither under a tenancy, nor to assert a right *in rem*, and that Article 16(1) therefore did not apply. The counterclaim was essentially one *in personam*, and it did not matter that immovable property was somehow involved in the action, nor that issues of fact and law analogous to those properly under Article 16(1) would inevitably arise.

Jurisdiction is normally determined by the facts stated in the claim

3–105   This conclusion that jurisdiction is to be examined purely on the facts of the plaintiff's claim is supported in a different context to Article 16 by decisions of the European Court of Justice in a number of cases on Article 5(1), dealing with jurisdiction in contract cases. In *Effer v. Kantner*,[89] the Court held that the plaintiff could invoke the jurisdiction of the courts of the place of performance of an alleged contract, even if the very existence of the contract relied on was in dispute, with the qualification that the trial court was not bound to take those allegations at face value but could investigate their factual basis to the extent necessary to accept or decline jurisdiction.

---

[84] The contract was for the provision of holiday services, with accommodation being only part of the package. Ironically, one of the complaints in *Hacker v. Euro-Relais* (that the holiday home was only half the advertised size) seems precisely the sort of issue requiring "checks, inquiries and expert assessments which must be carried out on the spot" contemplated by *Sanders v. van der Putte*.

[85] Case C–294/92 [1994] E.C.R. I–1717. See para. 2–125.

[86] Italics in the original, underlining added.

[87] To the same effect see Mischo A.-G. in Case 115/88 *Reichert v. Dresdner Bank (No. 1)* [1990] E.C.R. 27 agreeing that "The right *in rem* must be the actual *cause* of the action. The object of the action must be to obtain a ruling with effect *erga omnes* on the title to the property in question."

[88] Case C–292/93 [1994] E.C.R. I–2535.

[89] Case 38/81 [1982] E.C.R. 825; [1984] 2 C.M.L.R. 667.

An analogy may also be drawn with contract cases under Article 5(1) in so far as the latter gives jurisdiction to the courts "for the place of performance of the obligation in question." If Article 5(1) were concerned with the real underlying issues in the case, one might suppose that one would be encouraged to attempt to identify the court having the closest and most real connection with the contract.[90] That might involve interpreting the Article in a cognate sense to that of the place of "characteristic performance" of the contract under the Rome Contracts Convention,[91] or at least taking into account the principal contractual obligation(s) of each party. However, the case law of the Court rejects any approach based on subjective evaluation of connecting factors in this context. The accepted interpretation is that "the obligation in question" is "that which corresponds to the contractual right on which the plaintiff's action is based."[92] It follows that by choosing an appropriate obligation upon which to sue, the plaintiff may select his forum.[93] This has apparently become such a source of abuse that drastic revision or even outright abolition of Article 5(1) has been proposed.[94]

3–106 Two relevant conclusions may be drawn from the cases on Article 5(1). First, they confirm the remorselessly mechanical application of the Convention: in the interests of legal certainty its rules are to be applied without deviation even though "in certain cases [they] may have the effect of conferring jurisdiction on a court which has no connection with the dispute. . . ."[95] Secondly, *Custom Made Commercial v. Stawa* confirms in its own context that to establish jurisdiction one looks solely to the plaintiff's claim, regardless of any defence, and *a fortiori* that any exercise in balancing the relative importance of issues is prohibited:

> "The use of criteria other than that of the place of performance, where that confers jurisdiction on a court which has no connection with the case, might jeopardize the possibility of foreseeing which court will have jurisdiction and for that reason be incompatible with the aim of the Convention.
>
> The effect of accepting as the sole criterion of jurisdiction the existence of a connecting factor between the facts at issue in a dispute and a particular court would be to oblige the court before which the dispute is brought to consider other factors, in particular

---

[90] *i.e.* the court of the objective proper law, in English terms.

[91] As to which see para. 7–16.

[92] Case 288/92 *Custom Made Commercial v. Stawa* [1994] E.C.R. I–2913 following Case 14/76 *De Bloos v. Bouyer* [1976] E.C.R. 1497; [1977] C.M.L.R. 60.

[93] In the context of Art. 5(1) alone, the Brussels Convention admits a doctrine of ancillary jurisdiction: Case 266/85 *Shenavai v. Kreischer* [1987] E.C.R. 239; [1987] 3 C.M.L.R. 782. However, although *Shenavai* contemplates that a national court should apply the maxim *accessorium sequitur principale* this is no more than a challenge to the pleader. Any court, it seems, can assert that whichever obligation is to be performed within its own jurisdiction is the principal one, and all others subsidiary.

[94] See the Lord Chancellor's Department's Consultation Paper *The Operation of the Brussels and Lugano Conventions* (1997), paras 30 to 32 and sources there cited.

[95] Case 288/92 *Custom Made Commercial v. Stawa*, above.

the pleas relied on by the defendant, in order to determine whether such a connection exists and would thus render Article 5(1) nugatory.

Such an examination would also be contrary to the purposes and spirit of the Convention, which requires an interpretation of Article 5 enabling the national court to rule on its own jurisdiction without being compelled to consider the substance of the case (see Case 34/82 *Peters v. ZNAV* [1983] ECR 987, paragraph 17)."[96]

3–107   Cases in tort under Article 5(3) are to similar effect. It was once suggested in *Reinwater*[97] that jurisdiction should be determined according to which place had the most significant relationship to the tort. That was rejected by Capotorti A.-G. because of its inconsistency with legal certainty:

> "It would also be difficult to reconcile adoption of a criterion of the 'most significant connexion' with the intention of the Convention to make it easy to determine the court having jurisdiction, on the basis of clear, precise and sufficiently objective criteria which could thus be applied uniformly in all the States adhering to the Convention. In this respect insufficient assurances are afforded by a criterion, such as that referred to above, which does not lend itself to abstract defintion and which tends to rely upon the subjective appraisal of the court."

What applies to Article 5 in the interests of legal certainty surely applies *a fortiori* to Article 16, where the court must decline of its own motion to enter the prohibited territory. Again, in *Shevill v. Press Alliance*,[98] it was suggested in argument that a claim in the nature of one for invasion of privacy should only be allowed to be brought before the courts of the place where the main harm suffered by the victim arose.[99] This was again rejected by Darmon A.-G. in the following terms:

> "Attractive though that approach may be, and although the court must ascertain whether it has jurisdiction *ratione materiae*, I do not think that the intention of the Convention was to bind the court's jurisdiction to an assessment of the substance of the dispute; it is based upon an objective, impersonal view of the link of proximity, which cannot vary according to the specific nature of a given case."

---

[96] *ibid.*

[97] Case 21/76 *Bier v. Mines de Potasse d'Alsace* [1976] E.C.R. 1735; [1977] 1 C.M.L.R. 284.

[98] Case C–68/93 [1995] E.C.R. I–415.

[99] By analogy with the treatment of principal and subsidiary contractual claims under Article 5(1) proposed in Case 266/85 *Shenavai v. Kreischer* [1987] E.C.R. 239; [1987] 3 C.M.L.R. 782.

The treatment of preliminary or incidental questions and the exclusive jurisdictions

The remaining point on which *Coin Controls v. Suzo*[1] is open to criticism in law is its treatment of "preliminary or incidental matters" as they are called in the Jenard Report. The concept of "preliminary" or "incidental" questions does appear in the Brussels Convention in Title III on Recognition and Enforcement,[2] but this is not a context which throws much light on the relationship between Articles 16 and 19,[3] where the use of the expression is admittedly a gloss by Jenard. The concept of legitimately investigating an otherwise non-justiciable issue as an incidental matter is already known to English law, for instance in *Tito v. Wadell*,[4] but care needs to be taken not to import purely English law into the Convention without justification. The Brussels Convention and the Jenard Report were compiled without reference to English law, and the treatment of incidental questions in the latter is pervaded with factors which have no application under the Convention.

3–108

So far as the exclusive jurisdictions are concerned, Article 19 provides that a court of one contracting state shall decline jurisdiction of its own motion when it is "seised of a claim which is *principally* concerned with a matter over which the courts of another Contracting State have exclusive jurisdiction by virtue of Article 16." By implication—and even if one agrees with Laddie J. that Article 19 is concerned with issues raised by either party, as opposed to the claim as such—the court so seised need not decline jurisdiction if the matter within the exclusive jurisdiction of the other court is not something with which the action is principally concerned. Although no decision of the European Court of Justice has expressly interpreted what is meant by "principally concerned," the answer is implicit in several of the cases on the Article 16 jurisdictions from *Sanders v. van der Putte*[5] onwards.

There is a distinction to be drawn between a preliminary issue or question which it is necessary for the court to resolve in order to do justice between the parties in a dispute over which it has or may have substantive jurisdiction, and one on which the court is asked to grant relief. The latter is a "claim" in the language of Article 19 and if Article 16 is contravened then the court cannot entertain it, no matter how relatively insignificant it may be in the litigation considered as a whole. The Brussels Convention has no doctrine of accessory or ancillary jurisdiction: every claim must stand on its own and have a jurisdictional basis in the Convention.[6] The form of words used by Jenard suggests that the court may consider, and if necessary rule on, the preliminary or

3–109

---

[1] [1997] F.S.R. 660 (Laddie J.).

[2] See para. 3–112, below.

[3] Other than to demonstrate that an "incidental question" may be determinative. See Art. 26 and para. 3–112.

[4] [1970] Ch. 106 (Megarry J.).

[5] Case 73/77 [1997] E.C.R. 2383; [1978] 1 C.M.L.R. 331. See para. 3–101 above.

[6] Case 189/87 *Kalfelis v. Schroeder* [1998] E.C.R. 5565 applied in *Kitechnology BV v. Unicor GmbH* [1995] F.S.R. 763; [1994] I.L.Pr. 568. CA.

incidental question but that it was never contemplated that the court should grant any relief in connection with the matter within the other court's jurisdiction.

3–110   For example, the plaintiff's title to property might depend on an assignment which was alleged to be *ultra vires* and so perhaps within the exclusive jurisdiction of another court under Article 16(2). It might be alleged by way of defence that the action was not properly authorised on behalf of the plaintiff, or even that the plaintiff company had ceased to exist. There would be nothing to prevent the court addressing such questions of personal capacity or corporate *vires*, but with purely *inter partes* effect. A situation of this sort which might well arise in intellectual property litigation is exemplified by *Presentaciones Musicales S.A. v. Secunda*.[7] The facts were that English solicitors issued a writ for copyright infringement in *The Jimi Hendrix Tapes* on behalf of a Panamanian company. Some three years later, the defendant discovered that the company has been dissolved 10 months before the issue of the writ, and applied to strike out the action. The Court of Appeal held that as a matter of Panamanian law the company had not wholly ceased to exist, that its liquidators had validly ratified the action of the solicitors, and that the action should be allowed to proceed in their name. Suppose now that the plaintiff company had existed under the law of another Brussels Convention contracting state: copyright infringement is governed by the normal rules of the Convention, the internal affairs of corporations are one of the exclusive jurisdictions[8] and the winding up of insolvent companies is outside the scope of the Convention altogether,[9] but the court could not avoid deciding these latter two issues as preliminary or incidental matters to the copyright claim.[10]

3–111   As another example, questions of personal status are wholly outside the scope of the Convention,[10a] but liability to pay maintenance is within the Convention,[10b] and if the plaintiff and defendant were never married or had now divorced then that is likely to be a complete defence to the claim.[10c] Obviously, the existence or not of the marriage can if necessary be investigated as a preliminary or incidental matter, although the court seised of the maintenance case might not have had jurisdiction to declare that the parties were or were not married. At the level of general personal jurisdiction too, the domicile of a party who is a natural person

---

[7] [1994] Ch. 271; [1994] 2 W.L.R. 660, CA. See also *KEDS TM* [1993] F.S.R. 72 (Vinelott J.) where both parties claimed under assignments executed on behalf of a dissolved New Jersey corporation.

[8] Art. 16(2).

[9] Art. 1(2), proviso 2.

[10] An issue not addressed by the Court of Appeal was devolution of the copyright on the liquidation of the plaintiff company. This could conceivably have removed the plaintiffs' title (as opposed to their capacity to instruct solicitors to sue) and would likewise have raised issues outside the scope of the Brussels Convention.

[10a] Art. 1, proviso 1.

[10b] Confirmed by implication from Art. 5(2) and the Jenard report thereon.

[10c] Compare Case 145/86 *Hoffmann v. Kreig* [1988] E.C.R. 645, deciding that a subsequent divorce rendered a previous obligation to pay maintenance unenforceable.

may depend on marital status.[10d] Domicile in this sense might be relevant to any civil claim against that defendant, however far removed from claims in family law. So one may have the situation that although a court has no jurisdiction under the Convention to rule whether a person is married or not, it may well have to deal with that very issue as an "incidental question," and its ultimate judgment will not be vitiated by the fact that in reaching it, it seemed to trespass on matters reserved to another court. Conversely, the ruling of the court on the incidental quesiton will not be a "judgment" to which the recognition and enforcement provisions of the Convention apply, and it will not constitute *res judicata* in the other contracting states.

Preliminary questions and matters outside the Convention

Title III of the Convention on Recognition and Enforcement does **3–112** have some bearing on the nature and treatment of preliminary questions falling outside the scope of the Convention altogether. The relevant provision is mentioned here essentially for completeness, and it is not suggested that it assists more than slightly in understanding the different circumstances of Article 19. Article 1(1) provides that the Convention does not apply to the status or legal capacity of natural persons, rights in property arising out of a matrimonial relationship, wills and succession. The Jenard Report on Article 5(2) noted the probability of a claim for maintenance being complicated by the existence of a preliminary issue of affiliation,[11] the latter being outside the scope of the Convention. The problem of treating personal status as a preliminary issue is expressly addressed in the context of recognition and enforcement by Article 27(4) which reads:

> A judgment shall not be recognised: . . . If the court of the State of origin, in order to arrive at its judgment, has decided a preliminary question concerning the status or legal capacity of natural persons, rights in property arising out of a matrimonial relationship, wills or succession in a way that conflicts with a rule of the private international law of the State in which recognition is sought, unless the same result would have been reached by the application of the rules of private international law of that State.

[10d] This was more apparent under the original Convention, before the San Sebastian Convention deleted the former third paragraph of Art. 53. Art. 5(2) is deliberately framed to confer jurisdiction on the courts of the domicile *or habitual residence* of the plaintiff; one assumes precisely because the domicile of the deserted wife might otherwise be that of her absconding husband.

[11] A further illustration of the point that the preliminary issue may be determinative of the substantive one, and may even be the main bone of contention. Compare Case 295/95 *Farrell v. Long* [1997] I.L.Pr. 243; [1997] All E.R. (E.C.) 449 interpreting Art. 5(2) to hold that proceedings for maintenance of an illegitimate child could be brought by the mother in Ireland against a Belgian-domiciled defendant alleged to be the father; although there was no previous order for maintenance or finding of paternity. Paternity was denied, and that issue in its own right was outside the scope of the Convention.

3–113   It is implicit in Article 27(4) that in other circumstances the enforcing court cannot review the originating court's treatment of the preliminary question and the normal rule of Article 29 applies, although *ex hypothesi* the jurisdiction of the originating court over the preliminary question as such may not have been founded on the Convention and the preliminary question may have been answered in a way offensive in some way to the law of the state where recognition is sought. However it does not follow that preliminary questions falling within Article 16 are governed by the same principle. There is nothing inherently objectionable in a court deciding questions of marital or personal status, marital property, or wills and succession with extraterritorial effect. Indeed, it is highly desirable that such issues should be resolved on a worldwide basis once and for all. The Brussels Convention has no policy against foreign judgments on such issues being recognised; it merely leaves this to existing or future specialised conventions or future Community legislation. In comparison, the effect of Article 28 (first paragraph) obliges the foreign court to refuse recognition to a judgment originally rendered in breach of Articles 16 and 19, so the court cannot ignore the question of whether any preliminary or incidental issue was properly characterised as such, unless this is considered to be a finding of fact which Article 28 (second paragraph) treats as conclusive.

E. THE POSSIBLE INTERPRETATIONS OF ARTICLE 16

The preferred solution in outline

3–114   If *Coin Controls v. Suzo*[12] is not the last word on the application of Article 16(4) to infringement actions, then what are the options? They may be summarised as follows[13]:

1. No extraterritorial jurisdiction at all when action is for infringement of a registered intellectual property right;
2. Jurisdiction over infringement unless and until validity is put in issue (the solution in *Coin Controls v. Suzo* itself).
3. Jurisdiction only over infringement as such; no jurisdiction over the issue of validity;
4. Jurisdiction over infringement and over invalidity as a defence *inter partes*;
5. Jurisdiction over infringement, validity and over counterclaims for revocation *in rem*.

3–115   Of these, the solution proposed by the author in 1985 as the one to which fewest objections may be made and which is now repeated in the

---

[12] [1997] F.S.R. 660 (Laddie J.).
[13] With the exception of options creating a special regime for provisional measures under Art. 24, as to which see paras 3–23 *et seq*, above.

present work is the fourth: a court seised of an action for infringement of a foreign patent or other registered intellectual property right may entertain the action and allow the defendant to raise invalidity by way of defence and with *inter partes* effect, but may not entertain a counterclaim for revocation or grant an order purporting to have effect *in rem*.[14] This is the solution expressly adopted by the *Landgericht Dusseldorf* in one case[15] and implicitly adopted by the Dutch courts in many, although the latter are complicated by the special nature of *kort geding* proceedings.[16] It is not necessarily the solution the present author would have preferred if the issue had been *res integra* in 1968; but given the provisions of the Convention itself, the terms of the Jenard Report and the jurisprudence of the European Court of Justice, it is suggested that it combines submission to legal authority with justice to the parties rather better than do the alternatives. Admittedly it involves a considerable inroad into traditional notions of comity, sovereignty and territoriality; but it is the Convention itself which gives those considerations less than paramount importance.

Option 1: No extraterritorial jurisdiction at all when action is for infringement

One possibility which may certainly be rejected with confidence is that **3–116** patent infringement actions automatically fall within Article 16(4). The Jenard Report explicitly states the opposite, and the passage in question from Jenard was approved by the European Court of Justice in *Duijnstee v. Goderbauer*.[17] It would be inconsistent with the express terms of Article 16(4), and with the often-expressed principle that Article 16 should be interpreted narrowly.

The quotations from *Chiron v. Organon Teknika; Chiron v. Murex (No. 10)*[18] and *Plastus Kreativ v. Minnesota Mining & Manufacturing*[19] set out at paragraph 3–53 above as well as the *dictum* of Dillon L.J. in *Molnlycke v. Procter & Gamble (No. 4)*[20] suggest that the English courts might once have welcomed any valid basis for refusing jurisdiction over actions for infringement of foreign patents. However, in *Coin Controls v. Suzo*[21] Laddie J. rejected the twin arguments that validity was inherently in issue in any patent infringement action; or that Article 16 applied *ab initio* because validity might, and probably would, be put in issue:

"As I have said, validity is frequently in issue, and sometimes the most important issue, in English patent infringement proceedings.

---

[14] Wadlow, "Intellectual Property and the Judgments Convention" (1985) 10 E.L. Rev. 305, some material from which is incorporated in this section.
[15] See para. 1–40.
[16] See paras 1–28 *et seq.*
[17] Case 288/82 [1983] E.C.R. 3663; [1985] 1 C.M.L.R. 220.
[18] [1994] F.S.R. 325 (Aldous J.).
[19] [1995] R.P.C. 438 (Aldous J.).
[20] [1992] R.P.C. 21, CA.
[21] [1997] F.S.R. 660 (Laddie J.).

This is now enshrined in s. 74(1)(a) of the Patents Act, 1977. We have always taken the view that you cannot infringe an invalid patent. This was restated by Aldous J. in the passage from *Plastus* quoted above. However the fact that the defendant can challenge validity does not mean that he will. In *Plastus* he did not. Until he does, only infringement is in issue and the approach in *Pearce* applies. The court cannot decline jurisdiction on the basis of mere suspicions as to what defence may be run."

3–117 Although this line of persuasive authority has been rejected by Laddie J. in *Coin Controls v. Suzo*, it may still be worthwhile to examine the practical implications of holding that infringement *per se* is within the exclusive jurisdictions of Article 16(4), if only to confirm that such an interpretation should be repudiated. Likewise, if actions for infringement of United Kingdom patents are to be strictly confined, consistently with Convention obligations, to United Kingdom courts, then virtually the only option would be to hold that the mere possibility of validity being put in issue automatically brings all infringement actions within the scope of Article 16(4).[21a] This interpretation, if correct, would also be the only one which would consistently allow United Kingdom courts to refuse to recognise and enforce foreign extraterritorial injunctions such as those granted by the Dutch courts, since breach of Article 16 provides one of the few occasions on which the enforcing court can review the jurisdiction of the court making the order sought to be enforced.

3–118 The consequences on this hypothesis would include the following. Most obviously, the infringement action could only ever be commenced in the courts of the state of registration. That is a conclusion which the English courts and perhaps others would probably welcome, but when the implications are followed through it can hardly be what the Convention intended. On this interpretation, if the infringement action were commenced outside England, perhaps in the member state where the defendant was domiciled, then all the consequences of contravention of Article 16 would follow even if validity was never called into question at all. So if an action for infringement of an English patent were commenced in France against a French-domiciled parallel importer, and the defendant failed to enter an appearance, then the combined effect of Articles 16(4) and 20 would be to oblige the court seised to refuse to enter a default judgment, and to declare that it had no jurisdiction, although *ex hypothesi* the validity of the English patent would not be in issue. If the defendant did appear, and expressly conceded validity, then the French court would still have to apply Article 19 and decline jurisdiction. The French court could not even allow judgment for the plaintiff to be entered by consent, since Articles 16 and 19 override Articles 17 and 18. If judgment were inadvertently given in any such

---

[21a] As a separate matter, there is an argument (considered and rejected at para. 2–139 above) to the effect that infringement of European patents is not justiciable on an extraterritorial basis, but even if this were sound it could not apply to patents obtained by the national route or to other national registered intellectual property rights.

circumstances, then Article 28 would preclude it from being recognised, even on a discretionary basis, although by now the original proceedings would have come to an end without any challenge in them to the validity of the English patent. All these conclusions may be acceptable on policy grounds, but it would be a travesty of the Convention to .say that proceedings in which validity was never in issue at all should be treated for the purposes of Article 16(4) on the same footing as ones in which it was the sole (or predominant) issue. The same is true *a fortiori* if one departs from *Coin Controls v. Suzo* and understands Article 19 in terms of claims, rather than issues.

If an infringement action as such were inherently within Article 16(4), **3–119** then it is suggested that the same would have to be true of an action for a declaration of non-infringement, especially as the European Court of Justice has held in *Gubisch v. Palumbo*[22] that where there is an action for a negative declaration and one to impose liability on the same facts the two are governed by the strict *lis alibi pendens* rule of Article 21. In *The Tatry*,[23] the European Court of Justice also held that an action for a declaration of non-liability by one party was "for the same cause of action" as a claim for damages by the opposite party, so as to fall under the *lis pendens* rule of Article 21 even though one action was *in rem* and the other *in personam*. In *Plastus Kreativ v. 3M*[24], the action in England for a declaration of non-infringement in respect of French and German patents was treated as falling outside the Convention, since the defendant patentee was domiciled in America. This is surely correct, but if the action for a declaration had been within the exclusive jurisdiction then Article 16(4) would have applied regardless of the defendants' domicile and under Article 19 the court should have struck out the action of its own motion without needing to consider its propriety under domestic law.

Returning to the implications for ordinary patent infringement action **3–120** in England, and the absurdities come thick and fast. Article 16 does not just exclude jurisdiction, it is one of the provisions of the Convention that creates jurisdiction where none might otherwise exist. From the hypothesis under consideration, it would follow that there would never be any need to rely on Article 5(3) or 6(1) to found jurisdiction against an alleged infringer domiciled in another contracting state. More serious are the consequences which would arise as against a defendant not domiciled in a contracting state. English practice is that service of a concurrent writ for patent infringement outside the jurisdiction on a defendant domiciled in a non-contracting state requires leave and can be set aside on the application of the defendant if the case is not within RSC, Ord. 11 or if the application for leave was irregular. However, Article 16 expressly applies, and directly confers jurisdiction, "regardless of domicile" so that if it applies to patent infringement actions from the outset, then an action could be commenced against a Japanese company

[22] Case 144/86 [1987] E.C.R. 4861.
[23] Case C–406/92 [1994] I–E.C.R. 5439.
[24] Above.

and the writ served in Japan without leave[25] and without the Japanese company having any grounds on which it could contest the jurisdiction of the English court.[26]

In short, this option was rightly rejected in *Coin Controls v. Suzo*.

Option 2: Jurisdiction over infringement unless and until validity is put in issue

3–121   This was the preferred solution in *Coin Controls v. Suzo*[27] and is dealt with in detail at paragraph 3–81 *et seq*, above.

Option 3: Jurisdiction only over infringement as such

3–122   The next possibility is that a court seised by virtue of Article 2 or Article 5(3) has jurisdiction to entertain the infringement action as such but must assume the patent to be valid. If the defendant wanted to challenge validity, he would have to do so in separate proceedings in the country where the patent was registered, whose courts would have exclusive jurisdiction under Article 16(4). This corresponds to the situation under German internal law, where issues of infringement and validity are never considered together.[28] Infringement actions are heard by specified District Courts (*Landgerichte*) with appeals to Regional Courts of Appeal (*Oberlandesgerichte*) and thence to the Supreme Court (*Bundesgerichthof*). Validity cannot be put in issue in the infringement proceedings before the *Landgericht*, and the defendant must commence separate nullity proceedings in the Federal Patent Court in Munich (the *Bundespatentgericht*) for nullification of the patent. A similar functional division applies in Austria, though there is no further regional division of jurisdiction over infringement and all patent infringement actions are heard in Vienna.

3–123   The bifurcated treatment of invalidity in Germany might suggest that where an action for infringement of a German patent is brought before the courts of another contracting state, then there would be no prejudice to the defendant and no affront to international comity in allowing the infringement action to proceed and requiring the defendant to challenge validity in Germany. Laddie J. in *Coin Controls v. Suzo*[29] considered this

[25] *Napp Laboratories v. Pfizer Inc* [1993] F.S.R. 150 (Hoffmann J.) applying RSC, Ord. 11, r. 1(2)(a) confirms that leave to serve out is not required in cases falling within Art. 16. See now RSC, Ord. 104, r. 24.

[26] It might be asked if a plaintiff could bring his infringement action within Art. 16(4) by including a plea for a declaration that his patent was valid and infringed (Patents Act 1977, s. 61(1)(e)). Probably not, because a claim for a declaration of validity cannot be free-standing (s. 74(2)), and the writ would still not be *principally* concerned with validity or registration. Moreover, the declaration sought would be *in personam*, and would not have effect *erga omnes* as Art. 16 requires.

[27] [1997] F.S.R. 660 (Laddie J.).

[28] This will change if the Community Patent Convention ever enters force, and the Landgericht Dusseldorf has already decided that it may entertain an action for infringement of an English patent and allow invalidity to be raised, so following English rather than German practice. See para. 1–40.

[29] [1997] F.S.R. 660 (Laddie J.).

argument in respect of the German patent sued on, and rejected it. In any event, the reasoning applies directly only to two of the 15 Brussels Convention contracting states and does not readily lend itself by analogy to the others, or to registered intellectual property rights other than patents. Laddie J. observed:

> "At one stage I was attracted to the argument that in Germany questions of validity and infringement are dealt with by separate courts. Therefore it is easier to treat them as discrete and severable claims. It follows that at least in respect of foreign claims 1 and 2, it would be permissible to retain the issue of infringement here. But in the end I have come to the conclusion that this point is bad. The fact that, for constitutional reasons, different courts deal with these issues in Germany does not alter the fact that there, as here, there is in the end only one question; 'has the defendant infringed a valid claim?' "

This approach previously had one other attraction in that it corresponded fairly closely to the scheme of the Community Patent Convention in its original (1975) form, and in *Duijnstee v. Goderbauer*[30] the European Court of Justice attached importance to interpreting the Brussels Convention consistently with the European and Community patent conventions. However, the enforcement provisions of the Community Patent Convention itself were radically overhauled by the 1985 Luxembourg Agreement and Protocol on Litigation, and the option under discussion here no longer corresponds to the Community Patent Convention as revised.[31] One of the conclusions to draw from the Luxembourg Agreement is that considerations of international comity which in 1975 precluded national courts from ruling on the validity of Community patents in any circumstances, had lost much of their force by 1985.   3–124

From every point of view other than international comity, this interpretation of Article 16(4) is an unattractive one. The "golden rule" for jurisdiction under the Brussels Convention, except for consumer contracts, insurance and a few other situations, is that the interests of the defendant come first. To require the defendant either to concede validity or to bring a separate revocation action in a foreign country would be quite contrary to this principle. In practice, a defendant would probably be at a greater disadvantage defending an infringement action in the state where he was domiciled—or where he was sued under Article 5(3) as interpreted in *Shevill*[32]—and conducting a revocation action in another, than he would be in defending one single action in a court of the foreign state where the patent was in force.   3–125

It is another cardinal principle of the Brussels Convention that its provisions should be interpreted so as to avoid a multiplicity of   3–126

[30] Case 288/82 [1983] E.C.R. 3663; [1985] 1 C.M.L.R. 220.
[31] See Chaps 4 and 5.
[32] Case C–68/93 [1995] E.C.R. I–415.

proceedings and especially the possibility of courts in different member states giving judgments which are irreconcilable. According to the decision of the European Court of Justice in *Hoffmann v. Krieg*,[33] judgments are irreconcilable if they entail legal consequences that are mutually exclusive. This would clearly apply to one court granting an injunction and damages for infringement of a patent which another court decided should be revoked for invalidity.[34] Mere inconsistency in result or reasoning does not amount to irreconcilablity in this sense, so two judgments would not necessarily be irreconcilable simply because they gave different interpretations to the patent claims, but this situation too is obviously undesirable and potentially unjust. There is a procedural problem here as well in that it is implicit in the Convention that the court first seised of a matter cannot abstain from deciding it to wait for the decision of some other court. The defendant could bring a revocation action in the state where the patent was in force, but there is no express basis in the Convention for the court hearing the infringement action to stay its own proceedings pending the outcome. As well as the possibility of the two courts giving inconsistent constructions to the patent, it is uncertain that a finding of infringement in the first action would effectively be pre-empted or reversed by a finding of invalidity in the second.

Whether revocation in one state defeats judgment on infringement in another

3–127   A conflict between a finding of infringement in the court of the defendant's domicile, and revocation of the patent in the state of registration might give rise to more problems than may appear at first sight. In the absence of any provision allowing the infringement action to be stayed, or to depend on the outcome of the revocation action, the defendant might on one reading of the Convention be faced with an award of damages for infringement and an injunction which could be enforced in any member state where the defendant had assets, except the one in which the patent had formerly been in force. Defendants are most likely to have assets in the state of their domicile, and *ex hypothesi* that will not be the state where the patent was formerly registered.

3–128   This is because by Article 27(3) a judgment "shall not be recognised if it is irreconcilable with a judgment given in a dispute between the same parties *in the State in which recognition is sought*." Article 27(3), being a derogation from the general principle of full faith and credit, is presumably to be interpreted narrowly. As confirmed by the European Court of Justice in *Solo Kleinmotoren v. Boch*,[35] Articles 27 and 28 list exhaustively all the grounds on which recognition can be refused. If this

---

[33] Case 145/86 [1988] E.C.R. 645.

[34] Unless the revocation was only with prospective effect, as might well happen with a trade mark invalid because of non-use or other supervening circumstances. Prospective revocation of patents was previously known in Dutch law, but is no longer a problem.

[35] Case C–414/92 [1994] E.C.R. I–2237.

is the situation then the court hearing the infringement action might come to a decision against the defendant which was unjust (because the patent was infringed but invalid) but which could still be enforced against the defendant's assets in the state of the defendant's domicile and every other contracting state except the one where the patent had once been in force and had now been revoked. Finally, the defendant would be at risk even in that state if the patent were revoked at the suit of a third party, since the judgment, though irreconcilable, would not have been given in a dispute "between the same parties" as Article 27(3) requires.

If this obviously undesirable situation is to be avoided then a **3–129** distinction will have to be drawn with the reasoning of the European Court of Justice in *Hoffmann v. Krieg*,[36] where the Court held that an order for maintenance made by a German court ceased to be enforceable in the Netherlands under Article 27(3) once a decree of divorce had been pronounced in the Netherlands, although it was still assumed to be enforceable in Germany. Article 27(3) was central to the result because the Convention did not require the Dutch divorce to be recognised in Germany, and under German law the German maintenance order might well have been unaffected by a Dutch order dissolving a German marriage between two German nationals. One might rhetorically ask if the German maintenance order would still have been enforceable in France, say, notwithstanding the Dutch divorce; or whether the divorce would have cancelled out the maintenance order wherever recognition was sought outside Germany. Probably the former, assuming Article 27(3) is to receive a strict interpretation. Private parties can frequently arrange their affairs so that they have no assets in the jurisdiction of a foreign court, but large businesses are more vulnerable.

Two points of distinction may be advanced compared to *Hoffmann v.* **3–130** *Krieg*. One is the fact that a judgment revoking a patent is one *in rem* as opposed to one merely *in personam*, whereas Article 27(3) appears to be concerned with the latter. The other is that divorce is altogether outside the scope of the Convention and there is no Convention obligation for a divorce in one contracting state to be recognised in another; whereas revocation of a patent by a court of competent exclusive jurisdiction must be recognised in all contracting states without formality. Presumably the draftsmen of the Convention intended revocation of a national registered intellectual property right to have some sort of uniform effect throughout the member states pursuant to Title III, since otherwise it was pointless for the Convention to apply to revocation proceedings at all, and they could equally well have been excluded from its scope altogether. An order for revocation must therefore be recognised *in rem* in all contracting states, or it would be meaningless to speak of recognising the judgment for revocation at all outside the state where it was given.

Finally, there may be a distinction to be drawn between a past award **3–131** of damages and a continuing injunction. In English practice, subsequent

---

[36] Case 145/86 [1988] E.C.R. 645.

revocation of a patent does not exonerate a previously unsuccessful defendant from paying damages,[37] though the injunction obviously no longer applies once the patent has gone. The injunction would equally fall away if the patent had expired by effluxion of time or for non-payment of renewal fees. To this extent, what matters even in a Convention case is not so much that the patent has been revoked by a judgment, but that it has ceased to exist at all. However, while this frees the defendant from future enforcement of any injunction which may have been granted, it leaves open the question of whether orders for damages, costs or past breaches of an injunction could still be enforced.

Option 4: Invalidity as a defence *inter partes*

3-132   The fourth possibility, and the one which it is suggested causes the fewest difficulties overall, is that a court seised of an action for infringement of a foreign patent or other registered intellectual property right may allow the defendant to raise validity by way of defence, at least if its internal law so permits, but may not entertain a counterclaim for revocation or grant an order purporting to have effect *in rem*. It is implicit in the Convention that a court need not altogether refuse to consider a matter normally reserved to another court under Article 16, because Article 19 provides that a court must declare of its own motion that it has no jurisdiction where the claim is *principally* concerned with a matter over which the courts of another contracting state have exclusive jurisdiction by virtue of Article 16. Elsewhere it is suggested that Article 19 means what it says in referring to the "claim," rather than to the issues which may be raised by any party to the litigation.[38] As the Jenard Report notes, the court is not obliged to declare of its own motion that it has no jurisdiction if the matter within the jurisdiction of the other court is raised as a "preliminary or incidental matter." It is also implicit that the court has no discretion: either it must refuse to hear the case altogether if it is principally concerned with a matter under Article 16, or it must hear and decide the whole case, incidental question and all, as the court first seised under Article 22.

3-133   This suggestion has the advantage of consistency with the treatment of the distinction between counterclaims and defences in the decision of the European Court of Justice in *Danvaern v. Otterbeck*,[39] where the Court ruled that the absence of jurisdiction to entertain a counterclaim under Article 6(3) was not relevant to the extent that a defendant raised, simply as a defence, a claim which he had against the plaintiff. Article 6(3) applied only to claims by defendants seeking the pronouncement of a separate judgment or decree. According to *Danvaern v. Otterbeck*, the defences which may be raised and the conditions under which they may be raised are governed by national law; to which one must add that

---

[37] *Poulton v. Adjustable Cover and Boiler Block Company* (1908) 25 R.P.C. 661 (Parker J.).
[38] See para. 3–93, above.
[39] Case C–341/93 [1995] E.C.R. I–2053.

national law is not allowed to discriminate on grounds of nationality or nullify the effect of the Convention. In the United Kingdom, invalidity is a defence to an action for patent infringement and can be raised as such without needing to counterclaim for revocation of the patent, though making a counterclaim is universal practice if validity is challenged. On this analysis, the question of the validity or invalidity of a foreign patent could be decided by the court as a preliminary or incidental matter within the meaning of Jenard's comments on Article 19 and it would not matter that jurisdiction over validity was within the exclusive jurisdiction of another court under Article 16(4). All that would be precluded would be a *claim* by the defendant, by way of counterclaim, for an order that the patent be revoked or declared invalid.

It is unfortunate that the question of validity in a patent infringement **3–134** action falls squarely between the forms of words used in Article 19 and the Jenard Report. The action as such cannot be said to be *principally* concerned with validity, but as the judgment of Laddie J. in *Coin Controls v. Suzo*[40] shows, it is instinctively hard to dismiss validity as a "preliminary or incidental matter" except in the most technical sense. However, it is suggested that the problem is one of terminology rather than substance. The expression "preliminary or incidental matter" does not appear in Article 19 of the Convention, but if it did it would almost certainly be given an independent meaning, which need not depend on the relative importance of the issue so described to the other issues in the litigation. Article 26 already uses the term "incidental question" in a context which makes it clear that the question so described may be determinative. Given the tendency of the Court to give a restrictive interpretation to Article 16 and to safeguard the procedural rights of the defendant as a high priority, it is quite likely that the Court would give a strict interpretation to the word "principally" and minimise the importance of the gloss put on it by Jenard. There are signs of this already in the cases on Article 16(1). If one understands Article 19 in terms of claims rather than issues the conceptual problem of entertaining foreign infringement actions is minimised, even if the result may not be universally welcome.

Precedents for deciding invalidity with *inter partes* effect

In other contexts, there is already some authority that an English court **3–135** may investigate the validity of a foreign patent or registered intellectual property right as an incidental matter under the recognised exception to the *Mocambique* rule.[41] Parker J. was prepared to do so in *Comiot v. Eadie and Williams*,[42] although in the event the case was decided without his expressing any opinion as to the validity of the French patent at the

[40] [1997] F.S.R. 660 (Laddie J.).
[41] The rule in *British South Africa Co v. Companhia do Mocambique* [1893] A.C. 602, HL. See paras 6–48 *et seq*. It is not suggested that the scope of the exception under English law is of any assistance in defining that under Art. 19.
[42] (1911) 28 R.P.C. 687 (Parker J.).

centre of a contract dispute. In *Apple Corps v. Apple Computer*[43] the majority opinion in the Court of Appeal was that the court could have investigated the validity of various foreign trade marks, had the issue been relevant and properly pleaded.

3–136 The further suggestion that a United Kingdom court may entertain an action for infringement of a registered intellectual property right which may be invalid but which it has no power to revoke is an unfamiliar one, but not entirely unprecedented.[44] The Patents, Designs and Trade Marks Act 1883 (s. 90) gave jurisdiction to rectify the Register of Trade Marks to the English High Court, but was silent as to whether the superior courts of Scotland and Ireland were intended to enjoy concurrent jurisdiction. The situation was complicated by the fact that English practice at the time was to require the validity of a trade mark registration to be put in issue by way of separate proceedings on an originating notice of motion. Invalidity of the registration was not a defence as such, and rectification of the Register could not be sought by counterclaim. The Irish High Court held in *Bayer v. Connell Bros*[45] that it had no jurisdiction over the validity of trade marks registered in England, so that a counterclaim for rectification could not be made in Irish infringement proceedings. However, the infringement action as such was allowed to proceed and judgment was given for the plaintiffs. The defendant were offered, but did not take, the opportunity to apply to rectify the mark in the English courts. In contrast, the Court of Session held in *Dewar v. Dewar*[46] that whatever the true construction of section 90 on its own power to rectify the Register, it did have jurisdiction to entertain an action for infringement in which the validity of the mark was put in issue by way of defence. This decision was followed in *Dawson v. Stewart*[47] where objection was unsuccessfully taken to the jurisdiction of the Court of Session although the validity of the pursuer's registration was not in issue. On the facts, the court found for the defenders in both cases on the ground that their marks were sufficiently distinct.

3–137 None of these authorities are likely to have been present to the minds of Jenard's Committee when it was drafting Article 16, but an outline understanding of patent litigation procedure in the original six contracting states prior to 1968 confirms that a finding of invalidity with purely *inter partes* effect would have been within the contemplation of the draftsmen, and goes some way to explaining why Article 16(4) was not expected to cause problems in actual practice. Broadly speaking, the original six contracting states could be divided into countries with an

---

[43] [1991] 3 C.M.L.R. 49, CA.

[44] There still remains at least the theoretical possibility of the defendant in a patent infringement action putting validity in issue in his defence, but not counterclaiming for revocation.

[45] (1897) 14 R.P.C. 257; (1899) 16 R.P.C. 157 (CA, Ireland).

[46] (1900) 17 R.P.C. 341 (SC, IH).

[47] (1905) 22 R.P.C. 250 (SC, OH). See also *Cowie Bros & Co v. Herbert* 14 R.P.C. 43; 14 R.P.C. 436 (SC, OH).

examination system (German and the Netherlands) and those with a registration system (France, Italy and Belgium).[48]

In the former, a single court had exclusive jurisdiction over patent **3–138** validity but infringement actions as such could be brought in a number of regional or district courts. The German system had substantially the same strictly bifurcated procedure as exists today, with infringement proceedings as such taking place before designated *Landgerichte* and nullity proceedings taking place before the *Bundespatentgericht* in Munich. The Dutch system[49] was that all district courts had jurisdiction over infringement actions but only the Hague Disctict Court had jurisdiction over nullity actions, which took effect *erge omnes* but with prospective effect only. Dutch and German courts hearing infringement actions were obliged to assume the patent to be valid, but had a discretion to stay their proceedings pending the outcome of any nullity action. The Dutch Patent Office was famously the strictest in the world and a Dutch patent, once granted, was rarely invalidated. The German Patent Office also set a high standard of patentability. In both examination countries, therefore, Jenard's Committee could justifiably assume that different jurisdictional regimes for infringement and validity would cause no problems.

In the registration countries of France,[50] Italy[51] and Belgium, patent **3–139** validity could be raised as a defence to an infringement action before a district court,[52] but a finding of invalidity in an infringement action had effect only *inter partes* unless the public prosecutor was a party to the proceedings, which was exceptional. In normal civil proceedings between the patent proprietor and an alleged infringer, a finding of invalidity did not result in the patent being revoked and was not binding in future litigation against other defendants. In respect of France and Italy prior to 1978 and 1979, Mangini[53] comments:

---

[48] See Strobele "The Impact of Decisions by Patent Authorities on Courts of General Jurisdiction in Various Patent Systems" (1975) 6 I.I.C. 243 which summarises patent litigation procedure in the early 1970's in most European countries and the USA; and Stauder, "The Practical Significance of Infringement and Revocation Proceedings in the Federal Republic of Germany, France, Italy and the United Kingdom" (1983) 14 I.I.C. 793 reporting and commenting on a survey into patent litigation practice in the period 1972 to 1974. See also Stauder, "Die Anwendung des EWG-Gerichtssands- und Vollstreckungs-ubereinkommens auf Klagen im gewerblichen Rechtsschutz und Urheberrecht" [1976] GRUR Int 465 at 514; Mangini, "The Legal Framework for Infringement and Revocation Proceedings in Patent Matters in the Contracting States of the European Patent Convention" (1983) 14 I.I.C. 776.

[49] Stroblele, *op. cit*; Report of the House of Lords Select Committee on the European Communities: *A European Community Patent* (1986), evidence. p. 172.

[50] French procedure was reformed in 1978 to allow counterclaims for revocation with *erga omnes* effect. See Vianes, "The Reform of French Patent Legislation" [1979] *Industrial Property* 220 as well as the sections on French procedure in Strobele. *op. cit*.: Mangini. *op. cit.*, and Stauder. *op. cit.*

[51] Strobele, *op. cit.*; Mangini, *op. cit.*; Stauder, *op. cit.*; Ubertazzi, "Der Pat-entverletzungsstreit in Italien" [1981] *Mitteilungen der deutschen Patentanwälte* 119. Italian law was reformed in 1979 to give decisions of invalidity *erga omnes* effect.

[52] A *tribunal de grande instance* in France, a *tribunale* in Italy. These are the normal civil courts for substantial claims.

[53] *op. cit.*

"The French patent system is basically similar to the Italian one, for which it served as a model. For France as well the most interesting innovation has been introduced by the Act of July 14, 1978, which dispenses with the *inter partes* effect of decisions asserting the invalidity (also partial) of patent (Sec. 50bis of the Patent Act). As in the Italian system, in fact, the traditional solution allows the patentee to claim infringement despite an invalidity decision rendered in a previous proceeding against a person not having intervened in it; this was inappropriate in so far as it was prejudicial to the certainty of the legal relationships. In several cases, in fact, the validity of the same patent was differently decided upon at different times and by different courts. In France, too, however, the *erga omnes* effect (now having become general) of the decisions concerning the validity of a patent, works only one way: in other words, even after the above-mentioned reform, the decisions declaring the validity of a patent are effective only *inter partes*."

3–140   And for Italy:

"With respect to the subjective limits of the invalidity decisions, one of the most important changes introduced by the 1979 Act deserves to be given mention here. Under the previous wording of the Act, Secs. 78(1) and 79 were interpreted by the unanimous case law and by the majority of scholars as ascribing absolute effect (*erga omnes*) to a decision declaring the invalidity or the loss of rights of a patent, only in the event it had been rendered following an action taken by the public prosecutor of his own motion or if the action had been brought by a private party, but the decision having been rendered according to the conclusions of the public prosecutor.

In any other case it was a common notion that the decison should be effective only *inter partes* (theory of the so called 'double level of effectiveness')."

The Jenard Committee, therefore, could legitimately overlook the possibility of a defendant counterclaiming for revocation in the English sense, or a raising a defence of invalidity with *erge omnes* effect. Those became problems only with the accession of new contracting states, or the reform of patent law in the original states to turn what was previously a defence *in personam* into a binding judgment of invalidity *in rem*.

3–141   Before going on to consider practical objections to the option currently under consideration, one fallacy needs to be laid to rest: there is nothing inherently objectionable in the conclusion that an English court may decide in favour of a defendant that a registered intellectual property right is invalid, yet be unable to revoke it. That is already the situation, at least in principle, under domestic law. Invalidity may be raised as a defence in a patent infringement action and there is no obligation to counterclaim. If, contrary to almost invariable practice, an English court found itself seised of an infringement action in which there was a successful defence of invalidity but no counterclaim for revocation then it is hard to see any basis on which it could revoke a British patent, or on which any third party, not privy to the litigation, could rely on the *inter partes* finding of invalidity as *res judicata* in his favour.[54] Probably the most the court could do is follow the course which commended itself to Aldous J. in *Autopia Terakat v. Gwent Auto*[55] by making a declaration that certain claims were invalid and ordering the declaration to be entered on the Register.

Finally, the treatment of invalidity in United States law long corres-   **3–142** ponded to that in France and Italy. Invalidity could be raised as a defence in an infringement action (or as part of the claim in a declaratory action) but a finding of invalidity in *inter partes* litigation was not binding in subsequent litigation against another defendant: *Triplett v. Lowell.*[56] The rule, though not unworkable,[57] was obviously less than ideal in a country as litigious as America and in 1970 the Supreme Court held in *Blonder-Tongue v. University of Illinois*[58] that a declaratory judgment of invalidity rendered after the patentee had had a full and fair opportunity to litigate the validity of his patent created an estoppel in favour of the world at large, so that a declaratory judgment of invalidity was all but equivalent in effect to revocation.

Objections to option 4: amendment and effect of invalidity proceedings elsewhere

The main objection to this fourth option is likely to be that it   **3–143** represents an unacceptable intrusion into the sovereignty and economic welfare of a foreign state. That is certainly how it would have appeared to Aldous J., to judge from his observations in *Plastus v. 3M*.[59] However, once it is conceded that the Brussels Convention contemplates jurisdiction over actions for infringement of foreign registered intellectual property rights in at least some circumstances, then the issue ceases to be one of principle and becomes one merely of degree and perhaps even of expediency.

Another attractive but fallacious argument is embodied in the dictum   **3–144** by Aldous J. in *Plastus v. 3M* that "no man can infringe an invalid patent." This is rhetoric rather than reality,[60] and once it has been

---

[54] There have been suggestions that the court could revoke a patent of its own motion but they seem to have come to nothing. The high point is *Natural Colour Kinematograph v. Bioschemes* (1915) 32 R.P.C. 256, HL *per* Lord Parker but it is doubtful if even this is still the law. Compare Patents Act 1977, s. 72(1).

[55] [1991] F.S.R. 517 (Aldous J.).

[56] (1936) 297 U.S. 638, S.C. of U.S.A..

[57] One of the reasons advanced for retaining *Triplett v. Lowell* was the extreme divergence between the district courts of the various circuits, among which the most inept and inexperienced at trying infringement actions were generally the most hostile to patentees. Johnston, "The Draft European Patent Convention—A Commentary" (1963) 1 C.M.L.R. 17 proposed litigating European (*sc.* Community) patents on the American model, presumably with similar considerations in mind.

[58] (1970) 402 U.S. 313, S.C. of U.S.A..

[59] [1995] R.P.C. 438 (Aldous J.).

[60] After *Chiron v. Murex (No. 13)* [1996] F.S.R. 578 the defendants Murex were driven into receivership by the damages awarded against them for infringement of a patent which Aldous J. himself had held to be partially invalid.

rejected as an argument against entertaining infringement actions at all, it has no further relevance. Quite apart from the old law of licensee estoppel, invalidity is only a defence if it is raised as such, and it is not unusual for patents to be held invalid but for relief to be granted on the patent as amended. However, consideration of this issue does lead to a more serious problem, which is how the court of one contracting state should deal with an argument by the plaintiff in an infringement action that although his patent may be invalid in the form in which it stands, amendment to cure the defect should be allowed and would enable the plaintiff to obtain an injunction and perhaps recover damages.

3–145   Under the interpretation of Article 16(4) currently under consideration the court certainly could not allow amendment of a foreign patent, and it is perhaps unacceptably quixotic for it to imagine itself exercising a discretion which it did not in fact possess. Even so, the practical objection is not perhaps as serious as it might appear at first sight. The importance of amendment in English litigation is very largely an historical consequence of the literal technique of interpretation of patent claims practised in English law. Amendment seems to be much less of an issue in Continental jurisdictions, if it is an issue at all; perhaps because the more flexible the definition of the invention, the less need there has been to amend the precise terms of the claims. The other comment is that any inability to consider whether invalid claims might be rescued by amendment can only be to the detriment of the plaintiff. No one compelled him to sue outside the country of registration, and it is not drastically unfair that by exercising his choice of forum for his own advantage he should be at risk of suffering some corresponding detriment.

3–146   The other main disadvantages of this approach are also practical rather than ones of fundamental principle. As with any of the interpretations of the Convention which allow actions to be brought outside the state in which the patent is registered, it would apparently still be possible for the defendant to commence separate revocation proceedings in the appropriate national court or patent office. These would not be proceedings "involving the same cause of action" as the infringement action so as to require the revocation action to be stayed or dismissed under Article 21, and although they would apparently be a "related action" for the purposes of Article 22 it is unlikely that the revocation action would be stayed voluntarily because the court hearing the infringement action could not order revocation and to that extent would enjoy less than full jurisdiction; and because the court or patent office in the country of registration would almost certainly consider itself obliged to decide the question of validity as it affected the public generally.

3–147   On this basis it is possible that the court of the defendant's domicile might find the patent valid and infringed while in the country of registration it might be revoked before or after the decision in the infringement action. Would Article 27(3) then mean that the judgment of infringement would be unenforceable in the country of registration? In England the answer is not necessarily that it would. In *Poulton v.*

Adjustable Cover and Boiler Block Company[61] the defendant lost an infringement action and counterclaim for revocation but subsequently had the patent revoked on grounds not previously raised. Notwithstanding the proven and retrospective invalidity of the patent he was still ordered to pay the damages awarded in the infringement action.

Another problem is that it is against the public interest for patents to remain in force and on the register after they have been found invalid. However, there is a balance to be struck between the public interest in removing invalid patents from the register, and the public interest in subjecting the register exclusively to the jurisdiction of national courts. Some such tension is inherent in a system which combines any degree of extraterritorial infringement jurisdiction with Article 16(4). In the last resort, this option is no more offensive to the public interest than allowing the parties to take a multinational patent dispute to a single international arbitration able to decide infringement and invalidity with *inter partes* effect on a Continental or even Global scale.

Option 5: Jurisdiction also over counterclaims

The most radical and intrusive interpretation of Article 16(4) in the context of an infringement action would be to say that the court seised of an action for patent infringement, for instance under Article 2 or 5(3), could not only entertain the action as such but could also assume jurisdiction over any counterclaim for revocation, and if necessary revoke the patent and order the national patent office in question to remove it from the register. It is suggested that this would plainly be in breach of Article 16(4) on any credible interpretation of the relationship of the latter to the rest of the Brussels Convention. The Article cannot be concerned only with free-standing petitions or actions for revocation, and jurisdiction over a counterclaim is determined, subject to Article 6(3), in the same way as if the counterclaim were an action in its own right. In particular, the fact that consent or submission cannot override Article 16 means that there is no scope for the argument that the plaintiff implicitly invited the counterclaim by suing for infringement, thereby creating a jurisdiction which would not otherwise exist. In *Lieber v. Göbel*[62] it was taken for granted that jurisdiction over a counterclaim alleged to fall within Article 16(1) was to be decided in the same way as for an independent action. It also made no difference that the plaintiff only objected to the court's jurisdiction to hear the counterclaim on appeal.   **3–148**

If any such order were made then it would clearly be contrary to established notions of comity and the relevant national patent office would certainly refuse to give effect to it under Article 28 for breach of Article 16.[63] In principle the European Court of Justice would ultimately   **3–149**

---

[61] (1908) 25 R.P.C. 661 (Parker J.).

[62] Case C–292/93 [1994] E.C.R. I–2535.

[63] Art. 28 provides that a judgment "shall not be recognised" if it conflicts, *inter alia*, with Art. 16. The public policy of exception of Art. 27(1) may appear to be relevant, but see para. 8–125.

be able to decide what the patent office ought to do, but in practice it is hard to imagine any defendant being sufficiently concerned about the state of the patent register to take the case to appeal when he already had a finding of invalidity in his own favour, and the possibility of requesting a preliminary ruling only arises on appeal.

3–150 Fundamental problems also arise as to whether the court hearing the infringement action could hear a counterclaim for revocation if it lacked jurisdiction over the plaintiff by virtue of domicile under Article 2. The question of whether Article 6(3) or Article 16 prevails when a counterclaim is within the exclusive jurisdiction of another court is considered at paragraph 2–66, where it is suggested that Article 6(3) is subject to Article 16. Whether or not this is the case there is another obstacle to allowing a counterclaim for revocation under Article 6(3) in the requirement that the counterclaim should be on "the facts on which the original claim was based." Article 6(3) appears to require a closer connection between action and counterclaim than the concept of "related actions" for Article 22 or under English internal law. Unless one admits that validity was the basis of the original claim (which would have brought it within Article 16 in the first place) it is unrealistic to say that a counterclaim for revocation is ever based on the same facts as the infringement action.

The possible interpretations: their pro's and con's summarised

3–151 Assuming that infringement actions as such are within the terms of the Brussels Convention, and that *Coin Controls v. Suzo*[64] cannot be taken as the last word on the application of Article 16(4), then what are the options? They are summarised in the following table with the major characteristic pro's and con's of each.[65]

---

[64] [1997] F.S.R. 660 (Laddie J.).
[65] With the proviso that what is a pro to some may be a con to others.

Pro	Con
Refuse jurisdiction even over infringement as such	
Most consistent with international comity and pre-existing practice; Plaintiff and defendant know where they stand; No scope for forum shopping; Validity and infringement will be tried together (but only for one country) by single and most *conveniens* court.	Plainly wrong on the text of the Brussels Convention, Jenard and case law of the European Court of Justice; Effectively removes intellectual property infringement actions from the scope of the Brussels Convention, except for enforcement; No scope for multilateral infringement proceedings even if favoured by both parties; Has unacceptable implications for jurisdiction in infringement actions against non-Convention domiciled defendants; Inconsistent with Dutch and German practice; Inconsistent with judgments of Lloyd J. in *Pearce v. Ove Arup*, Laddie J. in *Coin Controls v. Suzo* and the Court of Appeal in *Fort Dodge v. Akzo Nobel.*
Refuse jurisdiction if validity put in issue	
Complies scrupulously with Articles 16(4) and 19; Consistent with one reading of Jenard; Preserves one aspect of international comity; Allows pan-European infringement proceedings in some circumstances; Pan-European jurisdiction cannot be imposed on the defendant; Favoured by Laddie J. in *Coin Controls v. Suzo* and by Laddie J. and the Court of Appeal in *Fort Dodge v. Akzo Nobel.*	Interprets Articles 16(4) and 19 too generously for provisions which are derogations; Inconsistent with spirit of Article 18; Arguably inconsistent with bulk of jurisprudence on Article 16(1); Neither plaintiff nor the court know where they stand at least until defence served, and possibly long afterwards; Other courts are embarrassed in applying Articles 21 and 22; No pan-European jurisdiction, even by consent, if validity a real issue; but a charter for unscrupulous defendants with no real attack on validity; Jurisdiction at risk of being displaced at least at any time up to trial; if not, then defendant prejudiced; Contrary to jurisprudence and practice of Dutch and German courts.

Pro	Con
Try infringement but not validity	
Respects Articles 16(4) and 19 and one aspect of international comity;	Highly unfair and prejudicial to defendant;
Some possibility of international jurisdiction and relief;	Contravenes *Danvaern v. Otterbeck*;
Jurisdiction of infringement court does not depend on outside or supervening event (though procedure, timetable and outcome ought to);	Creates multiplicity of proceedings;
	Substantial risks of inconsistency of interpretation and legal reasoning as a result of validity and infringement being split;
Corresponds to German national practice and pre-1968 Dutch practice;	Uncertain that court can stay own infringement proceedings pending foreign nullity proceedings;
Corresponds to 1975 Community Patent Convention.	Uncertain that final infringement judgment would be set aside by nullity in all circumstances;
	Rejected in context of Community Patent Convention;
	Rejected by Laddie J. in *Coin Controls v. Suzo*;
	The worst of all worlds.
Try infringement and invalidity as a defence *inter partes*	
Interprets Articles 16(4) and 19 narrowly, consistently with Court policy;	Interpretation of Article 16(4) and 19 too radical for Laddie J. in *Coin Controls v. Suzo* and for Laddie J. and the Court of Appeal in *Fort Dodge v. Akzo Nobel*;
Does not wholly ignore comity;	Takes liberties with international comity;
Invalidity as an *inter partes* defence known in pre-1968 French and Italian law;	Possibility of *in personam* finding of invalidity;
Validity and infringement will be tried together;	Hard to deal with discretionary amendment;
Protects substantive and procedural rights of defendant;	*Res judicata* effect uncertain, especially for third parties.
Corresponds more closely (as between parties) to 1985/9 Community Patent Convention;	
Corresponds to current Dutch practice, in fact and possibly in legal analysis;	
Corresponds to current German practice in the one Brussels Convention case to date.	
Try infringement action and counterclaim for revocation	
Validity and infringement will be tried together;	Drives a coach and horses through Articles 16(4) and 19;
Discretionary amendment issues could be addressed (though court will not be used to dealing with them);	Inconsistent with comity and *ordre public*;
	Almost certainly inconsistent with Jenard;
Public and third parties will know where they stand (though only if purported revocation is recognised).	National patent offices would certainly refuse to recognise judgment *in rem* and would be entitled to do so by virtue of Article 28;
	More objectionable than the previous option in theory, and likely to be no better in practice.

CHAPTER 4

COMMUNITY PATENTS, TRADE MARKS AND DESIGNS: THE INTERNATIONAL FRAMEWORK

A. HISTORICAL INTRODUCTION

The nature of Community patents, trade marks and designs

4–01   Since April 1, 1996 it has been possible to apply for registration of a Community trade mark effective throughout the common market and the first registrations of Community trade marks were announced on September 14, 1997. Unlike most previous attempts to simplify the international protection of intellectual property rights, the application matures into a single registration with a unitary character defined by Community law, rather than a bundle of national intellectual property rights each governed by a different system of law. The legislative basis is the Community Trade Mark Regulation[1] which establishes an "Office for Harmonisation of the Internal Market (trade marks and designs)" with power to register Community trade marks. The same Office will, in due course, grant Community registered designs.

4–02   In contrast, the Community Patent Convention has existed since 1975, but unlike the Community Trade Mark Regulation and the European Patent Convention it is not in force. The Convention, if and when it comes into force, will provide for the granting by the European Patent Office of a single patent valid for the whole of the European Community.[2] The Community Patent Convention is to be distinguished from the European Patent Convention, under which the European Patent Office entertains a single application for a "European patent" which, if granted, takes effect as a bundle of national patents for as many contracting states as are designated.

4–03   All these "Community" intellectual property rights are unitary rights for the whole of the European Union, existing by virtue of autonomous Community law and enforceable or revocable for the whole of the territory of the Union in a single action. The same will apply in due course to Community plant variety rights. This international character distinguishes them from traditional national intellectual property rights (including European patents) and requires a new international framework to deal with the unfamiliar situation of intellectual property rights being granted, litigated, enforced and invalidated on a Continental scale.

[1] Council Regulation 40/94 on the Community Trade Mark (December 20, 1993) [1994] O.J. L11/1.
[2] The E.C. Commission has now proposed to implement the Community patent by way of Regulation: see the *Green Paper on the Community Patent and the Patent System in Europe* COM(97) 31 final of June 24, 1997 and see para. 1–69, above.

The background to the Community Patent Convention, Community Trade Mark Regulation, etc.

In 1959, the then six member states of the European Community set **4–04**
up working parties in the fields of patents, trade marks and designs. In
1962, the working party responsible for patents, chaired by Dr Kurt
Haertel, published a Preliminary Draft Convention Relating to a European Patent Law which contemplated the establishment of a "European
Patent Office" as a Community institution, which would grant "European patents" on a Community-wide basis and with a unitary and
autonomous character. A European Patent Court would exercise final
instance jurisdiction. Work on this scheme was suspended between 1964
and 1969, and when it resumed it was on the basis that there would be
two parallel conventions: one open to any European state and providing
a centralised procedure for granting independent national patents in its
contracting states, the other confined to Community member states and
leading to a single European patent for the Common Market.[3]

The former proposal led to the publication of First and Second **4–05**
Preliminary Draft Conventions for a European System for the Grant of
Patents in 1970 and 1971 with explanatory reports. A diplomatic
conference was held at Munich in 1973 attended by delegations from 21
Western European states as participants; and the E.C. Commission, the
Council of Europe and various interested international and non-
governmental organisations as observers. This conference resulted in the
European Patent Convention of October 5, 1973 which entered into
force on October 7, 1977. The second parallel convention in contempla-
tion was rather slower to proceed, but preliminary draft Conventions
were published in 1970 and 1972. A draft Convention for the European
Patent for the Common Market was published in 1973 and a diplomatic
conference was held at Luxembourg in 1975.[4] The 1975 Luxembourg
Conference adopted the Convention for the European Patent for the
Common Market and related texts on December 15, 1975. Unlike the
Munich Conference, only the member states of the European Communities and the E.C. Commission attended the 1975 Conference as
participants with other interested states and organisations as observers.

The 1975 Luxembourg Conference had never expected that the **4–06**
Community Patent Convention (as it was generally called) would be
implemented immediately, but even so, progress in ratifying the Convention was unacceptably slow and Denmark and Ireland were unable to
ratify for constitutional reasons. The 1975 Convention had also provided
for a working party to be set up to make revised proposals for the
enforcement of Community patents. A second diplomatic conference
was held in Luxembourg in 1985 attended, as participants, by the

---

[3] My thanks go to Richard Pavry for his diligence in obtaining copies of the published
travaux préparatoires to the European and Community patent conventions.
[4] For a U.K. insight into the 1975 Conference and subsequent developments, there are
first-hand accounts from several participants in the Report of the House of Lords Select
Committee on the European Communities: *A European Community Patent* (1986).

Commission, the 10 member states of the Community and Spain and Portugal, which were to join the Community in 1986. Other states and organisations were present as observers. This conference adopted a new Protocol on Litigation and a Protocol on the Common Appeal Court which, together with the Community Patent Convention and a Protocol on Amendments to the latter, formed the major parts of a new Agreement relating to Community Patents. However the conference allowed old disputes about working languages and money to be reopened, and failed to resolve the constitutional problems of Denmark and Ireland or agree a timetable for the implementation of the Convention. The latter was postponed to a third Luxembourg conference in 1989, when it was decided that if all else failed, the Convention would come into force initially for less than the whole Community. That conference adopted with minimal further changes the Agreement relating to Community Patents (which now consolidated the 1985 amendments to the Community Patent Convention with the 1975 text), a Protocol on entry into force and a Joint Declaration. Notwithstanding the 1989 compromise, the Community Patent Convention still has not entered into force. A further diplomatic conference at Lisbon in 1992 failed to solve the outstanding problems and decided against recommending that the Convention should initially enter into force for less than all 12 of the then member states of the Community.[5]

4–07   The patents working party of 1962 had been the only one of the three to make substantial progress. In 1973, however, progress on the European Patent Convention encouraged the Commission to publish a Preliminary Draft Convention for a European Trade Mark as it stood in 1964, when work had halted, but the proposed European Trade Mark was not immediately taken any further. In 1976 the Commission published a Memorandum on the Creation of an EEC Trade Mark[6] and a working paper on its power to do so in 1979.[7] In 1980 the Commission published a formal proposal for a Council Regulation on the Community Trade Mark and in 1984 it published a revised draft. Political problems relating to the working languages of the Community Trade Mark Office, and its location, delayed implementation but the Regulation was finally adopted, with many revisions, on December 20, 1993.

4–08   The rest of this section describes in more detail how the institutional provisions of these various proposals developed with time, and their relationship with the Community legal order.[8] The current state of the

---

[5] See Scordamaglia, "The Common Appeal Court and the Future of the Community Patent Following the Luxembourg Conference" part I (1991) 22 I.I.C. 334 and part II (1991) 22 I.I.C. 458; Neukom, "What Price the Community Patent?" [1992] E.I.P.R. 111. The E.C. Commission has now proposed to implement the Community patent by way of Regulation: see n. 2, and see para. 1–69 above.

[6] *Bulletin of the European Communities*, Supplement 8/76. See para. 4–23 below.

[7] [1980] E.I.P.R. 120 with comments by Morcom at [1980] E.I.P.R. 359.

[8] In view of the sheer number of the various draft instruments referred to below, and the fact that they have all along since been superseded, as has the original 1975 version of the Community Patent Convention, it is not considered worthwhile to give references to individual articles except for instruments currently in force, or for the draft in the case of the Design Regulation.

institutional law of the Community patent and trade mark is described in detail in Sections B and C respectively.

In comparison to patents and trade marks, Community registered **4-09** designs and plant variety rights have had relatively short histories and controversy has centred on substantive law. A Commission Green Paper on designs was published in 1991, and a draft Regulation in 1993. At the time of writing, progress on the Design Regulation appears to have become stalled until a political wrangle over the treatment of spare parts in the parallel Designs Directive is resolved. A draft Regulation on Plant Variety Rights was published in 1990, with a revised draft in 1993, and the Regulation on Community Plant Variety Rights was adopted on July 27, 1994.[9]

Early proposals leading to the Community Patent Convention[10]

The original 1962 Draft Convention Relating to a European Patent **4-10** Law[11] would have created a European Patent Office[12] and a European Patent Court. The latter might have been independent, or attached to another existing international court, presumably the European Court of Justice. The Office would grant European patents, which would have a unitary and autonomous character and which would exist according to a common system of law known as European patent law. A complication is that there would have been both "provisional patents," examined only for obvious lack of novelty or patentability, and "final patents" which would have undergone a more thorough examination on application by the patentee within five years after grant of the provisional patent. Patent protection would begin on publication of the provisional patent, but a judgment against infringement could not be issued until confirmation of the provisional patent into a final patent. Appeals by applicants against decisions of the Examining Divisions would lie to Boards of Appeal with a limited further right of appeal the European Patent Court.

[9] Council Regulation 2100/94 on the Community Plant Variety Right (July, 27, 1994) [1994] O.J. L277/1. For the substantive law of all these Community intellectual property rights (except the Community Patent) see Tritton, *Intellectual Property in Europe* (1996).

[10] See generally Oudemans, *The Draft European Patent Convention* (1963); Singer, "The European Patent Enters a New Phase" (1970) 1 I.I.C. 19 and annex; Haertel, "The Draft Conventions for the European System for the Grant of Patents and for the European Patent for the Common Market" (1970) 1 I.I.C. 289 and (1971) Ind. Prop. 82; van Empel, "European Patent Conventions" (1972) 9 C.M.L.R. 13; Thompson, "The Draft Convention for a European Patent" (1973) 22 I.C.L.Q. 51; Ladas, *Patents, Trademarks and Related Rights: National and International Protection* (1975), Chaps. 19 and 20; Pennington ed., *European Patents at the Crossroads* (1976); Report of the House of Lords Select Committee on the European Communities: *A European Community Patent* (1986); and Benyamini, *Patent Infringement in the European Community* (1993), Chap. 2 which gives further citations.

[11] Published in an unofficial English translation by HMSO. Oudemans, *The Draft European Patent Convention* (1963) contains the French and (unofficial) English texts and a commentary.

[12] In what follows, it should be borne in mind that these early proposals correspond more closely to the *Community* Patent Convention, and not to the *European* Patent Convention. The terminology may confuse.

4–11   Applications for revocation of a granted European patent would always be made to the European Patent Office. There was no opposition procedure as such, either before or after grant, and national courts had no jurisdiction at all over validity. Applications for revocation of a "final" European Patent would be heard by a Revocation Board, from which there would be a general right of appeal on fact and law to the European Patent Court. The European Patent Office could also entertain applications for declarations of non-infringement and there was provision for Revocation Boards to act by consent as "arbitration tribunals" on the scope of protection of a European patent with appeal to the European Patent Court. Apart from these provisions, the Office did not have any infringement jurisdiction.

4–12   Infringement actions as such were to be heard by national courts, but the national court had no jurisdiction over validity and a defendant either had to commence revocation proceedings in the Office or concede validity. Infringement proceedings would normally be stayed pending a final decision on revocation. The national court could make what was, in effect, a reference for a preliminary ruling on a point of law to the European Patent Court and in the case of a court of last resort was obliged to do so. A national court could also require the European Patent Office to deliver a technical opinion on the patent in question. Apart from these provisions, infringement and validity were essentially to be bifurcated on the German model with separate first instance jurisdiction and separate lines of appeal.[13]

4–13   The proposals in the 1962 draft effectively lapsed,[14] but First and Second Preliminary Draft Conventions for the European Patent for the Common Market were published[15] with brief reports in 1970 and 1972, in parallel with preliminary drafts for what became the European Patent

[13] See Johnston, "The Draft European Patent Convention—A Commentary" (1963) 1 C.M.L.R. 17; Haardt, "Infringement Procedure According to the Draft Convention Relating to a European Patent Law" (1963) 1 C.M.L.R. 202; Froschmeier "Some Aspects of the Draft Convention Relating to a European Patent Law" (1963) 12 I.C.L.Q. 886. The first two criticise the proposed litigation procedure from opposite perspectives, though both agree that a convention drafted principally by representatives of national patent offices might be expected to be deficient in its proposals for substantive patent law and litigation procedure. Johnston (an English patent Q.C.) insists that the defendant must be allowed to challenge validity (though only with *inter partes* effect) by way of defence in infringement proceedings without having to commence revocation proceedings in a central office. Haardt (a Dutch professor) would preserve the exclusive jurisdiction of the office over validity, but opposes any stay of infringement actions pending office revocation proceedings and offers the opinion that the defendant in an infringement action would hardly be harmed by the court entering judgment against him while the revocation was still unresolved.

[14] According to Savignon's *Report on the First Preliminary Draft Convention for the European Patent for the Common Market* in 1970, there was a 1965 draft which Savignon's working party used as a basis for the 1970 Preliminary Draft Convention. The present Author has been unable to trace this, but it must have been similar to the 1962 draft since Savignon's 1970 draft gives the Article numbers of the 1965 draft for the purposes of comparison and they correspond closely to the 1962 draft, though not so closely as to suggest that the 1962 and 1965 drafts were identical.

[15] Both were published in English by HMSO as *Patents in the Common Market*.

Convention. It was assumed that the latter would already be in force and the European Patent Office functioning before the Community patent became a reality. For present purposes no distinction need be made between the first and second preliminary drafts and they have a common numbering scheme. Compared to the 1962 draft, the proposed European Patent Court was abandoned and its functions divided between the European Court of Justice and appellate boards in the European Patent Office. There was an even more emphatic division of responsibility than before between national courts, which would determine infringement, and the Office, which would decide validity. Only at the level of the European Court of Justice might a single court ever be seised of both issues, and that would be a result of pure coincidence.

The European Patent Office was to be given special organs for the **4–14** Community patent in the form of a Patent Administration Division, Revocation Divisions and Revocation Boards. Application, examination and opposition would not be affected except that designation of any one Community state automatically operated as an application for a Community patent. In the case of Community patents alone, applications for revocation could be made to the Revocation Divisions[16] with a general right of appeal to the Revocation Boards. A limited further right of appeal to the European Court of Justice existed for substantial infringement of formal and procedural rules, or for infringement of the Convention and provisions made under it if a higher decision was necessary to ensure uniformity of law or to decide a point of fundamental importance.

The Office was to have no jurisdiction over infringement. National **4–15** courts had jurisdiction over infringement actions as such, but had no jurisdiction over validity and were obliged to treat the patent as valid until it had been revoked. Infringement proceedings would normally be stayed pending a decision on validity. There was provision for national courts hearing infringement actions to request preliminary rulings on the Convention and implementing legislation from the European Court of Justice, and a reference was compulsory by courts of last resort.

These proposals were reproduced without major variations in the **4–16** Draft Convention for the European Patent for the Common Market which was the basic text for discussion at the 1975 Luxembourg Diplomatic Conference.[17] The right of appeal to the European Court of Justice from the Revocation Boards was slightly widened. One new proposal in that draft which did not proceed any further was that the European Patent Office, when it upheld a Community patent, should automatically give an opinion on the extent of protection of the patent if there were infringement proceedings in a national court which had been stayed pending its decision on validity.

---

[16] The second preliminary draft convention, Art. 59a, precluded lodging an application for revocation during the opposition period or while an opposition was pending. The provisions of the European Patent Convention dealing with oppositions were among the last to be finalised.

[17] The 1973 Draft with some further amendments.

Litigation under the original Community Patent Convention[18]

4–17   The Community Patent Convention as adopted in 1975 quite closely followed these proposals.[19] No single court was intended to have jurisdiction over both the infringement and the validity of Community patents. Infringement actions had to be brought before national courts, but validity could only be determined by the European Patent Office. If a defendant to an infringement action wished to contest the validity of the Community patent, he would have had to commence separate revocation proceedings in the EPO, pending which the infringement action would have been stayed.[20] At the time the Convention was signed, this may have seemed the best compromise between respecting the interests of litigants and entrusting the validity of Community patents to a single Community institution, but it was always clear that the solution would involve additional expense and delay because of the separation of proceedings between two institutions in different countries. It was also likely that different and possibly contradictory interpretations of a single patent might be given by the different institutions and that on matters of infringement national courts in the various member states would be influenced by their existing practices and might differ significantly from one another despite applying a law which was supposed to be uniform.[21] Recognising these problems and the fact that no Community patents were likely to be granted for some years, the signatories provided for a working party to be established to propose a protocol on the litigation of Community patents which was intended to be implemented within 10 years of the Community Patent Convention itself.

---

[18] This paragraph and those that follow incorporate material from Wadlow, "The Community Patent Appeal Court" (1986) 11 E.L. Rev. 295.

[19] For litigation procedure under the 1975 Convention and the underlying policy decisions see Ellis, "Trying Infringement Actions" in Pennington, ed., *European Patents at the Crossroads* (1976) and Stauder "The Future of Patent Infringement Proceedings in Europe" (1975) 6 I.I.C. 168.

[20] The U.K. insisted on a reservation, contained in Art. 90 of the 1975 Community Patent Convention, which in effect allowed the trial court limited jurisdiction to rule on the validity of the Community patent; but only by consent and with relief being confined to the one contracting state. A previous decision of the EPO upholding validity was binding on its facts. Art. 90 was to have effect for 15 years at most. See the Report of the House of Lords Select Committee on the European Communities: *A European Community Patent* (1986).

[21] Though the European Patent Convention, Art. 25, already provided a mechanism independent of the Community Patent Convention for the European Patent Office to deliver a "technical opinion" at the request of a competent national court trying an infringement or revocation action. It was in the discretion of the national trial court whether to request such an opinion, and what effect to give to it; and in practice the Article has been used rarely, if at all. Since Art. 25 provides for the opinion to be delivered by an Examining Division it would necessarily be delivered by a different organ of the EPO to that entertaining revocation proceedings under the Community Patent Convention.

The Protocol on Litigation

The working party was faced with three conflicting objectives.[22] The **4–18** first was that the Community patent should truly be one for the whole of the common market, so that it was essential not only that it should be created, revoked and amended for the Community as a whole and not state-by-state as for the European Patent, but also that it should be interpreted uniformly throughout the Community despite the differing legal traditions of the member states. The second was that the enforcement of Community patents should not be prohibitively expensive, unfair to one party, or inconsistent with the principles of existing Community law such as the Brussels Convention. The third was to ensure that the Protocol was constitutionally acceptable to all the member states and was not seen as requiring an unacceptable loss or transference of sovereignty. The original scheme of the Community Patent Convention was biased towards the third of these objectives at the expense of causing an unacceptable degree of inconvenience to the parties, especially the defendant, and without really solving the problem of different interpretations being given to the patent itself or the infringement provisions of the Community Patent Convention in different courts. The revised Protocol reflected the fact that most member states were by then prepared to accept that a national court, as opposed to a Community institution, could not only enforce the Community patent throughout the common market but could also revoke or amend it *in toto*. A patent proprietor would in principle be able to bring one action in one court in respect of infringements in all member states, but always at the risk of that court revoking his patent in its entirety if it were found invalid.

The major institutional innovation of the 1985 Protocol on Litigation **4–19** was intended to be the establishment of a Community Patent Appeal Court (the "Common Appeal Court" or more conveniently COPAC) which would hear appeals directly from first instance courts in member states. COPAC was to be a new Community institution rather than a division of the European Patent Office or the European Court of Justice and would wholly supersede existing national courts of second instance in the application of the law of Community patents. The second instance jurisdiction of COPAC allowed the working party to entrust defences of invalidity as well as issues of infringement, at first instance, to national courts which would have power to enforce, or revoke, the Community patent for the whole common market. The supplementary role of the European Patent Office—in addition to granting Community patents and hearing oppositions—was effectively reduced to deciding freestanding revocation or limitation proceedings, from which an appeal would also lie to COPAC.

---

[22] See the Scordamaglia Report, the Report of the House of Lords Select Committee on the European Communities: *A European Community Patent* (1986), and Stauder, "Thoughts on the Development of the European Patent Infringement Procedures" [1980] E.I.P.R. 253 for progress between 1975 and 1985. See also Haardt, "The Setting Up of a Court of Appeal for Community Patents" (1985) 16 I.I.C. 332.

4-20   The scheme, adopted by the Luxembourg Diplomatic Conference in 1985 and affirmed in 1989, offered three advantages over its predecessor: it was reasonably fair as between plaintiff and defendant, it made the litigation of a Community patent at first instance no more expensive or difficult in principle than that of a national or European patent, and it went a long way to ensuring that the law of Community patents would genuinely be uniform in practice as well as theory. Its disadvantages were that patent proprietors were expected to entrust the validity of Community patents in their entirety to a number of first instance courts in which they could not reasonably be expected to have any confidence; the need for a new and unproven Community institution in the form of COPAC; and the possibility that Community patent cases taken to appeal would be slow, expensive and unpredictable—even in comparison to exisitng practice. These disadvantages were thought to be more than compensated for by the relative simplicity of first instance procedure compared to that originally proposed in the 1975 Convention and above all by the fact that multiple infringement actions in the various member states would no longer be necessary.

Related documentation: the Scordamaglia Report

4-21   A commentary on the Community Patent Convention and its related texts was prepared by Sig. Vincenzo Scordamaglia who supervised the secretariat of the three inter-governmental conferences in 1975, 1985 and 1989 and was responsible for the *travaux préparatoires*. Compared to, say, the Jenard and Schlosser Reports on the Brussels Convention the Scordamaglia Report is not as significant as an authority in its own right. It covered a very wide range of issues of both substantive and procedural law; there is no express legislative reference to its use and it is less readily available, though once found it is much more accessible than the *travaux préparatoires* themselves. None the less, the Report is an invaluable aid to understanding an extremely complicated series of negotiations and there are places where consideration of the bare text of the Agreement relating to Community Patents itself, without the Report or the *travaux préparatoires*, might easily lead to an interpretation which was not that intended.

4-22   The Scordamaglia Report summarised the scheme of the Protocol on Litigation and its expected advantages as follows:

> "The Agreement also made major changes to the 1975 Convention on the question of reviewing patent validity.
>
> The strict division between revocation actions—before the EPO departments—and infringement actions—to be heard by national courts—has been dropped and replaced by a litigation system which should be so effective as to constitute one of the major pluses of the Community patent.
>
> There will be two ways of reviewing a patent's validity:
> — a direct action before the EPO revocation divisions, or
> — a counterclaim for revocation by the defendant in an infringement action.

In both cases the ruling may be challenged before the Common Appeal Court as the body of second and final instance on validity.

No other plea for revocation can be entertained, and if such a plea is made the court in question must consider the patent as valid.

The other EPO procedure is for limitation. This enables the patent proprietor to surrender some of the scope of his protection to ward off reactions from third parties, with the guarantee of a procedure enabling the EPO to find in the public interest that the patent as limited continues to meet the conditions for patentability.

The system of litigation thus established, and particularly the Protocol on Litigation which is an integral part of the Agreement, provides effective protection against infringement. Every Contracting State designates one or more specialised courts, the 'Community patent courts' of first and second instance, with territorial and substantive jurisdiction over all infringement actions relating to Community patents.

Precise rules on international jurisdiction enable the State whose courts have jurisdiction to be identified in each case. The patent proprietor has a choice between the jurisdiction in which infringement occurred or was threatened and another jurisdiction, as a rule that of the defendant's domicile. This second jurisdiction—readily establishable by means of supplementary criteria even if the defendant is not domiciled within the Community—has the great advantage that the court's substantive jurisdiction then covers any act of infringement committed or threatened within the territory of any Contracting State. The rulings of a Community patent court of first instance are appealable, in accordance with its national law, to the Community patent court of second instance. At this stage the appeal procedure divides into two:

— the main part, involving the patent's effects and validity, is heard by the Common Appeal Court whose ruling is not challengeable in any subsequent proceedings,

— the national part, involving any other forms of appeal, penalties (prohibition of acts of infringement, damages etc.) and court costs, is handled by the national court.

The ruling of the Community patent court of second instance is in turn appealable under national law, but not in respect of any matters decided by the Common Appeal Court.

The provisional and protective measures which are very important for patent protection may be ordered by any court with jurisdiction under national law, but the Community patent courts with general jurisdiction may order measures effective also in the other Contracting States.

The judgments of Community patent courts, and the provisional and protective measures, are recognised and enforced in the other Contracting States in accordance with the 1968 Brussels Convention on Jurisdiction and Enforcement applicable to all civil and commercial matters."

The origins and development of the Community Trade Mark Regulation

4–23   The origin of the Community Trade Mark Regulation is ultimately the Preliminary Draft Convention for a European Trade Mark of 1964.[23] This would have established a European Trade Mark Office and a European Trade Mark Court. The latter might have been independent, or attached to another existing international court—presumably either the European Court of Justice or the European Patent Court contemplated by the contemporary Preliminary Draft Patent Convention. European trade marks would be granted by the European Trade Mark Office after examination on both absolute and relative grounds and would have a unitary and autonomous effect throughout the Community. The Office would entertain oppositions, but only by national intellectual property offices of contracting states[24] or by proprietors of prior trade marks and other prior rights. There would be a right of appeal to Boards of Appeal, with a limited further right of appeal to the European Trade Mark Court for violation of essential formal and procedural rules, or for violation of the Convention or Regulations when a higher decision was necessary to ensure uniformity of law or to decide a point of fundamental importance.

4–24   Both infringement and invalidity would normally be dealt with at first instance in national courts. The Office had jurisdiction over oppositions as such and applications for declarations of non-infringement, but it had no other contentious first instance jurisdiction. The court hearing the infringement action had jurisdiction to hear a counterclaim for a declaration that the European trade mark was invalid or had lapsed.[25] National courts also had first instance jurisdiction to entertain applications for declarations of lapse or for revocation of European trade marks. National courts hearing infringement proceedings could make references for preliminary rulings to the European Trade Mark Court and were obliged to do so in the case of courts of last instance.

4–25   The treatment of appeals in the preliminary draft convention is particularly interesting. Appeals in respect of validity would lie from national courts hearing applications or counterclaims for revocation or lapse directly and exclusively to the European Trade Mark Office, where they would be heard by Revocation Boards. There would be a limited right of further appeal from the Revocation Boards to the European Trade Mark Court in the same circumstances as from a Board of Appeal. Appeals on the issue of infringement were not separately provided for, and would be to national courts of second instance. The possibility (or requirement, in the case of a court of final instance) of the

---

[23] Although work on the draft was abandoned in 1964, it was only published in 1973. See van Empel "Now a Trade Mark for Europe?" (1975) 12 C.M.L.R. 27.

[24] And then only on absolute grounds of invalidity.

[25] A complication for trade marks was that, within a state, jurisdiction over infringement and validity might be split between different courts but in any event jurisdiction over validity was kept at national level. In the case of the 1962 preliminary draft for patents, the court hearing the infringement action never had jurisdiction to determine validity but had to defer to the EPO.

national court making a preliminary reference to the European Trade Mark Court would provide a measure of uniformity in respect of the issues of infringement.

In 1976 the Commission published a detailed *Memorandum on the Creation of an EEC Trade Mark*.[26] Section D.XIII[27] dealt relatively briefly with cancellation and invalidity proceedings and section D.XVI[28] dealt with infringement actions. So far as invalidity and cancellation were concerned, the Memorandum acknowledged that the proposals of the 1964 draft needed to be reconsidered, not least because of the objections to an essentially administrative body hearing appeals from national courts. Instead, the Memorandum proposed to keep the jurisdiction of national courts completely separate from that of the proposed EEC Trade Mark Office. The latter would have exclusive jurisdiction over invalidity with *erga omnes* effect and only the Office would be able to remove a mark from the Register. It was left as an open question whether national courts would have jurisdiction to declare a trade mark invalid with *inter partes* effect in the context of an infringement action.[29] In any event the European Court of Justice would have appellate jurisdiction over the EEC Trade Mark Office, and would hear preliminary references from national courts.

4–26

Section D.XVI of the 1976 Memorandum on enforcement in infringement actions essentially repeated the proposals of the 1964 draft with the proviso that they needed to be adapted to conform to the 1968 Brussels Convention. In view of the new proposals of Section D.XIII, the Memorandum also proposed that further consideration should be given to whether invalidity should be allowed to be raised as a defence or counterclaim in infringement proceedings. The Memorandum concluded that there were no overriding objections to allowing a defence that the EEC trade mark was invalid.

4–27

The 1976 Memorandum had not gone so far as to propose that national trade marks should be abolished, but it had certainly contemplated that national trade mark systems might be wholly superceded by the EEC system after a transitional period. In 1979 the Commission responded to criticisms of the 1976 Memorandum by publishing a Working Paper.[30] The Working Paper argued that the 1964 proposal for a European Trade Mark *Convention* based on the original proposals of the committee of experts in 1960 was not inconsistent with the constitutional propriety of a *Regulation* under Article 235 E.C.; and that neither

4–28

---

[26] Doc. SEC(76) 2462, final July 7th, 1976, Supplement 8/76 to the *Bulletin of the European Communities*; also published at (1976) 7 I.I.C. 367. The proposal was for a Community Trade Mark Regulation, but at this stage there was no draft Regulation as such. See Beier, "Objectives and Guiding Principles of European Trade Mark Law" (1977) 8 I.I.C. 1; van Empel, "The EEC Trade Mark Memorandum" (1978) 15 C.M.L.R. 55.

[27] Paras 133–134.

[28] Paras 155–158.

[29] The Memorandum refers to the national court deciding the "legal force of the EEC Trade Mark" which is presumably a euphemism for its validity. Compare Section D.XVI below and Art. 90 of the 1975 Community Patent Convention.

[30] Commission Working Paper *Community Trade Mark—Power of EEC Commission to Enact CTM Regulation* III/D/1294/79 also published in edited form at [1980] E.I.P.R. 120.

harmonisation of national laws by Directive nor a separate international convention would be adequate.

4–29   The first draft Regulation for the Community Trade Mark of 1980 abandoned many of the 1964 proposals. It retained the Community Trade Mark Office which would examine applications on absolute grounds only. The Office would also hear pre-grant oppositions on relative grounds, from which an appeal would lie to Boards of Appeal with a limited further appeal on law only to the European Court of Justice for want of jurisdiction, infringement of an essential procedural requirement, infringement of the Treaty of Rome, the Regulation or other applicable law (except national law), or for misuse of power.

4–30   The Office had concurrent jurisdiction with national courts to entertain applications for revocation or invalidation. Infringement actions, counterclaims for revocation or invalidation or applications for revocation or invalidation could all be made to national courts with appeals to national second instance courts in the usual way. There were provisions for either the Office or a national court to stay its proceedings to avoid multiplicity. A national court could require a party to submit the issue of validity to the Office, but apart from this and the general jurisdiction of the European Court of Justice under Article 177 E.C. there was little attempt to provide any mechanism for centralisation or for ensuring uniformity of decisions. In particular, there was no central appeal court and the Office would have no role in appeals from national courts. The validity of a Community trade mark would be determined either by a succession of Community institutions starting with the Opposition or Cancellation Divisions of the Office, or by successive national courts, with little possibility of interaction between the two hierarchies and with the choice between the two probably lying with the first person to challenge validity. The relevant provisions were largely carried over into the 1984 draft Regulation and correspond quite closely to the position under the Community Trade Mark Regulation as it is in force.[31]

The case law of the European Court of Justice

4–31   It is notable that the Community was initially uncharacteristically hesitant in legislating for intellectual property.[32] Drafts for the Community patent and trade mark in the 1960's contemplated that Community-wide rights could only be created pursuant to specific new treaties between the member states and with national intellectual property rights continuing to exist in parallel. Even in the area of harmonisation of law, which might seem less controversial, the Community was relatively passive. The Strasbourg Convention on the Unification of Certain Points of Substantive Patent Law was concluded within the Council of Europe. The European Patent Convention was

[31] The principal difference is that only the Office can entertain free-standing revocation or invalidation proceedings.

[32] For literature, now of historical interest only, see citations above and in Benyamini, *Patent Infringement in the European Community* (1993), Chap. 2.

negotiated by the member states individually, with the Community having the same observer status as the Council of Europe or WIPO. In 1975, the adoption of the Community Patent Convention implicitly acknowledged that the same result could not be achieved by Regulation. In 1979, the Commission felt that the Community's competence to create a European Trade Mark System was sufficiently uncertain or controversial to be suitable material for a working paper.[33] It is not until after this 1979 paper that one finds the Community simultaneously making concrete proposals for the creation of Community-wide intellectual property rights by Regulation, and for the harmonisation of existing national intellectual property law by Directive. This route, rather than that of ad hoc conventions, was followed for trade marks, designs and plant variety rights[34] and has now been proposed for patents in place of the unratified Community Patent Convention.[35] Harmonisation on its own has been pursued for copyright, supplementary protection certificates, semiconductor topologies, databases, biotechnological inventions and much more.

Since the Community was relatively slow to legislate in the field of substantive intellectual property law, the case law of the European Court of Justice on its competence to do so is predominantly recent. In Opinion 1/94 *Re the Uruguay Round Treaties*[36] the Court dealt with the power of the Community to enter into international treaties relating to intellectual property. For present purposes, the treaty of interest is the Agreement on Trade Related Aspects of Intellectual Property Rights or TRIPs. The World Trade Organisation Agreement and related treaties, including TRIPs, had been signed by the 12 individual member states as well as by the Commission. The Commission claimed it had exclusive competence to conclude the WTO Agreement and that the member states should not have signed. It applied for opinions from the European Court of Justice as to whether it had competence to conclude the WTO Agreement, and in particular TRIPs, and whether its competence as to the latter was exclusive. The Court rejected the Commission's claim to sole competence, and did not expressly answer whether it was jointly competent with the member states. The degree of harmonisation of intellectual property rights already achieved within the Community would not be prejudiced by the member states continuing to participate

4–32

---

[33] "Community Trade Mark: Power of the EEC Commission to Enact CTM Regulation" [1980] E.I.P.R. 120 reproducing Commission Working Paper III/D/1294/79. See also Hobbs, "Community Trade Mark Regulation: Validity a Massive Gamble" [1979] E.I.P.R. 231 and Morcom, "The Legitimacy of a European Trade Mark System" [1980] E.I.P.R. 359. It should be borne in mind that the original Commission proposals were more radical in their effect on national rights than the Community Trade Mark Regulation as adopted.

[34] Reading between the lines of the 1979 Working Paper, it is obvious that the Commission was determined the outflank the difficulties which had arisen from the fact that the Community Patent Convention was an international treaty in its own right, and so to play down the original reasons for proceeding by that route and not by Community secondary legislation.

[35] See the *Green Paper on the Community Patent and the Patent System in Europe* COM(97) 31 final of June 24, 1997 and see para. 1–69 above.

[36] [1994] E.C.R. I–5267; [1995] 1 C.M.L.R. 205.

in international negotiations. However, in reaching this conclusion the Court confirmed that the Community had power to create new rights as well as to harmonise national intellectual property law, and cited the Community Trade Mark Regulation as an example:

> "It should be noted here that, at the level of internal legislation, the Community is competent, in the field of intellectual property, to harmonise national laws pursuant to Articles 100 and 100a and may use Article 235 as the basis for creating new rights superimposed on national rights, as it did in Council Regulation 40/94 on the Community trade mark. Those measures are subject to voting rules (unanimity in the case of Articles 100 and 235) or rules of procedure (consultation of the Parliament in the case of Articles 100 and 235, the joint decision-making procedure in the case of Article 100a) which are different from those applicable under Article 113.
>
> If the Community were to be recognised as having exclusive competence to enter into agreements with non-member countries to harmonise the protection of intellectual property and, at the same time, to achieve harmonisation at Community level, the Community institutions would be able to escape the internal constraints to which they are subject in relation to procedures and to rules as to voting."

4–33 The reasoning of the Court in Opinion 1/94 *Re the Uruguay Round Treaties* was amplified in *Spain v. Council (Supplementary Protection Certificates)*[37] where the Kingdom of Spain challenged the Supplementary Protection Certificate Regulation,[38] requiring member states to grant the proprietors of certain pharmaceutical patents equivalent protection for a period after the patent expired, to compensate for regulatory delays in marketing. The challenge went both to the competence of the Community in intellectual property generally, and to the fact that supplementary protection certificates were patents in all but name.

> "[T]he Court must examine whether Articles 222 and 36 of the EEC Treaty reserve the power to regulate substantive patent law for the national legislature, thereby excluding any Community action in the matter.
>
> In that respect, the Court held in its judgment in *Commission v. United Kingdom*, cited above (paragraphs 16 and 17), that, as Community law stands, the provisions on patents have not yet been the subject of unification at Community level or in the context of approximation of laws and that, in those circumstances, it is for the national legislature to determine the conditions and rules regarding the protection conferred by patents.

[37] Case C–350/92 [1995] E.C.R. I–1985.
[38] Council Regulation 1768/92 on the Creation of a Supplementary Protection Certificate for Medicinal Products (June 18, 1992) [1992] O.J. L182/1.

However, it added that the provisions of the Treaty—and in particular Article 222, which provides that the Treaty does not in any way prejudice the rules in Member States governing the system of property ownership—cannot be interpreted as reserving to the national legislature, in relation to industrial and commercial property, the power to adopt measures which would adversely affect the principle of free movement of goods within the common market as provided for and regulated by the Treaty (paragraph 18 of the same judgment).

Thus, far from endorsing the argument that rules concerning the very existence of industrial property rights fall within the sole jurisdiction of the national legislature, the Court was anticipating the unification of patent provisions or harmonization of the relevant national legislation.

The Court followed similar reasoning in relation to Article 36 of the Treaty. That provides, in particular, that the provisions of Articles 30 to 34 shall not preclude prohibitions or restrictions justified on grounds of the protection of industrial and commercial property, but that such prohibitions or restrictions shall not constitute a means of arbitrary discrimination or a disguised restriction on trade between Member States.

In its judgment in Case 35/76 *Simmenthal v. Italian Minister for Finance* [1976] ECR 1871, paragraph 14, the Court held that Article 36 is not designed to reserve certain matters to the exclusive jurisdiction of Member States but permits national laws to derogate from the principle of the free movement of goods to the extent to which such derogation is and continues to be justified for the attainment of the objectives referred to in that article.

It follows that neither Article 222 nor Article 36 of the Treaty reserves a power to regulate substantive patent law to the national legislature, to the exclusion of any Community action in the matter."

Prospects for the Community Trade Mark and Community Patent

Spain v. Council[39] confirms (if only *obiter*) that the Community Trade Mark Regulation is *intra vires*, and it is a matter of fact that the Community Trade Mark Office is operational, and receiving a far greater volume of applications than it had expected. Since the Community Trade Mark competes with national trade marks issued on individual national applications or centrally through the Madrid Protocol, it may be assumed that industry has weighed the advantages of a single registration against the disadvantages and concluded that the Community system is at least worth a try. **4–34**

In contrast, it may be doubted if the Community Patent Convention in its present form will ever be implemented. The case law of the European **4–35**

[39] Case C–350/92 [1995] E.C.R. I–1985.

Court of Justice as it has developed over the past two decades has proved that the continuing existence of national patents need not be inconsistent with the functioning of the single market. Industry is unimpressed with a system which appears markedly more expensive than at present, especially in translation costs, without obvious countervailing advantages. The European Patent Office is successful to a degree that could hardly have been predicted in 1975, and the system is perceived to work reasonably well in its present form. Such problems as it has would not be removed by bringing the Community Patent Convention into effect alongside it. The political difficulties of deciding on a seat for the proposed Common Appeal Court, allocating revenue and expenses, and reopening the issue of the number of working languages in the EPO remain as intractable as ever, and become no easier with every new entrant to the Community.

4–36   That being the case, it may be asked whether it can possibly be worthwhile to comment upon a body of law which will not be in force in the foreseeable future, or perhaps at all. So far as the substantive law of infringement and validity of the Community patent is concerned, such reservations are probably valid.[40] However, what might be called the private international law of the Community patent substantially corresponds to that of the Community trade mark, and applications for Community trade marks are actually being processed by the Community Trade Mark Office. Litigation to enforce Community trade marks will certainly be a reality well before the end of the decade. Not much further away, litigation over Community plant variety rights and Community designs will be in prospect and will follow a very similar plan. To describe the respective systems for enforcing Community patents and Community trade marks in parallel does not involve a substantial amount of wasted effort and enables the development of the law to be followed through what is essentially a single process of evolution, with the policy decisions underlying the Community Trade Mark Regulation being put into their historical perspective.

4–37   Finally, the constitutional law of the Community may have developed to the point where the Community Patent Convention as such is unnecessary.[41] There is little doubt that until well after 1975 there was a preconception that intellectual property rights in general, and patents especially, involved the exercise of national sovereignty to a degree which precluded radical innovation through normal Community legislation and required the conclusion of a separate treaty in the form of the Community Patent Convention. That preconception has been laid to rest by the Opinion of the European Court of Justice in *Re the Uruguay Round Treaties*[42] and its decision in *Spain v. Council (Supplementary*

---

[40] Though Benyamini, *Patent Infringement in the European Community* (1993) is invaluable as an exercise in comparative patent law.

[41] The E.C. Commission now relies on these developments in the European Court of Justice in proposing to create a Community patent by way of Regulation under Art. 235. See the *Green Paper on the Community Patent and the Patent System in Europe* COM (97) 31 final of June 24, 1997 and see para. 1–69 above.

[42] Opinion 1/94 [1994] E.C.R. I–5267; [1995] 1 C.M.L.R. 205.

Protection Certificates),[43] following which the general competence of the Community to legislate anywhere in the field of intellectual property is no longer in question. In the result, as much of the Community Patent Convention as is still considered worth implementing could probably now be enacted by way of Regulation, as the Green Paper proposes, perhaps with minor consequential amendments to the Brussels Convention[44] and the internal application of the European Patent Convention.[45] The only outstanding problem is the inability to create a new Community patent appeal court corresponding to COPAC, and although that is regretted by the present author the Green Paper is able to present it as an advantage. The proposals of the Green Paper would radically overhaul the institutions of the Community patent described in the present chapter,[46] but would leave much of the subject matter of Chapter 5 untouched.

B. THE INSTITUTIONS OF THE COMMUNITY PATENT CONVENTION[47]

The European Patent Office

The main institution of the Community Patent Convention in its day to day application would be the European Patent Office, which would grant Community patents[48] and entertain oppositions as it does at present under the European Patent Convention.[49] However, the Office would not become *functus officio*, as it does now, after the opposition

4–38

---

[43] Case C–350/92 [1995] E.C.R. I–1985.

[44] Which could be done by Community legislation and would not require a diplomatic conference: Brussels Convention, Art. 57(3).

[45] The terms of Art. 142(1) of the European Patent Convention contemplate a "special agreement" between a group of states, but even if this precludes creation of such a group by Regulation the necessary special agreement need in principle be no more complex or difficult to agree than that amending EPC Art. 63; and far simpler than the Community Patent Convention itself.

[46] And both the Green Paper options amount to a reversion in whole or part to the scheme of the original 1975 Community Patent Convention.

[47] This section deals with the 1989 Community Patent Convention. The Community Patent Convention and the Protocol on the Settlement of Litigation Concerning the Infringement and Validity of Community Patents both form part of the Agreement Relating to Community Patents (89/695) published at [1989] O.J. L401/1 and as Cm. 1452. A more convenient source is Booy and Horton, *Sweet & Maxwell's E.C. Intellectual Property Materials* (1994). There will be major changes if the *Green Paper on the Community Patent and the Patent System in Europe* COM(97) 31 final of June 24, 1997 is implemented in either of its variants. In particular, there is no provision for COPAC under the Green Paper and the jurisdiction of the EPO would probably be extended, with appeals lying from it to the Court of First Instance. See para. 1–69 above.

[48] Community Patent Convention, Art. 2(1). Art. 142 of the European Patent Convention contemplates the grant of unitary patents for any group of contracting states.

[49] The Community Patent Convention does not make special provision for oppositions, but it acknowledges them.

period had expired or any opposition had run its course.[50] The Office would continue to have jurisdiction throughout the life of a Community patent[51] to entertain applications for revocation[52] or amendment[53] (limitation) and proceedings for licences of right.[54] The Office would also maintain the Register of Community Patents[55] and accept renewal fees, notifications of change of ownership and the like. To perform these tasks, new special departments within the EPO would be set up, in the form of a Patent Administration Division and one or more Revocation Divisions.[56]

4–39 The 1975 Community Patent Convention originally gave the European Patent Office exclusive first instance jurisdiction over the validity of Community patents, with national courts having jurisdiction solely in respect of infringement in a manner reminiscent of German law. The 1985 Luxembourg Protocol on Litigation as confirmed in 1989 deprived it of much of this jurisdiction and provided instead for actions for infringement and counterclaims for revocation to be tried together by the same court, both at first instance and on appeal. National courts would have jurisdiction to revoke as well as to enforce Community patents throughout the common market. Prospective defendants, however, would still only be able to take the initiative on validity by commencing opposition or revocation proceedings in the EPO, depending on whether or not the opposition period had expired.

4–40 The European Patent Office is not a Community institution, and its functions under the Community Patent Convention would give it an unusual composite status. All members of the European Communities are members of the European Patent Convention, but Switzerland, Monaco and Liechtenstein are members of the European Patent Convention without being current or prospective members of the European Communities, so the European and Community aspects of its functions could not simply be merged even if this were felt to be desirable. The institutional structure of the EPO would also vary according to whether it was acting with respect to European or Community patents, since the Patent Administration Division and Revocation Divisions would be concerned solely with Community patents and would be subject to a special Select Committee of the Administrative Council of the European Patent Organisation.[57] Appeals from the Patent Administration Division

[50] After the proceedings in the EPO which gave rise to *Lenzing's European Patent* [1997] R.P.C. 245 the former proprietors, Lenzing, twice applied to the Technical Board of Appeal for it to reopen its procedure but the Board refused to do so. The issue of whether the Boards of Appeal are wholly *functus officio* after giving judgment is now pending before the Enlarged Board of Appeal of the EPO in Case G1/97 *ETA/Watch*.

[51] And beyond, since Community Patent Convention, Art. 55(3) permits applications for revocation to be filed although the Community patent has lapsed.

[52] Community Patent Convention, Art. 55.

[53] *ibid.*, Art. 51.

[54] *ibid.*, Art. 43(5).

[55] *ibid.*, Art. 63.

[56] *ibid.*, Art. 4 and 6 to 8 relying on European Patent Convention, Art. 143. There are to be Implementing Regulations, not dealt with in this work.

[57] *ibid.*, Arts 4, 6 to 8, 11 to 19 and European Patent Convention, Art. 145.

and Revocation Divisions would lie to COPAC[58] and not to the EPO's own Boards of Appeal.[59] The Boards of Appeal would continue to have jurisdiction in appeals from the Examining and Opposition Divisions and their decisions would not be subject to any further appeal.

The Common Appeal Court (COPAC)[60]

The major institutional innovation of the Protocol on Litigation was **4-41** intended to be the establishment of a Community Patent Appeal Court[61] (the "Common Appeal Court" or more conveniently COPAC) which would hear appeals directly from first instance courts in member states[62] and from Revocation Divisions in the European Patent Office.[63] The role of COPAC is stated as being to "ensure uniform interpretation of [the Agreement relating to Community Patents] and of the provisions enacted in implementation thereof, to the extent to which they are not national provisions.[64] It performs the functions assigned to it by the Protocol on Litigation.[65] COPAC would be a new Community institution rather than a division of the European Court of Justice or the European Patent Office and would wholly supersede existing national courts of second instance in the application of the law of Community patents. The following description necessarily proceeds on the basis that COPAC will indeed be created.[66]

COPAC is to be a new and independent Community institution with **4-42** its own seat,[67] president,[68] judiciary,[69] rules of procedure,[70] personnel[71] and budget.[72] It is to be represented and managed by its President[73] and administered by an Administrative Committee of members appointed by the contracting states and the Commission.[74]

After a transitional period[75] it is intended that COPAC will have a **4-43** permanent, full time judiciary with at least as many judges as there are

---

[58] The "Community Patent Appeal Court" to be established by the Protocol on Litigation to the Community Patent Convention: see below.

[59] Protocol on Litigation, Art. 28.

[60] This paragraph and those that follow incorporate material from Wadlow, "The Community Patent Appeal Court" (1986) 11 E.L. Rev. 295. See also Haardt, "The Setting Up of a Court of Appeal for Community Patents" (1985) 16 I.I.C. 332; Scordamaglia, "The Common Appeal Court and the Future of the Community Patent Following the Luxembourg Conference" part I (1991) 22 I.I.C. 334 and part II (1991) 22 I.I.C. 458.

[61] Protocol on Litigation, Art. 2.

[62] Protocol on Litigation, Art. 22.

[63] Protocol on Litigation, Art. 28. COPAC would also hear appeals from the Patent Administration Division.

[64] Agreement relating to Community Patents, Art. 5. See also Protocol on Litigation, Art. 26.

[65] Protocol on Litigation, Art. 2(1).

[66] Since this is uncertain, less detail is given here as to how COPAC would operate.

[67] To be determined pursuant to Protocol on Litigation, Art. 2(2).

[68] Protocol on Litigation, Art. 7.

[69] *ibid.*, Art. 5.

[70] *ibid.*, Art. 12.

[71] Protocol on the Statute of the Common Appeal Court, Art. 7.

[72] Protocol on Litigation, Art. 10.

[73] *ibid.*, Arts 3(3) and 8.

[74] *ibid.*, Art. 9.

[75] *ibid.*, Art. 39.

contracting states.[76] The judges are required to possess experience in patent law and the qualifications for appointment to judicial office in their home state.[77] They are to be appointed for renewable terms of six years by the representatives of the governments of the contracting states.[78] COPAC may sit in plenary session of at least half the court or in chambers of at least three judges, in either case with an uneven number of judges sitting.[79] One judge is to act as rapporteur,[80] but there is no provision corresponding to that for the Advocates-General before the European Court of Justice. Parties are not entitled to object to the composition of the bench on the ground of nationality.[81] Parties must be represented before COPAC by a lawyer qualified to act before a court of a contracting state, who may be assisted by a technical adviser who is a patent agent qualified to practice before the European Patent Office or a national patent office of a contracting state.[82] The technical adviser may address the court.

4–44   COPAC procedure is to consist of a written stage in which pleadings and documentary evidence are exchanged and a public oral stage.[83] There is provision for COPAC to require the parties to produce documents and supply information,[84] to allow the introduction of fresh evidence,[85] and to take evidence on oath and under penalty for default from witnesses and experts at the court itself or on commission under letters rogatory.[86] COPAC may also entrust any person or body to give an expert opinion.[87] COPAC may examine the experts, witnesses and the parties themselves at the hearing.[88] The implication seems to be that its procedure may be inquisitorial to a much greater extent than in the Boards of Appeal of the EPO or the English Court of Appeal. The oral stage also consists of the presentation of the report of the judge acting as rapporteur and the arguments of lawyers and technical advisers. COPAC is to have a procedure for allowing interventions by persons establishing an interest in the result of a case before the court, but the intervening

[76] Protocol on Litigation, Art. 5.

[77] *ibid.*. Art. 6.

[78] *ibid.*

[79] Protocol on Litigation, Art. 5(3); Protocol on the Statute of the Common Appeal Court, Art. 10.

[80] Protocol on the Statute of the Common Appeal Court, Art. 13.

[81] Protocol on the Statute of the Common Appeal Court, Art. 11.

[82] Protocol on the Statute of the Common Appeal Court, Art. 12. Parties represented by a European patent attorney in the EPO will have engage additional representation on the appeal to COPAC. The Scordamaglia Report, para. 68, noted this, but makes it clear that the consensus of the Luxembourg Diplomatic Conference was that because COPAC was a court, there could be no exception to the requirement of representation by a lawyer. The Report of the House of Lords Select Committee on the European Communities: *A European Community Patent* (1986) regrets the resulting cost and inconvenience to appellants from EPO decisions.

[83] Protocol on the Statute of the Common Appeal Court, Arts 13 and 22.

[84] *ibid.*, Art. 14.

[85] *ibid.*, Art. 15.

[86] *ibid.*, Art. 17 *et seq.*

[87] *ibid.*, Art. 16.

[88] *ibid.*, Art. 23.

party is limited to supporting the submissions of an existing party.[89] COPAC is not entirely *functus officio* when it has given judgment, because an application may be made to have it construed[90] or revised.[91]

The European Court of Justice exercises some supervisory jurisdiction **4–45** over COPAC, primarily by way of COPAC being required to make preliminary references to the Court on the interpretation of the Agreement relating to Community Patents and its annexed texts whenever there is a risk of their being interpreted inconsistently with the E.C. Treaty.[92] There is also a procedure, reminiscent of that under Article 4 of the 1971 Protocol to the Brussels Convention, under which the Commission or a member state can request the European Court of Justice to give an opinion on a ruling by COPAC, though without affecting the rights of the parties *inter se*.[93] It is also the European Court of Justice, rather than COPAC itself, which rules on questions of jurisdiction by way of a preliminary reference from a national appellate court.[94] The decisions of COPAC, however, are final in the sense of being binding in further proceedings of the case[95] and there is no appeal from its findings.

COPAC and the other alternatives considered

COPAC is to some extent a composite body, taking over and **4–46** combining aspects of the jurisdictions which in the 1975 Community Patent Convention were divided between appellate Revocation Boards in the European Patent Office and the European Court of Justice. The Scordamaglia Report summarises the nature of COPAC and the two alternatives which were under consideration and were rejected in favour of an entirely new and independent body:

"The other body common to the Contracting States established by the ACP is the Community patent appeal court.

Under public international law, the CAC constitutes a new international organisation established by the States parties to the Agreement relating to Community Patents. During the preparatory work, two other possibilities were also considered, but then ruled out mainly for political reasons.

The first was to set up the CAC as a special department of the EPO, but guaranteed the complete independence from EPO management which its judicial nature would require. This was the solution adopted for the Boards of Appeal established by the EPC. However, it was felt that it would be awkward to incorporate into an

---

[89] Protocol on the Statute of the Common Appeal Court, Art. 29.
[90] *ibid.*, Art. 31.
[91] Protocol on the Statute of the Common Appeal Court, Art. 32, referring to the law of the state from which the reference was made.
[92] Agreement relating to Community Patents, Art. 2(2).
[93] *ibid.*, Art. 2(3).
[94] *ibid.*, Art. 3.
[95] Protocol on Litigation, Art. 27.

essentially administrative body like the EPO a court whose main function would be to decide appeals against decisions taken at first instance by national courts of the Contracting States.

The second alternative was to attach the CAC to the EC Court of Justice, as had been done with the Court of First Instance provided for in Art. 168a of the EEC Treaty. This idea was dropped as well: it would probably have meant revising the EEC Treaty, as did the Single European Act inserting *inter alia* Art. 168a into the EEC Treaty.

The only remaining solution was thus to set up an autonomous international organisation. Taking this course meant having to adopt a number of institutional provisions in the Prot. Lit., Prot. Stat. and Prot. Imm. concerning the CAC. These are broadly modelled on the corresponding provisions regarding the EC Court of Justice and the European Patent Organisation."

Community patent courts of first and second instance

4-47   The contracting states are obliged to designate courts of first and second instance in their respective territories which are referred to as Community patent courts.[96] The name is somewhat misleading, because they are not Community institutions and they need not be exclusively concerned with Community patents (COPAC, conversely, is not a "Community patent court" in the sense of the Protocol on Litigation). In the case of Community patent courts of second instance they are not even intended to have any effective jurisdiction over Community patents. In practice first and second instance courts in each contracting state which already have jurisdiction over normal patent infringement actions appear to have been designated as Community patent courts and will exercise their new jurisdiction concurrently with the old. The personal, territorial and subject matter jurisdiction of Community patent courts of first instance is described in Chapter 5. It is notable that national patent offices have no place in this scheme even in those countries where they had concurrent jurisdiction over infringement, or concurrent or exclusive jurisdiction over the validity of national patents. Conversely, the trial and appeal courts of Germany and, subsequently, Austria would have to exercise a jurisdiction over validity which they never had under national law.

4-48   There may be several Community patent courts of first or even second instance for a state, each with local jurisdiction determined by national law. In the case of the United Kingdom alone, there are Community patents courts of first instance with concurrent local jurisdiction, since as well as the geographical division between England, Scotland and Northern Ireland, the Patents County Court has been designated as a Community patent court of first instance for England in addition to the High Court.[97] The judges of Community patent courts are required to

---

[96] Protocol on Litigation, Art. 1.

[97] *Quaere* whether this complies with the obligation to designate as limited a number of Community patent courts as possible.

possess experience of patent law,[98] a requirement which may cause difficulties for small jurisdictions such as Scotland and Northern Ireland. The failure to distinguish between first and second instance courts in Article 31 is particularly curious, since Community patent courts of second instance have no effective jurisdiction over issues of Community patent law and one does not need a bench of patent specialists to refer an appeal lock, stock and barrel to COPAC. One wonders if any consequences in private law arise if a court exercising the jurisdiction of a Community patent court demonstrably does not consist of suitably experienced patent lawyers.

National courts in their capacity as Community patent courts are to apply the Community Patent Convention and the Protocol on Litigation.[99] In general the Brussels Convention on Jurisdiction and Enforcement also applies where the Protocol is silent.[1] On matters not covered by these sources, the national courts are to apply national law including their own rules of private international law.[2] There is considerable scope for a Community patent court to have to apply the national laws of other Community states. Normal local rules of procedure appropriate to the type of action in question are followed except to the limited extent that the Convention or Protocol require otherwise.[3] The national court is obliged to record the evidence given and the other essentials of the oral proceedings, and the intention is clearly that COPAC should not be impeded in evaluating all the evidence and argument in the case and should not be confined to the formal record of the first instance decision.[4]

4–49

The mandatory referral to COPAC

An appeal lies from the Community patent court of first instance (the national trial court) to the corresponding Community patent court of second instance in the same country.[5] National law determines the circumstances under which an appeal may be lodged.[6] The jurisdiction of the national appeal court is extremely limited because it must refer all substantive matters of Community patent law to the Common Appeal Court (COPAC),[7] unless the appeal concerns interlocutory relief.[8]

4–50

Although the Protocol on Litigation hesitates to speak in terms of an appeal from the Community patent court of first instance to COPAC,

4–51

---

[98] Protocol on Litigation, Art. 31. Looking at the list of courts in the Annex to the Protocol on Litigation, this can only be intended to apply to judges of Community patent courts *in their capacity as such* though even on that construction it is all but pointless in the case of appellate courts.

[99] Protocol on Litigation, Art. 31(1).

[1] *ibid.*, Art. 13. See Chap. 5.

[2] *ibid.*, Art. 32(2).

[3] *ibid.*, Art. 33.

[4] *ibid.*, Art. 33(3).

[5] *ibid.*, Art. 21(1).

[6] *ibid.*, Art. 21(2). The terms of Art. 21(1) probably exclude making such appeals discretionary or subject to leave, as does Art. 32 of TRIPs.

[7] *ibid.*, Art. 22.

[8] *ibid.*, Art. 36(3).

the reality is that any appeal is bifurcated. All issues of Community patent law are referred almost automatically to COPAC without the national court having any discretion. Issues of national law, if there are any, remain within the jurisdiction of the Community patent court of second instance. It is worth emphasising that the referral to COPAC is neither a third tier of appeal nor a preliminary reference in the sense of Article 177 E.C.

4-52   COPAC has exclusive jurisdiction over all matters of fact and law relating to the effects of the Community patent or application so far as national law is not involved, and the validity of the Community patent if it has been put in issue in a counterclaim.[9] Although COPAC is the main authority on the construction of the Community Patent Convention its role is far wider than this may suggest at first sight. On appeal COPAC has exclusive jurisdiction over the validity of the patent, the construction of its claims and whether it has been infringed. Most importantly COPAC is fully entitled to differ from the national court of first instance on matters of pure fact, apparently even if the national appeal court would have been bound to accept them. Article 24 provides that COPAC "shall examine all the issues of which it is seized and give a ruling on fact and law." The extensive power of COPAC to admit new evidence is indicative of this, and is far wider than English practice in the Court of Appeal. On infringement the exclusive jurisdiction of COPAC covers all the central questions normally arising in patent litigation including whether the patent claims cover the defendant's product, article or process, whether any act of the defendant constituted an infringement, and whether exhaustion of rights or any of the other enumerated defences in the Community Patent Convention applies. In all these respects COPAC decides not only how the Convention is to be construed but also how it applies to the facts of the individual case in all its detail.

4-53   The national appeal court—the Community patent court of second instance—retains jurisdiction over any causes of action which do not involve Community patents, and aspects of the Community patent action itself which involve purely national law.[10] The latter category might include questions of the liability of directors and defences of acquiescence or statutory limitation. Somewhat surprisingly, the national appeal court also apparently retains jurisdiction over questions of general Community law not to be found in the Community Patent Convention and Protocol on Litigation themselves. It may voluntarily refer such questions to the European Court of Justice under Article 177 E.C. but not, apparently, to COPAC. The national appeal court may only continue its own proceedings to the extent that the decision of COPAC

[9] Protocol on Litigation, Arts 22 and 24.
[10] Not necessarily the national law of the court in question. For instance, evaluation of damages will almost always require an exercise in comparative law because of the Protocol on Litigation, Art. 35(2), and some defences may have to be dealt with on a country by country basis. One might have thought that COPAC was better qualified to conduct this sort of exercise.

is not prejudged,[11] and in any event may not give a final judgment before COPAC.[12] The Protocol takes no account of the fact that a successful defence under national law might dispose of the action and render continuing proceedings before COPAC otiose. So far as the appeal raises questions within the exclusive jurisdiction of COPAC, the national appeal court is obliged to stay its own proceedings and refer the issues to COPAC for judgment. It may do so without an oral hearing and in practice one would expect the stay and referral to take place automatically once an appeal had been filed.[13]

COPAC in the Community legal order

COPAC applies Community law as embodied in the 1989 **4–54** Luxembourg Agreement relating to Community Patents and in particular the Community Patent Convention itself and the Protocol on Litigation.[14] COPAC does not concern itself with, or attempt to apply, purely national law.[15] Subject to this and the following observations, COPAC is obliged to examine and rule on all matters of fact and law in the case.[16] The extent to which COPAC is expected to rule on general Community law is problematical, since although its express jurisdiction is confined to the Community Patent Convention and related instruments (and Community enactments thereunder) it can hardly consider them in a vacuum. To ensure that the E.C. Treaty remains paramount[17] and to preserve the uniformity of the Community legal order COPAC is therefore obliged to make a reference to the European Court for a preliminary ruling whenever there is a risk of the Agreement and its texts being interpreted in a way inconsistent with the E.C. Treaty.[18] In case this is not sufficient, the Commission, or a member state, may request the European Court to give a ruling when it considers that a final decision of COPAC fails to comply with these obligations under Article 2(1) or (2) of the Agreement.[19] This procedure has no effect as between the parties to the case. The only express provision as to procedure before the European Court on this reference is that member states and the Commission may submit written statements or observations.

The relatively straightforward arrangement of COPAC acting as a **4–55** second and final instance court with jurisdiction over all aspects of Community patent law and subject only to the European Court of Justice is complicated by two further provisions of limited and in some respects uncertain scope and by the possibility of an action on a

---

[11] Protocol on Litigation, Art. 23(2).
[12] *ibid.*, Art. 23(3).
[13] *ibid.*, Art. 23(1).
[14] *ibid.*, Art. 26.
[15] Agreement relating to Community Patents, Art. 5, proviso and by implication.
[16] Protocol on Litigation, Art. 24.
[17] Agreement relating to Community Patents, Art. 2(1).
[18] *ibid.*, Art. 2(2).
[19] *ibid.*, Art. 2(3).

Community patent raising issues of Community law over which COPAC would not have jurisdiction. The first of these provisions is to the effect that questions as to the interpretation of the provisions on jurisdiction in the Community Patent Convention and the Protocol on Litigation are not assigned to COPAC, but are for the European Court to decide on a procedure similar to an Article 177 reference except that it may be invoked only by an appellate court of a contracting state, whether or not it is a Community patent court.[20] Only the designated highest courts of a state, in the United Kingdom the House of Lords, are obliged to make such a reference and then only if they consider it necessary.

4–56 The second qualification to the general scheme is that COPAC has jurisdiction to give a preliminary ruling on the interpretation of the Agreement in respect of matters *not* falling within its exclusive jurisdiction, or on the validity and interpretation of Community legislation implementing the Agreement.[21] Apparently any court of a member state, at whatever level and whether or not it is a Community patent court may request such a ruling, as may a national patent office in exercising its jurisdiction over a Community patent on matters relating to ownership or compulsory licensing. A reference is obligatory in the case of a court of last resort.

4–57 This raises the question of whether a Community patent court of first instance trying an action for infringement of a Community patent may make a preliminary reference and bring the case before COPAC without waiting for an appeal. The answer is almost certainly that it cannot, because where the *exclusive* jurisdiction of COPAC is concerned it is only a Community patent court of second instance that can and must make a referral, in which event COPAC becomes seised of the whole case. Article 30 (1)(a) of the Protocol on Litigation expressly prevents COPAC entertaining a preliminary reference in respect of a matter falling within its exclusive jurisdiction defined by Article 22. It would be productive of duplication and inconsistency if a first instance court could request a preliminary ruling from COPAC on a single abstract question of law separated from its surrounding facts, and if the same case should then go to COPAC on appeal for a full ruling on all aspects of fact and law.

4–58 The Protocol on Litigation seems to have assumed, dubiously, that the only issues of Community law likely to arise in a Community patent case may be dealt with exclusively under the Convention and related legislation. COPAC does not exist to interpret the E.C. Treaty, the Brussels or Rome Conventions or other general sources of Community law. The problem is compounded if actions for infringement of Community patents and national patents are combined. In so far as a case independently raises matters of general Community law, for instance under

---

[20] Agreement relating to Community Patents, Art. 3. A closer analogy is to the 1971 Protocol to the Brussels Convention.

[21] Protocol on Litigation, Art. 30 implementing Agreement relating to Community Patents, Art. 5. The preliminary reference procedure is likely to be far less important than COPAC's role as an appeal court.

Articles 30 and 36, or 85 and 86 of the E.C. Treaty, COPAC appears to have no jurisdiction and the national courts retain their discretion to make a preliminary reference to the European Court of Justice or decide the point themselves. The Agreement relating to Community Patents is expressly subordinate to the E.C. Treaty, but in some respects it may have been left behind by developments in general Community law. The provisions for national reservations on the grant of compulsory licences,[22] for instance, are probably inconsistent with the decision of the European Court of Justice in *Commission v. United Kingdom and Italy (Compulsory Patent Licences)*.[23] Exhaustion of rights and national defences of prior use or personal possession are other areas where the consensus view embodied in the Convention is not beyond question.

It is clear that national courts in their capacity as Community patent courts, whether of first or second instance, cannot request a preliminary ruling from the European Court of Justice on the interpretation of the Community Patent Convention, the Protocol on Litigation, or subordinate Community legislation there under unless the issue is one of jurisdiction.[24] Those are exclusively matters for COPAC.[25] However, the making of a reference to COPAC does not apparently relieve the national appeal court of responsibility for questions of general Community law of wider relevance than the Community Patent Convention and Protocol, and the national court presumably retains its discretion or duty (if a final court) to refer such questions to the European Court of Justice for a preliminary ruling under Article 177 E.C. so far as they are not within the jurisdiction of COPAC. Conversely, although a Community patent court of first instance has only a very limited power to make a voluntary reference to COPAC, it is apparently not deprived of its right to request a preliminary ruling from the European Court under Article 177 on matters of general Community law.

4–59

---

[22] Community Patent Convention, Art. 83.

[23] Joined Cases C–235/89 and 30/90 [1992] 1 E.C.R. 777; [1992] 2 C.M.L.R. 709. The Scordamaglia Report, para. 21, itself contemplates that Art. 83 may be incompatible with general Community law.

[24] Agreement relating to Community Patents, Art. 3.

[25] Benyamini, *Patent Infringement in the European Community* (1993), p. 25 argues that although it is obviously convenient for references to the European Court of Justice always to go via COPAC, the Agreement relating to Community Patents does not purport to amend Art. 177 E.C. so as to deprive national courts of their power to make a reference. The Scordamaglia Report at para. 22 is consistent with his view. The answer is that Art. 2 of the Agreement is misleading, and that what is contemplated is not an Art. 177 reference properly so called but one under an analogous but *sui generis* procedure. The jurisdiction of the European Court of Justice under Art. 177 is not curtailed, because the Agreement is a separate treaty comparable to the Brussels or Rome Conventions and in the absence of express provisions the Court would have no jurisdiction to entertain a preliminary reference from anywhere. See Arnull, "Refurbishing the Judicial Architecture of the European Community" (1994) 43 I.C.L.Q. 296 at 310. However, Benyamini's comments would be valid, and fatal to COPAC's exclusive jurisdiction, if the Community patent were to be implemented by Regulation as is now proposed.

Effect of the COPAC judgment

4–60   The judgment of COPAC is binding between the parties in the further proceedings in the case.[26] It is then for the national court to award remedies,[27] other than revocation or amendment (limitation) of the patent which is ordered by COPAC itself.[28] The Protocol does not deal separately with the case of COPAC hearing an appeal from a court which had jurisdiction only because of an infringing act committed or threatened in its territorial jurisdiction. If COPAC finds infringement and upholds the patent, then any relief granted by the national court will still be confined to its own national territory. Presumably in these circumstances the COPAC judgment as to infringement does not automatically bind even the same parties in actions in other states. A decision of COPAC to revoke (or amend) a patent is always effective for the whole common market.

4–61   If a Community patent is revoked the consequences are clear, but if it is maintained in force major uncertainties arise which the Protocol scarcely answers. The problems centre around the extent to which a decision of a national court or COPAC on the interpretation or validity of a Community patent is binding, and upon whom. The Protocol provides that the decision of COPAC is binding in further proceedings in the case, but no more. This leaves a number of major questions: to what extent is the rejection by a national court or COPAC of a particular attack on the validity of a Community patent binding in other proceedings, possibly between different parties and before different national courts; and to what extent is the established interpretation of the patent, especially its claims, binding on another court or between different parties. To give an example, a national trial court or COPAC may have rejected an attack on the patentability of an invention based on a particular piece of prior art, and found that a particular machine falls within the scope of the patent. If the patentee were to sue another infringer in a different national court for the use of the same type of machine, and the defendant were to rely on the same prior art, then to what extent are these findings of fact by the first national court or COPAC binding or influential? The provisions for related actions to be stayed contemplate that uniformity between different national courts is desirable, but there is no explicit mechanism for achieving it, and the possibility of a third party intervening before COPAC only goes some way towards solving the problem. Until COPAC itself develops some jurisprudence on these questions, without much concrete guidance from the Convention or the Protocol, they will apparently be left to discretion and national doctrines of estoppel and precedent which are far from uniform and ill-adapted for the new situation.

[26] Protocol on Litigation, Art. 27.
[27] *ibid.*, Art. 35.
[28] *ibid.*, Art. 25(2).

Further proceeding in the national courts

If the national legal system in question has three or more tiers of   **4–62**
courts then a further appeal is possible on questions not exclusively
reserved to COPAC,[29] but the decision of COPAC is binding on the
court of third instance.[30]

C. THE INSTITUTIONS OF THE COMMUNITY TRADE MARK, DESIGN AND PLANT VARIETY RIGHT

The Community Trade Mark and Designs Office (OHIM)

The institutional framework of the Community trade mark is simpler   **4–63**
than that for the Community patent, and unlike the latter its institutions
are actually in being or due to be designated as such within the
foreseeable future.

The Community Trade Mark Regulation[31] establishes, by Article 2, an   **4–64**
"Office for Harmonisation of the Internal Market (trade marks and
designs)." It is referred to in the Regulation as "the Office" but it will
also be referred to here as "OHIM," the "Community Trade Mark
Office" or the "Community Design Office," according to the context and
its function.[32] Title XII of the Regulation deals with the legal status and
organisation of the Office. It is a body of the Community and has legal
personality.[33] The Office has a President, who is its formal representative
and manager,[34] and an Administrative Board of members from each
member state and the Commission.[35] The Office is situated in Spain at
Alicante.[36] There are implementing regulations or rules for the Office[37]
and its Boards of Appeal.[38]

---

[29] Protocol on Litigation, Art. 29.

[30] *ibid.*, Art. 27.

[31] Council Regulation 40/94 on the Community Trade Mark (December 20, 1993) [1994] O.J. L11/1 reprinted in Booy and Horton, *Sweet & Maxwell's E.C. Intellectual Property Materials* (1994). The Regulation was slightly amended by Council Regulation 3288/94 (December 22, 1994) [1994] O.J. L349/83 to comply with TRIPs and the consolidated text is printed in issue 1/95, p. 50 of the OHIM O.J. in five languages. See Franzosi, ed., *European Community Trade Mark* (1997) and especially the chapter by Scordamaglia, "Jurisdiction and Procedure in Legal Actions Relating to Community Trade Marks"; Annand and Norman, *Blackstone's Guide to the Community Trade Mark* (1998).

[32] The Spanish acronym OAMI, for *Oficina de Armonization del Mercado Interior* has more charm than the English OHIM.

[33] Community Trade Mark Regulation, Art. 111(1).

[34] *ibid.*, Art. 111(3) and 119.

[35] *ibid.*, Arts 121 *et seq.*

[36] Statement by the Council and the Commission of October 29, 1993, published on January 14, 1994 [1994] O.J. L11/36.

[37] Commission Regulation 2868/95 of December 13, 1995 [1995] O.J. L303/1. Rules 15 to 22 deal with opposition procedure; rules 37 to 41 with revocation and invalidity proceedings; rules 48 to 51 deal with appeals.

[38] Commission Regulation 216/96 of February 5, 1996 [1996] O.J. L28/11.

4–65   The Office comprises examiners, Opposition Divisions, Cancellation Divisions, an Administration of Trade Marks and Legal Division and Boards of Appeals.[39] The Opposition and Cancellation Divisions are separate entities, the first hearing oppositions as such and the second hearing applications for revocation or declaration of invalidity. It is implicit that an Opposition Division will normally include the examiner,[40] but members of Cancellation Divisions may not have taken part in previous examination or opposition proceedings.[41] Opposition Divisions and Cancellation Divisions must each contain at least one legally qualified member.[42] Boards of Appeal consisting of three members, at least two of whom must be legally qualified, hear appeals from all these divisions and from the examiners.[43] Members of the Boards of Appeal are independent and must not have taken part in the decision under appeal.[44] They cannot also be examiners or members of the other divisions.[45] There is no provision for an Enlarged Board of Appeal either in terms of enhanced status or even by way of a board sitting with more than three members. The role of the Enlarged Board of Appeal of the European Patent Office in providing guidance and consistency is taken instead by the Court of First Instance of the European Court of Justice.

OHIM in the Community legal order and the roles of the European Court of Justice

4–66   Contentious proceedings in the Office are either by way of opposition, before an Opposition Division,[46] or by way of an application for revocation or declaration of invalidity before a Cancellation Division.[47] Oppositions can only be filed on the relative grounds of Article 8, by parties claiming earlier rights, and within three months after publication of the application.[48] Registration does not take place until the opposition period has expired, and any opposition has been rejected by a definitive decision.[49] Applications for revocation or invalidity are to be the normal way of challenging validity at any time after registration, and any grounds available to the applicant can be raised.

4–67   Appeals lie to the Boards of Appeal of OHIM from decisions of the Opposition Divisions and Cancellation Divisions.[50] They have suspensive effect.[51] The time for filing notice of an appeal is two months from the

[39] Community Trade Mark Regulation, Arts 125 *et seq.*

[40] Art. 132(1) provides that two of the three members of the Opposition Division should not have taken part in examining the application. Oppositions in OHIM take place before registration.

[41] Community Trade Mark Regulation, Art. 132(1).

[42] *ibid.*, Arts 127 and 129.

[43] *ibid.*, Art. 130.

[44] *ibid.*, Arts 131 and 132.

[45] *ibid.*, Art. 131(2).

[46] *ibid.*, Art. 42.

[47] *ibid.*, Art. 55.

[48] *ibid.*, Art. 42(1).

[49] *ibid.*, Art. 45.

[50] *ibid.*, Art. 57. Also from the examiners and the Administration Division.

[51] *ibid.*, Art. 57(1).

date of notification of the decision appealed from and written grounds must be filed within four months from the same date.[52] Interlocutory appeals are possible only if the order so provides, otherwise the interlocutory decision can only be appealed together with the final decision.[53] The Boards of Appeal may exercise all the powers of the division appealed from or may remit the case for further proceedings.[54]

Decisions of the Boards of Appeal are not strictly open to appeal but may be challenged by way of actions before the European Court of Justice.[55] The recitals to the Regulation state that such actions will in fact be brought before the Court of First Instance.[56] Actions may be brought on grounds of lack of competence, infringement of an essential procedural requirement, infringement of the E.C. Treaty or the Community Trade Mark Regulation, or of any rule of law relating to their application or to misuse of power.[57] They have suspensive effect.[58] The time limit for bringing an action is two months from notification of the decision of the Board of Appeal.[59] Actions in respect of errors of fact by the Board of Appeal seem to be excluded in principle, but could perhaps be characterised as arising from a misinterpretation of the Regulation or as a violation of an essential procedural requirement. The Court can annul or vary the contested decision and OHIM is obliged to take the necessary steps to comply with it.[60] A further appeal on points of law only lies from the Court of First Instance to the European Court of Justice itself.

4–68

OHIM as the Community Designs Office

The institutional structure of the Office may be expected to be similar in its capacity as the Community Designs Office, except that for designs there are to be Invalidity Divisions[61] which correspond to the Cancellation Divisions. Examination by the Office *ex parte* is purely formal, with provision for *inter partes* proceedings by way of a single procedure for an application for a declaration of invalidity at any time after registration.[62]

4–69

[52] Community Trade Mark Regulation, Art. 59.
[53] *ibid.*, Art. 57(2).
[54] *ibid.*, Art. 62.
[55] *ibid.*, Art. 63.
[56] In accordance with Council Decision 88/591 of October 24, 1988. Amendments to the Rules of Procedure of the Court of First Instance to deal with intellectual property matters are published at [1995] O.J. L172/3. A new Title 4 consisting of Arts 130 to 136 is inserted.
[57] Community Trade Mark Regulation, Art. 63(2).
[58] *ibid.*, Art. 62(3).
[59] *ibid.*, Art. 63(5).
[60] *ibid.*, Art. 63(3) and (5).
[61] Draft Community Design Regulation, Art. 116. The draft "Regulation on the Community Design" of December 3, 1993 COM(93) 342 final is printed at [1994] O.J. C29/20 and reproduced in Booy and Horton, *Sweet & Maxwell's E.C. Intellectual Property Materials* (1994). See the Commission's *Green Paper on the Legal Protection of Industrial Design* (1991); Franzozi, ed., *European Design Protection* (1996), and especially the commentary by Scordamaglia on the litigation proposals.
[62] Draft Regulation, Art. 56. In contrast to trade marks, there is no pre-registration opposition and, indeed, the application is not even published. In contrast to patents, there is no special post-grant opposition procedure as distinct from a normal application for a declaration of invalidity.

There is provision for intervention not only by assumed infringers, as in European Patent Office oppositions, but also by the E.C. Commission and member states.[63] Appeals lie to internal Boards of Appeal, whose decisions may be challenged by action in the Court of First Instance as in the case of Community trade marks. The Explanatory Memorandum of the Commission emphasises "how important it is for users of the Community Trade Mark and Design systems to be presented with an absolutely unitary appeal mechanism."

Community trade mark courts of first and second instance

4–70   Member states are obliged to designate as limited a number as possible of national courts of first and second instance which are to be called "Community trade mark courts" and which will exercise the functions assigned to them under the Community Trade Mark Regulation.[64] As with Community patent courts, these are not Community institutions but national courts exercising a particular jurisdiction and applying Community law.[65]

4–71   Community trade mark courts hear actions for infringement[66] and for declarations of non-infringement (if permitted under national law) and counterclaims for revocation or invalidation.[67] Actions for compensation in respect of the rights conferred by publication of the application are also within their jurisdiction, apparently whether or not such actions are otherwise allowed under national law. This may have surprising importance because infringement actions as such cannot be commenced until after registration, and registration is likely to be delayed significantly in many cases by the pre-registration opposition procedure in OHIM and any appeals. Community trade mark courts do not in general have jurisdiction to entertain attacks on the validity of the Community trade mark except by way of counterclaim.[68] Validity cannot be put in issue at all in an action for a declaration of non-infringement.[69] The personal, territorial and subject matter jurisdiction of Community trade mark courts of first instance is described in Chapter 5. Unless otherwise provided for in the Regulation, Community trade mark courts apply the procedural law of the forum as appropriate to actions relating to national trade marks.[70]

4–72   The requirement to limit the number of Community trade mark courts in a given member state will have a significant effect in Civil law

[63] Draft Regulation, Art. 58. The Community Trade Mark Regulation does not have provision for assumed infringers to intervene in oppositions, and the special nature of trade mark oppositions means that intervention would not often serve any useful purpose.
[64] Art. 91.
[65] The meeting of the Council adopting the Regulation recorded in its minutes that "The Council and the Commission consider that the functions assigned by the Regulation to Community trade mark courts cover only infringement and validity actions together with the provisional, including protective, measures referred to in Article 99."
[66] Including threatened infringement, if such actions are permitted under national law.
[67] Art. 92.
[68] Art. 95(1). There is a very limited exception in Art. 95(3).
[69] Art. 95(2).
[70] Art. 97(3).

jurisdictions with highly decentralised court systems, since in contrast to patents there has been much less progress to date in assigning trade mark litigation to specialist courts. In contrast to the position under the Community Patent Convention again, there is no express requirement for their judges to be experienced in trade mark law but some *de facto* specialisation is implicit from the intention to concentrate litigation in a few courts. Lists of Community trade mark courts with details of their territorial jurisdiction must be given by the member states to the Commission within three years of the Community Trade Mark Regulation entering into force and will be published in the Official Journal of the E.C.[71] Designations of Community trade mark courts can be modified from time to time.[72] Pending notification, national courts with appropriate local and subject matter jurisdiction over national trade marks will have the same jurisdiction over Community trade marks.[73]

Appeals lie to the appropriate Community trade mark court of second instance, which has the same jurisdiction as the court appealed from.[74] The Community Trade Mark Regulation provides that "an appeal . . . shall lie" in respect of matters within Article 92 and this probably precludes national legislation from making such appeals discretionary or subject to leave. Otherwise, the conditions under which an appeal may be lodged are determined in accordance with the national law of the forum.[75]   **4–73**

Unlike Community patent courts of second instance, Community trade mark courts of second instance exercise real jurisdiction over all aspects of the action and counterclaim. There is no provision for any reference of issues of infringement and validity to any central Community court or institution. The Community trade mark court of second instance is fully seised of all issues of Community trade mark law, as well as any issues of national law or general Community law which arise.   **4–74**

Appeals to a third level court (if any) are governed by national law.[76] Curiously, the third instance court does not fall within the definition of a "Community trade mark court" and there is something of a lacuna as to what jurisdiction it exercises over Community trade mark law, and what effect is to be given to its judgments.[77] A comparison with Article 29 of the Protocol on Litigation to the Community Patent Convention confirms that the third instance appeal is not intended to be confined to issues of national law, as it would be in the case of an appeal from a Community patent court of second instance. There is no special provision in the Regulation for references to the European Court of Justice under Article 177 E.C. Although both third tier appeals and Article 177   **4–75**

[71] Art. 91(2) and (4). Presumably there will also be publication in the OHIM O.J.
[72] Art. 91(3).
[73] Art. 91(5).
[74] Art. 101(1).
[75] Art. 101(2).
[76] Art. 101(3).
[77] If the third tier court was a *Cour de Cassation* in the French sense then any operative order could be attributed to the second instance court to which the case would be referred for further proceedings if the appeal *en cassation* was allowed.

references are possible, they may be expected to be rare once the first few such decisions have set precedents. In the typical action, the decision of the Community trade mark court of second instance will be the final word for the whole Community on the validity of the Community trade mark and its effects *inter partes*.

Community design courts

4–76   The provisions of the draft Community Design Regulation provide for Community design courts in virtually identical terms to the provisions for Community trade mark courts.[78] Community design courts will also have jurisdiction to entertain actions for declarations of invalidity of *unregistered* Community designs,[79] which are outside the jurisdiction of OHIM. There is no provision for actions for compensation prior to grant, because the Community registered design will only be published when registered and so the Regulation does not confer any such rights.

Voluntary remission of issue of validity to OHIM

4–77   Article 96(7) of the Community Trade Mark Regulation provides that a Community trade mark court hearing a counterclaim for revocation or invalidation may request the defendant to submit an application for revocation or invalidation to OHIM within a set time, failing which the counterclaim is deemed to be withdrawn. The order may only be made on the application of the plaintiff and after hearing the other parties.

Community plant variety rights

4–78   The Community Plant Variety Office[80] has a similar structure and place in the Community legal order to OHIM, but the strict separation of validity and infringement between the Office and national courts is more reminiscent of the original 1975 Community Patent Convention. The draft Plant Variety Regulation was proposed to be based on Article 43 E.C. and the competence of the Community to implement the Common Agricultural Policy, but the final Regulation[81] is based on Article 235 E.C. like those for trade marks and designs.

4–79   The Office examines applications for the grant of Community plant variety rights. There is provision for pre-grant objections to be filed on limited grounds and for the objector to become a party to the application.[82] The Office has exclusive jurisdiction to entertain applications

---

[78] Arts 84 *et seq.* of the draft Regulation. The Explanatory Memorandum of the Commission refers to the (draft) Community Trade Mark Regulation and emphasises the importance of unitary rules.

[79] Draft Art. 85(c).

[80] Established by the Regulation on Community Plant Variety Rights, Art. 4. The Office is at Brussels.

[81] Council Regulation 2100/94 of July 27th, 1994 on Community Plant Variety Rights [1994] O.J. L227/1.

[82] Art. 59. Written observations may be filed against applications for Community or European patents, or Community trade marks, but the person making the observations does not become a party.

for nullity[83] or cancellation[84] of Community plant variety rights. Appeals lie to Boards of Appeal within the Office[85] and thence by way of further appeal to the European Court of Justice.[86]

The Plant Variety Regulation does not require the member states to **4-80** designate courts corresponding to Community patent, trade mark or design courts. Competent courts in member states[87] are given jurisdiction over infringement actions according to rules similar to those for Community patents and trade marks.[88] However, national courts have no jurisdiction over validity in any circumstances. They cannot even entertain counterclaims for revocation or cancellation. They must assume the plant variety right to be valid,[89] but may stay their proceedings to await the outcome of nullity or cancellation proceedings in the Office.[90]

D. PATENT AND TRADE MARK ENFORCEMENT: AN INSTITUTIONAL COMPARISON

First instance and interlocutory jurisdiction and procedure: closely comparable

First instance procedure under the Protocol on Litigation to the **4-81** Community Patent Convention and the Community Trade Mark Regulation is very similar. In both cases one finds that national courts designated as Community patent courts or Community trade mark courts have jurisdiction over both infringement and validity, but only if invalidity is raised on a counterclaim for revocation. In both cases, the national court can in general enforce or revoke the Community patent or trade mark for the whole of the Community. National courts cannot entertain free-standing applications for revocation; and invalidity cannot generally be pleaded as a pure defence or raised at all in an action for a declaration of non-infringement. The rules as to personal and territorial jurisdiction are virtually identical.

In the case of interlocutory relief, enforcement of Community patents **4-82** and trade marks is even more closely comparable because COPAC has no role in the grant or refusal of interlocutory remedies, so Community patent courts of second instance have the same comprehensive appellate jurisdiction in this respect as Community trade mark courts of second instance.

---

[83] Art. 20.
[84] Art. 21.
[85] Arts 45 *et seq.* and 67 *et seq.*
[86] Art. 73. The appeal is to the Court of First Instance.
[87] Including Lugano Convention member states, according to the letter of Art. 101. See para. 5–51.
[88] Art. 101, except for the problematic allocation of jurisdiction to the courts of Lugano. Convention contracting states, noted above.
[89] Art. 105.
[90] Art. 106(2).

Jurisdiction and procedure in OHIM and the EPO

4–83   At first instance, again, the jurisdiction of OHIM and the EPO is quite closely comparable. Only OHIM, in its capacity as the Community Trade Mark Office, hears pre-grant oppositions and the EPO has a special opposition procedure in the nine months following grant, but both have exclusive jurisdiction to hear free-standing applications for revocation during the life of the patent or trade mark. In both cases, central attack on the patent or mark in the relevant Office is the only way of challenging validity, unless one is prepared to wait to be sued by the proprietor.

Procedure on appeal shows significant differences. In the case of Community trade marks, appeals always lie to internal Boards of Appeal of OHIM. In the case of Community patents, appeals in oppositions are to a Board of Appeal of the EPO but in applications for revocation appeals go directly to COPAC. Another relevant distinction is that only OHIM has a third and fourth tier. Appeals in both oppositions and applications for revocation lie, in all but name, from the Boards of Appeals of OHIM to the Court of First Instance and thence to the European Court of Justice. In the case of the EPO, the decisions of the EPO's own Boards of Appeal and COPAC are final, but in appeals on applications for revocation COPAC can make a preliminary reference to the European Court of Justice.[91]

Second instance jurisdiction: the absence of a Community Trade Mark Appeal Court

4–84   The most striking institutional difference between the Community Patent Convention and the Community Trade Mark Regulation is the absence of any central appellate Community court for ensuring uniformity between the various national courts with first instance jurisdiction over trade mark infringement.[92] There is no "Community Trade Mark Appeal Court" corresponding to COPAC. In so far as appeals from the Office are concerned, the Court of First Instance of the European Communities will doubtless develop a body of jurisprudence on questions of validity, but it remains to be seen if national courts will actually pay more than lip service to its decisions in the absence of any effective mechanism to compel them to do so. As far as infringement is concerned, there is no prospect of any uniform body of case law developing at all except to the limited extent that the European Court of Justice may give preliminary rulings under Article 177 E.C..

4–85   Actions before the Court of First instance will doubtless provide a comprehensive means of judicial review against the Boards of Appeal of

---

[91] If the *Green Paper on the Community Patent and the Patent System in Europe* COM(97) 31 final of June 24, 1997 is implemented, then the procedure for revocation of Community patents is bound to correspond far more closely to procedure in and on appeal from OHIM, though with one fewer tier. See para. 1–69, above.

[92] Again, implementation of the Green Paper, *ibid.*, would remove this difference.

OHIM and will be a powerful influence in ensuring that oppositions and applications for revocation or invalidation before OHIM are decided according to a common Community standard of validity. Oppositions are likely to be numerous, because the *ex parte* examination performed by OHIM is confined to absolute grounds of invalidity and the opposition procedure will provide the first opportunity for other trade mark proprietors to raise any of the relative grounds affecting them. However, there is no such centralising function for the Court of First Instance in relation to infringement actions and counterclaims for revocation or invalidation in national courts, which is where it is far more likely to be needed. OHIM, after all, is a Community institution unburdened by settled national preconceptions of trade mark law and its Boards of Appeal would probably achieve a substantial degree of consistency even in the absence of recourse to the Court of First Instance.

Such mechanisms as there are for ensuring uniformity are mainly **4–86** voluntary. Since the Community Trade Mark Regulation is an ordinary piece of secondary Community legislation a Community trade mark court of first or second instance can make a voluntary reference to the European Court of Justice under Article 177 of the E.C. Treaty, but only on matters of law. A Community trade mark court may stay a counterclaim for revocation or invalidity so that the defendant can apply for the issue to be determined in the Office,[93] but this is not compulsory and leaves the question of infringement to be dealt with by the national court.

Is the different treatment of patents and trade marks justified?

A central Community trade mark appeal court was never a feature of **4–87** the drafts for the Community Trade Mark Regulation in 1980 and 1984. What is perhaps more surprising, is that the proposed creation of COPAC by the 1985 amendments to the Community Patent Convention did not have any influence in the field of Community trade marks.[94] Whether this was the result of a conscious decision that trade marks were different, a reaction to the problems of implementing the Community Patent Convention, or simply the force of inertia is impossible to say. Perhaps the most likely explanation is that the terms in which the Court of First Instance was eventually constituted under Article 168a E.C. in 1988 permitted it to hear appeals from Community institutions, such as OHIM, but expressly precluded it from hearing references (and *a foritori* appeals) from national courts. In the result, there was no existing court which could exercise functions corresponding to those of COPAC, and no realistic prospect of creating one.

Some plausible reasons can be tendered for saying that a central court **4–88** for Community trade marks is not needed, but their underlying assumption is that substantial non-uniformity of trade mark protection in fact

---

[93] Community Trade Mark Regulation, Art. 96(7).
[94] The creation of COPAC was in contemplation at least as early as 1980: Stauder, "Thoughts on the Development of the European Patent Infringement Procedures" [1980] E.I.P.R. 253.

can continue to be tolerated. Trade marks are not monopoly rights in the same sense as patents, so the revocation of invalid registrations is of less importance to the public interest as a whole. Conversely, Community trade marks which are revoked can be converted into national applications without loss of seniority, so the proprietor does not suffer to the same extent from having put all his eggs into one basket.[95] It might be said that trade mark law is inherently less difficult than patent law and that technical or scientific understanding is not needed, removing two reasons for a centralised specialist court.

4-89   Even if all this were true, however, there is every reason to suppose that for the foreseeable future Community trade mark courts in different member states will come to such radically different decisions on the facts that true harmonisation will be thwarted and forum shopping encouraged to an unacceptable extent. First, trade marks, unlike patents, are highly susceptible to differences in language, culture and pronunciation, as is reflected in the diversity from one state to another of trade marks in use or registered. Secondly, national trade mark law is far less thoroughly harmonised than for patents. Harmonisation of many points of substantive patent law occurred for most Community member states in the 1960's or 1970's as a result of the Strasbourg Convention and the European Patent Convention, yet national differences in the approach to such basic questions as infringement and inventive step are still manifest after 20 years or more. Harmonisation of trade mark law has only just commenced, but it is already clear that interpretation of the Trade Mark Directive[96] is heavily coloured by previous national practice. Absent a strong central court capable of deciding issues of fact as well as abstract principles of law, there is no reason to hope that issues such as the degree of confusing similarity between *Scholler Nucki* and *Lucky Whip* will be decided with anything approaching consistency.[97]

---

[95] Community Trade Mark Regulation, Arts 108 *et seq.*

[96] Council Directive 89/104 of December 21, 1988 to Approximate the Laws of Member States relating to Trade Marks [1989] O.J. L40/1.

[97] The example given by Jacobs A-G in Case C–10/89 *SA CNL-Sucal NV v. HAG GF AG (HAG II)* [1990] E.C.R. I–3711; [1990] 3 C.M.L.R. 571.

CHAPTER 5

COMMUNITY PATENTS, TRADE MARKS AND DESIGNS: THE ACTION FOR INFRINGEMENT

A. COMMUNITY PATENTS, TRADE MARKS AND DESIGNS: A NEARLY UNIFORM SYSTEM OF JURISDICTION AT FIRST INSTANCE

Introduction: parallel treatment of the regimes in the present chapter

Any treatment of Community patents, trade marks, designs and plant variety rights at once faces the problem that although the provisions as to enforcement at first instance are virtually the same in all four cases, one still has to refer to four different legal instruments, each with a different numbering scheme and each with slight, but sometimes significant, differences in wording. Of these four instruments, three are Regulations and one is a Convention in its own right with an annexed Protocol.[1] One is in force,[2] one is final but not yet fully implemented,[3] one is still in draft[4] and one has a definitive text but uncertain prospects for implementation.[5] The practical problem for the author is how to preserve the essential simplicity and uniformity of the underlying scheme, while allowing practitioners access to the individual provisions relating to any particular Community intellectual property right.[6]

5–01

The solution adopted in the present chapter is to present the commentary on the Community patent and Community trade mark essentially in parallel, with footnotes or further paragraphs dealing with

5–02

---

[1] The Community Patent Convention and the Protocol on the Settlement of Litigation Concerning the Infringement and Validity of Community Patents, which both form part of the Agreement relating to Community Patents (89/695) published at [1989] O.J. L401/1 and as Cm. 1452. A more convenient source for these and for the Trade Mark and (draft) Design regulations is Booy and Horton, *Sweet & Maxwell's E.C. Intellectual Property Materials* (1994). The Agreement is also printed in several major texts on patent law. See also Benyamini, *Patent Infringement in the European Community* (1993); Report of the House of Lords Select Committee on the European Communities: *A European Community Patent* (1986), especially App. 3; Haardt "The Setting Up of a Court of Appeal for Community Patents" (1985) 16 I.I.C. 332; Wadlow, "The Community Patent Appeal Court" (1986) 11 E.L. Rev. 295; Foglia, "Procedural Aspects of Litigation Relating to Community Patents" (1991) I.I.C. 970; Scordamaglia, "The Common Appeal Court and the Future of the Community Patent Following the Luxembourg Conference" part I (1991) 22 I.I.C. 334 and part II (1991) 22 I.I.C. 458; Young and Birss, "Forum Shopping under the Community Patent Convention" [1992] E.I.P.R. 361.

[2] Council Regulation 40/94 on the Community Trade Mark (December 20, 1993) [1994] O.J. L11/1. The Regulation was slightly amended by Council Regulation 3288/94 (December 22, 1994) [1994] O.J. L349/83 to comply with TRIPs and the consolidated text is printed in issue 1/95 p. 50 of the OHIM O.J. in five languages. See Franzosi, ed., *European Community Trade Mark* (1997); Annand and Norman, *Blackstone's Guide to the Community Trade Mark* (1998). See also Jenkins, "Forum Shopping under the Community Trade Mark Regulation" [1996] February *Trademark World* 24.

[3] Council Regulation 2100/94 (July 27, 1994) [1994] O.J. L227/1 on Community Plant Variety Rights.

[4] The draft Design Regulation. Proposed Regulation [1994] O.J. C29/20. See Franzosi, ed., *European Design Protection* (1996).

[5] The Agreement relating to Community Patents. See also the E.C. Commission *Green Paper on the Community Patent and the Patent System in Europe* COM(97) 31 final of June 24, 1997 and see para. 1–69 above.

[6] The actual legislation is set out in four parallel columns in the Appendix to this book.

Community designs to the extent that they require separate treatment. Community plant variety rights are of such specialised interest that they are mentioned only to the extent that their regime presents particularly interesting features. This is admittedly a compromise. The Community Trade Mark Regulation is the only one of these instruments which is actually in force, so it would be wrong not to give it full treatment. That might suggest that the chapter could be simplified by presenting the law principally in terms of the Community trade mark, with the Community patent relegated to the same status as the Community design. This solution has been rejected for two reasons. One is that the Community patent, if and when implemented,[7] may be expected to be of even greater importance than the Community trade mark, let alone the Community design or plant variety right. The second and perhaps more fundamental reason is that the other three Community intellectual property rights all draw heavily on the scheme for jurisdiction and enforcement devised over a period of almost three decades for the Community patent, and it is easiest to explain that scheme in its original context and by reference to materials which are specifically concerned with patents. The Community patent is also, at least for the time being, better documented than the others.[8]

Principal differences in enforcement between Community patents, trade marks and designs

5–03   The principal difference between the Protocol on Litigation to the Community Patent Convention on the one hand, and the Community Trade Mark Regulation on the other is the absence of a central appeal court corresponding to COPAC.[9] The absence of a central court is also a feature of the Plant Variety Regulation and the draft Design Regulation. Otherwise, it is the similarities between the four schemes which are most striking. Unlike the others, the draft Design Regulation has to deal with unregistered as well as registered rights and it contains one provision missing from its predecessors, facilitating a challenge to the validity of a Community Registered Design in interlocutory proceedings without a formal counterclaim for revocation.[10]

The jurisdiction scheme of the Community Patent Convention summarised

5–04   The Scordamaglia Report[11] on the Community Patent Convention summarises the intent of the Protocol on Litigation as follows:

[7] The possibility of implementing the Community patent, this time by Regulation rather than Convention, has been revived. See above n. 5.

[8] Nothing yet available for the Community trade mark corresponds to the Scordamaglia Report, the House of Lords Report, *op. cit.* or Benyamini *op. cit.*

[9] Institutional matters, which is where the differences are mainly to be found, are treated in Chap. 4, above. See now the E.C. Green Paper, above n. 5, which would remove even this difference. The fact that the detailed jurisdictional and procedural rules of the Community Patent Convention were easily applied to the Community trade mark, plant variety right and design, indicates that they would not require much amendment to cope with the proposed Community Patent Regulation.

[10] Art. 94(2) of the Draft Regulation.

[11] Para. 175. See para. 4–21, above.

"The negotiators were particularly anxious that the patent proprietor should be provided with a single court which could hear any action for infringement committed or threatened in the Contracting States. At the same time, precautions had to be taken to ensure that, given the differences in substantive and procedural law in those States, plaintiffs were not induced to opt for the courts of a particular State to the defendant's detriment. To prevent this practice, known as 'forum shopping,' Art. 14(1) to (3) Prot. Lit. has laid down a set of criteria for identifying a single Contracting State whose courts are assigned jurisdiction over infringements committed throughout the Contracting States (Art. 17(1) Prot. Lit.).

The courts, chosen in the following order, are those of the Contracting State

— in which the defendant is domiciled (ordinary jurisdiction under Art. 2 of the Brussels Convention),
— in which the defendant has an establishment,
— in which the plaintiff is domiciled,
— in which the plaintiff has an establishment,
— in which the CAC[12] has its seat.

Alternatively, the plaintiff may choose a court in the Contracting State in which the acts of infringement have been committed or threatened (Art. 14(5) Prot. Lit.), in which case the territorial jurisdiction of this court will be limited to acts committed or threatened on the territory of the State in which it is situated (Art. 17(2) Prot. Lit.)."

Substantially the same provisions apply, and for the same reasons, to the other three Community intellectual property rights: trade marks, designs and plant variety rights. The rest of the present chapter explains these provisions in detail, and examines how well the intentions of the negotiators have been realised.

B. THE RELEVANT BODIES OF LAW: COMMUNITY LAW AND NATIONAL LAW

Introduction and summary

Although the Community patent has an "autonomous" and "unitary" character,[13] an action for infringement of a Community patent is likely to involve at least three and possibly more independent but interconnected bodies of law: Community law in several manifestations, the national law of the court hearing the action (*lex fori*) and the national law of the place   5–05

---

[12] Common Appeal Court or COPAC.
[13] Community Patent Convention, Art. 2(2) and 2(3). The Community trade mark is "unitary" but not in terms "autonomous" (Community Trade Mark Regulation, Art. 2) although it deserves that description as much as does the Community patent.

or places of infringement (*lex loci delicti commissi*) so far as different. To over-simplify, perhaps: the substantive law of infringement and validity is principally that of the Community Patent Convention itself and the Convention defines which courts have jurisdiction; procedural law (other than as to jurisdiction) is principally that of the forum; and the law relating to remedies principally that of the place or places of infringement.[14] Substantially the same division applies to the Community trade mark. In both cases, there are also rules for identifying the system of national law which governs the Community patent or trade mark as an object of property.[15]

5–06   The Community Patent Convention and Community Trade Mark Regulation are subordinate to the E.C. Treaty itself, and in the event of any conflict the Treaty would prevail.[16] Since they were both drafted with the general law of the European Communities in mind, such conflicts are hardly to be expected but the possibility is recognised and is not entirely academic. The case law of the European Court of Justice is dynamic and constantly evolving, in contrast to a legislative text which is fixed at a single point in time and which—so far as it purports to be declaratory—may represent no more than a summary of how the law was understood to its draftsmen.

5–07   The *lex fori* is relevant to an action for infringement of a Community patent or trade mark in at least three respects. The Community patent or trade mark court is to apply its own national law (including its private international law) on matters not covered by the Convention or Regulation, and it always applies its own procedural law. However, the Convention and Regulation also sometimes make express reference to national law in defining the rights of the parties or the powers and duties of Community patent or trade mark courts, so that, for instance, the power of a court to entertain a *quia timet* action or an action for a declaration for non-infringement, may, as a matter of Community law, be defined by reference to its ability to hear such proceedings under its national law.

5–08   The *lex loci delicti commissi* can be relevant either because the Convention or Regulation expressly requires it to be applied; or, perhaps more frequently, because the application of the private international law of the forum leads to an issue being governed on a state-by-state basis by the *lex loci delicti commissi*, rather than on an E.C.-wide basis by the *lex fori*. The Protocol on Litigation and the Community Trade Mark Regulation expressly provide that final sanctions other than the mandatory injunction are to be governed by the law of the contracting state in which the infringements were committed or threatened. Since one court may have jurisdiction over infringements committed throughout the Community, it follows that a complex exercise in comparative law may be necessary in evaluating damages.

[14] For a more detailed account of the relationship between the various systems of law in the context of the Community patent, see Benyamini, *op.cit.* Chap. 4.
[15] See para. 5–25, below.
[16] Art. 2(1) of the Agreement relating to Community Patents. In the case of the Community trade mark, the conclusion follows from the status of the Regulation.

In addition to general Community law and the autonomous law of the **5–09** Community Patent Convention or Trade Mark Regulation themselves, two bodies of public international law deserve specific mention. The first is the Brussels Convention on Jurisdiction and the Enforcement of Judgments. The Protocol on Litigation and the Community Trade Mark Regulation both provide that the Brussels Convention applies to litigation on Community patents and trade marks except to the extent that it is excluded. The detailed rules on jurisdiction are themselves based on the Brussels Convention scheme, and decisions of the European Court of Justice under the Convention would almost certainly apply to corresponding provisions of the Protocol or Regulation framed in the same terms. Conversely, the Protocol on Litigation has already been relied on by the Advocates-General in the European Court of Justice as providing an analogy for interpreting the Brussels Convention.[17] Secondly, the European Court of Justice has recognised that the E.C. Treaty itself is subject to certain overriding principles, such as the recognition of fundamental human rights, which have the status of *jus cogens* in public international law. The extent of application of the principle has still to be defined, but it must equally well apply to secondary Community legislation and relatively subordinate treaties such as the Community Patent Convention.

The Community Patent Convention, Protocol on Litigation and **5–10** Community Trade Mark Regulation frequently refer to "national law," as distinct from Community law, as if a single ascertainable and well-defined body of national law were in contemplation. As has been seen, some issues are referred expressly to the *lex loci delicti commissi* or the law of the patent or trade mark as an object of property, but this is comparatively rare. The normal technique is to refer to the *lex fori*, but including the rules of private international law of the forum. The preference for the *lex fori* over the *lex loci delicti commissi* has two obvious advantages which are conducive to legal certainty: one system of law applies instead of up to 15, and it is a body of law with which the court will be familiar. Unfortunately, the proviso more than eliminates both these advantages; not least because it fails to take into account the fact that the private international law of infringement is everywhere all but non-existent.[18] To conclude, whether confidently or hesitantly, that a particular question is governed by the *lex fori* is only half the battle, since unless the question is unambiguously one of the procedure the *lex fori* itself could send it off in almost any direction to be decided by one system of law or many.[19]

---

[17] In Case 68/93 *Shevill v. Presse Alliance* [1995] E.C.R. I–415.

[18] No national courts, even in the Netherlands, can be said to have a settled body of jurisprudence. The most obvious suggestion, that the normal private international law of tort applies, is itself highly controversial.

[19] Benyamini, *op. cit.*, suggests "Arguably, the resort to national rules of private international law may be discarded on the ground that there are no such rules which are directly relevant to infringement of Community patents in another Contracting State." But a problem is not so easily converted into an opportunity.

Law relating to infringement

5–11　　The Community Patent Convention and Community Trade Mark Regulation respectively define the "effects" of the Community patent or trade mark, by which is meant the acts which Community law prohibits as infringements.[20] Community law also contains exhaustive lists of the grounds on which a Community patent or trade mark may be found to be invalid. However, questions of liability for infringement cannot be determined solely by Community law, and national law also plays a part.

5–12　　Article 34(1) of the Community Patent Convention provides that "The effects of a Community patent shall be governed solely by the provisions of this Convention. In other respects, infringement of a Community patent shall be governed by the national law relating to infringement of a national patent, in accordance with and subject to the provisions of the Protocol on Litigation." The Protocol on Litigation provides at Article 32 "On all matters not covered by the Agreement relating to Community Patents, a Community patent court shall apply its national law, including its private international law."

5–13　　The Committee of the Whole at the 1975 Luxembourg Diplomatic Conference, in considering what was then Article 38, recorded[21]:

> "The Committee of the Whole noted that Article 38 (36) only dealt with the effects as regards patent law of the Community patent and that national provisions governing acts constituting infringement would continue to apply, for example in respect of tort."

5–14　　The Scordamaglia Report does not provide any further help in explaining what issues might be left to national law, but the distinction seems to be that the question of whether a particular act amounts to an infringement is always and exclusively a matter for Community law; but that whether a particular person is liable for infringement is a matter for national law to the extent that the Community Patent Convention or Protocol on Litigation fail to provide uniform rules.[22] So for an infringing act committed in England, for example, liability for infringement by joint tortfeasorship would still be a matter for English law. The same distinction between the effects of a Community trade mark—which are exclusively a matter of Community law—and liability for infringement, which is partly for national law, is to be found in the Community Trade Mark Regulation.[23]

5–15　　The relationship between the Community Patent Convention and national law may, however, have more radical effects on the existing law of infringement than appears at first sight. The Community Patent

---

[20] Since all Community patents are also European patents, Chap. III of Pt II of the European Patent Convention ("Effects of the European patent . . .") applies, in particular Arts 64 and 69.

[21] Minutes of the 1975 Luxembourg Diplomatic Conference para. 425, p. 282.

[22] See Benyamini, *op. cit.*

[23] Community Trade Mark Regulation, Arts 14(1) and 97(2).

Convention itself incorporates by reference part of the substantive law of the European Patent Convention.[24] This oblique technique for requiring Community patent courts to give effect to the European Patent Convention may not appear to be significant, since the latter is effective in any event by virtue of incorporation into national law, but it does in fact require a reassessment of the relationship between the two. The European Patent Convention does not, as such, have the force of law in the United Kingdom.[25] Unlike the Community Patent Convention, the European Patent Convention is not part of the Community legal order[26]: it has always existed separately, its membership has not corresponded to that of the Community in either fact or intention; its institutions are not Community institutions and their decisions are not subject to the European Court of Justice. Since the two conventions fall to be construed according to different cannons and against different factual backgrounds, a provision in the one does not necessarily have the same legal effects as an identically worded provision in the other.[27]

For the United Kingdom, probably the most significant point arising **5–16** from the incorporation of the European Patent Convention into the Community Patent Convention concerns the respective scope of protection of European and Community patents. Article 69 of the European Patent Convention and the Protocol on its Interpretation define in fairly general terms how the scope of protection of a European patent is to be ascertained. Since it is self-evident that different national courts have continued to decide questions of infringement according to standards which are not identical, the question has arisen as to whether any such variation is consistent with the Protocol on Interpretation. Recent English case law is to the effect that the European Patent Convention does not define a single "European" test for infringement but allows each contracting state to follow its own *via media* consistently with the Protocol.[28] As a matter of public international law this is almost certainly

---

[24] Art. 2(3) of the Community Patent Convention provides that those provisions of the European Patent Convention which are binding upon every European Patent shall be deemed to be provisions of the Community Patent Convention.

[25] The Patents Act 1977 enacts certain provisions of the EPC or CPC in language "framed as to have, as nearly as practicable, the same effects . . . as the corresponding provisions" of the EPC and CPC: s. 130(7).

[26] Case 35/87 *Thetford v. Fiamma* [1988] E.C.R. 3585; [1988] 3 C.M.L.R. 540, *per* Mischo A.-G.

[27] Compare the treatment of the E.C.-Portugal free trade agreement in Case 270/80 *Polydor v. Harlequin* [1982] E.C.R. 329; [1982] 1 C.M.L.R. 677; Opinion 1/91 *First EEA Case* [1991] E.C.R. 6079 on the EEA Agreement; and the treatment of the domestic application of the Modified Brussels Convention under Sched. 4 of the Civil Jurisdiction and Judgments Act 1982 in Case C–346/93 *Kleinwort Benson v. City of Glasgow* [1995] E.C.R. I–615; [1995] All E.R. (E.C.) 514. For confirmation that two texts may have different meanings, though verbally identical, see Borges, "Pierre Menard, Author of the *Quixote*" in *Labyrinths* (1964).

[28] *Kastner v. Rizla* [1995] R.P.C. 585, CA and *Assidoman Multipack v. The Mead Corp* [1995] R.P.C. 321; [1995] F.S.R. 225 not following *PLG Research v. Ardon* [1995] R.P.C. 287; [1995] F.S.R. 116, CA. In English law, an international treaty (unless part of the Community legal order) creates obligations only on the plane of public international law

correct: so far as harmonisation of substantive law is concerned, the European Patent Convention has more in common with old-style treaties such as the Paris or Berne Conventions which set general standards for protection but do not require precise uniformity in implementation. If this were wrong, then any failure by the United Kingdom to implement the Protocol on Interpretation properly would be a breach of its public international law obligations but would not affect private rights.

5–17   In contrast, the Community Patent Convention, once in force, will be part of the "new legal order" of the European Communities and will have to be given effect as such. Article 2, providing that Community patents are unitary and autonomous, that they shall have equal effect throughout the Community, and that they shall be subject only to the provisions of the Community Patent Convention itself and the European Patent Convention, is hardly consistent with even minimal deviations from a single standard of infringement. Article 34 leads to the same conclusion, since the "effects" of the Community patent "which shall be governed solely by the provisions of this Convention" must be defined in terms of what infringes. Though English law as stated in *Catnic*[29] or *Improver*[30] may well be consistent with Article 69 of the European Patent Convention, it by no means follows that either English law or any other existing body of national law corresponds to the single standard contemplated by the Community Patent Convention.[31]

Law relating to defences

5–18   No single body of law can be said to govern defences to an action for infringement of a Community patent or trade mark. Both instruments are subordinate to the E.C. treaty itself and it is possible for a defence to exist under general Community law,[32] without being specifically recognised by the draftsmen of the Convention or the Regulation—whether because it was outside their terms of reference, or because of developments in the general law. The Community Patent Convention and Community Trade Mark Regulation themselves enumerate some defences, such as exhaustion of rights, which are clearly to be applied as a matter of Community law.[33] The definition of the "effects" of a

and does not affect private rights except to the extent that it may be incorporated into domestic law by legislation. In many Continental jurisdictions, however, treaties are capable of being self-executing and do not necessarily require transposition into domestic law. This may account, in part, for the difference between the English view that a "European patent" is no more than a bundle of national patents, and the view sometimes expressed on the Continent that it has a partial degree of unitary and autonomous character, intermediate between ordinary national patents and Community patents.

[29] *Catnic Components v. Hill & Smith* [1981] F.S.R. 60; [1982] R.P.C. 183, HL.
[30] *Improver Corp v. Remington* [1990] F.S.R. 181 (Hoffmann J.).
[31] Similar comments may apply to validity, though national differences in interpretation of the EPC have been less conspicuous. The problem is less marked for trade marks because harmonisation of national law is much more recent, and has been effected by E.C. legislation to which the European Court of Justice may in time give a consistent and binding interpretation.
[32] For example, breaches by the plaintiff of Art. 85 or 86 E.C.
[33] Community Patent Convention, Art. 28; Community Trade Mark Regulation, Art. 13.

Community patent implicitly and in some cases expressly creates corresponding defences or limitations, such as experimental or non-commercial use, which must be governed by uniform Community law.[34] Likewise, the Community Trade Mark Regulation exempts certain *bona fide* uses of a Community trade mark from liability for infringement.[35]

In some cases, a defence existing as a matter of Community law can only be defined by reference to national law. The Community Patent Convention recognises prior rights resulting from national patents or applications.[36] The Convention also expressly provides that national law is to apply to the specific defences of prior use and prior personal possession of an invention, so that a defendant may have a defence in some member states, but not in all, according to the use he made of the invention and the vagaries of national law.[37] The Community Trade Mark Regulation recognises a defence of prior local rights, which need not arise from registration, and the existence and scope of these inevitably requires the application of national law.[38]   **5–19**

Where Community law is silent, the existence and scope of any defences to infringement are presumably determined by the application of the law of the state of the Community patent or trade mark court hearing the action, including its private international law.[39] Depending on that law, this might result either in a defence being decided according to a single system of law, not necessarily the *lex fori*, or in the defence having to be evaluated on a state-by-state basis. A defence that the defendant was licensed, for instance, would almost certainly be decided according to the applicable law of the contract relied on,[40] but an alleged defence of estoppel or acquiescence does not have any obvious single system of law to govern it. Conversely, a defence of breach of national competition law (as opposed to Community law) would have to be decided on a state-by-state basis. Unfortunately, the private international law of defences to intellectual property infringement actions is universally non-existent, because none but the Dutch courts have any experience of hearing actions in respect of infringements abroad. Defences going solely to remedies other than the mandatory final injunction[41] are presumably applied on a state-by-state basis as a result of the application of Article 35(2) of the Protocol on Litigation or Article 98(2) of the Community Trade Mark Regulation.   **5–20**

A major problem arises with the widely recognised defence of innocent infringement. It is reasonably clear from the *travaux préparatoires* to the Community Patent Convention that a deliberate decision was   **5–21**

---

[34] Community Patent Convention, Art. 27.
[35] Community Trade Mark Regulation, Art. 12.
[36] Community Patent Convention, Art. 36.
[37] Community Patent Convention, Art. 37. The Scordamaglia Report (para. 109) regrets the departures of Art. 36 and 37 from the principle of a uniform and autonomous Community patent law.
[38] Community Trade Mark Regulation, Art. 107.
[39] Community Patent Convention, Art. 34; Protocol on Litigation, Art. 32; Community Trade Mark Regulation, Art. 14.
[40] See Chap. 7.
[41] See para. 5–146, below.

taken not to make liability for infringement dependent on the defendant's state of mind, except in the limited cases expressly provided for by Articles 25 and 26. Early drafts referred the question of "complicity or the requirement of fraudulent intent" to national law,[42] without any corresponding provision appearing in either the 1975 or 1985 texts of the Community Patent Convention.[43] Likewise, the Community Trade Mark Regulation treats *bona fides* as relevant only in the context of Article 12, and does not make liability for infringement dependent on the defendant's state of mind in any other way. It ought to follow that defences of innocence, by whatever name, existing under national law cannot as a matter of principle provide a complete defence to an action for infringement of a Community patent or trade mark.[44] The problem which remains is whether a national law which recognises innocence as a defence to a specific remedy, in particular damages, is preserved by Article 35(2) of the Protocol on Litigation[45] or Article 98(2) of the Community Trade Mark Regulation. Neither interpretation is entirely satisfactory. If innocence is not a defence to damages, then liability for patent infringement under the Convention is far more draconian than under the domestic law of the majority of member states.[46] If it is, then one has the paradoxical position that a defendant may be worse off in a country which purports to recognise innocence as a defence to infringement as such, than in one where it is only a defence to a remedy.

Invalidity, whether raised on its own in the relevant Office or as a defence on a counterclaim to infringement proceedings in a national court, is with a few minor and narrowly defined exceptions, wholly governed by Community law.[47]

Law of procedure

5–22   Civil procedure is among the least harmonised areas of law in the European Communities and is likely to remain so for the foreseeable future. Procedure in patent cases, especially, also has to deal with particular issues not relevant in other areas of law. The Protocol on Litigation to the Community Patent Convention and the Community

---

[42] Art. 20b(2) of the 1962 draft; Art. 12(1) of the 1970 and 1972 drafts corresponds. The Basic Text discussed at the Luxembourg Diplomatic Conference in 1975 lacked this provision, and the issue was not apparently revisited.

[43] See Benyamini, *op. cit.*, 4.4.1.

[44] Benyamini cites Art. 51 of the French patent law, under which a person other than a manufacturer is not liable at all for acts committed unknowingly and in good faith. See also Bouju, ed., *Patent Infringement Litigation Penalties* (1989) for a comparative survey.

[45] Such defences are widely recognised, though with much variation in their scope and availability. See Benyamini, *loc. cit.*, and Bouju, *op. cit.* The Community Plant Variety Regulation, Art. 94(2), makes liability for damages depend on the presence and degree of negligence in the German manner.

[46] This is the solution preferred by Benyamini, *op. cit.*, but if the member states intended such a drastic departure from a widely recognised consensus one would have expected express language.

[47] Although national law may govern incidental questions, such as whether a disclosure was made in confidence or whether the plaintiff is not the true owner.

Trade Mark Regulation contain detailed rules for determining jurisdiction and some relating to other aspects of procedure, such as stays of pending proceedings. Otherwise the Protocol and Regulation adopt the only feasible approach in the circumstances which is to say that procedure is governed by the *lex fori*. Article 33(1) of the Protocol on Litigation provides: "Unless otherwise specified in the Agreement relating to Community Patents, a Community patent court shall apply the rules of procedure governing the same type of action relating to a national patent in the Contracting State where it has its seat." Article 97(3) is to the same effect for the Community Trade Mark Regulation.

Law of remedies

The right to a permanent injunction after trial is governed by **5–23** Community law. For both Community patents and trade marks, it is provided that where the court finds that the defendant has infringed or threatened to infringe the plaintiffs' rights, it shall, unless there are special reasons to the contrary, make an order prohibiting the defendant from proceeding with the acts which infringed or would have infringed.[48] The trial court is also obliged to take whatever measures are appropriate under its national law to ensure that the order is complied with. Apart from the mandatory injunction, the Community patent or trade mark court is obliged to apply the law of the member state in which the acts of infringement or threatened infringement were committed, including its private international law.[49] This most obviously applies to the pecuniary remedies of damages or an account of profits.[50] It follows, at least in principle, that an exercise in comparative law will be required whenever there has been infringement on a sufficiently large scale and in several countries.[51] Bouju (who includes some non-E.C. states in his survey) comments on the extreme diversity of the principles and methods of assessing damages and the fact that no country has a clear and precise method for the assessment of monetary damages. Limitation periods for accrued damages, the liability of innocent infringers and the ability of licensees to recover also differ widely.

The 1975 Luxembourg Diplomatic Conference on the Community **5–24** Patent Convention recognised the desirability of a uniform law as to remedies, but rejected this as a practical proposition in the short term[52]:

"The AIPPI delegation had proposed . . . that the reference to national law in Article 38 (36) should be replaced by Community

---

[48] Protocol on Litigation, Art. 35(1); Community Trade Mark Regulation, Art. 98(1).

[49] Protocol on Litigation, Art. 35(2); Community Trade Mark Regulation, Art. 98(2).

[50] Damages are universally available. An account of profits, if available at all, may be regarded either as a remedy for infringement or for a separate cause of action in unjust enrichment.

[51] For patents there is a comparative survey of remedies in Bouju, ed., *Patent Infringement Litigation Penalties* (1989). See also Karnell, "Computation of Damages for Patent Infringement . . . A Comparative Law Overview" [1997] I.P.Q. 92.

[52] Minutes of the 1975 Luxembourg Diplomatic Conference, para. 424, p. 282. Art. 38 corresponds to Art. 34 of the 1989 Community Patent Convention.

rules on civil sanctions for infringement, penal sanctions being dealt with by Article 75 (79).

Working Party I had considered this proposal favourably, but felt that the time was not yet ripe for laying down uniform Community remedies in this respect. Moreover, attention had been drawn to the draft Resolution on future litigation of Community patents, and to the statement by the Commission . . . referring to its current work in relation to the establishment of uniform rules on choice of law for contractual and noncontractual obligations, rights *in rem* and intellectual property.

The Committee of the Whole confirmed that the proposal by the AIPPI delegation could not be adopted at present, and took note of a request by the AIPPI delegation that this proposal be taken into account when the Resolution on future litigation of Community patents was implemented and by the Commission in its work."

The law of the Community patent or trade mark as an object of property

5–25   A Community patent or trade mark as an object of property has its principal characteristics defined by Community law.[53] In particular, the unitary character of the patent or trade mark means that it can be assigned or otherwise dealt with only as a whole,[54] although both Community patents and trade marks can be licensed in whole or in part, as to scope or territory.[55] Transfers of Community patents[56] and trade marks[57] must be in writing and, unless the result of a judgment, require the signatures of the parties. Transfers are not effective against third parties until registered.[58] Applications for Community patents and trade marks are subject to the same regime as Community patents and trade marks which have been granted.[59] This is in contrast to an application for a European patent, which (even at the application stage) is subject in each contracting state to the law of that state applicable to national patent applications.[60]

[53] Community Patent Convention, Pt II, Chap. IV comprising Arts 38 to 44; Community Trade Mark Regulation, Tit. II, s. 4 comprising Arts 16 to 24. The term *lex situs* is potentially misleading in relation to Community patents and trade marks: it is only in residual cases that the *situs* of the register will necessarily correspond to the law of the patent or trade mark as an object of property.

[54] Community Patent Convention, Art. 38(1); Community Trade Mark Regulation, Art. 16(1).

[55] Community Patent Convention, Art. 42; Community Trade Mark Regulation, Art. 22.

[56] Community Patent Convention, Art. 39(1). The Scordamaglia Report (para. 111) explains that "transfer" is intended to include succession on death as well as assignment *inter vivos*.

[57] Community Trade Mark Regulation, Art. 17(3), providing that any transfer not meeting the requirements of writing and signature is to be "void".

[58] Community Patent Convention, Art. 39(3); Community Trade Mark Regulation, Art. 23(1). Third parties taking with notice are not protected.

[59] Community Patent Convention, Art. 44; Community Trade Mark Regulation, Art. 24.

[60] Art. 148 of the European Patent Convention disapplies the normal rule of Art. 74 EPC.

In the case of a Community trade mark, it is stated expressly that it **5–26** may be assigned separately from the undertaking (*sc.* of the proprietor) and in respect of some or all of the goods or services for which it is registered[61]; that a transfer of the whole undertaking includes the transfer of the Community trade mark[62]; and that the Community trade mark may be given as security or made the subject of rights *in rem*.[63] These rules are more liberal than might have applied, in some countries, according to domestic law. However, the Office must refuse to register a transfer if it is clear from the transfer documents that as a result of it the trade mark would be likely to mislead the public as to the nature, quality or geographical origin of the goods or services.[64]

To the extent that its nature as an object of property is not **5–27** exhaustively defined by Community law, a Community patent or trade mark is treated as a national patent or trade mark registered in a member state identified according to specified rules applied to the entry in the relevant Community Register at Munich or Alicante.[65] This does not cause it to lose its unitary character, because the Community patent or trade mark as an entity continues to be governed by a single system of law, albeit the national law of a particular member state.[66] The provisions of the Community Patent Convention and Community Trade Mark Regulation in this respect are broadly similar in effect, but differ in wording and detail. The major difference is that the law of a Community patent is defined from the outset once and for all,[67] whereas the Community Trade Mark Regulation appears to contemplate that the law of a Community trade mark may change from time to time. In both cases, the relevant rules have to be applied in strict sequence until one of them yields the law of a member state. In the case of Community patents,[68] the relevant national law so identified also determines by analogy, but with Community-wide effect, whether or not a particular kind of right in a patent is effective only after registration in the Register

---

[61] Community Trade Mark Regulation, Art. 16(1).

[62] Community Trade Mark Regulation, Art. 17(2), subject to agreement to the contrary (determined by the applicable law of the agreement, not by the law of the Community trade mark) or where circumstances clearly dictate otherwise. The same applies *mutatis mutandis* to an agreement to transfer.

[63] Community Trade Mark Regulation, Art. 19.

[64] Community Trade Mark Regulation, Art. 17(4). The Office may require the registration to be limited to goods or services in respect of which the mark is not likely to mislead.

[65] Community Patent Convention, Act. 38(1), Community Trade Mark Regulation, Art. 16(1), see below. For Community patent applications, note that Art. 74 of the European Patent Convention does not apply and a single system of law governs the application as a whole.

[66] This is in contrast to the European Patent Convention, Arts 2(2) and 74.

[67] The Minutes of the 1975 Luxembourg Diplomatic Conference, para. 426, make it clear that there was some concern that the proprietor might change the law applicable to the patent.

[68] There is no corresponding provision in the Community Trade Mark Regulation. Presumably Art. 23 constitutes a complete code.

of Community Patents.[69] It is not possible for either a Community patent or a Community trade mark to be governed, as an object of property, by the law of a non-member state.

5–28 For a Community patent, the relevant member state is determined according to Article 38 of the Community Patent Convention at the date of filing the European patent application and is defined by an entry in the Register of European Patents for the residence or principal place of business of the applicant[70]; failing that a place of business of the applicant[71]; or failing that the place of business of the applicant's representative.[72] If none of these apply, the law is that of Germany.[73] In the case of the Community trade mark, the applicable national law is to be determined from the Register of Community trade marks at the "relevant date" according to where the proprietor has his seat or domicile,[74] or, failing that, where the proprietor has an establishment.[75] If neither of the foregoing yields a result, Spanish law applies.[76]

5–29 The courts of the member state determined by the foregoing rules have exclusive jurisdiction in respect of proceedings to levy execution against a Community trade mark,[77] or to enforce judgments, etc., against a Community patent.[78] Jurisdiction in bankruptcy proceedings and the like is, for a transitional period, determined according to the member state in which proceedings are first brought.[79]

5–30 The law for Community designs is similar to that for trade marks, except that in the case of unregistered Community designs the law of the design as an object of property has to be determined according to where the proprietor actually has his seat, domicile or establishment on the relevant date, since there is no register.[80] The law for Community plant variety rights more closely resembles that for Community patents, except that it is to be ascertained at the "relevant date" rather than the date of application.[81]

---

[69] Community Patent Convention, Art. 38(4). The Scordamaglia Report, para. 110, gives the example of a lien against a patent, which, as a matter of Dutch law, is effective only once registered. If the application of Art. 38(1) led to a Community patent having to be being treated as a national patent for the Netherlands, the relevant provisions of Dutch national law would apply by virtue of Art. 38(4).

[70] Community Patent Convention, Art. 38(1)(a).

[71] Community Patent Convention, Art. 38(1)(b). The question is not whether the applicant had a place of business in a member state as a matter of fact, but whether a place of business in a member state is entered as such in the Register.

[72] Community Patent Convention, Art. 38(1)(c). The representative whose name is entered first is the only one to count. In contrast to the previous two rules, the address of the representative apparently need not have appeared on the Register for Art. 38(1)(c) to apply.

[73] Community Patent Convention, Art. 38(2). There are special rules in Art. 28(3) for co-proprietors.

[74] Community Trade Mark Regulation, Art. 16(1)(a).

[75] Community Trade Mark Regulation, Art. 16(1)(b).

[76] Community Trade Mark Regulation, Art. 16(2). There are special rules in Art. 16(3) for co-proprietors.

[77] Community Trade Mark Regulation, Art. 20.

[78] Community Patent Convention, Art. 40.

[79] Community Patent Convention, Art. 41; Community Trade Mark Regulation, Art. 21.

[80] Draft Design Regulation, Art. 29.

[81] Community Plant Variety Regulation, Art. 22.

C. INCORPORATION AND EXCLUSION OF THE BRUSSELS CONVENTION IN THE PROTOCOL ON LITIGATION AND THE COMMUNITY TRADE MARK REGULATION

Relationship to the Brussels Convention: Articles 13 and 90[82]

By Articles 13 and 90 respectively, the Protocol on Litigation and the Community Trade Mark Regulation are both expressed to incorporate the provisions of the Brussels Convention on Jurisdiction and Enforcement of Judgments except to the extent that the Brussels Convention is excluded or modified.[83] The Scordamaglia Report explains the relationship in the context of the Community Patent Convention[84]:

> "The Brussels Convention applies to all legal decisions in civil and commercial matters. Art. 13 Prot. Lit. thus exists purely for information purposes, in common with Art. 66 CPC which states the principle that the Brussels Convention applies to all other civil actions relating to Community patents. At the same time, these provisions were made necessary by the fact that the Protocol on Litigation and the CPC lay down explicit exceptions to the Brussels Convention."

5–31

In the case of the Community Patent Convention, Article 57(1) of the Brussels Convention contemplates that the member states may conclude separate conventions relating to particular matters, with different rules as to jurisdiction than the Brussels Convention.[85] The Community Trade Mark Regulation relies on the derogation for future legislative acts of institutions of the Communities contained in Article 57(3).[86]

5–32

Brussels Convention provisions excluded or modified

Both the Protocol on Litigation and the Community Trade Mark Regulation exclude certain provisions of the Brussels Convention. These are Articles 2, 4, 5(1), (3), (4), (5) and 24. Articles 17 and 18 apply with one express modification and one which is implicit.[87] The Scordamaglia Report comments in the following general terms on the Articles of the Brussels Convention which are excluded:

5–33

---

[82] The form "Articles 13 and 90" or even "Article 13/90" is used here as a convenient shorthand for "Article 13 of the Protocol on Litigation and Article 90 of the Community Trade Mark Regulation."

[83] Draft Design Regulation, Art. 83 corresponds. For the Community Plant Variety Regulation, see para. 5–51.

[84] Para. 172.

[85] Scordamaglia Report, para. 174.

[86] This causes complications in how references to the European Court of Justice are to be made: see para. 5–52.

[87] The latter arises from treating establishment on a par with domicile: see para. 5–42.

"The Protocol on Litigation has established uniform rules equally applicable where defendants are domiciled in a third country, whereas in such cases the Brussels Convention refers to the provisions of national law, even where they differ. Art. 13(2) Prot. Lit. excludes the application of Articles 2, 4 and 5, point 3, of the Brussels Convention, replacing them with the independent provisions of Art. 14 Prot. Lit.

The non-application of Article 5, points 1, 4 and 5, of the Brussels Convention was intended as a precaution to prevent the plaintiff from circumventing the rules of international jurisdiction applicable to infringement by disguising his suit as proceedings to obtain the performance of a contract (point 1), as an action arising out of the operations of a branch, agency or other establishment (point 5) or as a civil claim for damages relating to criminal proceedings (point 4)."

5–34 Although Article 2 of the Brussels Convention—its principal jurisdiction-creating provision—is excluded by both the Protocol and the Regulation, both re-enact in their own language the basic rule that a defendant domiciled in a state of the Community should be sued in the courts of the contracting state where he is domiciled. To this extent, the exclusion of Article 2 is less radical than might appear. Article 3 of the Brussels Convention is not expressly disapplied or modified, but must be read so that defendants domiciled in a contracting state can only be sued according to the rules of jurisdiction set out in the Protocol on Litigation or the Community Trade Mark Regulation as well as Title II of the Brussels Convention as modified.

5–35 The effect of excluding Article 4 of the Brussels Convention is that jurisdiction over defendants domiciled outside the contracting states is also always governed by uniform Community rules, rather than by the application of the national law of the forum, as would be the case under the Brussels Convention. As the Scordamaglia Report puts it: "The Protocol on Litigation has established uniform rules equally applicable where defendants are domiciled in a third country, whereas in such cases the Brussels Convention refers to the provisions of national law even where they differ." It follows that national rules on extraterritorial jurisdiction have no place in the scheme of the Community patent or trade mark, whether the defendant is domiciled in a member state or not, and that the Protocol on Litigation and Community Trade Mark Regulation each constitutes a complete code as to jurisdiction.

5–36 The otherwise puzzling exclusion of Article 5(1) of the Brussels Convention is expressly *ex abundati cautela* in case someone should disguise an infringement action so heavily as to pass for one in contract. However, it would not be unusual in a dispute between licensor and licensee for genuine claims to be framed simultaneously in tort, for infringement, and in contract, for breach of the licence. This raises the question of whether the contractual claim would be governed, in the case of a patent licence, by the Protocol on Litigation or the unmodified Brussels Convention. Articles 13(2) and 14 of the Protocol on Litigation apply to "proceedings governed by this Protocol" which seems to exclude contractual claims, even if the subject matter of the contract is a Community patent. Since contractual claims would be outside the jurisdiction of Community patent courts of first instance in their capacity as such, the answer seems to be that the claim under the licence could possibly be heard by the Community patent court, but only under any parallel jurisdiction it might have in the general law and with the unmodified Brussels Convention scheme applying. The same reasoning applies *mutatis mutandis* to Community Trade Marks.

The exclusion of Article 5(3) is important as it would otherwise give **5–37** jurisdiction in tort to the courts of the place of infringement as "the place where the harmful event occurred," but Articles 14(5) and 93(5) give jurisdiction based on the place of infringement instead, though relief is territorially limited.[88] Article 5(4) applies to civil relief ordered in criminal proceedings, for which there is no corresponding provision in the Protocol on Litigation or Community Trade Mark Regulation. Apart from the fact that criminal prosecution for patent infringement, at least, is very rare anywhere in Europe, allowing non-specialist criminal courts to exercise any such jurisdiction would be contrary to the scheme of assigning infringement litigation to a limited number of designated civil courts.[89] Article 5(5) would otherwise give jurisdiction on matters "arising out of the operation of a branch, agency or other establishment" to the courts where the branch, (etc.), was situated. The Article has been interpreted restrictively by the European Court of Justice, and the treatment of "establishments" under the Protocol on Litigation and the Community Trade Mark Regulation is rather different.[90]

Finally—so far as the excluded articles are concerned—interlocutory **5–38** injunctions and the like are particularly important in intellectual property infringement actions. Both the Protocol on Litigation and the Community Trade Mark Regulation contain more detailed provisions as to "provisional, including protective measures" than does the excluded Article 24 of the Brussels Convention.[91]

Provisions as to jurisdiction at variance with the Brussels Convention

The golden rule of the Brussels Convention—that defendants **5–39** domiciled in the Community should be sued in the courts of the contracting state where they are domiciled—is preserved in the Protocol on Litigation and the Community Trade Mark Regulation. However, the rules which come into operation if the golden rule is inapplicable show some quite radical departures from the scheme and policy of the Brussels Convention.

---

[88] See para. 5–136.

[89] Though Art. 74 of the Community Patent Convention provides for national penal sanctions (if any) to apply to Community patents as to national ones. In any but the clearest cases, and if any arise, the criminal court might be well advised to invoke the preliminary reference procedure of Art. 30 of the Protocol on Litigation.

[90] See paras 5–42 *et seq.* and 5–70 *et seq.*

[91] See para. 5–141.

5-40   If the defendant is not domiciled in the Community, but has an establishment in it, then proceedings for infringement of a Community patent or trade mark are to be brought in the courts of the state of the establishment. This is not to equate establishment with domicile, because the defendant's establishment only becomes relevant if he is not domiciled in the Community: the plaintiff does not have the option of choosing between domicile and establishment as the basis for jurisdiction. The Brussels Convention itself pays very little attention to establishment: Article 5(5) permits actions "arising out of the operations of a branch, agency or other establishment" to be brought in the courts of the place where the branch, (etc.), is situated but the Article has received a restrictive interpretation and the word "establishment" in the Protocol on Litigation alludes to a different origin in the form of Article 3 of the Paris Convention.[92] The Protocol on Litigation and Community Trade Mark Regulation are in any event different in that the jurisdiction they create is not concurrent with that of the defendant's domicile, as it is for Article 5(5). On the other hand, if jurisdiction based on place of establishment exists at all, it is perfectly general and is not confined to acts arising out of, or even connected with, the operations of the establishment. In other respects, the Protocol on Litigation and Community Trade Mark Regulation go some way to assimilating establishment to domicile, though not to the extent that the two may be regarded as interchangeable.[93]

5-41   A more radical departure from the Brussels Convention arises where the defendant has neither his domicile nor an establishment in the Community. The Brussels Convention typically leaves questions of jurisdiction to national law if the defendant is not domiciled in a member state. In contrast, the Protocol on Litigation and the Community Trade Mark Regulation confer jurisdiction on the courts of the plaintiff's domicile (or failing that, his establishment) if that is within the Community. Since such defendants are *ex hypothesi* domiciled outside the Community the Scordamaglia Report may be literally correct to say that the Agreement relating to Community Patents "is in complete harmony with the Brussels Convention in making no provision for these jurisdictions[94] to be used against defendants domiciled on the territory of a Contracting State"[95] but the Brussels Convention emphatically rejects jurisdiction by reason of *forum actoris*, as the European Court of Justice has many times affirmed. The fallback jurisdictional provision, that in the absence of any other connecting factor, jurisdiction rests with the

---

[92] See para. 5–70.
[93] Art. 33(3) of the Protocol on Litigation and Art. 90(2)(c) of the Community Trade Mark Regulation.
[94] *sc*. Arts 13(2) and (3) of the Protocol on Litigation.
[95] Scordamaglia Report, para. 177. It has to be said that the Brussels Convention displays no policy of protecting the legitimate interests of defendants domiciled outside the contracting states, and in some respects it treats them very badly. See Briggs & Rees, *Civil Jurisdiction and Judgments* (2nd ed., 1997), para. 7.04 remarking that such a defendant "is at the mercy of those jurisdictional rules which are deemed to be no longer fit to be used against Europeans."

courts of the seat of COPAC or the Community Trade Mark Office, has no counterpart in the Brussels Convention but cannot be said to be contrary to its spirit.

Title II of the Brussels Convention as adapted

In applying Title II of the Brussels Convention[96] to Community patents and trade marks, Article 33(3) of the Protocol on Litigation and Article 90(2)(c) of the Community Trade Mark Regulation provide that provisions applicable to persons domiciled in a contracting state shall also be applicable to persons not so domiciled but having an "establishment" therein. Taking account of the fact that some of the provisions of Title II of the Convention are excluded altogether, and others are independent of domicile, the main practical effects of this provision are as follows:　　5–42

Article 2 of the Brussels Convention is irrelevant because it is one of those excluded. Article 3 prevents the so-called exorbitant grounds of jurisdiction under existing national law being invoked against defendants domiciled in the Community, and defendants with an establishment will be similarly protected.[97] Article 4 and those provisions of Article 5 which might otherwise be relevant are also excluded.　　5–43

Article 6 is of importance, because Article 6(1) gives jurisdiction over multiple defendants and Article 6(3) applies to counterclaims.[98] In its application to Community patents and trade marks, Article 6(1) will have the effect that persons domiciled or with an establishment in a contracting state may be sued, irrespective of the place of their domicile or establishment, in the courts of the place where any defendant is domiciled. What is less clear on the face of the provision, is whether it was intended that a defendant, either domiciled in a contracting state or having an establishment in one, might also be sued in a court which has jurisdiction solely by virtue of another defendant's place of establishment.[99] This broader interpretation is confirmed by the commentary in the Scordamaglia Report[1]:　　5–44

> "Art. 13(3) Prot. Lit. extends the application of the jurisdiction provisions of the Brussels Convention beyond persons domiciled in

[96] Consisting of Art 2 to 24 inclusive, collectively entitled "Jurisdiction."

[97] Though it is not obvious why the national exorbitant grounds should ever be relevant to anyone, since the Protocol, or Regulation, defines a complete code as to jurisdiction. The exclusion of the Brussels Convention, Art. 4 means that none of the national grounds, exorbitant or not, are available to be used against defendants not domiciled in a contracting state.

[98] The mandatory counterclaim for revocation is dealt with by Art. 15(1)(d) of the Protocol on Litigation and Arts 92(d) and 96 of the Community Trade Mark Regulation. It is doubtful in any event if a counterclaim for revocation is "a counterclaim arising from the same . . . facts on which the original claim was based" so as to fall within Art. 6(3) of the Brussels Convention.

[99] Art. 6(1) is clearly inapplicable if jurisdiction over the other defendant(s) is based on the plaintiff's domicile or place of establishment, the place of infringement, or the seat of the relevant Community institution.

[1] Para. 180.

273

a Contracting State to include those with an establishment there. The main purpose of this provision is to enable proceedings to be brought before the court having jurisdiction over the domicile or establishment of any one of a plurality of defendants (Art. 6, point 1), and to allow agreements conferring jurisdiction in accordance with Art. 17 to be concluded when one of the parties at least has an establishment in a Contracting State. In this respect too the Protocol enhances the harmonising effect of the Brussels Convention."

5–45　Articles 6a to 15 are unlikely to be relevant to infringement actions, and to the extent that Article 16 is relevant at all, it expressly depends on neither domicile nor establishment. Article 17, allowing prorogation of jurisdiction by advance agreement between one or more parties domiciled in a contracting state, will apply equally when one or more parties has an establishment in a contracting state. If none of the parties has its domicile or an establishment in a contracting state, then the proviso to Article 17 will mean that no court other than that chosen may accept jurisdiction unless the chosen court has declined it. Articles 18 and 19 do not depend on domicile.

5–46　The modified application of Article 20 is complicated, since in some circumstances it may benefit the defendant with an establishment in a contracting state and in other circumstances it would be to his disadvantage. The original Article in the Brussels Convention protects defendants domiciled in a contracting state against unjustified default judgments by providing that where a defendant domiciled in one contracting state is sued in the courts of another contracting state and does not enter an appearance, the court must declare of its own motion that it has no jurisdiction unless its jurisdiction is derived from the Brussels Convention. Clearly, defendants not domiciled in a contracting state but having an establishment in it are protected if they are sued for infringement in the courts of a place other than where they have an establishment, but if the court where they are sued concludes that they have an establishment within its jurisdiction, then it may enter a judgment in default of appearance and need not declare that it has no jurisdiction. The remaining Articles of Title II do not depend on domicile.

Prorogation of jurisdiction: Articles 17 and 18

5–47　Articles 17 and 18 of the Brussels Convention respectively allow the parties to confer jurisdiction by advance agreement, or by submission, on a court which would not otherwise be competent. The modification effected by Articles 13(2) of the Protocol on Litigation and 90(2)(b) of the Community Trade Mark Regulation is that the first instance court so chosen must be a Community patent court or Community trade mark court as the case may be. Neither advance agreement nor entry of an appearance by the defendant can confer jurisdiction on a court which is not a Community patent court or a Community trade mark court.[2]

"The alternative jurisdictions under Art. 14(1) to (3) and (5) Prot. Lit. are not exclusive. The parties are at liberty, in accordance with the principles of civil law, to extend jurisdiction to a court of another State and to confer on it exclusive jurisdiction. The prorogation may be explicit, being based on an agreement conferring jurisdiction, or implicit, where the defendant tacitly accepts it by entering an appearance before a court which would not otherwise have jurisdiction.

Art. 14(4) Prot. Lit. refers to Arts. 17 and 18 of the Brussels Convention, but restricts the parties' freedom to extend jurisdiction. An agreement conferring jurisdiction or the defendant's tacit acceptance of a court which would not otherwise have jurisdiction is only admissible if it is a Community patent court. The purpose of this is to ensure a high level of competence on the part of the judges."[3]

Article 17 of the Brussels Convention is also implicitly modified by   **5–48** Article 33(3) of the Protocol on Litigation and Article 90(2)(c) of the Community Trade Mark Regulation so that parties with a establishment in the Community are treated on a par with parties domiciled there. This means that an effective exclusive choice of court clause will have full effect if any party to the agreement is domiciled, or has an establishment in, the Community. The fallback provision—that the courts of other contracting states have no jurisdiction unless the court or courts chosen have declined jurisdiction—will only apply if no party to the agreement has a domicile or establishment in a member state.

The application of the unmodified Brussels Convention

Apart from Title II, the provisions of the Brussels Convention apply to   **5–49** actions for infringement of Community patents and trade marks in unmodified form, so as to require, for instance, judgments of a competent Community patent or trade mark court to be recognised and enforced throughout the Community. Judgments revoking or amending a Community patent, or revoking or invalidating a Community trade mark would in any event take effect *in rem* under Articles 20 of the Protocol on Litigation and Article 54 of the Community Trade Mark Regulation respectively. However, the application of the enforcement provisions of the Brussels Convention is important in respect of injunctions, whether interlocutory or final, pecuniary relief and costs.

---

[2] In the case of Art. 18 as modified, there is a problem as to the territorial extent of jurisdiction conferred by entry of an appearance before a Community patent or trade mark court: see para. 5–84. Note also that courts which are not Community patent or trade mark courts have some jurisdiction to grant provisional and protective measures, though only with national effect.

[3] Scordamaglia Report para. 176.

5–50   The decisions of COPAC take effect directly by virtue of the Agreement relating to Community Patents, and not the Brussels Convention, since it is not a "court or tribunal of a member state" within the terms of Article 25 of the latter. Likewise, decisions of the European Patent Office take effect under the European Patent Convention or the Community Patent Convention. Awards of costs in the European Patent Office or on appeal to COPAC are enforceable under Article 104(3) of the European Patent Convention which is made applicable to revocation proceedings under the Community Patent Convention by Article 60(3) of the latter.

Enforcement proceedings relating to judgments, etc., against a Community Patent as an object of property are governed by Article 40 of the Community Patent Convention. Article 20(2) of the Community Trade Mark Regulation corresponds.[4]

The Community Plant Variety Regulation

5–51   A major and inexplicable difference between the Plant Variety Right Regulation and the others is that the Lugano Convention, rather than the Brussels Convention, is deemed to apply to infringement proceedings to the extent that the Regulation does not contain its own specific rules.[5] This potentially creates major conceptual difficulties, since the Lugano Convention is not part of the Community legal order[6] and the European Court of Justice has no power to interpret it.[7] Switzerland, Liechtenstein, Norway and Iceland are members of the Lugano Convention without being members of the Brussels Convention or the European Communities. It is therefore impossible to understand how the Plant Variety Right Regulation can have effect in so far as it provides, for instance, that proceedings for infringement shall be brought in the "Member State or other Contracting Party to the Lugano Convention in which the defendant is domiciled."[8]

Problems with references to the European Court of Justice

5–52   In the case of Community trade marks, designs and plant variety rights a problem may arise when a court in a member state wishes to make a reference to the European Court of Justice on a matter relating to

---

[4] See para. 5–25.
[5] Art. 101.
[6] One may even wonder whether the draftsman misunderstood the nature of the Lugano Convention. Otherwise, the only credible explanation lies in the objections of the EFTA states to jurisdiction over persons domiciled in their territories being subjected to a regime which was different to and more onerous than that under the Lugano Convention. If so, the solution may be more troublesome than the problem. The objections of the EFTA states to the Community Patent Convention and the Community Trade Mark Regulation were never resolved.
[7] cf. Opinion 1/91 *First EEA Case* [1991] E.C.R. 6079.
[8] Art. 101(2)(a).

jurisdiction or the recognition and enforcement of judgments.[9] The problem may be illustrated with regard to a question of jurisdiction under the Community Trade Mark Regulation.

The Community Trade Mark Regulation employs three legislative techniques to allocate jurisdiction: it provides for the Brussels Convention to apply except in so far as modified or excluded, it modifies certain provisions of the Convention in their application to Community trade marks and it contains its own specific rules. This is all as permitted by Article 57(3) of the Brussels Convention. The problem arises from the fact that the jurisdiction of the European Court of Justice to entertain preliminary references derives from Article 177 E.C. in the case of the Regulation, but from Article 1 of the 1971 Protocol on Interpretation in the case of the Brussels Convention. The problem is compounded by the fact that an Article 177 reference may be made by any court or tribunal of a member state, but a reference under the Brussels Convention can only be made by an appellate court. What, therefore, is to happen if a first instance court attempts to refer a complicated question as to its jurisdiction? Does the European Court of Justice interpret only those provisions which are specific to the Regulation, or does it adopt an all-or-nothing approach and either refuse to accept the reference altogether or answer every question, in effect interpreting pure Brussels Convention provisions under Article 177 E.C. on the basis that they have been incorporated by reference? No solution is obviously satisfactory. **5–53**

The situation becomes even more bizarre in the case of the Community Plant Variety Rights Regulation, which unlike the other two regulations purports to incorporate the general provisions of the Lugano Convention rather than the Brussels Convention.[10] The Lugano Convention may in terms be virtually identical to the Brussels Convention, but it is a separate treaty in public international law and it does not form part of the Community legal order. Switzerland, Iceland, Norway and Liechtenstein are members of the Lugano Convention without being members of the Brussels Convention or the European Communities. The European Court of Justice has no jurisdiction to interpret the Lugano Convention,[11] and its decisions on the interpretation of the Brussels Convention are strictly speaking not binding in interpreting the former.[12] Either the Regulation confers on the Court a previously unheard of jurisdiction to interpret the Lugano Convention by the back **5–54**

---

[9] The problem does not arise in the case of the Community Patent Convention, since Community patent courts of first instance cannot make preliminary references under either the Brussels Convention or the special provisions of the Protocol on Litigation. In both cases, the reference to the European Court of Justice would be made by an appellate court.

[10] Community Plant Variety Rights Regulation, Art. 101(1). See para. 5–51, above.

[11] Jenard and Moller Report, paras 110 *et seq.*

[12] Though the preamble to Protocol 2 to the Lugano Convention recites that decisions of the European Court of Justice under the Brussels Convention were taken into account.

door under Article 177 E.C., or any preliminary reference would in all probability be abortive.[13]

5–55   What is even more remarkable is that the application of Article 101(2) of the Regulation may result in an action for infringement of a Community plant variety right being assigned to a court of a state which is not a member state of the European Communities, but which is given jurisdiction over infringements in all member states! Whether the Regulation can confer jurisdiction in this way must be open to question, but in any event the non-member-state court cannot apply for a preliminary ruling by any existing procedure.

D. JURISDICTION UNDER THE PROTOCOL TO THE COMMUNITY PATENT CONVENTION AND THE COMMUNITY TRADE MARK REGULATION

Introduction: Article 14 (patents) and Article 93 (trade marks)

5–56   Actions for infringement of Community patents and Community trade marks are subject to virtually identical rules as to jurisdiction. Both are governed by a scheme based on the Brussels Convention, but not identical to it, under which the principal connecting factor recognised is the defendant's domicile. If the defendant is domiciled in a member state of the Community, then, with some exceptions, he *must* be sued in the courts of the state in which he is domiciled. In contrast to the Brussels Convention, the Community Patent Convention and Community Trade Mark Regulation also recognise the presence of an "establishment" in the Community as relevant to jurisdiction, and if a defendant not domiciled in the Community has an establishment in a member state he must be sued there.

5–57   If neither the defendant's domicile nor any place of establishment is in the Community, then (subject to the same exceptions) the plaintiff must sue in the courts of the place where the plaintiff is domiciled, if he is domiciled in the Community, or where he has an establishment, if not. This again is contrary to the policy of the Brussels Convention, which avoids giving jurisdiction to the courts of the plaintiff's domicile except in rare circumstances and which generally leaves questions of jurisdiction to existing national law when the defendant is not domiciled in the Community. The fallback position where neither party is domiciled or established in the Community is that the courts of the place where COPAC or the Community Trade Mark Office is situated (as the case may be) have jurisdiction.[14] All these rules are mandatory, and must be

---

[13] The Court could hold that the purported inclusion of the Lugano Convention (as modified) was wholly ineffective, so that the unmodified Brussels Convention applied. The final drastic possibility is that the Court would hold that "Lugano" actually means "Brussels" and interpret the Regulation accordingly.

[14] The Community Trade Mark Office has its domicile in Alicante; COPAC does not yet have a proposed seat.

applied in strict sequence. Once one of them yields a result, it is impossible to rely on a subsequent rule which might seem more favourable.[15]

By way of exception to this strict scheme, the parties may agree to confer jurisdiction on any Community patent court or Community trade mark court. The defendant is also deemed to submit to the jurisdiction of any Community patent court or Community trade mark court by entering an appearance, otherwise than to contest the jurisdiction of that court. Neither provision can confer jurisdiction on a court which is not a Community patent court or Community trade mark court.   **5–58**

Finally, and irrespective of either party's domicile or place of establishment, a defendant may always be sued in the courts of a place where he has actually infringed (or in some cases, depending on national law, threatened to infringe) the Community patent or trade mark, but in that case the court's jurisdiction as to infringement is confined to its own territory.   **5–59**

The hybrid parentage of Articles 14 and 93

In view of the uncertainties in the interpretation of Articles 14 and 93 respectively, it may be helpful to trace the relevant provisions on jurisdiction from the first draft of what was to become the Community Patent Convention. Article 174(1) of the 1962 draft[16] referred the question of jurisdiction to national law: "Actions for infringement of a European patent shall be dealt with by the national courts of the Contracting State, who are competent, *ratione loci et ratione materiae*, as in the case of actions for infringement of a national patent."[17] In the 1970 and 1972 drafts the corresponding provision, now Article 72, was substantially the same but with a note stating that the Article would have to be re-examined in the light of the 1968 Brussels Convention. Between 1972 and 1975 progress on the draft Community Patent Convention was in abeyance while the European Patent Convention was finalised and signed at Munich in 1973.   **5–60**

The scheme of giving exclusive jurisdiction against defendants not domiciled in the Community to the courts of the plaintiff's domicile or place of establishment was derived from the Protocol on Jurisdiction and Recognition to the European Patent Convention.[18] The Protocol governs entitlement proceedings prior to grant, which the European Patent   **5–61**

---

[15] Though the rules appear to favour the defendant, or at least to be even-handed as between plaintiff and defendant, the reality is that the plaintiff can often choose which of several defendants to sue and can assign the Community patent or trade mark to an affiliate in a more favourable jurisdiction. See para. 5–154.

[16] The preliminary Draft Convention Relating to European Patent Law.

[17] The same wording was used, *mutatis mutandis*, in Art. 156(1) of the preliminary draft Convention for a European Trade Mark in 1973.

[18] The Protocol on Jurisdiction and the Recognition of Decisions in respect of the Right to Grant of a European Patent to give it its full title. The AIPPI and UNICE submissions to the 1975 Luxembourg Diplomatic Conference expressly referred to making the Community Patent Convention consistent with the Protocol on Recognition.

Office has no jurisdiction to entertain.[19] The Protocol provides that if the applicant for a European patent has his residence or principal place of business within one of the contracting states, then entitlement proceedings must be brought against him there,[20] if not, then if the party claiming the right to grant of the European patent has his residence or principal place of business within one of the contracting states then the courts of that state have exclusive jurisdiction,[21] and if neither applies then the German courts have exclusive jurisdiction.[22] This aspect of the Protocol on Recognition was itself a last-minute improvisation agreed at the Munich Diplomatic Conference: the draft Protocol had given jurisdiction in all cases against non-Convention applicants to the courts of Germany as the seat of the European Patent Office, regardless of whether the plaintiff had a domicile or place of establishment in one of the contracting states or not.[23] The Munich Diplomatic Conference does not seem to have paid any attention to the relationship of the Protocol to the Brussels Convention: after all, the latter is specifically part of the Community legal order and the very reason for the European Patent Convention was that it was intended to be open to non-Community states. Twenty-one European states attended the Munich Conference, compared to a Community recently increased to nine of which only the original six were then members of the Brussels Convention.

5–62   When work on the Community Patent Convention resumed at the Luxembourg Diplomatic Conference in 1975, the relevant provision was Article 69 of the draft Convention which provided for the Brussels Convention to apply to all actions relating to Community patents,[24] except that actions for infringement against a defendant who had neither his residence nor his principal place of business in the Community could also[25] be brought before the courts of the contracting state in which the Community patent had been infringed.[26]

5–63   These proposals were considerably re-worked at the Conference[27] in line with submissions made by the AIPPI, CIFE, UNICE and the Commission of the European Communities. The provisions as to first instance jurisdiction over infringement in the Community Patent Convention as adopted at the Luxembourg Conference in 1975 substantially correspond to the situation today. Article 68 gave effect to the Brussels

---

[19] For commentary on the Protocol, see para. 2–130.

[20] Protocol on Jurisdiction and Recognition, Art. 2. In the interests of simplicity, provisions relating to employees and jurisdiction by consent are omitted.

[21] Art. 3.

[22] Art. 6.

[23] Minutes of the Munich Diplomatic Conference, para. 3006.

[24] What is said applies only to infringement proceedings as such. A major feature of the 1975 Convention was that the European Patent Office had exclusive jurisdiction over the issue of validity. A new Art. 16(6) would have been inserted in the Brussels Convention to allocate exclusive jurisdiction for compulsory licences and the like.

[25] Art. 4 of the Brussels Convention would have allowed defendants domiciled outside the contracting states to be sued under whatever national rules of extraterritorial jurisdiction could be brought to bear on them.

[26] A further proviso (Art. 69(3)(b)) gave residual jurisdiction in other cases to Germany.

[27] Minutes of the Luxembourg Diplomatic Conference, paras 438 to 451.

Convention except as varied or excluded. Article 69(1) provided for Community-wide jurisdiction to vest in the courts of the contracting state in which the defendant was resident or had an establishment; failing that the courts for the contracting state where the plaintiff was resident or had an establishment; and the courts of residual jurisdiction were those of Germany. Article 69(2) gave concurrent but territorially limited jurisdiction to the courts where an infringement was committed, irrespective of the residence or establishment of any party. There was extensive discussion as to the choice of wording between "residence" on its own as corresponding to "domicile" in the Brussels Convention; "residence or principal place of business," "establishment," "industrial or commercial establishment" and "real and effective establishment" before the final version was accepted.

When it came to the revision of the Community Patent Convention at the second Luxembourg Conference in 1985 the provisions as to first instance jurisdiction were re-worded and incorporated into a separate Protocol on Litigation, but remained very similar in practical effect. It was at this point that "domicile" was substituted for "residence" but "establishment" remained as a separate basis for jurisdiction. The major innovation of the 1985 Conference was the decision to create a new Common Appeal Court, COPAC, and the corresponding abandonment of split first instance jurisdiction over infringement and validity.[28] If the idea of reverting to the scheme of the Protocol on Jurisdiction to the European Patent Convention was ever in contemplation, then the impracticality of giving wholesale jurisdiction to the courts of the seat of COPAC in every action against a defendant neither domiciled, nor with an establishment in the Community, would have been brought home to the negotiating parties by the Merger Treaty of 1965,[29] under which it was more than arguable that COPAC would be bound to have its seat in the Grand-Duchy of Luxembourg.[30] The third Luxembourg Conference in 1989 substantially retained the 1985 scheme, though with slightly different numbering. **5–64**

The jurisdiction provisions of the Community Trade Mark Regulation, Community Regulation on Plant Varieties and the draft Community Design Regulation are recognisably those of the Protocol on Litigation to the Community Patent Convention with surprisingly few further developments. The original Preliminary Draft Convention for a European Trade Mark of 1964 (published in 1973) had provisions for jurisdiction in infringement actions at Articles 156 *et seq.* generally corresponding to Articles 174 *et seq.* of the 1962 Preliminary Draft Convention relating to a European Patent Law, except that the court hearing the infringement action also had jurisdiction to hear a counterclaim for a declaration that the European trade mark was invalid or **5–65**

---

[28] See Chap. 4.

[29] Decision of the Representatives of the Governments of the Member States on the Provisional Location of Certain Institutions and Departments of the Communities, Art. 3.

[30] The Scordamaglia Report at para. 54 notes the claim of Luxembourg to be the seat of COPAC, as does the Report of the House of Lords Select Committee on the European Communities: *A European Community Patent* (1986).

had lapsed.[31] Since national courts also had jurisdiction to entertain applications for lapse or revocation of European trade marks it was necessary to make provision for jurisdiction over trade mark proprietors. Article 128 provided that, subject to agreement, competence *ratione loci* was decided by the place of the defendant's residence or registered office, if within the Community; failing that the place of business of his registered agent on the Register of European Trade Marks; and as a last resort the courts of the place of the European Trade Mark Office.

5–66   The provisions of the 1980 draft Regulation on the Community Trade Mark relating to jurisdiction in infringement actions are found at Article 74(1) and (2) which are virtually identical to Article 69(1) and (2) of the 1975 Community Patent Convention.[32] The 1984 draft made no changes to these provisions,[33] but abandoned a curious proposal previously in Article 74(3) of the 1980 draft that an injunction against the infringing use of another Community trade mark, though in principle Community-wide, should only have effect in a member state where infringement had occurred. Article 74(3) of the 1984 draft provided that the court should order the infringing mark or sign not be used anywhere within the Community, and that provisional measures should be ordered similarly. The 1984 draft also introduced an Article 74(4) allowing the infringement court to ask the Office for advisory opinions. Between 1984 and 1993, when the Community Trade Mark Regulation was adopted, the Protocol on Litigation to the Community Patent Convention superseded the 1975 Convention and the jurisdiction provisions of the Regulation itself are modelled on the former, except for the absence of a second tier Community court.

Domicile

5–67   The principal connecting factor which determines jurisdiction is the domicile of a party, generally the defendant. Both the Protocol on Litigation and the Community Trade Mark Regulation clearly intend that domicile should be determined according to the same rules as under the Brussels Convention.[34] The Brussels Convention itself, at Article 52, provides that domicile is to be decided according to the internal law of the state where the defendant is putatively domiciled. Domicile is one of the few concepts of importance under the Brussels Convention which does not have an independent meaning, except to the extent that Article 53 of the Convention provides that the "seat" of a company or association is to be treated as its domicile.[35]

---

[31] A complication for trade marks was that, within a state, jurisdiction over infringement and validity might be split between different courts but in any event jurisdiction over validity was kept at national level. In the case of the 1962 preliminary draft for patents, the court hearing the infringement action never had jurisdiction to determine validity but had to defer to the EPO.

[32] The draft Trade Mark Regulation uses "habitual residence" instead of "residence" in the Community Patent Convention.

[33] Except that it introduced a new Art. 73a expressly applying the Brussels Convention.

[34] See para. 179 of the Scordamaglia Report, quoted at para. 5–72, below.

[35] See para. 2–43.

Complications arise under English law because two concepts of **5–68**
"domicile" exist in parallel. The Civil Jurisdiction and Judgments Act
1982 contains detailed provisions at section 42 for determining the
domicile and seat of a corporation for the purposes of implementing
the Brussels Convention, and corresponding provisions for ascertaining
the domicile of individuals at section 41. However, the common law
concept of domicile—which can produce radically different results to
that under the Civil Jurisdiction and Judgments Act 1982—continues to
apply for other purposes. It would clearly make sense for the statutory
definition of domicile to apply to the Protocol on Litigation and the
Community Trade Mark Regulation, though it is less clear that sections
41 and 42 of the Civil Jurisdiction and Judgments Act 1982 can strictly
be interpreted so as to achieve this result. For companies, there are
fewer difficulties because the Brussels Convention expressly provides
that a company is domiciled where it has its seat, and since the concept
of "seat" is unknown by that name to the common law[36] there is no
antecedent meaning which might be at variance with section 42. The
problem, if there is one, would largely be confined to the relatively
uncommon case of infringement proceedings being brought against
individuals of uncertain domicile.

It is worth noting that both the Protocol on Litigation and the **5–69**
Community Trade Mark Regulation refer to proceedings being brought
in the "courts of the Contracting State" where the defendant or plaintiff
is domiciled or has an establishment, in contrast to some (incorporated)
provisions of the Brussels Convention which refer to the "place" of
domicile or establishment. The difference is whether internal allocation
of jurisdiction within a contracting state with a decentralised legal system
is a matter for Community or domestic law.

Establishment in a member state

The other connecting factor recognised by the Protocol on Litigation **5–70**
and the Community Trade Mark Regulation is where the defendant or
the plaintiff has an "establishment" in the forum. It would be an
exaggeration to say that this goes so far as to equate place of establishment with domicile, but if a defendant not domiciled in the Community
has an establishment in a member state, then he must be sued in the
courts of that state, and Title II of the Brussels Convention is deemed to
apply to persons with an establishment in a contracting state as if they
were domiciled therein. Conversely, if the defendant is neither domiciled
nor with an establishment in the Community, and the plaintiff is not
domiciled in it, then the plaintiff must sue, if possible, in a member state
where he has an establishment. These rules are relaxed to the extent that
suit can always be brought in a state where there is an actual infringement, but at the price of confining the scope of relief to that one state.

It is worth emphasising again that Article 14 of the Protocol on **5–71**
Litigation and Article 93 of the Community Trade Mark Regulation

[36] Schlosser Report, para. 75(e).

each provide a rigid and mandatory set of rules which must be applied in strict sequence. Once one of their provisions yields a result by identifying a court with general jurisdiction, it is impossible to go on to consider any of the subsequent ones. The plaintiff does not have the opportunity, or at least not in theory, to pick and choose among the various jurisdiction-allocating paragraphs of either article so as to confer jurisdiction on the court he favours. The only exception not dependent on the defendant's co-operation is that the plaintiff may always sue in the courts of the place of infringement, but in that case there is no extra-territorial jurisdiction. The strict sequential application of the rules as to jurisdiction applies even if it is unknown in advance whether a given rule is satisfied or not, for instance because the defendant is known not to be domiciled in the Community, but it is uncertain whether or not he has an establishment in any member state. In this situation, which will not be uncommon, the plaintiff cannot avoid the risk that whichever court he sues in will turn out not to have jurisdiction. All that can be said is that if the defendant enters a defence on the merits, he will be deemed to have waived any objection to jurisdiction.

5–72   In contrast to domicile, the term "establishment" is not one which is defined in the Brussels Convention and it is used only in the context of the operations of a "branch, agency or other establishment."[37] At first sight, "establishment" in Article 14 of the Protocol on Litigation and Article 93 of the Community Trade Mark Regulation might be supposed to bear the same meaning as it does in the Brussels Convention. However, the *travaux préparatoires* to the Community Patent Convention make it clear that this was not the intention underlying Article 14.[38] The Scordamaglia Report comments:

> "The concept of domicile used in Art. 14 Prot. Lit. must be interpreted in the light of Articles 52 and 53 of the Brussels Convention, the seat of companies and legal persons being considered as the domicile.
>
> The concept of establishment, however, is not defined and the courts will have to interpret it, although it was not intended to be given a different meaning to that suggested by Art. 38(1)(b) CPC or Art. 3 of the Paris Convention."[39]

5–73   In any event, the context of Article 5(5) of the Brussels Convention is very different to that of Article 14. In the former, there are three interrelated reasons why the precise meaning of "establishment" is not

---

[37] Arts 5(5), 8 (insurance) and 13 (consumer contracts). The latter two Articles deem a party, for certain purposes, to be domiciled in a state where he has a branch, agency or other establishment.

[38] See para. 5–60, above.

[39] Scordamaglia Report, para. 179. Art. 3 of the Paris Convention provides: "Nationals of countries outside the Union who are domiciled or who have real and effective industrial or commercial establishments in the territory of one of the countries of the Union shall be treated in the same manner as nationals of the countries of the Union."

of very much importance. First, Article 5(5) applies only against a defendant domiciled in a contracting state, and in that case jurisdiction under Article 5(5) will always co-exist with jurisdiction under Article 2, and possibly with jurisdiction under Article 5(1) or 5(3). This is expressly one reason why the European Court of Justice has given Article 5(5) a relatively narrow interpretation. Secondly, the presence of an establishment never defeats jurisdiction under one of the other heads. Finally, Article 5(5) contains its own self-limiting mechanism: since it applies only to litigation "arising out of the operations" of that branch, etc., the existence and operations of the branch must by definition be fundamental to the dispute and known to the opposite party no matter how small, obscure or inactive it may be. In any event, the Article 5(5) has been given a restrictive interpretation and is not of much importance in practice.[40]

This is in contrast to the position under the Protocol on Litigation and the Community Trade Mark Regulation where the presence of an establishment anywhere in the Community is of crucial importance in actions against defendants not domiciled in a contracting state. Not only does the presence of an establishment confer general jurisdiction on a court which would not otherwise enjoy it, but in the absence of such domicile or establishment, a Community-domiciled plaintiff will find itself in the ideal position of being able to sue in its home territory, or of having almost unlimited scope for forum shopping by being able to assign (or perhaps even license) the patent or trade mark to a connected person domiciled or established in the most favoured jurisdiction. The result is thoroughly unsatisfactory: jurisdiction can wholly depend on an imprecise and undefined concept and on facts which it may be all but impossible to resolve. The potential for abuse on both sides is manifest. **5–74**

It is implicit for Article 14 that a defendant or plaintiff may have establishments in more than one contracting state, and in that case the plaintiff may choose which to sue in.[41] An American bank or hotel chain, for instance, may well have an establishment in every major European city. If so, it might be sued in Helsinki for an infringement only committed in Lisbon, and the injunction would be effective throughout the Community from Dublin to Athens. An establishment probably does not have to be very substantial to qualify as such, although a commercial agency, distributor or representative office probably would not count. A subsidiary would not necessarily count as an establishment, but its corporate status would not prevent it being one if it actually fulfilled that role. It is unclear whether, or in what circumstances, a single office may simultaneously be an establishment of several related companies, for instance all the members of a corporate group. **5–75**

---

[40] See para. 2–53, for the cases on Art. 5(5).
[41] *Mutatis mutandis* if the plaintiff has multiple establishments and Art. 14(2) applies. Domicile in two contracting states is also possible for a company incorporated in one but managed from another.

The meaning of "establishment" and Article 5(5) of the Brussels Convention

5–76   Although the derivation of the concept of an "establishment" is actually from Article 3 of the Paris Convention, in the absence of better authority the cases on Article 5(5) of the Brussels Convention may still be of interest in understanding the meaning of the term for the purposes of Article 14 of the Community Patent Convention and Article 93 of the Community Trade Mark Regulation.[42] Article 5(5) provides:

> "A person domiciled in a contracting state may, in another contracting state, be sued— . . . As regards a dispute arising out of the operations of a branch, agency or other establishment, in the courts for the place in which the branch, agency or other establishment is situated."

5–77   In applying the cases on Article 5(5), however, certain differences should be borne in mind. The first is concerned simply with the terms of the respective provisions: Article 14 is not confined to actions against Convention-domiciled parties; the existence of an establishment of the plaintiff is as capable of conferring jurisdiction in the specified circumstances as one of the defendant; and the action does not have to "arise out of" the operations of the establishment. The latter requirement, irrelevant in Article 14, has perhaps coloured the interpretation of Article 5(5) in some cases, notably *Somafer v. Saar-Ferngas*.[43] A related point is that although the European Court of Justice in *Somafer* acknowledged that Article 5(5) can apply to non-contractual liability, the cases actually decided have all been in contract.

5–78   Another factor influencing the Court's interpretation of Article 5(5) has been that jurisdiction under the latter always exists simultaneously with jurisdiction based on the defendant's domicile, and this is expressly one reason why the Court has given Article 5(5) a relatively narrow interpretation as a derogation from the general rule of Article 2. In contrast, the place of establishment of a party will either be altogether irrelevant for Article 14 of the Community Patent Convention or it will be the sole non-consensual basis for Community-wide jurisdiction. Article 14 is not a derogation from anything: it is the fundamental, if multi-faceted, rule. The distinction between "branch, agency or other establishment" in Article 5(5) and "establishment" *simpliciter* in the Community Patent Convention and the Community Trade Mark Regulation is probably of little importance. If anything, "establishment" on its own might bear a wider meaning than in Article 5(5) of the Brussels Convention since in the latter context it has expressly been interpreted as *eijusdem generis* with "branch" and "agency."[44] Every branch is probably also an establishment. Not every agency in the popular sense

---

[42] See para. 2–53, above.
[43] Case 33/78 [1978] E.C.R. 2183; [1979] 1 C.M.L.R. 490.
[44] Case 14/76 *de Bloos v. Bouyer* [1976] E.C.R. 1497; [1977] 1 C.M.L.R. 60.

would be an establishment, but Article 5(5) has never applied to agencies which are independent.

With these provisos in mind, the term "branch, agency or other **5–79** establishment" has been interpreted by the European Court of Justice in the context of Article 5(5) to mean a entity which is subject to the direction and control of its (foreign) head office, thereby excluding normal commercial agents, independent distributors and the like. Conversely, the "establishment" must have at least the appearance of permanence and be equipped to do business and conclude contracts without the need for third parties to deal direct with its head office. A purely representative office, or a temporary presence at an exhibition, for instance, would not be an establishment within the meaning of the Article. A "branch, agency or other establishment" can be, and frequently is, a separate corporate entity to the principal or parent and need not be a subsidiary or under the same ownership.

Finally, whereas Article 5(5) gives jurisdiction to the courts of the "place" where the branch, etc. is situated, Article 14 gives jurisdiction to the courts of the "Contracting State" where the establishment is situated, leaving internal allocation of jurisdiction to domestic law.

The relationship between jurisdiction and scope of relief: Article 17/94

There is an important distinction between jurisdiction based solely on **5–80** the place of infringement under Article 14(5), and jurisdiction based on any of the other grounds. Article 17 of the Protocol on Litigation provides that a Community patent court whose jurisdiction is based on Articles 14(1) to (4) has jurisdiction over acts of infringement committed or threatened in the territory of any of the contracting states. However, if jurisdiction is based on Article 14(5), its territorial jurisdiction is confined to acts committed or threatened in the territory of the state in which it is situated. In the latter case, the restriction on jurisdiction applies both to past and future infringements. The court whose jurisdiction is based only on Article 14(5) cannot investigate whether there have been infringements outside its own territorial jurisdiction, and cannot grant extraterritorial relief. Article 94 of the Community Trade Mark Regulation is substantially identical. The court's jurisdiction to entertain a counterclaim for revocation or invalidity is always the same regardless of the basis of jurisdiction over infringement, and if the counterclaim is successful the Community patent or trade mark has to be revoked in its entirety. There is no symmetry between the relief which can be granted in the infringement action, and that on the counterclaim.

A further restriction on the practical utility of Article 14(5) or 93(5) is **5–81** that there is no provision for joining additional defendants, since Article 6(1) of the Brussels Convention as adapted applies only if jurisdiction against the principal defendant is based on domicile or establishment, and if that were the case then there would be no need to rely on Article 14(5) or 93(5) in the first place. Since the plaintiff is expected to stake the very existence of his Community patent or trade mark for the whole of Europe against the benefit of an injunction against one defendant, and effective only in one state, it may be expected that reliance on Article 14(5) or 93(5) will be infrequent.

5–82   The Scordamaglia Report comments:

> "Community patent courts hearing proceedings under any of the jurisdictional criteria listed in Art. 14(1) to (4) Prot. Lit. have jurisdiction in respect of acts of infringement committed or threatened on the territory of any Contracting State (centralised jurisdiction) (Art. 17(1) Prot. Lit.), whereas those sitting on the basis of *forum delicti commissi* (Art. 14(5) Prot. Lit.) may only hear proceedings concerning acts of infringement committed or threatened on the territory of the State in which the court is situated (Art. 17(2) Prot. Lit.).
>
> The choice between these alternative jurisdictions is left to the plaintiff, who will decide what tactics he wishes to adopt in the proceedings. Any Community patent court with jurisdiction in respect of infringement actions may also hear counterclaims for revocation, whatever its territorial jurisdiction."[45]

5–83   This distinction between the effects of jurisdiction based on domicile or establishment and jurisdiction based on place of infringement was created by Working Party II for the first Luxembourg Diplomatic Conference in 1975 in response to proposals from the AIPPI, UNICE, CIFE and the Commission of the European Communities.[46] In the previous draft Convention, Article 5(3) of the Brussels Convention would have applied against defendants domiciled in a contracting state and national law, supplemented by Article 69(3)(a) of the draft Convention, would have provided jurisdiction over defendants not domiciled or having a principal place of business in a contracting state. Relatively little discussion was given to this aspect of the new proposals, beyond clarifying that "where paragraph 2 [of Article 69] applied, an order prohibiting acts of infringement would have effect solely in the Member State in which the court was situated. Only where paragraph 1 applied could such an order have effect throughout the Community."[47] Subject to this explanation, the proposals of the Working Party were adopted.

The problem of submission by entry of an appearance

5–84   There is an unresolved conflict between Article 14(4)(b) and Article 17(2) in the case of the Protocol on Litigation which also arises for the corresponding Articles of the Community Trade Mark Regulation. Once the defendant "enters an appearance" otherwise than to contest the jurisdiction, Article 18 of the Brussels Convention is applied by Article 14(4)(b) of the Protocol on Litigation so as to confer jurisdiction on the Community patent court in which the action is pending, even if another

---

[45] Scordamaglia Report, para. 187.
[46] Minutes of the 1975 Luxembourg Diplomatic Conference, paras 440 *et seq.*
[47] *ibid.*, para. 445.

Community patent court would otherwise have (exclusive) jurisdiction under paragraphs 1 to 3 of Article 14. Unlike Article 14(5), territorial jurisdiction based on Article 14(4) extends across the whole Community. Once unrestricted jurisdiction exists under Article 14(4)(b), does it matter that the jurisdiction (if any) of that particular court could only originally have been based on Article 14(5) with restricted territorial effect? The same problem arises *mutatis mutandis* for the Community trade mark.

There are two possible answers, and neither is obviously satisfactory: **5–85** the first is that if jurisdiction was originally asserted under Article 14(5), then the plaintiff is bound by his reliance on that paragraph and nothing short of express agreement by the defendant can render the latter susceptible to extraterritorial relief. This seems the more sensible option in practice, but it fails to explain why Article 17(1) failed to distinguish the case of Article 14(4)(a) from that of Article 14(4)(b), as it could easily have done. It also produces the curious result that once the defendant enters an appearance, perhaps through inadvertence, the plaintiff is better off for having sued in a Community patent court which had no jurisdiction at all, rather than one with limited jurisdiction under Article 14(5). A literal reading suggests that the effect of Article 17(2) is limited, in effect, to default judgments, since in other cases the defendant would have filed a defence and Article 14(4)(b) would operate. Such a narrow interpretation may seem unreasonable but need not necessarily be contrary to the presumed intention of the contracting states, since protecting defendants against default judgments in states with which they have no substantial connection would be a legitimate objective and consistent with the Brussels Convention.

A complicating factor is provided by Article 36(2) in that a Com- **5–86** munity patent court having jurisdiction under one of paragraphs 1 to 4 of Article 14, and *only* such a court, has jurisdiction to grant provisional and protective measures effective in any contracting state. It seems unfair to the defendant sued under Article 14(5) to require him to elect between submitting to a default judgment in respect of one territory, and rendering himself liable to a pan-European interlocutory injunction (from a court which is not that of his domicile, and which would not otherwise have jurisdiction to grant it) if he defended the action on the merits.[48]

Personal and subject matter jurisdiction: Article 14/93 as jurisdiction-creating or as jurisdiction-allocating?

The jurisdiction of Community Patent courts of first instance is **5–87** defined by reference to the subject matter of the proceedings in question and the presence of specified connecting factors which assign jurisdiction over a defendant to a specific court. Articles 13 ("Application of the Convention on Jurisdiction and Judgments") and 14 ("Jurisdiction")

---

[48] See further para. 5–154.

constitute Part II of the Protocol on Litigation and are collectively headed "Provisions on International Jurisdiction and Enforcement." From these articles it seems that every legal or natural person in the Universe is subject to the jurisdiction of a Community patent court of first instance, from the Llama of a Tibetan monastery to an unused shelf-company in Delaware, irrespective of whether they had ever committed or threatened any infringement or have any connection at all with Europe.

5–88 To English eyes this is a surprising conclusion, since one is used to a relatively high standard of proof being required to support extraterritorial assumption of jurisdiction. A party seeking leave for service of the writ outside the jurisdiction must demonstrate a good arguable case on the merits,[49] and there is still room for leave to be refused on discretionary grounds corresponding to *forum non conveniens*. This would suggest that questions of personal jurisdiction under Articles 13 and 14 ought not to be separated from the treatment of subject matter jurisdiction under Articles 15 ("Jurisdiction over Infringement and Validity") and 17 ("Territorial Jurisdiction"), which are placed in Part III of the Protocol on Litigation under the collective heading "First Instance."

5–89 However, the treatment of exorbitant jurisdiction in the civil law does not necessarily lead to the same conclusion. *Forum non conveniens*, despite its Latin name, is not a civil law doctrine and jurisdiction based solely on the plaintiff's nationality or domicile is widely recognised. Specifically, Article 14 of the French Civil Code, which has been adopted in other civil law jurisdictions, has been interpreted as meaning that a French national may always sue a foreigner in the French courts, regardless of the absence of any other connection with the subject matter of the proceedings.[50] To return to English law, the practical question is whether an allegedly unjustified or even abusive action by a plaintiff domiciled (or with an establishment) in England against a defendant without a domicile or establishment anywhere in the Community can be attacked under RSC, Ord. 11 or only on the more unfavourable ground of Ord. 18. The answer probably lies in the exclusion of Article 4 of the Brussels Convention and the fact that the Protocol on Litigation or the Community Trade Mark Regulation each form a complete code as to jurisdiction. The domestic rules on extraterritorial jurisdiction are equally irrelevant whether the defendant is domiciled in a contracting state or not, so if the Protocol or Regulation provide for the English courts to have jurisdiction then that is conclusive.

The same question arises for infringement of the Community trade mark, except that the structure of the Community Trade Mark Regulation is more logical with all the relevant Articles coming under Title X "Jurisdiction and Procedure in Legal Actions Relating to Community Trade Marks."

---

[49] *Seaconsar v. Bank Markazi Jomhouri Islami Iran* [1994] A.C. 438, H.L.
[50] See Art. 3 of the Brussels Convention and the commentary in the Jenard Report.

E. TYPES OF ACTION PERMITTED AND *LOCUS STANDI* TO SUE

Categories of action permitted: Community patents

The Protocol on Litigation gives the Community patent courts of first **5–90** instance exclusive jurisdiction over the following categories of legal proceedings: proceedings for actual infringement of a Community patent[51] and in respect of threatened infringements[52]; proceedings for compensation for use of the invention between publication and grant[53]; proceedings for a declaration of non-infringement[54]; and counterclaims for revocation.[55] Only infringement actions properly so called, actions for pre-grant compensation under Article 32(1)[56] and counterclaims for revocation must be entertained—*quia timet* actions and actions for declarations of non-infringement are allowed only if permitted under national law. A noteworthy exception to the jurisdiction of Community patent courts of first instance is that they cannot entertain proceedings for the revocation of a Community patent, except by way of counterclaim,[57] nor can the validity of a Community patent be put in issue at all in proceedings for a declaration of non-infringement.[58] The Community patent court of first instance is obliged to treat the Community patent as valid unless there is a counterclaim for revocation.[59]

Categories of action permitted: Community trade marks

The Community Trade Mark Regulation provides that Community **5–91** trade mark courts are to have exclusive jurisdiction over actions for infringement of the Community trade mark[60]; for threatened infringement if permitted under national law[61]; for declarations of non-infringement if permitted under national law[62]; and for "reasonable compensation" in respect of would-be infringing acts occurring between publication of the application and grant.[63] The validity of a Community trade mark cannot in general be put in issue except by counterclaim,[64]

[51] Protocol on Litigation, Art. 15(1)(a).
[52] *ibid.*
[53] Art. 15(1)(c).
[54] Art. 15(1)(b).
[55] Art. 15(1)(d) and (2).
[56] Unlike Art. 15(1)(a) and (b), Art. 15(1)(c) contains no qualification referring to national law, but this does not necessarily mean that the Community patent court must entertain such actions prior to grant, contrary to the present position in the U.K. In any event, Art. 18 would require a stay of proceedings. See Benyamini, *op. cit.*, para. 13.1.2.[f].
[57] Art. 15(2). Applications for revocation as such are within the exclusive jurisdiction of the European Patent Office under Art. 55 of the Community Patent Convention.
[58] Art. 15(4).
[59] Art. 15(2).
[60] Community Trade Mark Regulation, Art. 92(a).
[61] *ibid.*
[62] Art. 92(b).
[63] Art. 92(c).
[64] With exceptions for non-use or prior rights, which can be raised by way of defence: Art. 95(3).

and cannot be challenged at all in an action for a declaration of non-infringement.[65] The Community trade mark court is obliged to treat the Community trade mark as valid unless there is a counterclaim for revocation or for a declaration of invalidity.[66]

5–92   In comparison with Article 15 of the Protocol on Litigation, Article 92 omits the words "of first instance" between "courts" and "shall have exclusive jurisdiction." This corresponds to the fact that Community trade mark courts of second instance will decide issues of infringement and validity, whereas Community patent courts of second instance have to refer these issues to COPAC.

Categories of action permitted: Community designs

5–93   Two factors complicate the treatment of jurisdiction in relation to Community designs: the fact that the draft Community Design Regulation creates unregistered design rights as well as Community registered designs administered by OHIM, and the fact that the validity of the latter can be challenged by way of a defence to an interlocutory injunction without needing to file a counterclaim for revocation.[67] Since OHIM has no jurisdiction over unregistered rights, their validity can be challenged by an action for a declaration of invalidity in national courts as well as by counterclaim to an infringement action. Otherwise, the law is generally similar to that for Community trade marks. There is no action for pre-grant compensation, because Community design applications are not published as such.

Locus standi of the plaintiff under the Community Patent Convention

5–94   The Agreement relating to Community Patents is silent as to who may commence proceedings for infringement of a Community patent. Self-evidently, the registered proprietor may do so, and the unitary nature of the Community patent means that ownership must be the same for the whole of the Community.[68] Apart from that, there are broadly three possible interpretations of the Protocol on Litigation: that the Protocol defines an occupied field and does not permit actions by anyone except the proprietor; that *locus standi* is entirely left to national law; or that actions by licensees and perhaps others are permitted as a matter of Community law by implication from Article 15(3) or by analogy with the Community Trade Mark Regulation. The question is important not only in its own right, but because any increase in the number of possible plaintiffs correspondingly increases the number of choices of forum against defendants outside the Community.

[65] Community Trade Mark Regulation, Art. 95(2).
[66] Art. 95(1).
[67] Draft Regulation, Art. 94(2).
[68] Co-ownership of a Community patent is possible (Community Patent Convention, Art. 23(2)) and may create opportunities for forum shopping. *Locus standi* is probably governed by the law of the Community patent as an object of property.

The first of these three may almost certainly be rejected. Article 42 of **5–95** the Community Patent Convention permits contractual licensing, which may be exclusive or non-exclusive and for the whole or part of the territories for which the Community patent is effective. Licences of right and compulsory licences are provided for by Articles 43 and 45 to 47. National law may permit licensees and others to sue for infringement, at least in certain circumstances.[69] If actions by persons other than the proprietor are not permitted by the Convention, then there would be a plain inconsistency with Article 15(3) of the Protocol on Litigation, which provides that where there is a counterclaim for revocation, the patent proprietor may be joined as a party to the action in accordance with national law if he is not one already. This obviously contemplates that a properly constituted infringement action can be commenced without the proprietor being a plaintiff.

The commentary in the Scordamaglia Report confirms that actions by **5–96** plaintiffs other than the proprietor are contemplated, but without saying whether Community or national law governs the issue:

"If an infringement action is brought by a licensee or the proprietor of a right *in rem* in respect of the patent, the patent proprietor must be informed and may be joined as a party to the action in accordance with *lex fori* (art. 15(3) Prot. Lit.)."[70]

If the matter is one for national law, then there is the further question **5–97** of which body of national law applies. The possible answers are that the question is decided on a Community-wide basis by either the *lex fori* or by the law governing the Community patent as an object of property[71]; or that the private international law of the forum may refer the question state-by-state to *lex loci delicti commissi*. As a separate matter, the ability of the licensee to recover pecuniary remedies may fall to be decided under Article 35(2) of the Protocol on Litigation on a state-by-state basis according to the *lex loci delicti commissi*. The Community Patent Convention itself does not answer these questions, and any recourse to existing national law is frustrated by the fact that there has never previously been any need to distinguish between the *lex situs*, the *lex fori* and the *lex loci delicti commissi*, because in practice the three have almost always been one and the same.

A final question, if actions by licensees and others are allowed in **5–98** principle, concerns the effect of non-registration of the licence, etc., on the licensee's ability to sue, and, separately, to recover damages. In the case of contractual licences, Article 42(3) of the Community Patent Convention deems Article 39(2) and (3) to apply *mutatis mutandis*, so that a licence only affects third parties after registration in the Register of Community Patents. In the case of other rights, such as rights *in rem*,

---

[69] *e.g.* Patents Act 1977, s. 67.
[70] Para. 184.

[71] In the interests of legal certainty the latter is perhaps preferable, but this is no more than personal preference.

the answer is probably determined by Article 39(2) in favour of the law of the patent as an object of property,[72] but even this conclusion is not beyond doubt since Article 35(2) of the Protocol on Litigation could conceivably require the application of the *lex loci delicti commissi*.

Locus standi in trade mark and design infringement actions

5–99   The Community Trade Mark Regulation presents fewer problems of interpretation in this respect. Contractual licensing is expressly permitted by Article 22(1), irrespective of the position under pre-existing national law. Article 22(3) contemplates that any licensee may bring proceedings for infringement of a Community trade mark provided that the proprietor consents. An exclusive licensee is in a better position: he can bring infringement proceedings, presumably in his own name, if the proprietor of the trade mark does not do so himself within a reasonable period after a formal notice requiring him to do so. These provisions are without prejudice to any agreement to the contrary in the licence agreement.

5–100   Article 22(4) of the Regulation provides that a licensee may intervene in infringement proceedings brought by the proprietor in order to claim compensation for damage suffered by him. Conversely, if an infringement action is commenced by a plaintiff other than the proprietor, the proprietor is entitled to be informed if a counterclaim is brought for invalidation of the trade mark and he may be joined as a party in accordance with national law.[73]

5–101   The rights of licensees to commence proceedings in their own name, or intervene in proceedings brought by the proprietor, are dependent on the licence being registered. Article 23(1) of the Community Trade Mark Regulation provides that licences are among the legal acts which do not have effect against third parties until after entry in the Register. The exception in the second sentence of Article 23(1) does not apply in terms, since an infringer, even if he had notice of the licence, is not a third party acquiring rights in the trade mark. It should be borne in mind that a licence, whether exclusive or non-exclusive, can be for any territory, so that a licensee-plaintiff may not be entitled to sue, or recover compensation, for all member states. A licensee in one jurisdiction might even be an infringer in another.

The relevant provisions of the draft Community Design Regulation correspond to those of the Trade Mark Regulation.

Joinder of parallel causes of action under national law

5–102   The Agreement relating to Community Patents is silent as to joinder of other causes of action in an action for infringement of a Community patent. Broadly, the following situations may be distinguished: the

[72] Community Patent Convention, Art. 38(4).
[73] Community Trade Mark Regulation, Art. 96(3); "national law" in this context must be the *lex fori*. Absent a counterclaim, the proprietor has no express right to intervene and the licence agreement should take account of this.

plaintiff may have both national and Community patents for the same invention[74]; he may have several patents, Community or national, for related inventions or unrelated inventions which are infringed at the same time; he may have causes of action which are wholly unrelated to patent infringement, such as for breach of confidence, breach of contract or infringement of other intellectual property rights; and he may have causes of action which depend on there being an infringement of a Community patent, but which have a separate existence in law. Conspiracy to injure by unlawful means might be an example of the latter in English law, unfair competition or unjust enrichment in some civil law jurisdictions.[75]

Early drafts for the Community Patent Convention expressly stated that it was "without prejudice to the provisions of national law enabling the proprietor . . . to bring actions other than those based on patent law"[76] or that "other actions may be brought by the proprietor of a Community patent on the basis of the provisions of national law relating in particular to civil offences and unfair competition."[77] These provisions were omitted from the draft used at the 1975 Luxembourg Diplomatic Conference and from the 1975 Community Patent Convention itself.[78] Nonetheless, it is suggested that the provisions in the early drafts were only present *ex abundanti cautela* and that, with one exception, the Community Patent Convention does not affect parallel national causes of action. In any event, COPAC has no jurisdiction over such causes of action and on appeal they would be determined by the Community patent court of second instance.

5–103

The exception concerns acts which are expressly excluded from liability under the Community Patent Convention, either by way of a limitation on the effects of the patent, or because of the terms in which infringement is defined. A supplier of staple commercial products, for instance, is not liable for infringement unless they are supplied as an inducement to infringe. Where the policy of the Convention is clear, as in this case, it is suggested that a doctrine or cause of action otherwise available under national law ought not to be invoked if it has the effect of making the supplier liable when he would not have been liable under Article 26,[79] unless there are factors outside the scope of the Community Patent Convention which justify the imposition of liability.

5–104

The Community Trade Mark Regulation is more explicit in its treatment of parallel national causes of action. Early drafts were

5–105

---

[74] This should be rare, but the situation is possible while an opposition against the Community patent is pending: Community Patent Convention, Art. 75.

[75] In *Union Carbide v. B.P. Chemicals (No. 2)* [1998] F.S.R. 1, Jacob J. held that in English law a claim for unjust enrichment did not lie as an independent cause of action against an infringer of a patent.

[76] 1962 draft Art. 20b(1).

[77] 1970/2 draft Art. 13.

[78] See Benyamini *op. cit.*, paras 4.1 and 4.6. The issue is the mirror image of that of innocent infringement which had a similar legislative history, see para. 282 of the Minutes of the 1975 Luxembourg Diplomatic Conference.

[79] This would be to subvert an apparent limitation of the Community Patent Convention, according to Cornish, *Intellectual Property* (3rd ed., 1996), para. 6–18.

criticised for the extent to which national trade mark and common law rights were supplanted, and the Regulation as adopted is tolerant of the continuing existence of national trade mark registrations and causes of action based on laws of unfair competition or passing-off. Recital (5) provides that "the Community law relating to trade marks nevertheless does not replace the laws of the Member States on trade marks; . . . it would not in fact appear to be justified to require undertakings to apply for registration of their trade marks as Community trade marks; . . . national trade marks continue to be necessary for those undertakings which do not want protection of their trade marks at Community level." Article 14(2) of the Regulation provides that it "shall not prevent actions concerning a Community trade mark being brought under the law of Member States relating in particular to civil liability and unfair competition." The draft Community Design Regulation expressly permits actions under national or Community laws relating to "trademarks or other distinctive signs, patents and utility models, typefaces, civil liability and unfair competition."[80] Designs may also enjoy simultaneous copyright protection.[81]

5–106   Neither the Community Patent Convention nor the Community Trade Mark Regulation deals expressly with what happens if Community and national infringement actions are brought together. Community patent courts and Community trade mark courts, despite their name, are existing national courts and there is no reason why they should not exercise any concurrent jurisdiction they may have over national causes of action. There is, however, no implication that a court seized of an action on a Community intellectual property right can entertain related actions under domestic or foreign law unless it can independently derive jurisdiction over every such cause of action from the Brussels Convention or national law.[82] Given the differences between the Brussels Convention and the Protocol on Litigation or the Community Trade Mark Regulation, especially against defendants domiciled outside the Community, this will not always be the case.

F. RELATED PROCEEDINGS, MANDATORY AND DISCRETIONARY STAYS

Introduction

5–107   The Brussels Convention deals with the possibility of different courts being simultaneously seised of actions in respect of the same cause of action or related actions. The relevant Articles, 21 and 22, are applied to the Protocol on Litigation and the Community Trade Mark Regulation without modification. Briefly, when proceedings are brought on the same

---

[80] Draft Art. 100.
[81] Draft Art. 100(2) and (3).
[82] Compare para. 2–68 on the general law under the Brussels Convention.

cause of action in the courts of different contracting states, then any court other than the court first seised *must* at once stay its own proceedings of its own motion and *must* decline jurisdiction once the jurisdiction of the first court has been established. When "related actions" are brought in the courts of different contracting states, then any court other than the court first seised *may* stay its own proceedings or decline jurisdiction in favour of the first court.[83] However, the Protocol and Regulation also have to deal with the possibility of proceedings being carried on simultaneously in one or more national courts and in the European Patent Office or the Community Trade Mark Office. Articles 21 and 22 of the Brussels Convention would not apply in this case, because although the relevant Office may conceivably be a "court or tribunal" within the meaning of the Brussels Convention,[84] neither Office is a court *of a contracting state* since both are international rather than national institutions.[85]

Patents: actions for compensation prior to grant

Article 32(1) of the Community Patent Convention gives the applicant for a Community patent the right to recover reasonable compensation for use of the invention between the date of publication of the application and the date of grant of the patent.[86] Since the right to recover under Article 32 depends both on whether any patent is ever granted, and on the form of the granted claims, Article 18 of the Protocol on Litigation provides that judgment may only be given after the European Patent Office has granted or refused the application.[87] It is implicit from Article 18 that such proceedings may be commenced before grant, but it is uncertain whether the combined effect of Article 18 and Article 15(1)(c) is that such proceedings must be entertained before grant, irrespective of national law and practice to the contrary. There is no procedure for putting the validity of a European patent application in issue while it is still at the application stage, either in the Office or in court.[88]   **5–108**

The interaction of Article 18 with the remaining provisions of the Protocol on Litigation is complicated and not entirely satisfactory. In terms, Article 18 allows judgment to be entered for the proprietor the day on or after the Community patent issues, even though the validity of the patent may be in doubt. The defendant cannot immediately file a   **5–109**

---

[83] For further commentary on Arts 21 and 22 of the Brussels Convention see para. 8–11.

[84] The Brussels Convention applies to civil and commercial matters "whatever the nature of the court or tribunal," (Art. 1) though in many of their functions the EPO and OHIM may be regarded as exercising an administrative, rather than judicial, function.

[85] Art. 21 could, in any event, only apply to invalidity proceedings because neither the EPO nor OHIM has any jurisdiction over infringement. It is assumed that Art. 21 applies to counterclaims as it does to actions.

[86] There are complicated provisions in Art. 32(2) to (4) relating to translations.

[87] The Community Patent Convention, Art. 73 also requires a stay *mutatis mutandis*, but applies only to proceedings not covered by the Protocol on Litigation.

[88] The defendant might file written observations pursuant to EPC Art. 115, but that is all.

counterclaim for revocation because of the combined effect of Article 15(2) of the Protocol on Litigation and Article 55(2) of the Community Patent Convention, considered below. Absent a counterclaim, the court must assume the patent to be valid.[89] Presumably, the defendant should oppose in the European Patent Office and request a further stay of the proceedings for compensation pursuant to Article 34(1) of the Protocol on Litigation. If judgment is entered for the plaintiff, and is enforced, then subsequent revocation of the patent by either the Office or a Community patent court probably does not affect it.[90]

No counterclaim during opposition period or pending opposition in EPO

5–110   The combined effect of Article 15(2) of the Protocol on Litigation and Article 55(2) of the Community Patent Convention is that a counterclaim for revocation may not be filed on any of the normal grounds of invalidity while the Community patent is under opposition in the European Patent Office, or before the opposition period has expired.[91] It is irrelevant whether or not the defendant in the infringement action is an opponent in the EPO. In contrast to the general provisions for stays of related proceedings, no residual discretion is allowed to the court seised of the infringement proceedings to proceed with the counterclaim even in special circumstances and it is the filing of the counterclaim as such which is prohibited. Since the counterclaim cannot even be filed, Article 15(2) of the Protocol on Litigation applies and the court is obliged to treat the Community patent as valid.[92]

Opposition proceedings in the European Patent Office are to be distinguished from revocation proceedings and proceedings by the patentee for limitation (amendment) of the patent. These are governed by the same rules as for proceedings in other Community patent courts and COPAC.

Parallel pending proceedings in another Community patent court or for revocation in the EPO

5–111   Article 34 of the Protocol on Litigation deals with related proceedings concerning Community patents and complements Articles 21 and 22 of the Brussels Convention. If the validity of the Community patent is

[89] Protocol on Litigation, Art. 15(2).
[90] Community Patent Convention Art. 33(2). This depends on reading "decision on infringement" as covering a decision on rights under Art. 32, as is probably intended, although in other contexts a distinction is drawn between infringement *strictu sensu* and Art. 32.
[91] Community Patent Convention, Art. 55(2) does not apply to two relatively minor grounds of invalidity: non-entitlement (Art. 56(1)(e)) and prior national rights (Arts 36 and 56(1)(f)).
[92] This is capable of causing major problems. See para. 5–130. According to the evidence of the Chartered Institute of Patent Agents, published in the Report of the House of Lords Select Committee on the European Communities: *A European Community Patent* (1986), strenuous efforts made by the U.K. delegation at the 1985 Luxembourg Conference to correct this anomaly met with indifference from the others.

already in issue before another Community patent court, COPAC or the EPO,[93] then a Community patent court hearing a subsequent action for actual or threatened infringement, or for pre-grant compensation, or a counterclaim for revocation, must stay its own proceedings on the application of one of the parties, and after hearing the other parties, unless there are special grounds for continuing the action. Article 34 applies even if validity is not in issue in the subsequent action, but expressly does not apply to applications for declarations of non-infringement. There is no provision for the court to stay its proceedings of its own motion, although in the case of pending opposition proceedings before the EPO Article 55(2) of the Community Patent Convention as applied by Article 15(2) of the Protocol on Litigation would automatically prevent the filing of a counterclaim.

By Article 34(2) of the Protocol on Litigation the EPO is obliged to **5–112** stay revocation or limitation proceedings in similar circumstances and on the application of a party, unless there are special grounds, when the validity of the patent is already in issue before a Community patent court or COPAC. This does not apply to oppositions, which are never at risk of being stayed, because validity cannot be challenged in a Community patent court by counterclaim if an opposition is pending in the EPO or before the opposition period has expired.[94] Within the EPO, limitation proceedings are always stayed pending determination of a later-filed application for revocation.[95]

Trade marks: pending oppositions in OHIM and actions for compensation prior to registration

In contrast to the situation in the European Patent Office, oppositions **5–113** in the Community Trade Mark Office take place before registration and a mark cannot be registered until the three month opposition period has expired, or until any opposition has finally been dismissed. *Ex parte* examination of applications for Community trade marks will examine only for compliance with the absolute grounds of validity and any relative grounds will have to be raised in opposition proceedings by those entitled to the relevant earlier rights. It is therefore to be expected that a substantial proportion of applications will be opposed[96] and that this, together with the unfamiliarity of the procedure, the unexpectedly high level of applications to the Office, and the possibility of third and fourth level appeals to the Court of First Instance and the European Court of Justice are likely to make oppositions even more protracted than in the European Patent Office. In the result it is quite likely that Community trade mark applicants will find that actual registration is

[93] Art. 34 applies when proceedings for opposition, revocation or limitation (amendment) are pending in the EPO.
[94] See para. 5–110, above.
[95] Community Patent Convention, Art. 51(5).
[96] Early indications are that about one quarter of applicants are being opposed: [1997] October *M.I.P.* p. 4.

delayed by perhaps five years or more from acceptance, while the opposition procedure is exhausted,[97] and even longer if there are further appeals.

5–114 In these circumstances the ability of the trade mark applicant to commence legal proceedings prior to registration may be important. Article 9(3) of the Community Trade Mark Regulation provides that the rights conferred by a Community trade mark shall prevail against third parties from the date of registration of the trade mark, but that reasonable compensation may be claimed in respect of matters occurring after the date of publication of the application, which would be prohibited after registration. Article 92(3) gives Community trade mark courts exclusive jurisdiction over actions pursuant to Article 9(3) and, in contrast to the terms of Articles 9(1) and (2), does not make jurisdiction over such actions dependent on whether they are permitted in national law. The implication that actions can be brought under Article 9(3) prior to registration is confirmed by the closing provision of Article 9(3) itself, prohibiting the court seised from deciding on the merits until the registration has been published.[98] It is also of interest that Article 99 expressly contemplates the grant of provisional and protective measures in respect of a Community trade mark application. Since the only right existing prior to registration is a bare right to recover compensation, it presumably follows that the provisional measures in contemplation are analogous to *Anton Piller* or *Mareva* relief, to secure the ultimate recovery of damages, and do not extend to the grant of an ordinary interlocutory injunction.

5–115 Apart from the tailpiece to Article 9(3) itself, there are no express provisions dealing with the effect of a pending opposition in the Community Trade Mark Office on litigation under Article 9(3). Article 100, which obliges a national court to stay its own proceedings pending the outcome of an earlier application for revocation or a declaration of invalidity in the Office, does not in terms apply when there is an earlier opposition pending.[99] The application of Articles 95 and 96 may also be problematical. The general rule of Article 95 is that the court must treat a Community trade mark as valid unless and until its validity is put in issue by counterclaim, but it seems unlikely that one can counterclaim under Article 96 for revocation or invalidation of something that does not yet exist,[1] and neither a literal nor a purposive construction of

---

[97] Multiple oppositions could protract this even further. In contrast to opposition procedure in the EPO, oppositions will not necessarily be heard together, but a "pathfinder" opposition may proceed while the others are stayed: Rule 21(2). If the pathfinder opposition fails, the others will have to be determined (or abandoned) before the mark can be registered.

[98] As with the corresponding provisions of the Community Patent Convention and Protocol on Litigation, see para. 5–108, above, it is unclear whether these Articles are permissive or mandatory.

[99] Conversely, nothing obliges the Office to stay an opposition in the perhaps unlikely event of validity being put in issue in legal proceedings commenced after advertisement of the application, but before the opposition period expired.

[1] It would be surprising if one could counterclaim in a national court at a point in time at which the Office could not entertain revocation proceedings.

Article 95(1) leads to the conclusion that the court should treat a mere pending application as valid, especially if it is under opposition.

Article 95(3) does provide that in the actions referred to in Article 5–116 92(a) and (c), the latter being the action for pre-registration compensation, a plea relating to revocation or invalidity made otherwise than by counterclaim is admissible in so far as the defendant claims that the mark could be revoked for lack of use or could be declared invalid on account of an earlier right of the defendant.[2] The latter is the only ground on which the defendant could have opposed, so the practical result is that regardless of whether a counterclaim may be filed at this point he can defend on the basis of the same relative grounds of invalidity as he would have been able to raise in opposition proceedings in the Office. There is no provision in the Community Trade Mark Regulation for intervention in oppositions by assumed infringers, so if the three month opposition period has expired the defendant cannot challenge validity in the Office unless and until the mark is registered and an application can be made to a Cancellation Division.

Article 96(2) provides that a Community trade mark court shall reject 5–117 a counterclaim for revocation or invalidation if a decision taken by the Office "relating to the same subject matter and cause of action and involving the same parties" has become final. There appears to be no distinction between opposition and revocation proceedings in this respect, except for the fact that the relative grounds which an opponent could raise in the Office can also be raised by way of a simple defence in infringement proceedings and do not have to be the subject of a counterclaim. It is hard to imagine why there should be any relevant distinction between what is *res judicata* for the purpose of a counterclaim, and what is *res judicata* for a defence as such raising exactly the same issues. Subject to what is probably a defect in drafting, it seems to follow that decisions of the Office in trade mark oppositions create an issue estoppel between the parties so that grounds decided against the opponent in the Office cannot be re-litigated in court. The provision is redundant if the decision is against the applicant, since in that case registration would be refused and there would be no mark to revoke.

Pending revocation in OHIM or proceedings in another Community trade mark court

The provisions of the Community Trade Mark Regulation dealing 5–118 with simultaneous proceedings after registration are similar but not quite identical to those for Community patents. They are more flexible, and there is never any prohibition on filing a counterclaim. In comparison to the position for Community patents, it should be borne in mind that oppositions in the Community Trade Mark Office take place before grant, so that a full infringement action as such can never be co-pending

---

[2] Of course, an action for pre-grant compensation can be brought post-grant, as in existing U.K. practice, so it cannot be assumed that Art. 95(3) is specifically contemplating pre-grant proceedings.

with an opposition.[3] Once the trade mark is registered, it is immediately open to central attack in the Office by way of an application for revocation or a declaration of invalidity and there is no period corresponding to that under Article 55(2) of the Community Patent Convention. Since the period for lodging opposition is quite short at three months, and the provisions of the Community Trade Mark Regulation are relatively limiting as to who can oppose and on what grounds, an application for revocation or invalidation immediately after registration is a real possibility.

5–119 The relevant provision is Article 100(1) which provides that where the validity of a Community trade mark is already in issue in a counterclaim before another Community trade mark court, or where an application for revocation or invalidation has already been filed at the Community Trade Mark Office, the court shall stay its proceedings unless there are special grounds for continuing. Several points are worth noting. What is contemplated is a stay of the proceedings as a whole: there is nothing expressly preventing a counterclaim being filed but absent special circumstances neither the action nor the counterclaim is to proceed. The stay is not automatic but it can be imposed of the court's own motion or on the application of one of the parties, though in either case only after the parties have had an opportunity to be heard. This gives, at least indirectly, some discretion as to how far the action is allowed to proceed before the stay comes into force. Applications for a declaration of non-infringement are not to be stayed, but validity cannot be put in issue in them anyway. There is again no express provision for the case where the defendant in an infringement action does not intend to challenge validity, although that might come within the general concept of "special grounds" and the implication from the treatment of declaratory actions is that there is no objection in principle to such an action being decided without waiting for the decision on validity of the Office or the other Community trade mark court.

5–120 Conversely, Article 100(2) provides in similar terms that the Office should in general stay its own proceedings for revocation or a declaration of invalidity if validity has already been put in issue by counterclaim in a Community trade mark court. The provisions as to hearing the parties are similar, except that there is also provision for one of the parties before the Community trade mark court to apply to the court to stay its own proceedings in favour of those in the Office, which the court may do after hearing the other parties. This is in addition to the power the court has under Article 96(7) on the application of the trade mark proprietor to require, in effect, a defendant to commence proceedings in the Office rather than pursuing a counterclaim.

A Community trade mark court which stays its own proceedings pursuant to Article 100(1) or (2) to await a decision of the Office expressly has the power to grant provisional and protective measures for the duration of the stay.

---

[3] For actions for compensation prior to registration, which can co-exist with an opposition, see para. 5–113, above.

Res judicata in the European Patent Office or another Community patent court

If the European Patent Office finally revokes a patent in opposition **5–121** proceedings then its decision takes effect *in rem* and cannot be challenged in any national court.[4] If an opposition fails, then it is generally considered that the opponent is not estopped from raising the same, unsuccessful, grounds of opposition in national proceedings, although opinions differ as to how much weight to give to the decision of the Office. So far as the Community Patent Convention is concerned, there is no express provision as to whether an unsuccessful opponent or applicant for revocation in the Office is estopped from raising the same grounds in a subsequent counterclaim in national infringement proceedings. Nor is there any express provision for whether or in what circumstances the Office is bound by its own previous decisions, as might arise if a patent was unsuccessfully opposed, and then made the subject of revocation proceedings.

The Community Patent Convention is likewise completely silent as to **5–122** *res judicata* between two Community patent courts of first instance; or between COPAC and a Community patent court; or in consecutive cases before COPAC. Even a decision of COPAC is, in terms, only binding in further proceedings in the same case. Uniformity of decisions is obviously desirable, especially once an issue has been decided by COPAC, but the question seems to be left wholly to national law.

Res judicata and judgments *in rem* relating to Community trade marks

A decision revoking the registration of a Community trade mark is not **5–123** necessarily fully retrospective and proceedings for accrued damages might conceivably continue.[5] Otherwise, a decision of either OHIM or a Community trade mark court revoking the Community trade mark or declaring it to be invalid,[6] which has become final, takes effect *in rem* and necessarily terminates any other pending proceedings. In the case of decisions of a Board of Appeal, the decision is not final until the time for bringing an action in the Court of First Instance has expired, or while one is pending.[7] A decision on infringement which has become final and has been enforced is not affected by the retroactive nature of a subsequent decision of revocation or invalidity.[8]

The Community Trade Mark Regulation contains slightly more **5–124** detailed provisions than the Protocol on Litigation as to the effects *inter partes* of Office decisions which do not have effect *in rem*. Article 96(2)

---

[4] *Lenzing's European Patent* [1997] R.P.C. 245 (Jacob J.). See also Cook, "Judicial Review of the EPO and the Direct Effect of TRIPs in the European Community" [1997] E.I.P.R. 367.
[5] Art. 54(1).
[6] Art. 54(2).
[7] Art. 62(3).
[8] Art. 54(3)(a).

provides that a Community trade mark court shall reject a counterclaim for revocation or invalidation if a decision of the Office "relating to the same subject matter and cause of action and involving the same parties" has become final. There appears to be no distinction between opposition and revocation proceedings in this respect. In other words, decisions of the Office create an issue estoppel between the parties and grounds decided against the opponent or application for revocation in the Office cannot be re-litigated in court. The provision is redundant if the decision is against the proprietor, since there is no occasion to reject a counterclaim if the mark has been revoked. Article 55(3) correspondingly provides that an application to the Office for revocation or a declaration of invalidity shall be inadmissible if an application between the same parties relating to the same subject matter and cause of action has been finally adjudicated upon by a national court of a member state. The draft Community Design Regulation contains similar provisions.

Articles 105(2) and (3) deal with the possibility of parallel actions based on national and Community trade marks being brought before different courts and implement the principle *nemo debet bis vexare pro eiadem causam.*

G. PROCEDURE AT FIRST INSTANCE

General

5–125   In general, the Community patent or trade mark court of first instance applies its own normal rules of procedure and evidence appropriate to actions for infringement of national patents or trade marks except to the extent that the Community Patent Convention, the Protocol on Litigation or the Community Trade Mark Regulation otherwise requires.[9]

The mandatory counterclaim

5–126   Article 15(2) of the Protocol on Litigation has the effect that a defendant to an infringement action wishing to challenge the validity of the Community patent sued on must do so by a counterclaim for revocation. In contrast to the situation in England, invalidity cannot be raised simply as a defence. In the absence of a counterclaim, Community patent courts must assume that the Community patent is valid. Substantially the same principle applies to infringement of Community trade marks—with two exceptions—but the treatment of Community designs is slightly different.

5–127   The Scordamaglia Report comments[9a]:

> "Community patent courts must assume that a Community patent is valid (Art. 15(2) Prot. Lit.).

---

[9] Protocol on Litigation, Art. 33; Community Trade Mark Regulation, Art. 97(3).
[9a] para. 185.

Where an assumed infringer files a plea for revocation as a means of defence, restricting his plea to rejection of the infringement action without requesting a ruling on the patent's validity with *erga omnes* effect, a Community patent court is obliged to reject the plea and treat the patent as valid without being able to enter into the merits of the case.

The defendant must therefore enter a plea for revocation of the Community patent in the form of a counterclaim if the Community patent court is to be in a position to rule on the validity of the patent with *erga omnes* effect.

The same grounds for revocation may be invoked in a counterclaim as in direct proceedings before the special departments of the EPO (Art. 56(1) CPC). Art. 55(1) CPC sets out limits concerning the person entitled to institute proceedings. Art. 55(2), (3) and (6) CPC also applies (cf. point 157 above)."

Essentially the same principle applies to the Community trade mark, except that the defence of lack of use of the mark can be raised without a counterclaim. So can the defence that the trade mark is invalid as a result of earlier rights of the defendant. Other grounds of invalidity must be raised by a counterclaim for revocation or a declaration of invalidity. **5–128**

The Community Trade Mark Regulation distinguishes between two categories of counterclaim where the Protocol on Litigation has only one. There are counterclaims for "revocation" and those for a "declaration of invalidity." The Community trade mark court has exclusive jurisdiction over both categories of counterclaim,[10] irrespective of the situation under domestic law, and the appropriate counterclaim is the only way for the validity of the registration to be put in issue in the infringement action.[11] The distinction between the two is that the Regulation uses the term "application for revocation" in respect of invalidating factors arising after grant:[12] as when the mark has not been used for five years, has become generic or misleading, or the proprietor no longer qualifies. The Regulation uses "application for declaration of invalidity" if the mark could originally have been refused registration on absolute[13] or relative grounds[14] or if the applicant acted in bad faith.[15] Despite the terminology, a declaration of invalidity takes effect *in rem* with fully retrospective effect and amounts to revocation in all but name.[16] Revocation so called prima facie takes effect from the date of the application or counterclaim, but may have effect from an earlier date on which one of the grounds for revocation occurred if either party so requests.[17] **5–129**

[10] Community Trade Mark Regulation, Arts 92(d) and 96.
[11] Art. 95(1).
[12] Community Trade Mark Regulation, Art. 50.
[13] Art. 51.
[14] Art. 52.
[15] Art. 51.
[16] Art. 54(2).
[17] Art. 54(1).

Some problems of the mandatory counterclaim and the presumption of validity

5–130   The requirement of the Community Patent Convention to put validity in issue by counterclaim or not at all, and the corresponding obligation on the court to treat the Community patent as valid in the absence of a counterclaim, may cause difficulties and even injustice in a number of circumstances, typically in situations where the plaintiff seeks some kind of interlocutory or summary relief when the validity of the patent is in doubt but the defendant is for some reason unable to counterclaim.[18] This situation is addressed expressly in the case of the Community Registered Design, but the lacuna remains for the Community patent and to a lesser extent for the Community trade mark.

5–131   The problem is most pronounced where a Community patent is under opposition in the European Patent Office or the nine month opposition period has not yet expired. About one European patent in twenty is opposed, but patents which are worth opposing are perhaps the most likely to be litigated. The period for entering opposition is nine months, and during this period no defendant anywhere can counterclaim for revocation even if an infringement action for summary or interlocutory relief was commenced on the very day the patent was granted.[19] An opposition typically lasts two years at first instance and a further two years on appeal, but oppositions can last much longer, especially if there are many opponents, or if the Technical Board of Appeal makes a reference to the enlarged Board of Appeal or remits the case to the Opposition Division for further proceedings. Pending oppositions are likely to be further prolonged in the circumstances under consideration by the intervention of defendants as assumed infringers pursuant to Article 105 of the European Patent Convention.

5–132   One can understand, even if one does not entirely support, the policy that any opposition should be finally determined before national courts are allowed to rule on the validity of the same patent; and the interests of the defendant are protected to some extent by his right to oppose within the nine month period or subsequently to intervene in the opposition as an assumed infringer. What is incomprehensible is the conclusion that national courts should be obliged to treat the patent as valid until the nine month opposition period is up, or the opposition has run its course, simply because of the existence of a procedural bar to the defendant making a counterclaim for revocation. The presumption applies without exception no matter how unrealistic it may be in fact: the Opposition Division or Board of Appeal may have issued a non-binding

---

[18] For example, filing a counterclaim would probably operate as a submission to the jurisdiction, so a defendant sued on an invalid patent in a court arguably having no jurisdiction could not safely challenge validity until the jurisdiction issue had been determined against him. Meanwhile, the court might have granted a preliminary injunction on the assumption that the patent was valid.

[19] It is fortunate that "self-oppositions" are no longer allowed, or the proprietor could make his Community patent counterclaim-proof for at least the first few years after grant.

but persuasive interim opinion of invalidity; the patentee may have admitted that his claims are too wide and have submitted radical limitations; corresponding national patents may have been revoked,[20] perhaps even by the same court; or an appeal against a first instance order for revocation in the EPO may obviously be hopeless. Notwithstanding any or all of these, the court seised of the infringement action apparently has no alternative but to assume the Community patent to be valid.

Although the terms of Article 15(2) are strong, it is not entirely clear **5–133** how widely the presumption of validity is intended to apply in practice, and the effect of the Article can only be understood in conjunction with Article 34 which imposes a near-mandatory stay on infringement actions when the validity of the patent in suit is already in issue in the European Patent Office. Broadly, three questions arise: on an application for summary judgment, what is the combined effect of the ban on filing a counterclaim and the resulting presumption of validity;[21] does an application for an interlocutory injunction have to be dealt with on the presumption that the patent in suit is valid or can the court form its own judgment;[22] and on an application to stay the action, perhaps on terms, should the court take the presumption of validity into account? A further complication in the case of interlocutory injunctions is that COPAC has no role in the granting or refusal of provisional and protective measures.[23]

Remittal of validity to OHIM

Article 96(7) of the Community Trade Mark Regulation provides that **5–134** a Community trade mark court hearing a counterclaim for revocation or invalidity may stay the counterclaim and request the defendant to apply to the Community Trade Mark Office for revocation or a declaration of invalidity within a set time limit. The stay of the counterclaim can only be made on the application of the proprietor and after hearing the other parties. If the defendant does not apply to the Office within the set time his counterclaim is deemed to be withdrawn. There is no corresponding provision for Community patents.

---

[20] National patents can coexist with a Community patent for the same invention until the opposition period has expired or any opposition has been finally determined in favour of maintaining the Community patent: Community Patent Convention, Art. 75 (1).

[21] During the nine month opposition period, and assuming no opposition has been filed, the defendant cannot file a counterclaim but Art. 34(2) of the Protocol on Litigation does not apply and the court is under no obligation to stay its proceedings. In principle, it could enter summary judgment for the plaintiff, although this would obviously be too unjust to contemplate if the defendant genuinely preferred to challenge validity in the national court rather than the European Patent Office.

[22] Given the practice under *American Cyanamid v. Ethicon* [1975] A.C. 396, HL this might not be thought to make much difference, but *Cyanamid* is unpopular, and courts abroad which grant interlocutory injunctions can and do take validity into account.

[23] Protocol on Litigation, Art. 36(3).

Appeal procedure

5–135   Appeals from decisions of Community patent courts of first instance go to the corresponding national Community patent court of second instance, but unless the appeal concerns interlocutory relief the latter must refer all issues of Community patent law to COPAC for determination. Community trade mark courts of second instance, in contrast, determine all issues in the case. Appeal procedure is discussed in Chapter 4.

H. REMEDIES AND TERRITORIAL SCOPE OF RELIEF

The relation of scope of relief to basis of jurisdiction

5–136   A fundamental principle of both the Protocol on Litigation and the Community Trade Mark Regulation is that the territorial scope of relief which may be granted by a Community patent or trade mark court depends on the basis on which it has jurisdiction. The normal rule is that the court may grant relief for the whole of the Community. This applies if jurisdiction derives from heads (1) to (4) of Article 14 of the Protocol on Litigation or Article 93 of the Regulation: the domicile or place of establishment of the defendant; the domicile or place of establishment of the plaintiff; the seat of COPAC or OHIM; agreement or entry of an appearance. Although it is not stated expressly, it is presumably intended that where the court has jurisdiction over any one defendant by virtue of his domicile or place of establishment, then jurisdiction over any co-defendants joined pursuant to Article 6(1) of the Brussels Convention is coextensive with that over the principal defendant.

5–137   The only remaining independent ground of jurisdiction is that of head (5) of either Article: actual or threatened infringement in the member state where the action is brought. In the latter case alone, jurisdiction is confined to relief in respect of acts threatened or committed in that state. The territorial restriction on jurisdiction in this case is twofold. The court cannot investigate or grant relief in respect of acts committed or threatened outside the state in which it is situated, and any injunction granted will have effect only for that state and not for the Community as a whole. The territorial jurisdiction of a court in this respect is defined on a state-by-state basis, and not according to any more limited territorial jurisdiction the court may have within a member state. So, for example, the Protocol and Regulation do not prevent the High Court or the Court of Session from granting relief in these circumstances for the whole of the United Kingdom.

5–138   Regardless of the basis on which a Community patent or trade mark court has jurisdiction over infringement, its jurisdiction on a counterclaim always extends to revoking the Community patent or trade mark for the whole Community. The plaintiff who sues in a court with limited territorial jurisdiction in respect of the injunction and damages does not, as a *quid pro quo*, receive any more favourable treatment in respect of validity. Actions for declarations of non-infringement cannot be brought under Articles 14(5) or 93(5) so the declaration will always have Community-wide effect. The right to reasonable compensation between publication of the application and grant is governed by the same principles as for damages for infringement.

There is a problem with counterclaims for relief other than revocation or invalidation. For instance, an action for a declaration of non-infringement may be met with infringement proceedings as such, or one infringement action may trigger a counterclaim for infringement in response. Article 6(3) of the Brussels Convention allows a person domiciled in a contracting state to be sued on a counterclaim arising from the same facts on which the original claim was based, in the court where the original claim was pending. Article 6(3) is deemed to be incorporated in both the Protocol on Litigation and the Community Trade Mark Regulation so as to apply to persons with an establishment in a contracting state as if they were domiciled. Supposing that there is no independent basis on which the court could assert jurisdiction over the plaintiff, then there appear to be two inconsistent possibilities. One is that the court's jurisdiction over the plaintiff on the counterclaim corresponds to that on the claim, so that both parties, or neither, would be subject to Community-wide relief. The other is to say that the plaintiff is always deemed to submit to the jurisdiction of the court he sues in, so that by analogy with head (4) of Article 14 or 93, he is always subject to Community-wide relief on a counterclaim even if his claim is based on head (5) and confined to local relief. The uncertainty of the position and the possible absence of reciprocity are reasons for avoiding this situation. **5–139**

Another situation not addressed by the Protocol or Regulation concerns actions brought by plaintiffs other than the proprietor, whose rights may not extend to the whole territory of the Community patent or trade mark. Licences may be for any geographical territory, and actions by licensees are contemplated expressly by the Community Trade Mark Regulation and implicitly by the Protocol on Litigation. Presumably, unless the proprietor is made a party, the territorial scope of any relief cannot exceed that for which the licensee has rights. **5–140**

Interlocutory remedies: provisional and protective measures

Community patent or trade mark courts which have jurisdiction under heads (1) to (4) of Article 14 of the Protocol on Ligation or Article 93 of the Community Trade Mark Regulation have general jurisdiction to grant provisional, including protective, measures with effect for all contracting states. It is expressly stated that no other courts have such jurisdiction. Since there are quite wide national differences in what provisional and protective remedies are available, and in what circumstances, it is unfortunate that the Protocol and Regulation are not more specific on these questions.[24] **5–141**

[24] See the Report of the House of Lords Select Committee on the European Communities: *A European Community Patent* (1986), and especially the passage quoted at para. 5–153.

5–142   The expression "measures which . . . are applicable in the territory of any Contracting State" could perhaps be read as a way of defining the provisional and protective measures in contemplation, but if so it is ambiguous and leads to absurdities on either interpretation. Does it mean measures which are universally available, or measures which are available in at least one state?[25] If the latter, does it make sense that a German plaintiff should be able to ask a French court to invoke a remedy which is only known to the law of Sweden, but which is proposed to be executed at premises in Spain owned by an Italian defendant? If the former, then perhaps no preliminary measures could ever be granted at all, or at least not without an elaborate preliminary exercise in comparative law. The simplest though open-ended explanation is that the expression leaves the nature of the measures in question undefined and simply means that the court can impose them for any, or all, of the contracting states, as justice demands. A Community-wide injunction is only mandatory after trial.

5–143   The applicability of extraterritorial provisional and protective measures is expressly subject to any necessary procedure for recognition and enforcement pursuant to Title III of the Brussels Convention. In context, the main practical consequence of this is that *ex parte* measures will not be enforceable outside the state in which they are granted. That is an important safeguard for defendants but it is subject to two qualifications. One is that a defendant may be served in sufficient time for the exception for *ex parte* orders not to arise, but without his really being able to arrange his defence effectively at short notice before an unfamiliar foreign court. The other is that although an *ex parte* order is not enforceable outside the jurisdiction of the court which made it, that does not mean that an extraterritorial *ex parte* order is in any way ineffective or invalid. If the defendant has assets against which the *ex parte* order can be enforced without recourse to the mechanism of the Brussels Convention, then he may have no choice in practice but to obey it.

5–144   The Protocol and Regulation also provide that application may be made to the courts of a member state, whether or not they are Community patent or trade mark courts, for such provisional, including protective, measures as are available under national law in respect of a national patent or trade mark. This may be done even if a Community patent or trade mark court in another country has exclusive jurisdiction over the substance of the matter. There is no requirement that the court should be able to assert any jurisdiction under Article 14(5) or 93(5), and indeed that would be inconsistent with the fact that a national court granting local provisional and protective measures under Article 36(1) or 99(1) need not even be a Community patent or trade mark court at all. In many cases there would be no scope for granting local interlocutory relief unless there was an actual or threatened infringement, but a *Mareva* injunction, for instance, might genuinely be needed wherever the defendant happened to have a bank account.

---

[25] The question is canvassed by Young and Birss, "Forum Shopping under the Community Patent Convention" [1992] E.I.P.R. 361.

COPAC has no role in the grant or refusal of provisional and protective measures so that Community patent courts of second instance will find themselves in the unusual position of disposing of all aspects of an appeal, including infringement and validity if those are in issue. In the case of Community trade marks, there is no central court corresponding to COPAC so that procedure on appeal will be the same whether or not any relief was final or interlocutory.

5–145

The mandatory final injunction

For both Community patents and trade marks, it is provided that where the court finds that the defendant has infringed or threatened to infringe the plaintiffs' rights, it shall, unless there are special reasons to the contrary, make an order prohibiting the defendant from proceeding with the acts which infringed or would have infringed.[26] The trial court is also obliged to take whatever measures are appropriate under its national law to ensure that the order is complied with. This broadly corresponds to English practice, except that an English final injunction is normally granted in general terms without reference to actual or threatened infringements.[27] Even in the case of trivial, isolated or discontinued infringements it would seem that the plaintiff is prima facie entitled to an injunction, although one might not have been awarded under previous English practice.

5–146

Final remedies other than the mandatory injunction; compensation

Apart from the mandatory injunction, the Community patent or trade mark court is obliged to apply the law of the member state in which the acts of infringement or threatened infringement were committed, including its private international law.[28] This most obviously applies to the pecuniary remedies of damages or an account of profits.[29] It follows, at least in principle, that an exercise in comparative law will be required whenever there has been infringement on a sufficiently large scale and in several countries.[30]

It is unclear whether delivery up (or destruction) is a remedy in its own right, so as to be applied on a state-by-state basis, or whether it is a measure "aimed at ensuring that this prohibition [the injunction] is complied with" so that, for patents, Article 35(1) rather than 35(2)

5–147

---

[26] Protocol on Litigation, Art. 35(1); Community Trade Mark Regulation, Art. 98(1).

[27] *Quaere* whether the court can grant an injunction wider than that provided for in Art. 35(1) of the Protocol on Litigation or Art. 98(1) of the Community Trade Mark Regulation, and if so whether it may do so on a national, E.C.-wide or state-by-state basis.

[28] Protocol on Litigation, Art. 35(2); Community Trade Mark Regulation, Art. 98(2).

[29] Damages are universally available. An account of profits, if available at all, may be regarded either as a remedy for infringement or for a separate cause of action in unjust enrichment.

[30] For patents there is a comparative survey of remedies in Bouju, ed., *Patent Infringement Litigation Penalties* (1989). See also Karnell, "Computation of Damages for Patent Infringement . . . A Comparative Law Overview" [1997] I.P.Q. 92.

applies. Otherwise, the only final remedy widely available (though not in England) is an order for publication of the judgment. In the interests of simplicity it is to be hoped that costs, whether lawyers' or court fees, are always to be awarded according to the *lex fori*, though even this is not beyond doubt where, as in Germany, recoverable costs are tied to the value of the infringing acts.

I. FORUM SHOPPING: THEORY AND REALITY

The policy of the Protocol on Litigation and its underlying assumptions

5–148   At first sight, each of Article 14 of the Protocol on Litigation and Article 93 of the Community Trade Mark Regulation provides a rigid and inflexible set of rules for assigning litigation over a Community patent to a single court with minimal opportunity for the plaintiff to steer the litigation towards a preferred jurisdiction. As the Scordamaglia Report acknowledges, the Protocol on Litigation was drafted on the basis that "precautions had to be taken to ensure that, given the differences in substantive and procedural law in those States, plaintiffs were not induced to opt for the courts of a particular State to the defendant's detriment" and the report goes on to say that it was expressly to prevent "forum shopping" that the Protocol on Litigation laid down a set of criteria for identifying a single Contracting State whose courts are assigned jurisdiction over infringements committed throughout Europe. The only express qualifications to this policy either depend on the co-operation of the defendant, or prejudice the plaintiff by removing the benefit of Community-wide jurisdiction over infringement, without which the Community Patent Convention, at least, loses its main attraction.[31]

5–149   On closer analysis, it will be seen that this policy is erroneous in at least three respects: forum shopping is not necessarily undesirable or undertaken for improper motives; the attractiveness of the Community Patent Convention scheme to industry depends on a degree of forum shopping being permitted; and, perhaps fortunately, the opportunities for forum shopping in reality are far greater than the Report allows. One suspects that an unstated reason for the approach of the Protocol on Litigation was not so much to protect defendants, as to protect national and regional interests and prevent Community patent litigation gravitating in its entirety to no more than half a dozen courts of known capability, as would certainly happen if the wishes of litigants, plaintiffs and defendants alike, prevailed.[32]

---

[31] Young and Birss, "Forum Shopping under the Community Patent Convention" [1992] E.I.P.R. 361.

[32] A prospect foreseen, and deplored, by Peter Ford of the EPO in his evidence to the House of Lords Select Committee on the European Communities: *A European Community Patent* (1986).

Differences in law and procedure are not the only, or even the **5–150** principal, cause of forum shopping. In France, Germany and Italy patent litigation is already assigned to about seven to 10 first instance courts on a regional basis. In each case, one finds that a single court (Paris, Dusseldorf or Milan) accounts for half or more of all national patent litigation, that two or three courts account for most of the rest, and that the remainder hardly exercise their patent jurisdiction at all. Since substantive law is the same throughout each state, and procedural law differs only very slightly at most, something else must account for such a marked imbalance. Since the pattern is not transient, it cannot simply be the presence of judges who tend favour the plaintiff. The implication is simply that plaintiffs are often prepared to forgo the home advantage of suing in their local court and will entrust their litigation to courts of known experience and competence.

A glance at the Annex to the Protocol on Litigation shows that the **5–151** three dozen identified Community patent courts of first instance vary enormously in their experience of patent litigation, both from one state to another and within single jurisdictions. The Community Patent Convention purports to offer two answers to this imbalance. One is the requirement that there should be "as limited a number as possible" of Community patent courts in each contracting state,[33] and that the judges of Community patent courts "shall be persons who possess experience of patent law."[34] The other is that COPAC is supposed to provide a uniform and reliable standard of justice on appeal. As to the first, the principle has obviously been compromised in favour of regional interests[35] and the belief that no state is too small to have at least one Community patent court. The standard of experience must be a low one if the High Court of Northern Ireland, for example, or the *Tribunal di Cagliari*, are genuinely considered to meet it. COPAC itself will not prove its mettle for several years after the Community Patent Convention comes into force. The Community Trade Mark Regulation has no central court corresponding to COPAC.

The Protocol on Litigation makes most sense if one assumes that it **5–152** was drafted on the basis that infringement normally only occurs in one place, that there is typically only one possible plaintiff and one defendant and that both are single companies rather than members of corporate groups, that manufacturers deal directly with consumers, that even counterfeiters will make no efforts to evade service of proceedings or defeat enforcement of a judgment, that it is equally satisfactory for patent litigation to take six months or six years, that neither party will

[33] Protocol on Litigation, Art. 1 and Annex.
[34] Art. 31.
[35] A total of 36 first instance courts are designated by name for 10 contracting states (not including Spain and Portugal) to which must now be added the Patents County Court in England, courts in former East Germany and the courts of Spain, Portugal, Austria, Finland and Sweden. Evidence to the House of Lords (House of Lords Select Committee on the European Communities: *A European Community Patent* (1986) Q. 43) noted that even this was the result of compromise, without which there might have been up to 100 Community patent courts in some countries.

attempt to procure any procedural advantage over the other and that if the application of Article 14 points to a court which no litigant would chose of his own free will then the parties will either put up with the situation cheerfully or agree to confer jurisdiction on another Community patent court. On these assumptions, the Protocol on Litigation adequately fulfils the stated intentions of its draftsmen and is of negligible interest to industry; on any others, it is a less straightforward but much more viable piece of legislation.

The House of Lords on forum shopping

5–153   In view of the suspicion of forum shopping expressed in the Scordamaglia Report, it is perhaps surprising that the practice is actually encouraged by many unnecessary uncertainties in the application of the Community Patent Convention and Protocol on Litigation, most of which are also to be found in the Community Trade Mark Regulation. The Select Committee on the European Communities of the House of Lords identified many of the problem areas[36]:

> "A jurisdictional system which allows a plaintiff some choice among courts in which to start proceedings for enforcement of a unitary right inevitably presents some opportunity for 'forum shopping.' Witnesses to the Committee took different views of how likely this would be, or indeed how undesirable.[37] Today, in patent matters, there is often a choice of courts—as where alleged infringements of a patent occur in different parts of a country for which different courts have jurisdiction or, more generally, where there are parallel patents in different countries and infringements are alleged in each of them. Moreover, it is not uncommon to treat the outcome of proceedings in one jurisdiction as deciding the dispute internationally. If the place for such proceedings is selected because of the skill and experience of the court, or the expedition or cheapness of litigation there, the choice will doubtless be beneficial to both parties. It is only if, as between different courts, one or other side will predictably be placed in a more advantageous position that a serious problem emerges. Indeed, such a prospect would be a serious defect, whether or not the plaintiff is in a position to influence the outcome by choosing his court.
>
> There are several opportunities for choosing a forum within the proposed CPC system; the two most likely cases are as follows:
> (i) in relation to a defendant who has a domicile in a Member State, only the courts of that state may be used if a Community-wide order is to be obtained; but action may also be brought (for that territory alone) in any state where infringement is allegedly occurring;

[36] Report of the House of Lords Select Committee on the European Communities: *A European Community Patent* (1986); App. 3, para. 12.
[37] Internal references and citations omitted.

(ii) in relation to a non-EEC defendant, a Community-wide order may be obtained in the courts of any state where he has an establishment, or the proceedings may be brought in a place of infringement. Thus it will not be possible to take a defendant to court in a distant territory with which he has no connection.

The proposed system ultimately provides a safeguard against variations by the overall jurisdiction of COPAC and indeed this is an important part of the court's *raison d'etre*. But, as already noted, this supervisory function is not available in interlocutory proceedings.[38] Yet if interim injunctions are available relatively readily is a particular jurisdiction, the ability to proceed there may have major commercial implications, for much intellectual property litigation is not taken beyond the interlocutory stage. As has already been pointed out, the legal basis for the granting of such relief may well vary between Member States. The consequences could be most undesirable. In the Committee's view, the contracting states should explore the possibility of a further protocol to the Convention which would establish a common set of rules for the granting of such relief.

A separate problem affecting interlocutory relief concerns the applicable law, since it is a matter on which a Community patent court is to apply its national law, including its private international law. Article 36(1) gives jurisdiction to a court in any contracting state to grant such provisional relief 'as may be available under the laws of that State in respect of a national patent,' and from this it may be inferred that Community patent courts with regular jurisdiction under the litigation protocol are likewise to apply their national patent law to the issue. It is plainly the sensible choice of law in respect of proceedings which may have to be very expeditious. But the rule deserves to be explicitly stated.

The Protocol on Litigation gives one court (usually that of the defendant's domicile or place of establishment) the power to make interlocutory orders effective throughout the Community. To be able to procure such an order in an appropriate case is one of the most striking advantages that will attach to the Community patent. The Committee are on balance persuaded that it is a development which should be part of the new proposal, even though the grant of the order is to be a matter entirely for the courts of the country concerned. At the same time they are conscious that, unwisely used, the order could injure defendants unfairly and that the injustice could be of an order which could not truly be compensated for through machinery such as cross-undertakings in damages. They certainly agree with those witnesses who stressed that interlocutory orders should have extra-territorial effect only if made in proceedings *inter partes*. This appears to follow from the interpretation

---

[38] Nor, one might now add, in proceedings under the Community Trade Mark Regulation. The idea of COPAC extending its Community-wide jurisdiction to intellectual property generally appealed to the House of Lords, but not, apparently, to the other member states.

given to a similar provision in the Judgments Convention by the European Court. However, the Committee are of the view that, on so important a matter, it is desirable that the rule should be stated explicitly in the Protocol on Litigation."

Opportunities for forum shopping in theory and practice

5–154   The Community Patent Convention and Community Trade Mark Regulation expressly contemplate a limited degree of forum shopping, principally by allowing the proprietor to sue anywhere where there has been an actual infringement. However the option is deliberately made unattractive by the fact that the court can only grant relief for its own national territory. Since the validity of the Community patent or trade mark will still be at stake for the whole Community, this option is likely to be one of last resort for any but the most optimistic plaintiff. The Convention and Regulation are rather more generous in the scope for forum shopping at the interlocutory stage. National provisional and protective measures without extraterritorial effect can be granted by any court, whether or not it is a Community patent or trade mark court, and whether or not it has any jurisdiction at all over the substance of the case. Depending on the facts, a well-chosen application for interlocutory relief might have a wholly disproportionate effect outside the jurisdiction of the court making the order, at little immediate cost or risk to the plaintiff.

5–155   The main technique for forum shopping is likely to result from the inclusion of Article 6(1) of the Brussels Convention in both the Protocol on Litigation and the Community Trade Mark Regulation. In the case of widely-traded consumer goods, at least, it will almost always be possible to find an infringer such as a wholesale dealer or retailer who is domiciled or who has an establishment in whichever state is considered to be the preferred forum. If this defendant is sued pursuant to Article 14(1) of the Protocol on Litigation or Article 93(1) of the Regulation, then it would be a straightforward application of Article 6(1) to join as an additional defendant his supplier, hypothetically domiciled or established in another contracting state which presents less favourable opportunities. The chain of supply could then be followed upwards to the manufacturer or principal importer, as long as that defendant was domiciled or established in a member state. More controversially, since the application of Article 6(1) is still uncertain, other dealers domiciled or established in other member states could quite conceivably be joined as defendants in some jurisdictions even if they would not be liable as joint tortfeasors in the English sense.

5–156   This use of Article 6(1) might be regarded as abusive and it was almost certainly not contemplated by the draftsmen of the Protocol or Regulation, but it is already more than a mere hypothetical possibility or an attempt to create unreal problems. In Dutch patent infringement actions one routinely finds a list of perhaps a dozen defendants, with only one being domiciled in the Netherlands, and the Dutch courts regard the presence of a single Dutch infringer as giving them wholesale jurisdiction to grant extraterritorial relief against them all.[39] It does not seem to matter, either in theory or in practice, that the Dutch defendant may be an insignificant infringer in his own right or a relatively small cog in a corporate machine governed from elsewhere. Article 6(1) does not import the doctrine of *forum non conveniens* into the Brussels Convention.

There are two broad sets of circumstances where Article 6(1) of the **5–157** Brussels Convention is unlikely to be useful. One is typically where goods are sold directly from manufacturer to end-user, as with capital goods. Whether the end-user infringes is perhaps academic, since few businesses are prepared to sue their own customers, actual or potential. The other is where the defendant one wishes to sue is neither domiciled nor established in a member state. The latter at least presents a trivial exercise for the forum shopper, since if the proprietor is not already domiciled or established in his favoured jurisdiction then he can simply transfer the Community patent or trade mark to a connected party with the desired domicile. Variants on this technique which give virtually unlimited scope for forum-shopping as against non-Community defendants would exploit the possibility of co-proprietors or licensees suing in the courts of their own domicile.

The last and most cynical form of forum-shopping is simply to sue in **5–158** the preferred court and ignore the fact that it does not have jurisdiction to grant the relief sought. That may seem too blatant a tactic to have any prospect of success, but in fact a number of uncertainties combine to make it an option which requires separate consideration. As long as the chosen court is a Community patent court or trade mark court of first instance, then any original defect in its jurisdiction will be cured once the defendant enters an appearance to defend on the merits. The Protocol on Litigation takes pride in the claim that if its rules of jurisdiction are rigid and inflexible, they are at least definite and easy to apply. In reality, jurisdiction based on a place of establishment of either party is quite often likely to be open to argument, and if the plaintiff relies on his own alleged establishment then only he will be in possession of the facts. A defendant may irrevocably submit to a court which does not objectively have jurisdiction by inadvertently or prematurely defending on the merits.

The position of the defendant is particularly serious if interlocutory **5–159** relief is sought, or if the defendant is already subject to an *ex parte* order. A defence to an application for an interlocutory injunction might normally involve challenging the jurisdiction, denying infringement, attacking validity and raising discretionary factors such as urgency or the balance of convenience. It is by no means certain that a defendant can raise any but the first of these, even in interlocutory proceedings, without being deemed to have submitted to the jurisdiction pursuant to Article 14(4)(b) of the Protocol on Litigation or 93(4)(b) of the Community

---

[39] See para. 1–28 but see now para. 1–54.

Trade Mark Regulation.[40] This is most obviously the case for validity, which is presumed in favour of the plaintiff unless and until the defendant counterclaims, and it is hard to see how he can counterclaim and challenge jurisdiction simultaneously. What is worse for the defendant is that even a successful attack on jurisdiction under the Protocol or Regulation would not prevent the court granting such provisional measures as are available under its national law, though without extraterritorial effect. The result is virtually to force the defendant to challenge the grant of the provisional measures on the merits, regardless of whether this involves conceding the question of jurisdiction.

5–160   The one point on which the Convention and Regulation undoubtedly achieve their stated objective is in providing no useful scope for forum shopping by the prospective defendant. In particular, the application for a declaration of non-infringement cannot be used as a vehicle for challenging validity in a national court as opposed to the relevant Office.

---

[40] Though the case law of the European Court of Justice under the Brussels Convention does allow a defence on the merits to be filed at the same time as a challenge to jurisdiction, without prejudice to the latter: Cases 150/80 *Elefanten Schuh v. Jacqmain* [1981] E.C.R. 1593; [1982] 3 C.M.L.R. 1 and 27/81 *Rohr v. Ossberger* [1981] E.C.R. 2431; [1982] 3 C.M.L.R. 29. It is uncertain how far the same reasoning will be applied under the Protocol and the Regulation, and especially to counterclaims for revocation.

CHAPTER 6

ENFORCEMENT OF FOREIGN INTELLECTUAL PROPERTY RIGHTS UNDER DOMESTIC LAW

A. INTRODUCTION

The scope of the chapter

6–01   This chapter deals with two principal questions which can arise under domestic law if a plaintiff attempts to bring an action on a foreign intellectual property right in England.[1] First, it has to be decided

---

[1] Dicey and Morris, *The Conflict of Laws* (12th ed., 1993); Cheshire and North's *Private International Law* (12th ed., 1992); Wolff, *Private International Law* (2nd ed., 1962). See also Arnold, "Can One Sue in England for Infringement of Foreign Intellectual Property Rights" [1990] E.I.P.R. 254; Carter, "Foreign Copyright Laws not Justiciable" in "Decisions of British Courts during 1990 Involving Questions of Public or Private International Law" [1990] B.Y.I.L. 377 at 400; Floyd and Purvis, "Can an English Court Restrain Infringement of a Foreign Patent?" [1995] E.I.P.R. 110; Cornish, "Intellectual Property

whether the action ought to be allowed to proceed at all. That depends on the jurisdiction of the English court to hear it and on whether it is possible in any circumstances for it to grant relief. Even if the English court has jurisdiction in the narrow sense, it might decline to proceed with the action for discretionary reasons such as comity or *forum non conveniens*. Because the term *jurisdiction* is generally used in English law primarily in the sense of personal jurisdiction over a defendant, it is convenient and increasingly common to use the term *justiciability* to denote the question of whether or not the English court could or should assert jurisdiction over the subject matter of the dispute.

If the action is allowed to proceed to trial on the merits then the second question which arises is what system of law should be applied by the English court. It might be thought that the only law relevant to matters of substance would be that of the country of infringement, and this is the situation which will normally apply in the future under the Private International Law (Miscellaneous Provisions) Act 1995. It might also be thought that the two issues of justiciability and choice of law were entirely separate. In the past, however, English private international law has required the cumulative application of English law and the relevant foreign law, and greater prominence was given to English law. The prevailing opinion has been that the operation of this rule prevented intellectual property infringement actions ever having any prospect of succeeding, so that the choice of law rule effectively preempted any separate discussion of justiciability. **6–02**

It has to be said that there are very few reported cases, either in the United Kingdom or elsewhere in the common law world, in which any attempt has been made to enforce foreign proprietary intellectual property rights prior to the Brussels Convention. Those that are known have been uniformly unsuccessful. The only relevant area of law where actions have been brought with success in respect of wrongful acts abroad is for passing-off. **6–03**

Four explanations may be advanced for the fact that actions on foreign intellectual property rights are virtually unknown at common law: **6–04**

Infringement and Private International Law: Changing the Common Law Approach" [1996] GRUR Int. 285; Jooris, "Infringement of Foreign Copyright and the Jurisdiction of the English Courts" [1996] E.I.P.R. 127; Austin, "The Infringement of Foreign Intellectual Property Rights" (1997) 113 L.Q.R. 321; Howell, "Intellectual Property, Private International Law and Issues of Territoriality" (1997) 13 *Canadian Intellectual Property Review* 209. The major intellectual property textbooks have relatively little to say about private international law but see Cornish, *Intellectual Property* (3rd ed., 1996), paras 2–71 *et seq.*; *Copinger and Skone James on Copyright* (13th ed. 1991), para. 11–31; Laddie, Prescott and Victoria, *The Modern Law of Copyright* (2nd ed., 1995), para. 24.19; Stewart *International Copyright and Neighbouring Rights* (2nd ed., 1989), Chap. 3; Victoria *et al.*, *Encyclopaedia of United Kingdom and European Patent Law* para. 10–501 *et seq.*; Wadlow, *The Law of Passing-off* (2nd ed., 1995), para. 4.50.

1. The first branch of the "double actionability" rule in *Phillips v. Eyre*[2] formerly meant that any such action would inevitably fail[3];
2. Such actions are not justiciable in England because of the application of the *Mocambique*[4] rule to intellectual property[5];
3. Justiciability exists, but jurisdiction would be declined for reasons of discretion, international comity, *forum non conveniens* or the like[6]; and
4. The underlying reason is simply the reluctance of the courts, litigants or their advisors to innovate.

6–05   The first of these is given pride of place because it has been accepted by *Dicey and Morris*,[7] several other commentators, and the Law Commission.[8] It has undoubtedly been influential in the past decade or so,[9] though its importance in its own right has perhaps been exaggerated. It is said to be justified by the rule in *Phillips v. Eyre* itself and by the only common law cases to have considered the matter. Both justifications are in fact questionable, and unless the theory has some other ground for its acceptance then any reasons for not entertaining actions based on foreign intellectual property rights may have to be sought elsewhere.[10] It is, in any event, obsolete with the passing of the Private International Law (Miscellaneous Provisions) Act 1995.

6–06   The second explanation is in fact supported by the original Australian authority normally cited to support the strict double-actionability theory,[11] but may only apply to patents and similar registered rights. At any rate, the rule should be understood as one of public policy, and as such its validity deserves to be reconsidered as times and international relations change. The third may perhaps explain why the only known action on a foreign copyright was unsuccessful.[12] If none of these reasons apply then foreign intellectual property rights could presumably be enforced in the English courts, even in cases not governed by the Brussels Convention, despite the fact that there is apparently no reported instance of this having happened to date. The absence of cases

---

[2] (1870) L.R. 6 Q.B. 1. The application of the rule to conclude that infringement actions on foreign intellectual property rights are bound to fail will sometimes be referred to as the "strict double actionability theory," as other interpretations which do not lead to this conclusion are possible. See para. 6–107.

[3] See paras 6–71 *et seq.*, below.

[4] The rule in *Companhia do Mocambique v. British South Africa Co* [1893] A.C. 602, HL. This is the same as the rule which distinguishes "local" and "transitory" actions.

[5] See paras 6–48 *et seq.*, and paras 6–114 *et seq.*, below.

[6] See para. 6–148, below.

[7] Dicey and Morris, *The Conflict of Laws* (12th ed., 1993), pp 1515 *et seq.*

[8] In its Working Paper (No. 87) *Private International Law—Choice of Law in Tort and Delict* (1984), para. 1.13 citing *Potter v. Broken Hill*, below.

[9] As a result of the decision of Browne-Wilkinson V.-C. in *Def Lepp v. Stuart Brown* [1986] R.P.C. 273.

[10] See para. 6–93.

[11] *Potter v. Broken Hill* (1906) 3 C.L.R. 479 (High Court of Australia) *affirming* [1905] V.L.R. 612.

[12] *Morocco Bound Syndicate v. Harris* [1895] 1 Ch. 534 (Kekewich J.).

may therefore have been the result of nothing more than conservatism, lack of imagination or a long-standing misconception of the law.

Two rules known by name: *Mocambique* and *Phillips v. Eyre*

Although the rules established in the cases of *Phillips v. Eyre*[13] and **6–07** *British South Africa Co v. Compania do Mocambique*[14] are subject to extensive commentaries later in the present chapter, each is of such pervasive relevance that it is convenient to summarise them here. The statement of the rule in *Phillips v. Eyre* is invariably taken from the judgment of Willes J. speaking for the Exchequer Chamber:

> "As a general rule, in order to found a suit in England for a wrong alleged to have been committed abroad, two conditions must be fulfilled. First, the wrong must be of such a character that it would have been actionable if committed in England. . . . Secondly, the act must not have been justifiable by the law of the place where it was done."

Thus the rule applies English and foreign law cumulatively, but with a **6–08** different emphasis on each. The first branch of the rule requires "the wrong" to be actionable if committed in England, and this means that the plaintiff should have an identifiable cause of action in tort under English law to which there would be no defence, had the facts occurred in England. Under the second branch, the defendant is not liable if the act would have been "justifiable" where it was committed. In *Boys v. Chaplin*[15] the House of Lords decided that the plaintiff can only satisfy the second branch by showing that he has a civil cause of action of some sort, though not necessarily in tort, in the country where the act took place. *Boys v. Chaplin* also recognised the existence of exceptions to the general rule, under which a single system of law may govern.

The *Mocambique* rule is purely one of justiciability, rather than choice **6–09** of law. In *Hesperides Hotels v. Aegean Turkish Holidays*[16] Lord Wilberforce approved the summary by *Dicey and Morris* of the *Mocambique* rule in its classic application to land:

> "The rule in the *Moçambique* case can be conveniently stated in the form in which it is generally accepted, viz., in Dicey & Morris, The Conflict of Laws, rule 79. I quote from the 9th ed. (1973), but it appears as rule 53 in the same form (except for one letter) in the 3rd ed. (1922) edited by Professor Dicey himself and Dr. Berriedale Keith.
>
> 'Subject to the exceptions hereinafter mentioned, the court has no jurisdiction to entertain an action for (1) the determination

---

[13] (1870) L.R. 6 Q.B. 1. The "double actionability" rule.
[14] [1893] A.C. 602, HL. This is the rule distinguishing "local" and "transitory" actions, only the latter being justiciable in England.
[15] [1971] A.C. 356, HL.
[16] [1979] A.C. 508, HL.

of the title to, or the right to the possession of, any immovable situate out of England (foreign land); or (2) the recovery of damages for trespass to such immovable.'"

6–10   The more controversial application of the *Mocambique* rule to intellectual property is considered in detail later.[17] However, it is of historical interest that the case which may claim to be the origin in English law of the underlying principle on which the *Mocambique* case rests was, in a broad sense, concerned with a foreign patent.[18] As Lord Wilberforce said in *Buttes Oil & Gas v. Hammer*[19]:

"In my opinion there is, and for long has been, such a general principle, starting in English law, adopted and generalised in the law of the United States of America which is effective and compelling in English courts. This principle is not one of discretion, but is inherent in the very nature of the judicial process.

The first trace of it is in the 17th century in *Blad v. Bamfield* (1674) 3 Swan. 604, 607. The record of the decision from Lord Nottingham's manuscript contains this passage:

'. . . the plaintiff hath proved letters patent from the King of Denmark for the sole trade of Iceland; a seizure by virtue of that patent; a sentence upon that seizure; a confirmation of that sentence by the Chancellor of Denmark; an execution of that sentence after confirmation; and a payment of two-thirds to the king of Denmark after that execution. Now, after all this, to send it to a trial at law, where either the court must pretend to judge of the validity of the king's letters patent in Denmark, or of the exposition and meaning of the articles of peace; or that a common jury should try whether the English have a right to trade in Iceland, is monstrous and absurd.'

Lord Nottingham records that 'I thought fit to put an end to [the case]' and he decreed that the plaintiff should have a perpetual injunction to stay the defendant's suit at law—a decision clearly on justiciability, and not merely on defence."

The double actionability rule of *Phillips v. Eyre* and the principle of territoriality

6–11   Although the rule of judicial abstention stated by Lord Wilberforce in *Buttes Oil & Gas v. Hammer*[20] and the rule of double actionability are completely separate, there is an interaction between them which is

---

[17] See paras 6–48 *et seq.*, below.
[18] *Blad's Case*; *Blad v. Bamfield* (1673) 36 E.R. 991 and (1674) 36 E.R. 992 (Lord Nottingham L.C.). The patent was one granted by the King of Denmark to Blad conferring trading privileges in Iceland, rather than a patent for an invention in the modern sense. The suit in Equity by Blad was for a common injunction to stay a suit by Bamfield at law, in which the latter claimed that the patent was invalid as contrary to Articles of Peace between England and Denmark, and sought to recover in respect of goods of his that had been seized.
[19] [1982] A.C. 888, HL.
[20] [1982] A.C. 888, HL.

particularly acute in the case of intellectual property. In fact, the very name of the double actionability rule was something of a misnomer for most of its life; and even now the rule is misunderstood if it is thought that it treats the *lex loci* and the *lex fori* on an equal footing, simply requiring the cumulative application of both. The relationship of the two in the sense that *Phillips v. Eyre*[21] was originally understood is summarised by Lord Pearson in *Boys v. Chaplin*[22]:

"The act must take its character of wrongfulness from the law of the place: it must not be justifiable under the law of the place: if it is 'valid and unquestionable by the law of the place, it cannot, so far as civil liability is concerned, be drawn in question elsewhere.' But Willes J. does not say that the wrongful act has to be actionable, or to give a cause of action for damages, according to the law of the place. The actionability is by the *lex fori*: 'the wrong must be of such a character that it would have been actionable if committed in England.' The second condition has to be read in the light of what has gone before. The act referred to is one which is wrongful according to the law of the place in which it is committed. But there is no requirement that it must be actionable by the law of that place as well as by the law of England: double actionability is not required. The requirement is that the act must not be justifiable by the law of the place. The reason for that must be that a person could not fairly be held liable in damages for doing something which in the place where it was done was either originally lawful or made lawful by retrospective legislation."

Up to that point, it might be said that Lord Pearson was in the minority in continuing to interpret *Phillips v. Eyre* in this sense, and that *Boys v. Chaplin* has generally been understood to require civil actionability, though not necessarily in tort, under the *lex loci* as well as the *lex fori*. However, the next passage from his speech remains valid in principle under any accepted interpretation of *Phillips v. Eyre*: **6–12**

"Willes J.'s statement of the conditions which have to be fulfilled (. . .) shows that in such a case the substantive law of England plays the dominant role, determining the cause of action, whereas the law of the place in which the act was committed plays a subordinate role, in that it may provide a justification."

This leads to the paradox that if an English court were to apply the rule in *Phillips v. Eyre* to a foreign intellectual property infringement, it **6–13**

---

[21] (1870) L.R. 6 Q.B. 1.

[22] [1971] A.C. 356 at 406, HL. Although the speeches of the five law lords differed in many respects, the relative subordination of the *lex loci* is common ground between them, the differences being the degree to which it is subordinate. Lord Pearson's speech has not been the most influential subsequently, and although it is used to illustrate the problem stated in the text, nothing for present purposes turns on which reading of *Boys v. Chaplin* is preferred.

would in fact find itself applying substantive British intellectual property law to acts wholly occuring within a foreign sovereign state, with the role of the foreign law being reduced to that of providing "justification" or not for the defendant's actions. In the case of the registered intellectual property rights, one likely justification would be the invalidity of the rights in question, so that the English court would be bound, in the interests of fairness to the defendant, to investigate the lawfulness of the acts of an administrative organ of a foreign sovereign state. But it is the first of these that would be the more significant violation of the principle of territoriality. It is one thing to enforce the intellectual property laws of another country—though that is controversial enough— it is quite another to apply one's own laws to transactions in that country, under colour of a rule of private international law. As Professor Cornish put it in his memorandum to the House of Lords during the passage of the Private International Law (Miscellaneous Provisions) Act 1995[23]:

> "So long as English PIL[24] dealt with the choice of law for tort or delict claims by a rule of double actionability which was designed to identify those cases where English law could be applied to events which were[25] partly or wholly foreign, it made no sense to include infringements of foreign IP within that category. Territoriality required that an infringement in France be dealt with by French law, not by English law. The courts duly refused to contemplate proceedings in England relating to such an act. Either they said that IP could not fit the double actionality test or else they said that[26] infringement was a 'local' as distinct from a 'transitory' issue (by analogy to the rule for title to land laid down in the *Mozambique* case). (Both explanations in my view obfuscate rather than clarify)."

6–14   The English cases cited by Professor Cornish and discussed later in this chapter have, perhaps, worked towards this conclusion from a number of different starting points and without offering any single statement of principle which is entirely satisfactory. In particular, it is potentially misleading to discuss the double actionability rule as if its application turned on the absence of extraterritorial effect in British intellectual property legislation.[27] None the less, the underlying rationale is clear: the former obligation to apply the so-called double actionability rule necessitated total judicial abstention from adjudicating on alleged infringements of foreign intellectual property, and it was of secondary

---

[23] *Proceedings of the Special Public Bill Committee* HL Paper 36 (1995), evidence, p. 64.
[24] The supernumerary word "is" in the original text is omitted.
[25] The text reads "where".
[26] The supernumerary word "if" in the original text is omitted.
[27] The common law tort of passing-off is not extraterritorial, but actions in respect of passing off abroad have succeeded. Patent, trade mark and copyright infringement were all once actionable at common law, but foreign infringements were no more actionable in England then than now.

importance how this was achieved: whether as an example of the *Mocambique* rule, as one aspect of the "other public law" exception, as a nominally discretionary application of principles of comity or *forum non conveniens*, or by application of the double actionability rule itself to conclude that the action cannot succeed. It is suggested later that the best formulation is probably in terms of an expanded *Mocambique* rule justified in terms of policy rather than procedure, though that is to a large extent a matter of personal preference. All the same, there is a certain elegance in turning the double actionability rule against itself, so as to invoke the rule itself to justify striking out *in limine* an action which would inevitably lead to unacceptable results if the rule was actually applied to the facts of the case. The rule is both the problem, and one source of the solution.

The relationship of this chapter to the Brussels Convention

Special attention needs to be given to cases to which the Brussels **6–15** Convention applies. In principle, the Brussels Convention does not affect national rules of conflict of laws,[28] so the Private International Law (Miscellaneous Provisions) Act 1995 applies to determine the applicable law in Brussels Convention cases just as much as in cases to which the Convention applies does not apply. However, Article 16(4) of the Convention contains its own code as to whether or not intellectual property actions are justiciable, and the *Mocambique* rule is therefore superceded in cases to which the Convention applies.[29] It has also been decided that the former rule of double actionability in intellectual property cases is inconsistent with the Convention,[30] but the point is of declining importance since it applies only to causes of action which accrued before the 1995 Act came into force.

Passing-off, unfair competition and breach of confidence

Passing-off differs from the other intellectual property torts in that it **6–16** has never been subject to the *Mocambique* rule, and actions in respect of passing off abroad have been brought successfully in England[31] and Scotland[32] with the double actionability rule applying. In the latter case, an express comparison was drawn between passing-off and trade mark infringement, with only the former being justiciable outside the state

---

[28] See para. 2–33, above for the general rule, and para. 6–104 below for the exception recognised by Lloyd J. in *Pearce v. Ove Arup* [1997] F.S.R. 641.

[29] See paras 6–63 *et seq.*, below.

[30] *Pearce v. Ove Arup* [1997] F.S.R. 641, see para. 6–104, below.

[31] *John Walker v. Ost* [1970] R.P.C. 489 (Foster J.); *Alfred Dunhill v. Sunoptic* [1979] F.S.R. 337, CA. See Wadlow, *The Law of Passing-Off* (2nd ed., 1995), para. 4.50 and supplement.

[32] *James Burrough Distillers v. Speymalt Whisky Distributors* [1991] R.P.C. 130 (SC, OH). In Ireland, the double actionability rule was applied in *An Bord Trachtala v. Waterford Foods* [1994] F.S.R. 316 where an action in respect of alleged passing-off in England was held to be admissible but failed on the facts.

where the infringing acts took place. The double actionability rule would previously have prevented successful actions in England under broader civil law doctrines of unfair competition with no counterpart at common law. The position under the 1995 Act is considered at paragraphs 6–19 *et seq.*

6–17 Passing-off also has a doctrine under which the export of goods from the United Kingdom to a market where they will deceive is regarded as actionable in its own right, irrespective of liability or not under local law.[33] This doctrine of "instruments of deception" is not an application of private international law principles, since liability is determined solely according to English (or Scottish) law and the tort is deemed to be complete once the goods leave the jurisdiction.[34]

6–18 The action for breach of confidence is wholly anomalous in that it is not characterised as a tort at all in English law, but as breach of an equitable obligation.[35] As such, the double actionability rule almost certainly never applied, but it is uncertain how the applicable law of a foreign or multinational breach of confidence is to be ascertained. There is no reason to suppose that the *Mocambique* rule applies to actions for breach of confidence. Although the High Court of Australia in the *Spycatcher*[36] litigation refused to entertain an action for breach of confidence on the ground that it was being asked to enforce a foreign public law, analogous to a penal or revenue law, the decision expressly turned on the special nature of the confidential relationship between the defendant Peter Wright and the Crown, and has no application to ordinary private actions in respect of trade secrets or personal confidences.

B. THE PRIVATE INTERNATIONAL LAW (MISCELLANEOUS PROVISIONS) ACT 1995

Introduction: the Act summarised

6–19 Actions for infringement of foreign intellectual property rights, with the exception of the action for breach of confidence,[37] are now governed by the provisions of the Private International Law (Miscellaneous Provisions) Act 1995.[38] The Act implements, with some modifications,

---

[33] See, *e.g.*, *Modus Vivendi v. British Products Sanmex* [1996] F.S.R. 790 (Knox J.) and Wadlow, *op. cit.*, para. 4.49.

[34] *William Grant v. Glen Katrine Bonded Warehouse* [1995] S.L.T. 936, expressly distinguishing the principle from that in *Phillips v. Eyre*.

[35] See paras 6–123 *et seq.*, below.

[36] *Attorney General v. Heinemann Publishers* [1989] 2 F.S.R. 631.

[37] As to which see para. 6–163, below.

[38] See Morse, "Torts in Private International Law: a New Statutory Framework" (1996) 45 I.C.L.Q. 888. Pt III of the Act was brought into force on May 1, 1996 by The Private International Law (Miscellaneous Provisions) Act 1995 Commencement Order 1996 (S.I. 1996 No. 995) which is subject to the transitional provisions of s. 14 of the Act.

the proposals of the English and Scottish Law Commissions for choice of law in tort.[39] It abolishes the former rule of "double actionability," otherwise known as the rule in *Phillips v. Eyre*,[40] in favour of the simple application in most cases of the law of the place where the tort occurred. However, the *lex loci delicti commissi* itself may be displaced in favour of the "proper law of the tort" (although that phrase is not used in the Act) if there are sufficiently important factors connecting the tort with another country. In the application of the Act to intellectual property, the normal and perhaps invariable rule will be that the *lex loci delicti commissi* applies unmodified.[41]

Because the 1995 Act is so new, almost all previous discussion of the   **6–20** application of English private international law to intellectual property infringement actions took place in the context of the requirement of double actionability under *Phillips v. Eyre*. However, it is impossible simply to ignore the old authorities and start with a clean slate. A case principally decided in terms of double actionability may contain valuable material on issues which remain relevant today, but which cannot properly be understood outside their original context. In particular, the rather mechanical application of the double actionability requirement so as to conclude that an infringement action on a foreign intellectual property right could never succeed, disguised the fact that but for *Phillips v. Eyre*, the courts would have had to consider the legitimacy of entertaining such actions from the point of view of justiciability, comity and *forum non conveniens*. Of the relatively few decisions in point, several do address these issues as well as the application of the rule in *Phillips v. Eyre*. It is therefore still necessary to discuss the old common law position in almost as much detail as if it still applied, as it does to defamation claims and—to a diminishing extent—in common law jurisdictions outside the United Kingdom.[42]

The legislative history of the 1995 Act

Although the Private International Law (Miscellaneous Provisions)   **6–21** Act 1995 was the outcome of a lengthy process of consultation and debate within the Law Commissions, next to no express consideration seems to have been given to intellectual property.[43] In the course of its examination in the House of Lords, Lord Wilberforce raised the question of how the Act would apply to intellectual property rights and

---

[39] The Law Commission and The Scottish Law Commission, *Private International Law Choice of Law in Tort and Delict* (1990) (Law Com. No. 193; Scot. Law. Com. No. 129).

[40] (1870) L.R. 6 Q.B. 1.

[41] See the informal briefing document by the draftsman of the Bill, Mr A. J. Hogarth, printed at *Proceedings of the Special Public Bill Committee* HL Paper 36 (1995), written evidence, p. 64.

[42] See paras 6–71 *et seq.*, below.

[43] Intellectual property was briefly mentioned at an early stage, but not in the final report: Law Commission (Working Paper No. 87) and The Scottish Law Commission (Consultative Memorandum No. 62) *Private International Law—Choice of Law in Tort and Delict* (1984).

this resulted in the production of a supplementary memorandum by Professor Beatson of the English Law Commission (with the assistance, *inter alia*, of Jacob J.) and an annex by Professor Cornish. Although these observations are not equivalent to a ministerial statement within the rule of *Pepper v. Hart*,[44] they are of interest in their own right as illustrating the expected effects of the Bill as understood by the Member of the Law Commission responsible for the final report. As summarised by Professor Beatson these are[45]:

"(i) UK legislation will continue to apply to all alleged infringements of UK intellectual property rights (hereafter 'IP' rights) within the UK . . .

 (ii) UK legislation will continue to have no application to alleged infringements outside the UK of IP rights conferred by UK legislation because of its territorial limitations: . . .

 (iii) In the case of alleged infringements of IP rights conferred by foreign laws outside the UK—

 (a) the Bill would make it possible for an English or Scottish Court with jurisdiction to apply . . . the law of the place where the alleged infringement occurred . . ., but

 (b) it is possible that the court would decline jurisdiction by applying the 'local rather than transitory' action principle, particularly where the issue primarily concerns the ownership of a foreign IP right . . . and

 (c) in cases not governed by the Brussels or Lugano Conventions, it is likely that *forum non conveniens*, which is not affected by the Bill, would be invoked. . . .

 (d) in cases governed by the Brussels Convention, jurisdiction in proceedings concerned with the validity or registration of IP rights is restricted to the courts of the state concerned. . . ."

6–22   The memorandum then explained these conclusions in more detail. Regarding actions in the United Kingdom for infringement of foreign intellectual property rights, the memorandum summarised the existing state of the law with regard to acts within and outside the United Kingdom and continued:

"If Part III of the PIL Bill is enacted, with regard to Lord Wilberforce's Q 168,[46] the result would not be that such an act

[44] [1993] A.C. 593, HL.

[45] Supplementary Memorandum from Professor Jack Beatson, "Intellectual Property and Part III of the Private International Law (Miscellaneous Provisions) Bill" in *Proceedings of the Special Public Bill Committee* HL Paper 36 (1995), minutes of evidence, p. 61. References to paragraphs of the Bill are omitted.

[46] Which reads: "United Kingdom law only relates to British copyright therefore it is not a breach of United Kingdom law if somebody commits a breach of United Kingdom copyright in France. Dicey deals with this really in some length. I am not quite sure what your position about it is or what the Bill's position is? Is the result of the Bill that in future a breach in France or Germany of United Kingdom copyright or United Kingdom patent would be suable on in England under the general applicable law clause or would it be let out by some other provision? . . ." HL Paper, p. 53.

would be a breach of the UK copyright or patent because, for the reasons given above, an act in another country (say in France or Germany) does not constitute a breach of the territorially limited UK statutes. The alleged infringement may well, however, constitute a breach of the comparable French or German IP right and the result of enacting Part III would mean that in principle it would be open to a UK court to apply the law of the place where the alleged infringement occurred (under clause 11(1)).

The result in practice in UK jurisdictions is likely to depend on whether the Brussels or Lugano conventions apply. Where they do not apply, it is likely, in the light of what was said in *Conan Doyle*, that the court would decline jurisdiction on the basis of the inappropriateness of proceedings here; i.e. *forum non conveniens* would be invoked. Nothing in the Bill affects the ability of the court to do this. Where the Brussels Convention does apply, if the issue is the validity of a registered right it is (Art 16(4)) the exclusive preserve of the courts of that country. In other cases the court may very exceptionally use its indigenous rules (e.g. on abuse of process) to exclude an admissible claim.

From a policy point of view the possibility of the application of a foreign law in respect of an alleged infringement of a foreign IP right in the foreign country should not give rise to concern. In the case of passing off it already happens albeit within the framework of the double actionability rule. The statutory regimes governing other IP rights derive from international conventions which means that many such rights are broadly harmonised throughout many countries. The conventions acknowledge the principle of territoriality since they apply the 'principle of national treatment' (Paris Convention of Industrial Property, Art 2(1); Berne Convention on Literary and Artistic Works, Art 5). This means that any right owner who is a national of a convention member state, or who first publishes in a member state, is entitled in every other member state to the same protection as the nationals of that state. Thus the countries which are party to a convention offer the citizens of other convention states the same treatment as nationals and this is in effect an implied *lex loci delicti* approach (i.e. clause 11 of the Bill conforms to this). See generally Stephen Stewart Q.C., *International Copyright and Neighbouring Rights* (1989) esp. para. 3.28. There are also signs that other countries, including neighbouring European jurisdictions, are becoming more willing to take jurisdiction to adjudicate upon foreign infringements suits (on Holland, see Brinkhof, [1994] 8 EIPR 360).

Professor W. R. Cornish considers that there are a number of **6–23** reasons for admitting such actions here (see pp 2–3 of the Annex to this note). In particular he points to the increasingly international trade in goods and services protected by IP and electronic dissemination of copyright material across borders as giving rise to the need for fora in which multinational infringement can be determined and enforced. The example of a defendant who does business (e.g. supplying pirated copies of books, films or records) in one or more foreign states without himself setting up any office or branch there is, in my respectful submission, particularly telling. Mr Justice Jacob concludes that 'it seems unavoidable that we should assume jurisdiction over foreign (or at least other European Union state) IP infringements given what is happening in Europe. If we do not the Continental Europeans will simply take over.'

Lord Wilberforce (Q 168, Q 173 and Q 174) raised the question of the effect of clause 9(2) on these questions. Clause 9(2) is subject to clause 13(4). In Q 174 his Lordship raised the scenario of French law saying 'Never mind what English law says, it is actionable in French courts to sue in respect of a foreign breach of a UK copyright'. First, the scenario of a French court wishing to treat an act in France as an infringement of UK copyright might be thought unlikely in view of the territorial character of IP rights and the fact that it is probable that the alleged infringement in France would constitute a breach of the comparable French IP right. On the assumption, however, that it did occur, this would not mean that, under the Bill, the English court would apply the French view of the ambit of the UK statute. To give effect to a statute in circumstances in which UK law states it does not apply would, it is submitted, 'prejudice the operation of [a] rule of law which . . . has effect notwithstanding the rules of private international law . . .'. The territorial principle means that it is the rule of UK law that the foreign act is not an infringement of UK law. In this context it would be desirable to consider whether an amendment to clause 13(4) along the lines suggested by Professor McLean is required to make it clear that the clause is only concerned with UK mandatory rules."

As a separate matter, media interests succeeded in restoring to the Bill the preservation of double actionability in defamation actions, which had been proposed by the Law Commissions but omitted from the Bill as originally introduced.[47]

The old rule of *Phillips v. Eyre* abolished

6–24   The former rule of double actionability stated in *Phillips v. Eyre*[48] and affirmed with some qualifications in *Boys v. Chaplin*,[49] and the common law exceptions to it recognised in the latter and in *Red Sea Insurance v. Bouygues*,[50] are abolished by the 1995 Act for actions in tort other than defamation actions:

[47] See para. 6–42.
[48] (1870) L.R. 6 Q.B. 1.
[49] [1971] A.C. 356, HL.
[50] [1995] A.C. 190, PC.

Section 10. Abolition of certain common law rules

The rules of the common law, in so far as they—

(a) require actionability under both the law of the forum and the law of another country for the purpose of determining whether a tort or delict is actionable; or

(b) allow (as an exception from the rules falling within paragraph (a) above) for the law of a single country to be applied for the purpose of determining the issues, or any of the issues, arising in the case in question,

are hereby abolished so far as they apply to any claim in tort or delict which is not excluded from the operation of this Part by section 13 below.

The new law under the Act

The new rules for the private international law of tort are contained in **6–25** Part III of the Act. The sections likely to be relevant to intellectual property infringement actions are the following. Section 9 defines the purpose of the Act in identifying the applicable law:

Section 9: Purpose of Part III

(1) The rules in this Part apply for choosing the law (in this Part referred to as "the applicable law") to be used for determining issues relating to tort or (for the purposes of the law of Scotland) delict.

(2) The characterisation for the purposes of private international law of issues arising in a claim as issues relating to tort or delict is a matter for the courts of the forum.

(3) The rules in this Part do not apply in relation to issues arising in any claim excluded from the operation of this Part by section 13 below.

(4) The applicable law shall be used for determining the issues arising in a claim, including in particular the question whether an actionable tort or delict has occurred.

(5) The applicable law to be used for determining the issues arising in a claim shall exclude any choice of law rules forming part of the law of the country or countries concerned.

(6) For the avoidance of doubt (and without prejudice to the operation of section 14 below) this Part applies in relation to events occurring in the forum as it applies in relation to events occurring in any other country.

(7) In this Part as it extends to any country within the United Kingdom, "the forum" means England and Wales, Scotland or Northern Ireland, as the case may be.

(8) In this Part "delict" includes quasi-delict.

The general rule is that the *lex loci delicti* is the applicable law. Section 11 of the 1995 Act provides:

Section 11. Choice of applicable law: the general rule

(1) The general rule is that the applicable law is the law of the country in which the events constituting the tort or delict in question occur.

(2) Where elements of those events occur in different countries, the applicable law under the general rule is to be taken as being—

    (a) (. . .)[51]

    (b) for a cause of action in respect of damage to property, the law of the country where the property was when it was damaged; and

    (c) in any other case, the law of the country in which the most significant element or elements of those events occurred.

Section 11 applied in *Waterford Wedgwood v. Nagli*

6–26   To date, only one reported case has applied section 11 in the context of intellectual property. In *Waterford Wedgwood v. David Nagli*[51a] the plaintiffs sued for trade mark infringement and passing-off in respect of dealings by the defendants in counterfeit Waterford crystal, and applied for summary judgment. The defendants had purchased crystal from an intermediary for sale to an American company and it was shipped from Ireland to Spain, where it was repackaged, and then shipped onwards from Bilbao to the United States, but via Felixstowe. The purchasers inspected the goods at Bilbao and on arrival at New York, and on each occasion were assured that the goods, their packaging and marks, were genuine.

So far as trade mark infringement was concerned, no questions of private international law arose and the plaintiffs were awarded summary judgment on one claim, relating to the counterfeit goods in transit which had passed through Felixstowe on their way to New York. Turning to the passing-off claims, the Vice-Chancellor described the facts as showing the clearest case of passing off imaginable. Though the defendant was conceded to have acted innocently, he had expressly represented to his own customers and to their intended customers that the counterfeit goods were genuine. The terms of certain invoices and letters describing the goods as "Waterford" were not conclusive, because at their dates the counterfeit goods had not been appropriated to the contract, but clear misrepresentations had been made in this respect when the goods were at Bilbao and later in New York. The question therefore arose as to the law to apply to these misrepresentations:

> "This raises the question whether the passing off is a tort to which English law is applicable. If it is not, if the applicable law is the law

---

[51] Provisions relating to personal injury are omitted. Those relating to damage to property are retained *ex abundanti cautela*, although it is to be doubted if they apply to intellectual property.

[51a] [1998] F.S.R. 92 (Scott V.-C.).

of Spain or the law of New York, evidence of the requisite foreign law would be necessary in order to establish that the acts relied on as constituting the tort were indeed tortious under the foreign law in question. Since there is no evidence of foreign law before the Court, the case would not be one for summary judgment. This proper law difficulty seems to me to be the only point standing in the way of summary judgment for the plaintiffs on their passing-off claim.

The identification of the country whose law is applicable to the alleged tortious acts of which a plaintiff complains is often a matter of difficulty. The rules to be applied are now to be found in sections 11 and 12 of the Private International Law (Miscellaneous Provisions) Act 1995."

The Vice-Chancellor went on to hold that the events constituting the tort had occurred in Spain and New York, but not in England. Although there were some connections with England and with English law, it would not have been right to give summary judgment on the basis that English law applied. Nor was it possible to give summary judgment under Spanish and/or New York law, when the relevant foreign law had not been pleaded or put in evidence. In the result, the application for summary judgment on the passing-off claim failed. **6–27**

"It seems to me that 'the events constituting the tort or delict' (see section 11 of the 1995 Act) occurred in Spain and in New York but not in England. Under the section 11 general rule, therefore, the applicable law would not be the law of England. It might, however, be argued that because the crystal was passed off in Spain for the purpose of satisfying the purchaser under an English contract, and was appropriated to the English contract before being exported to and passed off in New York, it would be 'substantially more appropriate for the applicable law . . .' to be the law of England (see section 12 *ibid.*). However, neither counsel has addressed me on the effect of sections 11 and 12 of the 1995 Act on the facts of this case. A conclusion that the law of this country is the proper law applicable to the passing off that took place in Spain and in New York cannot possibly be reached on this summary judgment application. For these reasons I have come to the conclusion that the plaintiffs' application for summary judgment for passing off must fail. This is, in many ways, an unfortunate conclusion. It seems to me almost certain that the events in Bilbao whereby the counterfeit crystal was represented to be genuine crystal would be as delictual in Spain as they would have been tortious in England. The same applies to the passing-off that took place in New York. But the plaintiffs have not pleaded any reliance on foreign law and have not placed before me any evidence of the relevant rules of Spanish or New York law. It would not be right for me to give summary judgment against the defendants on a point of foreign law neither pleaded nor supported by evidence."

The rationale for applying the *lex loci delicti*

6–28   The Working Paper by the Law Commission and the Scottish Law Commission had proposed two alternatives to replace double actionability: either the *lex loci delicti commissi* with exceptions, or the "proper law of the tort" as identified by the preponderance of connecting factors in the same sense as in contract law.[52] The 1990 Report of the two Law Commissions[53] favoured the *lex loci* with certain presumptions and exceptions, and this policy preference was carried over into the Bill and subsequently into the Act. Although relatively little consideration was given to intellectual property prior to the Bill being introduced, the practical effect of the Act is to give effect to the principle of territoriality since the only law relevant to the substantive issues will henceforth be the *lex loci*, which will necessarily correspond to the law of the protecting state.

6–29   The memorandum by Professor Cornish produced in response to a question by Lord Wilberforce summarised the intent of the Bill and the reason for the application of the *lex loci delicti* in intellectual property cases, there being no legitimate scope for the application of any other system of law:

> "The Bill abolishes the rule of double actionability and the 'single country' exception to it. It substitutes a general rule that the applicable law is the *lex loci delicti* (Cl 11(1)).[54] This is the territoriality principle and it is essential that it should continue to apply to IP infringements. There should be no scope for displacement under Cl 12. As to 'cross-border' activities, dealt with in Cl 11(2), IP legislation and rules relating to joint tortfeasorship, authorising commission etc, define fairly precisely the acts which constitute infringement and require them to occur within the territory. This settles whether contributory acts towards the eventual infringement (making the patented invention, reproducing the copyright book etc), fall within the territorial scope of a local IP law."

The 1995 Act the *Mocambique* Rule

6–30   As a separate matter to the application of the *lex loci delicti*, the memorandum by Professor Cornish went on to consider whether infringements of foreign intellectual property rights ought to be justiciable in the United Kingdom:

> "The question remains whether, despite the general change to an application of the *lex loci delicti* (in line with what has long been the

---

[52] Law Commission (Working Paper No. 87) and The Scottish Law Commission (Consultative Memorandum No. 62) *Private International Law—Choice of Law in Tort and Delict* (1984).

[53] The Law Commission and The Scottish Law Commission, *Private International Law Choice of Law in Tort and Delict* (1990) (Law Com. No. 193; Scot. Law Com. No. 129).

[54] The numbering of sections in the Act corresponds.

necessary rule for IP), there should still be an exclusion of actions in the UK courts for acts committed in another country and alleged to be infringements of that country's IP laws."

The memorandum went on to list five reasons why actions for infringement of foreign intellectual property rights ought to be entertained in the future, which might be summarised as the increasing trade in goods and services protected by intellectual property; standardisation of intellectual property protection though international conventions such as TRIPs; piratical defendants infringing in states where they had no local assets; the implications of the Brussels Convention and the example set by the Dutch courts in particular. The memorandum favoured dealing with foreign invalidity by a discretionary stay of United Kingdom infringement proceedings. Professor Cornish therefore proposed an amendment which would have had the effect of abolishing the application of the *Mocambique*[55] rule to intellectual property infringement actions:

> "[T]o take account of the desirability of applying Cl. 11 to intellectual property infringement actions, it is desirable to ensure that the rule excluding 'local' actions is abolished, as well as that requiring double actionability. If this is not done, the 'local action' exception might be held to remain in force by virtue of Cl 13(4) (the scope of 'in the particular circumstances' is not clear)."

However, no such amendment was made, and the Act as passed includes section 14 (2) which provides "Nothing in this Part affects any rules of law (including rules of private international law) except those abolished by section 10 above" as well as subsection (4) providing "This Part has effect without prejudice to the operation of any rule of law which either has effect notwithstanding the rules of private international law applicable in the particular circumstances or modifies the rules of private international law that would otherwise be so applicable." In the result, there seems little doubt that as much as the *Mocambique* rule as had not already been abolished by Civil Jurisdiction and Judgments Act 1982, s. 30, or the United Kingdom's accession to the Brussels Convention continues to apply. In *Pearce v. Ove Arup*[56] (to which the 1995 Act did not apply) Lloyd J. held that the rule would have applied to an action for foreign copyright infringement, but for the effects of the Brussels Convention.[57] In the patent case of *Coin Controls v. Suzo*[58] (to which the 1995 Act did apply) Laddie J. clearly agreed, although in that case the *Mocambique* rule was supplanted by Article 16(4) of the Brussels Convention.[59]

6-31

6-32

---

[55] The rule in *Compania do Mocambique v. British South Africa Co* [1893] A.C. 602, HL.
[56] [1997] F.S.R. 641 (Lloyd J.).
[57] See para. 6–104, below.
[58] [1997] F.S.R. 660 (Laddie J.).
[59] See para. 6–63, below.

Application of the "proper law of the tort:" section 12

6–33   The normal rule that the applicable law is the law of the place where the tort was committed may be displaced in certain circumstances in favour of another system of law with which the tort has a closer connection. This is the effect of section 12 of the 1995 Act, which provides:

> **Section 12. Choice of applicable law: displacement of the general rule**
>
> (1) If it appears, in all the circumstances, from a comparison of—
>> (a) the significance of the factors which connect a tort or delict with the country whose law would be the applicable law under the general rule; and
>> (b) the significance of any factors connecting the tort or delict with another country,
>> that it is substantially more appropriate for the applicable law for determining the issues arising in the case, or any of those issues, to be the law of the other country, the general rule is displaced and the applicable law for determining those issues or that issue (as the case may be) is the law of that other country.
>
> (2) The factors that may be taken into account as connecting a tort or delict with a country for the purposes of this section include, in particular, factors relating to the parties, to any of the events which constitute the tort or delict in question or to any of the circumstances or consequences of those events.

6–34   To summarise, the section requires a comparison to be performed between the significance of the factors connecting the tort with the country where the tort occurred and those connecting the tort with another country. The relevant connection is in terms with a country, rather than a system of law as such. The factors allowed to be taken into account include ones relating to the parties, to any of the events constituting the tort or to any of the circumstances or consequences of those events. The statutory list is probably not intended to be exhaustive. The *lex loci* is displaced if these connecting factors make it "substantially more appropriate" to apply the other system of law. Although a balancing exercise is obviously required, the Act does not appear to contemplate any overt exercise of discretion: once the comparison has been performed the terms of the Act appear to be mandatory. The section contemplates that different issues relating to a single tort may be governed by different systems of law, either as a result of some issues having their most substantial connection with the *lex loci*, or as a result of different issues each having their own proper law.[60]

6–35   The Law Commission Report gives some examples of when it contemplates that the proper law of the tort should displace the *lex loci*

---

[60] This is contrary to the proposals of the Law Commission, who recommended against providing for *depecage*.

delicti: when the latter was fortuitous, as for an air disaster; when the parties had a common pre-existing connection or relationship, as with a group of holidaymakers abroad; and generally where every factor other than the place of the tort pointed to a particular system of law, as in *Boys v. Chaplin* itself. These are mostly uncontentious, but they illustrate that the application of the "proper law of the tort" to displace the *lex loci delicti* was not envisaged in circumstances comparable to the typical intellectual property infringement action. The Law Commission Report considered, and rejected, creating a separate rule for the economic torts, partly because of difficulties in distinguishing economic torts from others.

The "proper law" in unfair competition cases

The one area of intellectual property for which section 12 deserves **6–36** detailed consideration is unfair competition, including actions for passing-off. Historically, there has been some tendency (and not only in the United Kingdom) for courts to apply national law to competition between their own nationals, even if the competition takes place abroad.[61] Sometimes this is done expressly as a matter of policy, sometimes without even realising what is being done. The doctrine of liability for exports of "instruments of deception" in the English law of passing-off has this effect in practice, although it has never been understood in terms of private international law. The registration of trade marks for the export trade is another example.

One suggestion which may need to be firmly repudiated is that "unfairness" in competition is a universal concept which can be applied as well by one court as by another. In some cases, there has been an unwillingness to accept that what is unfair and even illegal in one market may be perfectly acceptable, legally and ethically, in another. Comparative advertising, for example, is regarded in some legal systems as inherently unfair, in others as an essential part of the competitive process. Even Article 10 *bis* of the Paris Convention, which provides in broad terms that member states are obliged to provide effective protection against acts of unfair competition, predominantly leaves it to individual states to decide what acts constitute unfair competition, and what remedies are available.

It is therefore suggested that the starting point for ascertaining the **6–37** "proper law" applicable to acts of alleged unfair competition is that the fairness of competition cannot simply be judged as between plaintiff and defendant. Acts of competition, whether fair or unfair, affect consumers as well as other competitors in the market. It is for each state to draw the line between competitive conduct which is permitted or encouraged in its own territory and that which is actionable. This will result in the "proper law" almost invariably corresponding to the *lex loci delicti*. Even the briefest comparative examination of national unfair competition laws

---

[61] For example, *An Bord Trachtala v. Waterford Foods* [1994] F.S.R. 316 (Ireland).

shows that they differ very markedly, both in content and underlying policy, between almost completely *laissez-faire* and highly interventionist.

Ulmer[62] comments:

> "The principles of the [Paris] Convention as regards conflict of laws are thus basically in harmony with the rules of private international law on the application of the *lex loci delicti commissi*. Here we find, however, the tendency of the courts to apply domestic law in as comprehensive a manner as possible for the protection of national traders. Thus for example in German and Italian case-law an infringement committed within the country has repeatedly been assumed both in cases in which the act of competition was directed abroad from within the country and in cases in which the effects of the damage occurred within the country. In the case-law there is also to be found the concept that national traders in their mutual competition are also bound abroad by national law; this concept has been put forward in the legal literature, especially by Nussbaum.
>
> Such tendency towards an extensive application of national law is not altogether unproblematic. It fails to take account of the fact *inter alia* that national traders must be allowed the opportunity to adapt their competitive behaviour abroad to the rules applicable there. In more recent writings therefore the question is raised where is the main area of violation of traders' interest? Attempts are being made to establish the 'proper law of the tort' for competition law. In my view it will not be possible to answer the question uniformly for all acts of unfair competition. At all events however, it seems adequate, even from the point of view of consumer protection, that in the case of acts of competition which serve the purpose of advertising, the law of the country is applied in which influence is brought to bear upon consumers, especially persuasion by means of the mass media such as the press, radio, television etc. In the case of such acts of competition as bribery of employees and enticement to betray secrets the central point must be sought within the country in which the disturbance of the business activities of the competitor takes place."

6–38   There are perhaps three circumstances in which the application of a proper law other than the *lex loci delicti* might deserve further consideration. The first corresponds to that mentioned in the concluding passage above, where the act of unfair competition might be regarded in English law as procurement of a breach of contract or as creating liability in equity for breach of confidence or a fiduciary obligation. Only the former would be characterised as tortious. Another is where two parties with a common personal law compete in a relatively undeveloped market which has no effective law of unfair competition. It is of interest that several of

---

[62] Ulmer, *Intellectual Property Rights and the Conflict of Laws* (1978), p. 19, citations omitted.

the early English cases on the export of "instruments of deception" fell into this category, and that if English law had not been applied then the parties would have competed according to the law of the jungle. This situation will become increasingly uncommon as economies develop and international conventions such as TRIPs take effect. The third is where there is international or even global competition between two or more businesses with a common personal law. Applying a single proper law to their competitive relationship in its entirety has the superficial attraction of simplicity and relative legal certainty, but it is suggested that the consequent infringement of the right of every state to regulate competition in its own market is unacceptable.

A complicating factor is that in so far as a claim under a foreign law of **6–39** unfair competition may be based on disparagement of the plaintiff, or perhaps in certain cases of inaccurate comparative advertising, it might be said to correspond to injurious falsehood in English law so that section 13(2)(b) of the 1995 Act would exclude the operation of section 12 altogether, leaving the old common law rules to apply. Perhaps, if the case was one of those suitable for the application of a single system of law as the proper law of the tort, then the common law could reach the same result as under section 12 by applying one of the recognised exceptions to the double actionability rule.

Section 12 in other cases

It remains to ask whether there are any other circumstances in which **6–40** it would be right to invoke section 12 so as to displace the law of the country in which the tort occurred in favour of a system of law with which the tort had a closer connection: in other words to identify and apply "the proper law of the tort" for infringements of the nominate intellectual property rights in general. In some respects this would be tempting. Actions for infringement of intellectual property rights frequently have international ramifications which would be simplified enormously by the application of a single system of law, by a single court, to the dispute in its totality. However, it is suggested that the attractions of this approach are illusory and that there are very few occasions, if any, in which section 12 would apply in this field. The violation of comity and the principle of territoriality which would be involved in an English court saying, for instance, that infringement of a Dutch patent or trade mark, in the Netherlands, should be governed by any system of law other than the law of the Netherlands, is not to be contemplated.

Apart from unfair competition, considered in the preceding para- **6–41** graph, it is suggested that there are very few circumstances in which there is any reason for applying a proper law other than the *lex loci delicti* in actions for infringement of intellectual property. One possible application of section 12 might be to claims in tort entirely ancillary to non-tortious claims under a different system of law, for instance in contract. At first sight, another might be to actions for breach of confidence in several jurisdictions where there was an antecedent confidential relationship governed by a single system of law. However, breach of confidence is not characterised in English law as a tort, so section 9(2) would probably operate to exclude the claim from the 1995 Act altogether, even if the action were characterised as tortious under the putative proper law.

Defamation and injurious falsehood: section 13

6–42   By sections 9(3), 10 and 13(1) the common law, which will generally mean the old rule of double actionability, continues to apply to defamation claims. By section 13(2)(a) a defamation claim is deemed to include, *inter alia*, a claim for malicious falsehood and by section 13(2)(b) it also includes a claim under the law of any country "corresponding to or otherwise in the nature of" one of the types of claim enumerated in section 13(2)(a). The application of section 13 to intellectual property infringement actions is clearly peripheral at most and is likely to be confined in practice to the occasional claim for injurious falsehood. However, actions for unfair competition under systems of law which recognise this as a nominate tort may involve claims for commercial disparagement or inaccurate comparative advertising which could be said to correspond to injurious falsehood in English law. To that extent, section 13 rather than sections 11 or 12 might apply to those issues in the claim.

6–43   It has been suggested that actions for infringement of rights of privacy, recognised in many jurisdictions, might be analogous to defamation claims and therefore within the section. This is too simplistic an approach. For example, Prosser's classic formulation of American law is that actionable invasions of non-constitutional privacy fall under four heads: intrusion into the plaintiff's personal seclusion or private affairs, public disclosure of embarrassing private facts, publicity placing the plaintiff in a false light, and appropriation for commercial advantage of the plaintiff's name or likeness.[63] Of these, only "false light" is perhaps analogous to defamation, and since any liability under American law would be subject to the Constitutional protection for freedom of the press under the First Amendment, it is not obvious why double actionability should also be necessary to protect the legitimate interests of media defendants. *A fortiori* actions by celebrities or personalities for infringement of the right of publicity recognised in both civil and common law jurisdictions abroad ought not to fall within section 13.

6–44   This conclusion in respect of privacy is supported by the Parliamentary history of the Bill. The Law Commissions' joint report cited invasion of rights of privacy as an example of a foreign tort not recognised in this country but despite this the tort (unlike defamation proper) received no special treatment in the Act. Lord Lester attempted to introduce an amendment which would have retained the double actionability rule for claims "based upon a law for the protection of reputation, self-esteem, privacy or confidentiality"[64] but it was withdrawn after opposition from

---

[63] Prosser "Privacy" (1960) 48 California Law Rev. 383.

[64] *Hansard* HL Vol. 562 Col. 1410 (March 27, 1995). The intention of the proposed amendment was expressly to cover "foreign laws of privacy of a kind unrecognised by common law or statute law in this country."

the Lord Chancellor and other peers. Even this attempted amendment would not by any means have covered every kind of actionable invasion of privacy under foreign law, and as the law stands a claim for invasion of privacy would have to be one "corresponding to" a claim for defamation for section 13 to apply. Of course, there might also be cases where the public policy exception of section 14(3)(a) would exclude the application of foreign privacy law, but as Lord Hailsham pointed out,[65] a right to privacy subject to public interest exceptions is recognised by the European Convention on Human Rights.[66]

The comparison contemplated by the Act is apparently to be per- **6–45** formed in the abstract, so that the question is whether the foreign claim is inherently in the nature of a claim in defamation or injurious falsehood, rather than whether the facts of the foreign claim would support an English defamation or injurious falsehood action.[67] So, for instance, if an author were to complain of a travesty of one of his works being published under his name, then a claim by him for false attribution of authorship or infringement of his moral rights under the relevant foreign law would be governed by the general rule of section 11, even if the attributed publication was sufficiently scurrilous for there to be the possibility of concurrent liability in defamation.

Public policy and other exceptions: section 14

Section 14 contains a numbers of savings and exceptions: **6–46**

(1) Nothing in this Part applies to acts or omissions giving rise to a claim which occur before the commencement of this Part.

(2) Nothing in this Part affects any rules of law (including rules of private international law) except those abolished by section 10 above.

(3) Without prejudice to the generality of subsection (2) above, nothing in this Part—

(a) authorises the application of the law of a country outside the forum as the applicable law for determining issues arising in any claim in so far as to do so—

  (i) would conflict with principles of public policy; or

  (ii) would give effect to such a penal, revenue or other public law as would not otherwise be enforceable under the law of the forum; or

(b) affects any rules of evidence, pleading or practice or authorises questions of procedure in any proceedings to be

---

[65] *ibid.*, Col. 1415.

[66] Art. 8(1): "Everyone has the right to respect for his private and family life, his home and his correspondence." Art. 10 protects the right to freedom of expression "subject to such formalities, conditions, restrictions or penalties as are prescribed by law and are necessary in a democratic society, . . . for the protection of the reputation or rights of others. . ."

[67] A comparison which applied the exception only in factual situations where the plaintiff would have had a cause of action for defamation or the like in England would obviously deprive the section of any practical effect.

> determined otherwise than in accordance with the law of the forum.
>
> (4) This Part has effect without prejudice to the operation of any rule of law which either has effect notwithstanding the rules of private international law applicable in the particular circumstances or modifies the rules of private international law that would otherwise be so applicable.

6–47   Of these, section 14(1) provides that the Act has no retrospective effect on accrued causes of action[68] and subsection (2) preserves the *Mocambique* rule in so far as not otherwise abolished.[69] Subsection (3) disapplies the *lex loci* or other applicable law where its application would be contrary to public policy and expressly preserves the rule against foreign penal, revenue or "other public" laws. Except to the limited and controversial extent to which the "other public" category embraces the action for breach of confidence in state secrets,[70] it is doubtful if this or subsection (4) is likely to have any application to intellectual property.[71] Subsection (3) also expressly provides that procedural questions remain exclusively in the preserve of the *lex fori*.

C. JUSTICIABILITY OF ACTIONS ON FOREIGN INTELLECTUAL PROPERTY RIGHTS: *TYBURN v. DOYLE* AND THE *MOCAMBIQUE* RULE

Introduction: the concept of justiciability

6–48   There is a long-standing doctrine in English law that the courts will not entertain actions which would involve investigating the acts of foreign sovereign states.[72] The principle is quite separate from that of sovereign immunity and it applies equally to cases between private litigants. One manifestation of the principle which has the status of a nominate rule in its own right is that actions for trespass to foreign land are not justiciable in the courts of the United Kingdom.[73] The principle, which is known as the *Mocambique* rule, has been applied to actions for infringement of intellectual property rights and no distinction is made

---

[68] Although in the copyright case of *Pearce v. Ove Arup* [1997] F.S.R. 641 Lloyd J. applied the *lex loci deliciti* to a pre-Act cause of action so as to comply with the Brussels Convention. See para. 6–104. One effect of sub. (4) is that to the extent that the Convention modifies any rule of private international law, its effect is not reversed by the Act.

[69] Alternatively, it might be said that the rule is preserved by sub. (4).

[70] See para. 6–163.

[71] The question of invasion of privacy is considered above at para. 6–42 where it is suggested that such foreign laws and their application need not be contrary to English public policy.

[72] *Buttes Oil and Gas v. Hammer* [1982] A.C. 888, HL. See para. 6–114, below.

[73] *Companhia do Mocambique v. British South Africa Co* [1893] A.C. 602, HL.

between registered and unregistered rights, although the rule does not apply to the action for passing-off. The rule was partly abolished in relation to foreign land by the Civil Jurisdiction and Judgments Act 1982, s. 30, but the partial repeal has been held not to affect its continuing application to intellectual property.[74] The *Mocambique* rule is to be distinguished from that of double actionability, and unlike the latter has survived the enactment of the Private International Law (Miscellaneous Provisions) Act 1995.[75] On the other hand, it has been held that the rule has no application in cases to which the Brussels Convention applies.[76]

The present section offers a relatively uncritical account of what might **6–49** be called the orthodox approach to justiciability, exemplified by the judgment of Vinelott J. in *Tyburn v. Conan Doyle*.[77] The following section examines the application of the double actionability rule prior to the Private International Law (Miscellaneous Provisions) Act 1995. In the last of this group of three sections the development of the law is re-examined from its origin in the *Mocambique* case and the Australian case of *Potter v. Broken Hill*[78] and a different analysis to *Tyburn v. Conan Doyle* is advanced. Although that section is critical of several aspects of the judgment in *Tyburn v. Conan Doyle*, there remains much to be said in favour of the latter. First, even if the *Mocambique* rule may have been misunderstood in *Tyburn v. Conan Doyle*, it was still vastly preferable to decide the issue of justiciability as such, rather than approaching it indirectly by relying on the implications of the double-actionability rule as in *Def Lep v. Stuart Brown*.[79] Whether jurisdiction over actions for infringement of foreign intellectual property rights is to be accepted or declined, the issue is squarely one of justiciability rather than choice of law and should be addressed as such. Secondly, the actual decision in *Tyburn v. Conan Doyle* is almost certainly correct, at the very least as an exercise of discretion. Finally, the preferred analysis of justiciability has very much the same effect in practice as that in *Tyburn v. Conan Doyle*, though distinguishing between registered and unregistered rights and preserving a greater degree of flexibility for the future.

Tyburn v. Conan Doyle: the facts and judgment

In *Tyburn v. Conan Doyle*[80] the plaintiffs were a film production **6–50** company who had produced a film, *The Abbot's Cry*, incorporating the characters Sherlock Holmes and Doctor Watson, but which was otherwise completely original. Copyright in all Sir Arthur Conan Doyle's works had expired in the United Kingdom, but for the United States the

---

[74] See para. 6–68, below.
[75] See para. 6–63, below.
[76] See para. 6–63, below.
[77] [1990] R.P.C. 185 (Vinelott J.).
[78] (1906) 3 C.L.R. 479 (High Court of Australia) *affirming* [1905] V.L.R. 612.
[79] [1986] R.P.C. 273 (Browne-Wilkinson V.-C.).
[80] [1990] R.P.C. 185 (Vinelott J.).

defendant Lady Bromet, the only surviving child of Sir Arthur Conan Doyle, was registered as copyright owner for the last 14 of his 60 works. From past experience, the plaintiffs expected that the defendant would assert that the film infringed her rights under American law and that any such threats would be sufficient to prevent distribution there. Since there was no way to compel the defendant to bring an action in the USA, or to obtain a declaratory judgment there, they sued in England for a declaration that the proposed distribution in the United States of America would not infringe any American copyright of the defendant or be in breach of American unfair competition or trade mark laws. They also sought an injunction restraining the defendant from asserting to any third party that she was entitled to prevent the distribution of the film in the United States. The defendant was English and was subject to the personal jurisdiction of the High Court.

6–51   Vinelott J. held on the authority of *Companhia do Mocambique v. British South Africa Co*[81] that he had no jurisdiction to grant the declaration or injunction sought. The *Mocambique* rule, in its normal formulation, may be summarised as it was by Lord Wilberforce in *Hesperides Hotels v. Aegean Turkish Holidays*[82] in a passage cited by Vinelott J.:

> "The rule in the *Moçambique* case can be conveniently stated in the form in which it is generally accepted, viz., in Dicey & Morris, *The Conflict of Laws*, rule 79. I quote from the 9th edition (1973), but it appears as rule 53 in the same form (except for one letter) in the 3rd edition (1922) edited by Professor Dicey himself and Dr. Berriedale Keith. 'Subject to the exceptions hereinafter mentioned, the court has no jurisdiction to entertain an action for (1) the determination of the title to, or the right to the possession of, any immovable situate out of England (foreign land); or (2) the recovery of damages for trespass to such immovable.' The exceptions later mentioned relate to actions in equity (*Penn v. Lord Baltimore* (1750) 1 Ves. Sen. 444) and other special cases on which reliance cannot be placed in this appeal."

6–52   However in *Tyburn*, Vinelott J. held that the rule was not confined to foreign land, or to immovable property properly so called. Quoting from the speeches in *Mocambique*, he concluded that it was the distinction between "local" and "transitory" actions which was the very *ratio* of *Mocambique*, rather than a mere historical prelude:

> "Lord Herschell L.C. gave the leading speech. Lord Morris expressed his agreement with it. Much of that speech is concerned with the history of the distinction between transitory and local actions and the consequence of that distinction in domestic law.

[81] [1893] A.C. 602, HL.
[82] [1979] A.C. 508, HL.

However, at p. 621, he cited with approval a passage in the judgement of Buller J. in *Doulson v. Matthews* (1792) 4 Durn. & E. 503, 504:

> "It is now too late for us to inquire whether it were wise or politic to make a distinction between transitory and local actions: it is sufficient for the courts that the law has settled the distinction, and that an action *quare clausum fregit* is local. We may try actions here which are in their nature transitory, though arising out of a transaction abroad, but not such as are in their nature local."

Lord Herschell L.C. added:

> "In saying that we may not try actions here arising out of transactions abroad which are in their nature local, I do not think that the learned judge was referring to the mere technical difficulty of there being no venue in this country in which these transactions could be laid, but to the fact that our courts did not exercise jurisdiction in matters arising abroad 'which were in their nature local.' The case of *Doulson v. Matthews* has ever since been regarded as law, and I do not think it has been considered as founded merely on the technical difficulty that in this country a local venue was requisite in a local action."

He concluded, at p. 629 "that the grounds upon which the courts have hitherto refused to exercise jurisdiction in actions of trespass to lands situate abroad were substantial and not technical . . ." and that the distinction had not, accordingly been affected by the Judicature Acts.

Lord Halsbury, having cited a passage in Story's *Conflict of Laws*, 8th ed. (1883), pp. 770–771, section 553 in which Vattel's *Law of Nations* (1797) is cited added, at p. 631:   **6–53**

> "That very learned lawyer proceeds to point out that the distinction between local and transitory actions is one which is known to the common law."

And then, after a review of earlier authorities, he concluded, at p. 632:

> "Where therefore the actual place of, for instance, a debt or contract was alleged (though contrary to the fact) to be some place in England, the defendant was not at liberty to deny that the place alleged was in England, since in such matters the place was immaterial. But wherever the place was material, as the unvarying current of authorities establishes that it was in all controversies relating to land, the defendant might traverse the place, and, even if he did not, if it appeared in proof that the place was out of England, the plaintiff was nonsuited."

Lord Macnaghten concurred in the motion reversing the decision of the Court of Appeal.

Mr. Rayner James' submission was that the analysis of the distinction between transitory and local actions, although relied on to justify the conclusion that an action bringing into issue the title to or for damages for trespass to foreign land would not be entertained in the English courts, should not be given any wider scope. He submitted that the decision of the House of Lords in the *Moçambique* case has always been treated as restricted to actions bringing into issue title to, or for damages for trespass to, land."

6–54   Rejecting the latter submission, this reading of *Mocambique* led to two further questions: given that the rule applied to all "local" actions, then how did it affect an action for copyright infringement; and was intellectual property "immovable property" in the sense of section 30 of the Civil Jurisdiction and Judgments Act 1982 which created a statutory exception to the *Mocambique* rule?

Intellectual property as quasi-immovable property: "local" and "transitory" actions

6–55   The interpretation of the *Mocambique* rule given by Vinelott J. relied in two respects on a decision of the High Court of Australia in the case of *Potter v. Broken Hill*.[83] In the first place, *Potter v. Broken Hill* was said to support the conclusion that the relevant distinction was between local and transitory actions; and as *Potter v. Broken Hill* was itself a case about infringement of "foreign" patent he took it as providing the answer to whether patent infringement (and hence copyright infringement) would have been a local action prior to the Judicature Act. After mentioning section 30 of the Civil Jurisdiction and Judgments Act 1982 he continued:

> "However, in *Potter v. Broken Hill Proprietary Co. Ltd.* (1906) 3 C.L.R. 479, the High Court of Australia—Griffiths C.J., Barton and O'Connor JJ.—held that the rule applies when the validity of or infringement of a patent is in issue; they held that the validity of a patent granted in exercise of the sovereign power conferred on the state of New South Wales was not justiciable in the courts of the state of Victoria.
> Griffiths C.J. having referred to Lord Herschell's description of the right conferred by a patent as "the right to exclude others from manufacturing in a particular way, and using a particular invention." (see *Steers v. Rogers* [1893] A.C. 232, 235) and to a similar description of a patent in the United States case of *Bloomer v. McQuewan* (1852) 14 How. 539 said, at p. 494:
> > "There is no doubt also, that this franchise or monopoly has no effective operation beyond the territory of the state under whose laws it is granted and exercised. In this respect it partakes of the nature of an immovable as distinguished from a movable. It is true that the distinction between movables and immovables by writers on international law has never, so far as

---

[83] (1906) 3 C.L.R. 479 (High Court of Australia) *affirming* [1905] V.L.R. 612.

I know, been expressly applied to the case of patent rights. Yet there can be no doubt that, as the right is the creation of the state, the title to it must devolve, as in the case of land, according to the laws imposed by the state. In two important particulars, therefore, it is analogous to an immovable. It differs from an immovable in that it is neither itself visible nor appurtenant to any particular thing that is visible and fixed within the state. It may perhaps be regarded as, in a sense, pertinent to the whole territory."

(. . .)

Barton and O'Connor JJ. similarly treated the question as concluded by the *Moçambique* decision. O'Connor J. said, at p. 510:
"The principles of international law, which systematises the comity of nations, generally recognises that the courts of a country will not inquire into the validity of the acts of a foreign state, except subject to certain well known limitations. The principles upon which the limitations rest are concisely stated as follows in [*Moçambique* [1982] 2 Q.B. 358, 395] by Lord Esher M.R. in his judgment at the Queen's Bench Division—a judgment which was afterwards upheld in the Court of Appeal. 'With regard, then, to acts done within the territory of a nation, all are agreed that such nation has without more jurisdiction to determine the resulting rights growing out of those acts; but, with regard to acts done outside its territory it has no jurisdiction to determine the resulting rights growing out of those acts, unless such jurisdiction has been allowed to it by the comity of nations.' For instance, the courts of most nations will refuse to adjudicate upon claims of title to foreign land in proceedings founded upon an alleged invasion of the proprietary rights attached to it."

It is accepted by Mr. Rayner James that no distinction can be drawn for this purpose between patent rights, copyright and rights of trade marks and other intellectual property rights."

And Vinelott J. went on to cite with approval a second Australian decision, *Norbert Steinhart v. Meth*,[84] which had applied *Potter v. Broken Hill* and *Mocambique* to a statutory "threats action" under the Australian Patents Act.   **6–56**

Tyburn v. Conan Doyle[85] does not decide that intellectual property rights are "immovable property" in the strict sense of the *Mocambique* rule, and although Vinelott J. dealt with the issue only briefly, he implicitly rejected the argument that section 30 of the Civil Jurisdiction and Judgments Act 1982 applied to anything other than land.

[84] (1960) 105 C.L.R. 440 (Fullagar J., High Court of Australia).
[85] [1990] R.P.C. 185 (Vinelott J.).

Cases subsequent to *Tyburn v. Conan Doyle*

6–57   Several cases subsequent to *Tyburn v. Conan Doyle*[86] have considered Vinelott J.'s decision in the context of intellectual property infringement actions or commented on it in *obiter dicta*. In *LA Gear v. Whelan*[87] Mummery J. referred with approval to *Tyburn* in deciding that English proceedings for trade mark infringement were not for the same cause of action as a pending action for passing-off in Ireland, so as to require the former to be stayed in accordance with Article 21 of the Brussels Convention. In *Plastus v. 3M*[88] Aldous J. obviously approved of the result and the reasoning but found it unnecessary to decide whether *Tyburn* was so plainly right that the contrary could not be argued, because claims for declarations of non-infringement in respect of French and German patents were inadmissible and would be struck out on other grounds. In a more recent New Zealand case, *Atkinson Footwear v. Hodgskin*,[89] an injunction was granted against importation of boots from China into New Zealand, but the court refused to enjoin alleged infringement of the plaintiffs' corresponding Australian copyrights.

6–58   On the other hand, a willingness to give a more restrictive interpretation to the rule in the *British South Africa* case was shown by the Court of Appeal in *Apple Corps v. Apple Computer*,[90] although the observations of Neill and Nicholls L.JJ. on the question are *obiter*. The facts were that the plaintiffs sued to enforce a trade mark delimitation agreement which incorporated a clause preventing the defendants from challenging the plaintiffs' worldwide trade mark registrations. In breach of the agreement, the defendants commenced opposition or cancellation proceedings in a number of countries and argued that the no-challenge clause was invalid as being in breach of competition law: whether English common law of restraint of trade as the proper law of the contract, Article 85 E.C., or the domestic laws of the individual states. At trial, the defendants sought to adduce evidence that the trade marks in nine countries were invalid, principally for non-use, but the trial judge held that the point was not open to them on the pleadings and refused leave to raise it by rejoinder.

6–59   The Court of Appeal dismissed the defendants' appeal on these points, holding that the validity of the trade marks had not been put in issue; that if it had, particulars of the grounds of invalidity and of foreign law should have been given; that the validity or not of the registrations was not a relevant issue in the case; and that Ferris J.'s exercise of his discretion was correct. For present purposes, what is principally of interest is the attitude of the Court of Appeal to the argument that the

---

[86] *ibid.*
[87] [1991] F.S.R. 670 (Mummery J.).
[88] [1995] R.P.C. 438 (Aldous J.).
[89] (1994) 31 I.P.R. 186 (Tipping J., High Court of New Zealand).
[90] [1991] 3 C.M.L.R. 49, CA. It is noticeable that otherwise comprehensive reviews of cases subsequent to *Tyburn* either omit *Apple* altogether, or cite it only for a *dictum* of Ferris J. Presumably the Court of Appeal has suffered for being reported only in the C.M.L.R.

validity of the overseas trade marks was not justiciable in England. Although this was one of the grounds on which Ferris J. based his judgment, the observations in the Court of Appeal are *obiter*. Neill L.J. ostensibly left the issue open but in terms which are unsympathetic to the argument:

"It was argued on behalf of Apple that the issue of the validity of their trade marks in the nine countries other than the United Kingdom identified in the schedule to the draft rejoinder was not justiciable in England. In summary the argument was to the following effect:

(a) Subject to certain limited exceptions the court has no jurisdiction to entertain proceedings which are principally concerned with a question of the title to, or the right to possession of, immovable property situated outside England.

(b) This rule, which is based on the decision of the House of Lords in *British South Africa Company v. The Companhia de Mocambique*, applies not only to realty but also to property rights in letters patent (*Potter v. Broken Hill Proprietary Company Ltd*) and to rights of copyright (*Tyburn Productions Ltd v. Doyle*). Accordingly the rule plainly applies to trade mark rights.

(c) In the present case the limited exceptions to the rule, as explained by Lord Herschell in the *Moçambique* case have no application.

(d) The draft rejoinder therefore raises issues which the court has no jurisdiction to try and accordingly leave to serve it should be refused.

I have considered this argument and I have taken account of the fact that it was accepted by the judge and formed one of the two grounds on which he refused Computer's application. I have come to the conclusion, however, that it would not be right on an interlocutory appeal of this nature to attempt to define the precise ambit of the exceptions to the *Moçambique* rule. The rule has not escaped criticism. Furthermore, if the enforceability of the 1981 agreement depended, either under English domestic law or by reason of the provisions of Article 85, on the validity of Apple's foreign trade marks, I would be reluctant to be driven to the conclusion that this issue of validity was not justiciable. I therefore propose to express no view on this aspect of the case."

Nicholls L.J. principally dealt with arguments based on foreign **6–60** competition law but added:

"I add only one further comment. Having regard to the foregoing it is unnecessary for me to decide the question whether, as to foreign trade marks, the cancellation issue is justiciable in this country in this action. However, I am not to be taken as accepting the judge's view on this. The established but much-criticised *Moçambique* rule is not to be extended. I am far from persuaded that, had the

351

cancellation issue been relevant in the present action, it could not properly be regarded as incidental to the principal issues and is such within the equally well established exception to the rule."

6–61   The third member of the Court of Appeal, Taylor L.J., had nothing to say on this point. When the first instance hearing resumed after the Court of Appeal judgment, the defendants once again raised the issue of justiciability in another context, arguing that principle of *Mocambique* and *Tyburn* applied to the no-challenge clauses by analogy, as it did to the trade mark registrations themselves. Ferris J. rejected the argument[90a]:

> "Mr. Carr's argument was to this effect. There is no difference in the principles applicable to a trade mark granted by the law of a particular country and to land situate in that country. A trade mark is a strictly local item of property. The law of the country which grants a trade mark must govern all the incidents which attach to that mark. If that law, like the law of the United Kingdom, renders the trade mark not absolute but defeasible (e.g. by being liable to cancellation on grounds of non-use or because it is or has become a deceptive or confusing mark), the law of another country cannot be invoked in order to render the mark indefeasible.
>
> Up to this point it appears to me that Mr. Carr's argument has considerable force. It may be dangerous to press too far the analogy between a trade mark right, or other item of intellectual property, and land. But there can be no doubt that the English court has no power to enlarge the scope of, for example, an Australian or a German trade mark under Australian or German law, or to pronounce for or against a challenge to any such mark under the relevant law in any way which operates *in rem*.

6–62
> It is at the next stage that, in my judgment, Mr. Carr's argument runs into difficulty. He said that if a trade mark proprietor enters into a contract with another person whereby that other person agrees not to challenge the mark, the proprietor thereby extends the rights attached to the mark, because what was previously defensible has become less defensible or, if the party who agrees not to challenge is the only likely challenger, practicably indefeasible. If the law of the place which granted the mark allows this to be done there is no problem. But if the law of the mark does not allow this to be done it will be objectionable for the contract to be enforced by the courts of some other country because those courts would then be enlarging the rights given to the proprietor of the mark.
>
> In my judgment there are two objections to this argument. First, the country which enforces the no challenge agreement will not be enlarging the rights of the trade mark proprietor at all in any legal sense. Those rights will remain exactly as they are under the law of

---

[90a] [1992] F.S.R. 631 at 470 (Ferris J.).

the grant. The party who has agreed not to challenge the mark will not have deprived himself of his standing to make a challenge. If he challenges in defiance of his agreement the question whether his challenge will be allowed to proceed in the appropriate tribunals of the country of grant will depend upon the law of that country, including its rules as to conflicts of law. But the courts of a different country may have jurisdiction over a party who has agreed not to challenge and may be able to act *in personam* against him so as to compel him to keep his bargain. If they do this they will not alter the incidents attached to the mark in the hands of its proprietor. In economic terms the mark may become more valuable or effective, but in my judgment this is not something which ought to prevent a court which has such jurisdiction from exercising that jurisdiction, nor is it a reason why, so far as this country is concerned, a new rule of private international law should be devised in order to deal with the position.

The second objection to the defendants' argument is that the no challenge obligation is, in any event, a personal obligation derived exclusively from contract, not a proprietary right attached to the trade mark. In my judgment it would be wrong to apply a rule different from that generally applicable to contractual obligations on the basis of a fiction that what is being dealt with is the proprietary rights of the trade mark owner.

Mr. Carr sought to put substantially the same argument in a somewhat different form by treating a right to challenge a trade mark given by the law of the country of grant as a right which can only be surrendered in accordance with the law of the country of grant. In my judgment this too involves an erroneous approach. It requires a personal contractual obligation to be treated as if it were the surrender or grant of an item of property of a strictly territorial nature. In my view it is no such thing."

Pearce v. Ove Arup and *Coin Controls v. Suzo*: the Brussels Convention

The final pair of cases to consider *Tyburn v. Conan Doyle*[91] do so in the context of the Brussels Convention. In *Pearce v. Ove Arup*[92] the plaintiff sued for alleged infringement of architectural drawings by the construction of a building, the Kunsthal, in Rotterdam. Lloyd J. held that whatever the position under the general law would have been, under the Brussels Convention the claim was justiciable although on the facts it was bound to fail because of the lack of similarities between the plaintiff's plans and the Kunsthal itself. The defendants had unsuccessfully argued that the action should be struck out because it was bound to fail either under the *Mocambique* rule as applied in *Tyburn v. Doyle,* or under the double actionability rule of *Phillips v. Eyre.*[93] After

6–63

[91] [1990] R.P.C. 185 (Vinelott J.).
[92] [1997] F.S.R. 641 (Lloyd J.).
[93] (1870) L.R. 6 Q.B. 1.

considering section 30 of the Civil Jurisdiction and Judgments Act 1982 and holding that it did not apply to intellectual property, Lloyd J. went on to deal with the effect of the Brussels Convention. Articles 16(1) and (4) were in some respects similar to the *Mocambique* rule, since they gave exclusive jurisdiction in certain cases to the courts of the state where land was situated or registered intellectual property rights existed, but they did not apply to copyright. That left the question of whether the continuing existence of the double actionability and *Mocambique* rules was consistent with the Convention:

"On the one hand it is said that the national rules relied on are conditions of admissibility which have nothing to do with the designation of the court which is to have jurisdiction and which are therefore left by the Convention to the application of national law, just as the Convention would leave unaffected rules such as about Acts of State. On the other hand it is said that the operation of the rules relied on here (unlike rules as to Acts of State) would impair the effectiveness of the Convention and they must therefore be overridden, although only so far as is necessary to allow Article 2 to have its full effect.

The English rules would have a similar effect to Article 16(4) as regards excluding jurisdiction from English courts, but in a wider range of cases, not being limited to registrable rights. However that point by itself does not necessarily demonstrate that the English rules are incompatible with the Convention. The Convention applies to all Contracting States, and I know not what the local law of other Contracting States may have said on this point. If any of them would otherwise have permitted an action within the scope of Article 16(4) to be brought in a State other than that of the registration of the relevant right, that rule would be automatically overridden by the article. It is true that this Article derives from the same policy as the English rule of territoriality, as mentioned by the House of Lords in the *Moçambique* case and by Vinelott J. in *Tyburn Productions v. Conan Doyle*, but that does not of itself mean that the Article is the only permissible extent of such an exclusionary rule."

6–64   After considering the various English and Scottish cases in which *Tyburn v. Conan Doyle* had been considered and approved, Lloyd J. continued:

"So far as I know this is the first English case in which the point put to me has been argued. The comments of judges that I have cited and referred to show a reluctance to accept jurisdiction in relation to the infringement of foreign intellectual property rights. There may well be sound policy reasons for that reluctance, including a judge's natural hesitation at having to decide, possibly in the absence of national decisions, what some unclear provision of foreign law means. I note that in the Schlosser report, at paragraph

78, it is remarked that under the Convention the Contracting States are not only entitled to exercise jurisdiction in accordance with the provisions laid down in Title 2; they are also obliged to do so. It is not, therefore, a case in which this court has a discretion, to which such policy considerations are relevant: either the case is not justiciable, because of the *Moçambique* rule and Rule 203, or it must be accepted because Article 2 prevails."

Finally, he concluded that in the cases to which it applied, the Convention prevailed over the *Mocambique* rule: **6–65**

"My conclusion on this point is that the Convention does require an English court to accept jurisdiction where an action is brought against an English domiciled Defendant (with or without other defendants) for breach of a Dutch copyright, and to hear that action on the merits, and thus overrides, so far as is necessary for that purpose, both Rule 203 and the *Moçambique* rule, even though neither of them is a rule as to jurisdiction. Each of them, to the extent that they would preclude the English court from hearing such an action, would in my judgment impair the effectiveness of the Convention by frustrating the operation of the basic rule in Article 2, and must therefore give way in order to allow the jurisdictional rules of the Convention to have their proper effect. The position is quite different from other exclusionary rules, such as Acts of State, because both Rule 203 and the *Moçambique* rule proceed on the clear premise that the English courts are not a suitable forum for such an action whereas the courts of another country are appropriate. It seems to me that, where that other country is another Contracting State, this is a position which subverts the policy and provisions of the Convention. To borrow a phrase from another area of Community law, although they are not rules as to jurisdiction, they are 'measures having an equivalent effect' to rules of jurisdiction, and are inconsistent with the mandatory effect of the Convention and its basic rule as to domicile-based jurisdiction in article 2."

The other case to consider *Tyburn v. Conan Doyle* in the context of the Brussels Convention is the patent case of *Coin Controls v. Suzo*.[94] So far as the general law was concerned, Laddie J. rejected the submissions that the *Moçambique* and double actionability rules were two aspects of one underlying rule,[95] and held that patents were not immovable property in the sense of section 30 of the Civil Jurisdiction and Judgments Act 1982. That led to the conclusion that: **6–66**

"If the *Moçambique* rule has been destroyed or limited in relation to patent and similar rights, that must be as a result of our

---

[94] [1997] F.S.R. 660 (Laddie J.).
[95] The argument being that the Private International Law (Miscellaneous Provisions) Act 1995, by then in force, had abolished the *Mocambique* rule along with double actionability.

adherence to the Brussels convention, not because of the 1982 and 1995 Acts. It follows that, in the absence of any change in our law brought about by the convention, the three foreign claims are not justiciable here and I would order them to be struck out of the plaintiffs pleadings."

6–67   Going on to consider the latter point, Laddie J. followed the decision of Lloyd J. in *Pearce v. Ove Arup*, though he went on to hold that the action in respect of foreign patents was excluded by Article 16(4) of the Convention. So far as the *Mocambique* rule itself was concerned, its status as a rule of justiciability as opposed to one of jurisdiction did not save it. The Convention could and did force the courts of a contracting state to entertain and determine foreign infringement proceedings, though they would not have been justiciable under domestic law.[96]

Section 30 of the Civil Jurisdiction and Judgments Act 1982

6–68   After the decision of the House of Lords in *Hesperides Hotels v. Aegean Turkish Holidays*[97] and their Lordships' refusal to qualify the *Mocambique* rule for cases in which title to the foreign property was not in issue, legislation was passed in the form of section 30 of the Civil Jurisdiction and Judgments Act 1982 creating an exception to the rule. Section 30 provides:

> (1) The jurisdiction of any court in England and Wales or Northern Ireland to entertain proceedings for trespass to, or any other tort affecting, immovable property shall extend to cases in which the property in question is situated outside that part of the United Kingdom unless the proceedings are principally concerned with a question of the title, or the right to possession of, that property.
>
> (2) Subsection (1) has effect subject to the 1968 Convention and the Lugano Convention and the provisions set out in Schedule 4.

6–69   If the *Mocambique* rule prima facie applies to intellectual property, then the question arises as to whether section 30 does too. This has consistently been answered in the negative, on the basis that intellectual property is not immovable property properly so called. Vinelott J. reached this conclusion in *Tyburn v. Conan Doyle*[98] itself, on the strength

---

[96] In *Fort Dodge v. Akzo Nobel* [1998] F.S.R. 222, the Court of Appeal (affirming Laddie J.) approved of both *Pearce v. Ove Arup* [1997] F.S.R. 641 and *Coin Controls v. Suzo* [1997] F.S.R. 660, in their application of Arts 2, 5 and 16 of the Brussels Convention. The compatibility of the Brussels Convention with either of the two common law rules discussed here was not directly addressed, but the Court of Appeal would surely have said so, had they disagreed.

[97] [1979] A.C. 508, HL.

[98] [1990] R.P.C. 185 (Vinelott J.).

of *Potter v. Broken Hill.*[99] and the reasoning has been applied since. In *Pearce v. Ove Arup*,[1] Lloyd J. observed:

"The *Moçambique* rule has been modified by section 30 of the Civil Jurisdiction and Judgments Act 1982. This however provides only that the jurisdiction of the English court to entertain proceedings for trespass to, or any other tort affecting, immovable property extends to cases in which the property is situated outside the United Kingdom unless the proceedings are principally concerned with the question of the title to, or the right to possession of, that property. The categorisation of an intangible right such as a copyright as either movable or immovable is not straightforward, and is described by Dicey and Morris (at page 918) as an illogical distinction. In any event it is difficult to regard it as immovable property under English conflict of laws rules. In Australia a patent has been held to be analogous to an immovable, so as to fall within the scope of the *Moçambique* rule: *Potter v. Broken Hill Pty. Co. Ltd.* (1906) 3 CLR 479; it does not follow, and that court did not decide, that it is to be classified as an immovable for all conflict of laws purposes. Nor did Vinelott J. so decide in *Tyburn Productions*. According to Dicey & Morris intangibles are classified as movables even though, from their very nature, they cannot be moved. If they are not immovables, section 30, even though in force from 1st January 1987, does not assist the Plaintiff to overcome the constraints of the *Moçambique* rule."

And the same argument was raised without success before Laddie J. in **6–70** *Coin Controls v. Suzo*[2]:

"In the alternative, Mr. Silverleaf argued that intellectual property is properly to be regarded as an immovable for the purposes of determining whether the court has jurisdiction and that the court is accordingly given jurisdiction by s. 30 of the Civil Jurisdiction and Judgments Act, 1982. . .

His reasoning was as follows. The *Moçambique* rule is based on the fact that land is an immovable. It is because of this that the English courts have held that there is no jurisdiction. That rule has then been applied to oust the jurisdiction of the English (and Australian) courts to determine foreign intellectual property claims by analogy. He said that in those circumstances it would be wrong and illogical to treat such rights as analogous to immoveables for

---

[99] (1906) 3 C.L.R. 479 (High Court of Australia) *affirming* [1905] V.L.R. 612. "Immovable property" has no single, precise meaning and it can hardly be said that the orthodox cannons of construction require a U.K. statute of 1982 to be construed by reference to an obscure Australian court decision of 1906; but by now the question of what s. 30 of the 1982 Act intended has become academic.

[1] [1997] F.S.R. 641 (Lloyd J.).
[2] [1997] F.S.R. 660 (Laddie J.).

the purpose of application of the rule but then to ignore the analogy for the purposes of its statutory removal.

As attractive as this argument is, I am not persuaded it is right. In *Potter v. Broken Hill* Griffiths C.J. stated that a patent was 'analogous to an immovable' and I accept that the *Moçambique* rule has been applied to intellectual property rights by analogy. But that fact emphasises that, whatever the similarities may be, patents and other intellectual property rights are not accurately described as immovables. The same view was expressed by Lloyd J. in *Pearce v. Ove Arup Partnership Ltd and Others* (7 March, 1997—unreported). Since s.30 of the 1982 Act only applies to immovables and that expression does not cover intellectual property rights, it has no bearing on the issues I have to determine."

D. INFRINGEMENT ACTIONS AND THE LIKE DECLINING JURISDICTION ON CHOICE OF LAW GROUNDS

Choice of law at common law before the 1995 Act: *Phillips v. Eyre*

6–71   In cases to which English law applies unmodified by the Brussels Convention, the *Mocambique* rule,[3] as applied in *Tyburn v. Conan Doyle*,[4] provides a complete and self-sufficient explanation why actions on foreign intellectual property rights are not justiciable here; and there is logically no opportunity to invoke any rule of the conflict of laws, and no need to look in that direction for a further reason for declining jurisdiction. However, although the question of justiciability ought logically to be completely separate from that of which law the court should apply if it does entertain the action, in practice the two questions have become entangled through the operation of the former common law choice of law rule which was understood as preventing the action having any prospect of succeeding. The way the law has developed is far from satisfactory: not only have rules of justiciability and choice of law been confused with one another, but attention initially focused inappropriately on the latter; disguising the proper characterisation of the underlying problem and creating unnecessary uncertainty when the Private International Law (Miscellaneous Provisions) Act 1995 was introduced.[5]

6–72   Prior to the enactment of the Private International Law (Miscellaneous Provisions) Act 1995 the classic statement of English private international law as it applied to torts was to be found in the judgment of Willes J. speaking for the Exchequer Chamber in the case of *Phillips v. Eyre*[6]:

[3] *Companhia do Mocambique v. British South Africa Co* [1893] A.C. 602, HL.
[4] [1990] R.P.C. 185 (Vinelott J.).
[5] *Coin Controls v. Suzo* [1997] F.S.R. 660.
[6] (1870) L.R. 6 Q.B. 1.

"As a general rule, in order to found a suit in England for a wrong alleged to have been committed abroad, two conditions must be fulfilled. First, the wrong must be of such a character that it would have been actionable if committed in England. . . Secondly, the act must not have been justifiable by the law of the place where it was done."

The rule thus contemplated a two stage application of English and foreign law in that order. The first branch of the rule required that "the wrong" should be actionable if committed in England, and this meant that the plaintiff should have had an identifiable cause of action in tort under English law to which there would be no defence, had the facts occurred in England. The second branch dealt with situations where English law was more generous to the plaintiff than the foreign law. Under this head, the defendant avoided liability if "the act" would have been "justifiable" where it was committed. Different judicial interpretations have been given to the word "justifiable", and for many years the leading authority was the Court of Appeal's decision in *Machado v. Fontes*[7] to the effect that the plaintiff could recover in England if the act complained of was tortious here, even if it gave rise only to criminal liability where it was committed and the plaintiff had no civil remedies under the *lex loci delicti commissi*. In the decision of the House of Lords in *Boys v. Chaplin*[8] this interpretation was finally rejected, and to the limited extent that *Phillips v. Eyre* still applies today the law is that the plaintiff can only satisfy its second branch by showing that he has a civil cause of action of some sort, though not necessarily in tort, in the country where the act took place. *Boys v. Chaplin* and the later decision of the Privy Council in *Red Sea Insurance v. Bouygues*,[9] also recognised that there were exceptions to the double actionability rule, but the applicability of any of these exceptions to intellectual property has only recently—and inconclusively—been considered judicially.[10]

6–73

It was the principle that English and foreign law had to be applied cumulatively under the former rule in *Phillips v. Eyre* that was argued to be crucial in deciding whether a claim for infringement of a foreign intellectual property right ought to be allowed to go to trial at all, because it could be said that any particular act of infringement would be actionable only under one legal system and perfectly lawful under the other, so that the action would be doomed to failure. This argument was accepted in the first of the modern cases on infringement of foreign intellectual property rights, *Def Lepp v. Stuart-Brown*,[11] and came to be regarded as the principal obstacle to enforcing foreign intellectual property rights in the United Kingdom.

6–74

With the repeal of the rule in *Phillips v. Eyre* by the Private International Law (Miscellaneous Provisions) Act 1995, it might be

6–75

[7] [1897] 2 Q.B. 231, CA.
[8] [1971] A.C. 356, HL.
[9] [1995] A.C. 190, PC.
[10] In *Pearce v. Ove Arup* [1997] F.S.R. 641, see para. 6–101 below.
[11] [1986] R.P.C. 273 (Browne-Wilkinson V.-C.).

hoped that *Def Lepp v. Stuart-Brown*, and the short line of cases represented by it, is now of historical interest only. With hindsight, double actionablity was, at most, no more than a subsidiary reason for declining jurisdiction in these cases. The *Mocambique* rule, which has not been abolished, continues to have the same practical effect in cases which are governed by the 1995 Act but which are outside the Brussels Convention.

The Australian background: *Potter v. Broken Hill*

6–76   The origin of the strict application of the double-actionablity theory to intellectual property infringement actions is ultimately the old Australian case of *Potter v. Broken Hill*.[12] The latter was approved in the more recent Australian case of *Norbert Steinhardt v. Meth*,[13] and followed at least indirectly in the English cases of *Def Lepp v. Stuart-Brown*[14] and *Tyburn v. Doyle*[15] and the Scottish case of *James Burrough v. Speymalt*.[16] One might even suppose that *Potter v. Broken Hill* was by now sufficiently subsumed into English law not to require any extensive commentary in its own right; but *Potter v. Broken Hill* has suffered too much already from over-simplification or even ignorance of the original decisions,[17] and deserves a proper commentary in its own right.[18]

6–77   The facts of *Potter v. Broken Hill* were that the plaintiff sued in Victoria claiming relief for infringement of a New South Wales patent at the defendants' mines in New South Wales, and alleging a separate infringement of the Victorian patent in Victoria.[19] The defendants put the validity of both patents in issue and pleaded that the Victorian courts had no jurisdiction over the alleged infringement in New South Wales. The latter question was referred on a demurrer to the Full Court of the Supreme Court of Victoria, and was subsequently appealed to the High Court of Australia. The arguments for the defendants were that the

---

[12] (1906) 3 C.L.R. 479 (High Court of Australia) *affirming* [1905] V.L.R. 612.

[13] (1960) 105 C.L.R. 440 (Fullagar J., High Court of Australia).

[14] [1986] R.P.C. 273 (Browne-Wilkinson V.-C.).

[15] [1990] R.P.C. 185 (Vinelott J.).

[16] [1991] R.P.C. 130 (SC, OH).

[17] The case was reported in both the Supreme Court of Victoria, and on appeal to the High Court of Australia. In each court all three judges delivered full reasoned opinions, and in the Supreme Court of Victoria the reasoning of the three judges differed significantly. Since the V.L.R.'s and C.L.R.'s for the first decade of the present century are not widely available in England, it is hardly surprising that many commentators give the impression of having used secondary materials. Occasionally there is internal evidence of this.

[18] The present paragraphs deals with *Potter v. Broken Hill* in terms of double actionability. For a commentary on how *Potter v. Broken Hill* applied the *Mocambique* rule, see para. 6–117, below.

[19] Prior to federation and the enactment of the Patents Act 1903 (Commonwealth) pursuant to s. 51 (xviii) of the Australian Constitution patents were granted by the individual states under colonial legislation generally corresponding to English law. See Ricketson, *The Law of Intellectual Property* (1984), para. 46.23. The reason for suing in Victoria was apparently a doctrine, long since defunct, that a corporation had to be sued in the state in which it was incorporated.

Victorian court had no jurisdiction at all, but that if it did then the plaintiff had no cause of action because under the rule in *Phillips v. Eyre*[20] the action was bound to fail irrespective of its merits. The three judges of the Victorian Supreme Court were split in their decision with two finding for the defendant on differing grounds and one finding for the plaintiff.

The viability of the plaintiff's cause of action turned on the require-   **6–78**
ment in the judgment of Willes J. in *Phillips v. Eyre* that "the wrong must be of such a character that it would have been actionable if committed in England". In the Supreme Court of Victoria A'Beckett J. (dissenting) interpreted these words as requiring only that the foreign right of action should be of a type known to the law of the state where the action had been brought. Patent infringement being a recognised tort in Victoria, there was therefore no reason not to allow an action for the infringement of a New South Wales patent.[21] Hood J. in the judgment which has most influenced later courts and commentators rejected this approach:

> "The only question debated before us upon which our decision is asked is whether or not an infringement in New South Wales of a New South Wales patent affords a cause of action of which this court will take cognizance... The defendant's argument is put in two ways. It was argued first that the plaintiff's cause of action is purely local, and so cannot be tried in this Court; and second, that this Court cannot try an action for tort committed outside its jurisdiction, unless the very act complained of is wrong by the foreign law and also by our own.
>
> I propose to deal first with the latter branch of the defendant's objection. Two rules are usually cited on this point, as laid down by Willes, J.—*Phillips v. Eyre*—but only the first is of importance here. The rule is that 'the wrong must be of such a character that it would have been actionable if committed in England.' The dispute has turned on the meaning of those words. The plaintiff contends that the rule includes cases where the foreign tort is of such a character that this court would give relief in an analogous case. The other view is that the very act complained of must be a tort in both countries."

After rejecting the relevance of American law as being based on   **6–79**
different principles and considering a number of English writers and authorities, Hood J. went on conclude:

> "The act which is wrong by the foreign law must be such that if done in England it would be actionable. The plaintiff reads the rule without the words 'if committed,' and makes the word 'actionable'

---

[20] (1870) L.R. 6 Q.B. 1.
[21] This is plainly wrong. The classic counter-example is that a defendant sued in England for a libel published abroad can rely on any defence known to English law.

refer rather to the character or class of the act rather than to the act itself. The defendant's objection is therefore sustained on the second branch, in my opinion, because the act of the defendant— viz., 'using and working' certain alleged inventions in New South Wales—even though it be a wrong by the law of that State, would not be actionable if committed here."

6–80   The third judge, Hodges J., also found for the defendant, but by application of the *Mocambique* rule and he deliberately expressed no opinion on the point addressed by Hood J. Since Hood J. expressly agreed with Hodges J., and A'Beckett J. dissented, the *ratio decidendi* of the Victorian court can only be that the *Mocambique* rule applied and rendered the action on the New South Wales patent non-justiciable. On appeal all three judges of the High Court of Australia agreed in finding that the Victorian court altogether lacked jurisdiction because of the application of the *Mocambique* rule, and did not find it necessary to refer to *Phillips v. Eyre* at all.

Reception of *Potter v. Broken Hill* (1): *Norbert Steinhardt v. Meth*

6–81   At first sight the judgment of Hood J. in *Potter v. Broken Hill*[22] gains some additional weight from having been approved by another Australian judge in the case of *Norbert Steinhardt v. Meth*.[23] This was not an infringement case, but what is conveniently known as a "threats" action. Both the English[24] and the Australian[25] patents acts have long provided that it is a tort, actionable by any person aggrieved, to threaten to sue for patent infringement unless there is a valid patent which is in fact infringed by the acts in respect of which the threat was made.

6–82   The plaintiff in *Norbert Steinhardt v. Meth* was an English Company which claimed that the American defendants had contravened the Australian Patents Act by threatening them and a prospective Australian customer with proceedings for infringement of an Australian patent. So far as the threat to the Australian customer was concerned, no problems of private international law arose. The threat to the English plaintiff was more problematical. The threat was contained in a letter posted in the United States to the plaintiff company in England and it threatened infringement proceedings in various countries including Australia. The questions before the judge were therefore whether the Australian statute

---

[22] (1906) 3 C.L.R. 479 (High Court of Australia) *affirming* [1905] V.L.R. 612.

[23] (1960) 105 C.L.R. 440 (Fullagar J., High Court of Australia). This case is probably responsible for *Potter v. Broken Hill* starting on the path to acceptance among English lawyers, assisted by the 8th (1967) edition of *Dicey and Morris*. See Austin, *op. cit.*, n. 17.

[24] The English Act in force at the time was the Patents Act 1949, s. 65. The Patents Act 1977, s. 70 now corresponds, see para. 6–153, below. The action for groundless threats was originally introduced by the Patents, Designs and Trade Marks Act 1883, s. 32.

[25] The relevant Australian provision in force at the time was the Patents Act 1952 (Commonwealth), s. 121. The original provision in Australian law was the Patents Act 1909 (Commonwealth), s. 90A. See Ricketson, *The Law of Intellectual Property* (1984), para. 50.34.

had been contravened by a threat communicated in England when the threat was to sue in Australia for infringement of an Australian patent,[26] or, if not, whether a tort had been committed in England which was actionable in Australia.

Fullagar J. seems to have taken it for self-evident that if no action **6–83** could be brought in Australia for infringement of an English patent, then no action could be brought in Australia on a statutory "threat" made in England, even if the threat expressly related to an Australian patent rather than an English one. It was in this context that Fullagar J. observed: "It is not unlawful to threaten in England to infringe an Australian patent, or to threaten in Australia to infringe an English patent." Quite so, but this is to confuse infringement as such, threats to infringe, and the statutory "threats action." It is not even unlawful to threaten in England to infringe an English patent; and a threat to commit the tort of patent infringement is actionable *quia timet*, not because it is a wrong in itself.[27] The "threats action" as such is for a *sui generis* tort which happens to involve a real patent in the majority of cases, but need not do so. The two types of "threat" are really totally dissimilar. To this extent at least, the reasoning in *Norbert Steinhardt v. Meth* is plainly wrong and of very little weight in so far as it supports the judgment of Hood J. in *Potter v. Broken Hill* and the strict double-actionability theory.

Nor does it help that the judge attempted to justify treating threats **6–84** actions and infringement actions on the same footing by saying that threats actions almost always developed into full infringement actions. So they do, and this would certainly justify an Australian court in exercising its discretion and refusing to hear an action for a threat to sue for infringement of an English patent (supposing the action were otherwise admissible); but it would hardly prevent an Australian court hearing an action on a threat, wherever made, to sue on an Australian patent in Australia. The Australian court plainly has jurisdiction over infringement and the validity of the Australian patent and is, after all, the court best placed to decide those issues if and when they arise, and whether as an incidental question or on a counterclaim for infringement.[28]

The short and simple ground on which Fullagar J. could have decided **6–85** this aspect of the case, and to which he did briefly allude, was that the threat was "justified" in England in the sense of the second limb of *Phillips v. Eyre*[29] because there was no reason to suppose that the English Patents Act[30] was intended to provide a remedy in respect of threats— whether made in England or elsewhere—of proceedings in foreign

---

[26] As to which see para. 6–153.

[27] There is no reason why the defendant's intention to infringe should not be evidenced by a threat made anywhere in the world, provided it shows an intention to infringe in England.

[28] This in fact happened in *Norbert Steinhardt v. Meth* itself, since the plaintiffs were also able to plead a threat uttered within Australia.

[29] (1870) L.R. 6 Q.B. 1.

[30] Patents Act 1949, s. 65.

courts for infringement of foreign patents. The plaintiff therefore had no plausible cause of action under English law in the first place, and consideration of any other factor ought to have been unnecessary so far as private international law was concerned. There was never any need for *Norbert Steinhardt v. Meth* to have considered *Potter v. Broken Hill* at all and the approval of the judgment of Hood J. is entirely *obiter*.

Reception of *Potter v. Broken Hill* in England: *Def Lepp* and *Tyburn v. Conan Doyle*

6–86   In modern English intellectual property law, the first case to mention *Potter v. Broken Hill*[31] was *Def Lepp Music v. Stuart-Brown*,[32] though as the reference appears to have been something of an afterthought it is perhaps more convenient to start with the judgment of Vinelott J. in *Tyburn v. Conan Doyle*,[33] where the decision of Browne-Wilkinson V.-C. in the former case is summarised and provided with an explanation. Referring first to *Potter v. Broken Hill* and *Norbert Steinhardt v. Meth*,[34] Vinelott J. commented:

> "These decisions are not of course binding on me. I should nonetheless be reluctant to decline to follow decisions of the High Court of Australia reached after very full argument unless I felt convinced that they do not reflect the law of England or that circumstances have so changed as a result of social or economic developments or statutory intervention that the rule should now be confined to actions in which title to land is in issue. Moreover, the application of the rule to intellectual property rights of this nature can I think be supported by other authority.
>
> It should be noted first that Willes J. giving the judgment of the Exchequer Chamber in *Phillips v. Eyre* (1870) L.R. 6 Q.B. 1, 28, stated the rule in the following terms:
>> 'there are restrictions in respect of locality which exclude some foreign causes of action altogether, namely, those which would be local if they arose in England, such as trespass to land . . . and even with respect to those not falling within that description our courts do not undertake universal jurisdiction.'
>
> Lord Herschell [1893] A.C. 602, 621, similarly founded his decision on a distinction between transitory actions and 'actions here arising out of transactions abroad which are in their nature local.' He did not in terms restrict it to actions claiming title to or damages for trespass to land."

6–87   To that point, the Australian cases were understood by Vinelott J. in terms of the majority *ratio* of *Potter v. Broken Hill*, to the effect that the

---

[31] (1906) 3 C.L.R. 479 (High Court of Australia) *affirming* [1905] V.L.R. 612. *Potter v. Broken Hill* was alluded to in *Hesperides Hotels v. Aegean Turkish Holidays* [1979] A.C. 508, but only for the proposition that the *Mocambique* rule had been adopted in Australia.

[32] [1986] R.P.C. 273 (Browne-Wilkinson V.-C.).

[33] [1990] R.P.C. 185 (Vinelott J.).

[34] (1960) 105 C.L.R. 440 (Fullagar J, High Court of Australia).

Mocambique rule applied to intellectual property. However, Vinelott J. went on to find support for his conclusion in recent English law:

"The two Australian decisions are I think also supported by the recent decision of Sir Nicolas Browne-Wilkinson V.-C. in *Def Lepp Music v. Stuart-Brown* [1986] R.P.C. 273. In that case one question was whether the plaintiffs could bring themselves within the 'double actionability' rule which is stated in Dicey & Morris, *The Conflict of Laws*, 10th ed. (1980), p. 935, rule 172, in the following terms:
'(1) As a general rule, an act done in a foreign country is a tort and actionable as such in England, only if it is both (a) actionable as a tort according to English law, or in other words is an act which, if done in England, would be a tort; and (b) actionable according to the law of the foreign country where it was done.
This rule (then numbered 158), as very similarly stated in the 8th ed. (1967), p. 919, was approved by Lord Hodson in *Boys v. Chaplin* [1971] A.C. 356, 374.
In the *Def Lepp* case [1986] R.P.C. 273 the plaintiffs claimed to be the owners of the United Kingdom copyright in a tape recording. It was said that the sixth defendant, a company incorporated and resident in Luxembourg, had manufactured records from the recording and had sold them to the eighth defendant, a Dutch company, and that the eighth defendant in turn had sold them to the ninth defendant who had imported a number of them into the United Kingdom. Leave to serve the sixth and eighth defendants having been obtained ex parte they applied to set aside the order granting leave or alternatively to strike out the claim as against themselves.
The evidence before the court was that the manufacture took place outside the United Kingdom and that the sales by the sixth defendant to the eighth defendant and by the eighth defendant to the ninth defendant took place outside the United Kingdom and that the eighth defendant had not imported the records into the United Kingdom. The Vice-Chancellor accordingly treated the plaintiffs' primary claim as a claim for infringement of a United Kingdom copyright by acts done outside the United Kingdom. He held that that claim was bound to fail. He said, at p. 275: 'only acts done in the United Kingdom constitute infringement either direct or indirect of such right.'
However, counsel for the plaintiffs, Mr. Rubin, also relied on rule 172. The judgment of the Vice-Chancellor, after citing rule 172, records, at p. 276: 'Mr. Rubin says that it is common ground that under the law of Luxembourg and Holland the making of the records and their sale constitute legal wrongs.' As I understand it there was no allegation in the statement of claim that these acts constituted legal wrongs and no evidence of Dutch or Luxembourg law. However, the Vice-Chancellor went on to dismiss this further contention on the ground that even if these acts had constituted

legal wrongs under Dutch and Luxembourg law they would not have been justiciable in the English courts."

Def Lepp v. Stuart-Brown in more detail, and *Speymalt*

6–88   The relevant facts of *Def Lepp Music v. Stuart-Brown*[35] are as summarised by Vinelott J. in *Tyburn v. Conan Doyle.*[36] Unfortunately, as Vinelott J. noted, it is hard to understand precisely what the plaintiffs' case was or how it was pleaded; and it is also unclear why the highest the plaintiffs felt they could put their case in respect of the acts alleged in Luxembourg and the Netherlands was that they were "not justifiable in Luxembourg . . . (or) Holland" or were "legal wrongs," rather than pleading that they were actionable infringements of copyright under local law. Commentaries on *Def Lepp* generally assume that the plaintiffs were obliquely asserting infringement of Dutch and Luxembourg copyrights; but the plaintiffs may not have been the owners of copyright in either country, in which case the question arises as to who (if anyone) could sue under Dutch or Luxembourg law, and for what cause of action, if any. For the Netherlands, at least, there is reason to believe that the ambivalence of the statement of claim was deliberate. Prior to 1993 (when it acceded to the 1961 Rome Convention for the Protection of Performers, Producers of Phonograms and Broadcasting Organisations) Netherlands law did not recognise copyright is sound recordings as such, though a degree of protection was available under the general law of unfair competition.[37] If there was no civil liability in the Netherlands at all, then as a matter of English law the plaintiffs could only have succeeded on this aspect of their case on an interpretation of *Phillips v. Eyre*[38] no less generous to them than that in *Machado v. Fontes.*[39]

6–89   Four possible causes of action may be postulated against the foreign defendants. First, there appears to have been a somewhat speculative but otherwise unexceptionable allegation of joint tortfeasorship under which all nine defendants were alleged to be engaged in a common design to infringe the United Kingdom copyright. By 1986 this form of pleading was becoming routine, and it was the normal way in which jurisdiction was obtained over foreign defendants who had not actually infringed within the jurisdiction.[40] Under this doctrine, the foreign defendants could very easily have been liable for infringements actually committed in the United Kingdom by the English defendants, notwithstanding that

---

[35] [1986] R.P.C. 273 (Browne-Wilkison V.-C.).

[36] [1990] R.P.C. 185 (Vinelott J.).

[37] See Sterling, *Intellectual Property Rights in Sound Recordings, Film and Video* (1992), para. 37.70. The cases cited by Sterling as establishing liability for unfair competition post-date 1986.

[38] (1870) L.R. 6 Q.B. 1.

[39] [1897] 2 Q.B. 231, CA, overruled in *Boys v. Chaplin* [1971] A.C. 356, HL.

[40] For example, *Electric Furnace v. Selas* [1987] R.P.C. 23, CA, a patent case. However, both the nature of the cause of action against the foreign defendants and the manner of pleading it may have been unfamiliar enough to confuse Browne-Wilkinson V.-C. as to precisely what was being alleged.

any overt acts by the foreign defendants may wholly have taken place abroad. Secondly, there may have been an allegation that the foreign defendants had infringed the Copyright Act 1956 by "authorising"—though abroad—acts of infringement by the English defendants in the United Kingdom.[41] Neither of these causes of action would have required foreign law to be pleaded at all, so one must assume that as a separate matter the plaintiffs alleged that the foreign reproduction of the tape in Luxembourg and sale of records in the Netherlands were wrongful (in some sense) by local law so as to be actionable in England under *Phillips v. Eyre*. Finally, there may have been a plea that the foreign defendants were liable as importers of the infringing records, which again would not have required any legal liability under foreign law although it would have required proof that making the tape and records would have infringed, had those acts taken place in the United Kingdom, and that the defendants had the necessary knowledge and intent.[42]

This analysis suggests that a case could almost certainly have been pleaded against the sixth and eighth defendants to justify service of the writ out of the jurisdiction without relying in terms on any infringements allegedly committed abroad. However, it was this aspect of the claim which Browne-Wilkinson V.-C. regarded as underlying the whole case, and which he rejected. After summarising the pleadings, the Vice-Chancellor continued: **6–90**

> "Accordingly, the claim on its face is a claim for infringement of the United Kingdom copyright in 'First Strike' by acts done by the sixth and eighth defendants wholly outside the United Kingdom. The sixth and eighth defendants claim that acts done by them outside the United Kingdom cannot constitute breaches of the United Kingdom copyright in the tapes. Accordingly, no cause of action is disclosed against them.
>
> The draughtsman of the Copyright Act 1956 scrupulously ensures that at no stage does the Act have any application outside the United Kingdom and the other countries to which the Act extends (which do not include Holland or Luxembourg). Thus in section 1 'copyright' is defined as meaning 'the exclusive right . . . to do, and to authorise other persons to do, certain acts in relation to that work in the United Kingdom . . .'. It then defines such acts as being the acts restricted by the copyright, Section 1(2) provides that 'the copyright in a work is infringed by any person who (without authority) does, or authorises another person to do, any of the said acts in relation to the work in the United Kingdom . . .'. Section 5 deals with infringement by importation sale and other dealings, but

[41] In *ABKCO Music & Records v. Music Collection* [1995] R.P.C. 657, CA the Court of Appeal interpreted the Copyright, Designs and Patents Act 1988, s. 16(2) as meaning that there was liability when an act of infringement in the U.K. was authorised from abroad.

[42] According to the judge "there is no allegation that either the sixth defendant or the eighth defendant themselves did the importing" but that need not be conclusive, because one may be liable without having done the act oneself.

expressly limits such infringement to cases of importation 'into the United Kingdom' or sale and other dealings 'in the United Kingdom'. So far as copyright in sound recordings is concerned, copyright is created by section 12, and section 16 sub section (2) and (3) deal with the importation of, and dealings with, copies of such recordings, again in both cases the importation and dealing being expressly limited to acts done in the United Kingdom.

It is therefore clear that copyright under the English Act is strictly defined in terms of territory. The intangible right which is copyright is merely a right to do certain acts exclusively in the United Kingdom: only acts done in the United Kingdom constitute infringement either direct or indirect of such right."

6–91   It was *Def Lepp v. Stuart Brown* and *Norbert Steinhardt v. Meth*,[43] rather than *Tyburn v. Conan Doyle*,[44] which were followed by the Court of Session in *James Burrough v. Speymalt*,[45] where claims in respect of alleged trade mark infringement in Italy were struck out. Claims for passing-off in Italy were allowed to go to trial. That case specifically held that the requirement of double actionability was not satisfied by different plaintiffs holding parallel registered intellectual property rights in the two jurisdictions.[46] Lord Coulsfield would apparently have gone further, and would have held that the action in relation to the Italian trade mark would have failed even if the marks had been vested in the same person, but although *Speymalt* is sometimes cited for that proposition it is only *obiter*.[47] No strictly comparable issue had arisen in *Def Lepp v. Stuart-Brown*, because there had been no express claim of infringement of any Dutch or Luxembourg copyrights of the plaintiffs.

"If the requirement of double actionability applies in the sense explained by Lord President Cooper in *McElroy v. McAllister*, it seems clear that the petitioners cannot maintain an action for interdict in the present case on the simple ground that the Italian and the United Kingdom trade marks are held by different proprietors. As the Lord President pointed out, it is necessary to ask: 'On whom does the *lex loci* confer a right of action, and for what?' Italian law confers a right of action only on the second named petitioners, who have no right to sue for any infringement in

---

[43] (1960) 105 C.L.R. 440 (Fullagar J., High Court of Australia).

[44] [1990] R.P.C. 185 (Vinelott J.).

[45] [1991] R.P.C. 130 (SC, OH); see Kaye, "International Trade Mark Infringement: Territorially Defined Torts and the Double Actionability Rule" [1990] E.I.P.R. 28.

[46] The first petitioners (*James Burrough*) were the registered proprietors of the U.K. mark; the second petitioners (*D Johnston*) were the registered proprietors of the Italian mark. *Quaere* which of the two would have had *locus standi* to sue for passing-off in each country.

[47] On the actual facts, this is an entirely uncontroversial application of *McElroy v. McAllister* [1949] S.C. 110. Lord Wilberforce in *Boys v. Chaplin* [1971] A.C. 351 also expressly required that the cause of action must vest in the same person under both the *lex loci* and the *lex fori*.

Scotland. It seems to be that this consideration alone, defeats the petitioners' claim in the present case.

Further, even if the Italian and the UK trade marks were held by the same person, I do not think that that would be sufficient to satisfy the double actionability rule. No authority directly in point was cited, but there are, I think, a number of relevant authorities concerned with the nature of the rights created by trade marks, patents and copyrights, which, for this purpose, may all be treated as similar."

And after citing *Dicey and Morris, BASF v. Basle Chemical Works*,[48] **6–92**
Def Lepp v. Stuart-Brown and *Norbert Steinhardt v. Meth* he concluded:

"The legislation governing patents, copyrights and trade marks is common to Scotland and England and there is no reason not to follow the guidance which can be obtained from these authorities. They all emphasise the strictly territorial character of rights such as trade marks. In a case such as the present, therefore, the petitioners cannot meet the requirement of showing that the acts complained of are actionable according to the law of the forum because they would only be so actionable if they had been done in the United Kingdom. Putting the matter another way, the effect, in my opinion, is that the *jus actionis* for breach of an Italian trade mark is a different *jus actionis* from that for breach of a United Kingdom trade mark. Each *jus actionis* is separately derived from a statutory privilege which the trade mark holder has in the territory in question and is strictly confined to that territory. It follows in my view, that the fact that a person holds trade marks in each of two separate countries does not satisfy the requirement of double actionability in a case such as the present."

Territoriality, justiciability and double-actionability distinguished

Returning to *Def Lepp v. Stuart-Brown*,[49] the criticism to which it is **6–93**
open is that it treated what was really a question of justiciability as one of choice of law. The key to understanding the way in which the Vice-Chancellor interpreted the law is the passage in which he concluded that the first limb of *Phillips v. Eyre*[50] could never be satisfied:

"The only wrong under English law that he[51] can rely on for this purpose is breach of the statutory rights conferred by the Copyright Act 1956 and particularly section 1(1). Those rights do not extend to render unlawful anything done outside the United Kingdom. His right under English law is a statutory right, not a tort at common

---

[48] [1898] A.C. 200, HL.
[49] [1986] R.P.C. 273 (Browne-Wilkinson V.-C.).
[50] (1870) L.R. 6 Q.B. 1.
[51] *sc.* Counsel for the plaintiffs.

law. No common law rule of international law can confer on a litigant a right under English law that he would not otherwise possess. The words of rule 172(1)(a) are derived from *The Halley* (1868) L.R. 2 P.C. 198: for myself I do not understand what is added by the phrase 'in other words is an act which, if done in England, would be a tort'. But what is clear in any event is that the acts complained of by the plaintiffs in the present case do not fall within the first part of rule 172(1)(a) i.e. on no basis are they actionable as a tort in England.

Having once applied rule 172 to establish which law is applicable and found that the applicable law is the law of England, the question must be whether under English law those acts constitute an actionable wrong. For that purpose, if under English law the plaintiff's right is to complain of acts done in England alone (the place of the doing of the act being of the very essence of the claim) it could not be right for the trial judge to proceed on the footing that acts in fact done abroad were done in the United Kingdom. In other words, although for the purpose of establishing what is the appropriate law the acts may have to be deemed to have been done in England, on the trial of the substantive case the court must be bound to have regard to the actual facts not to any deemed facts."

6–94   This is essentially to treat the first limb of *Phillips v. Eyre* as a rule of justiciability or jurisdiction, for which there is some historical and academic support. In *Boys v. Chaplin* in the Court of Appeal, Diplock L.J. too would have characterised the first head of *Phillips v. Eyre* as a rule of jurisdiction, rather than as one of conflict of laws, and would have understood it in much the same way as the Vice-Chancellor[52]:

"He [Willes J.] then goes on to discuss the limitations upon the jurisdiction of the English courts to entertain what he calls 'foreign causes of action' which, in the context of what has gone before, clearly refers to actions brought to enforce the civil liability arising under the law of a foreign place from an act done in that place. This in my view is what he meant by 'a suit in England for a wrong alleged to have been committed abroad' in the passage which was cited in *Machado v. Fontes* and has been reproduced in Lord Upjohn's judgment in this appeal. This is borne out by the terms in which the first condition is expressed:
    'the wrong must be of such a character that it would have been actionable if committed in England,'
not, it is to be noted, the 'act' or the 'foreign transaction.'
    This first condition states what is strictly a rule of jurisdiction comparable to that whereby English courts decline jurisdiction over actions relating to foreign land to which Willes J. also refers in the same passage. It is a rule of public policy that our courts do not

---

[52] [1968] 2 Q.B. 1, CA. Lord Upjohn sat in the Court of Appeal.

hear and determine liability for acts of a kind which are not regarded as giving rise to liability in tort in England, notwithstanding that such acts give rise to civil liability under a foreign system of law and could be the subject of a foreign judgment which would be recognised here.

The second condition is of a rather different character. It does not express what today would be called a rule of 'jurisdiction'; but a rule about choice of law."

However Diplock L.J. was in a minority in the Court of Appeal, and his interpretation failed to find favour with the Law Lords when the case went to the House of Lords. Whatever its intrinsic attractions, it cannot now be regarded as an orthodox statement of English law.[53]   **6–95**

The significance of the notional transfer to England

What is actually contemplated by the first limb of the rule in *Phillip v. Eyre*[54] as it is generally understood is paraphrased by Hancock "It envisages a surreptitious transplanting of the operative facts of the case to the soil of the forum in order to consider what would have been their legal effect had that been their original location."[55] This does not depend on whether liability arises from statute or common law, still less on whether the relevant English law is territorial or not. Nor (except for torts to immovable property as such) is there one law for torts "connected with a particular place" and another for torts which might occur anywhere: that would be to introduce from the *Mocambique* rule a distinction analogous but not identical to that between local and transitory actions, which is irrelevant for choice of law purposes. In so far as intellectual property torts may be said to be connected with a particular place, this means no more than that they are connected with a particular national legal system, and that is equally true for every tort imaginable. There is no universal or international law of tort. That is perhaps why Vinelott J. in *Tyburn v. Conan Doyle*[56] attributed to *Def Lepp v. Stuart-Brown*[57] an intention which was not necessarily precisely what Browne-Wilkinson V.-C. actually had in mind.   **6–96**

"It is I think clear that in characterising the alleged infringements as acts 'the place of the doing of' which was 'of the very essence of the

[53] Some of the speeches in the House of Lords might be said to be ambiguous, but the speech of Lord Wilberforce, which has carried the most weight since, clearly does not regard the first limb of *Phillips v. Eyre* as a rule of jurisdiction.
[54] (1870) L.R. 6 Q.B. 1.
[55] Hancock, "Torts in the Conflict of Laws: The First Rule in *Phillips v. Eyre*" (1940) 3 *University of Toronto L.J.* 400. Hancock's concern is to demonstrate that this is not what Willes J. intended, but his paraphrase corresponds to what is still the generally held view. Hancock expressly prefers the meaning which A'Beckett J. attributed to *Phillips v. Eyre* in *Potter v. Broken Hill*. For present purposes, the question is whether the existence of an intellectual property right is one of the "operative facts" which is notionally transplanted.
[56] [1990] R.P.C. 185 (Vinelott J.).
[57] [1986] R.P.C. 273 (Browne-Wilkinson V.-C.).

claim' the Vice-Chancellor had in mind the distinction drawn in the *Moçambique* case [1893] A.C. 602 and in *Potter v. Broken Hill Proprietary Co. Ltd.*, 3 C.L.R. 479 between transitory actions and actions such as are in their nature local. *Potter v. Broken Hill Proprietary Co. Ltd.* and *Nobert Steinhardt & Son Ltd. v. Meth*, 105 C.L.R. 440 had both been cited to him. In my judgment, although the *Def Lepp* case [1986] R.P.C. 273 is complicated by the claim that acts done outside the United Kingdom constituted infringement of United Kingdom copyright and by reliance on rule 172, it is authority for the proposition that a claim that acts done outside the United Kingdom constitute an infringement of the copyright law of a foreign country is not justiciable in the English courts. The first limb of rule 172 cannot be satisfied because an infringement of a foreign copyright cannot constitute a tort under English law; the fact that the act complained of if done in England would have constituted a breach of an English copyright law if any is then irrelevant; for the locality of the act is inseparable from the wrong."

6–97   As *Dicey and Morris* itself emphasises (in the context of dismissing the suggestion that the first branch of *Phillips v. Eyre* is a rule of jurisdiction, not of choice of law) "Willes J. did not say that the wrong must be actionable by English law; he said it must be of such a character that it would have been actionable if committed in England—a very different proposition."[58]

6–98   It follows that it is impossible simply "to have regard to actual facts and not to deemed facts" as Browne-Wilkinson V.-C. would have preferred, since it is inherent to *Phillips v. Eyre* that facts which actually took place abroad are treated as if they had taken place in England, and the only live question is the extent to which the actual facts are imported, varied, deemed or discarded in the process. Ignoring this deliberate artificiality renders *Phillips v. Eyre* unworkable, as may be seen from an example based on *Hesperides Hotels v. Aegean Turkish Holidays*.[59] In that case, the dispossessed proprietors of an hotel in Northern Cyprus brought an action for conspiracy to trespass against the new occupiers of the hotel. The House of Lords held that the conspiracy claim in relation to trespass to land was barred by the *Mocambique* rule, but that the claim in relation to trespass to chattels could proceed. Subsequently, the Civil Jurisdiction and Judgments Act 1982, s. 30, disapplied the *Mocambique* rule in precisely these circumstances. Now suppose that the operative facts occurred after 1982 and that section 30 of the 1982 Act applied. Self-evidently, Parliament cannot have intended that the action the proprietors were now allowed to bring would fail *in limine* because of the rule in *Phillips v. Eyre*. But in that case far more than in any intellectual property infringement action it would be true to say that the place of the doing of the act was "of the very essence of the

---

[58] Dicey and Morris, *The Conflict of Laws* (12th ed., 1993), p. 1488.
[59] [1979] A.C. 508, HL.

claim." The acts of trespass to land and to the chattels on the land are inextricably connected not just with a whole country and its legal system, but with the very piece of land which is the plaintiff's. Had the same acts been done perhaps 100 yards away, there might have been no trespass.

There are two routes by which one may avoid the consequences of the **6–99** application of the double actionability rule to the facts of *Hesperides Hotels*[60]: the preferable solution is to say that where one is truely dealing with a tort to property "for which the place of the doing of the act is of the very essence of the claim", then there is only one system of law which has any credible claim to be the applicable law of the tort and that is the *lex situs* which must correspond to the *lex loci delicti commissi*. The law of England, or any other foreign law, has no business saying whether a particular act is a trespass to land in Cyprus, or an infringement of Dutch copyright. It may also be true that the English courts have no business saying whether an act done in Cyprus or the Netherlands is a trespass or an infringement by the standards of local law, but that is a matter of justiciability rather than applicable law.

However, although the *lex situs* in its capacity as such governs torts **6–100** relating to foreign immovable property, the question remains of whether intellectual property is immovable property for the purposes of this choice of law rule.[61] The second alternative, which may now be confirmed on the authorities, is that English law is flexible enough for the *lex loci delicti commissi* to be applied on its own; even if the rule for the application of the *lex situs* in its capacity as such is though to be confined to claims relating to immovable property in the sense of land.

The exceptions to double actionability: *Red Sea v. Bouygues*

At the time *Def Lepp v. Stuart-Brown*[62] and *Tyburn v. Conan Doyle*[63] **6–101** were decided, it was generally accepted on the authority of *Boys v. Chaplin*[64] that there were exceptions of undetermined scope to the strict application of the double actionability rule to claims in tort. What was less clear, was whether there were any circumstances in which a tort claim as such—as opposed to individual issues—might be decided solely according to the *lex loci delicti*, a situation which had not specifically been addressed in *Boys v. Chaplin*. In *Red Sea Insurance v. Bouygues*[65] the Privy Council held that the whole of a claim could be governed by

---

[60] Though it may be wrong to conclude that the double actionability rule is wholly unworkable in this situation. It cannot conceivably matter that the plaintiffs do not in fact have any hotel in England (would Hilton have a cause of action, when Hesperides did not?) nor that an act done in Cyprus cannot damage either land or chattels in England. See para. 6–107.

[61] Whether intellectual property is movable or immovable seems to depend entirely on the context in which the question arises.

[62] [1986] R.P.C. 273 (Browne-Wilkinson V.-C.).

[63] [1990] R.P.C. 185 (Vinelott J.).

[64] [1971] A.C. 356, HL.

[65] [1995] 1 A.C. 190, PC. The claim was for alleged negligence for which the counter-claimant could have recovered under the law of Saudi Arabia (the *lex loci*) but not under the law of Hong Long (the *lex fori*).

the *lex loci delicti*, where all or virtually all of the significant factors were in favour of it[66]:

> "In *Boys v. Chaplin* the application of the exception enabled the plaintiff to rely on the *lex fori* and to exclude the limited measure of damages imposed by the *lex loci delicti*. Can the exception be relied on to enable a plaintiff to rely on the *lex loci delicti*. If his claim would not be actionable under the *lex fori*? There is obviously a difference between a court being able to apply its own law exclusively and it being required to apply exclusively another legal system. This, however, is not necessarily fatal to the contention that only the *lex loci delicti* be applied since the foreign law can be proved and it is clear that in appropriate cases the *lex loci delicti* can be applied to give a just result when the *lex fori* might not do so. In *Boys v. Chaplin* it is not suggested that the exception can be relied on only to exclude the *lex loci delicti* in favour of the *lex fori*. Their Lordships do not consider that the element of flexibility which exists is so limited. Whilst recognising that to do so is a departure from the strict rule in *The Halley*, L.R. 2 P.C. 193, they consider that in principle the exception can be applied in an appropriate case to enable a plaintiff to rely exclusively on the *lex loci delicti*. To limit the rule so as to enable an English court only to apply English law would be in conflict with the degree of flexibility envisaged by Lord Wilberforce, though the fact that the forum is being required to apply a foreign law in a situation where its own law would give no remedy will be a factor to be taken into account when the court decides whether to apply the exception.
>
> The second question is this. The present appeal is not based on an isolated issue (as was the case in *Boys v. Chaplin*). The contention put forward is that the whole case be decided according to the *lex loci delicti*. Although the cases may be rare where the exception should be applied to the whole case, their Lordships do not consider that to apply the exception to the whole case is in principle necessarily excluded. In their Lordships' view the exception is not limited to specific isolated issues but may apply to the whole claim, for example where all or virtually all of the significant factors are in favour of the *lex loci delicti*."

6–102   Once it is conceded that exceptions exist to the double actionability rule, then the argument of *Def Lepp v. Stuart-Brown* cannot be used as a surrogate rule of justiciability: even if one agrees with the analysis of the Vice-Chancellor that double actionability is always fatal to claims on foreign intellectual property rights, then that analysis can only be applied to strike out the action once one has first concluded that the connecting factors taken as a whole do not point to the sole application of the *lex*

---

[66] Although this was a decision of the Privy Council, there is little doubt that it would be regarded as declaratory of English law, but for the fact that the Private International Law (Miscellaneous Provisions) Act 1995 achieved much the same effect by statute.

loci delicti. The course actually taken in *Red Sea Insurance v. Bouygues* suggests that there is likely to be sufficient doubt on this point not to justify striking the action out at an early stage on the ground that the alleged tort would not have been actionable under the *lex fori.* That leaves one with two alternatives: either one must apply a true rule of justiciability (as was done in *Tyburn v. Conan Doyle,* dismissing the action under the *Mocambique* rule), or one must proceed at least sufficiently far with the facts of the case to identify the applicable law.

It is of interest that the judgment of Vinelott J. in *Tyburn v. Conan* **6–103**
Doyle already seems to have contemplated an exception to double actionability, and possibly the straightforward application of the *lex loci delicti:*

> "[I]t would in my judgment be an exercise in futility to allow these claims, which raise complex issues which may require a survey by the English courts with the assistance of experts of the laws of each of the states of the United States of America, to continue."

This passage can only contemplate the application of an exception to the double actionability rule, since if the rule applied there would be no need—and indeed no opportunity—to investigate American law. The English copyrights had expired and since the first head of *Phillips v. Eyre* could never be satisfied on any interpretation then *cadit quaestio* without reference to whether the proposed conduct would be "justifiable" in America or not.

Pearce v. Ove Arup as an application of *Red Sea v. Bouygues*

Intellectual property infringement actions, more than most, seem to be **6–104**
cases where "all or virtually all of the significant factors are in favour of the *lex loci delicti.*" The principle of territoriality certainly ought to preclude the *lex fori* from having any application to alleged infringements occurring on the territory and under the laws of a foreign sovereign state. This consideration provides an alternative ground for the decision of Lloyd J. in *Pearce v. Ove Arup*[67] which is perhaps more satisfactory than his invocation of Community law in the form of the Brussels Convention to override the double actionability rule.[68] In that case, in which the alleged cause of action for infringement of Dutch copyright had accrued before commencement of the Private International Law (Miscellaneous Provisions) Act 1995, Lloyd J. held that both the *Mocambique* rule of justiciability and the double actionability rule of *Phillips v. Eyre*[69] (Rule 203 in *Dicey and Morris*) were inconsistent with the Brussels Convention and were overridden by the latter as paramount Community law.[70] Although the *Red Sea* case was cited to Lloyd J. for

---

[67] [1997] F.S.R. 641 (Lloyd J.).
[68] See para. 3–49, above.
[69] (1870) L.R. 6 Q.B. 1.
[70] See the passage quoted at para. 6–63.

the proposition that Dutch law alone as the *lex loci deliciti* should apply purely as a matter of English private international law, he did not expressly decide that point:

> "The plaintiff says, however, that these rules have to be regarded as abrogated, or modified, in so far as they preclude the court from hearing an action which, in accordance with the Brussels Convention, may or must be brought in the English court. Mr. Speck for the plaintiff also says that rule 203 is not so inflexible as to preclude the present action in any event, and relies on *Red Sea Insurance Co. Ltd. v. Bouygues S.A.* [1995] 1 A.C. 190. However, it seems to me that only the Convention can enable him to overcome the *Moçambique* rule and, if it does so, it would also remove any problem presented by rule 203. I therefore do not need to consider the precise ambit of rule 203."

6–105   It is suggested elsewhere that Lloyd J. was right to conclude that the Convention could overcome the *Mocambique* rule; but the *Red Sea* case would have provided a better route to the conclusion that Dutch law alone applied to the substantive claim. The requirements for a provision of Community law to have direct effect in the sense of *Van Gend en Loos*[71] are threefold: it must be clear and unambiguous; it must be unconditional; and its operation must not be dependent on further action being taken by Community or national authorities.[72] In the present case, what distinguishes the *Mocambique* rule from that in *Phillips v. Eyre* is the third. If the *Mocambique* rule was inconsistent with the Convention then it had to go: the Court was right simply to ignore it and no further action was necessary. It is not so simple with the rule in *Phillips v. Eyre*. If one considers the application of this rule to be inconsistent with the Convention in a particular case, then one cannot simply ignore it, since that would leave one without any rule for the choice of law. Nor can one run a blue pencil though the part of the rule which requires actionability by English law, since a rule which asked no more than whether the act complained of was "justifiable" by the *lex loci delicti* would be absurd. Lloyd J. appreciated this:

> "One consequential issue which could arise from this is, where rule 203 is overridden, in relation to events to which the Act of 1995 does not apply, what is the choice of law? The answer is presumably the law of the protecting country, copyright arising under which is alleged to have been infringed (*lex protectionis*), here Dutch law, but that is not a matter which arises on this application. Although the

---

[71] Case 26/62 [1963] E.C.R. 1; [1963] C.M.L.R. 105. There is no doubt that provisions of the Brussels Convention are capable of having direct effect: Case 288/82 *Duijnstee v. Goderbauer* [1983] E.C.R. 3663; [1985] 1 C.M.L.R. 220.

[72] Taken in this form from Hartley, *The Foundations of European Community Law* (3rd ed., 1994) citing Dashwood, "The Principle of Direct Effect in European Community Law" (1978) 16 *Journal of Common Market Studies* 229.

plaintiff's case is challenged on the merits, to which I will turn next, there is no allegation of any particular proposition of Dutch copyright law diverse from English law by reference to which the merits are to be tested, nor any evidence of that law. I must therefore proceed on the basis that, for present purposes, there is no relevant difference between Dutch and English law and I do not have to decide which applies."

However, although Dutch law may have been the only candidate on the facts of the case, it cannot be said that application of the *lex loci delicti* was the only rule which could substitute for *Phillips v. Eyre*: there was a choice, and making that choice required further action at national or Community level to provide a rule for choice of law in intellectual property cases which complied with the Convention.[73] Since there was more than one way in which English law could be brought into line with Community law, it could not be certain that the doctrine of direct effect applied. However, the same result could equally well have been reached by applying Dutch law on its own as the *lex loci delicti* on the authority of the *Red Sea* case, and on that analysis there would never have been any inconsistency between the Brussels Convention and English choice of law rules so as to call for the application of *Van Gend en Loos*; except to remove the *Mocambique* rule.

6–106

Four versions of double actionability: What did *Potter v. Broken Hill* decide?

Potter v. Broken Hill[74] is often cited as if the mere existence of the double actionability rule inevitably led to the conclusion that an action for infringement of a foreign intellectual property right is bound to fail. That is to misunderstand the number of interpretations which can be given to the rule in the context of intellectual property. The problem is that the apparently simple formulation of Willes J. is fraught with latent ambiguity, and in any event is not to be interpreted as if it were a statute. The ambiguities centre on two phrases: what did Willes J. intend by referring to "the wrong," and does this include elements of foreign law as well as fact; and what did he mean by saying that it must be "of such a character" as to be actionable in England?

6–107

Now that double actionability has ceased to be the law in England, a definitive answer to these questions can be left to the dwindling number of Commonwealth lawyers to whom they are of direct concern.[75] The purpose of the present discussion is simply to say that once the question

6–108

[73] It should be noted that the rule in *Phillips v. Eyre* is not *per se* inconsistent with the Brussels Convention. It is only the application of the rule as in *Def Lepp v. Stuart-Brown* that is objectionable, because it is considered to preclude the English court from entertaining actions for which the Convention assigns them jurisdiction. This multiplies the number of ways in which the rule might be modified to remove the conflict.

[74] (1906) 3 C.L.R. 479 (High Court of Australia) *affirming* [1905] V.L.R. 612.

[75] Principally Australians, for whom *Phillips v. Eyre* is still the law. Canada now applies the *lex loci delicti*, and New Zealand would be expected to follow *Red Sea v. Bouygues*.

of choice of law is divorced from that of justiciability, then the application of double actionability to intellectual property is not as open and shut as has sometimes been assumed.[76] In descending order of severity to the plaintiff there are four alternative interpretations, which may be summarised as follows:

1. Double actionability requires that the self-same right of the plaintiff must actually be infringed in both jurisdictions simultaneously by the same act of the defendant: this is the only interpretation which leads to the conclusion that an action on a foreign intellectual property right can never succeed. This is how *Potter v. Broken Hill* has generally been understood, although there is no case for which this is the incontrovertible *ratio decidendi*.[77]

2. Double actionability is satisfied if the plaintiff has parallel intellectual property rights in both jurisdictions, such that the alleged infringement abroad would also be an infringement at home. This is sufficient to explain *Def Lepp v. Stuart-Brown*[78] (where no foreign copyright was pleaded), *Tyburn v. Conan Doyle*[79] (where no English copyright existed) and *James Burrough v. Speymalt*[80] (where the U.K. and Italian trade marks were vested in different plaintiffs). The interpretation has no policy attractions in the case of patents,[81] but it would not be entirely without merit for copyright infringement,[82] which may be important if the objections to entertaining actions on foreign patents apply with less force to foreign copyrights.[83]

[76] Two points should be borne in mind: first that the double actionability rule should not have to do double duty as a surrogate rule of justiciability; and secondly, that a rational policy-based approach to justiciability may lead to the conclusion that some foreign intellectual property actions should be entertained, and if so they should be given the benefit of a workable choice of law rule.

[77] In *Potter v. Broken Hill* the *ratio* was the *Mocambique* rule; in *Norbert Steinhardt v. Meth* it should have been the absence of actionability under the *lex loci delicti*; in *Tyburn v. Conan Doyle* the "wrong" was not, on any assumptions, actionable under the *lex fori*; in *Def Lepp v. Stuart-Brown* there was no plea that copyright even existed outside the *lex fori*; in *James Burrough v. Speymalt* the U.K. and Italian trade marks (and with them the causes of action for infringement) were vested in different persons.

[78] [1986] R.P.C. 273 (Browne-Wilkinson V.-C.).

[79] [1990] R.P.C. 185 (Vinelott J.).

[80] [1991] R.P.C. 130 (SC, OH).

[81] It makes the outcome depend on the entirely fortuitous questions of whether any corresponding English patent exists, is valid, is owned by the plaintiff and is infringed. However, the absence of policy attractions is not fatal if it is concluded that foreign patent infringement actions are non-justiciable for other reasons.

[82] The rule in *Phillips v. Eyre* would normally be satisfied in practice if the plaintiff owned corresponding copyrights in the forum and the country of infringement, as would often be the case absent an assignment, although the defendant could rely on any defence existing under either system of law. The Berne and Universal copyright conventions long ago harmonised many aspects of substantive copyright law to the extent that the application of *Phillips v. Eyre* in this sense would often be far simpler and less objectionable here than in many other fields of law where its application is comparatively routine.

[83] See para. 6–138.

3. Double actionability requires one to assume, if possible, that the plaintiff has a corresponding intellectual property right existing under the *lex fori*, so that the question is whether the acts which were actually performed abroad, would have infringed had they occurred within the jurisdiction. The defendant would have the benefit of any defence available under the *lex fori* (e.g. fair dealing or prior use), even if not available under the *lex loci delicti*. A fortiori, an action on a foreign intellectual property right of a type unknown to the *lex fori* would fail. This removes most of the arbitrariness and unpredictability of double actionability, while preserving the feature which most commends it to its supporters.
4. Double actionability is satisfied as the cause of action for that kind of infringement is known to the *lex fori*, so that the only effect of double actionability is to exclude actions unknown to United Kingdom law. This is the interpretation preferred by A'Beckett J. in *Potter v. Broken Hill*.

The first and strictest interpretation is in fact contradicted by the **6–109** treatment of the action for passing-off in English private international law. There is no doubt that acts committed abroad which would be actionable as passing-off if carried out in the United Kingdom, have been the basis of successful actions in England under the double actionability rule.[84] However, in English law the action for passing-off is regarded as protecting goodwill, and goodwill in the legal sense is a property right existing under English law[85] and just as localised as any patent or copyright.[86] An act of passing off in Italy cannot damage English (or Scottish) goodwill, any more than the same act can infringe a United Kingdom registered trade mark. In fact, to anyone other than a dedicated natural law theorist, whenever one applies the principle of double actionability to a violation of any personal or proprietary right, one is actually looking at two parallel rights which may or may not go by the same name, one existing under the *lex loci delicti* and one under the *lex fori*. Since it is settled law that the plaintiff's cause of action under the *lex loci delicti* need not be in tort at all, provided that there is liability under some head of civil law, it is hard to see as a matter of general principle how *Phillips v. Eyre* can bear the interpretation that the very act of the defendant must actually infringe the self-same right of the plaintiff under both the *lex fori* and the *lex loci delicti*.

If this analysis is correct, then there is at least the theoretical **6–110** possibility of double actionability being satisfied, according to which of

---

[84] *John Walker v. Ost* [1970] R.P.C. 489 (Scotch whisky in Ecuador); *Alfred Dunhill v. Sunoptic* [1979] F.S.R. 337, CA (sunglasses in Switzerland). See Wadlow, *The Law of Passing-off* (2nd ed., 1995), para. 4.50.

[85] See the judgment of Lord Evershed M.R. in *Adrema v. Custodian of Enemy Property* [1957] R.P.C. 49, CA, cited at Wadlow *op. cit.* para. 2.31.

[86] *Lecouturier v. Rey* [1910] A.C. 262, HL; *Star Industrial v. Yap Kwee Kor* [1976] F.S.R. 256, PC; *Anheuser-Busch v. Budejovicky Budvar* [1984] F.S.R. 413, CA. See Wadlow, *op. cit.* paras 2.31 *et seq.*

the other three interpretations one prefers. It is remarkable that in the whole of the judgment of Hood J. in *Potter v. Broken Hill*[87] there is no reference to the fact that if the defendants' operation at Broken Hill had been transported lock, stock and barrel to Victoria, then it more than arguably would have been actionable under Victorian law, and at the suit of the same plaintiff, since the plaintiff did indeed have a corresponding Victorian patent. Hood J. never decided that simultaneous actionability under parallel and equivalent intellectual property rights was insufficient for *Phillips v. Eyre*, since he never addressed the point. The omission is so remarkable that what *Potter v. Broken Hill* decided is easily misunderstood.[88]

6–111   One can only speculate why counsel for the plaintiff did not argue that double actionability was satisfied by the existence of a parallel Victorian patent, and instead risked their case by arguing for a more extreme interpretation of the rule. All one can say is that their argument found favour with A'Beckett J., so there may have been tactical reasons for eschewing the middle course. It is suggested that Hood J. was right to reject the approach of A'Beckett J. (the fourth option above), but that he went too far in the opposite direction. He stated, quite correctly, that an act in Victoria cannot infringe a New South Wales patent, but, more questionably, that the "very act" complained of must be actionable under the *lex fori*. That is to ignore the distinction Willes J. made between "the wrong" in the first branch of the rule, and "the act" in the second, as well as the element of abstraction which he introduced by saying that "the wrong must be of such a character that it would have been actionable if committed in England."

6–112   If the judgment of Hood J. were read literally, the private international law of torts would be confined to cases where the *lex fori* had extraterritorial effect, since only then could an act done abroad actually contravene both systems of law.[89] In Australia in 1905 it must have been particularly easy for a judge to contrast obviously local statutes with the supposedly universal common law: the "brooding omnipresence in the sky" of Holmes.[90] On this basis a common law right was perhaps thought to be the same wherever it was sought to be enforced, compared to a

[87] (1906) 3 C.L.R. 479 (High Court of Australia) *affirming* [1905] V.L.R. 612.
[88] Examples of the belief that the plaintiff could have had no corresponding Victorian patent are to be found in Morse, *Torts in Private International Law* (1978), p. 51; Arnold, *op. cit.*, and Floyd and Purvis, *op. cit.*
[89] It follows that the author does not agree with the analysis of Dutson, "The Internet, the Conflict of Laws, International Litigation and Intellectual Property" [1997] J.B.L. 495, to the effect that anything turns on the supposed difference between statutory and common law torts. The common law is no more extraterritorial than a statute, and if one is contemplating applying the tort law of a civil law country then *ex hypothesi* that law will derive from some form of legislation. Dutson's fallacy is to suppose that the common law of passing-off is not merely extraterritorial, but universal; and that although the English courts may require proof of actionability under foreign law, they are enforcing what is really an English law obligation.
[90] "The common law is not a brooding omnipresence in the sky but the articulate voice of some sovereign or quasi-sovereign that can be identified . . ." *Southern Pacific Co v. Jensen* (1917) 244 U.S. 205, SC of the U.S.A., *per* Holmes J., dissenting.

statutory right which was always local. If the courts of the forum and of the *locus delicti* both followed the common law then it was superficially reasonable to treat a common law right as being the very same right in each state, in contrast to a patent or other statutory right which arose in each state as a result of legislation conferring purely local rights.

The conclusion is that the first branch of the rule in *Phillips v. Eyre* **6–113** formerly meant neither that it was sufficient for the tort allegedly committed by the defendant to be known to English law, nor that the plaintiff had to show that he had some single legal right that was infringed in both jurisdictions. All the court should do is notionally transport the facts of the case to England with their surrounding circumstances and ask whether they would have been actionable here. It is an open question whether the surrounding circumstances notionally include the existence of the foreign intellectual property right. It may or may not turn out that the plaintiff's case fails there and then without having to consider the *lex loci*. What matters is that failure is not inevitable *ab initio*, so that the English court is not bound to refuse to hear the case on the ground that there is no cause of action on which relief could be granted.

E. POLICY ISSUES IN APPLYING THE *MOCAMBIQUE* RULE TO INTELLECTUAL PROPERTY: *TYBURN v. DOYLE* RECONSIDERED

Introduction

The thesis of the foregoing two sections is that the question of **6–114** whether actions on foreign intellectual property rights should be entertained in England is one which should be addressed directly as one of justiciability, rather than as an indirect consequence of a rule principally concerned with choice of law.[91] To date, it has been the *Mocambique* rule,[92] rather than the rule in *Phillips v. Eyre*,[93] which has been the predominant underlying reason preventing actions on foreign intellectual property rights being brought in England. The purpose of the present section is to re-examine more critically the process by which the *Mocambique* rule has been applied; bearing in mind that the rule need not apply equally to all the various categories of intellectual property rights, and that common law rules of private international law may change over time with developments in social or economic conditions or in international relations.

---

[91] See para. 6–107, above. For a deliberately uncritical exposition of the application of the *Mocambique* rule to intellectual property as propounded in *Tyburn v. Doyle* [1990] R.P.C. 185, see paras 6–48 *et seq.*, above. For the alternative explanation of *Tyburn v. Doyle* in terms of double actionability, see paras 6–86 *et seq.*, above.

[92] The rule in *Companhia do Mocambique v. British South Africa Co.* [1893] A.C. 602, HL.

[93] (1870) L.R. 6 Q.B. 1.

6–115   There is little doubt that the rule in *British South Africa v. Companhia do Mocambique*, "that much-criticised rule," as Lord Wilberforce described in *Buttes Oil & Gas v. Hammer*,[94] does have some sort of continuing existence, notwithstanding section 30 of the Civil Jurisdiction and Judgments Act 1982[95] and its probable inconsistency with the Brussels Convention in cases to which the latter applies.[96] The continuing effect and relevance of the *Mocambique* rule today in respect of property other than land depends on how one characterises it: does the pre-1875 classification of an action for infringement of foreign right as "local" or "transitory" conclusively determine for all time whether it is justiciable or not; or is the rule one which simply happens to have antecedents in the old distinction? Vinelott J. in *Tyburn v. Conan Doyle*[97] identified the question, and at first sight aligned himself with the former answer:

> "The central issue in this case is whether the distinction between transitory and local actions, which was considered by the House of Lords in *British South Africa Co. v. Companhia de Moçambique* [1893] A.C. 602, was fundamental to that decision and, if it was, whether an action raising questions as to the validity or infringement of patent rights, copyrights, rights of trade mark and other intellectual property rights are properly to be considered actions of a local nature; or whether that distinction was, as it were, an historical prologue setting out the basis of the narrower rule that the English courts will not entertain proceedings raising questions as to the title to, or for damages for trespass to, land."

6–116   It is suggested, however, that there is a third alternative which Vinelott J. did not expressly consider but which is actually more consistent with his reasoning and that of the Australian cases which he followed. This is that the *Mocambique* rule, properly understood, is simply one exemplification of a wider rule of international comity which does not depend on historical accident and is not confined to immovable property in the narrow sense of land, although that is the context in which it is most often likely to be invoked. The literal or historical reading of *Mocambique* preferred by Vinelott J. is one that had long been discarded by commentators and the courts. In any event, the bulk of Vinelott J.'s judgment belies his stated preference for the first alternative. Nowhere in it is there any consideration of whether actions for copyright infringement were "local" or "transitory" as those terms were used in domestic law prior to 1875 and the question in this form is all but ignored for the other intellectual property rights. Instead, what one finds is that Vinelott J. reasons backwards from the undesirability of entertaining actions on foreign patents, trade marks or copyrights to conclude that all such actions are "local" in the sense of *Mocambique*.

[94] [1982] A.C. 888, HL.
[95] See para. 6–68, above.
[96] See para. 6–63, above.
[97] [1990] R.P.C. 185 (Vinelott J.).

Carter[97a] offers the following comments on the real and ostensible reasons for the decision in *Tyburn v. Conan Doyle*:

"The decision in *Tyburn Productions v. Conan Doyle* would, therefore, seem to stand for the broad and general proposition that, in the light of the distinction between transitory and local actions, an English court is precluded from adjudicating upon title to, or rights relating to, foreign intellectual property.

The first enquiry which such a proposition may provoke is as to the actual meaning of the distinction between 'transitory' and 'local' actions. This elusive distinction has historically been the subject of much inconclusive debate. In 1792 Buller J in *Doulson v. Matthews*, having drily observed that it 'is now too late for us to inquire whether it were wise or politic to make a distinction between transitory and local actions', concluded: 'We may try actions here which are in their nature transitory, though arising out of a transaction abroad, but not such as are in their nature local'. These words were cited with approval in the *Moçambique* case by Lord Herschell LC, who took them to be indicative of 'the fact that our courts did not exercise jurisdiction in matters arising abroad "which were in their nature local".' But how is one to discover whether a matter is 'in its nature' local? Why, for example, is a breach abroad of a foreign copyright to be seen as being in its nature local, but the commission abroad of a tort or other civil wrong is not usually designated local in its nature? The distinction would in fact appear to turn, not on the intrinsic 'nature' of a matter, but rather upon the willingness of the courts of other countries to adjudicate upon it. There is here an element of circular reasoning. A legitimate enquiry is not as to whether the matter has some mystical quality which compels the courts of other countries to refrain from adjudication, but rather as to whether there are policy grounds indicating the desirability of such restraint by other countries. The response to this enquiry should be pragmatic not *a priori*."

The *Mocambique* rule applied to patents in *Potter v. Broken Hill*

The application of the *Mocambique* rule[98] to intellectual property first arose in Australia, in *Potter v. Broken Hill*.[99] That case was relied on by Vinelott J. in *Tyburn v. Conan Doyle*[1] as supporting his conclusion that the "local" versus "transitory" distinction was the express basis of the *Mocambique* rule and prevented the English courts deciding a question of infringement of United States copyrights. As a result of its citation in

6–117

[97a] Carter, "Decisions of British Courts during 1990 Involving Questions of Public or Private International Law" [1990] B.Y.B.I.L. 377 at 400.
[98] *Compania do Mocambique v. British South Africa Co.* [1893] A.C. 602, HL.
[99] (1906) 3 C.L.R. 479 (High Court of Australia) *affirming* [1905] V.L.R. 612.
[1] [1990] R.P.C. 185 (Vinelott J.).

Dicey and Morris, by Browne-Wilkinson V.-C. in *Def Lepp v. Stuart-Brown*,[2] and by Vinelott J. in *Tyburn v. Conan Doyle, Potter v. Broken Hill* has come to be accepted as equally applicable in English law. Yet the conclusions purportedly drawn from the case are sometimes so much at variance with what was actually decided that one may wonder how many of those relying on it have actually read the judgments.

6–118   In *Potter v. Broken Hill* the defendant was a company incorporated in the state of Victoria, which carried on business at the Broken Hill mine in New South Wales. The plaintiff had separate patents for the same invention in both New South Wales and Victoria[3] and claimed that the defendant had infringed the New South Wales patent at its Broken Hill mine, but could only be sued in Victoria where it was incorporated. The plaintiff sued in Victoria claiming relief for infringement of the New South Wales patent, and alleging a separate infringement of the Victorian patent in Victoria. The defendant put the validity of both patents in issue and pleaded that the Victorian courts had no jurisdiction over the alleged infringement in New South Wales. The latter question was referred on a demurrer to a Full Court of the Supreme Court of Victoria,[4] and on appeal to the High Court of Australia. The course the litigation then took is summarised by Griffith C.J. in the High Court of Australia:

> "The respondent also[5] sets up that the alleged cause of action for infringement is not justiciable in Victoria. The latter question was ordered to be argued before the Full Court. The points argued before that Court were, as stated by Hodges J., (a) That the Court had no jurisdiction over the cause of action, and, (b) That, if it had jurisdiction, the facts disclose no cause of action, inasmuch as to entitle the plaintiff to succeed he must show not only that the act was wrongful in New South Wales, but also that that very act, if it had been done in Victoria, would have been actionable. Hodges J thought that the action for the infringement of a patent is a local action as distinguished from a transitory action, since a violation of monopoly claimed could only take place within the territory where the monopoly existed. Hood J concurred in this view, and held also that the action failed on the ground that the act complained of, ie, the violation of a New South Wales monopoly, would not have been unlawful if done in Victoria. A'Beckett J was of a contrary opinion on both points. After the appeal had been argued before us on these points, we requested further argument on the question whether it is competent for the Courts of a State to examine into the validity of an act purporting to be done by the supreme

[2] [1986] R.P.C. 273 (Browne-Wilkinson V.-C.).
[3] Prior to federation and the enactment of the Patents Act 1903 (Commonwealth) pursuant to s. 51 (xviii) of the Australian Constitution, patents were granted by the individual states under colonial legislation generally corresponding to English law.
[4] As to which see para. 6–76, above.
[5] *sc.* in addition to defences of invalidity and non-infringement.

authority of another State in the exercise of its sovereign or quasi-sovereign powers. This question assumes, of course, that the grant of a patent is such an act. . . . There is apparently no decision of either the English or the American Courts directly in point and the question must be determined on principle."

As is implicit from the course the argument took, the High Court did **6–119** not regard the former distinction between local and transitory actions as determinative (as the majority had in the Supreme Court of Victoria) but treated the question as *res integra*, to be answered from first principles. Griffith C.J. went on to compare patent rights to conventional moveable and immoveable property and concluded that although a patent was incorporeal personal property it shared some characteristics with real property. In particular, although it was not visible or fixed at a particular place it could be said to be appurtenant to the whole territory for which it was granted, and it could devolve, as for land, only according to the laws of that state. The patent right was created by the exercise of the sovereign power of the state, and there was no distinction between the sovereignty of one Australian state *vis-a-vis* another and the sovereignty of a completely foreign country such as France. It was settled law that the courts of one state would not examine the acts of the government of another state done within its own borders, even if the courts of that other state could have done so. The only remaining question, therefore, was whether the grant of patent rights was such an act of government. Griffith C.J. concluded that it was. Having dismissed an argument that the patent in question was only purportedly granted by the Governor of New South Wales he went on to consider the substantial question, which was whether or not the grant of a patent right was an act of government within the rule exemplified by *Underhill v. Hernandez*[6]:

"The first objection requires more serious attention. There is, no doubt, for some purposes a great difference between an act of state, such as that involved in *Underhill v. Hernandez*, 168 U.S. 250 (which was an exercise of physical force) and the grant of a monopoly. But I apprehend that any exercise by *a de facto* repository of any power of sovereignty, which results in the creation of a right of property that can only be created by such an exercise, must be regarded as an act of the state itself. This appears to be the foundation of the doctrine referred to in the passage cited by Story J. from *Vattel*, and quoted both by Lord Herschell L.C. [1893] A.C. 602, 623, and Lord Halsbury, at p. 631, in *Moçambique*. 'The defendant's judge (that is, the competent judge), says he,' referring to Vattel, 'is the judge of the place where the defendant has his settled abode, or the judge of the place where the defendant is when any sudden difficulty

[6] "Every sovereign state is bound to respect the independence of every other sovereign state, and the courts of one country will not sit in judgment on the acts of the government of another done within its own territory." *per* Fuller C.J. 168 U.S. 250 at 252.

arises, provided it does not relate to an estate in land, or to a right annexed to such an estate. In such a case, inasmuch as property of this kind is to be held according to the laws of the country where it is situated, and as the right of granting it is vested in the ruler of the country, controversies relating to such property can only be decided in the state in which it depends.' (*Story, Conflict of Laws*, section 553). In *Chitty's* edition of *Vattel*, p. 173, the words 'as the right of granting it is vested' are translated as 'as the right of granting of possession is vested.' We have not had an opportunity of consulting the original text of *Vattel*, but I conceive that the variation in language makes no difference to the argument, which is, that the right of creating a title to such property as land, being vested in the ruler, that is in the sovereign power, of the country, controversies relating to such property can only be decided in the state in which the property is situated. The reason appears equally applicable to patent rights, which, as already pointed out, are created by a similar exercise of the sovereign power."

6–120   So the creation of patent rights was an exercise of the sovereign power of the state just as much as the grant of an estate in land, and the principles stated by Lord Esher M.R. and the Lord Chancellor in the *British South Africa* case applied whenever the courts of one country were called upon to inquire into the validity of the exercise of the powers of the government of another country in the creation of a right of property only capable of being enjoyed within that country. If the defendant was right and the patent was invalid then it followed that the New South Wales government must have acted mistakenly. Since the substantial question raised by the defendant was the validity of an act of the Government of New South Wales it followed that the case could only be dealt with by the courts of that state.

6–121   Barton J. and O'Connor J. delivered concurring judgments, though neither of them dwelt on the analogy between patents and land or whether or not patents were immovable property. O'Connor J. emphasised that there was no question of the power of New South Wales to grant patents being impleaded. Indeed, if it could have been alleged that the grant of the patent was wholly outside the jurisdiction of the state then there would have been a matter which the Victorian court could have investigated. Here, on the contrary, there was no doubt that the power to issue patents existed and the only question was whether an organ of the Government of New South Wales had in its discretion properly or improperly exercised an executive power vested in it.

Potter v. Broken Hill: **an aspect of international public policy . . .**

6–122   The perpetuation of the distinction between local and transitory actions made in *Potter v. Broken Hill*[7] and *Tyburn v. Conan Doyle*[8] can be understood in two different ways. The first, which is consistent with the

---

[7] (1906) 3 C.L.R. 479 (High Court of Australia) *affirming* [1905] V.L.R. 612.
[8] [1990] R.P.C. 185 (Vinelott J.).

analysis in *Potter v. Broken Hill* itself, is to say that the distinction is no more than a convenient verbal formulation on which to hang the real issue, which is whether or not it would be right, as a matter of public policy, to assert jurisdiction over foreign intellectual property rights. It provides a pretext for the court to address this issue without having to answer the vexed question of whether or not intellectual property rights are strictly speaking "immovable property" so as to fall within the express wording of the decision of the House of Lords in *British South Africa v. Companhia do Mocambique*[9] itself. On this basis, a local action is simply one to which *Mocambique* applies, a transitory action is one to which it does not.

In *Potter v. Broken Hill* itself, Barton J. was quite as explicit as Griffith C.J. that this was the real issue. He began his judgment: **6–123**

> "Though many cases were cited in which the distinction between local and transitory actions had been closely discussed, in my view, decisions as to what actions are local and what are transitory are not on the question really involved, although much learning may be found in the reports of such cases helping to throw light on the present question. That question, namely, whether the validity of a patent granted by the government of one country can be directly tested in the Court of another, is in this Empire one the answer to which depends, so far as we are concerned, on the limits which in the absence of legislative mandate, the Courts impose on their own jurisdiction in recognition of international comity."

On this analysis, and in terms of modern authority, *Potter v. Broken Hill* has rather more in common with *Buttes Oil & Gas v. Hammer*[10] than with *British South Africa v. Companhia do Mocambique*. In the former case, Lord Wilberforce examined the same line of authority as had the High Court of Australia, to conclude that in addition to the strict *Mocambique* rule there was a wider principle of judicial abstention in respect of the acts of a foreign sovereign state. The rule was best established when the acts in question were within its own territory, although it was not confined to that situation: **6–124**

> "So I think that the essential question is whether, apart from such particular rules as I have discussed, *viz.* those established by (a) the *Moçambique* [1893] A.C. 602 and *Hesperides* [1979] A.C. 508 cases and by (b) *Luther*'s case [1921] 3 K.B. 532 and *Princess Paley Olga v. Weisz* [1929] 1 K.B. 718, there exists in English law a more general principle that the courts will not adjudicate upon the transactions of foreign sovereign states. Though I would prefer to avoid argument on terminology, it seems desirable to consider this principle, if existing, not as a variety of 'act of state' but one for judicial restraint

[9] [1893] A.C. 602, HL.
[10] [1982] A.C. 888, HL.

or abstention. The respondents' argument was that although there may have been traces of such a general principle, it has now been crystallised into particular rules (such as those I have mentioned) within one of which the appellants must bring the case—or fail. The Nile, once separated into a multi-channel delta, cannot be reconstituted.

In my opinion there is, and for long has been, such a general principle, starting in English law, adopted and generalised in the law of the United States of America which is effective and compelling in English courts. This principle is not one of discretion, but is inherent in the very nature of the judicial process.

[. . .][11]

6–125 More clearly as a recognition of a general principle is *Duke of Brunswick v. King of Hanover* (1844) 6 Beav. 1; (1848) 2 H.L. Cas 1: a case in this House which is still authoritative and which has influenced the law both here and overseas. There are two elements in the case, not always clearly separated, that of sovereign immunity *ratione personae*, and that of immunity from jurisdiction *ratione materia*: it is the second that is relevant. I find the principle clearly stated that the courts in England will not adjudicate upon acts done abroad by virtue of sovereign authority. Thus Lord Cottenham L.C. states the question, quite apart from any personal immunity, as being whether the courts of this country can 'sit in judgment' upon the act of a sovereign, effected by virtue of his sovereign authority abroad. His decision is conveyed in the words, at p. 21:

'It is true, the bill states that the instrument was contrary to the laws of Hanover and Brunswick, but, notwithstanding that it is so stated, still if it is a sovereign act, then, whether it be according to law or not according to law, we cannot inquire into it.'

and he continues by distinguishing cases of private rights (cf. *Luther v. Sagor* [1921] 3 K.B. 532). He then said, at pp. 21–22:

'If it were a private transaction . . . then the law upon which the rights of individuals may depend, might have been a matter of fact to be inquired into . . . But . . . if it be a matter of sovereign authority, we cannot try the fact whether it be right or wrong.'

Lord Campbell is still more definite. The question he says, at p. 27, is 'as to the validity of an act of sovereignty,' and he expresses the view, at p. 26, that even if the Duke of Cambridge (i.e. not the sovereign) had been sued, 'it would equally have been a matter of state.'

6–126 It is justly said of this case, and of their Lordships' observations, that they are directed to the question whether a sovereign can be brought to account in this country in respect of sovereign acts, and that such general phrases as 'sitting in judgment on,' 'inquiring into'

---

[11] A passage referring to *Blad's Case*, omitted here, is quoted at para. 6–10, above.

or 'entertaining questions' must be read in their context. I agree that these phrases are not to be used without circumspection: the nature of the judgment, or inquiry or entertainment must be carefully analysed. It is also to be noted that the acts in question were performed within the territory of the sovereign concerned, reliance is placed on this in some passages: an argument on this I have already dealt with. These qualifications accepted, the case is nevertheless support, no doubt by reference to the issue in dispute, for a principle of non-justiciability by the English courts of a certain class of sovereign acts.

The discussion now shifts to the United States. *The Duke of Brunswick case*, 2 H.L.Cas. 1, was followed in *Underhill v. Hernandez* (1893) 65 Fed. 577. In the Supreme Court (1897) 168 U.S. 250, Fuller C.J. used the much-quoted words, at p. 252:

'Every sovereign state is bound to respect the independence of every other sovereign state, and the courts of one country will not sit in judgment on the acts of the government of another done within its own territory. Redress of grievances by reason of such acts must be obtained through the means open to be availed of by sovereign powers as between themselves.'

Again it is a just observation that the words 'sit in judgment' must be related primarily to the issue under discussion, viz., whether a remedy could be obtained in the United States for an alleged wrong committed by a foreign government in its own territory. But a principle is nevertheless stated."

. . . or an arcane rule of procedure?

The other interpretation—to which *Tyburn v. Conan Doyle*[12] in particular appears to lend itself—is that jurisdiction over intellectual property infringement actions is indeed strictly governed by the question of whether such actions were regarded as "local" or "transitory" prior to the abolition of the distinction in the Judicature Act, and that it is no more than a fortunate coincidence if a result compelled by the application of obscure procedural law abolished in the reign of Queen Victoria corresponds to that which the court would voluntarily adopt as a matter of contemporary public policy. **6–127**

The criticism to which *Tyburn v. Doyle* is legitimately subject is that this obscures the real basis for the decision. For a start, it is hopelessly anachronistic to assume, as Vinelott J. was invited to do, that all actions for infringement of proprietary intellectual property rights must be governed by the same criteria. The very idea of intellectual property as a unitary body of law is a late-twentieth century invention heavily influenced by Continental legal thought. Even the tendency of English law to group together patents, registered designs and trade marks owes much to the Patents, Designs and Trade Marks Act 1883 and the amalgamation of responsibility for registration in a single office, a development **6–128**

---

[12] [1990] R.P.C. 185 (Vinelott J.).

which can hardly affect a body of law which *ex hypothesi* must have been fixed prior to its abolition in the 1870's.

6–129   In some respects at least this lumping together of intellectual property rights can be shown to be obviously wrong, even without undertaking a detailed study of pre-Judicature Act procedure.[13] Vinelott J. expressly concluded that actions for infringement of foreign trade marks were excluded by the *Mocambique* rule, though he noted and approved the fact that actions for passing-off could be brought in respects of acts committed abroad. But this cannot depend on the one being a local action and the other transitory, since before 1875 the two actions were indistinguishable.[14] Again, *Norbert Steinhart v. Meth*[15] was relied on as having applied the strict *Mocambique* rule to a threats action, but since the threats action did not exist at all prior to the Judicature Act this cannot depend on its hypothetically having been local.[16] The antecedents of the statutory threats action are predominantly to be found in the common law action for injurious falsehood, which was almost certainly a transitory, rather than local, action in the pre-1875 classification.

6–130   The conclusion that patent infringement was a "local" action at common law is also open to doubt. There is very little case law addressing the issue and that which exists is contradictory and inconclusive. The High Court of Australia was much more careful in this respect than Vinelott J., who seems to have regarded the issue as conclusively determined in favour of the "local" action theory by the decision in *Potter v. Broken Hill*. In *Cameron v. Gray*[17] Lord Kenyon C.J. refused a motion to change the venue of an infringement action from London to Northumberland on the ground that "the plaintiff cannot make the proper and necessary affidavit that the cause of action arose wholly in Northumberland, and not elsewhere, when it is manifest that the substratum of the action, namely the patent, is at Westminster."[18] In *Brunton v. White*[19] a motion to change the venue from London to Lancashire was refused as there was no precedent to support it. However in *Bickford v. Skewes*,[20] venue was indeed changed, from London to Devon, and the action was tried at Exeter assizes. Since transfer of venue is the touchstone for whether actions are transitory or local, *Bickford v. Skewes* implies that patent infringement was not a local action.

---

[13] For the United States, Nimmer tentatively concludes that copyright actions were transitory whereas patent and trade mark actions were local: *Nimmer on Copyright* (1995), Vol. 3, para. 17.03.

[14] See *G.E. Trade Mark* [1973] R.P.C. 297, HL and Wadlow, *The Law of Passing-Off* (2nd ed., 1995), paras 1.05 *et seq*.

[15] (1960) 105 C.L.R. 440 (Fullaghar J., High Court of Australia). This case is probably responsible for *Potter v. Broken Hill* starting on the path to acceptance among English lawyers, assisted by the 8th (1967) edition of *Dicey & Morris*. See Austin, *op. cit.*, n. 17.

[16] For the origin and antecedents of the threats action see *Skinner v. Shrew* [1893] 1 Ch. 413, CA.

[17] (1795) 101 E.R. 596; 1 H.P.C. 407.

[18] If this substratum theory was correct, then all infringement actions should have been tried in London, though in reality examples of actions being tried at *nisi prius* are known.

[19] (1825) 1 H.P.C. 899.

[20] (1837) 1 W.P.C. 209 at 214 n. (e); 3 H.P.C. 233 at 241.

It is noteworthy that although *Cameron v. Gray* was cited to the High **6–131** Court of Australia by counsel in *Potter v. Broken Hill*, all the judges decided the case on the much broader ground that foreign patents *ought* to be governed by the same considerations as foreign land, and none of them thought it necessary to rely on *Cameron v. Gray* or to decide whether patent infringement actions had been local or transitory at common law. If the older cases and the textbooks cited to the High Court of Australia had also been cited to Vinelott J., would he have followed *Bickford v. Skewes* in preference to *Cameron v. Gray*, held that patent infringement actions had been transitory rather than local, and therefore that nothing decided in *British South Africa v. Companhia do Mocambique* prevented him from exercising jurisdiction? Almost certainly not, because despite the terms in which he expressed himself, Vinelott J. actually followed precisely the same train of thought as the High Court of Australia in reasoning backwards from the conclusion that foreign intellectual property infringement actions ought not to be justiciable in England, to the premise that they were "local" within the meaning of the *Mocambique* case. The mere possibility that on this issue *Tyburn v. Conan Doyle* was decided *per incuriam* simply emphasises the absurdity of basing modern decisions on an ancient rule about which nothing is certain except that it ought to be completely irrelevant.

Factors based on the exercise of sovereign power and the analogy with administrative law

At first sight it may appear rather exaggerated to describe the grant of **6–132** a patent as an "act of sovereignty," even though the majority of the High Court of Australia in *Potter v. Broken Hill*[21] were careful to avoid using the technical expression "act of state" and to make it clear that the jurisdiction of New South Wales to grant patents was not being challenged. Although the grant of a patent may not be a major exercise of a state's sovereign power in the sense of passing general legislation or conducting foreign policy, none the less it fits the description of "an act of sovereignty" rather more comfortably than many well-established examples of the rule that the acts of a foreign sovereign cannot be impleaded before an English court.

Patents and similar rights fall well within the general principles on **6–133** which the *British South Africa* case was decided. The question posed by Lord Esher M.R.[22] was whether the subject matter of the action was such that nations in general allowed foreign courts to adjudicate on it. Lord Esher answered this question in the negative for land, and it is abundantly clear, not least from Articles 16(1) and 16(4) of the Brussels Convention and the commentary in the Jenard report, that even today land and patent rights alike are not generally regarded as within the proper jurisdiction of foreign courts except to the extent that specific treaties permit.

[21] (1906) 3 C.L.R. 479 (High Court of Australia) *affirming* [1905] V.L.R. 612.
[22] [1892] 2 Q.B. 358 at 390, CA. Lord Esher M.R. dissented, but his view was upheld in the House of Lords [1893] A.C. 602, HL.

6–134   If one considers how the reasoning of *Potter v. Broken Hill* compares to the actual decision in *British South Africa Co v. Companhia do Mocambique*[23] it may be seen that the reasons advanced by the High Court of Australia apply in most cases with rather more force to patents than they do to land. The act of sovereignty which is indirectly called into question in cases of trespass to land is nominally the original grant of an estate in the land to one of the parties or his predecessor in title. In the *British South Africa* case there were in fact recent conflicting grants of land and trading privileges to the very parties in the case, but this was exceptional. In most cases involving foreign land the original grant will be little more than a legal fiction and any conceivable dispute will centre not on the propriety of the grant itself but on the subsequent devolution of the land or the loss or acquisition of rights by operation of law. Patents, in contrast, always result from the recent and deliberate exercise of sovereign power in favour of a particular individual, and the propriety of the grant is frequently a central issue which, unlike title in trespass, can be raised as a defence by anyone sued for infringement.

6–135   To avoid the objection that patents are granted in the exercise of sovereign power it might be suggested that a national patent office does nothing more than recognise and act on certain rights to which the applicant is already entitled under the relevant law, with the grant of the patent being dependent on compliance with all legal requirements as to novelty, inventive step and so on. On this hypothesis the only true exercise of the sovereign power is by the foreign legislature in enacting the conditions under which a person is entitled to a patent. Once these conditions have been specified, it may be suggested, the actual grant of the patent is not to be considered an act of sovereignty at all. The applicant is either entitled to a patent or he is not. The English court hearing an infringement action would automatically respect the sovereignty of the foreign legislature, but would do nothing objectionable in applying the foreign law to decide whether the patent in fact met the conditions prescribed for grant.[24]

6–136   This approach was rejected by the High Court of Australia in *Potter v. Broken Hill* and it is suggested that they were right to do so. It is impossible to challenge the validity of a patent without impugning the act of the office granting it. For patents, as for land, there are really at least two separate objections to the courts of one country assuming jurisdiction over rights existing under the legal system of another. One is the historical justification that such rights are for the sovereign to bestow or withdraw as it thinks fit; but the more contemporary and relevant is that entitlement to such rights is established by specially designated administrative or judicial bodies.[24a]

---

[23] [1893] A.C. 602, HL.

[24] For opposing views compare Arnold, "Can One Sue in England for Infringement of Foreign Intellectual Property Rights" [1990] E.I.P.R. 254 with Austin, "The Infringement of Foreign Intellectual Property Rights" (1997) 113 L.Q.R. 321.

[24a] For the proposition that there is no extraterritorial jurisdiction in administrative law, see Beloff and Mountfield, "The Territorial Limits of JR" [1997] *Judicial Review* 131, citing, *inter alia, Lenzing's European Patent* [1997] R.P.C. 245 (Jacob J.). Administrative law is expressly excluded from the scope of the Brussels Convention.

In the case of land, as for patents, most countries have some system of **6–137** registration under which title is proved by the existence of an entry in a public register. Anyone entitled as a matter of law to an interest in land is entitled to have an appropriate entry made in the register, and the function of the registry is not to create new rights in land but simply to record the creation, extinction or assignment of rights in accordance with the general law. For a court in another country to rule on rights to land situated in such a country would none the less be a violation of sovereignty, notwithstanding that the registry itself served a purely administrative function. It is an affront to sovereignty for a court in one country to review the propriety of purely administrative actions of organs of a foreign government, and in modern circumstances this is likely to be a far more valid reason for not inquiring into the ownership of foreign land (and *a fortiori* patents) than the theory that title to land ultimately depends on the state's exercise of its sovereign power. The fact that matters of this sort are not generally regarded as within the proper jurisdiction of foreign courts is shown by the exclusion of public and administrative law altogether from the scope of the Brussels Convention as well as by the recognition in Article 16(3) of exclusive jurisdiction over entries in public registers.

Which intellectual property rights does the *Mocambique* rule apply to?

Intellectual property actions cover a broad spectrum from those to **6–138** enforce purely common law rights, such as the action for passing-off, to those for infringement of state-granted monopolies such as patents or registered designs. On any view of the law, the application of private international law differs markedly according to the rights in question.[25] At the two ends of the scale the practical results for litigants are reasonably clear, although there is room for doubt as to how those results arise. Actions are permitted in England for passing-off abroad, and neither Vinelott J. in *Tyburn v. Conan Doyle*[26] nor Browne-Wilkinson V.-C. in *Def Lepp v. Stuart-Brown*[27] questioned the correctness of this. At the other extreme, nothing short of confining the *Mocambique* rule strictly to foreign land could credibly exclude foreign patent rights from its scope.

The principle of the *British South Africa* case[28] as understood in *Potter* **6–139** *v. Broken Hill*[29] ought to apply to all industrial property rights which are

[25] Even if one starts with the preconception that all intellectual property rights should receive the same treatment, one should bear in mind that "intellectual property" as a term embracing copyrights as well as the registered industrial property rights is a comparatively recent usage, especially in English law, and that in many respects (including their treatment in public international law) there is a natural dichotomy between copyrights and neighbouring rights on the one hand, and patents, trade marks and registered designs on the other.
[26] [1990] R.P.C. 185 (Vinelott J.), citing *Alfred Dunhill v. Sunoptic* [1979] F.S.R. 337, CA.
[27] [1986] R.P.C. 273 (Browne-Wilkinson V.-C.). A claim for passing-off abroad failed, but only because it was inadequately particularised and there was no evidence of foreign law.
[28] [1893] A.C. 602, HL.
[29] (1906) 3 C.L.R. 479 (High Court of Australia) *affirming* [1905] V.L.R. 612.

created upon registration and are potentially open to cancellation. There are fewer reasons why the same principle should apply to copyrights. Though this suggestion appears to be directly contradicted by the actual result in *Tyburn v. Conan Doyle*, that case proceeded throughout on the concession by the plaintiffs that actions for infringement of foreign copyright, trade marks and patents all stood or fell together. That concession, however, ignored the distinction between rights created by the exercise of sovereign power on an individual basis, and rights arising *ex lege* from legislation, the common law or self-executing treaty.[30] Alternatively, an analysis in terms of the legitimate interests of sovereign states in protecting essential national interests also suggests that copyrights[31] should receive different treatment to patents. Without wishing to understate the social, cultural or economic significance of copyright, it is not a monopoly right and it does not have the same potential for impact on national economies as patents do. The distinction is already reflected in international law, in that compulsory licensing of patents has always been permitted in the Paris Convention[32] (and even in TRIPs[33]), whereas the provisions for compulsory licensing of copyrights in the Berne Convention are confined to the single case of translations into the languages of developing countries.[34]

6–140   In all countries, now including even the United States, copyright arises *ex lege* without the need for any act on the part of the (prospective) copyright owner, or the state, which could bring matters of sovereignty into question. Because copyright invariably arises *ex lege* it does not exist by virtue of an act of sovereignty any more than any other legal right. It is also inappropriate to speak of a copyright being valid or invalid: copyright either exists or not and if it does exist then there is no question of arguing (as one might for a patent) that it was created in error and ought to be revoked. The only point of similarity between copyrights and patents or land is that in some countries (notably the United States) the ownership of copyrights is established by public registers kept by the state. Except where this is the case and ownership is the central issue, there seems to be no reason in principle why the English courts should invariably refuse to entertain an action on a foreign copyright *in limine*.

6–141   Two important reservations apply to the foregoing. First, quite apart from the question of whether subject-matter jurisdiction exists, it will always be necessary for there to be personal jurisdiction over the defendant obtained by valid service of the writ or pursuant to the Brussels Convention. Unless the defendant is physically present in England or incorporated here this is likely to be a major obstacle.

---

[30] The Brussels and Lugano Conventions may also be prayed in aid for the proposition that unregistered intellectual property rights are treated less sensitively than registered ones. Nothing in Art. 16 of the two conventions preserves exclusive jurisdiction in relation to copyright.

[31] And perhaps trade marks, if the crucial distinction is whether a true monopoly is involved.

[32] Paris Convention for the Protection of Industrial Property, Art. 5, s. A.

[33] Agreement on Trade Related Aspects of Intellectual Property Rights, Art. 31

[34] Berne Convention, Stockholm Protocol.

Secondly, where justiciability is at all doubtful it is only to be expected that the English court would be likely to exercise its discretion against hearing an action on a foreign intellectual property right unless there were very exceptional reasons for the plaintiff not suing in the country of infringement. Even if infringement of a foreign intellectual property right is technically justiciable in England, there are few circumstances in which the English courts would be *forum conveniens* for the claim.

Apparent examples of foreign copyrights enforced

At first sight, the proposition that copyright is different to the registered intellectual property rights might appear to have some support in authority. The two copyright infringement cases of *Baschet v. London Illustrated Standard*[35] and *Jonathan Cape v. Consolidated Press*[36] are sometimes given as examples of English courts enforcing foreign copyrights, but neither deserves this description. **6–142**

Baschet v. London Illustrated Standard was an action for an infringement of English copyright committed in England and tried before an English court. The only foreign elements were that the plaintiff was French and the pictures copied were of French origin.[37] Today there would be no suggestion that such a case involved more than a trivial application of private international law but in 1899 there was a complication. Copyright in works of foreign authorship, not first published in England, arose if at all under the provisions of the International Copyright Act 1886 which gave effect to the Berne Convention. Unlike present legislation, the 1886 Act partly defined the extent of protection under English law by reference to the law of the country where the work was produced. The Act provided that it should "not confer on any person any greater right or longer term of copyright in any work than that enjoyed in the foreign country in which such work was first produced."[38] On behalf of the defendants, it was argued that one effect of the Act was that the remedies available to the plaintiff could not exceed those available under French law, which was the relevant foreign law. Kekewich J. rejected this contention, holding that it was only the existence of copyright protection, and not the remedies for infringement, which was to be defined by reference to foreign law[39]: **6–143**

> "As I understand it, the principle is shortly this: A man cannot sue here in respect of a work published in the country of origin—in this

---

[35] [1900] 1 Ch. 73 (Kekewich J.).

[36] [1954] 1 W.L.R. 1313; [1954] 3 All E.R. 253 (Dankwerts J., QBD).

[37] Two of which were held by the Court of Appeal (in earlier proceedings, unreported) to be too indecent to be protected by an interlocutory injunction.

[38] International Copyright Act 1886, s. 2(3). The principle of dependent protection for copyright works was abolished, with a few unimportant exceptions, by Art. 5(2) of the Berne Convention adopted at the 1908 Berlin Conference. See Ricketson, *The Berne Convention for the Protection of Literary and Artistic Works: 1886–1986* (1987), paras 5.63 and 5.86.

[39] The Judge's conclusion is supported by *Scrutton on Copyright* (3rd ed., 1890); and is approved by Laddie, Prescott and Vitoria, *The Modern Law of Copyright and Designs* (2nd ed., 1995), para. 4.124, n. 4.

case France—unless he proves that he is entitled to protection in that country of origin; and, vice versa, a man cannot sue in France in respect of a work published in England unless he proves to the satisfaction of the French Court that he is entitled to sue in England as the country of origin.

But it is a very large step beyond that to say that, the right to sue once admitted, the plaintiff is to have no other remedies in the country in which he sues than he would have in the country of origin. Can it be contended that, sitting here as an English judge, I am only to apply the remedies of the French Court, and, vice versa, that the French Court can only grant English remedies, however out of place and inapplicable in that jurisdiction?

The remedy by injunction, the first remedy that an English plaintiff seeks, is unknown in France—an excellent example of the impracticability of that construction. As I read the section, 'any greater right' means any greater right of protection or of copyright, and the specific provision against a longer term being conferred by the Acts shews that no other limitation was intended. In other words, a copyright owner is only entitled to protection for the term which the country of origin gives him; but everything else is left open. I cannot believe that the Court has to consider the remedies of another country. It would be impossible to work two systems of jurisprudence together in that way. I therefore hold that the plaintiff is entitled to penalties."

6–144   Apart from this specific and limited provision, the author's rights in England were determined by the relevant English statute according to the nature of the work in question. It was never the case that the plaintiff was attempting to enforce a French copyright in England. The English copyright was the only right infringed, but the existence of the English copyright could only be confirmed after a reference to French law directed by the English statute. To this extent, therefore, English and foreign law were applied cumulatively in a manner deceptively reminiscent of *Phillips v. Eyre*,[40] but the only reason for doing this was that the English statute so provided.

6–145   *Baschet v. London Illustrated Standard* is representative of a principle also found in nineteenth-century patent law, to the effect that patent proprietors should not enjoy any greater rights in the United Kingdom than they did in their home territory. One such rule was that a British patent expired automatically as soon as an earlier corresponding foreign patent expired or was revoked. This also created what might be called a mirror image of *Phillips v. Eyre* in that an English action could in some circumstances be defended on the ground that the alleged infringement would be lawful abroad, but always because English domestic law defined the scope of English intellectual property with reference to foreign law.

[40] (1870) L.R. 6 Q.B. 1.

Jonathan Cape v. Consolidated Press[41] is rather more interesting. It was **6–146** an action for copyright infringement in Australia brought successfully in England without the judge or the parties apparently making any reference to either private international law or Australian domestic law at any stage. As with *Baschet*, however, the explanation of an apparently remarkable case lies in the obscurities of copyright legislation rather than in private international law. The case was heard in 1954, when copyright in both England and Australia was governed by the Copyright Act 1911. However, it was not just the case that the same Act was in force in both countries. The Act created a single, unitary copyright existing in all the countries of the Empire or Commonwealth to which it extended.

Sections 1(1) and 25(1) of the 1911 Act respectively provided:

1(1) Subject to the provisions of this Act, copyright shall subsist throughout the parts of His Majesty's dominions to which this Act extends. . . .

25(1) This Act . . . shall extend throughout His Majesty's dominions: Provided that it shall not extend to a self-governing dominion, unless declared by the Legislature of that dominion to be in force therein. . . .

In Australia, the Copyright Act 1912 (Commonwealth) declared the **6–147** 1911 Act to be in force in the Commonwealth with effect from July 1st, 1912. It is important to note that "this was not an exercise of the Commonwealth power to legislate with respect to copyright: the 1912 Act was simply a declaration that henceforth the 1911 United Kingdom Act operated within Australia of its own force . . ."[42] Thus—unless the copyright had been severed along national borders by the deliberate act of a previous owner—a truly international copyright existed. It was no more appropriate to speak of English and Australian copyrights than it would have been to speak of Yorkshire and Devonshire copyrights. In strong contrast to patents, the copyright existing in Australia was indeed the very same right as the copyright in England and the English judge was neither enforcing foreign law nor applying English law to a transaction governed by foreign law. Finally, the plaintiffs claimed only damages and a declaration, so no question arose of the judge being asked to grant an injunction with extraterritorial effect.

Tyburn v. Doyle as an exercise of discretion

There is a final aspect to *Tyburn v. Doyle*[43] which does not depend on **6–148** the *Mocambique* rule (on any of its interpretations) and which perhaps provides the safest justification for the result on the facts of the case.[44]

[41] [1954] 1 W.L.R. 1313; [1954] 3 All E.R. 253 (Dankwerts J., QBD).

[42] Ricketson *The Law of Intellectual Property* (1984), para. 4.63 citing *Gramophone Co v. Leo Feist* (1928) 41 C.L.R. 1 (Full Court of the High Court of Australia). Even after the 1911 Act was repealed in the U.K. (by the Copyright Act 1956) it continued in force in Australia until repealed and replaced by the Copyright Act 1968 (Commonwealth).

[43] [1990] R.P.C. 185 (Vinelott J.).

[44] However, it cannot be said that *Tyburn v. Conan Doyle* was an application of *forum non conveniens*, because it was common ground that there was no alternative forum to England.

Quite apart for the fact that the defendant had not asserted any claim of right, so as to entitle the plaintiff to claim a declaration of non-liability, there was no reason to suppose that any declaratory judgment would benefit the plaintiffs in the United States, which was the only place where it would matter:

> "In the instant case there is no evidence that, if the validity of the rights claimed were justiciable in the English courts, the decision of the English courts would be treated as binding on any of the states of the United States of America and it would in my judgment be an exercise in futility to allow these claims, which raise complex issues which may require a survey by the English courts with the assistance of experts of the laws of each of the states of the United States of America, to continue."

6–149   The editors of *Cheshire and North's Private International Law*[45] agree that this is the best justification for *Tyburn v. Conan Doyle*, rather than Vinelott J.'s attempt to apply the distinction between local and transitory actions:

> "This misunderstands the *Moçambique Case*, which was decided on a point of substance and not on the basis of a procedural distinction between *local* and *transitory* actions. The point of substance related to whether an English court could give an effective judgment. This too concerned Vinelott J. He concluded that, even if the action was justiciable in England, it would be an exercise in futility to allow the claims sought, since there was no evidence that any decision by an English court would be treated as binding in the United States. This provides a much better basis for the decision."

6–150   It is particularly interesting that the passage from Vinelott J.'s judgment necessarily contemplates a departure of some sort from the double actionability rule of *Phillips v. Eyre*,[46] since there would be no need to investigate American state law at all if the total absence of copyright protection for *Sherlock Holmes* in the United Kingdom would have caused the defendant's case to fail under the first limb of *Phillips v. Eyre*. The American courts could quite legitimately ignore an English declaratory judgment which purported to decide the case by applying American Federal or State law; but they would certainly refuse to recognise one which treated them as if they were still British colonies. Any declaration would be doubly futile if it purported to apply English law to conclude that the defendant had no cause of action in America.

6–151   The old case of *Morocco Bound Syndicate v. Harris*[47] is also probably best explained in terms of a discretionary refusal to grant equitable relief

---

[45] (12th, ed., 1992, by North and Fawcett), p. 263. This is also the view of Carter, *op. cit.*
[46] (1870) L.R. Q.B. 1.
[47] [1895] 1 Ch. 534 (Kekewich J.).

in circumstances where it would have been little better than futile. The plaintiffs were an English theatrical company with the exclusive European rights to a play. The defendants were another English company which was licensed to perform the play only in the English provinces. Despite that, the defendants announced their intention of performing it in Germany and other Continental countries, and left England on tour two days before the plaintiff's motion for an interlocutory injunction was heard. Germany was a member of the Berne Convention and there was expert evidence which the judge accepted that the defendants' performances would be actionable by the plaintiff in Germany.

Despite this Kekewich J. refused to grant an interlocutory injunction:

> "What I am asked to do is, not only to enforce the German law, but to enforce that law in Germany. . . . No doubt, it is part of the duty of an English court, in a proper case, to enforce German law—that is to say, enforce it in England; and the German courts will, similarly, enforce English law in Germany. But to enforce German law in Germany is no more a part of the duty or power of an English court than it is of a German court to enforce English law in England. If these defendants are not in England, they may set any such judgment at defiance, and unless they come to England there will be no means of enforcing it against them.
>
> Upon the grounds I have mentioned, I think that really I have no jurisdiction to grant an injunction, which is the only relief asked and the only thing which would be of any service to the plaintiffs."

Notwithstanding the troublesome use of the word "jurisdiction" there are some features of the judgment which imply that the case was one where the granting of an injunction was refused on essentially discretionary grounds. In the first place, the judge expressly agreed that it was part of the duty of an English court in a proper case to enforce German law in England, and *vice versa*. Secondly, he attached importance to the fact that the interlocutory injunction would be of no benefit to the plaintiffs because there was no way of enforcing it while the defendants were abroad. Why emphasise that the interlocutory injunction was the only relief asked for, if the court had no jurisdiction to grant any relief at all? Finally, it is interesting to note that despite the motion being dismissed the order for costs was for costs in the action, suggesting that the judge considered that the application for the interlocutory injunction had been properly made and that the plaintiff's case was not hopeless. The defendants had, after all, only left the jurisdiction after being served with the notice of motion. Although these indications are not conclusive, taken together they suggest that an interlocutory injunction against infringing the German copyrights might have been granted had the defendants still been in England and within the effective reach of the court.

6–152

Threats actions

6–153   In view of the decision of Fullagar J. in *Norbert Steinhardt v. Meth*,[48] and the unmerited influence it has had in England, further consideration needs to be given to whether the statutory "threats" action is—or ought to be—governed by the *Mocambique* rule. The conclusion is that there is no reason in principle why the English courts should not entertain an action in England, in respect of an otherwise actionable threat communicated abroad. Section 70 of the Patents Act 1977 provides, so far as relevant:

> (1) Where a person (whether or not the proprietor of, or entitled to any right in, a patent) by circulars, advertisements or otherwise threatens another person with proceedings for any infringement of a patent, a person aggrieved by the threats (whether or not he is the person to whom the threats are made) may, subject to subsection (4) below, bring proceedings in the court against the person making the threats, claiming any relief mentioned in subsection (3) below.
>
> (2) In any such proceedings the plaintiff or pursuer shall, if he proves that the threats were so made and satisfies the court that he is a person aggrieved by them, be entitled to the relief claimed unless—
>
> > (a) the defendant or defender proves that the acts in respect of which proceedings were threatened constitute or, if done, would constitute an infringement of a patent; and
> >
> > (b) the patent alleged to be infringed is not shown by the plaintiff or pursuer to be invalid in a relevant respect.
>
> (3) The said relief is—
>
> > (a) a declaration or declarator to the effect that the threats are unjustifiable;
> >
> > (b) an injunction or interdict against the continuance of the threats; and
> >
> > (c) damages in respect of any loss which the plaintiff or pursuer has sustained by the threats.
> >
> > (. . .)

6–154   A threats action is typically brought by a manufacturer or supplier in respect of threats of patent infringement proceedings made to customers of his, in which case it most closely resembles the common-law actions for injurious falsehood, intimidation and interference with contract; the object of the defendant being to stop the customer dealing with the plaintiff and his weapons being the cost and uncertainty of litigation and the assertion that the plaintiff's goods infringe. In this respect the action may be regarded in a broad sense as one for unfair competition; and in legal systems with a general law of unfair competition such unjustified

---

[48] (1960) 105 C.L.R. 440 (Fullagar J., High Court of Australia).

threats may be actionable despite the absence of a specific law corresponding to section 70 of the Patents Act 1977. However, the action can also be brought by the plaintiff in respect of threats addressed to himself, even if he has not been damaged by them. In this case the threats action becomes little more than a useful procedural device to allow the alleged infringer to litigate the scope and validity of the patent without waiting to be sued by the patentee. Although the defendant can justify his conduct by proving infringement, the plaintiff's cause of action in no way depends on the defendant actually having specified a patent alleged to be infringed, or indeed on his having a patent at all. Vague but effective threats made by a defendant who has no rights to enforce are a classic example of the need for the provision and are expressly contemplated by the Act.

In *Norbert Steinhardt v. Meth* itself the plaintiff was an English **6–155** company which claimed that the American defendants had contravened the Australian Patents Act by threatening them with proceedings for infringement of an Australian patent. The threat in question was made by a letter posted in the United States to the plaintiff company in England which threatened infringement proceedings in various countries including Australia. One question was therefore whether the Australian statute had been violated by a threat communicated in England where the threat was to sue in Australia for infringement of an Australian patent.[49] Fullagar J. held that the threat was "made" where and when it was received, and on the authority of *Egg Fillers v. Holed-Tite*[50] decided without further consideration that the Australian Act had not been contravened. This was a matter of construction of the Australian Act, but as the *Egg Fillers* case was decided solely on the question of service out of the jurisdiction it did not compel this conclusion. The court in *Norbert Steinhard v. Meth* undoubtedly had jurisdiction over the American defendant on other grounds and did not need to rely on the threat in the letter to England in applying the local equivalent of RSC, Ord. 11.

In English law, it is still uncertain whether threats to sue for **6–156** infringement of a United Kingdom patent are actionable here if communicated abroad. As a matter of policy, this would be desirable since it would otherwise be simple to evade section 70 of the Patents Act 1977 whenever a threatening letter sent abroad could be relied on to do the same damage as one addressed to a recipient in the United Kingdom. This suggestion would recognise section 70 of the Patents Act 1977 as one creating a tort of "double locality" in which acts committed abroad were legitimately within the territorial jurisdiction of the Act because of their intended effects in the United Kingdom.[51]

---

[49] There was also a threat to a prospective Australian customer which raised none of these problems. The threats action and a counterclaim duly went to trial.

[50] (1934) 51 R.P.C. 9 (Bennett J.).

[51] Compare *ABKCO Music & Records v. Music Collection* [1995] R.P.C. 657, CA where the Court of Appeal interpreted the Copyright, Designs and Patents Act 1988, s. 16(2) as meaning that there could be liability when an act of infringement in the U.K. was authorised from abroad.

6–157   The first decision in point is *Egg Fillers v. Holed-Tite*[52] where an order for leave to serve notice of the writ outside the jurisdiction on American defendants was discharged. The only ground relied on by the plaintiff under RSC, Ord. 11 was that a tort had allegedly been committed in the jurisdiction, but although the pleaded threats expressly related to infringement of United Kingdom patents by the importation of eggs in infringing packaging from Australia, there was no evidence stating where the threats had been made. The decision expressly rested on the inadequacy of the plaintiffs' evidence on this point and is not inconsistent with the possibility of a tort having been committed which would have been actionable if the court had had jurisdiction over the defendant on some other ground.

6–158   In *Johnson Electric v. Maubuchi-Motor*[53] the parties were in competition to supply small electric motors to the Black and Decker group. The defendants wrote threatening letters to Black and Decker representatives in England, France and the United States all of which clearly amounted to threats in respect, *inter alia*, of alleged infringement of certain United Kingdom patents. Whitford J. granted the plaintiffs an interlocutory injunction and refused to strike out the allegations in the statement of claim in respect of the threats communicated abroad. *Egg Fillers v. Holed-Tite* was expressly distinguished on the ground that it had only decided that the plaintiff there was not entitled to leave to serve out of the jurisdiction. It is suggested that the absence of express reasoning in *Johnson Electric v. Maubuchi-Motor* is less fatal than the manifestly erroneous reasoning of *Norbert Steinhardt v. Meth*, and that as a matter of policy *Johnson Electric v. Maubuchi-Motor* is to be preferred. Jacob J. is also believed to have granted an interlocutory injunction (possibly *ex parte*) against threats uttered abroad in *Big Smith Global v. Caterpillar*,[54] but details are lacking.

The changing landscape of comity

6–159   Once it is accepted that the rule against the justiciability of actions on foreign intellectual property rights is based on a principle of international comity, rather than a fixed procedural distinction between local and transitory actions, the possibility arises that a future case may be decided differently, as circumstances change. As Vinelott J. himself observed.[55]

> "I should nonetheless be reluctant to decline to follow decisions of the High Court of Australia reached after very full argument unless I felt convinced that they do not reflect the law of England *or that circumstances have so changed as a result of social or economic developments* or statutory intervention that the rule should now be confined to actions in which title to land is in issue."

[52] (1934) 51 R.P.C. 9 (Bennett J.).
[53] [1986] F.S.R. 280 (Whitford J.).
[54] *The Lawyer* July 30th, 1996.
[55] *Tyburn v. Conan Doyle* [1990] R.P.C. 185, emphasis added.

The degree to which perceptions of comity can change is illustrated by **6–160** one of the minor issues in *Potter v. Broken Hill*[56] itself. It was argued for the plaintiffs that it was doubtful that an action could be brought in New South Wales at all against a company incorporated in and managed from Victoria[57] even though the company carried on business in the former state. Today, exclusive jurisdiction over the internal constitutional affairs of corporations is widely recognised but the proposition that a company could only be sued in tort in the courts of the place where it was incorporated would be regarded as absurd.[58] However, it may have had more substance in the first decade of the twentieth century when it was perhaps still open to argument that the allegedly infringing acts might be *ultra vires* the company.[59] To that extent, the internal constitutional affairs of the company and its relationship with third parties may have seemed interrelated to an extent impossible to imagine today.

In English law, patents and corporations both received special treat- **6–161** ment in the Statute of Monopolies, and for two centuries thereafter incorporated companies were typically created by Royal Charter just as patents for inventions were granted under the Royal Prerogative. The charter defined the powers, obligations and immunities of the company and might grant it monopoly rights, especially in relation to foreign trade.[60] As with the grant of patents, incorporation was such a rare event that each individual occurrence was of economic significance. In the course of the nineteenth century, both incorporation and the grant of patents came to be governed by statute rather than the Royal Prerogative, and from being discretionary and exceptional both became matters of legal entitlement and administrative routine. Today, the once exceptional nature of incorporation is reflected only in very attenuated form in Article 16(2) of the Brussels Convention which preserves the rule that the internal constitutional affairs of companies are a matter for the exclusive jurisdiction of the courts of the place of incorporation, and that may owe as much to the unharmonised state of company law as to considerations of international comity.

It might be said that in the last decade of the twentieth century, to **6–162** require a patent or other intellectual property right to be litigated only in the country of grant, is as anachronistic as it was, a century ago, to expect a company to be sued only in the state of its incorporation. In his memorandum on the Private International Law (Miscellaneous Provisions) Bill to the House of Lords Select Committee,[61] Professor

---

[56] (1906) 3 C.L.R. 479 (High Court of Australia) *affirming* [1905] V.L.R. 612.

[57] [1905] V.L.R. 612 at 621.

[58] In *Burland v. Broxburn Oil Co* (1889) 6 R.P.C. 482 (Chitty J.) leave was granted to serve a Scottish defendant with a writ for infringement of a trade mark in England, although the contrary proposition was treated as not unarguable.

[59] *Campbell v. Paddington Corp* [1911] 1 K.B. 869 shows that a defence of *ultra vires* was considered worth arguing as a defence to a claim for public nuisance as late at 1911.

[60] In *East India Co v. Sandys* (1684) 1 H.P.C. 81 the plaintiff was incorporated by letters patent of Charles II which conferred on them a monopoly in trade with the East Indies.

[61] In *Proceedings of the Special Public Bill Committee* HL Paper 36 (1995), evidence, p. 64.

Cornish identified a number of policy reasons for admitting actions in the United Kingdom for acts committed in another country, alleged to be in infringement of that country's intellectual property laws: the increasing international trade in goods, services and information protected by intellectual property; progress in agreeing world wide minimum standards of intellectual property protection, and in particular TRIPs; the problem of international counterfeiters with no fixed place of establishment; the Brussels Convention; and the example set by the courts of the Netherlands.

Whether one looks at specific rights, the field of intellectual property as a whole, or at tendencies in the general law, there does seem to be a movement towards greater internationalisation and away from the territoriality principle in several of its manifestations. However, while this may be the direction of the trend it is equally clear that there is as yet no consensus at either the national, European or worldwide level that foreign intellectual property rights in general should be justiciable in the courts of another state. English judges invited to adjudicate on foreign intellectual property rights have declined to do so, or have done so with undisguised reluctance and only when compelled to do so by specific legislation. The *Mocambique* rule has been abolished in relation to foreign land where title is not in issue, but the abolition does not extend to intellectual property rights.[62] The Brussels Convention allows infringement actions on foreign intellectual property rights, but preserves, to an undetermined extent, exclusive jurisdiction over their validity. The European Community may have been given, by the Court of Justice, a general power to legislate for intellectual property which it did not imagine it possessed 30 years ago; but it has been slow to exercise it. Finally, the contracting states to TRIPs have accepted among themselves unprecedented obligations to harmonise their substantive intellectual property laws, but with nothing to displace the assumption that enforcement would continue to be on a territorial basis.

F. BREACH OF CONFIDENCE; *SPYCATCHER*

Breach of Confidence and the Private International Law Act 1995

6–163   The one aspect of intellectual property to which neither the *Mocambique* rule[63] not the Private International Law (Miscellaneous Provisions) Act 1995 applies is breach of confidence, which is not

---

[62] One may criticise *Tyburn v. Conan Doyle* and subsequent cases for their conservatism or for over-literal statutory interpretation, but their view of the law was implicitly confirmed when the Private International Law (Miscellaneous Provisions) Act 1995 failed to take the opportunity to amend s.30 of the Civil Jurisdiction and Judgments Act 1982 to apply it to intellectual property, as was suggested by Professor Cornish in his evidence to the House of Lords. In any event, an analogy with s. 30 of the 1982 Act would preserve the *Mocambique* rule whenever validity, title or subsistence was a central issue, which would be in practically every case.

[63] *Compania do Mocambique v. British South Africa Co* [1893] A.C. 602, H.L.

characterised as a tort in English law.[64] Section 9(2) of the 1995 Act provides: "The characterisation for the purposes of private international law of issues arising in a claim as issues relating to tort or delict is a matter for the courts of the forum." At first sight, this states the obvious and begs the question of which body of law the courts of the forum are to apply in characterising the claim: is it English (or Scottish) law, or do they apply the putative applicable law, under which liability for breach of confidence might conceivably be tortious? The legislative history confirms that foreign law has no application until the process of characterisation has been carried out. As the Lord Chancellor, Lord Mackay of Clashfern, said in Committee[65]:

"So far as the phrase 'for the purposes of private international law' is concerned, that clearly means the private international law of England, if it is the English court, or Scotland, if it is the Scottish court, and it is characterisation for that purpose that is in issue. That was certainly one of the difficulties that people found in the evidence about the clause as presently drafted. So it is not intended to have a vague, general reference to some body of law which is not distinct. It is our law about how these matters are characterised and putting into that law the rules of this part so far as the choosing is concerned. The characterisation will remain according to our rules of private international law."

It follows that the common law continues to apply to actions for breach of confidence unaffected by the 1995 Act, but the private international law of confidentiality is itself so undeveloped as to be almost totally indeterminate.

Spycatcher and the choice of law

To all intents and purposes, the issue of which system of law applies to **6–164** a breach of confidence with an international element is *res integra* in England and the common law world.[65a] *Union Carbide v. Naturin*[66] decided that it was at least arguable that it is actionable to import goods produced abroad in breach of confidence, but is best regarded as a matter of substantive English domestic law rather than private international law. The *Spycatcher* litigation in England, Scotland, Australia,

---

[64] *Kitechnology BV v. Unicor GmbH* [1995] F.S.R. 763; [1994] I.L.Pr. 568, C.A.

[65] *Official Report of the Committee on the Private International Law (Miscellaneous Provisions) Bill [HL]* Wednesday March 1 1995, col. 13. Again, it cannot be said that this passage is within the rule of *Pepper v. Hart*, although it clarifies the purpose of the Act. *Contra* Morse, "Torts in Private International Law: a New Statutory Framework" (1996) 45 I.C.L.Q. 888, who prefers the approach rejected by the Lord Chancellor.

[65a] See White, "Equitable Obligations in Private International Law: the Choice of Law" (1986) 11 *Sydney Law Rev.* 92 and Barnard, "Choice of Law and Equitable Wrongs: a Comparative Analysis" (1992) 51 C.L.J. 474, both of which consider the problem of breach of confidence in its wider context. Barnard includes a broader review of *Spycatcher* than is given here, and makes recommendations which are generally to be endorsed, see below.

[66] [1987] F.S.R. 538, CA. Followed in *Beecham v. Norton Healthcare* [1997] F.S.R. 81.

New Zealand and Hong Kong might have provided many opportunities for issues of private international law to arise, but for the most part they were allowed to go by default. This is perhaps not surprising, since the underlying equitable obligation of confidence is very similar in all common law jurisdictions. It was the application of that law to publications by members of the British security services which was controversial, whichever body of law one chose. The issue of enforcement of a foreign public law received much more prominence, but is logically separate to that of choice of law. Problems of choice of law cannot be avoided whenever there are two or more candidate legal systems, but it is hardly to be expected that the public law defence would arise in a typical commercial or private breach of confidence case.

6–165   The relevant facts for present purposes were that Peter Wright had worked for the British security services and on his retirement had emigrated to Australia where he wrote a book, *Spycatcher*, based on his personal experiences and incorporating information regarded by the United Kingdom Government as highly confidential.[67] The Attorney General sued Wright and his intended Australian publishers in the New South Wales Supreme Court before *Spycatcher* was published anywhere and was given undertakings pending trial. Before the Australian trial, the *Guardian* and *Observer* published in England articles on some of the allegations that *Spycatcher* was said to be likely to contain when published, though they denied having any access to the book or having received any material from the defendants in the Australian proceedings. The Australian action was dismissed, but the undertakings remained in force pending an appeal to the Court of Appeal of New South Wales. Articles in other newspapers appeared after the first instance New South Wales judgment and in the case of the *Independent*, the newspaper claimed to have had access to a manuscript copy of the book. *Spycatcher* was published in full in America, and two days before American publication the *Sunday Times* published the first of an intended series of extracts published under licence from Wright's Australian publishers but actually taken from a copy of the manuscript specially obtained by the *Sunday Times* in America. The Attorney General's appeal to the Court of Appeal of New South Wales failed, and at that point the undertakings lapsed. A final appeal to the High Court of Australia was also unsuccessful.

Spycatcher in Australia

6–166   In Australia, issues of choice of law were raised expressly in the Court of Appeal of New South Wales[68] and the High Court of Australia[69] but with inconclusive and inconsistent results. In the Supreme Court of New South Wales no consideration was given to choice of law. In the Court of

---

[67] In the English cases, it seems to have been taken for granted that writing *Spycatcher* as such amounted to a breach of confidence, independently of publication anywhere.
[68] [1989] 2 F.S.R. 349.
[69] [1989] 2 F.S.R. 631.

Appeal Kirby P. favoured applying the *lex fori* as such, but only in an *obiter dictum*: "as equity acts *in personam*, and as Wright has submitted to this jurisdiction, it would seem appropriate to apply here the law of this state. Nothing significant seems to turn on this point." McHugh J.A. dealt expressly with choice of law, but also came to the conclusion that it did not matter whether English or New South Wales[70] law governed. New South Wales law would not impose any higher standard of liability than English law, and under either system the plaintiff would have to prove that publication would be contrary to the public interest of the United Kingdom. *Obiter*, McHugh J.A. criticised the mechanical application of the *lex fori*. The judgment of Street C.J. is the least relevant for present purposes. Not only did he dissent, but he treated the right sought to be enforced by the United Kingdom Government as *sui generis* rather than as sounding in either contract or equity,[71] and would have invented a double actionability test rather similar to that in tort but with the *lex fori* playing a subordinate role.

In the High Court of Australia the majority dismissed the Attorney **6–167** General's appeal as being in substance an attempt to enforce the public law or policy of a foreign state, without expressly considering choice of law issues. The minority concurring judgment of Brennan J.[72] is more interesting. He would have regarded the Attorney General as relying on obligations validly arising under English law, but which the Australian courts would refuse to enforce as a matter of Australian public policy. Brennan J. identified as the "governing principle" of the case:

> "I have no doubt that, in the absence of a contrary statutory provision, an Australian court should refuse to enforce an obligation of confidence in an action brought for the purpose of protecting the intelligence secrets and confidential political information of a foreign government. I would identify this as the governing principle which applies whatever government might invoke the jurisdiction of the court and whatever be the source of the obligation of confidence which the government seeks to enforce."

And he went on to distinguish this from the source of the obligation of **6–168** confidence:

> "An obligation of confidence of the kind in issue in this case is likely to arise under the law of the plaintiff foreign state. In this case it was said that the obligation of confidence arose under the law of the United Kingdom, and that may well be so. Although the system of law which gives rise to the obligation of confidence is ultimately immaterial to the application of the governing principle[73] by an

---

[70] It is convenient to refer to Australian law, but strictly it was the law of New South Wales rather than that of the Commonwealth which was relevant.

[71] A right "not based on doctrines of contract or equity. It is a right of a different character . . ."

[72] [1989] 2 F.S.R. 644.

[73] Set out, above.

Australian court, the law which determines a domestic court's approach to the enforcement of obligations arising under foreign law is both consistent with and illustrative of the principle.

At the outset, a distinction can be drawn between two bases on which the court might refuse to enforce such an obligation of confidence though it is an obligation recognised by foreign law. The first basis is that it would be contrary to the public policy of the forum state to enforce the obligation; the second is that the court denies the capacity in international law of the relevant provision of the foreign law to give rise to the obligation sought to be enforced. The distinction is between a refusal to enforce what is recognised as an existing obligation and a denial of the existence of the obligation sought to be enforced. Sometimes the first basis is expressed as a rule that foreign laws offensive to the policy of the domestic law will not be enforced, domestic public policy prevailing over the offensive foreign law. [. . .]

Where the court refuses to enforce an obligation on the first basis, the court accepts the capacity of the foreign law to give rise to a legal obligation but declines to enforce the obligation inconsistently with the public policy of the domestic law. [. . .]

The second basis, unlike the first, denies the capacity of foreign law to govern the transaction which gives rise to the claimed obligation. Examples may be found in cases which refuse recognition of the efficacy of foreign laws which expropriate property situated outside the territory of the foreign country: see the cases reviewed by Lord Denning M.R. in *Attorney General (N.Z.) v. Ortiz.*

The first basis is material to the present case; the second is not. The problem is not whether the law of the United Kingdom gives rise to an obligation of confidence but whether the effect of applying the law which gives rise to the obligation would be inconsistent with the exigencies of public policy under the law of New South Wales."

It is implicit in this analysis that in a typical trade secret case, for instance, there would be nothing to prevent an Australian court enforcing obligations of confidence arising under English law, since this would not involve the direct or indirect enforcement of a foreign public law.

Spycatcher in England

6–169   The English litigation never addressed the issue of choice of law, it being assumed throughout that English law alone governed the liability of the defendants, principally English newspapers and their editors, in the various English proceedings.[74] Peter Wright himself was not a party to any of the English actions. Although issues of choice of law were never expressly addressed, any of the following rules would be consistent

---

[74] [1989] 2 F.S.R. *passim.*

with the way questions of liability were treated: (1) English law was applied by virtue of the presumption that it corresponds to the relevant foreign law. This seems the most plausible reason as the law of breach of confidence does not differ significantly in the various common law jurisdictions; (2) English law governed as the *lex fori*, regardless of any other connecting factors; (3) Wright's obligation of confidence to the Crown was governed by English law, which therefore governed the obligations of newspapers, etc., publishing information (allegedly) taken from *Spycatcher* with notice of the Crown's claim to confidence in it. This would not necessarily depend on Wright's own breach being governed by English law, though that is likely, nor would it depend on the newspapers acting in concert with Wright or on his authority; (4) unspecified connecting factors resulted in the obligations of the newspapers being governed by English law, regardless of the law governing the original relationship of confidence between the Crown and Wright.

Breach of confidence: the options for choice of law

In *Spycatcher*, the only systems of law canvassed in any jurisdiction **6–170** were English law as the law governing the confidential relationship between Wright and the Crown, and the *lex fori* whether that was English, Australian or New Zealand law. *A priori*, one ought not to assume that a single system of law need govern all the defendants in the various actions, or even all the issues in a single action. Three or perhaps four categories of defendants fall to be considered: Wright personally and those who had direct or indirect access to *Spycatcher* with his permission, such as his Australian and American publishers and the *Sunday Times*; those such as the *Independent* who claimed to have had access to *Spycatcher*, but in uncertain circumstances and possibly without Wright's authority; and those such as the *Observer* and the *Guardian* who published substantially the same allegedly confidential information as was in *Spycatcher*, but without deriving it from Wright. Issues which might at least in theory be subject to *depecage* are the existence and nature of the obligation of confidence, questions of breach and liability, the defences of public interest and iniquity, and the appropriateness of discretionary relief. There is also the question of whether to prefer a rule which leads to the application of a single system of law for the whole World or one which deals with liability for breach on a country by country basis.

With those reservations in mind, it is tentatively suggested that in the **6–171** present uncertain state of the law there are two credible rules for choice of law in breach of confidence cases and two which need to be mentioned, if only to be dismissed. They may be identified as the centre of gravity of the obligation, the tort analogy, the centre of gravity of the breach and the application of the *lex fori*.

The latter two may be dismissed for different reasons. The application **6–172** of the *lex fori*, is one hopes, altogether too self-centred to be credible as a rule of private international law today. The centre of gravity of the breach might at first sight be more attractive, although in practice it is quite likely to correspond to the *lex fori* because in the absence of a worldwide regime for recognition and enforcement of judgments, that is where litigation is most likely to be brought. However, the nature of breach of confidence means that the person in breach can very often determine for himself where the centre of gravity of the breach will be, and he could therefore take advantage of immunity under one system of law to legitimate the breach entirely. It may stick in the throat to say that nothing effective can be done about a traitor who defects and sells state secrets to the Russians, but that is no reason for saying that his legal liability in England and everywhere else in the world should be determined according to Russian law.

6–173   Of the other two possibilities, the centre of gravity of the obligation of confidence is the more attractive in respect of claims against the party to whom the confidential information was originally entrusted. Barnard's[75] recommendation is that:

> "As access to confidential information or to property for a specific purpose gives rise to the equitable relationship, and as this in turn gives rise to an equitable obligation and determines its scope, the law under which that access is gained should determine the existence of the equitable relationship and the scope of any obligations arising from it. Thus, the law under which access is gained will be the legal system which has the closest and most real connection with the equitable obligation, and should be recognised as its proper law and govern the existence, performance and breach of any fiduciary duties or equitable duties of confidence.
>
> A fiduciary or confidant may, of course, gain access to more than one specific piece of property or information in the course of the relationship; but the important question is where the initial access founding the opportunity for subsequent specific access was gained. So, where access has been gained under a contract of agency or employment, the proper law of that contract should determine all the agent's or employee's rights and duties in respect of the principal's property, including the scope of any equitable obligations. Where access has been gained by holding a corporate office, the law governing the acceptance of office should govern; in a partnership, the proper law of the partnership contract; and so on. Where access has not been gained by entry into a legal relationship—for example, where trade secrets have been obtained by industrial espionage—the law of the place where access is, in fact, obtained, should govern as a general rule. An exception may exist in those instances where the place of access is fortuitous, and on that account has a less significant connection with the claim. In such a case, it may be justifiable to depart from the primary focus on access, and to apply instead the parties' common personal law, if any.

[75] "Choice of Law and Equitable Wrongs: a Comparative Analysis" (1992) C.L.J. 474.

It is submitted that an approach referring issues of equitable wrong to the proper law of the obligation, to be identified on the basis of the above considerations, is consistent with the approach adopted in other areas of obligation, reflects the policies informing the area of equitable obligations, accommodates as far as possible the ideal of international uniformity in its practical outcome, produces results that are both effective and just, and is both flexible and sufficiently predictable."

The proposed rule has the further practical advantage that the law so identified will generally correspond to the applicable law of any contractual obligations,[76] so that where contractual and equitable obligations arise together—as happens quite often—they will be governed by the same single system of law. It will also normally result in any restitutionary claim being governed by the same system of law as the claim to an injunction, which is generally the more important head of relief. **6–174**

The final possibility, now that England has a private international law of tort for which it need not be embarrassed, is to apply the latter by analogy; though one problem is that the Private International Law (Miscellaneous Provisions) Act 1995 assigns the question of characterisation to the law—or at least to the courts—of the forum,[77] and breach of confidence is not characterised as a tort in English domestic law.[78] However, as against third party recipients of confidential information, it is suggested that the centre of gravity of the original obligation of confidence is irrelevant—they were not parties to it and might not even know about it—and that the tort analogy provides the better choice of law rule.[79] Against a third party recipient the tort analogy would lead to the application of English law alone (except as to any incidental questions) in so far as the breach of confidence for which the third party was alleged to be liable substantially occurred in England, and the *lex loci delicti commissi* would apply on a country-by-country basis in so far as the breaches occurred abroad. **6–175**

This would be consistent with the decision of the House of Lords in *Mustad v. Dosen*[80] in which the English defendants were the innocent and unknowing recipients of an alleged trade secret relating to the design of a machine for manufacturing fish hooks, communicated to them by Dosen, a former employee of the plaintiffs' predecessors in business. Details of the machine had been published by the plaintiffs in a patent application; and the decision of the House of Lords that what is **6–176**

---

[76] See *A-G v. Barker* [1990] 3 All E.R. 257.

[77] See para. 6–163, above.

[78] Of course, if the wrongful act takes place in the jurisdiction (as in *Mustad v. Dosen*, below) then English law would apply as the *lex loci delicti commissi* and the relevance of foreign law would be confined to incidental questions.

[79] According to one's point of view, the tort analogy may also be preferred to the centre of gravity of the obligation, even as against the original confidant. It depends on whether the predominant connecting factor is considered to be the obligation, or the breach and the damage caused by it.

[80] (1928) [1963] R.P.C. 41, HL.

published to the world in a patent specification, cannot be the subject matter of an action for breach of confidence, has always been regarded as an authoritative statement of English, rather than Norwegian, law. Conversely, the question of whether Dosen had been relieved of his obligations of confidence on the insolvency of his former employers (as he had been advised by competent Norwegian lawyers) seems to have been regarded as irrelevant.

6–177   This rule again has the advantage of consistency in analysis when the original confidant was under contractual as well as equitable obligations of confidence. A third party who knowingly receives confidential information cannot be liable in contract because of lack of privity, but he may be liable in tort for inducing a breach of contract. If his equitable liability is to be determined according to the same rules for choice of law as any liability in tort, then another desirable simplification will have been achieved.

THE PRIVATE INTERNATIONAL LAW OF INTELLECTUAL PROPERTY CONTRACTS

A. INTELLECTUAL PROPERTY CONTRACTS: GENERAL PRINCIPLES

Scope of the chapter

7–01   The present chapter is principally concerned with the issues of private international law which may arise when dealings with intellectual property rights have an international element. It assumes that an intellectual property right is already in existence, and does not in general address issues of initial ownership or entitlement. However, subsequent devolution of intellectual property rights is within the scope of the chapter, especially in the context of proving or getting in title for litigation or raising a defence.[1]

---

[1] See Ulmer, *Intellectual Property Rights and the Conflict of Laws* (1978). For the general private international law of contracts see Dicey and Morris, *The Conflict of Laws* (12th ed., 1993); Cheshire and North's *Private International Law* (12th ed., 1992). See also Meinhardt, "Conflict Avoidance in the Law of Patents and Trade Marks" (1956) 21 *Law and Contemporary Problems* 533; Plaisant, "The Exploitation of the Copyright and the

The Rome Convention and the Contracts (Applicable Law) Act 1990

For contracts made after April 1st, 1991, issues of private international **7–02** law are governed by the E.C. Convention on the Law Applicable to Contractual Obligations (the Rome Convention) which has the force of law in the United Kingdom by virtue of the Contracts (Applicable Law) Act 1990, s. 2. Whenever an English court has to decide the applicable law of a contract made after this date, even as an incidental matter, it must do so in accordance with the Rome Convention. Unlike the Brussels Convention, for example, the Rome Convention applies in full whether or not there is any connection at all with a member state of the European Communities, and for most purposes the old common law rules for choice of law in contract are wholly superseded. There are some issues and categories of contractual obligation to which the Rome Convention expressly does not apply, but contracts relating to intellectual property are not among them.[2]

The English and Continental approaches to choice of law in contract

The English approach to the proper law of a contract has historically **7–03** been to regard the parties' choice of law as determinative,[3] whether express or implied,[4] and in the absence of an express or implicit choice of proper law to identify the system of law with which the contract has the closest and most real connection.[5] This is done on a typically pragmatic basis by evaluating all the surrounding circumstances, without any predetermined hierarchy of importance being applied to the various connecting factors which might be relevant. *A fortiori*, the common law has never sought to identify one specific connecting factor which would be determinative of the proper law on its own. In English common law the proper law of a contract relating to intellectual property was

Conflict of Laws" (1962) 35 R.I.D.A. 62; Nimmer, "Who is the Copyright Owner When Laws Conflict" (1974) 5 I.I.C. 62; Finnegan, Irving and Stahl, "A Three-Country Conundrum in Conflict of Laws: What Law Governs when Ownership of a United States Patent is at Issue" [1979] *Annual of Industrial Property Law* 422; Modiano, "International Patent Licensing Agreements and Conflict of Laws" (1980) 2 *Northwestern Journal of International Law and Business* 11; Beier, "Conflict of Law Problems of Trademark License Agreements" (1982) I.I.C. 162; Kloss, "Copyrights and the Conflict of Laws" [1985] E.I.P.R. 15; Geller, "Harmonising Copyright Conflict Analyses" [1989] *Copyright* 49; Richards, "Ownership of Copyright: Some International Thoughts" (1989) 133 Sol.J. 1247; Stone, "Problems of International Film Distribution: Assignment and Licensing of Copyright and the Conflict of Laws" [1996] Ent. L.R. 62; Kurz, "Rechtswahl, Wahl des Gerichtsstands und Schiedgerichtsvereinbarungen in internationalen Technologielizen-vertragen" [1997] *Mitteilungen der deutchen Patentanwälte* 345.

[2] For the Rome Convention in general see Dicey and Morris, *op. cit.*; Cheshire and North, *op. cit.*; North, ed., *Contract Conflicts* (1982); Plender, *The European Contracts Convention* (1991); Kaye, *The New Private International Law of Contract of the European Community* (1993). See paras 7–16 *et seq.*

[3] *Vita Food Products Inc v. Unus Shipping Co* [1939] A.C 277, PC.

[4] *Amin Rasheed Shipping Corp. v. Kuwait Insurance Co* [1984] A.C. 50, HL.

[5] *Bonython v. Commonwealth of Australia* [1951] A.C. 201, PC; *Amin Rasheed Shipping Corp. v. Kuwait Insurance Co* [1984] A.C. 50 (Lord Wilberforce, HL).

determined according to the same principles as for any other contract.[6] If the parties had chosen a governing law then in the absence of compelling reasons of public policy that law would apply. If the parties had not made an express choice of law then the court had to ascertain the proper law of the contract on the basis of connecting factors with the various legal systems which might have been within the parties' contemplation. The country of the intellectual property right, if only one was involved, was clearly one relevant factor but there was no reason to treat it as conclusive.

7–04   By way of contrast, it has sometimes been suggested, and particularly by some Continental academic writers, that there should be a rigid set of rules for ascertaining the proper law of a contract relating to an intellectual property right in the absence of express choice, and in particular that the proper law of the contract should be the law of the protecting state in question.[7] This approach does not accord with English law or with the Rome Convention,[8] and its attractions are illusory. At first sight, it would apparently be an advantage for the proper law of an intellectual property agreement to be the same as that governing the creation, registration and enforcement of the right, but this is to ignore how contracts are used in reality. In the first place, contracts frequently cover more than one country, even the whole world, so that the rule could at best only be applicable to the case of a contract for only one country. Even in such cases the parties may well be assumed to prefer to have the contract governed, so far as they may, by a convenient and familiar system of law rather than by the possibly very unfamiliar contract law of the protecting state in question. It is not unknown for the licence territory to be defined without precision; and it is quite common for the territory to vary with time and to depend on supervening events, such as the grant, refusal or revocation of individual intellectual property rights, the exercise of options, or partial termination by either party.[9] What starts off as a licence of a recent United Kingdom patent application may turn into one for the whole world, perhaps even except for the United Kingdom itself if the parent application is refused.

7–05   Even where only one country is involved the rule proves unworkable in a number of atypical but commercially important cases. In the United States and the United Kingdom there is no unique system of contract law to associate with intellectual property rights created under national

---

[6] See paras 7–60 *et seq.*, below.

[7] See Ulmer, *Intellectual Property Rights and the Conflict of Laws*, paras 74 (copyright) and 145 (industrial property rights) and the sources therein cited. See also Cohen Jehoram, *Copyright Conflicts* (1977) for a comparative account of party autonomy in copyright law. Copyright aside, the principle of freedom of choice is generally accepted even by those who favour the mechanical application of rules to identify the proper or applicable law in the absence of choice.

[8] But the authors who favour the test of a single "decisive factor" may have won half a victory with the doctrine of "characteristic performance" under Art. 4(2) of the Rome Convention.

[9] Modiano, "International Patent Licensing Agreements and Conflict of Laws" (1980) 2 *Northwestern Journal of International Law and Business* 11 criticising Ulmer's proposed rule as to formal validity (Art. K(c), p. 101, *op. cit.*).

legislation. A contract relating to a United Kingdom patent, trade mark or copyright cannot be governed by United Kingdom contract law because there is no such thing, and English, Scottish or Northern Irish law might apply. Likewise in the United States all patents and copyrights, and the more important registered trade marks, exist under Federal law, but general contract law is the preserve of the individual states. Attempting to assign a proper law to a contract relating to an American patent, for instance, would still leave one with 50 different legal systems to choose from. Finally, truly international intellectual rights are already in existence in which a single and unitary right exists and is enforceable in several states. Again, there is no single body of contract law to be naturally associated with such a right. The Benelux trade mark is one existing example, and Community trade marks, designs and perhaps patents will follow.[10]

The Rome Convention tends more towards the common law approach, especially in its explicit acceptance of the parties' generally unrestricted freedom of choice of applicable law.[11] However, the Convention departs from the common law in trying to identify a single determinative connecting factor in the form of the "characteristic performance" of the contract, rather than providing in the first instance for all the individual connecting factors to be evaluated and given appropriate weights.[12] This otherwise unfamiliar concept derives from Swiss law. It assumes that there is generally a single characteristic obligation under the contract, other than the payment of money. English courts might well try to rely on Article 4(5) to excuse them from even attempting to identify the characteristic performance; some Continental courts might be happier with the concept. The Rome Convention is also at variance with the common law in allowing the "mandatory rules" of a country other than the forum to override the applicable law, in a sort of compulsory *depecage*. This particular set of provisions has not been fully implemented in the United Kingdom.[13]   7–06

The law of the protecting state

The applicable law of the contract, however, is not the only governing law. The inherent properties of an intellectual property right are defined by the system of law under which it exists. That system of law may provide, for instance, that the right is indivisible, incapable of being licensed, or even incapable of assignment.[14] In this respect one may have to consider not only the applicable law of the contract, but also the law governing each of the rights affected. There is, therefore, a two-stage approach: one must look at the applicable law of the contract to see   7–07

---

[10] For Community patents and trade marks as objects of property see para. 5–25.
[11] Art. 3, entitled "Freedom of Choice."
[12] Rome Convention, Art. 4(2).
[13] Art. 7(1) excluded by s. 2(2) of the Contracts (Applicable Law) Act 1990.
[14] See generally Ulmer, *Intellectual Property Rights and the Conflict of Laws*, paras 68 *et seq.* (copyright) and 141 (industrial property rights).

what the intent of the parties was, but one must also look at the law governing each of the rights in issue to see to what extent that intention can be put into practice for that particular right. This two-stage approach applies equally under the Rome Convention and at common law.

7–08   Problems arise when one has to deal with a rule of foreign law which cannot be characterised as an inherent attribute of the right, and which is at variance with English law (or whatever the proper or applicable law may be) as the applicable law of a contract relating to the right. Unless the purported transaction is so outrageous that English public policy overrides the proper law, there seems to be no mechanism to give effect in England to foreign legislation relating to the disposition of the right, no matter how reasonable or justifiable it may be. In *Apple Corps v. Apple Computer*[15] Hoffmann J. had to deal with an argument that a worldwide contractual no-challenge clause in a trade mark delimitation agreement expressly governed by English law and with an English exclusive jurisdiction clause was contrary to the law of various states where the ban was sought to be enforced. The issue dealt with in *Apple Corps v. Apple Computer* is not identical to that stated above, since it did not concern a purported disposition of intellectual property rights and the Rome Convention did not apply, but the reception of the argument would probably be the same.

> "Mr. Carr[16] invited me to construct a new rule of the English conflict of laws which would give effect to the putative foreign rules of unenforceability, despite the express choice of English law in the contract. This could be done, he said, by characterising the right to bring cancellation proceedings or file oppositions as aspects of the defensibility of a trade mark arising under the trade mark law of the foreign country, so that the question of whether such rights could be surrendered was intrinsic to the marks, rather like the question of whether property was assignable, and so was governed by the law creating the trade marks rather than the proper law of the contract. Alternatively, he suggested that recent cases, like *The Hollandia* [1983] A.C. 565, showed that English courts paid less respect than formerly to express choice of law clauses and that the validity of a 'no challenge' clause was so closely connected with the jurisdiction of the relevant trade mark that the question of its validity should, notwithstanding the express choice, be governed by the law of that jurisdiction. In the further alternative, he said that if neither of these routes was possible, the English court should acknowledge the paramount interest of the foreign country by declining jurisdiction to grant an injunction to enforce a 'no challenge' clause in respect of its trade marks.
>
> All these propositions are, to a greater or lesser extent, revolutionary. I admire the fertility of imagination with which they were

---

[15] [1992] R.P.C. 70 (Hoffmann J.). Subsequent proceedings [1991] 3 C.M.L.R. 49, CA; [1992] F.S.R. 431 (Ferris J.).

[16] Christopher Carr Q.C. for the defendants.

produced and I am far from saying that they are unarguable. But it would, in my judgment, be quite inappropriate to pronounce upon them at this stage, particularly when their factual foundation—the state of the foreign laws as to 'no challenge' agreement being a question of fact—is very much in dispute."

Just as the legitimacy of no-challenge clauses may differ from state to **7–09** state, so the individual countries whose laws created the right or rights the subject of a contract may have attached restrictions to the free disposal of those rights which in their view at least ought not to be circumvented by the express or implicit choice of another system of law to govern the contract. This is the issue of whether the "mandatory rules" of the country of protection can override the applicable law of the contract. Since the United Kingdom, unlike most of the other signatories to the Rome Convention, has chosen not to implement Article 7(1), the answer seems to be that to the extent that a restriction on free disposal is characterised as a "mandatory rule" rather than as an inherent attribute of the right, then unless it is for the protection of employees or consumers[17] the United Kingdom courts can and perhaps must ignore it if it conflicts with the applicable law.[18] Whether another country's mandatory rules can really be overridden by the applicable law in this way is another matter, since intellectual property rights are useful only to the extent that they can be enforced, and when it comes to enforcing them in the courts of the protecting state those courts are bound to insist, if they can, that their own mandatory rules should have been complied with.[19]

Law and equity

The importance of the law of the protecting state is, in practice, **7–10** further diminished by the fact that under English law it is possible for legal rights and equitable interests to be separated. A problem which frequently arises in practice is that the intent of the parties is clear enough, but that through ignorance of foreign law, failure to comply with formalities or for some other reason they have attempted a transaction which is ineffective or prohibited under the law governing the right. In this case, English law can recognise that the legal title to the right is unaffected, but can, if appropriate, regard the transferee as having an equitable interest in it corresponding as closely as possible to that which the parties intended to create. For example, a purported transfer of an intellectual property right which is defective in form may be treated as a

---

[17] Rome Convention, Arts 6(1) and 5(2) respectively.
[18] Art. 3(3) is unlikely to apply since the foreign nature of the intellectual property right would be a relevant connection with another country. Art. 9(6) does bind the United Kingdom but it only applies to mandatory requirements *as to form* in contracts relating to immovable property. See paras 7–32 and 7–85. It is far from certain that intellectual property is immovable property in the sense of the Convention and in any event other types of mandatory requirements are not affected.
[19] See para. 7–96.

valid and enforceable agreement to assign in due form if required, or if the assignment is altogether impossible on the terms intended it may be given effect as an equitable exclusive licence.[20] The same principle applies in a purely domestic context.[21]

7–11   As between the parties to the transaction the intervention of equity to give effect to their intentions may produce an acceptable result. However the position of the purely equitable assignee or licensee is not entirely satisfactory. His equitable interest is liable to be defeated at any time by a conflicting claim by a bona fide purchaser without notice. If obliged to enforce his rights against third parties in infringement proceedings he would probably have no *locus standi* at all in foreign countries without a doctrine of equity on the English model, and even in common law countries would be well advised to get in the legal title if it could still be found.

7–12   There are two more respects in which the position of the equitable rightholder is uncertain. If the foreign right in question is the subject of a legal code for registration and priority of interests and transactions then it is submitted that the English courts should give effect to that code even if it meant the equitable interest being defeated by a later transaction which was not in favour of a bona fide purchaser for value without notice. Secondly, restrictions on the transfer of rights which at first sight appear to be purely formal may exist for substantial reasons which equity ought not to subvert. For example, requirements for an agreement to be in writing, to be notarised, or to be in a special form may be intended to impress upon the weaker party the seriousness of the transaction and protect him from exploitation. If so, the intended transaction may have to be treated as wholly ineffective to create or pass even an equitable interest. In this case there may even be cause to depart from the normal rule that formal compliance with the proper law of the contract or the law of the place of execution is sufficient.[22]

The Brussels Convention and jurisdiction in contract cases

7–13   The Rome Convention governs the choice of the applicable law for a contract and various other matters of substantive law such as formal and material validity and in some respects the effects of the contract. The Rome Convention does not, as such, have anything to do with jurisdiction in contract disputes, except that two separate Protocols are intended to give the European Court of Justice jurisdiction to entertain preliminary references on the interpretation of the Convention.[23] For defendants domiciled in the Community, jurisdiction is governed by the Brussels Convention and will normally vest in the courts of the defendants'

---

[20] See paras 7–60 *et seq.*

[21] *Baxter International v. NPBI* (Jacob J., May 16, 1997).

[22] See para. 7–52.

[23] The First and Second Protocols on the Interpretation by the European Court of Justice of the European Communities of the Convention on the Law Applicable to Contractual Obligations. The Protocols are not yet in force.

domicile under Article 2, the courts of the "place of performance of the obligation in question" under Article 5(1), or the court chosen by the parties under Article 17. For defendants domiciled outside the Community, national law as modified by the Brussels Convention will apply. There is no doubt that essentially contractual disputes relating to intellectual property rights, including patents and other registered rights, fall under the general provisions of the Brussels Convention and not under the exclusive jurisdiction provisions of Article 16(4).[24] Equally, the Rome Convention applies where contractual matters arise as a preliminary or incidental matter, for instance where title is in issue in infringement proceedings or the defendant relies on a licence.

The European and Community patent conventions

A European Patent, once granted, takes effect as a bundle of national **7–14** patents each of which can devolve separately. The Protocol on Recognition[25] annexed to the European Patent Convention governs jurisdiction over claims to the benefit of a European patent, made while the application is still pending before the European Patent Office. Neither the Protocol on Recognition nor the European Patent Convention itself governs the substantive law of ownership of the European patent, nor the private international law issues which may arise in deciding which body of law does so. Claims to European patents once granted are dealt with on a state-by-state basis but fall within the general provisions of the Brussels Convention so that one court may have jurisdiction over all such claims under Article 2 or 5(1).

In contrast, Community patents and trade marks have a unitary and **7–15** autonomous nature[26] and are capable of being assigned only as a whole.[27] The relationship between national law and Community law as enacted in the Community Patent Convention or the Community Trade Mark Regulation is dealt with in Chapter 5.

B. THE ROME CONVENTION AND THE CONTRACTS (APPLICABLE LAW) ACT 1990

The Rome Convention

The Rome Convention is the name conveniently given to the Conven- **7–16** tion on the Law Applicable to Contractual Obligations[28] which was concluded by the contracting states of the European Community on June

---

[24] Case 288/82 *Duijnstee v. Goderbauer* [1983] E.C.R. 3663; [1985] 1 C.M.L.R. 220.

[25] The full title is the Protocol on Jurisdiction and Recognition of Decisions in respect of the Right to the Grant of a European Patent. See para. 2–132.

[26] Community Patent Convention, Art. 2(2) and (3); Community Trade Mark Regulation, Art. 1(2).

[27] Community Patent Convention, Art. 38; Community Trade Mark Regulation, Art. 16.

[28] Though the short title is rather less convenient for intellectual property practitioners than for others, who are not at risk of confusing it with the 1961 Rome Convention for the Protection of Performers, Phonograms and Broadcasting Organisations.

19, 1980.[29] The Convention may be regarded as a logical continuation of the process of harmonisation of private international law started by the Brussels Convention on Jurisdiction and the Enforcement of Judgments. A preliminary draft convention which was the predecessor of the Rome Convention was formally proposed in 1972 as the Convention on the Law Applicable to Contractual and Non-Contractual Obligations.[30] Harmonisation of the private international law of tort proved too ambitious, and in 1975 the working party confined its terms of reference to contract. The resulting draft Convention was finalised in 1979 and after being offered for comments from the member states was adopted and published in 1980. A commentary on the Convention by two members of the working party, Professors Mario Giuliano and Paul Lagarde was also published in 1980.[31] It may be referred to in interpreting the Convention,[32] and stands in the same relation to the Rome Convention as the Jenard Report does to the Brussels Convention. All texts of the Rome Convention are equally authentic.[33]

The Convention in the Community legal order

7–17   The Rome Convention is undoubtedly part of the Community legal order in a general sense, although unlike the Brussels Convention it was not concluded under Article 220 of the Treaty of Rome or any other express provision. The European Court of Justice was not originally given jurisdiction to interpret the Convention, though subsequently two Protocols on Interpretation were signed allowing appellate courts in member states to make preliminary references to the European Court of Justice.[34] References are not obligatory, even by courts of last resort. The Convention is subordinate to general Community law, and to both past

---

[29] For the Rome Convention in general see Dicey and Morris, *The Conflict of Laws* (12th ed., 1993); Cheshire and North's *Private International Law* (12th ed., 1992); North, (ed.), *Contract Conflicts* (1982); Plender, *The European Contracts Convention* (1991); Kaye, *The New Private International Law of Contract of the European Community* (1993). The text of the Convention is printed at [1980] O.J. L266/1 and as Sched. 1 to the Contracts (Applicable Law) Act 1990. It is also printed in *Butterworths' Jurisdiction, Foreign Judgments and Awards Handbook* (1994) and in Plender, *op. cit.*, and Kaye, *op. cit.* A simplified version of part of the present section was published as Wadlow "Intellectual Property and the Rome Contracts Convention" [1997] E.I.P.R. 11.

[30] Commission Document XIV/398/72; also printed in (1973) 21 Am. J. Comp. L. 587 and Ulmer, *Intellectual Property Rights and the Conflict of Laws*.

[31] [1980] O.J. C282/1. The Giuliano-Lagarde Report is also reproduced in Plender, *op. cit.*, Kaye, *op. cit.*, and *Butterworths' Jurisdiction, Foreign Judgments and Awards Handbook*.

[32] The Contracts (Applicable Law) Act 1990, s. 3(3)(a) so provides.

[33] The official texts are published at [1980] O.J. L266/1. The First Schedule to the Contracts (Applicable Law) Act 1990 sets out the English text "for ease of reference" (s. 2(4)) and does not confer any greater status on it. Kaye, *op.cit.*, contains the English, French, German, Dutch and Italian texts, Plender, *op.cit.*, sets out the English, French and German texts in parallel columns.

[34] The First and Second Protocols on the Interpretation by the European Court of Justice of the European Communities of the Convention on the Law Applicable to Contractual Obligations. The Protocols are not yet in force.

and future legislative acts of the Communities and harmonised national laws implementing them.[35]

The Contracts (Applicable Law) Act 1990

The Rome Convention was enacted into English domestic law by the **7–18** Contracts (Applicable Law) Act 1990. The Act follows the scheme of the Civil Jurisdiction and Judgments Act 1982 by providing, at section 2, that the Rome Convention (with some exceptions) and two related conventions or protocols are to have the force of law in the United Kingdom.[36] The English texts of the Conventions are set out in schedules to the Act. The Convention also applies to conflicts arising between the different parts of the United Kingdom.[37] As with the Brussels Convention, the Rome Convention is not to be interpreted in the way appropriate to domestic United Kingdom legislation but as an international treaty forming part of the Community legal order.[38] Indeed, unlike the Brussels Convention, this is expressly provided for by Article 18: "In the interpretation and application of the preceding uniform rules, regard shall be had to their international character and to the desirability of achieving uniformity in their interpretation and application."

Contracts to which the Act and the Rome Convention apply

The Contracts (Applicable Law) Act 1990 applies only to contracts **7–19** made after April 1, 1991.[39] For contracts made on or before that date, the old common law rules continue to apply.

By Article 1 of the Rome Convention, the rules of the Convention **7–20** apply to contractual obligations in any situation involving a choice between the law of different countries. In this situation, the Convention is mandatory and applies whether or not it leads to the application of the law of a contracting state.[40] The implication that the English courts will have to apply the Convention to contracts between parties neither of whom has any connection with the European Community, in respect of obligations to be performed elsewhere in the world (and so as to identify an applicable law which is not the law of any member state) was described as a "startling conclusion" by Lord Goff of Chieveley[41] and was criticised by Lord Wilberforce as well as Lord Goff in debate in the House of Lords. Application of the Convention to purely domestic

---

[35] Art. 20.

[36] Two sub-arts of the Convention are excluded: Arts 7(1) and 10(1)(e).

[37] s. 2(3) disapplying Art. 19(2).

[38] See the observations of Bingham L.J. in *Re Harrods (Buenos Aires) Ltd* [1992] Ch. 72; [1991] 3 W.L.R. 397; [1991] 4 All E.R. 334, CA quoted at para. 2–14.

[39] Art. 29(1), which was triggered by the ratification of the United Kingdom. The Act was brought into force by the Contracts (Applicable Law) Act 1990 (Commencement No. 1) Order 1991, S.I. 1991 No. 707. Art. 17 of the Rome Convention excludes retrospective effect.

[40] The combined effects of Arts 1(1) and 2.

[41] In his foreword to Plender, *op. cit.*

choice of law problems between different legal systems within the forum, for instance England and Scotland, is not mandatory but in the case of the United Kingdom has been enacted voluntarily by section 2(3) of the Contracts (Applicable Law) Act 1990.

7–21 Various matters are altogether excluded from the scope of the Convention by Article 1(2) but intellectual property is not among them and there is no reason to doubt that the Convention applies to contractual obligations relating to intellectual property rights. The Giuliano-Lagarde Report[42] notes that the original preliminary draft had expressly provided that property rights and intellectual property were not covered, but that was in the context of the law of non-contractual obligations and before the scope of the proposed convention was restricted to contract. For the Rome Convention itself, the Giuliano-Lagarde Report states that it was considered superfluous to make special provision for intellectual property. The result is that intellectual property rights *qua* property are unaffected by the Convention, but that the contractual aspects of agreements relating to intellectual property rights are governed by its general provisions.[43]

The "applicable" or proper law of the contract: introduction

7–22 The Rome Convention operates to identify the "applicable law" of a contract which in broad terms corresponds to the "proper law" under English common law. The basic principle is that of freedom of choice: if the parties have chosen the law by which their contract is to be governed, then that is the applicable law.[44] If not, then as in the common law the Court has to identify the system of law with which the contract has the closest connection.[45] Unlike the common law, however, the Rome Convention contains various presumptions of which the most important is to the effect that a contract is assumed to be most closely connected with the country where the party responsible for "the performance which is characteristic of the contract" has his habitual residence, central administration or place of business.[46] The justification for this is given in the Giuliano-Lagarde Report as:

> "Article 4(2) gives specific form and objectivity to the, in itself, too vague concept of 'closest connection'. At the same time it greatly simplifies the problem of determining the law applicable to the contract in default of choice by the parties. The place where the act was done becomes unimportant. There is no longer any need to determine where the contract was concluded, with all the difficulties and the problems of classification that arise in practice. Seeking the

---

[42] Commentary on Art. 1, para.2.

[43] See para. 7–32.

[44] Art. 3.

[45] Art. 4. Strictly speaking, the connection is with a country rather than a legal system, but Art. 19 achieves much the same effect.

[46] Art. 4(2).

place of performance or the different places of performance and classifying them becomes superfluous."

Whatever the validity of these advantages, the concept of a perfor- **7–23** mance characteristic of the contract is previously unknown to the common law, and a similar concept has already created problems of interpretation in the slightly different circumstances of Article 5(1) of the Brussels Convention. If the characteristic performance cannot be determined, then the presumption expressly does not apply, and in any event it can be overridden if the connecting factors taken as a whole point to a different system of law.[47]

Effects of the choice of applicable law

The applicable law of the contract governs the matters specified in **7–24** Article 10 of the Rome Convention, except that in the United Kingdom the consequences of nullity are governed by the general law of restitution. The United Kingdom entered a reservation to the Convention in this respect.[48]

Article 10

Scope of the applicable law

1. The law applicable to a contract by virtue of Articles 3 to 6 and 12 of this Convention shall govern in particular:
   (a) interpretation;
   (b) performance;
   (c) within the limits of the powers conferred on the court by its procedural law, the consequences of breach, including the assessment of damages in so far as it is governed by rules of law;
   (d) the various ways of extinguishing obligations, and prescription and limitation of actions;
   (e) the consequences of nullity of the contract.[49]
2. In relation to the manner of performance and the steps to be taken in the event of defective performance regard shall be had to the law of the country in which performance takes place.

Choice of the applicable law by the parties

The basic principle of the Rome Convention, as in the common law, is **7–25** that the parties are free to choose the applicable law of the contract.

---

[47] Art. 4(5).
[48] Contracts (Applicable Law) Act 1990, s. 2(2).
[49] Para. (1)(e) does not apply in the U.K.: Contracts (Applicable Law) Act 1990, s. 2(2).

Article 3

Freedom of choice

1. A contract shall be governed by the law chosen by the parties. The choice must be express or demonstrated with reasonable certainty by the terms of the contract or the circumstances of the case. By their choice the parties can select the law applicable to the whole or a part only of the contract.
2. The parties may at any time agree to subject the contract to a law other than that which previously governed it, whether as a result of an earlier choice under this Article or of other provisions of this Convention. Any variation by the parties of the law to be applied made after the conclusion of the contract shall not prejudice its formal validity under Article 9 or adversely affect the rights of third parties.
3. The fact that the parties have chosen a foreign law, whether or not accompanied by the choice of a foreign tribunal, shall not, where all the other elements relevant to the situation at the time of the choice are connected with one country only, prejudice the application of rules of the law of that country which cannot be derogated from by contract, hereinafter called "mandatory rules".
4. The existence and validity of the consent of the parties as to the choice of the applicable law shall be determined in accordance with the provisions of Articles 8, 9 and 11.

7–26　　As may be seen from Article 3, the choice of applicable law can be either express or implied. It is implicit—not least from Article 3(3)—that the parties can choose a law which has no intrinsic connection with the contract, and from Article 2 the chosen applicable law need not be the law of a contracting state. In other respects freedom of choice has some perhaps surprising consequences: *depecage* is expressly permitted and the proper law can be changed. It is not necessarily to be assumed that an implicit choice of proper law would be decided in the same way as at common law.

7–27　　The effect of Article 3(3) is complicated by the fact that another Convention provision preserving the effect of mandatory rules, Article 7(1), does not have the force of law in the United Kingdom. Article 3(3) is of much more limited scope and applies when *all* relevant objective connecting factors point to a single country with a system of law other than the chosen applicable law. In this situation, the "mandatory rules" of that country would prevail.[50]

---

[50] For "mandatory rules" see paras 7–85 *et seq.*

The applicable law in the absence of choice

In the absence of an express or reasonably certain implicit choice of **7–28** applicable law, the applicable law is to be determined according to Article 4 of the Rome Convention.

Article 4

Applicable law in the absence of choice

1. To the extent that the law applicable to the contract has not been chosen in accordance with Article 3, the contract shall be governed by the law of the country with which it is most closely connected. Nevertheless, a severable part of the contract which has a closer connection with another country may by way of exception be governed by the law of that other country.
2. Subject to the provisions of paragraph 5 of this Article, it shall be presumed that the contract is most closely connected with the country where the party who is to effect the performance which is characteristic of the contract has, at the time of conclusion of the contract, his habitual residence, or, in the case of a body corporate or unincorporate, its central administration. However, if the contract is entered into in the course of that party's trade or profession, that country shall be the country in which the principal place of business is situated or, where under the terms of the contract the performance is to be effected through a place of business other than the principal place of business, the country in which that other place of business is situated.
3. Notwithstanding the provisions of paragraph 2 of this Article, to the extent that the subject matter of the contract is a right in immovable property or a right to use immovable property it shall be presumed that the contract is most closely connected with the country where the immovable property is situated.
4. [. . .][51]
5. Paragraph 2 shall not apply if the characteristic performance cannot be determined, and the presumptions in paragraphs 2, 3 and 4 shall be disregarded if it appears from the circumstances as a whole that the contract is more closely connected with another country.

At first sight, the scheme of the Rome Convention and Article 4(1) **7–29** especially may seem to correspond to the well-established common law principle that the proper law of the contract is the system of law with which the contract has the closest and most real connection. However, the prominence given to Article 4(1) is deceptive. The general rule is in fact that of Article 4(2), which creates a universal but rebuttable presumption that a contract (other than one relating to "immovable

---

[51] Carriage of goods—omitted.

property" or the carriage of goods) is most closely connected with the country where the party responsible for the "performance characteristic of the contract" has his habitual residence, central administration or relevant place of business. This presumption, which has no counterpart in the common law, is displaced if the characteristic performance cannot be determined, or if it appears from the circumstances as a whole that the contract is more closely connected with a different system of law. Though the presumption created by Article 4(2) is not conclusive, it cannot simply be ignored. The Convention obviously intends that Article 4(2) will normally govern the choice of applicable law, that an attempt will always be made to identify the characteristic performance of the contract and the party responsible for performing it, and that the court will not simply ignore the question and go straight on to apply Article 5(5).[52]

7–30   The concept of "characteristic performance" is explained in the Giuliano-Lagarde Report in the following terms:

> "The kind of idea upon which paragraph 2 is based is certainly not entirely unknown to some specialists. It gives effect to a tendency which has been gaining ground both in legal writings and in case law in many countries in recent decades. The submission of the contract, in the absence of a choice by the parties, to the law appropriate to the characteristic performance defines the connecting factor of the contract from the inside, and not from the outside by elements unrelated to the essence of the obligation such as the nationality of the contracting parties or the place where the contract was concluded.
>
> In addition it is possible to relate the concept of characteristic performance to an even more general idea, namely the idea that his performance refers to the function which the legal relationship involved fulfils in the economic and social life of any country. The concept of characteristic performance essentially links the contract to the social and economic environment of which it will form a part.
>
> Identifying the characteristic performance of a contract obviously presents no difficulty in the case of unilateral contracts. By contrast, in bilateral (reciprocal) contracts whereby the parties undertake mutual reciprocal performance, the counterperformance by one of the parties in a modern economy usually takes the form of money. This is not, of course, the characteristic performance of the contract. It is the performance for which the payment is due, i.e. depending on the type of contract, the delivery of goods, the granting of the right to make use of an item of property, the provision of a service,

---

[52] Even if the English court were minded to do so, one must expect that in due course a body of decisions from Europe will define the "characteristic performance" of typical contracts with at least persuasive authority.

transport, insurance, banking operations, security, etc., which usually constitutes the centre of gravity and the socio-economic function of the contractual transaction."[53]

The "characteristic performance" in the sense of the Rome Convention should be distinguished from that of the "place of performance of the obligation in question" under Article 5(1) of the Brussels Convention.[54] The Rome Convention contemplates a single "characteristic obligation" for both parties alike and for the contract as a whole. Article 5(1) of the Brussels Convention is consistent with multiple obligations, since one looks only to the place of performance of the particular obligation which has been broken,[55] and the latter might be the payment of money.   **7–31**

Intellectual property is probably not "immovable property" for Article 4(3)

In the case of contracts relating to "immovable property," or to the use of immovable property, the effect of Article 4(3) of the Rome Convention is that the contract is prima facie presumed to be most closely connected with the country where the immovable property is situated. Article 4(5) makes it clear that the presumption is rebuttable, but in that case one is thrown directly back to the general rule of Article 4(1), and no occasion arises to attempt to identify the "characteristic performance" so as to apply the presumption of Article 4(2). In any event, Article 4(3) is subject to the parties' express choice of applicable law.   **7–32**

The question therefore arises as to whether intellectual property rights are "immovable property" for the purposes of the Rome Convention. The answer to this question also affects the application of Article 9(6)—mandatory requirements of form for contracts relating to immovable property—and at first sight it would be attractive to invoke Article 4(3) to avoid the need to ascertain the "characteristic performance" for intellectual property contracts while simultaneously identifying a provision other than Article 7(1) under which an English court could give effect to at least some of the mandatory rules of the law of the protecting   **7–33**

---

[53] Yet the Rome Convention does not even purport to give effect to this policy. A contract to build an airport for the Government of Ruritania is prima facie governed, not by Ruritanian law as the law of the place of performance of the characteristic obligation, but by English, French or German law according to the principal place of business of the successful contractor. The centre of gravity of a simple licence of a U.K. patent is the U.K., but the applicable law will presumably be the personal law of the licensor.

[54] Although in the context of employment contracts (and even before Art. 5(1) was amended) the European Court of Justice has preferred to identify the place of the characteristic performance of the employment relationship as a whole. See Case 133/81 *Ivenel v. Schwab* [1982] E.C.R. 1891; [1983] 1 C.M.L.R. 538 interpreting Art. 5(1) of the Brussels Convention by reference to Art. 6 of the Rome Convention.

[55] A second distinction is that the place of the characteristic performance, as opposed to the identity of the party responsible for it, is largely irrelevant under the Rome Convention.

state. The indications are, however, that intellectual property rights are not within the concept of "immovable property" as used in the Rome Convention.

7–34   The characterisation of intellectual property as movable or immovable in English domestic law is inconclusive,[56] because the Rome Convention is part of the Community legal order and the term must be given an independent meaning. For the same reason, the status of intellectual property as immovable property or not under the *lex situs* ought not to be relevant. An analogy with the Brussels Convention, which distinguishes between "rights *in rem* in immovable property" (Article 16(1)) and "patents, trade marks or other similar rights" (Article 16(4)) suggests that "immovable property" in both conventions is used in the relatively narrow but familiar sense of land.[57] Nothing in the Giuliano-Lagarde commentary on Article 4(3) or 9(6) of the Rome Convention or the case law or commentaries on Article 16(1) of the Brussels Convention suggests otherwise. A narrow interpretation would be appropriate for a provision which is in derogation from a more general rule. In any event, Article 4(3) would be unworkable in the common situation of intellectual property rights in many different countries being assigned or licensed under a single agreement.

7–35   The conclusion is reinforced by Ulmer's proposed treatment of intellectual property contracts in the light of the Preliminary Draft Convention on the Law Applicable to Contractual and Non-Contractual Obligations.[58] Although Article 6 of the preliminary draft Convention contained a special rule for contracts relating to immovable property corresponding to Article 4(3) of the Rome Convention, Ulmer expressly rejected the *lex situs* as the preferred applicable law for contracts relating to intellectual property rights in favour of the general rule of the draft Convention that the applicable law was presumed to be the law of the party responsible for the characteristic obligation. This is more than a simple policy preference: Ulmer does not even appear to have contemplated that intellectual property might be "immovable property" in the sense of Article 6 of the preliminary draft Convention.

The "characteristic performance" in simple intellectual property contracts

7–36   In the absence of a chosen applicable law and assuming Article 4(3) does not apply the effect of Article 4(2) of the Rome Convention in a

---

[56] As to which see para. 6–55.

[57] As all the texts of the Rome Convention are equally authentic it is always legitimate to refer to foreign language texts, and *a fortiori* to resolve any ambiguity in the English text. The French text of Art. 4(3) refers to the exception to Art. 4(2) applying "où le contrat a pour objet un droit réel immobilier ou un droit d'utilisation d'un immeuble" and the German text to "der Vertrag ein dingliches Recht an einem Grundstück oder ein Recht zur Nutzung eines Grundstücks zum Gegenstand hat."

[58] Ulmer, *Intellectual Property Rights and the Conflict of Laws*, paras 75 *et seq.* (copyright) and 146 *et seq.* (industrial property rights).

business context is to create a presumption that the applicable law is the law of the country where the party responsible for the "performance characteristic of the contract" has his relevant place of business, either his principal place of business or the place of business through which the contract is to be performed. In contrast to Article 5(1) of the Brussels Convention, with which Article 4(2) of the Rome Convention has some affinities, the place where the characteristic performance is to be carried out is not determinative, unless the contract itself stipulates performance though an establishment there, although it may be a relevant connecting factor if Article 4(2) does not apply. Article 4(2) therefore remains workable, at least in theory, as long as the characteristic performance can be identified, even if the place of the characteristic performance is uncertain or it is to be carried out in many different countries.[59]

In the present context the doctrine of characteristic performance is **7–37** seen at its simplest in the typical contract for assignment where one party pays a lump sum in consideration for the other assigning an intellectual property right. The assignment is the characteristic performance and the personal law of the assignor is prima facie the applicable law of the contract.

Ulmer's treatment of contracts in *Intellectual Property Rights and the* **7–38** *Conflict of Laws* observed that no predominant opinion had emerged as to where the "centre of gravity" for intellectual property contracts generally lay, for licence agreements especially, and went on to refer to the Preliminary Draft Convention on Obligations (the predecessor of the Rome Convention) in justifying the importance of the "characteristic obligation" of the contract to determine the applicable law.[60] It will be seen that the rule contemplated by Ulmer is virtually identical to that under Article 4(2):

> "The rules in question are based on the view that in the absence of an express or implied choice of law by the parties the agreement is governed by the law of the country with which it is most closely connected, and that in case of doubt this is to be the country in which the party who is to carry out the obligation which is characteristic of the contract has his habitual residence or—if the obligation relates to a business activity—his principal establishment or a subsidiary establishment by which the obligation is to be carried out. This rule may be applied without pitfalls to cases of assignment and licensing agreements in which the obligation of the grantee consists only in the payment of a sum of money. The assignment of

---

[59] The converse situation is possible. For example, if an American and a Japanese company agree jointly to set up a research and development project in France on the basis of complete mutual equality then neither party appears to be responsible for the characteristic performance but it is obvious where it is to take place. More generally, who is responsible for the characteristic performance of a partnership?

[60] See also Modiano, "International Patent Licensing Agreements and Conflict of Laws" (1980) 2 *Northwestern Journal of International Law and Business* 11 who better appreciates the complex realities of international patent licensing.

the industrial property right or the grant of the licence, as the case may be, then comprises the characteristic obligation of the contract. (. . .)[61]

A different assessment appears to be indicated, however, in the case of licensing agreements in which the licensee undertakes to exploit the industrial property right or in which he is granted an exclusive licence. In such cases it must be assumed in accordance with the third paragraph of Article 4 of the Preliminary Draft of the Convention on Obligations that the contract is more closely connected with the country in which the establishment of the licensee is situated."[62]

The "characteristic performance" in more complex cases

7–39   As may be seen from the foregoing, the identification of the characteristic performance is anything but straightforward once one ceases to be concerned with simple assignments of intellectual property rights or bare licences in which the whole of the consideration is in money, and even in the latter case there is room for controversy.[63] For example, a technology transfer agreement may equally well be regarded as a patent licence, in which case the licensor supplies the characteristic performance, or as an agreement to manufacture and market the licensed articles, in which case the licensee does so. If the agreement is a joint venture for collaborative research and development then the performance by each party seems equally characteristic.

7–40   Or again, a typical publishing contract may equally well be regarded as a licence of copyright from the author to the publisher for a royalty; or as an obligation on the author to write and deliver the manuscript; or as an obligation on the publisher to print and publish it. The payment of the royalty and any advance may be disregarded; but is the characteristic performance the copyright licence, the obligation to write the book or the obligation to publish it? If either of the first two, it is the author who is the person who is to effect the characteristic performance; if the latter, it is the publisher. Ulmer regards publication as the characteristic obligation so that the contract would prima facie be governed by the law of the publisher's principal place of business.[64] One may note in passing that one cannot simply assume that the party *receiving* any payment in money—in this case the author—must be providing the characteristic performance in return.

7–41   It may also be noted that this analysis of the "characteristic performance" in the context of publishing achieves the same preferred end result as the school of the single "decisive factor" about which Ulmer

---

[61] Ulmer, *op. cit.*, para. 146.
[62] Ulmer, *op. cit.*, para. 147.
[63] Modiano, *op. cit.*
[64] Ulmer, *op. cit.* para. 76.

writes: "In Germany it is not only the prevalent opinion in legal writings nbut also in case law it is the established principle that the decisive factor is the commercial centre of exploitation and thus the place of establishment of the publisher. The same view is found in French and Swiss legal writings."[65]

One incidental advantage of this approach is relative legal certainty. **7-42** Although there may be several authors, perhaps resident in different countries, there will normally only be one publisher and though the publisher may have several places of business it will normally be clear which one is principally responsible for publication.

Ulmer's suggestions for identifying "characteristic performance"

In the absence of decided cases on the application of Article 4(2) of **7-43** the Rome Convention to intellectual property contracts, it may be instructive—or at least diverting—to summarise the suggestions of Ulmer in *Intellectual Property Rights and the Conflict of Laws* which are based, in part, on a comparative survey of the treatment of typical intellectual property transactions in the private international law of the major European Community member states,[66] and partly on the direct application of proposed rules corresponding fairly closely to Articles 3 and 4 of the Rome Convention.[67] As will be seen, the characterisation of the transaction and the identification of the more important obligations under it crucially affect the identification of the party responsible for the characteristic performance and the choice of the applicable law.[68] Since terms such as to an obligation to work (or even one as important as exclusivity[69]) may be implied as well as express, and since an agreement with no express choice of law clause is quite likely to be poorly drafted, one may be forced into the logically untenable position of having to construe the agreement in order to ascertain its applicable law!

---

[65] Ulmer, *op. cit.*, para. 74, citations omitted.

[66] A more than Herculean task, given the paucity of decided cases and the multiplicity and inconsistency of academic opinions: see also Modiano, *op. cit.*, and Beier, "Conflict of Law Problems of Trademark License Agreements" (1982) I.I.C. 162.

[67] Except that *depecage* was not expressly contemplated in the preliminary draft used by Ulmer.

[68] For a further comparative treatment (principally of academic opinions) in the context of patent licence agreements see Modiano, *op. cit.*, who identifies a weak consensus to the effect that the licensor provides the characteristic performance, and criticises it forcefully. Academic opinion can be found for almost any *a priori* rule as to whose is the characteristic performance.

[69] *Morton-Norwich Products Inc v. Intercen Ltd (No. 2)* [1981] F.S.R. 337 (Graham J.) where a patent which was expressly exclusive in respect of manufacture was held to be exclusive by implication in respect of importation and sale. The Patent Office had previously reached the opposite conclusion in separate proceedings where that interpretation was advantageous to both parties to the licence.

7–44   **Table: summary of Ulmer's suggestions as to which party is responsible for the characteristic performance in intellectual property contracts.**[70]

Type of transaction	Party responsible for the "characteristic performance"
Simple assignment of one or more intellectual property rights	Assignor
Sale of business with intellectual property	Vendor
Bare (non-exclusive) patent licence	Licensor
Exclusive patent licence	Licensee[71]
Patent licence with obligation to work	Licensee
Patent and know-how licence with continuing technical support	Licensor
Patent pool	May depend on ownership of any "dominant" patent
Publishing agreement	Publisher
Trade mark licence	Licensee[72]

7–45   An advantage claimed by Ulmer for the doctrine of characteristic performance is that, although it may be difficult to decide between the law of one party's place of business and that of the other, at least the choice of law is always narrowed down to those two, and all other legal systems may be disregarded: "if, for example, a British manufacturer grants to a French manufacturer a licence for the exploitation of an industrial property right in Japan, the law of the contract is either British or French law, but not Japanese law." Quite apart from the possibility of either party or both performing its obligations through a branch in Japan or a third country, this is not necessarily the case. If the characteristic performance cannot be determined then Article 4(2) can only be ignored. Article 4(5) then operates and in accordance with Article 4(1) the applicable law will be that of the country with which the contract is most closely connected. This will not necessarily be either of the two systems of law which were under contemplation for Article 4(2), and in Ulmer's example it is at least theoretically possible that Japanese law or another system altogether would govern.

[70] Ulmer, *op. cit.*, paras 76 (copyright) *et seq.*, 147 *et seq.* (industrial property rights).

[71] *Quaere* whether the applicable law changes (as it may do, Rome Convention, Art. 3(2), which is foreshadowed in the Preliminary Draft Convention) when an exclusive licence becomes non-exclusive or vice-versa.

[72] On the basis that use of the mark may be essential to maintain its validity.

The relevant places: habitual residence, central administration and places of business

Having identified the characteristic performance of the contract and **7–46** the person responsible for it, the applicable law is presumed to be that of the country where that party has his habitual residence, central administration or relevant place of business. Contracts relating to intellectual property rights will generally be concluded between traders in their capacity as such, so the applicable law will be that of the country where the party responsible for the characteristic performance has his principal place of business unless the contract provides for the performance to be effected through another place of business, in which case the place of the latter determines the applicable law.[73] Apart from this, the actual place of performance of the characteristic obligation is, in itself, irrelevant. Contracts with parties who are not traders or professionals cannot entirely be ignored, for instance in publishing.[74] In that case, the relevant place is where the party responsible for the characteristic performance had his habitual residence at the time of conclusion of the contract, if an individual, or its central administration if a corporation or unincorporated association.

The Giuliano-Lagarde Report justifies and explains this system as **7–47** follows:

"As for the geographical location of the characteristic performance, it is quite natural that of the country in which the party liable for the performance is habitually resident or has his central administration (if a body corporate or unincorporate) or his place of business, according to whether the performance in question is in the course of his trade or profession or not, should prevail over the country of performance where, of course, the latter is a country other than that of habitual residence, central administration or the place of business. In the solution adopted by the Group the position is that only the place of habitual residence or of the central administration or of the place of business of the party providing the essential performance is decisive in locating the contract.

Thus, for example, in a banking contract the law of the country of the banking establishment with which the transaction is made will normally govern the contract. It is usually the case in a commercial contract of sale that the law of the vendor's place of business will govern the contract. To take another example, in an agency contract concluded in France between a Belgian commercial agent and a French company, the characteristic performance being that of the agent, the contract will be governed by Belgian law if the agent has his place of business in Belgium."

---

[73] Rome Convention, Art. 4(2).

[74] Individual employment contracts are governed by the terms of Art. 6. Consumer contracts, which will rarely be relevant in this context, are governed by Art. 5.

Residual cases: connecting factors and the identification of the applicable law

7–48   If there is no chosen applicable law, and if the "characteristic performance" analysis of Article 4(2) fails to yield a result, then the contract is to be governed by the law of the country with which it is most closely connected.[75] This situation corresponds to English law and the applicable law so chosen is likely to correspond to the proper law of the contract as determined by the common law.[76] This result can also be achieved if it appears from the circumstances as a whole that the contract is more closely identified with a country other than that identified by the application of the presumption in Article 4(2). It is possible for severable parts of the contract to be governed by different systems of law, but this is expected to be rare.[77]

7–49   By its very nature, the operation of Article 4(1) on its own is open-ended and the relevant connecting factors cannot be identified in advance. As a matter of general principle, the following factors at least are likely to be relevant in relation to intellectual property contracts: the domicile, residence or nationality of all parties, the *situs* of the principal or only right involved, perhaps the place and manner of execution, the language of the agreement and any special legal terminology, the presence of terms meaningful only under a particular system of law, the specified currency and place of payment for any moneys which are to be paid, any specified place of jurisdiction or arbitration, the proper law of any related agreement, and the place of performance of the contract if one can be identified. There is very little authority in English law as to whether any of these factors is most influential in any particular case. In *Redwood Music v. Francis Day & Hunter*[78] the domicile of the assignee (and publisher) was taken as determining the proper law for a number of copyright assignments, but the point appears not to have been argued and no other law had any strong claim. In the patent case of *G.A.F. Corp. v. Amchem Products*[79] the relevant factors overwhelmingly pointed to America, and it was irrelevant for English purposes whether the proper law was that of the state of Delaware or Pennsylvania.

Material and formal validity: Articles 8 and 9

7–50   As at common law, the Rome Convention provides for the material validity of a contract to be determined according to the applicable or proper law:

---

[75] Art. 4(5), referring back to Art. 4(1).

[76] There may be differences. For instance, English law would not take account of the behaviour of the parties after the contract had been executed but according to the Giuliano-Lagarde Report it is permissible to take into account factors arising after conclusion of the contract.

[77] Art. 4(1).

[78] [1978] R.P.C. 429 (Robert Goff J.); [1979] R.P.C. 385, CA; [1980] 2 All E.R. 817; [1981] R.P.C. 337, HL.

[79] [1975] 1 Lloyds L.R. 601, CA.

Article 8

Material validity

1. The existence and validity of a contract, or of any term of a contract, shall be determined by the law which would govern it under this Convention if the contract or term were valid.
2. Nevertheless a party may rely upon the law of the country in which he has his habitual residence to establish that he did not consent if it appears from the circumstances that it would not be reasonable to determine the effect of his conduct in accordance with the law specified in the preceding paragraph.

A contract is formally valid (with certain exceptions) if it was validly **7–51** executed according to the applicable law or the law of the place or places where it was made. This also corresponds to the position at common law.

Article 9

Formal validity

1. A contract concluded between persons who are in the same country is formally valid if it satisfies the formal requirements of the law which governs it under this Convention or of the law of the country where it is concluded.
2. A contract concluded between persons who are in different countries is formally valid if it satisfies the formal requirements of the law which governs it under this Convention or of the law of one of those countries.
3. Where a contract is concluded by an agent, the country in which the agent acts is the relevant country for the purposes of paragraphs 1 and 2.
4. An act intended to have legal effect relating to an existing or contemplated contract is formally valid if it satisfies the formal requirements of the law which under this Convention governs or would govern the contract or of the law of the country where the act was done.
5. (. . .) [consumer contracts]
6. Notwithstanding paragraphs 1 to 4 of this Article, a contract the subject matter of which is a right in immovable property or a right to use immovable property shall be subject to the mandatory requirements of form of the law of the country where the property is situated if by that law those requirements are imposed irrespective of the country where the contract is concluded and irrespective of the law governing the contract.

Formal validity of contracts relating to intellectual property

Only Article 9(6) requires further comment. In English law, all the **7–52** statutory intellectual property rights have modest requirements as to form for at least some categories of contracts relating to them. Typically,

437

licences can be in any form[80] but assignments must be in writing and signed by or for the assignor, or by both parties in the case of patents. It is suggested at paragraph 7–32 that intellectual property is probably not "immovable property" in the sense of the Rome Convention so that Article 9(6) would not apply. In any event, a distinction is once again to be drawn between the formal validity of a contract in the sense of its binding the parties, and its effectiveness or not as a conveyance in transferring the legal title to property rights good against the world. It is settled law in England that a contract relating to an intellectual property right which fails to comply with statutory requirements of form may be perfectly valid, effective and enforceable as a contract, but that it confers only an equitable interest until the requirements of form, and registration if necessary, have been complied with. The Rome Convention only deals with the contractual rights of the parties between themselves and Article 9(6) is therefore irrelevant, whether intellectual property falls within the concept of "immovable property" or not. In this respect, the treatment of intellectual property rights in United Kingdom law does not correspond to the treatment of contracts for the sale of land, and the language of the statutes is sometimes capable of misleading.

The statutory requirements of form for the three major intellectual property rights are as follows.

Copyright

7–53 The Copyright, Designs and Patents Act 1988, s. 90, requires assignments of copyright to be in writing and signed by or on behalf of the assignor but imposes no requirements of form for licences.

Assignment and licences

(1) Copyright is transmissible by assignment, by testamentary disposition or by operation of law, as personal or moveable property.

(2) An assignment or other transmission of copyright may be partial, that is, limited so as to apply—

    (a) to one or more, but not all, of the things the copyright owner has the exclusive right to do;

    (b) to part, but not the whole, of the period for which the copyright is to subsist.

(3) An assignment of copyright is not effective unless it is in writing signed by or on behalf of the assignor.

[. . .]

Registered Trade Marks

7–54 The provisions for assignments of trade marks are now similar, and are to be found in section 24 of the Trade Marks Act 1994. This represents a considerable simplification of the position under the Trade

---

[80] Though trade mark licences must be in writing, Trade Marks Act 1994, s. 28(2).

Marks Act 1938, and the characterisation of some of the old restrictions on assignment and licensing is fortunately now of little relevance.

Assignment, &c of registered trade mark

(1) A registered trade mark is transmissible by assignment, testamentary disposition or operation of law in the same way as other personal or moveable property. It is so transmissible either in connection with the goodwill of a business or independently.

(2) An assignment or other transmission of a registered trade mark may be partial, that is, limited so as to apply—
  (a) in relation to some but not all of the goods or services for which the trade mark is registered, or
  (b) in relation to use of the trade mark in a particular manner or a particular locality.

(3) An assignment of a registered trade mark, or an assent relating to a registered trade mark, is not effective unless it is in writing signed by or on behalf of the assignor or, as the case may be, a personal representative
  Except in Scotland, this requirement may be satisfied in a case where the assignor or personal representative is a body corporate by the affixing of its seal.

[. . .]

(6) Nothing in this Act shall be construed as affecting the assignment or other transmission of an unregistered trade mark as part of the goodwill of a business.

Unlike patents and copyrights, licences of trade marks are required to be in writing and signed by the licensor, though once again an oral licence would be effective in equity. **7–55**

Licensing of registered trade mark

(1) A licence to use a registered trade mark may be general or limited. A limited licence may, in particular, apply—
  (a) in relation to some but not all of the goods or services for which the trade mark is registered, or
  (b) in relation to use of the trade mark in a particular manner or a particular locality.

(2) A licence is not effective unless it is in writing signed by or on behalf of the grantor.
  Except in Scotland, this requirement may be satisfied in a case where the grantor is a body corporate by the affixing of its seal.

[. . .]

Patents

In the case of patents formal requirements are dealt with in section 30 of the Patents Act 1977. **7–56**

Nature of, and transactions in, patents and applications for patents

(1) Any patent or application for a patent is personal property (without being a thing in action), and any patent or any such application and rights in or under it may be transferred, created or granted in accordance with subsections (2) to (7) below.

(2) Subject to section 36(3) below,[81] any patent or any such application, or any right in it, may be assigned or mortgaged.

[. . .]

(6) Any of the following transactions, that is to say—

    (a) any assignment or mortgage of a patent or any such application, or any right in a patent or any such application;

    (b) any assent relating to any patent or any such application or right;

shall be void unless it is in writing and is signed by or on behalf of the parties to the transaction (or, in the case of an assent or other transaction by a personal representative, by or on behalf of the personal representative) or in the case of a body corporate is so signed or is under the seal of that body.

[. . .]

7–57 The requirement for signature by both parties, and not just the assignor, should be noted. Despite the use of the word "void" in section 30(6), there is no reason to doubt long-standing law that an oral or inadequately executed contract is valid as such in equity as an agreement to assign notwithstanding the absence of writing or signatures but that it is ineffective to transfer the legal title.[81a] Of course, the Patent Office would in any event require an assignment presented for registration under section 33 to comply with section 30(6). There is no longer any requirement for an assignment of a patent to be by deed.

Assignment of things in action: Article 12

7–58 Article 12 of the Rome Convention, with the uninformative title of "voluntary assignment," provides for the assignment of choses in action:

1. The mutual obligations of assignor and assignee under a voluntary assignment of a right against another person ("the debtor") shall be governed by the law which under this Convention applies to the contract between the assignor and assignee.

2. The law governing the right to which the assignment relates shall determine its assignability, the relationship between the assignee

---

[81] s. 36 deals with the rare situation of co-ownership.

[81a] Now confirmed in *Baxter International v. NPBI* (Jacob J., May 16, 1997, not yet reported). Jacob J. refused to strike out an action for patent infringement, although at the time the writ was issued the title of the (first) plaintiffs depended on two consecutive assignments, neither of which had been executed by the assignee. The defective assignments were treated as agreements to assign, conferring on the plaintiffs an immediate equitable title which had subsequently been pefected.

and the debtor, the conditions under which the assignment can be invoked against the debtor and any question whether the debtor's obligations have been discharged.

It is unclear whether this terminology is apt to cover intellectual **7–59** property, as opposed to contract debts and the like where there is an identifiable "debtor." However, the question is largely academic because Article 12 does no more than to state expressly in its own context two propositions which would already apply to assignments of intellectual property in any event: the applicable law of the assignment governs the contractual relationship between assignor and assignee whereas the law of the protecting state governs the proprietary aspects of the right and the effect of the assignment on third parties.[82]

Similar comments apply where an accrued cause of action is assigned, either in general terms or in respect of a particular infringement.

C. THE PRINCIPAL DECIDED CASES UNDER THE COMMON LAW

Why the problem is not common in the reported cases

The scheme of the Rome Convention applied by the Contracts **7–60** (Applicable Law) Act 1990 is sufficiently close in some respects to the traditional common law rules on the private international law of contract for the older cases still to be of interest.[83] The common law also continues to govern contracts entered into on or before April 1, 1991 so it will continue to be of importance for the foreseeable future when issues of title arise in litigation. It has to be said that reported cases in English law as it applies to intellectual property agreements with an international element have been rare, especially for rights other than copyright, but this does not mean that there are no problems for patent and trade mark owners. Likewise, what literature there is has tended to concentrate on copyright rather than the industrial property rights.[84]

---

[82] Compare *Macmillan Inc v. Bishopsgate Investment Trust Ltd* [1996] 1 W.L.R. 387, CA deciding that where there were conflicting assignments of shares in a New York company, the law of New York as the *lex situs* of the shares decided which party had the better title. It was not submitted that shares in a company fell under Art. 12.

[83] There are no relevant cases to date under the Rome Convention.

[84] Ulmer, *Intellectual Property Rights and the Conflict of Laws* (1978) covers both aspects but deals more extensively with copyright. See also: Cohen Jehoram, ed., *Copyright Contracts* (1977); Dietz, *Copyright Law in the European Community* (1978); *Nimmer on Copyright* (looseleaf); Nimmer, "Who is the Copyright Owner When Laws Conflict" (1974) 5 I.I.C. 62; Ulmer, "Some Thoughts on the law of Copyright Contracts" (1976) 7 I.I.C. 202; Black, "The Regulation of Copyright Contracts a Comparative View" [1980] E.I.P.R. 386; Kloss, "Copyrights and the Conflict of Laws" [1985] E.I.P.R. 15; Katzenberger, "Protection of the Author as the Weaker Party to a Contract under International Copyright Contract Law" (1988) 19 I.I.C. 731; Richards, "Ownership of Copyright: Some International Thoughts" (1989) 133 S.J. 1247; Geller, "Harmonising Copyright Conflict Analyses" [1989] *Copyright* 49; Stone, "Problems of International Film Distribution: Assignment and Licensing of Copyright and the Conflict of Laws" [1996] Ent. L.R. 62.

Perhaps copyright lawyers are more internationally minded, but what distinguishes copyright from other intellectual rights for present purposes is that copyright is not registered, and except in the publishing and media industries (and sometimes even there) all but the most important copyrights tend to be allowed to devolve in a very informal manner over a period of time which may be as long as a century or more. With no registrations, it is deceptively easy to think in terms of a worldwide copyright and overlook the fact that this is no more than a shorthand expression for a bundle of national copyrights. It is likely that the need, or at least the desirability, of registering assignments and licences of patents and trade marks (as well as the relatively short life of patents) has discouraged questions of private international law from surfacing.[85]

7–61   Despite these factors there are enough cases under English common law for the main principles to emerge clearly. What the cases confirm is that one must look to the law of the protecting state to establish the nature of the intellectual property rights in question and the attributes which cannot be separated from them. If the agreement covers more than one right then this has to be done separately for each state and each right. It is for each protecting state to define the rights created under its own law, and no foreign or domestic court or foreign legal system can confer any different rights on the proprietor. In particular, if the rights are of their nature inherently personal and inalienable then the application of a foreign law cannot make them otherwise. Since an English trade mark could not, at common law, be assigned in gross a contract purporting to assign the mark without the underlying business was wholly ineffective, although the proper law of the contract was Mexican law under which the transaction was said to the permissible.[86] Authors' moral rights are quite likely to fall in this category,[87] as may copyright itself where the author's economic and moral rights are regarded as inseparable.[88] Such rights are no more assignable, under whatever system of law, than an English peerage. Likewise is it for the law of the protecting state to decide if the right may be assigned in part as to locality, duration or scope.[89] If the right is inherently indivisible then a purported part assignment can only take effect as an exclusive licence in equity.

7–62   To the extent that the transaction intended by the parties is permitted by the legal system under which the right subsists, it is for the proper law of the contract to decide on the essential validity of the contract and

---

[85] Ulmer, *op. cit.*; Beier, "Conflict of Law Problems of Trademark License Agreements" (1982) I.I.C. 162; Modiano, "International Patent Licensing Agreements and Conflict of Laws" (1980) 2 *Northwestern Journal of International Law and Business* 11.

[86] *Pinto v. Badman* (1891) 8 R.P.C. 181, CA.

[87] Though one must distinguish between moral rights being inherently non-assignable, and the existence of a "mandatory rule" against assignment. The latter can be overriden. See para. 7–88.

[88] Ulmer, *Intellectual Property Rights and the Conflict of Laws* (1978), para. 59 gives Austria and Germany as examples.

[89] The foregoing principles are widely recognised and are not confined to English law: See Ulmer, *ibid.*, paras 65 *et seq.* (copyright) and 141 *et seq.* (industrial property rights).

determine its effects in accordance with the normal rules of interpretation.

Patents: *AG fur Cartonnagen v. Temler*

The decision of Sterling J. in *AG fur Cartonnagen Industrie v. Temler*[90] is remarkable for establishing, as early as 1900, all the central principles applicable to intellectual property contracts in English private international law.[91] The plaintiffs were a German company in a patent infringement action where the principal defence was that the defendant was the licensee or assignee of the inventor of the two patents under which the plaintiffs claimed. The inventor was a German who had devised a new method of making cardboard boxes, and the plaintiff company had been set up by him and others to exploit the invention. In the document corresponding to the memorandum and articles of association of the German company the inventor had undertaken to assign to the company any improvement patents, but in the case of the two United Kingdom patents in issue he had failed to do so and the German company had sued him in Germany, where they had obtained judgment. The history of the two English patents in the hands of the inventor is complex, but so far as relevant the defendant claimed to be the legal assignee for the Leicester area only of one patent from a person who had undoubtedly been a bona fide purchaser without notice of any rights of the German company, and to be entitled to licences under both patents under English default judgments against the inventor which appeared to have been obtained collusively and with notice of the German company's rights. The defendant was also taken to have had notice of those rights when it took the assignment of the Leicester patent from the intermediate owner.

7–63

Stirling J. not only took German law as governing the rights of the company and the inventor to the British patents *inter se*, but he regarded the decision of the German Imperial Court as being strong prima facie evidence of what their respective rights were under German law. However this was not simply a case of an English court recognising and enforcing a foreign judgment, not least because the defendant Temler had not been a party before the German courts. The logic of the decision was that the obligations of the inventor, and the rights of the company against him, were governed by German law because the contract was made in Germany, between German nationals, in the German language and with no evidence of any contrary intention. In modern terminology German law was the proper law of the contract even in so far as it governed the English patents. Normally German law would fall to be proven by expert evidence, but since none had been called and since the German judgment was in evidence it should be taken as establishing what German law was. Accordingly Stirling J. found that the company had always been entitled in equity to the two patents, and that

7–64

---

[90] (1900) 18 R.P.C. 447 (Stirling J.).
[91] Prior to the enactment of the Rome Convention.

the defendant could not rely on the licences to him because he had notice of the company's equitable rights, even though their legal title had not been perfected until later. For the Leicester area alone the situation was different. The intermediate purchaser had acquired a good title free from any encumbrance, and he had passed that on to Temler intact notwithstanding the company's equitable interest of which Temler had notice.

7–65   Noteworthy features of *Cartonnagen* case are that Stirling J. had no difficulty in regarding contractual rights to English patents as being governed by German law and justiciable by the German courts, but that the rights under the original German contract and the German judgement took effect only in equity until they were perfected by registration, so that the involvement of German law as the proper law of the contract did not detract from the need, under the English statute, to register those rights in order to obtain a full legal title good against the world. It has been suggested[92] that the case turned on the fact that the obligation of the inventor was contained in a document which was not a contract *simpliciter* because it formed the by-laws of a German company and had to be governed by German law. However, the judge regarded himself as following English precedent relevant to ordinary contracts and contemplated that the by-laws might not have been governed by German law had the parties chosen otherwise. The better view is that the case would have been decided the same way if the obligation had been contained in a normal commercial contract. German law and the German courts could decide whether the inventor or the company owned the patents, but while the inventor was still registered as proprietor any bona fide purchaser from him was still entitled to rely on the provisions of English law as to registration and priority.

More recent patent cases: *British Nylon v. ICI*, *Beecham v. BLISA* and *G.A.F. v. Amchem*

7–66   Contrary to some suggestions or preconceptions, there is nothing "special" about patents or other intellectual property rights to displace the normal rules that the essential validity and effects of a contract are governed by its proper law, and that the proper law is ascertained by the unrestricted express or implied choice of the parties or in default of that by identifying the system of law with which the contract has its closest and most real connection. In particular, there is no rule of law that any aspect of the contract, as such, must be governed by the law or laws of the protecting state or states of the patent or patents which constitute its subject matter.

7–67   An illustration is provided by the decision of the House of Lords in *Beecham v. Bristol Laboratories International SA*[93] where there was an action and counterclaim for declarations of rights under a patent licence

[92] Meinhardt, "Conflict Avoidance in the Law of Patents and Trade Marks" (1956) 21 Law and Contemporary Problems 533.
[93] [1978] R.P.C. 521, HL.

agreement (the "International Agreement") covering a Territory essentially consisting of the whole world except for the Commonwealth and the United States of America.[94] The agreement was expressly governed by English law. The High Court, Court of Appeal and House of Lords all held that the International Agreement did not confer any rights on the defendants to manufacture, use or sell amoxycillin anywhere in the Territory and granted Beecham declarations accordingly.[95] None of the judges was troubled by the fact that an agreement under English law governed the existence and terms of licences under Beecham's patent rights in very many foreign countries, though not the United Kingdom. The question of whether amoxycillin could be described as "an invention now existing" during the term of the International Agreement was decided entirely by reference to English law, including substantive patent law.

Nor does the decision of the Court of Appeal in *British Nylon Spinners* **7–68** *v. ICI*[96] cast more than slight uncertainty on the general proposition. ICI had been ordered by a New York court to assign back to du Pont a number of patents which it had acquired from du Pont and under which British Nylon Spinners were ICI's exclusive licensees. The exclusive licence to British Nylon Spinners was governed by English law[97] and covered patents in the United Kingdom, various Commonwealth countries and elsewhere. British Nylon Spinners had not been party to the New York proceedings. The Court of Appeal upheld the grant of an interlocutory injunction against ICI restraining it from parting with possession of the patents in breach of its contract with British Nylon Spinners. Evershed M.R. was initially troubled, *arguendo*, as to whether the court could grant relief in respect of the Commonwealth patents and it has been said of a passage in his judgment[98] that it "goes far to sustain the rule that the essential validity and effect of contracts to assign patents and to give licences thereunder are governed by the law of the country of protection, irrespective of the nationality or domicile of the parties."[99] On this basis, the Court of Appeal's willingness to protect the plaintiffs' position as licensees under the foreign patents can only be justified on the weak ground that the relevant foreign laws were presumed to correspond to English law. Evershed M.R. alluded to this, but distinguished this argument from that based on "the general

[94] A separate but contemporaneous agreement covered North America. Bristol were never licensed for the U.K.: *Beecham Group v. Bristol Laboratories Ltd* [1978] R.P.C. 153, HL.

[95] Bristol attempted to re-open the question of a licence for amoxycillin as a defence in various infringement proceedings abroad, but the world-wide litigation was settled.

[96] (1952) 69 R.P.C. 288, CA. See also para. 8–79.

[97] It is unclear whether English law was the proper law of the licence to B.N.S. by virtue of a choice of law clause or not. The licence sued on had superseded a sub-licence under a master licence expressly governed by Delaware law, but there is no reason why licence and sub-licence need have had the same proper law.

[98] *Loc. cit.* at p. 294, line 36, set out at para. 8–79.

[99] Meinhardt, "Conflict Avoidance in the Law of Patents and Trade Marks" (1956) 21 *Law and Contemporary Problems* 533. Meinhardt does not suggest that such a rule overrides an express choice of proper law.

contractual right which relates to all the patents and is derived from the (English) contract."[1]

7–69   Another decision of the Court of Appeal confirms that there is no objection to a contract relating to United Kingdom patents being governed by a foreign law and adjudicated upon by foreign courts. In *G.A.F. Corp. v. Amchem Products*[2] the parties, both American corporations, had concluded an agreement in America providing for the defendants to test herbicides proposed by the plaintiffs. The agreement seems not to have had an express choice of law clause, since Delaware and Pennsylvania were both canvassed as the proper law, but there was no doubt that the centre of gravity of the contract was in America and that the proper law was that of an American state. The defendants applied for patents in numerous countries, and the plaintiffs commenced proceedings in the United States and subsequently in France, Germany and England claiming proprietorship. The English action was concerned only with the United Kingdom patents, in respect of which a declaration of trust and ancillary relief were sought. The American action embraced all the patents and was further advanced. Megarry J. and the Court of Appeal set aside leave to serve the writ out of the jurisdiction and struck out the action, holding that England was *forum non conveniens* in comparison to the United States.

7–70   In *Chemidus Wavin v. Societe pour la Transformation et l'Exploitation des Resines Industrielle (TERI)*[3] the question of whether the plaintiffs had been guilty of a repudiatory breach of a licence of two French patents with an express choice of English law was dealt with, though only briefly, according to English law.[4]

Copyright: *Campbell Connelly v. Noble*

7–71   *AG fur Cartonnagen Industrie v. Temler*[5] and the foregoing cases apart, the relevant cases on the private international law of contracts relating to intellectual property are almost all to do with copyright, where the absence of a system for registration and the relative informality of many dealings creates situations in which title to an English copyright may have to be traced through transactions which at first sight have very little to do with England, or vice versa for foreign copyrights. The leading modern English decision is probably that of Wilberforce J. in *Campbell Connelly v. Noble.*[6] The defendant was a band leader and song writer who in 1943 had composed a song "The very thought of you," which he

---

[1] The main criticism of the judgment of Evershed M.R. is that he equates licence rights (which are not proprietary) with the patents themselves: see para. 8–79.

[2] [1975] 1 Lloyds L.R. 601, CA.

[3] [1977] F.S.R. 181, CA.

[4] The live issue was alleged breach of Art. 85 E.C.

[5] (1900) 18 R.P.C. 447 (Stirling J.).

[6] [1963] 1 W.L.R. 253; [1963] 1 All E.R. 237 (Wilberforce J.). Approved by Ulmer, *op. cit.*, para. 67 who cites to the same effect an unnamed case of April 29, 1954 in the Oberlandesgericht Munich. See also Stone, "Problems of International Film Distribution: Assignment and Licensing of Copyright and the Conflict of Laws" [1996] Ent. L.R. 62.

had sold to the plaintiffs, a firm of music publishers. The assignment of copyright was by an English contract in which the operative words were:

> "The composer hereby assigns to the publishers the full copyright for all countries in the musical composition entitled 'The very thought of you' including the title, words and music thereof in all countries for the period of copyright so far as is assignable by law, together with all rights therein which he now has or may hereafter become entitled to whether now or hereafter known. . ."

At the time the assignment was executed, the work had not been published in the Untied States, and there was therefore no subsisting statutory American federal copyright. The song was published and registered there in due course, and an American copyright came into existence for an initial term of 28 years. Under American copyright law as it was then in force, the author, if still alive, was entitled to renew the copyright for a further term of 28 years upon the expiry of the initial term.[7] The defendant did so and purported to assign the American copyright for the renewed term to a third party. The plaintiffs sued, in England, for a declaration that they were entitled to the renewal copyright and for damages.   **7–72**

Wilberforce J. found that under American Federal copyright law the renewal copyright was an item of property quite distinct from the original copyright, and one which required to be separately assigned if it was to pass to an assignee. He also found that under a decision of the United States Supreme Court[8] the right of an author to obtain the renewal copyright could be assigned by him before the expiration of the original copyright term. On these two findings as to the nature of the renewal copyright under American law he then proceeded to ask if the words of the assignment were appropriate to pass it. As the assignment was governed by English law, Wilberforce J. declined to take into account decisions of American courts on the wording appropriate to transfer the renewal copyright, under which the plaintiffs would possibly have failed to have established their right to the renewal copyright. He thereby drew a distinction between those provisions of American law governing the nature of the renewal copyright and the validity and effect of an assignment, which were binding in the case, and those on the form or construction of the assignment which were not.[9]   **7–73**

Applying these principles, Wilberforce J. found that the words of the assignment were of the most general nature and were obviously intended to cover every right of whatever nature in whatever country. Despite the fact that the United States was an important market for the song it was   **7–74**

---

[7] See Stone, *op. cit.*, regarding the complexities of the renewal right and specifically the problems arising from the *Rear Window* case: *Stewart v. Abend* (1990) 110 S.Ct. 1750. A contract by an author to assign his renewal right does not bind his estate so is ineffective if the author dies prior to the renewal right vesting in him.

[8] *Fred Fisher Music Co v. M Witmark & Sons* (1943) 318 U.S. 643, S.Ct.

[9] The issue appears to have been one of construction, rather than formal validity.

not reasonable to suppose that the parties would have attempted to deal with one particular foreign country in specific terms. He therefore found that the assignment conferred on the plaintiffs an equitable right against the composer to his renewal copyright the moment it accrued. As there was no request for an injunction or specific performance there was no need to consider the status of this equitable right as against the assignees of the renewal copyright, nor did the judge decide whether the plaintiffs were the legal owners of the renewal copyright.

7–75   It is interesting that Wilberforce J. was prepared to say that had the contract dealt solely with the United States, then he would have taken very much more seriously the argument that the words used were ineffective to assign the renewal copyright. This might be taken as implying that he would have applied the law of an American state as the proper law of the contract in those circumstances. Unfortunately the report does not make it clear whether the assignment was expressly governed by English law, or whether the judge found it to be governed by English law on the basis of connecting factors pointing to England. In either case, however, it is not necessary to conclude that the judge had proposed to apply American law to the hypothetical assignment of an American copyright alone. It is just as likely that he simply meant that had the parties had the rights for only one major country in mind then they would have used terms appropriate to that country, and that failure to convey expressly an important right obviously within the parties' contemplation should, as a matter of construction under English law, be taken as deliberate rather than accidental.

Copyright: *Lowe's v. Littler, Redwood Music v. Francis Day & Hunter* and *ZYX Music v. King*

7–76   *Lowe's Inc v. Littler*[10] is also a case involving an international copyright agreement but it of less importance than *Campbell Connelly v. Noble* because it turned almost entirely on aspects of contract law unconnected with intellectual property. The dispute was over the English rights to the operetta *The Merry Widow*. The authors and composer had granted sole rights throughout the world to a German agent under a contract governed by German law, and the agent had granted the English rights to an English producer under a contract governed by English law. The plaintiffs were the successors in title of the executors of the English producer, and the defendants the representatives of the authors and composer. The defendants claimed that the rights of the English producer were personal and had ceased on his death, both as a matter of construction of the English contract and because the German contract appointing the agent had not empowered him to grant transmissible interests in the copyrights. The Court of Appeal reviewed the evidence of German experts and concluded that the agent was authorised to grant transmissible interests, and that as a matter of construction of the English agreement with the producer he had done so.

[10] [1958] Ch. 650; [1958] 2 W.L.R. 787; [1958] 2 All E.R. 500, CA.

The opera had been written, and both contracts executed, before the **7–77** Copyright Act 1911 increased the term of copyright from seven to 50 years after the author's death. Transitional provisions in the 1911 Act governed the position of assignees in the extended term. Having decided as a matter of German law that the agent was able to assign the English copyright, and as a matter of English law that he had done so, the Court of Appeal looked solely to English law to determine the position of the assignee under the transitional provisions.

The next of these cases on international copyright agreements may be **7–78** regarded as the mirror image of the *Campbell Connelly* case.[11] In the latter, the question was whether an English contract was effective to assign American renewal copyright. In *Redwood Music v. Francis Day & Hunter*[12] English courts including the House of Lords had to decide whether assignments of American renewal copyrights under New York law were also effective to assign English reversionary copyrights existing under the Copyright Act 1911. Under the 1911 Act the copyright in certain works reverted to the legal personal representatives of the author 25 years after his death notwithstanding any agreement to the contrary, but the reversionary right itself could be assigned by the personal representatives even before it vested in possession. The existence of this reversionary right had largely been ignored by songwriters, their estates and their publishers until an enterprising American agent discovered its existence and took assignments from a large number of estates. The existing publishers of the songs in question found that in many cases their position was in doubt.

One of the arguments of the publishers, and the only one relevant **7–79** here, was that a number of agreements between the widows of deceased American songwriters and their publishers were in terms wide enough to assign the English reversionary right. Under American law it was the widow of the author, in her capacity as such, who was normally entitled to apply for the renewal copyright of 28 years if the author had died before the expiry of the original 28 year term of copyright. It was normal practice for publishers to obtain assignments of the renewal copyright from the widow, and to include a general sweeping-up clause assigning any foreign rights which might have been overlooked before.

The court in the *Redwood* case was presented with six agreements **7–80** concerning American renewal rights. In each case the widow was also the personal representative of the deceased author under English law. Goff J. found as a fact that each agreement was governed by the law of the state of New York, primarily on the ground that in each case the assignee was a New York company. In addition five of the six agreements were executed in New York and in four of them the widow was a New York resident. The judge received expert evidence on New York law and concluded that for a contract which was unambiguous the principles of construction were substantially the same as under English

[11] [1963] 1 W.L.R. 253; [1963] 1 All E.R. 237 (Wilberforce J.).
[12] [1978] R.P.C. 429 (Robert Goff J.); [1979] R.P.C. 385, CA; [1980] 2 All E.R. 817; [1981] R.P.C. 337, HL.

law. None of the contracts dealt specifically with the English reversionary copyrights and there was evidence that neither the publishers, nor, *a fortiori*, the widows, would have had the English copyrights in mind. One contract was conceded not to assign the English copyright and the trial judge construed each of the others as being worded in terms broad enough to assign the reversionary copyright held by the widow as personal representative under English law as well as the American renewal copyright. One contract was the subject of an appeal and both the Court of Appeal and the House of Lords found, as a matter of construction, that it did not pass the English copyright.

7–81   In *Western Front v. Vestron*[13] Peter Gibson J. held it was arguable that the parties had come to a concluded agreement to produce a film, but held that on motion for summary judgment it was impossible to ascertain its proper law[14] or decide whether it was a licence or partial assignment of copyright.

7–82   The principle is no different where a foreign contract between third parties falls to be construed as an incidental matter in litigation relating to English intellectual property rights. In *ZYX Music v. Chris King*[15] one defence was that the plaintiff's arrangement of an existing song had itself been made in breach of copyright. Lightman J. construed two contracts expressly governed by New York law and concluded—though with great difficulty because of the absence of expert assistance—that a third party, Harrick, did not have the right to license the plaintiff to make the arrangement so that there was a technical but immaterial breach.

> "It seems to me to the highest degree unsatisfactory that I should be called upon to decide without any assistance of experts on the relevant American law difficult questions of construction of agreements governed by a foreign law with a different copyright law regime, made between persons in one case neither of whom, and in the other case only one of whom, is a party to this action. But I must do the best I can."

Express choice of English law in relation to foreign rights or vice versa

7–83   There was an express choice of English law in *Beecham v. Bristol Laboratories International SA*[16] although the patent licence agreement in question was for a territory which excluded the United Kingdom. Although there was no choice of law clause in *Redwood Music v. Francis Day & Hunter*,[17] it necessarily follows from that case too that there is no inherent problem in a contract relating to a foreign intellectual property

---

[13] [1987] F.S.R. 66 (Peter Gibson J.).
[14] The report omits this aspect of the decision.
[15] [1995] F.S.R. 566 (Lightman J.). An appeal by one defendant (not yet reported) was dismissed without reference to this issue.
[16] [1978] R.P.C. 521, HL. Above, para. 7–67.
[17] [1978] R.P.C. 429 (Robert Goff J.); [1979] R.P.C. 385, CA; [1980] 2 All E.R. 817; [1981] R.P.C. 337, HL, above para. 7–78.

right being expressly governed by English law. More generally, there is no reason why the proper law, whether chosen expressly or by implication, or ascertained from objective factors, need correspond to the law of the protecting state of any intellectual property right involved. This is no more than an application of the general principle of *Vita Food v. Unus Shipping*.[18]

In *Acrow v. Rex Chainbelt*[19] a patent licence agreement from an **7–84** American company ("S.I.") to the English plaintiffs was expressly governed by English law. The territory was the United Kingdom, Scandinavia and some other (unspecified) countries. S.I. purported to determine the licence and induced two associated companies (the Rex companies) not to continue to supply an essential component, in breach of an implied term in the contract. Acrow initially obtained an interlocutory injunction against S.I. which that company refused to obey. The Court of Appeal held that the acts of S.I. were unlawful and a contempt of court, that the injunction against S.I. was consistent with international comity, and granted a further interlocutory injunction requiring the Rex Companies to resume supply. In *Chemidus Wavin v. Societe pour la Transformation et l'Exploitation des Resines Industrielle (TERI)*[20] there was a licence of two French patents with an express choice of English law. The plaintiffs obtained a default judgment in England for unpaid minimum royalties, and an application to set aside for alleged breach of Article 85 EEC was dismissed, as was an allegation that the plaintiffs themselves had been guilty of a repudiatory breach of the agreement. In *Chiron v. Organon Teknika (No. 2); Chiron v. Murex Diagnostics*[21] there was no objection in principle to licences of United Kingdom patents (under worldwide agreements) being expressly governed by New Jersey law but the choice of law could not frustrate the application of the Patents Act 1977, s. 44.[22]

D. OVERRIDING THE APPLICABLE LAW: "MANDATORY RULES" AND *ORDRE PUBLIC*

General

As well as the applicable law of the contract, other systems of law may **7–85** be relevant. The most important of these is likely to be the law of the protecting state for each of the intellectual property rights to which the contract relates. At the very least, this is the system of law which governs the intrinsic qualities of the rights the subject of the contract, which cannot as a matter of definition be overridden or varied by the

---

[18] [1939] A.C 277, PC.
[19] [1971] 1 W.L.R. 1676, CA.
[20] [1977] F.S.R. 181, CA.
[21] [1993] F.S.R. 567, CA *affirming* [1993] F.S.R. 234 (Aldous J.).
[22] See para. 7–137.

applicable law. However, the protecting state may also attach conditions or restrictions to the free disposition of its intellectual property rights which are intended to apply irrespective of the intention of the parties and perhaps irrespective of the applicable law of any contracts relating to such rights. These are called "mandatory rules" in the Rome Convention.[23] States other than the protecting state may also have a legitimate interest in imposing their own mandatory rules, for instance for the benefit of employees who are their nationals or to prevent restrictive practices affecting their economy, and the mandatory rules of different legal systems can conflict with one another as well as with the applicable law of the contract.

7–86   Several provisions of the Rome Convention allow or require the mandatory rules of one state to be given priority over the applicable law. The most general of these is Article 7(1) which allows effect to be given to the mandatory rules of a country "with which the situation has a close connection," if under the latter system of law, those rules "must be applied whatever the law applicable to the contract." Giving effect to another country's mandatory rules under Article 7(1) is discretionary and the court seised of the question is invited to consider the nature and purpose of the rules and the consequences of applying them or not. The Rome Convention allowed member states to make a reservation in respect of Article 7(1) and the United Kingdom took advantage of this, so that the Rome Convention was enacted into English law without this provision.[24]

7–87   The remaining provisions of the Rome Convention as to mandatory rules do have effect in English law. Where all relevant factors point to one system of law, the choice of another system as the applicable law cannot override the mandatory rules of the former system.[25] There are special provisions relating to mandatory rules in consumer or employment contracts and contracts relating to immovable property.[26] In any event, the courts of the forum are allowed to require compliance with their own mandatory rules[27] and in extreme cases can refuse to give effect to the applicable law or foreign mandatory rules in so far as they conflict with the *ordre public* of the forum.[28]

---

[23] For general treatments of "mandatory rules" see Dicey and Morris, *The Conflict of Laws* (12th ed., 1993); Cheshire and North's *Private International Law* (12th ed., 1992), Chap. 18; Plender, *The European Contracts Convention* (1991), Chap. 9; Kaye, *The New Private International Law of Contract of the European Community* (1993), Chap. 21; Hartley, "Beyond the Proper Law: Mandatory Rules under the Draft Convention on the Law Applicable to Contractual Obligations (1979) 4 E.L. Rev. 236; Jackson, "Mandatory Rules and Rules of 'Ordre Public'" in North, ed., *Contract Conflicts* (1982); Philip, "Mandatory Rules, Public Law and Choice of Law in the EEC Convention on the Law Applicable to Contractual Obligations" in North, *op. cit.*.

[24] Art. 7(1) is also inapplicable in Germany, Ireland and Luxembourg.

[25] Art. 3(3).

[26] Respectively Arts 5(2), 6(1) and 9(6). The latter applies only to mandatory rules as to form.

[27] Art. 7(1).

[28] Art. 16.

The relevant provisions of the Rome Convention

The provisions of the Rome Convention which give precedence to **7–88** "mandatory rules" are Articles 3(3), 5(2), 6(1), 7 and 9(6). Of these, Articles 3(3) and 7(1) and (2) are of general relevance, except that Article 7(1) is not in force for the United Kingdom:

Article 3(3)

[. . .]
3. The fact that the parties have chosen a foreign law, whether or not accompanied by the choice of a foreign tribunal, shall not, where all the other elements relevant to the situation at the time of the choice are connected with one country only, prejudice the application of rules of the law of that country which cannot be derogated from by contract, hereinafter called "mandatory rules."

Article 7

Mandatory rules

1. When applying under this Convention the law of a country, effect may be given to the mandatory rules of the law of another country with which the situation has a close connection, if and in so far as, under the law of the latter country, those rules must be applied whatever the law applicable to the contract. In considering whether to give effect to these mandatory rules, regard shall be had to their nature and purpose and to the consequences of their application or non-application.[29]
2. Nothing in this Convention shall restrict the application of the rules of the law of the forum in a situation where they are mandatory irrespective of the law otherwise applicable to the contract.

Articles 5 and 6 relate to consumer contracts and employment **7–89** contracts. The latter would be relevant where employee inventors or authors were protected by mandatory rules, the former is of marginal relevance to intellectual property but might need to be borne in mind, for instance, for licences included with sales of computer software to consumers.

Article 5

Certain consumer contracts

1. This Article applies to a contract the object of which is the supply of goods or services to a person ("the consumer") for a purpose which can be regarded as being outside his trade or

---

[29] Art. 7(1) does not apply in the U.K.

profession, or a contract for the provision of credit for that object.

2. Notwithstanding the provisions of Article 3, a choice of law made by the parties shall not have the result of depriving the consumer of the protection afforded to him by the mandatory rules of the law of the country in which he has his habitual residence:
    —if in that country the conclusion of the contract was preceded by a specific invitation addressed to him or by advertising, and he had taken in that country all the steps necessary on his part for the conclusion of the contract, or
    —if the other party or his agent received the consumer's order in that country, or
    —If the contract is for the sale of goods and the consumer travelled from that country to another country and there gave his order, provided that the consumer's journey was arranged by the seller for the purpose of inducing the consumer to buy.

3. Notwithstanding the provisions of Article 4, a contract to which this Article applies shall, in the absence of choice in accordance with Article 3, be governed by the law of the country in which the consumer has his habitual residence if it is entered into in the circumstances described in paragraph 2 of this Article.

[. . .]

Article 6(1)

Individual employment contracts

1. Notwithstanding the provisions of Article 3, in a contract of employment a choice of law made by the parties shall not have the result of depriving the employee of the protection afforded to him by the mandatory rules of the law which would be applicable under paragraph 2 in the absence of choice.

[. . .]

7–90   Finally Article 9(6) would be relevant if it were concluded that intellectual property is "immovable property" for the purposes of the Rome Convention.[30]

Article 9

[. . .]

6. Notwithstanding paragraphs 1 to 4 of this Article, a contract the subject matter of which is a right in immovable property or a right to use immovable property shall be subject to the mandatory requirements of form of the law of the country where the

---

[30] As to which see para. 7–32.

property is situated if by that law those requirements are imposed irrespective of the country where the contract is concluded and irrespective of the law governing the contract.

What are "mandatory rules"

The term "mandatory rules" is used by the Rome Convention to describe rules of law which are intended to override the contractual freedom of the parties and which are capable in at least some circumstances of taking effect irrespective of the parties' choice of applicable law. They are rules for which contracting out is either altogether impossible, or possible only in limited circumstances. As such, mandatory rules are not unknown to English law—for instance in employment and consumer protection legislation—but at common law there was no special treatment for foreign mandatory rules in English private international law unless the rule in question rendered performance of the contract unlawful under the *lex loci solutionis*.[31] The unfamiliarity of the concept in the context of intellectual property is shown by the *Apple*[32] litigation: a foreign rule of law rendering a contractual no-challenge clause ineffective might well be a "mandatory rule" but the English courts would nonetheless enforce the clause except where its performance was actually illegal. Mandatory rules may have that quality by their express terms or by implication[33]; they may be statutory or common law[34]; and their mandatory nature may be international or confined to domestic contracts.

On the latter point, the Rome Convention implicitly contemplates two categories of mandatory rules but fails to adopt terminology to distinguish them.[35] Article 3(3) defines "rules . . . which cannot be derogated from by contract, hereinafter called 'mandatory rules'." In this context, and that of Articles 5 and 6, a mandatory rule is simply a rule of national law which cannot be derogated from in a contract governed by the same system of law. Article 3(3) essentially says no more than that an abusive choice of applicable law cannot evade such mandatory rules, and

7-91

7-92

---

[31] The rule in *Ralli Bros v. Cia Naviera Sota y Anzar* [1920] All E.R. 427, CA.

[32] *Apple Corps v. Apple Computer* [1992] R.P.C. 70 (Hoffmann J.); subsequent proceedings [1991] 3 C.M.L.R. 49, CA; [1992] F.S.R. 431 (Ferris J.). The contract antedated the applicability of the Rome Convention.

[33] Dicey and Morris, *The Conflict of Laws* (12th ed., 1993), Rule 184 cites the employee compensation provisions of the Patents Act 1977, ss. 40 and 42, as likely to be mandatory even to contracts expressly governed by a foreign law, despite the absence of express words in the Act.

[34] For example, the common law rules against penalties or ouster of the jurisdiction of the courts; or the rule of licensee estoppel in patent law. Probably none of these are internationally mandatory. For the common law restraint of trade doctrine (which probably goes to essential validity) see para. 7-151. The Giuliano-Lagarde Report acknowledges the existence of common law mandatory rules in the commentary to Art. 7(1) and notes that the French text of the Rome Convention deliberately uses *"droit"* in preference to *"loi."*

[35] There is a difference in terminology in the French and German titles of Art. 7 compared to the text of Art. 3(3), but not in the English version.

it is not concerned with whether or not those rules would otherwise apply to international contracts with a bona fide choice of a foreign applicable law. Article 7 contemplates a different and narrower class of mandatory rules, as does Article 9(6) in its limited field of application. Article 7(1) expressly applies only to mandatory rules which "must be applied whatever the law applicable to the contract" and Article 7(2) to rules which "are mandatory irrespective of the law otherwise applicable to the contract." Under Articles 7(1) and 7(2) alike, what is contemplated is laws which are not only mandatory in the previous sense of overriding the parties' agreement, but also in the rather stronger sense that they are intended to apply irrespective of the applicable law of the contract and perhaps the presence of substantial connecting factors with a foreign legal system. Although there is no express term in the Rome Convention, the latter class may be referred to as "internationally mandatory rules."[36]

7–93   Commentators agree that there are two areas where mandatory rules are particularly important: to redress unequal bargaining power and to promote the social or economic policies of the state in question. Of these, the first is of obvious importance when one is dealing with mandatory rules affecting ownership of intellectual property rights as between employer and employee or the right of the employee to compensation. In some Continental jurisdictions, it is also of importance as between authors and those responsible for the commercial exploitation of copyright works, to which one might add that copyright is not a purely economic right but also has important social and cultural implications which might be subject to mandatory rules in the general public interest. Since patents and the other industrial property rights are all essentially economic and are capable of having a substantial impact on the public well-being, the scope for the application of mandatory rules under the second head is almost infinite.

Examples of restrictions which may be mandatory rules

7–94   Restrictions on the contractual freedom of intellectual property right owners may fall into any of the following categories, although no enumeration could be all-inclusive:

1. For their own protection individuals, especially authors but also inventors, may be protected from improvidently disposing of their rights, and in some cases prevented from disposing of certain rights at all[37];

---

[36] The term "overriding statutes" is also used but "internationally mandatory rules" is preferred both as being more general and as corresponding to the terms of the Rome Convention. In either case, there is no magic in the form of words chosen.

[37] Ulmer, "Some Thoughts on the law of Copyright Contracts" (1976) 7 I.I.C. 202; Cohen Jehoram, ed., *Copyright Contracts* (1977); Dietz, *Copyright Law in the European Community* (1978); Katzenberger, "Protection of the Author as the Weaker Party to a Contract under International Copyright Contract Law" (1988) 19 I.I.C. 731. For Patents Act 1977, s. 42 see para. 7–145.

2. Special protection for employees is common, sometimes in terms that expressly cannot be circumvented by contrary agreement or choice of law[38];
3. General competition law is likely to apply to intellectual property contracts, but in addition proprietors of patents, and to a lesser degree other intellectual property rights, may specifically be prevented from exploiting them abusively, for instance by insisting on tying contracts with licensees or customers[39];
4. There may be provision for compulsory licences and the like, to ensure that monopoly rights or contracts exploiting them do not operate against the public interest. This may indirectly restrict the ability of the proprietor to grant (or perform) an exclusive licence agreement;
5. Trade mark owners may be restricted or prevented from assigning their marks separately from the underlying business to which they relate and restricted or prevented from licensing them in circumstances regarded as misleading[40];
6. The general law on the fairness of contractual terms may apply to contracts relating to intellectual property.[41]

These are all what may be thought of as legitimate restrictions on contractual freedom, the justification for which would be generally accepted in principle even if there might be no consensus as to the appropriateness of one country's solution compared to another's. In contrast to these there may be restrictions which amount to an appropriation of the right for the economic advantage of the state or as an indirect form of censorship.[42]   **7–95**

Can the mandatory rules of the protecting state be ignored?

At first sight, the reservation entered by the United Kingdom in respect of Article 7(1) of the Rome Convention might suggest that United Kingdom courts can simply ignore foreign mandatory rules (except in the cases of Articles 3, 5, 6 and 9) as they did at common law, but that is to misunderstand the problem. For intellectual property there is inherently potential for conflict between the applicable law of the contract and the mandatory rules of other systems of law, in particular the law of the protecting state, and the non-implementation of Article 7(1) does not resolve this but simply deprives the courts of one tool for dealing with it.   **7–96**

---

[38] Finnegan, Irving and Stahl, "A Three-Country Conundrum in Conflict of Laws: What Law Governs when Ownership of a United States Patent is at Issue" [1979] *Annual of Industrial Property Law* 422.

[39] Patents Act 1977, s. 44. See *Chiron v. Organon Technika (No. 2)* [1993] F.S.R. 567, CA and para. 7–137. For restraint of trade see para. 7–151 and for Arts 85 and 86 EEC see para. 7–115.

[40] See para. 7–149.

[41] As in *St Albans Council v. ICL* [1997] F.S.R. 251, CA.

[42] *Bodley Head v. Flegon* [1972] R.P.C. 587 (Brightman J.), see para. 7–121.

7–97 In the past, the inherently territorial nature of intellectual property rights has meant that these potential conflicts between the applicable law of a contract, the *lex fori*, and the mandatory rules of the protecting state have tended not to become apparent. Intellectual property rights are pre-eminently rights in action, which are valuable only to the extent that others can be excluded from infringing them. The specific subject matter of any intellectual property right is ultimately no more than the right to litigate, and until recently it went without saying that litigation had to be brought in the courts of each country where an intellectual property right existed and was infringed. Under this system, it hardly mattered if the courts of a third country had purported to recognise a disposition of intellectual property rights which violated the mandatory rules of the protecting state: such a judgment would be ignored in the one state where it mattered, and would be useless elsewhere.

7–98 There are three reasons why this state of affairs can no longer be taken for granted. The first is that intellectual property rights are increasingly regarded as rights in gross, whose value does not entirely depend on whether they can be enforced in the courts or not. A registered trade mark may enable royalties to be transferred to a tax haven; a patent may advantageously be used as security for a loan from a Dutch bank, or to enable an otherwise anti-competitive agreement to be structured to fall within a block exemption. In the extreme case there are "merchandising rights" which may not be enforceable in the courts at all, but which are bought and sold for millions of pounds. In all these cases and many others ownership of the right in an abstract sense is commercially important, regardless of whether the putative owner would be regarded as owner when he came to litigate.

7–99 Secondly, it can no longer be assumed that infringement litigation will always be brought in the courts of the protecting state. Elsewhere, it is suggested that the Brussels Convention already permits at least some infringement actions to be brought on an extraterritorial basis.[43] If so, one will soon have the situation where a national court will be called upon to enforce rights which exist in other jurisdictions, and as to which ownership or licensing may be a crucial issue. *Jus tertii*, after all, is a defence to any infringement action but it is an even stronger defence for the defendant to be the owner of, or licensed under, the very right sued on. What is more, the admissibility of extraterritorial infringement actions under the Brussels Convention is perhaps clearest in the case of copyright infringement, which is where title is most often uncertain and mandatory rules especially prevalent, intrusive and diverse. Even for registered rights, the foreign register may not always provide a conclusive answer as to ownership or, especially, licence rights; and for unregistered rights such as copyright it is no answer at all.

7–100 Finally, an intermediate situation already exists. United Kingdom courts may be reluctant to entertain actions for infringement of foreign intellectual property rights, or to accept that foreign courts can adjudicate on infringement of United Kingdom rights, but it is beyond

[43] See Chaps. 1, 2 and 3.

argument that disputes which go solely to proprietorship are within the general provisions of the Brussels Convention so that the courts of the defendant's domicile, for instance, have extraterritorial jurisdiction to decide whether it is the plaintiff or the defendant who owns disputed patents throughout the European Communities, as in *Duijnstee v. Goderbauer*.[44] Under the Brussels Convention, such a judgment must be recognised in every member state without formalities and can be refused recognition only on very restricted grounds. It is implicit in *Duijnstee v. Goderbauer* that there is nothing special about patents to prevent recognition of a Dutch judgment that *D* or *G* as the case may be is the owner of a bundle of patents throughout Europe.

Suppose now that the English courts are validly seised of a contractual **7–101** dispute as to the ownership of patents or copyrights around Europe in which it is argued that the effect of the contract according to the applicable law contradicts the mandatory rules of some countries.[45] If the dispute were litigated elsewhere,[46] the court could invoke Article 7(1) and could hold, for instance, that the copyright in France was validly assigned, but that the German copyright was not, assuming that German mandatory rules were contravened and that the court decided to give them paramount effect. However, apart from Articles 3(3), 5(2), 6(1) and 9(6), English law has no mechanism to give effect to any relevant foreign mandatory rules, even on a discretionary basis, and would have to hold that the German copyright had been validly assigned along with the French one. Now move forward and suppose that the parties are litigating infringement in Germany, and that title is a live issue: does the German court have to recognise the English judgment ignoring the German mandatory rules, when it would have been bound to have come to the opposite conclusion had it applied its own law? Probably it must,[47] unless the mandatory rules in question are of such importance that the German court could invoke the *ordre public* exception to automatic recognition under Article 27(1) of the Brussels Convention.

Foreign mandatory rules in the *Apple* cases

An unusual example of a situation where foreign mandatory rules **7–102** relating to intellectual property were ignored, not only with impunity but with some benefit to the plaintiff, is provided by the *Apple* litigation.[48]

---

[44] Case 288/82 [1983] E.C.R. 3663; [1985] C.M.L.R. 220.

[45] Copyrights are not registered, and mandatory rules to protect the author are more intrusive and more diverse than for other intellectual property rights. See Ulmer, "Some Thoughts on the law of Copyright Contracts" (1976) 7 I.I.C. 202; Cohen Jehoram, ed., *Copyright Contracts* (1977); Dietz, *Copyright Law in the European Community* (1978); Black, *op. cit.*; Katzenberger, *op. cit.*. That is not to say that analogous problems cannot arise for other intellectual property rights.

[46] Other than in Germany, Ireland or Luxembourg which have all entered reservations in respect of Art. 7(1).

[47] Subject to Art. 27(3) of the Brussels Convention.

[48] [1992] R.P.C. 70 (Hoffmann J.). Subsequent proceedings [1991] 3 C.M.L.R. 49, CA; [1992] F.S.R. 431 (Ferris J.).

The defendants were parties to a contract governed by English law and with an English exclusive jurisdiction clause under which they had undertaken not to oppose or apply to cancel the plaintiffs' trade marks. In breach of the agreement they commenced cancellation or opposition proceedings in the United Kingdom, Germany, New Zealand and elsewhere. They did not deny breach, but claimed that the no-challenge clause was invalid. Hoffmann J. rejected an argument that to enforce the clause pending determination of its validity under the law of the various states where the ban was sought to be enforced was contrary to international comity, and granted a worldwide interlocutory injunction against the defendants proceeding with the cancellation proceedings.

7–103   The course of the litigation elsewhere in the world demonstrates what one might expect: that the courts of other countries where cancellation proceedings had been commenced held different views to those of Hoffmann J. as to whether the injunction unduly interfered with their jurisdiction; and did not necessarily appreciate the English doctrine that the principles of party autonomy and contractual certainty prevail over mandatory local legislation if the parties have made suitable choices of governing law and jurisdiction. In New Zealand, Apple Corps unsuccessfully applied to stay cancellation proceedings which had been commenced by Apple Computer:

"As I have already stated the New Zealand Court is the only Court vested with jurisdiction to make the orders sought by Apple Computer. Clause 3.2 of the 1981 Agreement prima facie is a bar to the Court exercising that jurisdiction. Whether the Court would nevertheless make the orders on the ground that the clause was contrary to New Zealand law and therefore not able to be invoked by Apple Corps must remain an issue for determination by the New Zealand Court. Whatever any foreign Court may decide is New Zealand law (for it is a question of fact) cannot bind this Court which must in the end make that determination for itself. Assuming for the purposes of argument that the English Court determined that the provisions of Clause 3.2 did not infringe New Zealand law, it if chose to do so Apple Computer could still pursue its present action here and invite the New Zealand Court to refuse to enforce the Clause which the Court would in all probability do if it determined enforcement was contrary to New Zealand law (Dicey & Morris *The Conflict of Laws*, 11th Edn. Rule 34 p. 472). In principle this Court would not enforce a contractual provision which was void and unenforceable under New Zealand law, neither do I think it would refuse to entertain a plea to that effect on the ground that a foreign Court had previously determined in favour of the provision. I doubt whether pleas of res judicata or estoppel would prevail, it being established law that the validity or invalidity of a contract is to be determined in accordance with the *lex fori*."[49]

[49] *Apple Corps v. Apple Computer* [1990] 2 N.Z.L.R. 598 (Henry J.).

In Germany too, Apple Corps applied to stay cancellation proceedings **7–104** without success and they were ordered to submit to the withdrawal of various international trade marks registered in Germany.[50] The German court was in no doubt that the no-challenge clause was invalid:

"The action for withdrawal of protection is a *'Popularklage'* which can be asserted by anybody. [Clause 3.2 of the 1981 Agreement] does not stand in the way of the action for a non-attack obligation of this kind does not stand in the way of a plea of lack of business activities. According to the rulings of the Federal Court of Justice, the principle of the relation between a trademark and the relevant business operations is one of the main principles of German trademark law and is therefore part of the *ordre public*. The non-attack agreement concluded by the parties is invalid pursuant to Sections 134, 138 German Civil Code (Baumbach/Hefermehl, *Warenzeichenrecht* 12th Edn, 11 WZG, annot. 70)."

The discretion to apply foreign mandatory rules

Putting aside for the time being the United Kingdom's reservation in **7–105** respect of Article 7(1) of the Rome Convention, one might have thought that the following principles would apply in principle in deciding whether to give a foreign mandatory rule priority over an inconsistent contractual provision permitted (or imposed) by the applicable law.

The first question is whether the rule in question is intended to be **7–106** internationally mandatory, or only mandatory in respect of contracts governed by the same system of law as the rule itself. This may be approached by imagining that the case was being tried in the courts of the state whose mandatory rule is in issue, since those courts may be assumed to have no discretion to disregard the mandatory rules of their own law but must decide as a matter of interpretation whether the rules apply in any given situation or not. In those circumstances, would those courts regard the rule as applying to a contract with a foreign applicable law and whatever other international aspects the contract under consideration had? Self-evidently, German courts regard their rule against no-challenge clauses in trade mark delimitation agreements as internationally mandatory.[51]

It is only if the rule is intended to be internationally mandatory that **7–107** the exercise of discretion arises. The Giuliano-Lagarde Report notes that there is no international consensus as to the nature and purpose of internationally mandatory rules. Article 7(1) is not, therefore, confined

---

[50] Judgment of the Landgericht Munich I Case No. 1 HKO 14679/89 (28.3.90). This information is taken from Hobbs, "Contractual Dealings and Overriding Legal Rights" (paper delivered at Herschel Smith Seminar on Intellectual Property and Private International Law, Cambridge, February 24, 1996). Translation by Gleiss Lutz Hootz Hirsch.

[51] See para. 7–104, above. The question might also be illustrated by the problem of whether the mandatory rules under which French law prevents an author surrendering his moral rights are intended to apply to foreign authors and foreign contracts. See para. 7–120.

to the application of internationally mandatory rules generally recognised as such. None the less, where such a *de facto* consensus exists, that would be a reason for exercising the court's discretion in favour of recognising the mandatory rule.[52] This could be shown by the existence of "similar laws existing in other countries or which serve a generally recognised interest."

7–108   It is suggested for the application of Article 7(1), in those countries where it is in force, that mandatory rules relating to intellectual property which are intended to promote competition, avoid restrictive practices and protect the economic interests of consumers are likely to qualify as ones which protect generally recognised interests. These interests are among those noted by the Giuliano-Lagarde Report in its commentary on Article 7(2). An uncontroversial addition would be rules protecting human rights, such as the right to free expression.

7–109   Rules which are bona fide in the interest of the general public of the protecting state are also relatively easy to deal with. Such rules are perhaps most likely to be found in trade mark law to prevent activities which might mislead the public as to the source of goods. National laws vary considerably in what they allow. Assignments may be allowed in gross, either freely or subject to formalities; or only with the goodwill of the business. Licences may be allowed without restriction, subject to registration and approval, or not at all. Restrictions in this category imposed by the law of the protecting state ought to be observed whatever the proper law of the contract and the intention of the parties. Giving effect to a prohibited transaction might in any event be counterproductive, as it could quite possibly invalidate the trade mark altogether.

Mandatory requirements of the forum

7–110   Article 7(2) of the Rome Convention preserves the internationally mandatory rules of the forum in the following terms:

> 2. Nothing in this Convention shall restrict the application of the rules of the law of the forum in a situation where they are mandatory irrespective of the law otherwise applicable to the contract.

7–111   The Article is essentially included *ex abundanti cautela*.[53] It permits, but does not require, the courts of the forum to continue to apply their own internationally mandatory rules as they would have done in the absence of the Convention. It seems to follow from the opening words "nothing in this Convention . . ." that the internationally mandatory rules of the forum may override not only the applicable law, but also the

---

[52] Laws for the direct protection of consumers and employees would be uncontroversial examples, but they are dealt with specifically in Arts 5 and 6 of the Rome Convention.
[53] See the commentary in the Giuliano-Lagarde Report which specifically mentions mandatory rules relating to competition.

mandatory rules of other countries which might otherwise have been applied by Articles 3(3), 5(2) or 6(1). All the latter are phrased in terms of the parties' choice of law being ineffective to override mandatory rules, so there is no contradiction in making them yield to the internationally mandatory rules of the forum.[54]

The application of Article 7(2) to United Kingdom intellectual property rights is considered below.[55]

Public policy: *"ordre public"*

It is not always easy to distinguish internationally mandatory rules as   **7–112**
such from rules of public policy or *ordre public*. However, the two receive separate treatment in the Rome Convention, in Articles 7(2) and 16 respectively, and the effect of the two Articles is very different. Article 7(2) preserves the internationally mandatory rules of the forum and in an English context has no greater effect than to confirm that the parties cannot, by adoption of a foreign law for the contract, frustrate the intention of Parliament.[56] This is part of the identification of the law or laws applicable to the contract, which leads to a sort of mandatory *depecage*. In contrast, Article 16 allows the court, in circumstances described in deliberately restrictive terms, to refuse to apply a rule of law otherwise specified by the Convention if the application of that rule is "manifestly incompatible" with the public policy of the forum. Article 16 therefore allows *ordre public* to override the applicable law, or any other inconsistent rule of law such as a mandatory rule of a third state which itself displaces the applicable law.

Article 16 reads:

> The application of a rule of the law of any country specified by this Convention may be refused only if such application is manifestly incompatible with the public policy (*"ordre public"*) of the forum.

Preservation of the French term in the English text of the Rome   **7–113**
Convention acknowledges that *"ordre public"* in the Civil law sense is a concept defying accurate translation into English. Presumably, whilst it is for each court to define its own national rules of *"ordre public,"* the term is to be given as uniform and restrictive an interpretation as is possible in the context of the Rome Convention, so that the description of a rule as one of *ordre public* or public policy in national law, outside the context of the Convention, is not conclusive. This corresponds to the recognised distinction in French law between *ordre public international* or *ordre public externe*, which is within the scope of Article 16, and *ordre public*

---

[54] Art. 7(2) provides no problem because it is discretionary. Compare *ordre public* under Art. 16, below.

[55] Paras 7–134 *et seq.*

[56] To the extent that common law rules may be internationally mandatory these would be preserved, but such rules might alternatively be regarded as ones of public policy, below.

interne, which is not. In any event, English courts have historically been even more reluctant to invoke public policy in cases with an international element than they have in purely domestic ones. The rule against restraint of trade already provides one example where contract terms are considered as contrary to public policy and refused effect in a domestic context, but not internationally.[57] It is worth emphasising that it is the *application* of a foreign rule in a particular case, and not the rule in the abstract, which must offend against *ordre public* if Article 16 is to be invoked.

7–114   The Giuliano-Lagarde Report comments

> "Article 16 contains a precise and restrictively worded reservation in favour of public policy (*'ordre public'*).
> First it is expressly stated that, in the abstract and taken as a whole, public policy is not to affect the law specified by the Convention. Public policy is only to be taken into account where a certain provision of the specified law, if applied in an actual case, would lead to consequences contrary to the public policy (*'ordre public'*) of the forum. It may therefore happen that a foreign law, which might in the abstract be held to be contrary to the public policy of the forum, could nevertheless be applied, if the actual result of its being applied does not in itself offend the public policy of the forum.
> Secondly, the result must be 'manifestly' incompatible with the public policy of the forum. This condition, which is to be found in all the Hague Conventions since 1956, requires the court to find special grounds for upholding an objection. Article 16 provides that it is the public policy of the forum which must be offended by the application of the specified law. It goes without saying that this expression includes Community public policy, which has become an integral part of the public policy (*'ordre public'*) of the Member States of the European Community."

Community law as mandatory rules or as *ordre public*

7–115   There are numerous examples of mandatory rules in general Community law. The Directive on unfair terms in consumer contracts[58] provides a rare example of rules which are expressed to be internationally mandatory. Others may be internationally mandatory by implication. Article 85 of the Treaty of Rome itself is self-evidently mandatory, and it is trite law that it applies whether or not the contract is governed by the law of a member state. Rules as fundamental as those of free competition and free movement of goods, services and persons probably also constitute part of the Community *ordre public*.

7–116   European Community law also contains a number of examples of mandatory rules in the field of intellectual property. These rules tend to

---

[57] See para. 7–151, below.
[58] Council Directive 93/13 of April 5, 1993, Art. 6(2).

be found at the interface of traditional copyright law and the new technologies. Three underlying policies may be discerned. First, for the benefit of authors, who may be given unwaivable or inalienable rights, economic as well as moral. Secondly, for the benefit of legitimate users of the material in question, who are likely be in a contractual relationship with the right owner and vulnerable to standard contractual terms purporting to withdraw the right. Finally, for simplifying the administration of rights, by imposing collective negotiation and administration on rightholders, users or both.[59]

Article 9(1) of the Computer Programs Directive[60] provides that "any contractual provisions contrary to Article 6 or to the exceptions provided for in Articles 5(2) and (3) shall be null and void." The decompilation right under Article 6 of the Directive is thus subject to a mandatory rule: the authorisation of the rightholder is not required for permitted decompilation by a licensee or other person authorised to use the program, and the policy of the Directive would be frustrated if the right could be withdrawn by contract. Articles 5(2) and 5(3) of the Directive respectively provide that a person entitled to use a computer program cannot be prevented from making a back-up copy or from observing, studying or testing the functioning of the program in specified circumstances. Article 5(2) expressly (and apparently redundantly) states in terms that the right to make a back-up copy cannot be prevented by contract whereas Article 5(3) is expressed in terms of the user having the right to observe, study or test, etc., without the authorisation of the rightholder. In the related field of database protection, Article 15 of the Database Directive[61] renders null and void any contractual term purporting to remove the right to make and use insubstantial extracts in accordance with Article 8. **7–117**

An example of a mandatory rule for the protection of authors and performers is found in Article 4 of the Rental and Lending Right Directive[62]. **7–118**

Article 4

Unwaivable right to equitable remuneration

1. Where an author or performer has transferred or assigned his rental right concerning a phonogram or an original or copy of a film to a phonogram or film producer, that author or performer shall retain the right to obtain an equitable remuneration for the rental.

---

[59] A similar policy is found in ss. 116 to 144 of the Copyright, Designs and Patents Act 1988.

[60] Council Directive 91/250 of May 14, 1991 on the Legal Protection of Computer Programs [1991] O.J. L122/42.

[61] Council Directive 96/9 on the Legal Protection of Databases [1996] O.J. L77/20.

[62] Council Directive 92/100 of November 19, 1992 [1992] O.J. L346/61 on Rental Right and on Lending Right and on Certain Rights Related to Copyright in the Field of Intellectual Property.

2. The right to obtain an equitable remuneration for rental cannot be waived by authors or performers.
3. The administration of this right to obtain an equitable remuneration may be entrusted to collecting societies representing authors or performers.
4. Member States may regulate whether and to what extent administration by collecting societies of the right to obtain an equitable remuneration may be imposed, as well as the question from whom this remuneration may be claimed or collected.

7–119   The mandatory nature of this right could not be more emphatic: the fact that the right to remuneration cannot be waived is expressed in the body of Article 4(2), in the title and in recital (15). From the wording in the recital that authors and performers "must retain the possibility to entrust the administration of this right to collecting societies representing them" there also appears to be a mandatory aspect to Article 4(3). Authors and performers cannot be deprived either of the remuneration right itself, or of the ancillary right to have it administered centrally. A third and final mandatory aspect is that member states can require administration of the remuneration right by collecting societies, depriving the author or performer of at least some of the freedom he would otherwise have had and imposing on him a relationship with a quasi-monopolistic body which he may hold in no higher regard than a commercial publisher.

7–120   A similar mandatory rule requiring exercise of the cable retransmission right only through collecting societies and deeming a society to be mandated to manage the rights of a party who has not transferred his rights to the society is to be found in Article 9 of the Satellite Broadcasting and Cable Retransmission Directive.[63] Notwithstanding Recital (16) stating that the Directive is based on the principle of contractual freedom, Articles 8 to 12 regulate the cable retransmission right pervasively. The rightholder cannot choose whether or not to license his rights, and he cannot license them personally but only through a collecting society; representation may be imposed on him both in administering his rights and in negotiating terms with users; his negotiators (or the opposite party) can unilaterally insist on mediation and the mediators' proposals are deemed to be accepted if not explicitly rejected.

State monopoly and censorship: *Bodley Head v. Flegon*

7–121   In contrast to mandatory rules which protect legitimate interests, no matter how controversially, *Bodley Head v. Flegon*[64] may be cited as an example of foreign mandatory rules which quite clearly do not deserve

---

[63] Council Directive 93/83 of September 27, 1993 [1993] O.J. L248/15 on the Coordination of Certain Rules Concerning Copyright and Rights Related to Copyright Applicable to Satellite Broadcasting and Cable Retransmission.

[64] [1972] R.P.C. 587 (Brightman J.); see Colfin, "Freedom of Expression and the Exploitation of Creative Rights: The Struggle for Expression by Dissident Authors" [1987] E.I.P.R. 18.

not to be enforced, although the treatment of the relevant Russian laws inevitably proceeded on a different conceptual basis to that of the Rome Convention since the case was decided at common law.

Bodley Head v. Flegon concerned Alexander Solzhenitsyn's novel **7–122** *August 1914*. The novel was written in the USSR before that country joined the Universal Copyright Convention, was never openly published there, but was circulated clandestinely. In January 1970 the author executed a power of attorney in favour of a Swiss lawyer authorising him to act as agent for his literary works outside Russia. The power of attorney was expressed to be governed by Swiss law, had been executed in Russia, and had been delivered by an intermediary in Switzerland. The attorney granted extensive publishing rights to a German publishing house in a contract under German law, and the plaintiffs in the English action claimed under them. The first open publication of the work was in France under licence from the German publishing house, and it was as a result of this publication that the author and his licensees claimed copyright protection in the United Kingdom and the other countries of the Berne Union.

The defendant made no claim to the work himself, but argued that it **7–123** was in the public domain as a result of *samizdat* publication in Russia; that to give effect to the agreements would be a breach of comity with the USSR; and that the purported grant of the power of attorney to the Swiss lawyer was invalid under Russian law because the author lacked capacity and was acting in violation of the state trading monopoly.

The judge's findings as to Russian law were that the author had **7–124** contractual capacity to appoint an attorney, but that the state had a monopoly of foreign trade and that the power of attorney would therefore have been void under Soviet law and the purported granting of it illegal. As a further consequence, the first publication of the work in France as a result of which the English copyright subsisted would have been regarded as tainted by illegality under Russian law. The cornerstone of Brightman J.'s judgment for the plaintiff was that the contract of agency had been made in Switzerland, was governed by Swiss law, and had no relevant connection with Russia.[65] It was therefore sufficient that under Swiss law the author had adequate contractual capacity and was not acting illegally.

Bodley Head v. Flegon raises questions of general importance in the **7–125** context of contracts dealing with intellectual property rights. First, what effect if any is to be given to purported restrictions on the ability of the proprietor freely to dispose of his rights. Neither *Bodley Head v. Flegon* itself nor the law of the Rome Convention seems to provide any universal solution. The answer may depend on whether the restriction is characterised as an inherent property of the right or as a foreign mandatory rule, as well as on the purpose of the rule and the interests it

---

[65] In other contexts it may be to the detriment of authors, as well as questionable in principle, to suggest that the country of their domicile or nationality, or where the work was produced, is not a relevant connecting factor when considering contracts relating to their works.

protects. Secondly, to what extent should one state give effect to laws reflecting the public policy of another state which may conflict with its own, and to what extent should it impose its own notions of public policy. In the context of the Rome Convention one looks to Article 7(1), in those countries where it is in force, Article 7(2) and Article 16.[66]

Inalienable rights: *droit moral* in French law

7-126   The problem epitomised by *Bodley Head v. Flegon* is that of copyright being invoked to prevent an author exploiting and publishing his works for reasons that have nothing to do with protecting him or the public interest as it is understood in the West, in marked contrast to the preamble to the Universal Copyright Convention which declares the intention of the contracting states "to ensure respect for the rights of the individual and encourage the development of literature, the sciences and the arts" and to "facilitate a wider dissemination of the works of the human mind." The effect of an author's copyright being expropriated in this way may not just be to deprive him of the fruits of his labour: it may even prevent the publication of his works on any terms, leaving him in a worse position than if copyright had never existed.[67]

7-127   In contrast, laws exist in several Continental European countries derogating from the principle of freedom of contract with the legitimate object of protecting authors as the weaker party, particularly in respect of their moral rights, which legislation may declare to be inalienable.[68] Such rules may be regarded, *a priori*, either as defining the inherent features of the copyright or moral rights, as rules of *ordre public*, or as mandatory rules relating to disposal of the rights. In the latter two cases the question arises of whether they are part of *ordre public interne* or *externe*, internationally mandatory or not. The possible answers are illustrated by two French cases on whether to give effect in France, to waivers or purported assignments of French moral rights, by non-French authors, in contracts not governed by French law.

7-128   In *Rowe v. Walt Disney*[69] the plaintiff, an American national resident in Paris, was one of two authors who had originally devised the idea of a film based on an aristocratic family of cats in Paris. Rowe was the sole author of the resulting draft story and screenplay, which eventually, and after much further development, became the Walt Disney film *Aristocats*.

---

[66] See paras 7–85 and 7–112.

[67] Compare the unsuccessful claim of the U.K. Government to be entitled to the copyright in George Blake's autobiography (a claim which depended on his former status as a Crown servant rather than the fact that he was a traitor) in *A.-G. v. Blake* (CA, December 16, 1997, not yet reported). The Crown's private law claim to ownership of the copyright failed at first instance and on appeal. A further public law claim arising from Blake's membership of the Intelligence Services was introduced on the invitation of the Court of Appeal and an injunction was granted to prevent Blake retaining the proceeds of his crime.

[68] See Ulmer, "Some Thoughts on the Law of Copyright Contracts" (1976) 7 I.I.C. 202; Cohen Jehoram, ed., *Copyright Contracts* (1977); Dietz, *Copyright Law in the European Community* (1978); Black, *op. cit.*; Katzenberger, *op. cit.*

[69] [1987] F.S.R. 36 (Cour d'Appel, Paris)

He had given his co-author a written assignment of his rights in a form expressly governed by English law,[70] but when the film proved to be an immense success he sought to have it set aside on various grounds.[71] He also claimed that although he had been given screen credit as an author, he was not identified in publicity material for the film or in a related book published by Hachette, and that these omissions infringed his inalienable right of paternity.

The first instance court found for the plaintiff solely in respect of his **7–129** right of paternity in the Hachette book and some derivative materials relating to the film. The Court of Appeal allowed the defendants' appeal in relation to the right of paternity, and otherwise upheld the first instance decision. In so doing, the Court of Appeal gave precedence to the law of the contract over French public policy as reflected in the inalienability of French moral rights.

> "This concept of French public policy can be applied only with the greatest degree of caution to the foreign law under which a contract relating to an author's rights was signed.
> The legal certainty of contracts would be destroyed if a party were allowed to ignore obligations entered into under the law of a specific country by availing itself of the contrasting law of another country."

Rowe v. Walt Disney implicitly treats the inalienablity of French moral **7–130** rights merely as part of *ordre public interne*, so that a foreign author could validly alienate even his French moral rights in a contract governed by foreign law. The same result was also reached by the Paris Court of Appeal in the *Asphalt Jungle* case, *Huston v. La Cinq*[72] but the decision was overturned by the French Supreme Court (Cour de Cassation) in favour of giving the rights of the author precedence over contractual certainty.[73]

In *Huston v. La Cinq*[74] the plaintiffs were the successors of John **7–131** Huston, the American director and co-author of the film *Asphalt Jungle*, and Ben Maddow, the co-author of the script. The film had been shot in black and white but subsequent technical developments allowed the production of a colourised version. The successors of MGM, the original producers of the film, had licensed the defendants to broadcast the

---

[70] An antecedent informal assignment was held also to be governed by English law on the basis of closest connection.

[71] All these failed, with both French courts applying the English doctrine of the laches and concluding that the plaintiff had knowingly delayed far too long in pursuing any complaint he might have had. There was no fraud, incapacity, undue influence, misrepresentation, conspiracy or restraint of trade.

[72] (1993) 22 I.I.C. 702. Edelman, "Applicable Legislation Regarding Exploitation of Colourized U.S. Films in France: The 'John Huston' Case" (1992) 23 I.I.C. 629.

[73] In the meantime, the United States had acceded to the Berne Convention with effect from March 1, 1989 which, unlike the Universal Copyright Convention, expressly recognises moral rights.

[74] (1993) 22 I.I.C. 702. Edelman, *op. cit.*

colourised film on French television. The plaintiffs claimed it infringed John Huston's right of integrity.

7-132   It was already established in French law that the doctrine of reciprocity did not apply to moral rights. A foreign author could have and enforce moral rights under French law irrespective of whether such rights were recognised in the country of origin. The first live question which arose was therefore whether authorship of the film was to be determined according to French law, under which Huston as director was the author; or under United States law, under which MGM was considered to be the author of the film as a "work for hire" and Huston as director had no special status. The second question was whether Huston's successors were precluded from objecting to the colourisation by virtue of employment contracts between Huston, his co-author, and MGM, governed by United States (Californian) law, which permitted adaptations. The Paris Court of Appeal answered both questions in favour of the defendants.[75] The French Supreme Court held that authorship was to be determined according to French law, so that Huston was the author, and that the nature of moral rights in French law as part of *ordre public* meant that the Paris Court of Appeal had been wrong to give overriding effect to the American contracts.[76]

7-133   The case was remitted to the Versailles Court of Appeal, which found for the plaintiffs and granted an injunction against *La Cinq* screening the colourised film.[77] Even so, there are two reasons why the decision is not entirely conclusive for future cases. First, the Versailles court held that the colourised film was not an "adaptation." Secondly, the infringement of the right of integrity was a particularly serious one because the decision to shoot *Asphalt Jungle* in black and white had been taken for artistic rather than technical reasons and contributed to the dramatic effect of the film.

E. ENGLISH MANDATORY RULES AND INTELLECTUAL PROPERTY

Introduction

7-134   The following paragraphs discuss some examples of English mandatory rules relevant to intellectual property, which already exist in legislation or at common law but are not necessarily recognised as such because of the unfamiliarity of the term and concept. Relatively few statutory mandatory rules are explicit as to whether or not they apply to contracts not governed by English (or Scottish) law[78]; in other words they

---

[75] Judgment of July 6, 1989. (1991) 22 I.I.C. 121.
[76] (1992) 23 I.I.C. 702; (1991) 147 R.I.D.A. 197.
[77] (1995) 164 R.I.D.A. 389.
[78] The Unfair Contract Terms Act 1977 is expressly internationally mandatory in some circumstances: s. 27. The Arbitration Act 1996, s. 4, is exemplary (and almost unprecedented) in stating which of its provisions are mandatory or non-mandatory.

may or may not be internationally mandatory by implication. This is ultimately a matter of construction of the statute and it is legitimate to perform an exercise in "interests analysis," not because there is any discretion in applying the rule, but to see whether Parliament might reasonably have intended the statute to apply to contracts with a foreign applicable law or to confine it to domestic contracts. The exercise may be trivial for contracts where the express choice of law is abusive, but it will be seen that English rules may as a matter of statutory construction be held to be internationally mandatory even in respect of contracts where the centre of gravity of the contract is abroad and the choice of a foreign applicable law is bona fide and objectively justifiable. The presumption against extraterritorial legislation is not decisive, because where contracts relating to United Kingdom intellectual property rights are concerned there is by definition at least one connecting factor pointing to the United Kingdom; and at least some potential for impact on the economic and social life of this country.

In asking whether a provision is internationally mandatory or manda- **7–135** tory only in respect of contracts governed by English law, it is suggested that a useful test is that of the officious bystander; or as Dillon L.J. put it in the context of an argument that section 44 of the Patents Act 1977 did not apply to contracts governed by foreign law:

> "If the language of subsection (1) of section 44 is thus subject to the restriction of the relationship to the United Kingdom patent, what sense does it make to bring in the further restriction that the contract or licence relating to the United Kingdom patent must be governed by United Kingdom law?"[79]

Patents (1): competition-oriented mandatory rules

Of all the intellectual property rights, patents are perceived as having **7–136** the greatest potential effect on competition and the economy in general, so it is not surprising that they are subject to a variety of mandatory rules, including what are in fact internationally mandatory rules, although English law has not previously known them by that name.

Section 44(1) of the Patents Act 1977 provides that certain terms of a **7–137** patent licence or contact for the supply of a patented product are to be void. The terms prohibited may be summarised as any conditions requiring the licensee or purchaser to purchase from the patentee, anything other than the patented product, or prohibiting him from using articles or a patented process supplied by another.[80] A further consequence is that by section 44(3) the existence of a contract containing a term void by virtue of section 44(1) is a defence to an action for infringement against anyone, even a third party. The section does not contain any express rules of private international law, though the obvious

---

[79] *Chiron v. Organon Technika (No. 2)* [1993] F.S.R. 567, CA.
[80] The actual provisions are more complicated and there are certain exceptions: s. 44(2), (4), (6).

conclusion that it does not apply to licences of foreign patents only, whatever the applicable law, follows from the definitions of "patent," "patented product" and "patented invention" in section 130(1) as well as from the presumption that Parliament does not use general words to legislate with extra-territorial effect.

7–138   In *Chiron v. Organon Teknika (No. 2)*[81] the defendants pleaded that the plaintiffs had entered into contracts containing terms prohibited by section 44(1). The plaintiffs sought leave to amend to plead that the terms were contained in contracts governed by New Jersey law, that New Jersey law would not give effect to section 44(1), and that consequently the clauses were not void and section 44(3) did not come into operation. Aldous J. refused leave for the plaintiffs' amendments and held that:

> "Section 44 is concerned with United Kingdom patents. It only applies to contracts for the supply of products covered by United Kingdom patents or licences to work such patents, or contracts relating to such supply or licence. If the agreement does relate to such events, and in so far as it purports to require or prohibit the matters set out in subsection (1) of section 44, that clause is void. Parliament has laid that down. It is irrelevant that the agreement is governed by foreign law. It is irrelevant that the foreign law does not contain a similar provision to section 44. It is not possible for me to hold that such requirements and prohibitions as are referred to in section 44 are not void, and then conclude I will not enforce them. So to hold would disregard the clear intention of Parliament."[82]

7–139   The Court of Appeal, affirming Aldous J., held that the section applied to the contracts governed by New Jersey law, even though this was far from being a case of an artificial choice of proper law with no genuine connection with the contract.[83] Any other result would frustrate the clear purpose of the section:

> "A person who obtains the privilege of monopoly protection under a United Kingdom patent and comes to a United Kingdom court to enforce the patent will not be allowed to do so if by a contract relating to the patent he has, in the eyes of the English court, abused his monopoly power under the United Kingdom patent by seeking, for instance, to extend the monopoly to exploit goods or processes for which he has no monopoly patent protection. If that is the object, it is wholly irrelevant what the proper law of the contract

---

[81] [1993] F.S.R. 567, CA *affirming* [1993] F.S.R. 234 (Aldous J.). See Binns, "Section 44 of the U.K. Patent Act 1977—Still Alive and Kicking" *Patent World* April 1994, 28. Both agreements antedated the Contracts (Applicable Law) Act 1990 so the Rome Convention did not apply.

[82] *per* Aldous J. *ibid*., p. 574.

[83] The agreements were worldwide, between American companies, and had no particular reference to the U.K.

is. It is the effect of the contract relative to the United Kingdom patent which is at the heart of the matter. If Mr. Pollock is right, the effect would be likely to be that section 44(3) could be invoked against patentees who are United Kingdom subjects or United Kingdom companies and who are therefore likely to make their contracts relating to their patents subject to United Kingdom law, but could not be evoked against patentees who are subjects of a foreign state or companies incorporated in a foreign state who are likely to make their contracts relative to their patents subject to the laws of their own state. Such a distinction must be, in my judgment, contrary to the purposes of the section."[84]

At trial, the section 44 defence was upheld in respect of one of two agreements,[85] but the plaintiffs had modified the agreements to remove the disputed terms and obtained summary judgment in fresh actions.[86] **7–140**

Section 45 of the Patents Act 1977 contains provisions allowing a party to terminate a patent licence or contract for the supply of a patented product on three months' notice after all the relevant patents existing at the date of the contract or licence have ceased to be in force, notwithstanding any contract term to the contrary. The section thereby effectively prohibits charging a royalty under a patent which has expired or been revoked. Section 58 of the Patents Act 1949 was to similar effect.[87] The section is clearly mandatory in a domestic context. By analogy with section 44, it probably applies regardless of the applicable law of the contract, though this cannot be deduced from the few cases in point.[88]

Under section 58 of the 1949 Act, *Advance Industries v. Frankfurther*[89] decided that where there was a licence in respect of both British and foreign patents, including improvement patents, the licence in respect of the British patents could be terminated three months after all the original British patents had expired and the presence of foreign patents was irrelevant: "This provision, [section 58] in my judgment, is to be exercised in relation to the patent monopoly conferred by British Letters Patent and neither extends to nor can be defeated by the existence of **7–141**

---

[84] *per* Dillon L.J. *ibid*.

[85] [1994] F.S.R. 202 (Aldous J.), *affirmed* [1996] F.S.R. 153, CA except to allow a cross appeal by Ortho Ltd who were not a party and whose cause of action was not tainted.

[86] *Quaere* what happens if the other party refuses to agree to the removal of a term which *ex hypothesi* is void according to English law, but perhaps not according to the applicable law.

[87] s. 58 of the 1949 Act also prevented licensees being locked into an agreement indefinitely at the original royalty by the successive addition of dubious or unwanted improvement patents. Now s. 45 of the 1977 Act allows for severability and revision of the licence terms.

[88] The two cases which follow (*Advance Industries v. Frankfurther* and *Hansen v. Magnavox Electronics*, below) leave the question of proper law open. There was an express choice of English law for the sub-licences at issue in *Bristol Repetition Ltd v. Fomento (Sterling Area) Ltd* [1961] R.P.C. 222 (Cross J.) but the case was decided on narrow grounds which should not apply under the current s. 45.

[89] [1958] R.P.C. 392 (Lloyd-Jacob J.).

patent monopolies conferred by other powers." However, the judge declined to decide what would happen to the remainder of the agreement. In *Hansen v. Magnavox Electronics*[90] Lord Denning M.R. in the Court of Appeal held that as a piece of domestic legislation section 58 applied only to United Kingdom patents and to contracts where the provisions relating to United Kingdom patents and foreign patents were clearly severable. A worldwide exclusive licence[91] (except for Continental Europe) was not severable, and so had not been determined by notice pursuant to section 58 after 1972, when the licensed United Kingdom patents had expired. Section 45(1) now expressly provides for severablity and section 45(3) (which was also new in the 1977 Act) allows for continuing contracts to be varied by the court after the original relevant patents have ceased to exist. The latter, at least, is a further example of a mandatory rule in its own right.

Patents (2): licences and licences of right

7–142   When patents are extended either through general legislation increasing the patent term, or for inadequate remuneration, or for war loss, the implications for existing licences have to be considered. The Patents Act 1977 extended "new existing patents" for four years subject to endorsement "licences of right" in the extended term. Schedule 1, paragraph 4(2) of the Act made provision for existing licences. Any licence in force immediately before the appointed day until the end of the original 16 year term was to continue in force until the patent expired but was to become non-exclusive, if previously exclusive, and was to be free of any payment to the patent proprietor. The latter provision expressly applied notwithstanding the terms of the licence and both provisions are probably internationally mandatory. There was also a general power under paragraph 4(4) for the Court to apportion any loss or liability arising from the extension of term.

7–143   In *National Research and Development Corporation v. Wellcome Foundation*[92] Aldous J. decided that United Kingdom patents registered in Hong Kong and Singapore had been extended along with the corresponding United Kingdom patent and that the licences in respect of those patents had also become royalty-free in the extended term.

7–144   A similar problem arises for supplementary protection certificates but the solution does not apparently involve replacing the provisions of existing licences with new mandatory rules. Article 5 of the Supplementary Protection Certificates Regulation[93] provides that the certificate "shall confer the same rights as conferred by the basic patent and shall

---

[90] [1977] R.P.C. 301, CA. Identifying the *ratio decidendi* is complicated by the fact that the majority disagreed between themselves as to the construction of the agreement, and Lord Denning allowed the appeal on a construction of s. 58 which had not been argued.

[91] The proper law of the licence is not stated in the report.

[92] [1991] F.S.R. 663 (Aldous J.).

[93] Council Regulation 1768/92 (of June 18, 1992) [1992] O.J. L182/1 concerning the Creation of a Supplementary Protection Certificate for Medicinal Products.

be subject to the same limitations and the same obligations." Presumably these general words preserve existing licence arrangements,[94] though the Regulation is less than ideally clear, if only because the alternative of a licensee under the patent being left with no rights under the certificate is too inconvenient and unjust for the Regulation to have contemplated it.

Patents (3): protection of employee-inventors

The Patents Act 1977 contains provisions regulating the ownership of **7–145** inventions as between employer and employee and providing for employee-inventors to be compensated for inventions of exceptional benefit to their employers. In summary, section 39(1) specifies the circumstances in which an invention is to belong to the employer, and by section 39(2) any other invention made by an employee is to belong to him. Where the invention belongs to the employer by virtue of section 39(1), the employee may none the less be entitled to compensation pursuant to section 40(1) if the patent for the invention is of "outstanding benefit to the employer." Section 40(2) applies where the employee has assigned the patent to the employer and allows the court to re-open the contract and award the employee additional compensation. This subsection expressly overrides any inconsistent contractual term: section 40(4).

Section 42 entitled "enforceablity of contracts relating to employee's **7–146** inventions" provides:

(1) This section applies to any contract (whenever made) relating to inventions made by an employee, being a contract entered into by him—
   (a) with the employer (alone or with another); or
   (b) with some other person at the request of the employer or in pursuance of the employee's contract of employment.
(2) Any term in a contract to which this section applies which diminishes the employee's rights in inventions of any description made by him after the appointed day and the date of the contract, or in or under patents for those inventions or applications for such patents, shall be unenforceable against him to the extent that it diminishes his rights in an invention of that description so made, or in or under a patent for such an invention or an application for any such patent.

[. . .]

The interpretation section for sections 39 to 42 is section 43 which **7–147** provides:

[. . .]

---

[94] *Research Corp's SPC* [1994] R.P.C. 667 decided that if the basic patent was subject to licences of right, then so was the SPC. However the licence of right under the patent had expired and a fresh application had to be made.

(2) Sections 39 to 42 above shall not apply to an invention made by an employee unless at the time he made the invention one of the following conditions was satisfied in his case, that is to say—

(a) he was mainly employed in the United Kingdom; or

(b) he was not mainly employed anywhere or his place of employment could not be determined, but his employer had a place of business in the United Kingdom to which the employee was attached, whether or not he was also attached elsewhere.

[. . .]

(4) Any references in sections 39 to 42 above to a patent and to a patent being granted are respectively references to a patent or other protection and to its being granted whether under the law of the United Kingdom or the law in force in any other country or under any treaty or international convention.

[. . .]

7–148   All these provisions are clearly mandatory in a domestic context but leave open the question of whether they are internationally mandatory as well. Whilst the legislation is not explicit, the editors of *Dicey and Morris*[95] suggest that sections 40 and 42 are likely also to be mandatory even to contracts expressly governed by a foreign law. In the light of section 43, this is clearly right: the Act applies to foreign patents as well as United Kingdom ones, and contains its own code as to which employment relationships it applies to, so it makes no sense to impose the additional and irrelevant criterion that the contract of employment should be governed by English law. However, for the purposes of the Rome Convention the distinction is of little importance, since Article 6(1) preserves for the employee the benefit of the mandatory rules of the law which would govern his employment contract in the absence of choice, and that law is identified by Article 6(2) in terms closely corresponding to section 43(2). Article 6(1), unlike Article 7(2), does not depend on the rules in question being mandatory irrespective of the law otherwise applicable to the contract.

Trade marks (1): licensing and assignments

7–149   Both at common law, and under statutes prior to the Trade Marks Act 1938, trade marks were in principle regarded as assignable only with the goodwill of the business in which they were used and there was no statutory provision for licensing. The Trade Marks Act 1938 liberalised assignments and licences to a limited extent and the Trade Marks Act 1994 removed the remaining substantive restrictions on free assignment[96] and licensing.[97] The restrictions remaining under the 1994 are clearly ones as to form.[98]

[95] *The Conflict of Laws* (12th ed., 1993); rule 184
[96] s. 24.
[97] s. 28.
[98] See para. 7–54.

For trade mark licences and assignments executed prior to the 1994   **7–150**
Act the question arises as to whether the restrictions in the 1938 Act and
its predecessors are internationally mandatory or not. Almost certainly,
they are. In the early case of *Pinto v. Badman*[99] the brand *El Destino* was
coined and first used by a Mexican cigar manufacturer who exported to
England. He sold the brand, but retained the factory and business. The
deed of sale was apparently governed by Mexican law. The purchaser
registered the mark in England and sued some counterfeiters for
infringement and passing-off. The Court of Appeal held that the
registration was invalid and they had no title to sue. Lord Esher said of
the assignment:

> "All that they sold therefore was the trade mark. They sold no part
> of the business of which the trade mark was an indication that it was
> their business, and a valuable business.
>
> Now, on the question as to whether they might sell the trade
> mark in that way in Mexico, I am inclined to assume that they
> might. What rights that would confer in Mexico I do not know.
> They having sold that right, when it comes to be exercised in
> England for the purpose of and by means of registration, the
> question, whether when that is shewn they can rely on that
> registration to give them the exclusive right in England, is a matter
> of English law; and, inasmuch as there was nothing sold but the
> right to the trade mark, I come to the conclusion that the law of
> England does not allow the purchaser of such a right, when he
> purchases the right only, to register that trade mark, the right to
> register which, as between himself and the seller, has passed to him,
> to register that so as to obtain, by virtue of the Trade Marks Act,
> the right to the exclusive use as against the public or as against any
> individual member of the public."

Trade marks (2): restraint of trade issues in delimitation agreements

Two cases have dealt with restraint of trade issues which arise in trade   **7–151**
mark delimitation agreements, either in respect of undertakings not to
use particular marks or in respect of obligations not to challenge the
validity of the other party's registrations. Neither of these cases was
decided under the Rome Convention. As will be seen, English law
characterises the doctrine of restraint of trade as going to the material or
essential of the contract, so that at common law and under the Rome
Convention alike it is the proper or applicable law of the contract which
determines whether terms of a contract in restraint of trade are valid.
Subject to that, English law does not recognise foreign mandatory rules
or foreign rules of public policy striking down agreements in restraint of
trade unless performance of the restriction would actually be unlawful
according to the *lex loci solutionis*.[1]

---

[99] (1891) 8 R.P.C. 181, CA.
[1] An application of the doctrine in *Ralli Bros v. Compania Naviera Sota y Aznar* [1920] 2
K.B. 287, CA.

7–152   In *Apple Corps v. Apple Computer*[2] the defendants alleged that field of use restrictions and no-challenge provisions in a trade mark delimitation agreement were unenforceable as being in restraint of trade, both under English law as the express proper law of the agreement, under Article 85 EEC and under various national laws.[3] The plaintiffs sued to enforce the agreement. Ferris J. held that foreign law of restraint of trade was irrelevant unless it made performance illegal, which was not alleged.[4] In *South African Breweries v. King*[5] South African law, as the proper law of the contract, had governed whether a 10 year non-competition covenant was valid. The fact that a party had agreed to surrender his common law freedom to carry on any trade he chose did not alter the fact that the obligation was a contractual one. On the facts, the restrictions were not contrary to English law or Article 85 EEC. In particular, there was no doctrine of English public policy against enforcing no-challenge clauses in trade mark delimitation agreements.

7–153   In *Fyffes v. Chiquita Brands International*[6] the parties had agreed that the (second) plaintiffs would not use the mark *Fyffes* in Continental Europe. The plaintiffs subsequently complained to the E.C. Commission that the agreement was invalid under Articles 85 and 86 EEC and applied to the English court for interlocutory injunctions restraining the defendants from enforcing their trade mark rights on the Continent, using the *Fyffes* marks there, or enforcing the non-use provisions of the agreement. The agreement was expressly governed by English law and it was the plaintiffs who were entitled to the *Fyffes* marks in the United Kingdom. Vinelott J. held that it was doubtful that the agreement gave rise to any unlawful restraint of trade, and that there was no precedent for the application of the doctrine of restraint of trade to an agreement wholly operating outside the jurisdiction of the English courts. He refused all the interlocutory injunctions requested by the plaintiffs and continued interlocutory injunctions already granted to the defendants restraining the plaintiffs from selling bananas under the *Fyffes* marks outside the United Kingdom or Ireland.

Copyright and neighbouring rights

7–154   In some Continental jurisdictions, there are comprehensive laws protecting authors in their dealings with employers, publishers, broadcasters and other businesses interested in exploiting their copyrights.[7]

---

[2] [1992] F.S.R. 431 (Ferris J.). For the facts of the case see paras 7–102 above, and 8–84 below.

[3] The Court of Appeal had previously decided against the defendants in respect of various other foreign legal systems [1991] 3 C.M.L.R. 49, CA.

[4] Or unless the performance was in England and was contrary to English public policy, covering the possibility of an abusive choice of proper law in an attempt to preserve a restriction effective in England.

[5] [1900] 1 Ch. 273, CA.

[6] [1993] F.S.R. 83 (Vinelott J.).

[7] Cohen Jehoram, ed., *Copyright Contracts* (1977); Dietz, *Copyright Law in the European Community* (1978); Ulmer, "Some Thoughts on the Law of Copyright Contracts" (1976) 7 I.I.C. 202; Black, "The Regulation of Copyright Conflicts: A Comparative View" [1980] E.I.P.R. 386; Katzenberger, "Protection of the Author as the Weaker Party to a Contract under International Copyright Contract Law" (1988) 19 I.I.C. 731.

Such rules are conspicuous by their absence in the United Kingdom, where the principle of unrestricted party autonomy applies almost without exception. Historically, there have been a few examples of mandatory rules in United Kingdom copyright law such as the creation of reversionary interests under the 1911 Act[8] which the author could not alienate *inter vivos*. Virtually the only currently valid exception is to be found in sections 116 to 144 of the Copyright, Designs and Patents Act 1988 providing extensive statutory regulation for copyright licensing through collective schemes. Moral rights under the Copyright, Designs and Patents Act 1988 can be waived but are not assignable,[9] though this is probably better regarded as an inherent quality of the rights rather than a mandatory rule as such.

The E.C. Copyright Term Directive[10] required member states to **7–155** extend the term of copyright protection for EEA nationals from the previous international norm of 50 years after death to the German term of 70 years after death.[11] One effect of the Directive is that works which had fallen into the public domain in most member states may re-enter copyright if they were still in copyright in at least one. This immediately raises a number of problems of title and contract law, none of which are addressed by the Directive, such as the effect of the extension of term on licences and whether the extended term vests in an assignee of the original copyright or in the successors of the author under the general law. Another provision capable of affecting existing contracts is Article 2(1), providing that the principal director of a cinematographic or audiovisual work is to be its author or one of its authors.

In United Kingdom law, the position is governed by the transitional **7–156** provisions of the Duration of Copyright and Rights in Performances Regulations 1995[12] which draw a distinction between extended copyright and revived copyright, according to whether copyright subsisted at the commencement date[13] or the work was in the public domain.[14] The general principle is that the benefit of the extended or revived term lies where it falls, notwithstanding that as between assignor and assignee, or licensor and licensee, it is a supervening event that cannot reasonably have been foreseen by either party. There are no special provisions for revision of existing contracts to take the new circumstances into account or for equitable redistribution of the benefit of the extended or revived copyright as between the estate of the author and the assignee or licensee of the copyright. An assignee fortunate enough to have taken an assignment of a copyright with a couple of years to run, valued on the basis of predicted cash flows, may get ten times what he bargained for.

---

[8] Copyright Act 1911, s. 5(2) proviso.

[9] Copyright, Designs and Patents Act 1988, s. 87 and 94.

[10] Council Directive 93/98 (of October 29, 1993) Harmonising the Term of Protection of Copyright and Certain Related Rights [1993] O.J. L290/9.

[11] The extension of term does not apply to rightholders who are not EEA nationals, except on the basis of reciprocity: Art. 7(2).

[12] S.I. 1995 No. 3297.

[13] January 1, 1996, Reg. 1(1).

[14] Regs 14 to 26 deal with copyright. Regs 27 to 35 deal *mutatis mutandis* with rights in performances and do not receive separate commentary here.

7–157   For extended copyright, Regulation 18 provides that the extended copyright is to belong to the person who was the copyright owner immediately before commencement, unless that person was entitled to less than the full term of the original copyright in which case the extended copyright becomes part of the reversionary interest. Regulation 19 provides that the person who owned the original copyright immediately before it expired is to own any revived copyright, except that if the previous owner died before commencement (if an individual) or ceased to exist (if a legal person) then the revived copyright vests in the author or his personal representatives as part of his estate.[15] Extended and revived copyrights can both be assigned or licensed prospectively by the prospective owner prior to the commencement date,[16] raising the question of whether general words in an agreement long antedating the commencement date and even the E.C. proposals can have this effect.

7–158   In the case of extended copyrights, any licence or agreement relating to exploitation, existing immediately before the commencement date, and which is not due to expire before the end of the original copyright period, is automatically continued in effect for the term of the extended copyright, subject to any agreement to the contrary.[17] There are no provisions for licences in respect of revived copyright, though the former licensee has the benefit of the general provisions for the protection of persons making arrangements to exploit works in the public domain.[18]

7–159   The one area of interest at common law is that several contracts between performers or composers of popular music and their agents or record companies have been struck down under a number of common law doctrines: the rule that contracts are not binding on minors unless for their advantage[19]; undue influence[20]; and the common law restraint of trade doctrine.[21] The first of these is obviously characterised as a rule relating to contractual capacity and is of declining relevance now that the age of majority is 18. Undue influence probably goes to essential validity and so would be governed by Article 8 of the Rome Convention, though in so far as undue influence is an equitable doctrine, it might apply irrespective of the applicable law.[22]

---

[15] In the case of a film, the revived copyright vests in the principal director or his personal representatives.

[16] *ibid.*, Reg. 20.

[17] Reg. 21.

[18] Regs 23 to 25.

[19] Compare *Chaplin v. Leslie Frewin (Publishers) Ltd* [1966] Ch 71; [1965] 3 All E.R. 764, CA.

[20] *O'Sullivan v. Management Agency and Music Ltd* [1985] Q.B. 428; [1985] 3 All E.R. 351, CA.

[21] *Schroeder Music Publishing Co v. Macaulay* [1974] 1 W.L.R. 1308; [1974] 3 All E.R. 616, HL.; *O'Sullivan v. Mangement Agency and Music Ltd supra; Zang Tumb Tuum Records v. Johnson* [1993] E.M.L.R. 61, CA. See Laddie, Prescott and Vitoria, *The Modern Law of Copyright and Designs* (2nd ed., 1995) paras 13.49 *et seq.*

[22] Restraint of trade is dealt with at para. 7–151, above.

CHAPTER 8

FOREIGN JUDGMENTS AND PROCEEDINGS

A. INTRODUCTION

Title III of the Brussels Convention and the distinction between recognition and enforcement

8–01   Title III of the Brussels Convention deals with recognition and enforcement of foreign judgments.[1] The two are treated separately, with Articles 26 to 30 dealing in terms with recognition and Articles 31 to 45 dealing with the mechanics of enforcement. The underlying principles, though, are virtually identical: if a judgment to which the Convention applies must be recognised then to all intents and purposes it is entitled to be enforced under a special simplified procedure. The general policy is that there should be free movement of judgments. Once a judgment has been granted, there are only very limited grounds on which recognition or enforcement can be denied. In particular, the merits of the case cannot be re-examined and the jurisdiction of the court granting the order sought to be enforced is almost beyond challenge. In legal theory, at least, the interests of the defendant will have been sufficiently protected prior to judgment being granted.[2] This alone is a radical change from the position under the common law and previous bilateral conventions.

8–02   Recognition is a wider concept than enforcement: a judgment cannot be enforced under the Convention unless it is entitled to recognition, but

[1] For the Brussels Convention in general and the rules as to jurisdiction, see Chap. 2. For literature on the Convention, see Chap. 2, n. 3. Briggs and Rees, *Civil Jurisdiction and Judgments* (2nd ed. 1997) is not only the most up to date of these but the best reference for the detailed issues of English law considered in this chapter. As with Chap. 2, the present chapter does not purport to do more than discuss the issues under the Convention which are specially relevant to intellectual property.

[2] Though defendants not domiciled in a contracting state are subject to the same regime for recognition and enforcement, without enjoying the procedural safeguards of Tit. II.

a judgment can be recognised although there is no question of its being enforced. Enforcement requires some sort of action by judicial authorities on the application of a party; whereas recognition is a status conferred by law on a foreign judgment from which certain consequences may flow. Recognition of a judgment means that it is accepted, without more, as defining the legal relationship of the parties in the matter to which it relates. As such, a judgment finding that a defendant is not liable is as much capable of recognition as one imposing liability, although only the latter gives rise to an obligation capable of enforcement. In this respect, the Brussels Convention creates a subtle but profound difference in the treatment of foreign judgments in intellectual property cases.[3]

Recognition and enforcement compared to the pre-Convention position

At common law, whether a foreign judgment was to be recognised or not depended on the doctrine of *res judicata*. A judgment might be recognised in this sense as defining the legal relationship between the parties, but that did not entitle the successful party to automatic enforcement of the judgment. Either a fresh English action could be commenced on the foreign judgment—as opposed to the original cause of action[4]—or one of a number of bilateral conventions might be invoked. However, one was likely to be interested in a foreign judgment only if there was some reason to enforce it in this country, or if it was determinative here under the doctrine of *res judicata*. As to the latter, the principle of territoriality has meant until very recently that there was no scope for cause of action estoppel, since a foreign court would never have ruled on an infringement justiciable in another state. It has only recently been suggested that the doctrine of issue estoppel might apply between infringement actions and the like in different states, so far without success.[5] **8–03**

So far as enforcement was concerned, there does not previously seem to have been much difficulty in practice in recovering damages for infringement against reputable European defendants even without invoking any bilateral convention. In any event, the bilateral conventions dealt only with enforcement of money judgments. From past experience, it was easy to think in terms of recognition and enforcement as all but synonymous and of interest only where there had been a finding of liability and an order for the payment of money. A finding of non-liability is inherently incapable of being enforced, so what is the point of recognising it? **8–04**

This misunderstanding may have led to an idea which was valid under the old law being carried over and unconsciously applied to cases under **8–05**

---

[3] The Lugano Convention contains similar rules for mutual recognition and enforcement between the EU and former EFTA states. It is not separately dealt with in this work.

[4] Civil Jurisdiction and Judgments Act 1982, s. 34.

[5] *Kirin-Amgen Inc v. Boehringer Mannheim GmbH* [1997] F.S.R. 289, CA. The possibility of issue estoppel arising in a suitable case was acknowledged by the Court of Appeal.

the Brussels Convention, where it is not only inapplicable but positively misleading. This is the preconception that if a defendant has won an infringement action, then it does not matter whether he won on the merits or on the issue of jurisdiction. He is happy as long as he is not liable, and his lawyers may take greater self-satisfaction from winning on a technicality. Under the Convention, however, a finding of non-liability is as much entitled to recognition as one of infringement. A defendant has a legitimate interest in insisting that a pan-European claim against him should be resolved in his favour on the merits, since that gives him the benefit of *res judicata* in all member states. A finding of lack of jurisdiction, on the other hand, simply means that the plaintiff is free to litigate the issues elsewhere.[6] Correspondingly, it sometimes appears to have been thought that difficult questions of jurisdiction could be stood over till later, perhaps to be examined as if part and parcel of the merits. For various reasons it is essential for jurisdiction to be decided one way or the other at the very start of the case: the plaintiff must know where he stands; the defendant must know whether defending on the merits is safe[7]; and courts in other jurisdictions called upon to apply Article 21 or 22 must know whether the English court considers itself to be validly seised of the action or not.

A topic of increasing if prospective significance

8–06   In the past, intellectual property practitioners have had little need to consider enforcement of foreign judgments in the United Kingdom or *vice versa*. Infringement actions are normally fought primarily for the injunction, not for damages, but the pre-existing bilateral conventions are concerned only with enforcement of money judgments. Enforcement of an injunction has always been a matter exclusively for the court granting it. Above all, it would have been taken for granted that any court order in an infringement action anywhere, whether for an injunction or damages, would have related only to infringement in that jurisdiction. If the only effect of Title III of the Brussels Convention had been to make money judgments more readily enforceable than previously then it could largely continue to be ignored in this field. Substantial European defendants might be made to pay up slightly more promptly, but the enforcement provisions would not normally need to be invoked against them. As against counterfeiters, it is doubtful if Title III does anything more in practice than to multiply the opportunities for throwing good money after bad.

8–07   In the general law, it would previously have been sound advice that a defendant subject to a foreign assertion of exorbitant jurisdiction was often better off suffering a default judgment to be entered against him than appearing before the foreign court and either disputing its jurisdiction or defending on the merits. Under the Convention, the opposite is

---

[6] Although the finding by the English court that it lacked jurisdiction, would, *pro tanto*, be entitled to recognition and would be binding in subsequent proceedings.

[7] Since, subject to Art. 16, defending on the merits amounts to a submission to the jurisdiction by virtue of Art. 18.

the case. A European defendant must consider the prospect of the order, even if granted in default, being enforced against its assets in its home territory. Any defendant, whether European or not, has to consider the prospect of the order being enforced against assets it may have anywhere in Europe. The result, as the Convention surely intended, is virtually to force the defendant to challenge the jurisdiction of the court in which he is sued or to defend on the merits. Once that court has ruled, there is next to no opportunity to re-open either question when the order comes to be enforced.

The main practical effect of Title III in the field of intellectual property **8–08** comes from a combination of three factors: the near-automatic recognition and enforcement of all *inter partes* orders including both interlocutory and final injunctions; the absence of any exceptional treatment for intellectual property infringement actions as such in Title II; and the opportunity—or excuse—the Convention provides for courts to grant extraterritorial injunctive relief in circumstances previously unheard of. It is the interaction of Title II with Title III that has made the ultimate destruction of the territoriality principle a real prospect. Hitherto, if a client had been sued for a pan-European injunction in the Dutch courts, one could safely say that unless the client had assets in the Netherlands then the safest course was probably to ignore the proceedings altogether, including any extraterritorial default injunction. In the present state of the law, that is no longer the case. Even if the Dutch court had exceeded its Convention jurisdiction in granting the order, there is very little scope for challenging it when it comes to be enforced. What is more, the order can equally well be enforced against assets anywhere in Europe.

There may be a preconception that the assumption of extraterritorial **8–09** jurisdiction in patent infringement proceedings at least, and especially under the *kort geding* procedure, is so abhorrent to international comity that there must be a way of refusing to recognise injunctions so granted. At first sight, a route to non-recognition might be found in the public policy exception of Article 27(1) or under Article 28 for non-compliance with Article 16(4). On closer analysis, however, the most that can be said for either argument is that a defendant who has breached an extra-territorial injunction might have a fall back defence under one of these provisions.[8] Neither Article can possibly be thought of as providing sufficient assurance of immunity to justify a decision not to defend or not to comply with any injunction once granted. The law itself is unclear, and the public policy exception at least involves an unpredictable exercise of discretion. There is probably no way of forcing the issue to be resolved in advance of an application by the plaintiff to enforce an order in his favour.[9] What is worse, from the point of view of the defendant, is that he can be certain of his position only if recognition and enforcement would be refused in every member state where he had assets, and that might be virtually the whole of Continental Europe.

[8] See paras 8–107 *et seq*, below.
[9] Subject to what may be decided following the reference to the European Court of Justice in *Fort Dodge v. Akzo Nobel* [1998] F.S.R. 222, CA; but see paras 8–64 and 8–96, below.

8–10   With the territoriality principle in one of its aspects under attack, the problem arises for the first time of dealing with multiple infringement proceedings in several jurisdictions. Previously, it would have been taken for granted that each court would be seised only of issues of infringement and validity arising in respect of its own national territory, so that the presence of litigation elsewhere on similar issues could be ignored. Under the Convention, one has to deal for the first time with the possibility of two or more courts simultaneously being seised of litigation relating to infringement on a pan-European scale.[10] Less radically, the Convention may have to be considered even when parallel national proceedings are in being simply in respect of infringement of parallel national intellectual property rights.[11]

It is not surprising that the attention of prospective defendants has turned to whether they can force litigation into a court of their preference, and this chapter also examines two possible mechanisms by which this might be attempted.[12]

B. *LIS ALIBI PENDENS* AND RELATED ACTIONS: COMPULSORY AND DISCRETIONARY STAYS

Introduction

8–11   Articles 21 and 22 of the Brussels Convention deal respectively with strict *lis alibi pendens* and related actions. In the case of the former, any proceedings other than those first commenced must be stayed until the court first seised has determined whether or not it has jurisdiction; and must be struck out once that court has decided it does have jurisdiction. The court subsequently seised cannot examine the jurisdiction of the court first seised and has to accept the determination by the latter.[13] In the case of Article 22, the court second seised has a discretion whether or not to stay its own proceedings pending the outcome of the proceedings in the court first seised. It may alternatively decline jurisdiction in order to facilitate the two actions being heard together by the court first seised, if the latter would have jurisdiction over both and permits consolidation of the two actions.[14] Article 22 does not permit the court first seised to decline jurisdiction in favour of a court subsequently seised, even if the latter alone would have jurisdiction over both actions. Article 22 does not confer jurisdiction where none otherwise exists.[15]

---

[10] The problem of *lis alibi pendens* under Art. 21, see paras 8–16 *et seq.*, below.

[11] Related actions and Art. 22, see paras 8–22 *et seq.*, below

[12] For pre-emptive declaratory actions see paras 8–28 *et seq.*, below; for anti-suit injunctions see paras 8–50 *et seq.*, below.

[13] Case C–351/89 *Overseas Union v. New Hampshire Insurance* [1991] E.C.R. I–3317.

[14] There is a recognised but unresolved problem with the wording of Art. 22, second paragraph. Surely the relevant question ought to be whether the law of the court first seised permits consolidation of the two actions.

[15] Case 150/80 *Elefanten Schuh v. Jacqmain* [1981] E.C.R. 1671; [1982] 3 C.M.L.R. 1.

Articles 21 and 22 respectively provide: **8–12**

Article 21

Where proceedings involving the same cause of action and between the same parties are brought in the courts of different Contracting States, any court other than the court first seised shall of its own motion stay its proceedings until such time as the jurisdiction of the court first seised is established.

Where the jurisdiction of the court first seised is established, any court other than the court first seised shall decline jurisdiction in favour of that court.

Article 22

Where related actions are brought in the courts of different Contracting States, any court other than the court first seised may, while the actions are pending at first instance, stay its proceedings.

A court other than the court first seised may also, on the application of one of the parties, decline jurisdiction if the law of that court permits the consolidation of related actions and the court first seised has jurisdiction over both actions.

For the purposes of this Article, actions are deemed to be related where they are so closely connected that it is expedient to hear and determine them together to avoid the risk of irreconcilable judgments resulting from separate proceedings.

According to the European Court of Justice, the intention of Articles **8–13** 21 and 22 alike is to "preclude, in so far as is possible and from the outset" the possibility of irreconcilable judgments in the sense of Article 27(3) being issued by different courts.[16] Subsequent case law has maintained the principle while widening its application, especially for Article 22. In *The Tatry*[17] the Court explained Articles 21 and 22 in the context of an action for a declaration of non-liability:

"It should be noted at the outset that the English version of Article 21 does not expressly distinguish between the concepts of 'object' and 'cause' of action. That language version must however be construed in the same manner as the majority of the other language versions in which that distinction is made (see the judgment in *Gubisch Maschinenfabrik v. Palumbo*, cited above, paragraph 14).

For the purposes of Article 21 of the Convention, the 'cause of action' comprises the facts and the rule of law relied on as the basis of the action.

Consequently, an action for a declaration of non-liability, such as that brought in the main proceedings in this case by the shipowners, and another action, such as that brought subsequently by the cargo

---

[16] Case 144/86 *Gubisch v. Palumbo* [1987] E.C.R. 4861.
[17] Case C–406/92 [1994] E.C.R. I–5439.

487

owners on the basis of shipping contracts which are separate but in identical terms, concerning the same cargo transported in bulk and damaged in the same circumstances, have the same cause of action.

The 'object of the action' for the purposes of Article 21 means the end the action has in view."

8–14   The Court went on to say of Article 22:

"The third paragraph of Article 22 provides that 'actions are deemed to be related where they are so closely connected that it is expedient to hear and determine them together to avoid the risk of irreconcilable judgments resulting from separate proceedings.'

The purpose of that provision is to avoid the risk of conflicting judgments and thus to facilitate the proper administration of justice in the Community (see the Report on the Convention on Jurisdiction and the enforcement of judgments in civil and commercial matters, OJ 1979 C 59, p. 1, and in particular at p. 41). Furthermore, since the expression 'related actions' does not have the same meaning in all the Member States, the third paragraph of Article 22 sets out the elements of a definition (same report, p. 42). It follows that the concept of related actions there defined must be given an independent interpretation.

In order to achieve proper administration of justice, that interpretation must be broad and cover all cases where there is a risk of conflicting decisions, even if the judgments can be separately enforced and their legal consequences are not mutually exclusive."

8–15   It follows that the final paragraph of Article 22 is broader than a literal reading would imply: actions may be related in the sense of Article 22 even though they do not involve the risk of irreconcilable judgments in the strict sense of Article 27(3) or as contemplated in *Hoffmann v. Krieg*.[18] The word "irreconcilable" implicitly has significantly different shades of meaning in the two Articles.

True *lis alibi pendens*: compulsory stay and dismissal of second action

8–16   Where the strict *lis alibi pendens* rule of Article 21 applies any court other than the court first seised must stay its own proceedings until the court first seised has determined whether or not it has jurisdiction; and must decline jurisdiction altogether once that court has decided that it does have jurisdiction.[19] In *Overseas Union v. New Hampshire Insurance*[20] the European Court of Justice decided that the Article is to be given a broad interpretation and that it applies regardless of the domicile of any party. The Court also decided in that case that the national court

[18] Case 145/86 [1988] E.C.R. 645.
[19] The two stage process, stay then dismissal, was introduced by the San Sebastian Convention.
[20] Case C–351/89 [1991] E.C.R. I–3317.

subsequently seised cannot anticipate the result of this exercise or purport to examine the jurisdiction of the court first seised; it must accept the determination of the latter in its own favour.[21] It is implicit that the court first seised must either decline jurisdiction promptly or entertain the action diligently and deliver judgment on the merits.[22] It has no residual discretion to decline jurisdiction in favour of another court under any doctrine akin to *forum non conveniens*, nor can it postpone indefinitely the question of its own jurisdiction. Of course, if the defendant in the court first seised simply enters a defence on the merits then that waives any original defect in jurisdiction[23] (other than for non-compliance with Article 16) and courts subsequently seised will know they must decline jurisdiction.

Article 21 applies where the "cause of action" is the same in the two proceedings. Perhaps no phrase is more redolent of the history of the common law but "cause of action" has an autonomous meaning under the Convention which is independent of the meaning it may have under any given national system of law.[24] No comprehensive definition as yet exists, but the case law of the European Court of Justice implies that for the *lis alibis pendens* rule to apply the respective claims do not have to be identical but the two actions must have the same *parties*[25]; the same *object*, in the sense of determining legal liability one way or the other; they must arise from the same *facts* and must apply the same *rule of law*.[26] If all these are present, then Article 21 applies even if the plaintiff in one action is the defendant in the other.[27] It is possible for complicated proceedings to be split into causes of action to which Article 21 applies, and ones which are affected only by Article 22 or not at all.[28] Likewise, in multi-party proceedings Article 21 may apply to some parties and claims but not to others.[29] In English intellectual property litigation to date, no decision has found Article 21 applicable.[30] In

8–17

---

[21] Different considerations arise to some extent under Art. 16, see below.

[22] This is not to say that the court first seised cannot stay its proceedings for good reason, but it cannot stay them with a view to allowing another court to take over.

[23] Art. 18. There is a recognised exception which allows a defence on the merits to be filed at the same time as a challenge to jurisdiction, without prejudice to the latter: Cases 150/80 *Elefanten Schuh v. Jacqmain* [1980] E.C.R. 1593; [1982] 3 C.M.L.R. 1 and 27/81 *Rohr v. Ossberger* [1981] E.C.R. 2431; [1982] 3 C.M.L.R. 29.

[24] Case 144/86 *Gubisch v. Palumbo* [1987] E.C.R. 4861 explaining Case 129/83 *Zelger v. Salinitri* [1984] E.C.R. 2397; [1985] 3 C.M.L.R. 366. The expression "cause of action" in the English text is also open to criticism as being a conflation of the distinct civil law concepts of *"objet"* and *"cause"* alluded to in the other authentic texts. See Case C–406/92 *The Tatry* [1994] E.C.R. I–5439, at para. 38.

[25] Art. 21 so provides in terms.

[26] Principally Case 144/86 *Gubisch v. Palumbo* [1987] E.C.R. 4861, but also Case C–351/89 *Overseas Union v. New Hampshire Insurance* [1991] E.C.R. I–3317 and Case C–406/92 *The Tatry* [1994] E.C.R. I–5439.

[27] Case 144/86 *Gubisch v. Palumbo* [1987] E.C.R. 4861; Case C–351/89 *Overseas Union v. New Hampshire Insurance* [1991] E.C.R. I–3317 and Case C–406/92 *The Tatry* [1994] E.C.R. I–5439. See paras 8–28 *et seq.*, below.

[28] Case C–406/92 *The Tatry* [1994] E.C.R. I–5439.

[29] *ibid.*

[30] See para. 8–24, below.

particular, the Article does not apply to the common situation of infringement actions proceeding in parallel in different jurisdictions where each court is seised only of infringements committed within its own territory and actionable under its own laws. If the courts first and second seised could eventually arrive at decisions which were inconsistent with one another without being irreconcilable in the narrow sense, no matter how divergent they might seem in result or reasoning, then Article 21 does not apply.[31]

8–18   The question of which court is first seised is answered by reference to national law, in that the law under which each set of proceedings was commenced determines, in respect of those proceedings, whether they were considered to have been commenced on the date the originating document was issued, or was served, or on some other date.[32] In England, it is now settled law for the purposes of the Convention that proceedings are not deemed to be commenced until the writ is actually served.[33] If the English writ has to be served abroad under the Hague Service Convention or through Consular channels then the prospect of the High Court being the court first seised depends entirely on reciprocity of reasoning by any competitive foreign court. The same rule supposedly prevails in most of the civil law systems of Continental Europe.[34] It remains an open question whether service on one defendant (perhaps in the jurisdiction) creates a *lis pendens* against other defendants who may not yet have been served.[35] The reasoning of *The Tatry*[36] suggests otherwise.[37]

[31] By implication from Case 144/86 *Gubisch v. Palumbo* [1987] E.C.R. 4861. See para 8–33, below. The *Epilady* litigation, for instance, did not result in judgments that were irreconcilable, no matter that almost every possible permutation on validity and infringement was reached by the various courts seised.

[32] Case 129/83 *Zelger v. Salinitri* [1984] E.C.R. 2397; [1985] 3 C.M.L.R. 366

[33] *Dresser (U.K.) Ltd v. Falcongate Freight Management Ltd* [1992] 1 Q.B. 502, CA; *Neste Chemicals v. DK Line, The Sargasso* [1994] 3 All E.R. 180; [1995] I.L.Pr. 553, CA. The latter decided, contrary to *dicta* in the former, that there are no exceptions to the general rule.

[34] According to Case 129/83 *Zelger v. Salinitri* [1984] E.C.R. 2397; [1985] 3 C.M.L.R. 366 most contracting states considered proceedings to be "definitively pending" only when they have been served. As against foreign defendants, however, proceedings may be deemed to be pending from the date the originating process is "served" on the local public prosecutor, as opposed to the date of actual service on the defendant abroad, which puts the English courts at a major disadvantage. There is now also the Convention on the Service in the Member States of the European Union of Judicial and Extrajudicial Documents in Civil or Commercial Matters (adopted pursuant to Art. K.3(2)(c) T.E.U.) of May 26, 1997 [1997] O.J. L261/1; [1997] I.L.Pr. 693; but it will be some time before it has any practical effect. Art. 9 provides (in general) that the date of service of the document pursuant to the Convention is the date on which it is served in accordance with the law of the member state addressed, rather than the law of the state of origin.

[35] *Gruppo Torras SA v. Sheik Mohammed al-Sabah* [1996] 1 Lloyds' Rep. 7, CA.

[36] Case C–406/92 [1994] E.C.R. I–5439.

[37] The conclusion is regretted by Briggs and Rees, *op. cit.*, but the temptation to join an easily served locally domiciled party as a nominal co-defendant might otherwise prove irresistible. As it is, the delays of service abroad are likely to mean that each of two courts seised at roughly the same time is likely to have jurisdiction over its own domiciliaries, but not over foreign-domiciled defendants. Since defendants are most quickly and easily served in their country of domicile, the practical result may be that Art. 21 reinforces Art. 2 at the expense of the various special jurisdictions.

The relationship of Article 21 to Articles 16 and 24

A potentially significant question for intellectual property practitioners **8–19** concerns the relationship of Article 21 to the exclusive jurisdictions of Article 16. The problem is that in the present state of the law there is no international consensus as to whether, or in what circumstances, infringement actions as such fall within Article 16(4).[38] Article 23 provides that where actions come within the exclusive jurisdiction of several courts, any court other than the court first seised shall decline jurisdiction in favour of that court.[39] However the problem is most acute where the court subsequently seised considers itself to have exclusive jurisdiction over the cause of action by virtue of Article 16(4), whereas the court first seised considers that the action falls outside Article 16 altogether so that it has jurisdiction under the general rules of the Convention.[40]

In *Overseas Union v. New Hampshire Insurance*[41] itself this situation **8–20** was apparently recognised as constituting an exception to the general rule that the court second seised cannot examine the jurisdiction of the court first seised, or was at least left open.[42] The conclusion follows by inference from Articles 16 and 23 and by analogy with Articles 28 and 34 which exceptionally permit and indeed require courts to refuse to recognise or enforce a judgment of a court in another member state on the ground that the latter purported to exercise jurisdiction in contravention of Article 16. If this is correct, and it is tentatively suggested that it is, then if the court second seised considers that it has exclusive jurisdiction over the cause of action then it should decline jurisdiction if and only if it considers that the court first seised had prior exclusive jurisdiction under Articles 16 and 23. If the court first seised can only claim jurisdiction under one of the general provisions of the Convention such as Articles 2 or 5 then no question of a stay arises and the obligation on the court second seised to exercise its exclusive jurisdiction under Article 16 should prevail over the normal rule of giving full faith and credit to the exercise of jurisdiction by the court first seised. If the court second seised is right, then any judgment by the court first seised would in any event be disentitled to international recognition.

[38] See paras 3–78 *et seq.*

[39] Art. 23 most obviously applies to the internal affairs of companies with two domiciles. It is hard to see how it could apply to intellectual property, except, perhaps, to Benelux trade marks and designs to the extent that the relevant trilateral convention does not govern jurisdiction. The various Community intellectual property rights have their own special regimes: see Chap. 5.

[40] This is the problem exemplified by *Fort Dodge v. Akzo Nobel* [1998] F.S.R. 222, CA; see para. 8–52, below.

[41] Case C–351/89 *Overseas Union v. New Hampshire Insurance* [1991] E.C.R. I–3317.

[42] The reply of the Court to the second question put by the English Court of Appeal began "Without prejudice to the case where the court second seised has exclusive jurisdiction . . . under Article 16. . . ." But there is no supporting passage in the judgment to explain what was meant. Van Gerven A.-G. left the point open. Different considerations ought to apply to "exclusive jurisdiction" under Art. 17 since breach of Art. 17 does not preclude recognition and enforcement.

8–21   Another problem arises where it is uncertain whether the court apparently first seised is, in fact, only purporting to exercise its jurisdiction to order provisional and protective measures under Article 24. Just as a court can order measures under Article 24 without being seised of the action as such, so it is suggested that a court in which subsequent main proceedings are commenced may consider itself to be the court first seised for the purposes of Article 21 notwithstanding the existence of Article 24 proceedings of earlier date in another court.[43] Any other interpretation would clearly frustrate the very purpose of Article 24. The problem in practice is that there may be a legitimate difference of opinion as to whether the court in which proceedings were first commenced was only exercising an Article 24 jurisdiction or regarded itself as the court first seised for the purposes of Article 21.[44]

Related actions: the discretionary stay

8–22   If the strict *lis alibi pendens* rule of Article 21 does not apply, then the court subsequently seised should go on to consider whether the proceedings before it and the court first seised are "related"; and if so whether it should stay or dismiss its own proceedings in the exercise of its discretion under Article 22. Article 22 is thus of much wider scope than Article 21, because neither the parties nor the cause of action need be the same, but in the present state of the law it is of relatively little importance in intellectual property infringement actions. This is because an English court is most unlikely to conclude that an action for infringement of United Kingdom intellectual property rights should ever be stayed pending the outcome of foreign proceedings which might be influential, but are unlikely to be determinative of every issue. That has long been the law in one situation outside Article 22 but analogous to it, in that infringement actions and even petitions for revocation are not stayed pending oppositions in the European Patent Office,[45] notwithstanding that a successful opposition may conclusively revoke the patent in suit and render the English proceedings otiose.[46]

8–23   As for the second possibility contemplated by Article 22, in the present state of the law the English courts would probably deny that

---

[43] To the extent that the Art. 24 proceedings were *ex parte*, they would not count for Art. 21 anyway if the latter depends on service.

[44] Compare the widespread English perception that the Dutch *kort geding* procedure derives its legitimacy from Art. 24, with the Dutch view that Art. 24 is of residual importance only compared to Arts 2 and 6(1).

[45] *Amersham International plc v. Corning Ltd* [1987] R.P.C. 53 (Falconer J.) and *Pall Corporation v. Commercial Hydraulics (Bedford) Ltd* [1989] R.P.C. 703; [1988] F.S.R. 274, CA. Arts 21 and 22 do not apply to the EPO because it is not a "court or tribunal of a member state."

[46] As in *Lenzing's European Patent* [1997] R.P.C. 245 (Jacob J.). This case also decided that the successful opponents in the EPO were entitled to recover their full costs as defendants in the infringement action when the latter was inevitably struck out, notwithstanding an argument by the plaintiff that there should be a set-off between the costs of the issue of infringement and the costs of the issue of validity. Jacob J. decided it was not unreasonable for the defendants/opponents to have challenged validity on two fronts.

cross-border consolidation of patent actions is possible at all, at least if validity is or will be in issue.[47] The same principle would probably be thought to apply to actions for infringement of the other registered intellectual property rights. Multinational passing-off or unfair competition actions might conceivably be consolidated, but the authorities to date are against the possibility on the grounds that legal, linguistic and cultural factors are too diverse.[48] Copyright infringement actions perhaps offer the best prospect for consolidation.

The English intellectual property cases on Articles 21 and 22

The English courts have not yet had to apply Articles 21 and 22 to **8–24** actions for patent or copyright infringement, but two cases have dealt with parallel trade mark and passing-off actions in two jurisdictions.

In *LA Gear v. Whelan*[49] the plaintiffs sought judgment in default of **8–25** defence in an English trade mark infringement and passing-off action, and the defendants sought to have the action struck out under Article 21 or stayed under Article 22 on the basis of an earlier action by the plaintiffs in Ireland for passing-off. Mummery J. held that the Irish action was not for infringement of the English trade mark and that the respective causes of action in passing-off were distinct. Article 21 therefore did not apply and although the two sets of proceedings were related in a broad sense it was inappropriate to order a stay.

The most recent case in point is *Mecklermedia v. DC Congress*[50] where **8–26** Jacob J. held that an action for passing-off in England should not be struck out or stayed as a result of the existence of a trade mark infringement action in Germany, in which the positions of the parties were reversed. The facts were that the plaintiffs claimed goodwill in England in relation to publishing and organising trade shows under the name *Internet World*. The defendants DC had also organised shows under the name *Internet World*, in Dusseldorf in 1996 and in Vienna in 1997 and they had promoted their shows in the United Kingdom. Although the defendant's activities actually took place abroad, the plaintiffs' United Kingdom goodwill stood to the damaged so there was a serious question of passing-off to be tried. Jacob J. first held that the passing-off action fell within Article 5(3) in that the "place where the harmful event occurred" was in England, where the plaintiffs' goodwill and reputation existed. All the elements of the tort—goodwill, misrepresentation and damage—would have to be made out in England. This was not such a case as *Dumez v. Hessische Landesbank*[51] where the harm relied on was only indirect or consequential. Even assuming the German

---

[47] *Coin Controls v. Suzo* [1997] F.S.R. 660 (Laddie J.) approved in *Fort Dodge v. Akzo Nobel* [1998] F.S.R. 222, CA.

[48] *Mecklermedia Corporation v. DC Congress* [1997] F.S.R. 627 (Jacob J.), below; and the *dictum* of Laddie J. in *Coin Controls v. Suzo* [1997] F.S.R. 660 (Laddie J.).

[49] [1991] F.S.R. 670 (Mummery J.).

[50] [1997] F.S.R. 627 (Jacob J.).

[51] Case C–220/88 [1990] E.C.R. 1–49.

courts could have entertained an action for passing-off in England, Articles 2 and 5(3) applied equally and gave the plaintiffs an option of where to sue.

8–27   The next question concerned the effect of pending proceedings for trade mark infringement in Germany in which DC were plaintiffs and Mecklermedia's licensees were defendants. Article 21 did not apply because the latter were not to be considered as the same party as Mecklermedia: the argument might have been tenable for a wholly-owned subsidiary, but not for an arm's length licensee which might have very different interests. Nor was the cause of action in Germany the same. The facts and law relevant to prove infringement of the German trade mark registration would be very different to those relevant in the English passing-off action. The same considerations led to the conclusion that the English action should not be stayed pursuant to Article 22. The action in Germany was not a "related action" in the sense of *The Tatry*,[52] since there was no risk of conflicting decisions in the legal sense. Without deciding whether first instance proceedings were still pending in Germany, or whether an English passing-off action could be litigated there, the most convenient forum for the passing-off action was England.

> "I certainly would not take either of those steps [staying or striking out] when I think, as I do, that normally the most convenient forum for deciding an English trade mark or passing off case is this court. In many cases a question of deceptive resemblance involving language may be involved. Then I think it would be very difficult for a court which uses a language other than English to form a reliable view on the question, especially if it was marginal. In this case the question of a deceptive resemblance hardly arises. But even so the German court would have to import both the evidence and law, whereas neither of those things would be necessary if the action proceeds here.
>
> It is submitted that it would be better if all questions were decided by a single court and that multiple litigation should be avoided. That as a generality is of course always true, but on the other hand when an enterprise wants to use a mark or word throughout the world (and that may include an internet address or domain name) it must take into account that in some places, if not others, there may be confusion. Here it is clear DC knew that Mecklermedia used the name 'Intenet World' and I do not think it is surprising that it is met with actions in places where confusion is considered likely."

In the result Jacob J. refused to set aside service, stay the action or decline jurisdiction.

---

[52] Case C–406/92 [1994] E.C.R. I–5439.

C. PRE-EMPTIVE NEGATIVE DECLARATIONS, ETC.

Actions for negative declarations; *lis alibi pendens*

An action for a negative declaration potentially has several attractions **8–28** under the Brussels Convention. First, it may genuinely be intended to allow a prospective defendant to establish his innocence on a pan-European or multinational basis. It should not be assumed that all declaratory actions are necessarily tactical, still less abusive. On the other hand, it may simply be an attempt at pre-emptive forum shopping by a prospective defendant intending to frustrate the expected plaintiff from commencing infringement proceedings in his own chosen court. The intention is to steer the litigation towards a court which the alleged infringer favours; whether because it is his home territory, or because it is more likely to find in his favour, because it does not readily grant interlocutory relief, or because it is unlikely to grant any relief at all until the far distant future.[53] Both these objectives require that the declaration sought should be extraterritorial in effect, which depends as much on local law as on the Brussels Convention. In the first case, the intention is to obtain a finding of non-liability which will be entitled to automatic recognition throughout the Brussels Convention contracting states. In the second, the principal purpose is to force any court subsequently seised of infringement proceedings properly so called to stay them under Article 21, whether the claim for infringement as such is extraterritorial or purely national.

The applicant for the declaration may have more modest ambitions. **8–29** He may prefer to fight proceedings in parallel in several jurisdictions and so may apply for a declaration with purely national effect. This should, under Article 21, prevent any foreign court asserting infringement jurisdiction over the United Kingdom even if it asserted extraterritorial jurisdiction over other member states for which no declaratory proceedings were pending. Article 21 has to be applied on a claim-by-claim, state-by-state, party-by-party basis. The other advantage of a declaration of non-infringement with purely local effect is that a favourable declaratory judgment will locally protect the hypothetical infringer against recognition and enforcement of the foreign judgment by virtue of Article 27(3), and this applies even if the foreign court—or the English court for that matter—ignored Article 21.

Even if an action for a declaration may be brought consistently with **8–30** the Brussels Convention and domestic law, it may be doubted if it provides much protection in practice. Article 21 does not prevent a foreign court exercising any jurisdiction it may have to grant preliminary and protective measures under Article 24, and the Dutch courts apparently regard this as justifying the grant of summary pan-European relief under their *kort geding* procedure,[54] even if there are declaratory

---

[53] See Franzosi, "Worldwide Patent Litigation and the Italian Torpedo" [1997] E.I.P.R. 382. This is especially the case for patent infringement where delays can be such that some courts are unlikely to grant any relief at all until long after the relevant patent has expired.

[54] This may be doubted. See paras 3–23 *et seq.*, but what matters for present purposes is that the Dutch court would almost certainly not stay its *kort geding* procedure.

proceedings pending elsewhere. Article 21 also expressly applies only where the parties to the two actions are the same. There may be some scope for saying that this requirement is not to be applied too literally,[55] but in the typical case there is probably even more scope for the natural plaintiff to pick and choose which infringers he sues, so that Article 21 will have no application. Article 22 would apply, but is discretionary, and a failed attempt at pre-emptive forum shopping by the natural defendant could hardly be expected to shame the court seised of the infringement action as such into abandoning its own proceedings.

8–31   A petition for revocation, or any other proceeding concerned solely with validity, is self-evidently not for the same cause of action as an action for infringement and has no pre-emptive effect under Article 21. At most, it might justify a discretionary stay or dismissal of foreign extraterritorial infringement proceedings under Article 22, but for that purpose it would need to be commenced before the latter, so that the foreign court seised of the infringement action would be the court second seised. Actual revocation would also protect the defendant locally against enforcement of a foreign judgment in the plaintiff's favour.[56] Any such proceedings would clearly be within Article 16(4), meaning that no extraterritorial relief could be sought. However, there would be no problems of jurisdiction as against the patent proprietor, no matter where domiciled, because jurisdiction would derive directly from Article 16(4).

8–32   In *Chiron v. Evans Medical*[57] Robert Walker J. held that an action for a declaration of non-infringement under the inherent jurisdiction was not within the exclusive jurisdiction defined by Article 16(4) of the Brussels Convention. This seems correct from first principles, especially as the validity of a United Kingdom patent cannot be put in issue in such proceedings.[58] There were separate pending proceedings for revocation.

The treatment of negative declarations under the Brussels Convention

8–33   The Brussels Convention contains no provisions dealing expressly with actions for negative declarations. On general principles, therefore, the availability or not of such actions is governed by national law and jurisdiction must be based on one of the provisions of the Convention, if the defendant is domiciled in a contracting state. The main interest of actions for negative declarations is the scope they give for a party arguably in breach to commence declaratory proceedings in a court convenient to him, thereby pre-empting proceedings by the opposite party. In three cases decided to date the European Court of Justice has,

[55] As was contemplated by Jacob J. in *Mecklermedia Corporation v. DC Congress* [1997] F.S.R. 627.
[56] Art. 27(3). See para. 3–143.
[57] [1996] F.S.R. 863 (Robert Walker J.).
[58] *Organon Teknika v. Hoffmann-La Roche* [1996] F.S.R. 383 (Jacob J.) applying Patents Act 1977, s. 74(2).

perhaps inadvertently, given judgments which are surprisingly accommodating to this tactic.[59]

The problem—or opportunity—arises from Article 21 of the Brussels Convention,[60] providing:

    8–34

> Where proceedings involving the same cause of action and between the same parties are brought in the courts of different Contracting States, any court other than the court first seised shall of its own motion stay its proceedings until such time as the jurisdiction of the court first seised is established.
>
> Where the jurisdiction of the court first seised is established, any court other than the court first seised shall decline jurisdiction in favour of that court.

In *Gubisch v. Palumbo*[61] there was a contract between a German company and an Italian resident for the sale of a machine to the latter. Palumbo commenced proceedings in Rome for various declarations to the effect that he was not bound by the contract, but Gubisch had already sued in Flensburg for payment of the contract price. Gubisch claimed that this gave rise to a situation of *lis alibi pendens* and applied to have the Italian proceedings struck out under Article 21. On a reference from the Italian Supreme Court, the European Court of Justice held that Article 21 covered a case where one party brought an action for rescission or discharge of a contract whilst an action by the other party to enforce the contract was pending. However *Gubisch v. Palumbo* did not in terms deal with the question of whether the Italian courts alone would have had jurisdiction if Palumbo had commenced his declaratory proceedings first, and this is the situation of greater interest in intellectual property litigation.

    8–35

The opposite situation arose and the question was answered in *The Tatry*[62] where there were parallel proceedings in the Dutch and English courts over damage to a cargo of soy bean oil carried on a ship, *The Tatry*. The first action to be commenced was in the Netherlands by the shipowners for declaratory judgments against the cargo owners that they were not liable for the damage. Subsequently, some cargo owners sued in England and arrested the *Maciej Rataj*, a sister ship of the *Tatry*. There were other proceedings by the cargo owners against the shipowners in the Netherlands. The Court of Appeal referred a number

    8–36

[59] Case 144/86 *Gubisch v. Palumbo* [1987] E.C.R. 4861; Case C–351/89 *Overseas Union v. New Hampshire Insurance* [1991] E.C.R. I–3317 and Case C–406/92 *The Tatry* [1994] E.C.R. I–5439.

[60] In Case C–351/89 *Overseas Union v. New Hampshire* [1991] I–E.C.R. 3317 it was held that the Article applies irrespective of the domicile of any party.

[61] Case 144/86 [1987] E.C.R. 4861. See also Case C–351/89 *Overseas Union v. New Hampshire* [1991] E.C.R. I–3317 where proceedings in France antedated an action for a declaratory judgment in England. The European Court of Justice held that the English Commercial Court had rightly stayed its own proceedings, and that it could not investigate the jurisdiction of the French court.

[62] Case C–406/92 [1994] E.C.R. I–5439.

of questions relating to the application of Articles 21 and 22 to the European Court of Justice and the Court held that the strict *lis alibi pendens* rule of Article 21 applied.

> "The question accordingly arises whether two actions have the same object when the first seeks a declaration that the plaintiff is not liable for damage as claimed by the defendants, while the second, commenced subsequently by those defendants, seeks on the contrary to have the plaintiff in the first action held liable for causing loss and ordered to pay damages.
>
> As to liability, the second action has the same object as the first, since the issue of liability is central to both actions. The fact that the plaintiff's pleadings are couched in negative terms in the first action whereas in the second action they are couched in positive terms by the defendant, who has become plaintiff, does not make the object of the dispute different.
>
> As to damages, the pleas in the second action are the natural consequence of those relating to the finding of liability and thus do not alter the principal object of the action. Furthermore, the fact that a party seeks a declaration that he is not liable for loss implies that he disputes any obligation to pay damages.
>
> In those circumstances, the answer to the fifth question is that, on a proper construction of Article 21 of the Convention, an action seeking to have the defendant held liable for causing loss and ordered to pay damages has the same cause of action and the same object as earlier proceedings brought by that defendant seeking a declaration that he is not liable for that loss."

8–37   On a subsidiary point, the Court held that Article 21 applied only in so far as the parties to the two actions were the same, and that the court second seised was not obliged to decline jurisdiction and discontinue its own proceedings in so far as different parties were involved.

If an action for a negative declaration is to proceed at all, then there must be jurisdiction over the defendant (the owner of the intellectual property right) under one of the general provisions of the Brussels Convention, probably by virtue of domicile.[63] It may seem from the Rules of Court that proceedings can always be served on the patent or trade mark proprietor at his registered address for service,[64] but as against defendants domiciled in a contracting state the Rules only

---

[63] *Boss Group Ltd v. Boss France SA* [1996] 4 All E.R. 970, [1996] I.L.Pr. 544, CA, notwithstanding, it is to be doubted if jurisdiction over an action for a negative declaration can be founded on Art. 5(3). In *Chiron v. Evans Medical* [1996] F.S.R. 863 Robert Walker J., *obiter*, doubted if the applicant for a declaration of non-infringement under the inherent jurisdiction could base jurisdiction on Art. 5(3). However, in the corresponding Dutch litigation the District Court of the Hague held that it had jurisdiction, *inter alia* under Art. 5(3), to grant a pan-European declaration of non-infringement: *Chiron v. Evans Medical* (May 14, 1997, reversed on appeal: January 22, 1998).

[64] RSC, Ord. 104, r. 24; Ord. 100, r. 5.

provide a convenient mechanism for service and cannot confer jurisdiction contrary to the terms of the Convention.[65] The value of the declaratory proceedings is also destroyed if they cannot be served before another court becomes seised of the infringement proceedings which they are intended to pre-empt.[66] Even so, it is an open question whether pre-emptive declaratory proceedings would prevent the Dutch courts from granting relief under their *kort geding* procedure; since any injunction so granted might be considered to be "provisional measures" within Article 24 to which the *lis alibi pendens* rule of Article 21 expressly does not apply.[67]

The limited availability of declaratory relief

In English law, a major problem with this tactic is the general rule that **8–38** there is no jurisdiction to grant a declaration of non-liability in the absence of an assertion of right by the person against whom the declaration is sought.[68] As Hoffmann J. said in *Barclays Bank v. Homan*[69] "a party against whom no claim has been formulated cannot sue for a declaration of non-liability. Subject to limitation periods and laches, the prospective plaintiff is entitled to decide for himself when he will bring his action." In the context of pan-European proceedings, there is the further problem that the assertion of rights would have to cover, at least by implication, all the jurisdictions in which declaratory relief was sought.[70] An express claim to pan-European relief in extraterritorial proceedings abroad, as occurred in *Organon Technika v. Hoffmann-La Roche*,[71] would certainly be sufficient, but problems then arise under Article 21 of the Brussels Convention and the United Kingdom declaratory proceedings would no longer be pre-emptive.

The situation is not greatly improved where there is a statutory **8–39** right to apply for a declaration of non-infringement, as under section 71 of the Patents Act 1977.[72] In the first place, the Act only applies in respect of the United Kingdom.[73] It does not provide a vehicle whereby

---

[65] As against a defendant domiciled in a contracting state, it is hard to see how the procedure of RSC, Ord. 104, r. 24 or Ord. 100, r. 5 can be effective except in the case of invalidity (justified by Art. 16(4)) and threats actions (Art. 5(3)). Declaratory actions, whether under statute or the inherent jurisdiction, enjoy no rule of special jurisdiction under the Convention.

[66] See para. 8–18. Art. 21 would then probably require them to be stayed, but if they proceeded they might still have some benefit under Art. 27(3), which applies irrespective of which proceedings were commenced or completed first.

[67] For whether *kort geding* injunctions fall within Art. 24, see paras 3–23 *et seq.*

[68] *North Eastern Marine Engineering v. Leeds Forge* (1906) 23 R.P.C. 96 (patent); *Wyko Group plc v. Cooper Roller Bearings Co Ltd* [1996] F.S.R. 126 (copyright) applying *Re Clay; Clay v. Booth* [1919] 1 Ch. 66 and *Barclays Bank v. Homan* [1993] B.C.L.C. 680.

[69] [1993] B.C.L.C. 680 (Hoffmann J.), *affirmed ibid.*, CA.

[70] *Plastus Kreativ v. 3M* [1995] R.P.C. 438 (Aldous J.).

[71] [1996] F.S.R. 383 (Jacob J.).

[72] There is no corresponding provision for the other registered intellectual property rights or for copyright.

[73] *Plastus Kreativ v. 3M* [1995] R.P.C. 438 (Aldous J.).

infringement or not of foreign patents can be litigated. Secondly, the Act requires the prospective applicant to give the patent proprietor full particulars of the relevant product or process. The right to apply for a declaration does not arise until the proprietor has "refused or failed" to give the acknowledgement. Whilst no particular period of time is specified by statute before proceedings can be commenced, the need to give any advance notice at all is inconsistent with the section being used pre-emptively. A further problem arising from the previous need to obtain leave to serve proceedings out of the jurisdiction has purportedly been removed by modifications to Rules of Court.[74]

8–40 Two cases demonstrate failed attempts to obtain declarations of non-liability in the United Kingdom, in respect of proposed acts abroad. In *Tyburn v. Conan Doyle*[75] the plaintiffs sought declarations that the proposed making of a film about *Sherlock Holmes* would not infringe various intellectual property rights in the character, supposedly owned by the defendant under United States law. The action was struck out, principally because the claim was non-justiciable but also because the defendant had not asserted her rights in respect of the film in question.[76] *Tyburn v. Conan Doyle* was not a Brussels Convention case, nor was *Plastus Kreativ v. 3M*[77] in which the plaintiffs sought declarations of non-infringement in respect of corresponding United Kingdom, French and German patents. The latter two claims were struck out, principally because no claim of right had been asserted under the French and German patents. A letter before action was construed as referring only to the United Kingdom.[78] Although Aldous J. clearly regarded infringement of the French and German patents as being inherently non-justiciable, this strictly speaking does not form part of the *ratio decidendi*.[79] The action for a declaration in respect of the United Kingdom patent was allowed to proceed under section 71 of the Patents Act 1977, but the latter was held not to apply to acts proposed to be done outside the United Kingdom.

8–41 In the general law, pre-emptive declaratory proceedings intended to seise one court of an action which would otherwise have been litigated

---

[74] Though *quaere* whether service under RSC, Ord. 104, r. 24 at the proprietor's registered address is effective if the proprietor is domiciled in a contracting state other than the U.K. Jurisdiction against Convention-domiciled defendants can only be based on one of the rules of the Convention (Art. 3), not merely on service of the originating process in a manner permitted by Rules of Court.

[75] [1990] R.P.C. 185 (Vinelott J.). See also paras 6–48 *et seq.*

[76] The reasoning that the plaintiff had to show that defendant had asserted rights without any bona fide belief in her entitlement to them is surely too strict unless it turns on the way the case was pleaded. It confuses the requirement of *Re Clay; Clay v. Booth* [1919] 1 Ch. 66 with the action for malicious falsehood and inappropriately imports a requirement from the latter into every action for a declaration.

[77] [1995] R.P.C. 438 (Aldous J.). See also paras 3–53 *et seq.*

[78] The factual matrix against which the letter would have been construed would, at the time, have included a strong presumption against the plaintiffs attempting to invoke any extraterritorial jurisdiction from the English courts.

[79] See para. 3–60.

elsewhere have been regarded with disfavour,[80] even to the extent of an anti-suit injunction being granted,[81] but there are signs that attitudes are changing.[82]

Joinder of foreign parties to declaratory actions in respect of United Kingdom rights

Three cases where declaratory relief was sought purely in relation to the United Kingdom are also relevant. Unfortunately, two of them reached opposite conclusions on very similar facts and cannot credibly be regarded as reconcilable in principle. The other leaves more questions open than it resolves. In *Biogen v. Medeva*[83] the defendants were sued for infringement of two United Kingdom patents. As well as defending and counter-claiming for revocation, in the normal manner, they sought a declaration that their vaccine did not infringe any valid claim of the plaintiff's two patents in suit and purported to add another company, SmithKline Beecham PLC, as defendants to the counterclaim.[84] The plaintiffs and SmithKline Beecham applied to strike out the relevant part of the counterclaim, and Medeva applied to amend to add another SmithKline Beecham company as defendant to the counterclaim,[85] and to give particulars of circumstances in which the two SmithKline Beecham companies were alleged to have claimed that they controlled the patents in suit and would assert them against Medeva.[86] The reason for joinder was admittedly to obtain discovery. Aldous J. struck out the pleading and refused the amendment. Distinguishing *Molnycke v. Procter & Gamble (No. 4)*,[87] he held that any dispute between Medeva and the SmithKline Beecham companies was theoretical, and that all the substantive issues would be decided in the dispute between Medeva and Biogen.

8–42

---

[80] For example *Camilla Cotton v. Granadex* [1976] 2 Lloyd's Rep. 10, HL; *Volvox Hollandia* [1988] 2 Lloyd's Rep. 361 at 371, CA; *First National Bank v. Union Bank of Switzerland* [1990] 1 Lloyd's Rep. 32, CA.

[81] *Sohio Supply Co v. Gatoil (USA) Inc* [1989] 1 Lloyd's Rep. 588, CA. An anti-suit injunction was granted restraining proceedings for a negative declaration in Texas, notwithstanding over 12 months delay. Art. 21 of the Brussels Convention was invoked, presumably by analogy. *Barclays Bank v. Homan* [1993] B.C.L.C. 680 above is an example of both anti-suit and declaratory relief being refused.

[82] *Boss Group Ltd v. Boss France SA* [1996] 4 All E.R. 970, [1996] I.L.Pr. 544, CA, where the Court of Appeal held that a plaintiff who denied that any exclusive distribution agreement for France existed at all, could rely on Art. 5(1) to sue in England for a declaration to that effect. On the face of the plaintiff's claim there was no contract, no obligation and no performance due anywhere, least of all in England. The court allowed the plaintiff to pull himself up by his own bootstraps, despite the fact that he claimed to be barefoot.

[83] [1993] R.P.C. 475 (Aldous J.).

[84] The declaration was sought under the inherent jurisdiction, rather than s. 71.

[85] SmithKline Beecham Biologicals SA, a Belgian company. ("SKBB").

[86] Though neither the original nor the amended pleading alleged that these were actionable threats in the sense of s. 70.

[87] [1992] R.P.C. 21, CA. In *Chiron v. Evans Medical*, below, Robert Walker J. found the relevant passage of *Biogen v. Medeva* "very puzzling."

"Although there is pleaded a claim of right by the SKB companies, the dispute is theoretical. The issue of infringement and validity will be decided in the action as constituted. The SKB companies will be bound by that result. The SKB companies do not have any claim in damages against Medeva and their interest is in the protection that injunctive relief will bring. Whether or not such relief is appropriate is the issue that will be decided between Biogen and Medeva. The theoretical nature of the dispute between Medeva and the companies is illustrated by the fact that whether or not the declaration is actually ordered is irrelevant to Medeva and the SKB companies. Provided the SKB companies give discovery, Medeva's purpose in seeking a declaration will in theory and in practice be achieved. That is different to other proceedings where, as in the Molnlycke case, the plaintiff has enforceable relief."

8–43   As to the joinder of the Belgian SmithKline Beecham company Aldous J. added:

"I also believe it relevant that Medeva seek to bring into the proceedings SKB Biologicals which is a foreign company. They believe, and I will assume rightly believe, that they do not need leave of the court to serve the proceedings on SKB Biologicals. Even so, I do not believe it right that foreign companies should be made to submit to the jurisdiction of the court unless there is a genuine and real dispute between the company and the plaintiff. There is no such dispute in this case. The only dispute is whether SKB Biologicals should give discovery. It is frivolous and vexatious to bring proceedings against a foreign company where the plaintiff has no real interest in the relief claimed and no interest in deciding the pleaded issues as between himself and the foreign company."

8–44   In *Organon Technika v. Hoffmann-La Roche*[88] the plaintiffs sought a declaration under the inherent jurisdiction of the court to the effect that sales in the United Kingdom did not infringe any valid claim of a patent which the defendants were asserting against the plaintiffs in the Netherlands, where a pan-European injunction had been sought in *kort geding* proceedings.[89] Jacob J. held that validity could not be put in issue in the declaration, but allowed the plaintiffs to amend to seek revocation. The jurisdiction of the court to entertain the declaratory action in the first place does not seem to have been questioned. The Lugano Convention would have applied, the defendants being domiciled in Switzerland, but nothing expressly turned on this. The judgment poses more questions than it answers: on what basis were Hoffmann-La Roche served with the

---

[88] [1996] F.S.R. 383 (Jacob J.).
[89] Although this does not appear from the judgment of Jacob J., the injunction was refused in strong terms and the refusal upheld on appeal.

writ in the declaratory proceedings[90]; and why did Article 21 not preclude the court from proceeding with the declaratory action?[91]

In *Chiron v. Evans Medical*[92] the facts were that the plaintiffs Chiron **8–45** sought a declaration under the inherent jurisdiction of the Court to the effect that their vaccines for whooping cough did not infringe a patent of which the defendants Evans were registered proprietors. Two other defendants were Murex, the parent company of Evans, and SmithKline Beecham Biologicals SA ("SKBB" again), a Belgian company which was the worldwide exclusive licensee under the patent. There was a separate petition for revocation. SKBB applied for service of the writ on them to be set aside and for them to be struck out as defendants, both on the grounds that there was no cause of action against SKBB for a declaration and for lack of jurisdiction under the Brussels Convention. Distinguishing *Biogen v. Medeva*,[93] Robert Walker J. observed:

"But it does seem to me that in the present case, reduced to its barest essentials, I find this. First, that proceedings for declaratory relief as to non-infringement are a well recognised procedure in appropriate circumstances and the inherent jurisdiction, as well as the jurisdiction under section 71, is well recognised. Secondly, that on the undisputed facts of this case Chiron is seeking to raise an issue of real importance on facts which are real and present and not either hypothetical or future. Thirdly, that Evans as proprietor of the patent is a natural defendant to such proceedings and has at no stage and in no way contended otherwise. Fourthly, that SKBB as a worldwide exclusive licensee, which has plainly taken a combative attitude to Chiron's claim, is also a natural defendant with a real interest in the relief sought.

Whatever the full explanation of what I have called the puzzling passage in the judgment of Aldous J. in *Biogen v. Medeva*,[94] I do not find in it anything to distract me from what I see as the natural conclusion from the four basic points that I have mentioned, that is that under English procedural rules and the practice of the English court as to declaratory relief SKBB is a proper party and not an improperly joined party to the claim for declaratory relief."

[90] This was prior to RSC, Ord. 104, r. 24 purporting to allow service in the U.K. Presumably the court had jurisdiction under Art. 18 of the Lugano Convention, but one still wonders on what basis Hoffmann-La Roche were originally served. The question is both procedural, and one of substantive jurisdiction.

[91] Possible suggestions are (1) that the Dutch *kort geding* proceedings were under Art. 24 so as not to require the application of Art. 21; or (2) that the Dutch proceedings were in breach of Art. 16(4) in so far as relief was sought in the U.K.; or (3) that the Dutch proceedings were not pending at first instance. If there was a problem under Art. 21 of the Lugano Convention, the court should have taken it of its own motion.

[92] [1996] F.S.R. 863 (Robert Walker J.).

[93] And criticising that judgment for failing to deal expressly with the position under the Brussels Convention, or with the fact that SKBB were exclusive licensees under the Biogen parents and so had a cause of action for infringement and for damages. As to the latter, Aldous J.'s reasoning is presumably that SKBB would have been estopped from suing once the *Biogen* action was over.

[94] [1993] R.P.C. 475, at 489, line 36 onwards, the first passage set out above.

8–46   It also followed that SKBB were properly joined under Article 6(1) of the Brussels Convention and had properly been served in Belgium without leave. An offer by SKBB to be bound by the decision between Chiron and Evans, if they were struck out from the case, was rejected by the plaintiffs and the judge. In the result, the action proceeded against SKBB.

Threats actions

8–47   The various statutory threats actions do not appear to offer the prospective defendant any better prospects for forum shopping than declaratory actions. Threats actions can be brought in respect of threatened proceedings for infringement of patents,[95] trade marks,[96] and registered and unregistered designs,[97] but not copyright. Although it may be an open question whether a threat uttered abroad is actionable in England,[98] there is no reason to doubt that the threat must be a threat to sue for infringement of a United Kingdom intellectual property right.[99] Even if the other prerequisites for a threats action are made out, therefore, an English threats action cannot pre-empt infringement litigation in the rest of Europe.

8–48   Although the point has not yet been decided, it is also suggested that a statutory threats action would not be in respect of "the same cause of action" as an action for infringement of the United Kingdom intellectual property right so as to require the latter to be stayed or struck out under Article 21. Consequently, commencement of a threats action in England would not pre-empt an infringement action abroad, even in respect of any infringement in the United Kingdom. The actions would almost certainly be related for the purposes of Article 22, but any stay of the second action would be discretionary.

8–49   One advantage of threats actions is that they are undoubtedly actions in tort, so that Article 5(3) applies and confers jurisdiction on the English courts against defendants domiciled in a contracting state. There seems no doubt that England is "the place where the harmful event occurred" in at least one of the senses of *Reinwater*,[1] since whatever the terms of the threat, and wherever it may be uttered, a threat to enforce a United Kingdom patent can only produce its intended consequences in the United Kingdom.

[95] Patents Act 1977, s. 70.

[96] Trade Marks Act 1994, s. 21.

[97] Registered Designs Act 1949, s. 26; Copyright, Designs and Patents Act 1988, s. 253.

[98] see para. 6–153. As a separate matter there seems no reason why a threat to sue abroad, to enforce a United Kingdom right, should not be actionable if the other requirements of the action are made out. Such threats are now credible, and perhaps more daunting than threats to sue at home.

[99] This follows from the definitions of "patent" (s. 130(1)) "registered trade mark" (s. 2) and "design right" (s. 213(1)) in the respective Acts. In the case of the Registered Designs Act 1949 the expression "right in a registered design" used in s. 26 and elsewhere is not a defined term but the intent is clear and the conclusion probably follows from s. 7.

[1] Case 21/76 *Bier v. Mines de Potasse d'Alsace* [1976] E.C.R. 1753; [1977] 1 C.M.L.R. 284.

D. ANTI-SUIT INJUNCTIONS AND SIMILAR RELIEF

The jurisdiction to grant injunctions against commencing, pursuing or enforcing litigation

In common law systems, jurisdiction exists to grant injunctions **8–50** restraining a person from commencing or prosecuting legal proceedings or from enforcing a judgment in their favour in certain circumstances where to do so would be oppressive to the applicant for the injunction.[2] There is no accepted term to describe such injunctions in English law, but "anti-suit injunction" is appropriate and may conveniently be imported from American law where it is well-known.[3] The jurisdiction exists in relation to both domestic and foreign litigation, but is more useful, as well as more controversial, where the litigation to be restrained takes place abroad. The applicant for an anti-suit injunction need not have, and typically does not have, any independent cause of action in England and it is not even fatal that the party sought to be restrained may have a valid cause of action within the jurisdiction of the foreign court. Since the injunction takes effect *in personam* the foreign court itself is supposed not to be directly affected and a fiction of comity is preserved, but the party enjoined is at risk of contempt of court if he disobeys the injunction and continues to prosecute the foreign litigation. The judgment of the foreign court would also be disentitled to recognition and enforcement in the United Kingdom in such circumstances.[4]

For present purposes, four topics need to be discussed: the treatment **8–51** of anti-suit injunctions in the general law; their compatibility with the Brussels Convention; the question of whether there is anything special about intellectual property litigation; and the circumstances in which anti-suit injunctions, if available, ought to be granted. Two subjects closely related to anti-suit injunctions in the narrow sense, and therefore dealt with in the present section, are the enforcement of no-challenge clauses abroad and the situation exemplified by *British Nylon Spinners v. ICI*[5] where the defendants were restrained from complying with a court order adverse to the plaintiffs' interests, made against them in proceedings to which the plaintiffs were not a party.

Fort Dodge v. Akzo Nobel

There is now one recent but inconclusive example of an attempt to **8–52** obtain an anti-suit injunction in the context of intellectual property litigation, and specifically with the aim of restraining extraterritorial

---

[2] See Wilson, "Anti-suit Injunctions" [1997] J.B.L. 424; Karet, "Suit, Anti-suit" [1998] E.I.P.R. 76. Anti-suit injunctions are unknown in the civil law, and although the Dutch courts have been invited to grant them, they have not done so: Willems, "Report on Recent Jurisprudence in the Netherlands" (1997) 28 I.I.C. 876.

[3] The old term "common injunction" might perhaps be revived; it originally meant an injunction to restrain proceedings in one of the English Common law courts. An early example is *Blad v. Bamfield* (1674) 36 E.R. 992 in which Lord Nottingham L.C. granted an injunction to stay a suit at law, in favour of the holder of a Danish "patent" which conferred a trading monopoly with Iceland.

[4] *Philip Alexander Securities and Futures v. Bamberger* [1997] I.L.Pr. 73, C.A., proposing to apply the public policy exception of Art. 27(1).

[5] (1952) 69 R.P.C. 288, CA. See para. 7–60.

patent infringement proceedings in the Netherlands, which is the only Brussels Convention contracting state in which pan-European injunctions against infringement are currently available. The facts of *Fort Dodge v. Akzo Nobel*[6] were that Akzo Nobel owned corresponding Dutch and United Kingdom patents, derived from the same European application, for canine parovirus vaccines which were licensed to the second defendants, Intervet. The petitioners in the English Patents Court were five companies in the American Home Products group. Three of the petitioners were English companies, one was an Australian company which had developed a competitive vaccine, and the fifth was a Dutch company. The vaccine of the Australian company had been marketed in the United Kingdom by the three English petitioners since 1991, and on a very small scale in the Netherlands by the fifth petitioner.

8–53   In April 1997 Akzo Nobel commenced infringement proceedings in the Netherlands against all five of the petitioners and another Dutch company under a new accelerated procedure which was expected to lead to a full trial in November 1997 and under which Akzo sought relief in respect of both the Dutch and United Kingdom patents.[7] It was not alleged that the United Kingdom companies had actively participated in any acts alleged to infringe the Dutch patents, but jurisdiction was asserted under Article 6(1) of the Brussels Convention. In September, the five American Home Products companies petitioned the Patents Court in England to revoke the United Kingdom patent, and it thereupon became common ground that the Dutch court would not grant any final relief in respect of the United Kingdom until after the petition had been determined. However, Akzo applied for an interlocutory injunction and interim damages in respect of the United Kingdom patent; and it was also common ground that the Dutch court would consider itself competent to grant such relief, notwithstanding the English petition. The petitioners applied for injunctions restraining the respondents Akzo and Intervet from (a) bringing or maintaining any action in the Netherlands in respect of alleged infringement of the United Kingdom patent in England; (b) permitting any licensee to do so; or (c) seeking to register or enforce any relief obtained in the Netherlands in respect of alleged infringement of the United Kingdom patent in England.[8] There was also originally an application, which was abandoned, for an order that the respondents should surrender the United Kingdom patent unless they discontinued the Dutch proceedings in so far as they related to infringement in the United Kingdom.

---

[6] [1998] F.S.R. 222, CA; see Karet, *op. cit.* and paras 1–51 and 1–54 above.

[7] This was not under the Dutch *kort geding* procedure which is essentially interlocutory, see para. 1–28, above, but a new procedure for an accelerated final hearing.

[8] One of several unresolved questions in *Fort Dodge v Akzo Nobel* is whether a petition for revocation of a patent was a suitable vehicle for applying for an anti-suit injunction. From the combined effect of RSC, Ord. 5, r. 5, Ord. 9 and Ord. 104 one might have thought not, at least in so far as the claim to final anti-suit relief was concerned. The procedure followed seems to have had the effect of obscuring whether the High Court had any *personal* jurisdiction over either respondent in respect of the anti-suit claim. See para. 8–96, below.

Laddie J. refused to grant the injunctions.[9] Distinguishing *Continental* **8–54**
Bank v. Aeakos Compania Naviera[10] and *The Angelic Grace*,[11] he held:

"I accept the argument that this court has the power, in suitable
circumstances, to order a party not to engage in or continue
proceedings before a foreign court. However, it appears to me that
it would be completely inappropriate for the High Court to do so
here. What I am being asked to do is to impose my view of the
construction of the Convention on the Dutch courts. I do not think
that would be an appropriate course to adopt. As Mr. Prescott QC,
who appeared for the respondents, put it in his skeleton argument,
if it were open for one national court to restrain a party from
seeking relief from another on the basis that the one didn't think
the other would get the law right, why could there not be a counter-
injunction? As a matter of comity the High Court should think long
and hard before taking any such step.

. . .

In my view there is a world of difference between restraining a
party from bringing or pursuing proceedings in a foreign court on
the ground that to do so would breach a valid agreement not to do
so and restraining the party on the ground that you do not trust the
foreign court to apply an international convention properly or to act
fairly."

The Court of Appeal dismissed the petitioners' expedited appeal, but **8–55**
referred a number of questions on Articles 6(1), 16(4), 19, 24 and 57 to
the European Court of Justice under the 1971 Protocol on Interpretation.[12] The Court agreed with the interpretation of the Brussels Convention adopted by Lloyd J. in *Pearce v. Ove Arup*[13] and Laddie J. in *Coin
Controls v. Suzo*,[14] but also agreed with Laddie J. at first instance that the
interpretation of the Convention was not *acte clair* and that an anti-suit
injunction should not be granted simply because the Dutch courts took a
different and more expansive view of their jurisdiction:

"The United Kingdom Courts have jurisdiction to prevent vexation
and oppression by persons subject to their jurisdiction. In particular,
the Courts are entitled to prevent persons domiciled in this country
from being submitted to vexatious or oppressive litigation whether
started or to be started in this country or another country. As was

[9] The Petition was dated September 22. The application for the injunction was heard on
October 14 and judgment was given on October 16. Judgment was given in the Court of
Appeal on October 27 after a hearing on October 20 and 21.
[10] [1994] 1 W.L.R. 588, CA.
[11] [1995] 1 Lloyd's Rep. 87, CA.,
[12] See para. 1–51, above, where the questions are set out. The Court of Appeal did not
refer any questions on the consistency of the anti-suit relief sought with the Brussels
Convention, which might be thought to be at least equally relevant and controversial.
[13] [1997] F.S.R. 641 (Lloyd J.).
[14] [1997] F.S.R. 660 (Laddie J.).

stated in the advice of the Privy Council in *Societe National Industrielle Aerospatiale v Lee Kui Tak* (1987) 1 A.C. 871, a Court can restrain a person from pursuing proceedings in a foreign Court where a remedy is available both in that foreign Court and this country, but will only do so if pursuit by the person 'would be vexatious or oppressive.' Further, since such an order indirectly affects the foreign Court, the jurisdiction must be exercised with caution and only if the ends of justice so require. We emphasise that injunctions granted for such purposes are directed against the vexatious party and not the courts of the other jurisdiction.

In the present case we have concluded that the dispute relating to the United Kingdom patent comes, by reason of Article 16(4), within the exclusive jurisdiction of the United Kingdom Patents Court. We have also concluded that the matter is not *'acte claire'*. In those circumstances we do not consider we would be justified in reaching a final conclusion that the pursuit, by Akzo, of the claim in the Dutch Courts in respect of the United Kingdom patent would be vexatious. It follows that we are not prepared to grant a final injunction at this time. The reference is necessary in order to decide whether final relief by way of injunction or declaration would be appropriate. We now therefore proceed to consider whether interim relief by way of injunction or otherwise would be appropriate pending the determination of the reference to the European Court.

Despite the fact that the relief would be directed against the respondents, we have in mind that it would indirectly affect the Dutch Court which has not yet considered what action, if any, would be appropriate. We have every confidence that the Dutch Court will, when deciding what to do, take into account that this Court will be referring to the European Court of Justice questions to elucidate how Articles 6, 16(4), 19 and 24 should be applied to the dispute. It will give proper weight to our conclusion that it would be wrong for this Court to anticipate the decision of the European Court. It will, we believe, also consider carefully the other views expressed in this judgment and, of course, the submissions of the parties and the facts. That being so we have come to the conclusion that justice does not require that this Court should grant any relief at this stage."

Anti-suit injunctions in the general law: *Aerospatiale*

8–56   The leading authority on the grant of anti-suit injunctions in the general law may now be taken to be the decision of the Privy Council in *Aerospatiale v. Lee Kui Jak*,[15] in which the opinion of the Board was delivered by Lord Goff of Chieveley.[16]

"The law relating to injunctions restraining a party from commencing or pursuing legal proceedings in a foreign jurisdiction has a long

[15] [1987] A.C. 871, PC.
[16] Citations of older cases are omitted.

history, stretching back at least as far as the early 19th century. From an early stage, certain basic principles emerged which are now beyond dispute. First, the jurisdiction is to be exercised when the 'ends of justice' require it . . . This fundamental principle has been reasserted in recent years, notably by Lord Scarman in *Castanho v. Brown & Root (U.K.) Ltd.* [1981] AC 557 and by Lord Diplock in *British Airways Board v. Laker Airways Ltd.* [1985] AC 58, 81. Second, where the court decides to grant an injunction restraining proceedings in a foreign court, its order is directed not against the foreign court but against the parties so proceeding or threatening to proceed . . . .

Third, it follows that an injunction will only be issued restraining a party who is amenable to the jurisdiction of the court, against whom an injunction will be an effective remedy . . .

Fourth, it has been emphasised on many occasions that, since such an order indirectly affects the foreign court, the jurisdiction is one which must be exercised with caution: . . . *Castanho v. Brown & Root (U.K.) Ltd* [1981] AC 557, 573, per Lord Scarman."

As Lord Goff went on to note, the actual circumstances in which anti-suit injunctions are appropriate are somewhat more controversial than these abstract statements of principle. There are three recognised categories where an injunction may be granted. First, where there are two or more available forums for trial, one of which is England, and the foreign litigation is in some sense oppressive.[17] Secondly, where the bringing of proceedings abroad is an invasion of a legal or equitable right not to be sued there. This is probably the most relevant and least controversial head in intellectual property, since it covers contractual exclusive jurisdiction and no-challenge clauses. Finally, where the bringing of proceedings abroad would be unconscionable. It is an open question whether the three categories are closed, since there are conflicting decisions from the House of Lords on the point. Given the potential breadth of the three heads and the extent to which they overlap, the latter point may perhaps be regarded as academic.   **8–57**

So far as the first head is concerned, the Privy Council in *Aerospatiale v. Lee Kui Jak* rejected the suggestion that the test for granting an injunction was the mirror image of staying English proceedings under the doctrine of *forum non conveniens*. A higher standard of prejudice was required to justify the indirect interference with the foreign court: **8–58**

"In the opinion of their Lordships, in a case such as the present where a remedy for a particular wrong is available both in the English (or, as here, the Brunei) court and in a foreign court, the English or Brunei court will, generally speaking, only restrain the

[17] *Airbus Industrie v. Patel* [1997] I.L.Pr. 230, CA has now decided that an anti-suit injunction may be granted to restrain oppressive litigation abroad even though the English courts have no jurisdiction over the substance of the dispute, and the natural forum is elsewhere.

plaintiff from pursuing proceedings in the foreign court if such pursuit would be vexatious or oppressive. This presupposes that, as a general rule, the English or Brunei court must conclude that it provides the natural forum for the trial of the action; and further, since the court is concerned with the ends of justice, that account must be taken not only of injustice to the defendant if the plaintiff is allowed to pursue the foreign proceedings, but also of injustice to the plaintiff if he is not allowed to do so. So the court will not grant an injunction if, by doing so, it will deprive the plaintiff of advantages in the foreign forum of which it would be unjust to deprive him."

The Brussels Convention (1): injunctions against commencement or prosecution of proceedings

8–59   The Brussels Convention is silent when it comes to anti-suit injunctions restraining the commencement or prosecution of litigation in a member state. Here, one is faced with a dilemma. The underlying policy of the Brussels Convention is undoubtedly one of "full faith and credit" between the member states: the courts of different contracting states should trust one another, and if a court errs in the application of the Convention, recourse should be to a higher court in the same state and eventually to the European Court of Justice. Any other procedure risks compromising the principle of legal certainty which is at the root of the Convention. If a court subsequently seised of an action must unquestioningly accept the jurisdiction of the court first seised in the circumstances contemplated by Article 21, as the European Court of Justice has held in *Overseas Union v. New Hampshire Insurance*,[18] then how can it legitimately take the more drastic step of enjoining a party before the latter court from invoking a jurisdiction which the foreign court considers itself to enjoy?

8–60   However, there is nothing in the express terms of the Brussels Convention preventing the grant of anti-suit injunctions against defendants over whom the court has jurisdiction consistently with the Convention itself: typically by virtue of domicile or a suitable choice-of-court clause in a contract.[19] In England, the current state of the law is that anti-suit injunctions are believed to be consistent in principle with the Brussels Convention, at least in some circumstances. That is the result reached by the Court of Appeal in *Continental Bank v. Aeakos Compania*

---

[18] Case C–351/89 [1991] E.C.R. I–3317. It is a major criticism of *Continental Bank v. Aeakos Naviera*, below, that the implications of this decision were not considered.

[19] *The Eras EIL Litigation* [1995] 1 Lloyd's Rep. 64 confirms that anti-suit injunctions are governed by the normal rules of Tit. II of the Brussels Convention, including Art. 6(1). Jurisdiction in *Philip Alexander Securities and Futures v. Bamberger*, below, can only have been based on the power to grant interlocutory relief in aid of English arbitration proceedings, which may have taken the anti-suit injunction outside the scope of the Convention as defined in Art. 1. It is uncertain on what basis jurisdiction was asserted in *Fort Dodge v. Akzo Nobel* [1998] F.S.R. 222, CA, see para. 8–96, below.

Naviera[20] where the plaintiffs obtained an injunction against the defendants prosecuting an action in Greece in breach of a term in a loan agreement conferring exclusive jurisdiction on the English courts. As a matter of principle this may be doubted, but until a case is taken to the House of Lords or European Court of Justice on the point *Continental Bank v. Aeakos Compania Naviera* must be taken to represent the law.[21]

In one respect at least some anti-suit injunctions in the context of intellectual property may be more easily reconciled with the Brussels Convention than is the case in the general law. One potential ground for granting an anti-suit injunction is that the foreign court has purported to assume jurisdiction over a claim within the exclusive jurisdiction of another court under Article 16.[22] Not only is such a breach of Article 16 a reason for refusing recognition to the judgment of the foreign court under Article 28, but *Overseas Union v. New Hampshire Insurance* itself expressly contains a saving for when the court second seised considers that the court first seised is in breach of Article 16.[23] *Fort Dodge v Akzo Nobel*[24] did not address this question—perhaps because the Court of Appeal accepted that two interpretations of Article 16 were possible—so the decision leaves open the question of whether an anti-suit injunction might ever be granted against proceedings in a foreign court which quite clearly did not have Convention jurisdiction.[25] **8–61**

Supposing that an English anti-suit injunction is ignored, and the foreign court goes on to decide the case against the English plaintiff on the merits, then presumably recognition and enforcement of the foreign judgment in England would be refused under the public policy exception of Article 27(1),[26] even if not as an irreconcilable judgment under Article 27(3). However, recognition and enforcement would still in theory be possible elsewhere in Europe where assets could be found.[27] The success of the anti-suit injunction may therefore ultimately depend on whether the plaintiff in the foreign proceedings can effectively be constrained to discontinue them, which may in turn raise the question of whether the **8–62**

---

[20] [1994] 1 W.L.R. 588, CA. Followed in *Aggeliki Charis v. Pagnan, The Angelic Grace* [1995] 1 Lloyd's Rep. 87, CA, where an injunction was granted to restrain Italian proceedings commenced in breach of an arbitration clause.

[21] For the question of whether anti-suit injunctions ought to be granted in Convention cases as a matter of comity, see para. 8–69, below.

[22] See para. 8–87, below.

[23] See para. 8–20, above.

[24] [1998] F.S.R. 222, CA.

[25] Although it might be said that making the reference presupposed that an anti-suit injunction would indeed be granted to protect the Art. 16 jurisdiction of the English courts in a sufficiently clear case: see para. 8–96, below.

[26] As proposed in *Philip Alexander Securities and Futures v. Bamberger* [1997] I.L.Pr. 73, CA. The Court of Appeal considered that the public policy exception of Art. 27(1) very clearly precluded enforcement of the German judgments by those German plaintiffs who were on notice of the interlocutory anti-suit injunctions, unless there was an excuse for non-compliance.

[27] It is hard to understand why Briggs and Rees, *op. cit.*, assert that the consequences of breach of an anti-suit injunction are internal to England and have no extraterritorial effect (*op. cit.*, para. 5.37), when they acknowledge that actions for anti-suit injunctions fall under the general rules of the Convention (*op. cit.*, para. 5.25).

anti-suit injunction can be enforced outside the United Kingdom. In the context of the Brussels Convention, an anti-suit injunction, whether final or interlocutory, is presumably a judgment in a civil or commercial matter like any other,[28] and as such is entitled to near-automatic recognition and enforcement in all other member states, including the one in which the litigation sought to be restrained is pending.[29] The latter at least, however, might be expected to invoke the public policy exception itself and refuse to recognise the injunction.

8–63   If the reasoning of the Court of Appeal in *Continental Bank v. Aeakos Compania Naviera* is correct, the main proceedings and the anti-suit proceedings are not "related actions" so as to give effect to Article 22. They are certainly not proceedings on the same cause of action in the sense of Article 21.

The Brussels Convention (2): injunctions against enforcement of a judgment

8–64   Injunctions against the enforcement of an order obtained in foreign litigation also need to be considered. Such injunctions are less common than those obtained prior to judgment in the foreign action, but are not unknown: *E.D. & F. Mann v. Haryanto (No. 2)*.[30] One of the three injunctions sought in *Fort Dodge v. Akzo Nobel*[31] would have restrained the Dutch plaintiffs from seeking to register or enforce any relief obtained in the Netherlands in respect of alleged infringement of the United Kingdom patent in England.[32] Such is the absence of delay in Dutch *kort geding* proceedings,[33] that unless the applicant for the injunction is well prepared in advance or acts exceptionally quickly this may be the only form of anti-suit relief useful to him. Orders prohibiting a party from *complying* with a court order, as in *British Nylon Spinners v. ICI*[34] may raise similar issues.

8–65   In this situation, and although the point was not considered in *Fort Dodge v. Akzo Nobel*, it does appear that it would contravene the express terms as well as the policy of the Brussels Convention to grant an injunction in England to restrain the enforcement in another member state of a judgment obtained in that or a third member state.[35] The relevant provision is Article 16(5) which gives exclusive jurisdiction,

---

[28] *Continental Bank v. Aeakos Compania Naviera* [1994] 1 W.L.R. 588, CA proceeds on that basis as does *The Eras EIL Litigation* [1995] 1 Lloyd's Rep. 64.

[29] For the consequences of this, see para. 8–74, below.

[30] [1991] 1 Lloyd's Rep. 429, CA.

[31] [1998] F.S.R. 222, CA.

[32] Presumably the order sought was intended to be extraterritorial, certainly it was not on its face confined to enjoining registration or enforcement in the U.K., and in many cases the latter on its own would be little better than useless.

[33] See para. 1–28, above. The Dutch proceedings in *Fort Dodge v. Akzo Nobel*, above, were not *kort geding*, but even so the time from commencement to expected trial was six or seven months. Two to three months is typical for *kort geding* as such.

[34] (1952) 69 R.P.C. 288, CA.

[35] Or to restrain the enforcement in another member state of an English judgment, if that situation ever arose.

regardless of domicile "in proceedings concerned with the enforcement of judgments,[36] [to] the courts of the Contracting State in which the judgment has been or is to be enforced." An injunction restraining enforcement of an order or judgment of a court in a member state would seem to fall squarely within the terms of Article 16(5), whether it was sought by the defendant in the main proceedings or a third party[37] affected by the judgment. Little further light is cast by the Jenard Report, which contains a very brief commentary on Article 16(5) but does not mention anti-suit injunctions, or by Schlosser, which has no commentary on Article 16(5) at all.

Article 16(5) has received some consideration in the case law of the **8-66** European Court of Justice, although not specifically in the context of anti-suit injunctions. In *AS-Autoteile v. Malhe*[38] the Court held that applications to oppose enforcement of a judgment (in that case under section 767 of the German Civil code) fell within the exclusive jurisdiction provisions of Article 16(5) but that it was not possible to plead as a set-off against the judgment sought to be enforced, a claim over which those courts had no independent jurisdiction. In *Reichert v. Dresdner Bank (No. 2)*[39] the Court gave a restrictive interpretation to Article 16(5) and held that it did not encompass the French *action paulienne*—a procedure used by creditors for setting aside a fraudulent disposition of property. Quoting the Jenard Report as if it had the force of law in its own right, the Court held that the *action paulienne* "does not aim to settle a dispute relating to 'the use of force or constraint, or the dispossession of movables and immovables in order to obtain the physical implementation of judgments and measures' and therefore it does not come within the scope of Article 16(5) of the Convention." In *Owens Bank v. Bracco*[40] the Court held that actions in England and Italy to enforce a judgment obtained in St Vincent were altogether outside the scope of the Convention so that neither Article 16(5) nor Articles 21, 22 or 23 applied.

It should follow that unless Article 16(5) is to be given a very **8-67** restrictive meaning, an anti-suit injunction against the enforcement of an order or judgment of a court of a member state cannot be sought on a pan-European or extraterritorial basis. *AS-Autoteile v. Malhe* supports the common-sense reading: opposing enforcement of a judgment is within the exclusive jurisdiction of the member state where the judgment is sought to be enforced. *Deutsche Genossenschaftsbank v. Brasserie du*

---

[36] Case C–129/92 *Owens Bank v. Bracco* [1994] E.C.R. I–117 interprets Art. 25 as meaning that "judgment," wherever it appears in the Convention, means "any judgment given by a court or tribunal of a member state" so that Art. 16(5) does not apply to non-member state judgments. Contra Lasok and Stone, *op. cit.*

[37] Compare Case 148/84 *Deutsche Genossenschaftsbank v. Brasserie du Pecheur* [1985] E.C.R. 1981; [1986] 2 C.M.L.R. 496. holding that Art. 36 of the Brussels Convention excluded any procedure allowing a third party to oppose enforcement of a judgment even where such a procedure was available under domestic law.

[38] Case 220/84 [1985] E.C.R. 2267; [1986] 3 C.M.L.R. 321.

[39] Case C–261/90 [1992] E.C.R. I–2149.

[40] Case C–129/92 [1994] E.C.R. I–117.

Pecheur[41] confirms that the procedure of Article 36 is a complete code and provides the only means of challenge.

8–68   The main argument to the contrary would seem to be that the Jenard Report explains Article 16(5) in terms which are inapplicable to anti-suit injunctions, but that is hardly surprising since the concept is only known in Anglo-American law and not to the law of any of six original contracting states. Even in England, anti-suit injunctions were all but unknown in practice at the time the Jenard Committee was working. It would be a travesty of purposive construction to say that injunctions against enforcement (if permissible at all) are outside Article 16(5) for that very reason. In a purely domestic context the possibility of an anti-suit injunction against enforcement is rather theoretical. The Brussels Convention clearly intends that any challenges to either recognition or enforcement should be made consistently with Title III of the Convention rather than in separate proceedings, but in any event the rights of the parties would be the same whichever procedure was taken.[42]

Comity issues under the Brussels Convention

8–69   Whether or not the grant of anti-suit injunctions is strictly compatible with the Brussels Convention as a matter of law, there is a growing realisation that foreign courts do regard the practice as an unacceptable interference with the exercise of their jurisdiction, so that as a matter of comity it may be particularly inappropriate to grant anti-suit injunctions in Brussels Convention cases.[43] This is the reasoning that underlies the refusal of Laddie J. and the Court of Appeal to grant anti-suit injunctions against Dutch patent infringement proceedings in *Fort Dodge v. Akzo Nobel.*[44]

8–70   In *Philip Alexander Securities and Futures v. Bamberger*[45] the Court of Appeal acknowledged that anti-suit injunctions previously granted in the course of the litigation had been ignored by the German courts, which had refused to allow the injunctions to be served. In several of these

---

[41] Case 148/84 [1985] E.C.R. 1981; [1986] 2 C.M.L.R. 496.

[42] Compare Case 42/76 *De Wolf v. Cox* [1976] E.C.R. 1759; [1977] 1 C.M.L.R. 12 holding that the procedure under Art. 31 is the only way of enforcing a judgment within the scope of the Convention (even if national law would otherwise provide more attractive alternatives) and Case 148/84 *Deutsche Genossenschaftsbank v. Brasserie du Pecheur* [1985] E.C.R. 1981; [1986] 2 C.M.L.R. 496, holding that Art. 36 is a complete code.

[43] *Contra The Angelic Grace* [1995] 1 Lloyd's Rep. 87 CA; especially *per* Millett L.J. Of course, jurisdiction under the Convention either exists or it does not, and on that point no question of comity or discretion can arise. However the court has a separate discretion to grant or refuse injunctive relief, especially at the interlocutory stage when it is most needed and most dangerous.

[44] [1998] F.S.R. 222, CA. See para. 8–52, above and para. 8–96, below.

[45] [1997] I.L.Pr. 73, CA. The litigation concerned futures and options contracts between an English firm and individual German investors, which the Germans had cause to regret. The agreements provided for arbitration in London, but the German plaintiffs claimed that the arbitration clauses were invalidated by German or E.C. consumer protection legislation. The Court of Appeal eventually agreed that they could not be compelled to arbitrate.

cases the German courts had gone on to deliver judgment on the merits. In one case German proceedings were still pending. The English plaintiffs applied for an anti-suit injunction against their continuance but it was refused at first instance both as a matter of discretion and because the German plaintiff was not obliged to submit to arbitration,[46] and this was upheld on appeal. The propriety of restraining the German proceedings therefore became academic, but Leggatt L.J. observed[47]:

"The practice of the courts in England to grant injunctions to restrain a defendant from prosecuting proceedings in another country may require reconsideration in the light of the facts of this case. The conventional view is that such an injunction only operates *in personam* with the consequence that the English courts do not and never have regarded themselves as interfering with the exercise by the foreign court of its jurisdiction. In cases where the defendant lives or has assets of substance in England that view may have some reality for there is reason to think that the injunction may be enforced so as to prevent proceedings taken in breach of it from reaching the foreign court. But in cases in which the defendant does not live in England and does not have assets here the injunction is unlikely to be enforceable except by the foreign court recognising and giving effect to the injunction or, where it refuses to do so, by this court refusing to recognise the order of the foreign court made without such recognition. In the present case the German courts regarded the injunctions as an infringement of their sovereignty and refused to permit them to be served in Germany. In addition they proceeded to give judgments on the merits. It was for that reason that the *amici curiae* were appointed in this case.[48] In practice that point has not been developed in these proceedings. But in future cases it may assume greater importance."

The German position in the same litigation was that service of the **8–71** interlocutory anti-suit injunctions did interfere with the jurisdiction of German courts and was not merely of interest to the parties *inter se*. The Dusseldorf Court of Appeal therefore refused to order the German Central Authority to serve the anti-suit injunctions when the Authority refused to do so pursuant to Article 13 of the 1965 Hague Convention on Service of Documents Abroad.[49]

"The purpose of the contested injunctions, in the form of antisuit injunctions, is provisionally to prevent the continuation of the

[46] Waller J. and the Court of Appeal also refused to grant declarations as to whether or not the German judgments were enforceable in England.
[47] Delivering the judgment of the Court. It is of interest that Leggatt L.J. was a member of the panel which expressed very different views in *The Angelic Grace* [1995] 1 Lloyd's Rep. 87, CA.
[48] And since the German investors could not be expected to appear.
[49] *Re The Enforcement of an English Anti-suit Injunction* [1997] I.L.Pr. 320 (Oberlandesgericht Dusseldorf). The case is the more important in the context of the present work because Dusseldorf is the *de facto* premier patent court in Germany.

actions which have been commenced in Germany before the Landgericht Krefeld by Mr G. in connection with the agreement of 28 July 1994, in order to safeguard the exclusive jurisdiction of the London Court of International Arbitration alleged by the petitioner.

However, such injunctions constitute an infringement of the jurisdiction of Germany because the German courts alone decide, in accordance with the procedural laws governing them and in accordance with existing international agreements, whether they are competent to adjudicate on a matter or whether they must respect the jurisdiction of another domestic or a foreign court (including arbitration courts). Furthermore, foreign courts cannot issue instructions as to whether and, if so, to what extent (in relation to time-limits and issues) a German court can and may take action in a particular case.

The fact that the contested antisuit injunctions are not directly addressed to the German State or German courts, but to Mr G. as the plaintiff in the actions already instituted by him and in potential further actions in Germany, cannot affect this decision, for the following reasons.

Firstly, under German procedural law, where proceedings have already been instituted the courts must rely on the co-operation of the parties. In particular, if the parties fail to co-operate, this may, for reasons which need not be considered in detail here, bring the action to a standstill, thus achieving the aim of the antisuit injunctions described above, so that the injunction addressed to the party is quite likely to influence directly the work of the German courts and is, in effect, equivalent under certain circumstances to an order addressed directly to the court (which would no doubt also be inadmissible according to the Anglo-Saxon concept of justice).

8–72

Quite apart from this, the sovereignty of Germany would also be generally infringed if, as in the present case, a foreign court issued instructions to the parties to an action before a German court as to how they are to act or to enter appearance and what applications they are to make. Judicial proceedings are guaranteed to be duly conducted in accordance with the rule of law only if the parties and their representatives are able, without any restriction, to place before the court all the facts they consider necessary for assessment by the court and to make the applications required by the procedural situation, and no further demonstration of this is necessary. These rights are safeguarded by the German procedural codes and, in many respects, by the Basic Law.[50] The courts must give effect to these rights. Instructions from foreign courts to the parties concerning the manner in which the proceedings are to be conducted and their subject-matter are likely to impede the German courts in fulfilling this task. Therefore the authorities who are responsible for handling requests for assistance, and who have to respect jurisdiction, cannot be permitted to forward or serve such instructions to or

[50] *sc*. The German Constitution.

on parties and in this way to allow foreign courts to influence the arrangements for and the course of pending judicial proceedings or to expose the parties concerned to the risk of punishment for contempt of court merely because they wish to exercise their rights which are safeguarded by German procedural law.

Like instructions concerning actions which are already pending, instructions from foreign courts purporting to prohibit certain proceedings before the German courts constitute interference with the sovereignty of Germany. The principle of free access to the German courts, which as such is an expression of state sovereignty and must be safeguarded by all state authorities, includes the right of every individual to refer to a court a matter of concern to him. The decision whether the proposed action is admissible is a matter for the German courts alone and cannot therefore be anticipated by instructions from foreign courts.

Finally, taking all the circumstances into consideration, it must be observed that the sole purpose of antisuit injunctions (whatever form they take and to whomsoever they are addressed) is to safeguard the alleged jurisdiction of the foreign court (in the present case, the London Court of International Arbitration) and therefore their very object is to interfere with the jurisdiction of the German courts, which themselves claim the right and have the obligation exclusively to determine whether they have jurisdiction in any particular case."

Although the English Court of Appeal refused to grant declarations **8–73** that the German orders in favour of the German plaintiffs were not enforceable in the United Kingdom,[51] their opinion was clearly that orders rendered in deliberate breach of the English anti-suit injunctions would not be enforced, even though there had been no formal service in Germany and notwithstanding that the anti-suit injunctions turned out to have been unjustified, since the Court of Appeal agreed with the German trial courts that the arbitration clauses were unenforceable by the plaintiffs in the English proceedings.

The implications of Article 26: is the interference with the foreign court in Brussels Convention cases direct or indirect?

The assumption on which anti-suit injunctions are granted in any field **8–74** of law is that the jurisdiction of the foreign court is not being directly interfered with. It is the litigant, and not the court, who is enjoined. However, the special nature of the Brussels Convention may require this assumption to be reviewed. What might be said is that Article 26, and

---

[51] *Quaere* whether enforceability can, in any event, be adjudicated upon other than in proceedings under Tit. III of the Convention. Case 148/84 *Deutsche Genossenschaftsbank v. Brasserie du Pecheur* [1985] E.C.R. 1981; [1986] 2 C.M.L.R. 496 (speaking of "an enforcement procedure which constitutes an autonomous and complete system") suggests otherwise.

the fact that the Convention does not distinguish injunctive orders from money judgments, converts what would otherwise be an indirect interference into a direct interference.[52]

8–75   An example in which English litigation is hypothetically subject to a foreign anti-suit injunction is perhaps more telling than one where the boot is on the other foot. Suppose that a court in a foreign member state (Ireland, perhaps) granted an injunction against a litigant commencing or prosecuting an action in England.[53] If the English court is obliged by Article 26 to recognise the judgment granting the injunction[54] without any special procedure being required, and without having any opportunity to review either the merits, or the exercise of jurisdiction by the Irish court; then how can it proceed with the litigation, even if the English court would regard itself as properly seised, and the party enjoined is prepared to risk contempt of the Irish court? It is not just the injunction as such that is entitled to recognition; so are the underlying findings of fact and law and the conclusions from them which make up the judgment. If it is conceded that antisuit injunctions are within the scope of the Brussels Convention at all then the English court can do so only if recognition would be contrary to public policy, and a court which is prepared to grant anti-suit injunctions itself can hardly be heard to say that they are contrary to public policy as a matter of principle.

8–76   There is a major distinction in this respect between anti-suit injunctions restraining litigation in Brussels Convention member states as compared to those restraining litigation in a non-member state such as the USA. In the case of the latter, the injunction takes effect *in personam* and binds only the litigant himself. The jurisdiction of the foreign court is not directly interfered with and the court can legitimately ignore the injunction. In Brussels Convention cases, the interference with the foreign legal process is inevitably that much more direct because of the obligation to afford the injunction automatic recognition. Returning to the example, if the English court must recognise the Irish anti-suit injunction, then the question of whether it may be enforced in England becomes redundant, since the defendant in the English proceedings may invoke Article 26, second paragraph, and have the question of recognition decided in the pending proceedings as a determinative incidental question under the expedited procedure.

---

[52] This argument is logically independent from the one that anti-suit injunctions are in any event inconsistent with the spirit of the Convention.

[53] The argument which follows is more telling if the anti-suit injunction is wholly pre-emptive, but similar arguments arise if the injunction is granted prior to the other court deciding whether or not it has jurisdiction.

[54] Assuming the anti-suit injunction was granted *inter partes*. If so, then the fact that it might be interlocutory would not detract from the obligation to recognise it. The German *Philip Alexander* case, above, does not seem to have considered whether the anti-suit injunctions were *ex parte* or *inter partes* for the purposes of the Brussels Convention, nor whether the Convention applied at all to anti-suit injunctions in aid of English arbitration proceedings. There had been an order for substituted service on the defendants (German plaintiffs) and they had certainly never appeared in the English proceedings.

Injunctions against foreign intellectual property litigation: introduction

Reported examples of anti-suit injunctions in the field of intellectual **8–77** property prior to *Fort Dodge v. Akzo Nobel*[55] are few, but in the broader sense they are not completely unknown. There is one example of a patent proprietor being restrained from complying with an order of a foreign court in this country and abroad[56]; one of a proprietor being restrained from prosecuting patent infringement proceedings abroad in breach of a settlement agreement[57]; one of interlocutory and final injunctions being granted to restrain foreign cancellation and opposition proceedings in breach of a trade mark delimitation agreement[58]; and one of a plaintiff in English proceedings for breach of confidence, breach of contract and passing-off being enjoined from prosecuting an action on the same facts in New York.[59] There is also an example of an anti-suit injunction being granted against a foreign action for breach of confidence, but as the obligations of confidence in question were expressly contractual in nature it is of marginal relevance for present purposes.[60]

These cases including *Fort Dodge v. Akzo Nobel* confirm that in the **8–78** present state of the law there is at least some scope for anti-suit injunctions in intellectual property cases, though leaving open the question of whether such injunctions are ever appropriate when the application for the injunction is not based on contract. Historically, there was never any scope for anti-suit injunctions under the first head of *Aerospatiale*[61] because the territoriality principle has meant that infringement actions have invariably been brought in the courts of the place of infringement as the natural, and indeed only, forum for the litigation; so that it would be impossible to assert oppression and the existence of an alternative forum. It is only recently that the District Court of the Hague, in particular, has begun to assert that it has jurisdiction to grant extraterritorial relief in respect of alleged infringement abroad, sometimes against defendants who have minimal connection with the Netherlands, and in proceedings which some would consider oppressive.

Are intellectual property rights special?

Because of an observation by Lord Evershed M.R., *British Nylon* **8–79** *Spinners v. ICI*[62] is sometimes cited as authority for the proposition that there is something special about British patents (and by implication

---

[55] [1998] F.S.R. 222, CA.
[56] *British Nylon Spinners v. ICI* (1952) 69 R.P.C. 288, CA, see para. 8–79, below.
[57] *Scripto Inc v. Fomento (Uruguay) SA* [1964] R.P.C. 113, see para. 8–83, below.
[58] *Apple Corps v. Apple Computer* [1992] R.P.C. 70 (Hoffmann J.) and [1992] F.S.R. 431 (Ferris J.) see paras 8–84 and 8–94, below.
[59] *Advanced Portfolio Technologies Inc v. Ainsworth* [1996] F.S.R. 217 (Harman J.), see para. 8–86, below.
[60] *Bank of Tokyo v. Karoon* [1987] A.C. 45 (note), CA. Similar comments apply to *X AG v. A Bank* [1983] 2 All E.R. 464.
[61] *Aerospatiale v. Lee Kui Jak* [1987] A.C. 871, PC: *i.e.* that there are two or more available forums for trial, one of which is England, and the foreign litigation is oppressive.
[62] (1952) 69 R.P.C. 288, CA.

other registered intellectual property rights) which makes any foreign judgment purporting to deal with them ineffective. The facts were that ICI, the defendant in anti-trust litigation in the United States, had been ordered by the New York District Court to assign back to du Pont a number of patents which it had acquired from du Pont and under which British Nylon Spinners were ICI's exclusive licensees. British Nylon Spinners were not party to the New York proceedings. The Court of Appeal upheld the grant of an interlocutory injunction against ICI restraining it from parting with possession of the patents in breach of its contract with British Nylon Spinners.

> "Now an English patent is a species of English property of the nature of a chose in action and peculiar in character. By English law it confers certain monopoly rights, exercisable in England, upon its proprietor. A person who has an enforceable right to a licence under an English patent appears therefore to me to have at least some kind of proprietary interest which it is the duty of our courts to protect.[63] And, certainly so far as the English patents are concerned, it seems to me with all deference to His Honour's judgment, to be an assertion of an extraterritorial jurisdiction which we do not recognise, for the American courts to make orders which would destroy or qualify those statutory rights belonging to an English national who is not subject to the jurisdiction of the American courts."

8-80   These grounds are too widely expressed and the judgment actually stands for the opposite proposition. Lord Evershed was equally prepared to regard the plaintiffs' purely contractual rights as a species of English property which it was not competent for the American courts to interfere with; but the real gravamen of the plaintiffs' complaint and the ground for granting the injunction was that they were adversely affected by an order made in proceedings to which they were not a party, by a court which did not even claim to have jurisdiction over them, which purported to compel ICI to act in breach of its contract with them. The New York judge himself had expressed reservations as to whether his order would be enforceable in England.

8-81   The relief actually granted in *British Nylon Spinners v. ICI* was quite as extraterritorial as the order of the New York court, but unlike that order was not vitiated by lack of personal jurisdiction or breach of natural justice. ICI were restrained from parting with possession of designated patents not only in the United Kingdom, but in certain Commonwealth countries and elsewhere. The possibility that this order was itself a breach of comity did concern Lord Evershed M.R. sufficiently for him to justify it in these terms:

[63] This is very dubious. It is trite law that a licensee as such does not enjoy proprietary rights. The most that one can say is that the plaintiffs, as exclusive licensees, were partially assimilated to the position of the registered proprietors; and even that depends on ignoring the fact that their licence was not registered.

"As regards the patents other than the English patents, Australian, Indian, New Zealand, South African, Irish or other patents, a possible distinction can, of course, be drawn; since the patents in those countries are a species of property in those countries and an effective right to use those patents would, if necessary, have to be asserted in those countries. But no special point has been made before us as regards those Australian and other non-English patents; and for the present purposes indeed I do not understand that it is suggested, if the injunction goes as regards the English patents, that it should not go to the full extent of the patents in the schedule. We must, in the absence of some evidence to the contrary, assume that the law in these other countries is the same as it is here, and, as I have already said, apart from what I might call the particular rights *quoad* the particular non-English patents, there remains the general contractual right which relates to all the patents and is derived from the (English) contract of December, 1946."

If the order needed to be justified at all, then these reasons are **8–82** inadequate and irrelevant. Issues of comity and proof of foreign law are completely separate, and consent *inter partes* could no more override the sovereign interests of foreign states than ICI's participation in the New York proceedings could bind British Nylon Spinners. The rule against a court adjudicating on certain kinds of matters relating to foreign patents is one of public policy and no more depends on the presence or absence of differences in substantive patent law than the *Mocambique*[64] rule turns on differences in real property law. If issues of comity arise, it is the duty of the court to resolve them so as to respect the sovereignty of the foreign state, whatever the parties say.[65] This is not to say that the decision in *British Nylon Spinners v. ICI* is wrong, either in refusing to apply the New York judgment or in granting extraterritorial relief. It is consistent with the line of authority represented by *Penn v. Baltimore*,[66] and, as Lord Evershed said:

"[T]here is no doubt that it is competent for the courts of a particular country, in a suit between persons who are either nationals or subjects of that country or are otherwise subject to its jurisdiction, to make orders *in personam* against one such party— directing it, for example, to do something or to refrain from doing something in another country affecting the other party to the action."

Enforcing settlement agreements and no-challenge clauses

There is authority for restraining foreign litigation relating to intellec- **8–83** tual property rights carried on in breach of an agreement which the English courts have jurisdiction to enforce. A "non-aggression pact" was

[64] *Companhia do Mocambique v. British South Africa Co* [1893] A.C. 602, HL.
[65] Without suggesting that the action was collusive, one wonders how enthusiastic ICI were to comply with an adverse order which they had previously resisted.
[66] (1750) Ves. Sen. 444, [1558–1774] All E.R. 99, LC.

enforced by injunction in *Scripto v. Fomento*,[67] with an English judge granting an interlocutory injunction restraining patent infringement proceedings against third parties in South Africa. The parties had concluded an agreement governed by English law under which they had agreed not to sue one another or their customers for infringement of certain designated patents relating to ball point pens, and the plaintiffs in the English proceedings alleged that South African proceedings against two retail dealers in their pens were in breach of the agreement. The defendants (plaintiffs in South Africa) argued that proceedings were consistent with a provision allowing patents relating to ink to be enforced. Although the South African action was said to be ready to come on for trial, Faulks J. held that the English plaintiffs had made out a prima facie case for an injunction and that the balance of convenience was in their favour. He granted an injunction enjoining the defendants "from proceeding with a claim based on alleged infringement of South African letters patent 857/1945 in two actions by them in the court of the Commissioner of Patents in the Republic of South Africa."

The *Apple* and *banana* cases

8–84   The issue of comity is at first sight rather more pronounced in the case of extraterritorial injunctions to enforce contractual no-challenge clauses, because the foreign state has a legitimate interest in purging its registers of invalid patents or trade marks in the interest of the public at large, and may treat no-challenge clauses as invalid or unenforceable.[68] Nonetheless, in *Apple Corps v. Apple Computer*[69] Hoffmann J. granted an interlocutory injunction against the defendants proceeding with applications to cancel the plaintiffs' registered trade marks anywhere in the World.[70] The defendants were parties to a contract governed by English law and with an English exclusive jurisdiction clause under which they had undertaken not to oppose or apply to cancel the plaintiffs' marks. In breach of the agreement they commenced cancellation or opposition proceedings in the United Kingdom, Germany and Sweden, and subsequently in Australia, New Zealand, Belgium, France, South Korea and Japan. They did not deny breach, but claimed that the agreement was invalid. At trial the various remaining attacks on the no-challenge clause failed and Ferris J. held that it was enforceable.[71]

8–85   The opposite situation to *Apple* arose in *Fyffes v. Chiquita*[72] where the plaintiffs' motion for an interlocutory injunction to restrain the defendants from using or enforcing certain "*Fyffes*" trade marks in Continental Europe was refused. The defendants were entitled to do both

---

[67] [1964] R.P.C. 113 (Faulks J., Vacation Judge).
[68] See para. 7–102 for the attitude of German and New Zealand courts in the *Apple* litigation.
[69] [1992] R.P.C. 70 (Hoffmann J.). See also [1991] 3 C.M.L.R. 49, C.A. and [1992] F.S.R. 431 (Ferris J.) and see para. 7–94 below.
[70] See the passages quoted at para. 7–08 above and para. 8–95, below.
[71] [1992] F.S.R. 431 (Ferris J.).
[72] [1993] F.S.R. 83 (Vinelott J.).

under the terms of a settlement and delimitation agreement, and an attack on the enforceability of the latter as a matter of competition law failed.[73]

The European Patent Office has held that it has no jurisdiction to refuse to entertain an opposition allegedly brought in breach of a no-challenge obligation.[74] The Office cannot enforce contracts or resolve disputes turning on national contract law.

Other circumstances in which an injunction may be granted

No-challenge clauses and settlement agreements may be regarded as a **8–86** special and particularly strong instance of right-not-be-sued cases. The same principle ought to apply where there is a contractual choice of exclusive jurisdiction or a submission to arbitration. In the present state of the law, both would justify anti-suit injunctions in appropriate cases. However, in the context of intellectual property litigation neither situation is common except in licence disputes, and these present different problems to infringement actions since Article 16(4) of the Brussels Convention does not even arguably apply. The only intellectual property case prior to *Fort Dodge v. Akzo Nobel*[75] in which an anti-suit injunction had been granted otherwise than on the basis of contractual agreement appears to be *Advanced Portfolio Technologies v. Ainsworth*,[76] where it was considered oppressive for a party who had initially commenced passing-off and breach of confidence proceedings in England to abandon those and sue in New York, notwithstanding that there had originally been a contractual submission to New York jurisdiction. The New York proceedings were restrained and a stay of the prior English proceedings refused.[77]

Of rather more interest is the question of *Fort Dodge v. Akzo Nobel* **8–87** itself, which is whether an anti-suit injunction can be granted where the foreign proceedings are, in the opinion of the English court, brought in breach of Article 16(4) of the Brussels Convention. Since the eventual outcome of *Fort Dodge v. Akzo Nobel* depends on a reference to the European Court of Justice, the question has to be addressed from first principles for the time being. Two arguments can be made in favour of allowing anti-suit injunctions to be granted in these circumstances. First, the current state of the law in England is that an anti-suit injunction can

---

[73] The defendant's cross-motion to restrain the plaintiffs from selling bananas under the *Fyffes* marks in Continental Europe was granted. The order can be understood simply as enforcing a term the delimitation agreement, rather than as extraterritorial enforcement of the marks themselves.

[74] *MW/No-challenge clause* O.J. EPO 12/1992, 747 (Opposition Division). The proprietor claimed that the no-challenge obligation arose from the fact that the opponent was its exclusive licensee. This was disputed, but the reasoning of the Opposition Division applies equally to express and uncontroverted no-challenge clauses.

[75] [1998] F.S.R. 222, CA.

[76] [1996] F.S.R. 217 (Harman J.).

[77] It is noteworthy that breach of confidence and passing-off were the only two causes of action in intellectual property to which the *Mocambique* rule was never applied.

be granted to enforce an exclusive choice-of-court clause under Article 17. In the scheme of the Brussels Convention, Articles 16 and 17 are both expressed to be exclusive jurisdictions, but Article 16 is considerably the stronger. Unlike Article 17, Article 16 cannot be overridden by appearance and breach of it is a ground for refusing recognition. As against this *a fortiori* argument, however, it has to be said that the reasoning of *Continental Bank v. Aeakos Compania Naviera*[78] is not based on the obligation of the foreign court to decline jurisdiction under Article 17, but on the fact that the defendant in the anti-suit proceedings has gone back on his contract. *The Angelic Grace*[79] is even more explicit in this respect and the distinction was recognised in *Fort Dodge v. Akzo Nobel*. This reasoning is consistent with the underlying principle that it is the litigant, rather than the foreign court, who is in the wrong and who is made subject to the injunction. This element of going back on a previous agreement is lacking in Article 16 cases, where the obligation to sue in a particular court arises from an external mandatory rule of law which expressly gives the parties no scope for contrary agreement.

8–88   Secondly, it might be said as a matter of Community law that Article 16 creates a right for the plaintiff (in the anti-suit proceedings) to be sued in the court specified by Article 16 and nowhere else; to which it might be added that commencement of proceedings in a court which *ex hypothesi* has no jurisdiction to entertain them is surely vexatious and oppressive.[80] As against this, the Convention provides its own mechanisms for resolving the problem and these are presumably intended to constitute a complete code. The foreign court arguably seised in breach of Article 16 must examine its jurisdiction of its own motion, and dismiss the proceedings pursuant to Article 19 if another court has exclusive jurisdiction. Even appellate courts must examine their jurisdiction *de novo*,[81] and if necessary make a reference to the European Court of Justice. Appearance by the defendant cannot, contrary to the normal rule of Article 18, waive the defect in jurisdiction. The right of other courts to re-examine the jurisdiction of a court seised in apparent breach of Article 16 is, exceptionally, preserved in the context of recognition and enforcement by Articles 28 and 34.

8–89   The background to the problem is that it is highly unlikely that any Convention court, no matter how unsophisticated, would entertain proceedings blatantly in breach of Article 16(4). What is more likely is that the English and foreign courts might bona fide differ as to the scope of the Article, as is currently the case between England and the

---

[78] [1994] 1 W.L.R. 588, CA.

[79] [1995] 1 Lloyd's Rep. 87, CA.

[80] See the claim by the plaintiff SCOR in *The Eras EIL Litigation* [1995] 1 Lloyd's Rep. 64, although that did not involve Art. 16. *Airbus Industrie v. Patel* [1997] I.L.Pr. 230, CA may, arguably, have proceeded on the basis that the plaintiff had a Convention right to be sued in France. An anti-suit injunction was granted restraining litigation in Texas although the natural forum was not England but France or India. Does *Airbus Industrie v. Patel* go so far as to imply that the English courts should protect the jurisdiction of other Convention courts as keenly as they do their own?

[81] Case 288/82 *Duijnstee v. Goderbauer* [1983] E.C.R. 3663; [1985] 1 C.M.L.R. 220.

Netherlands. Although the English courts may consider that infringement actions *per se* fall under Article 16(4) once validity is put in issue,[82] it can hardly be said in the present state of the law that any contrary view is so plainly wrong that the litigant in the foreign court ought to be enjoined. That is the conclusion reached by both Laddie J. and the Court of Appeal in *Fort Dodge v. Akzo Nobel*.

Moreover, if Article 16(4) actually deserves a narrow interpretation,[83] contrary to the prevailing English view, then any foreign proceedings actually in breach of the Article would be so nearly futile as to make it not worthwhile even to attempt to restrain them. What effect is to be given, say, to a Greek order purporting to revoke a United Kingdom patent? The United Kingdom courts and Patent Office would certainly and rightly refuse to recognise it and it would be a complete nullity in this country. Courts in other contracting states would also be obliged not to recognise it since Article 28, first paragraph, is mandatory and does not depend on the recognising court having exclusive jurisdiction itself. The only possible adverse effect of the purported order would be that if an order in other proceedings were made against an infringer who had assets only in Greece, then the infringer could perhaps protect himself locally by relying on Article 27(3). That seems a remote ground for enjoining the Greek proceedings *ab initio*. **8–90**

Apart from the international cases, there are a few English intellectual property cases in which anti-suit injunctions and the like have been granted (or refused) in a purely domestic context where no problems of comity arise. They may prove informative, if only by analogy.[84] In *Commercial Development v. Atkins*[85] the purchasers of a patent were entitled to an interlocutory injunction to restrain the assignor from applying for leave to withdraw an appeal against a first instance decision holding patent invalid. In *Rex Co v. Muirhead and The Comptroller*[86] the personal defendant (who was outside the jurisdiction) was restrained *ex parte* from proceeding with a patent application which allegedly involved his disclosing a secret process and the Comptroller was initially restrained from accepting or publishing the specification. On appeal, the injunction against Muirhead was continued and that against the Comptroller discharged. **8–91**

More recently, in *Sport International Bussum v. Hi-Tech Sports*[87] a mandatory injunction was granted to withdraw oppositions to certain pending United Kingdom trade mark applications, in breach of a delimitation agreement, despite argument that the agreement was anti-competitive; in *Sears v. Sears Roebuck*[88] an injunction was granted to **8–92**

[82] *Coin Controls v. Suzo* [1997] F.S.R. 660 (Laddie J.).
[83] As *Duijnstee v. Goderbauer*, above, suggests. For the possible interpretations of Art. 16(4) see paras 3–114 *et seq*.
[84] As well as the very early case of *Blad v. Bamfield* (1674) 36 E.R. 992 in which Lord Nottingham L.C. granted an injunction to stay a suit at law, in favour of the holder of a Danish "patent" which conferred a trading monopoly with Iceland.
[85] (1902) 19 R.P.C. 93, CA. A "pro-suit" injunction, so to speak, rather than an anti-suit.
[86] (1926) 44 R.P.C. 38, CA.
[87] [1990] F.S.R. 312 (Hirst J., QBD).
[88] [1993] F.S.R. 283 (Lindsay J.).

restrain the plaintiffs from pursuing rectification and opposition proceedings in the Trade Marks Registry pending the outcome of a passing-off action in the High Court; but in *Thames & Hudson v. Design and Artists Copyright Society*[89] the court refused to enjoin a criminal prosecution under the Copyright, Designs and Patents Act 1988 pending the outcome of civil declaratory proceedings.

8–93   In *Western Electric v. Racal-Milgo*[90] the fact that the defendants had tried, and failed, to obtain anti-suit relief in the United States was relevant to a decision to strike out certain defences to a patent infringement action which pleaded that the plaintiffs were in breach of American anti-trust law in trying to enforce their United Kingdom patents.

Interlocutory and final anti-suit relief

8–94   With anti-suit injunctions, the distinction between interlocutory and final relief is somewhat blurred, since even a final order does not normally purport to decide the merits of the underlying dispute. None the less, there is authority that *American Cyanamid*[91] applies to interlocutory anti-suit relief so that the plaintiff need not demonstrate more than an arguable case on the merits. This is not to be taken as casting doubt on the general principle that anti-suit relief should be granted with circumspection, because that arises independently from issues of international comity and irrespective of whether the plaintiff has a strong or weak case.

8–95   On the interlocutory hearing in *Apple Corps v. Apple Computer*,[92] Hoffmann J. held that the case was governed by *American Cyanamid* and that notwithstanding the implicit interference with foreign courts the balance of convenience overwhelmingly favoured the plaintiffs.

> "My conclusion is that there are serious and difficult questions to be determined at the trial; that if, pending trial, the defendants are allowed to push on with their foreign trade mark proceedings, the plaintiffs may suffer harm not easy capable of being compensatable in money; and that if the defendants were held up from prosecuting these proceedings for nine or 10 months until after trial they would suffer no clearly discernable prejudice. In those circumstances, I think that *prima facie* the injunction should be granted. Is this conclusion affected by the need for caution in enjoining foreign proceedings? The reason for such caution is because, although the order operates *in personam* against the particular defendant, it is indirectly an interference with the foreign court. That reason is particularly strong in a case in which the English jurisdiction is preferred on the ground that England is the natural forum and the

---

[89] [1995] F.S.R. 153 (Evans-Lombe J.).
[90] [1979] R.P.C. 514, CA.
[91] *American Cyanamid Co v. Ethicon* [1975] A.C. 396, HL.
[92] [1992] R.P.C. 70 (Hoffmann J.).

foreign court is conversely being rejected on the ground of its unsuitability as a forum. But in a case like this in which a party has expressly contracted not to sue, the argument that the order merely operates *in personam* is at its strongest. It involves no finding whatever about the suitability of the foreign forum but merely the universal principle that until some good contrary reason has been shown, men should be held to their bargains. I appreciate that Mr. Carr urges the existence of governmental interests in the foreign country in the prosecution of trade mark proceedings within their jurisdictions. The existence of those interests has, however, yet to be established, and the effect of the injunction would not be to deny them but, if Mr. Carr is right, merely to delay their implementation for a few months."

Fort Dodge v. Akzo Nobel reconsidered

From the point of view of the issues considered in the present chapter, there are a number of unsatisfactory aspects to *Fort Dodge v. Akzo Nobel*.[93] The first problem is with the basis on which the High Court asserted jurisdiction over Akzo Nobel and Intervet, which received no express consideration from either Laddie J. or the Court of Appeal. Self-evidently, it cannot have been on the basis of the "play away" rule of Article 2, since both were domiciled in the Netherlands. The High Court undoubtedly had jurisdiction over the Petition for Revocation as such under Article 16(4), but it is trite law that the Brussels Convention has no doctrine of accessory jurisdiction: every claim must stand on its own.[94] It is conceivable that Akzo and Intervet submitted to the jurisdiction pursuant to Article 18 by defending on the merits,[95] but one notes that the hearing before Laddie J. actually took place before the Answer to the Petition was due, and in a future case the defendant to the anti-suit application might not be co-operative.[96] That leaves two possibilities. One is that the High Court considered that it had jurisdiction under Article 24, although that is contradicted by the fact that the Court of Appeal, at least, clearly contemplated the grant of a final anti-suit injunction after completion of the preliminary reference.[97] The other is

8–96

---

[93] [1998] F.S.R. 222, CA. The treatment of the issues of substantive law is addressed in Chap. 3.

[94] See Case 189/87 *Kalfelis v. Schroeder* [1988] E.C.R. 5565 for the general principle and, in the context of one of the exclusive jurisdictions, Case 220/84 *AS-Autoteile v. Malhe* [1985] E.C.R. 2267; [1986] 3 C.M.L.R. 321. See para. 2–68.

[95] Conversely it is unclear whether any of the defendants in the Dutch proceedings had submitted to the jurisdiction of the Dutch court by defending on the merits. That could not have affected the question under Art. 16(4), which is expressly not subject to Art. 18, but it would have waived any defect in the application of Art. 6(1).

[96] And in so far as the application for the injunction against enforcement of any Dutch judgment was concerned, submission could not affect the question of whether Art. 16(5) applied to deprive the English courts of extraterritorial jurisdiction.

[97] If the sole basis for jurisdiction had been Art. 24 (which is controversial in its own right) then the Court of Appeal would have been *functus officio* after refusing interlocutory relief and there would have been no possibility of making a preliminary reference.

that the claim to anti-suit relief was considered to fall within Article 16(4) in its own right as "proceedings concerned with the registration or validity of patents." That would be a radical and unprecedented interpretation for a provision which is supposed to be interpreted narrowly as a derogation from a general rule, and one which one might think deserved a preliminary reference in its own right. It is unfortunate that a case in which so much criticism was made of Dutch practice in ignoring the "play away" rule, should have been silent as to the basis on which the English petitioners claimed to be able to play at home.

8–97   There are also reasons to doubt whether the correct questions were referred to the European Court of Justice by the Court of Appeal. In particular, it is noticeable that the questions were all ones relating to the interpretation of substantive jurisdictional provisions of the Brussels Convention as they applied to intellectual property infringement actions, rather than to the consistency or not of anti-suit relief with the Convention.[98]

8–98   Except in the very earliest cases on the Brussels Convention, the Court has adopted a consistent policy of answering preliminary references in the narrowest terms necessary to dispose of the actual case under consideration.[99] The terms of the reference in *Fort Dodge v. Akzo Nobel* are open to two related criticisms. First, that they completely ignore the question of whether the anti-suit relief sought could or should be granted, either on the facts of the case or in any circumstances. Secondly, that while they ask questions which urgently need to be answered by the European Court of Justice, and which could quite properly be referred by a Dutch second or final instance court in the proceedings by *Akzo Nobel* in the Netherlands; none the less those questions arguably did not need to be answered in order for the English courts to give judgment in *Fort Dodge v. Akzo Nobel* itself.

8–99   The references in respect of Articles 6, 16, 19, 24 and 57 all presuppose that if the Dutch courts are indeed misinterpreting those Articles, then the High Court could and perhaps should enjoin further proceedings in the Netherlands once the interpretation of the Articles had been sufficiently clarified. The assumptions underlying this are quite amazing: does the Court of Appeal contemplate—without the benefit of any preliminary ruling on the point—that in a case in which it considers breach of the Convention to be *acte clair* it may (a) enjoin foreign infringement proceedings which ought to be within the exclusive jurisdiction of the High Court under Article 16(4); (b) enjoin foreign interlocutory proceedings brought when no relevant proceedings seeking final relief are pending; or (c) enjoin foreign proceedings where the only objection to them is the misapplication of Article 6(1)?

8–100   As a matter of Community law, the first of these is perhaps arguable[1] but the second and third are scarcely credible. In terms of English, law

---

[98] The questions are set out at para. 1–51, above.

[99] The Court has also been prepared to refuse to answer at all when it considered that the preconditions for a reference were not met, most recently in Case C–346/93 *Kleinwort Benson v. City of Glasgow* [1995] E.C.R. I–615; [1995] All E.R. (E.C.) 514.

[1] See para. 8–61, above.

the Court of Appeal in *Fort Dodge v. Akzo Nobel* itself went no further than to say that an anti-suit injunction might be granted in Brussels Convention cases where the party sought to be enjoined was in breach of a contractual choice-of-court clause, a situation not remotely relevant to the instant case. As a matter of Community law even that may be doubted, but it by no means follows from either English or Community law that an anti-suit injunction could or should be granted to protect the exclusive jurisdiction of the court granting the injunction; let alone simply because a foreign court is asserting a jurisdiction it does not in fact possess. There is a serious prospect that the European Court of Justice will refuse to answer the questions put to it, with or without volunteering its opinion on the consistency of anti-suit relief with the Brussels Convention. At the very least, there is a marked difference between the actual need for a preliminary reference on the Article 16 question, and those on Articles 6(1) and 24.

Alternatively, it might be said that once the Articles have been given a **8–101** definitive interpretation by the European Court of Justice, then the Dutch courts themselves could be relied upon to discontinue their own proceedings or refuse relief as appropriate, and that no anti-suit relief from the High Court would be necessary. This is almost certainly true, but it reduces the necessity for a reference by the English courts to a circular argument: the English Court of Appeal makes the reference not for its own benefit, but so that the District Court of the Hague (which cannot make a reference) or perhaps the Hague Court of Appeal (which has a discretion) may be told what the law is. One might rhetorically ask what the High Court or the Court of Appeal would do if the European Court of Justice held that the Dutch courts clearly lacked jurisdiction and the District Court none the less granted judgment. Would it grant an anti-suit injunction against enforcement (which raises a completely new set of issues under Articles 16(5) and 36)[2]; would it conclude after all that it was powerless to do anything; or would the Court of Appeal make a further preliminary reference to answer the questions it should perhaps have referred first time round?

E. RECOGNITION AND ENFORCEMENT OF FOREIGN JUDGMENTS UNDER THE BRUSSELS CONVENTION

Introduction

The purpose for which the Brussels Convention was originally **8–102** adopted, as stated in Article 220 E.C., was "the simplification of formalities governing the reciprocal recognition and enforcement of judgments. . . ." In less formal terms, it provides for the free

---

[2] See para. 8–64, above.

movement of judgments within the Community.[3] The whole of the elaborate scheme of Title II is ultimately justified by this objective of facilitating the mutual recognition and judgments of courts in the contracting states with minimal formality. Article 26 provides:

> A judgment given in a Contracting State shall be recognised in the other Contracting States without any special procedure being required.
>
> Any interested party who raises the recognition of a judgment as the principal issue in a dispute may, in accordance with the procedures provided for in Sections 2 and 3 of this Title, apply for a decision that the judgment be recognized.
>
> If the outcome of proceedings in a court of a Contracting State depends on the determination of an incidental question of recognition that court shall have jurisdiction over that question.

8–103   Article 26 and the rest of Title III of the Brussels Convention apply only to judgments given by a court or tribunal of a member state. This follows from Article 25, as interpreted by the European Court of Justice in *Owens Bank v. Bracco*,[4] providing:

> For the purposes of this Convention, "judgment" means any judgment given by a court or tribunal of a Contracting State, whatever the judgment may be called, including a decree, order, decision or writ of execution, as well as the determination of costs or expenses by an officer of the court.

8–104   Title III applies regardless of the nationality or domicile of any party. Defendants domiciled outside the contracting states are equally at risk, in so far as they have assets in a contacting state, even though they do not enjoy the benefit of the various procedural rules protecting defendants domiciled in a contracting state from exorbitant or unjustified assertions of jurisdiction.[5] The Title applies whether the jurisdiction of the originating court was based on the Convention itself, or on its own internal law in the cases contemplated by Article 4.[6] The only exceptions

---

[3] Case 166/80 *Klomps v. Michel* [1981] E.C.R. 1593; [1982] 2 C.M.L.R. 773.

[4] Case C–129/92 [1994] E.C.R. I–117, interpreting Art. 25 as meaning that "judgment," wherever it occurs in the Convention, means a judgment of a court or tribunal of a member state. The style of the Convention is typically concise rather than verbose, but presumably the draftsman, lifting his pen from Art. 25, intended Arts 26, 30 and 31 to be tautologous (all refer to "a judgment given in a/another Contracting State") and Art. 27(5) to be absurd.

[5] A very limited degree of protection is provided for by Art. 59, which allows individual member states to enter into bilateral conventions with third states, protecting defendants domiciled in the latter from enforcement of judgment in which jurisdiction was originally based on one of the exorbitant grounds of Art. 3. Few such conventions exist.

[6] The situation is described as "little short of scandalous" by Briggs and Rees, *op. cit.*, who might have used stronger language had they had in mind some of the wider exercises of jurisdiction by the Dutch courts. The only protection for the non-Convention domiciled defendant is provided by Art. 59, which applies only to the limited extent that individual states have entered into separate conventions not to recognise certain exorbitant judgments.

are under Article 59; or where the subject matter of the proceedings is altogether outside the scope of the Convention as not being a "civil or commercial matter" or as falling within one of the excluded categories. *Inter partes* interlocutory orders are within the scope of the Convention and must be recognised and enforced, but *ex parte* orders are not.[7] In *EMI v. Modern Music*[8] Hobhouse J. therefore refused to register for enforcement an *ex parte* German order restraining the respondents (EMI) from various acts alleged to infringe the applicants' copyright. It was irrelevant that EMI had not taken steps to have the judgment set aside in Germany.

Consistently with the principle of free movement of judgments, there **8–105** is expressly very little scope for the enforcing court to review the assumption of jurisdiction by the originating court, and no scope at all for it to review its decision on the merits. Article 29 provides "Under no circumstances may a foreign judgment be reviewed as to its substance" and this is repeated in the context of enforcement by Article 34. The principle of Title III is that of giving "full faith and credit" to the judgments of courts in other contracting states, even if that policy is not stated in those very words.[9]

A judgment which is entitled to be recognised is entitled—so far as its **8–106** nature admits—to be enforced. There are provisions for enforcement to be stayed pending appeals in either the originating[10] or the enforcing court,[11] but otherwise entitlement to enforcement follows from entitlement to recognition, and enforcement may be refused only if recognition is refused on one of the limited number of grounds specified by the Convention. Of these, the most interesting to intellectual property practitioners are that recognition must be refused if the originating court assumed jurisdiction in breach of Article 16 or if recognition would be contrary to the *ordre public* of the recognising court. The latter exception is narrower than may appear at first sight.

Grounds for non-recognition: general

The grounds for non-recognition of a judgment under the Brussels **8–107** Convention are exhaustively[12] specified in Articles 27 and 28. They constitute a complete code, and are deliberately restrictive. The theory is that the defendant should almost always make any challenge to the jurisdiction of the originating court, or the validity of its decision, in that court or on appeal from it and should not have further opportunities to raise belated objections around Europe when the judgment comes to be enforced. Article 27 provides:

[7] Case 125/79 *Denilauler v. Couchet Freres* [1980] E.C.R. 1553; [1981] 1 C.M.L.R. 62.
[8] [1992] 1 Q.B. 115; [1992] I.L.Pr. 30 (Hobhouse J., QBD).
[9] For a discussion of *Fort Dodge v. Akzo Nobel* [1998] F.S.R. 222, CA in the context of whether an injunction can be granted against proceedings to recognise or enforce a judgment, see para. 8–64, above.
[10] Arts 30 and 38. The stay is discretionary.
[11] Art. 39. The stay is mandatory except for protective measures.
[12] Case C–414/92 *Solo Kleinmotoren v. Boch* [1994] E.C.R. I–2237.

A judgment shall not be recognized—

1. If such recognition is contrary to public policy in the State in which recognition is sought.
2. Where it was given in default of appearance, if the defendant was not duly served with the document which instituted the proceedings or with an equivalent document in sufficient time to enable him to arrange for his defence.
3. If the judgment is irreconcilable with a judgment given in a dispute between the same parties in the State in which recognition is sought.
4. If the court of the State of origin, in order to arrive at its judgment, has decided a preliminary question concerning the status or legal capacity of natural persons, rights in property arising out of a matrimonial relationship, wills or succession in a way that conflicts with a rule of the private international law of the State in which the recognition is sought, unless the same result would have been reached by the application of the rules of private international law of that State.
5. If the judgment is irreconcilable with an earlier judgment given in a noncontracting State involving the same cause of action and between the same parties, provided that this latter judgment fulfils the conditions necessary for its recognition in the State addressed.

8–108   Of these, Article 27(1) is considered in more detail at para. 8–125 below. Paragraph (2) does not raise any issues specific to intellectual property. In its jurisprudence, the European Court of Justice has insisted that its requirements must be strictly observed, so as to safeguard the rights of defendants.[13] Paragraph (3) is of interest in the present context mainly if a finding for the plaintiff in infringement proceedings in one state is inconsistent with a finding of invalidity in another. It is considered at paragraphs 3–143 above and paragraph 8–120 below. Paragraph (4) is of interest only for the implication that in all other circumstances the recognising court cannot refuse recognition simply because it objects to the application of the originating court's rules of private international law, or to the manner of determination of some other preliminary or incidental question. Paragraph (5) is unlikely to apply to intellectual property actions in the present state of the law.

Article 28 is relevant in the present context only if the originating court assumed jurisdiction in breach of Article 16. It is set out and considered at paragraph 8–109, below.

Non-recognition for breach of Article 16: Article 28

8–109   Article 28 exceptionally provides that in certain circumstances the recognising court can re-examine the jurisdiction of the originating court and must refuse recognition if the latter exceeded its jurisdiction under

[13] Case 166/80 *Klomps v. Michel* [1981] E.C.R. 1593; [1982] 2 C.M.L.R. 773; Case C–305/88 *Lancray v. Peters* [1990] E.C.R. I–2725; Case C–123/91 *Minalmet v. Brandeis* [1992] E.C.R. I–5661; Case C–78/95 *Hendrikman v. Magenta Druck* [1996] E.C.R. I–4943; [1996] All E.R. (E.C.) 944; [1996] I.L.Pr. 752.

the Convention. The obligation to refuse recognition arises only in the context of insurance contracts, consumer contracts and for the exclusive jurisdictions of Article 16. In all other cases, the jurisdiction of the originating court cannot be reviewed either directly, or indirectly by purporting to invoke the public policy exception of Article 27(1). Article 28 provides in terms:

> Moreover, a judgment shall not be recognized if it conflicts with the provisions of Sections 3, 4 or 5 of Title II, or in a case provided for in Article 59.
>
> In its examination of the grounds of jurisdiction referred to in the foregoing paragraph, the court or authority applied to shall be bound by the findings of fact on which the court of the State of origin based its jurisdiction.
>
> Subject to the provisions of the first paragraph, the jurisdiction of the court of the State of origin may not be reviewed; the test of public policy referred to in point 1 of Article 27 may not be applied to the rules relating to jurisdiction.

Section 5 of Title II is the only provision of interest for present **8–110** purposes, since it consists of Article 16 which defines the exclusive jurisdictions. It follows from Article 28 that if the originating court was wrongly seised in breach of Article 16 and failed to decline jurisdiction of its own motion pursuant to Article 19, then its judgment must be refused recognition in all other contracting states. As the Jenard Report notes in its commentary on Article 19, the latter Article reflects the fact that the exclusive jurisdictions are matters of public policy, and Article 28 reinforces this. The Report comments on Article 28:

> "The very strict rules of jurisdiction laid down in Title II, and the safeguards granted in Article 20 to defendants who do not enter an appearance, make it possible to dispense with any review, by the court in which recognition or enforcement is sought, of the jurisdiction of the court in which the original judgment was given.
>
> The absence of any review of the substance of the case implies complete confidence in the court of the State in which judgment was given; it is similarly to be assumed that that court correctly applied the rules of jurisdiction of the Convention. The absence of any review as to whether the court in which the judgment was given had jurisdiction avoids the possibility that an alleged failure to comply with those rules might again be raised as an issue at the enforcement stage. The only exceptions concern, first, the matters for which Title II lays down special rules of jurisdiction (insurance, instalment sales and loans) or exclusive rules, and which, as has been shown, are in the six countries either of a binding character or matters of public policy, and, secondly, the case provided for in Article 59; reference should be made to the commentary on that Article.
>
> . . .
>
> The last paragraph of Article 28 specifies that the rules of jurisdiction are not matters of public policy within the meaning of

Article 27; in other words, public policy is not to be used as a means of justifying a review of the jurisdiction of the court of origin. This again reflects the Committee's desire to limit so far as possible the concept of public policy."

Problems in the application of Article 28 to intellectual property

8–111 An example of a straightforward application of Article 28 would be if the originating court purported to revoke a patent or registered intellectual property right subsisting in another contracting state, or purported to rectify the latter state's Register, then the purported order would not be recognised anywhere outside the originating state. The obligation to refuse recognition arises regardless of whether or not the courts of the recognising state would themselves have had exclusive jurisdiction over the claim, although that is obviously the situation of most practical importance.

8–112 However, several problems arise in the application of Article 28 to intellectual property actions in the wider sense. The most significant is the absence of any international consensus as to whether, or when, infringement actions as such fall within Article 16. There is both a question of principle, as to whether infringement actions as such ever fall within Article 16, and a question of degree as to what is intended by Article 19 when a claim is partly but not principally concerned with one of the exclusive jurisdictions. In the present state of the law, all that the courts of any contracting state can do is apply their own understanding of the law as consistently as possible, whether in the context of assuming or refusing jurisdiction under Article 19, or of recognising foreign judgments or not under Article 28.[14] However, it is irrelevant that the originating court may wrongly have asserted that it had exclusive jurisdiction under Article 16, if Article 16 was in fact inapplicable.[15] The originating court may have misapplied Article 16, but it has not trespassed on the exclusive jurisdiction of any other court. Even if it actually had no jurisdiction at all under the Convention as properly understood, its judgment must still be recognised.

8–113 Article 19 contemplates that a court seised of a claim which is not "principally concerned" with a matter over which another court has exclusive jurisdiction, may entertain the action notwithstanding that it has to resolve a "preliminary or incidental" question which is prima facie within the exclusive jurisdiction of another court. An interpretation of the Convention which allowed that court to entertain the action, and then denied the resulting judgment international recognition under Article 28 is obviously to be avoided. Conversely, Article 28 contemplates that the recognising court is not bound by the decision of the originating court to proceed. The better view from the interrelationship

---

[14] For the divergence in opinions, see paras 1–28 *et seq.* and paras 3–78 *et seq.*

[15] It is conceivable, for instance, that a court might assert that an ordinary infringement action automatically fell under Art. 16(4) so as to confer jurisdiction irrespective of Arts 2 and 5(3).

of Articles 16, 19 and 28 is that the recognising court may perform a similar exercise to that of the originating court, and is not bound by the decision of the latter to press ahead, if that is in breach of Articles 16 and 19.[16] On the other hand the recognising court should not refuse recognition if it too concludes that the matter otherwise within the exclusive jurisdiction of a court other than the originating court did not constitute the principal subject matter of the claim. Once the Article 16 claim—or issue—is rightly characterised as an incidental matter, its presence does not prevent the judgment of the originating court being recognised. This is confirmed from the express presence of a very restricted right to refuse recognition on the basis of the originating court's treatment of an incidental question in the circumstances contemplated by Article 27(4). By implication, the general rule is that decisions on incidental matters do not vitiate.

There still remains the question of what material the recognising court **8–114** can take into account in deciding whether Article 16 was originally contravened or not. It is suggested elsewhere that Article 16 is indeed concerned only with the claim stated by the plaintiff, and not with the wider issues arising in the case.[17] If so, the task of the recognising court is greatly simplified. It need only look at the document corresponding to the statement of claim, and any findings of fact by the originating court on which the latter based its jurisdiction. The originating court's relevant findings of fact are binding on the recognising court.

Obviously, if Article 28 falls to be applied, it will be because the **8–115** originating court did consider that it had jurisdiction, but one cannot hypothesise to what extent this would have been based on actual findings of fact and to what extent on pleaded allegations. The decision of the European Court of Justice in *Effer v. Kantner*[18] contemplates that the claim does not have to be taken at face value. The originating court may therefore have investigated whether or not the necessary factual allegations had been made out.[19] The extent to which it did so is likely to depend on its interpretation of Article 16(4). Unlike some of the other heads of Article 16, there is not really much scope for factual dispute as to whether, on a narrow interpretation, exclusive jurisdiction under Article 16(4) exists.[20] The only factual pre-requisite for jurisdiction is that a registered intellectual property right should actually exist,[21] but that can be assumed from the fact that someone wants to challenge it and if no right existed, no question of recognition would arise. On a

---

[16] Subject to the recognising court being bound by the relevant findings of fact by the originating court, see below.

[17] See para. 3–93.

[18] Case 38/81 [1982] E.C.R. 825; [1984] 2 C.M.L.R. 667.

[19] This may be true *a fortiori* if one is dealing with a default judgment to which Art. 20 applies.

[20] Compare, for instance, Art. 16(1)(b) where jurisdiction depends on such factual issues as the purpose and term of the tenancy and the domicile of the parties, all of which might be disputed.

[21] Or have once existed. The wording of Art. 16 does not on its face exclude actions to revoke registered intellectual property rights which have lapsed or been surrendered.

broader interpretation of Article 16(4), as in *Coin Controls v. Suzo*,[22] a more wide-ranging factual inquiry might be called for.[23]

Whether judgments partially in breach of Article 16 are severable: Article 42

8–116   The present section contemplates that a judgment may at least arguably partly contravene Article 16.[24] The situation is not expressly dealt with in the Convention or the jurisprudence of the European Court of Justice. The only relevant provision appears to be Article 42 which provides that:

> Where a foreign judgment has been given in respect of several matters and enforcement cannot be authorized for all of them, the court shall authorize enforcement for one or more of them.
> An applicant may request partial enforcement of a judgment.

8–117   The obvious and uncontroversial application of Article 42 is to cases such as matrimonial litigation where only part of any judgment may be within the scope of the Brussels Convention,[25] and the remainder, though not entitled to enforcement, is not actually precluded from recognition. It does not follow from its terms that Article 42 allows the unobjectionable parts of a judgment to be severed from those that are prohibited from recognition, no matter how convenient that might be. However, the Jenard Report does lead to this conclusion. The Report comments:

> "The first paragraph of Article 42 empowers the court of the State in which enforcement is sought to authorize enforcement in respect of certain matters dealt with in a judgment and to refuse it in respect of others. As explained in the report annexed to the Benelux Treaty, which contains a similar provision, this discretion exists in all cases where a judgment deals with separate and independent heads of claim, and the decision on some of these is contrary to the public policy of the country in which enforcement is sought, while the decision on others is not."

[22] [1997] F.S.R. 660 (Laddie J.).
[23] This is one reason for questioning *Coin Controls v. Suzo* [1997] F.S.R. 660, see para. 3–100. The more wide-ranging the inquiry performed by the originating court prior to asserting jurisdiction, the less scope there is in practice for other courts to refuse recognition pursuant to Art. 28.
[24] A judgment may comprise more than one claim. It is arguable, on the strength of Art. 19 and the cases on Art. 16(1), that a claim is either wholly within Art. 16 or wholly outside it. It may seem odd that a plaintiff can remove a claim from the scope of Art. 16 by dressing it up as part of a wider claim, but that is what Case C–280/90 *Hacker v. Euro-Relais* [1992] E.C.R. I–1111 seems to contemplate.
[25] As in Case C–220/95 *van den Boogaard v. Laumen* [1997] I.L.Pr. 278, where Article 42 was of passing relevance to the question of whether, or to what extent, an order for a lump sum payment on divorce could be regarded as an order for maintenance within the Convention.

Although the Article applies in terms only to enforcement, and not to **8–118** recognition, and forms part of Section 2 of Title III, it is implicit from the Jenard Report that the portions of the judgment which may be enforced, must first be recognised. What is not recognised cannot be enforced. It follows that at least where there are "separate and independent heads of claim" in the sense of Jenard, recognition and enforcement should be denied only to those claims which contravene the public policy of the enforcing court, and not to the others. Although the Report speaks only in terms of non-recognition on public policy grounds the wording of Article 42 is perfectly general and it is suggested that it applies equally when the objection to recognition and enforcement arises under Article 28, especially as the Article 16 jurisdictions are simply one specific embodiment of a public policy rule.

This in turn raises the question of whether judgments on validity and **8–119** infringement are "separate and independent heads of claim" in the sense of Jenard. This may to some extent be a question of fact, depending on the interrelationship between the various claims, but prima facie a claim for a declaration that a patent is valid or not,[26] if permitted under national law, would appear to be separate and independent from the claim in relation to infringement itself.

Situations likely to arise in practice under Article 28

The practical application of Article 28 may differ according to the **8–120** nature of the foreign judgment putatively entitled to recognition. In the present uncertain state of the law, little more can be done than to identify some of the situations capable of arising in practice and offer some tentative suggestions.

Suppose that in a final judgment a foreign court finds on an **8–121** extraterritorial basis that a certain European patent is valid and infringed, and the court grants a pan-European injunction and damages accordingly. In the present state of the law,[27] the English courts would certainly regard the assumption of jurisdiction over validity as contrary to Article 16.[28] The finding of validity would not therefore be entitled to recognition in England, and the defendant would be free to petition for revocation, even on the grounds previously raised and rejected, without being met with a plea of *res judicata*.[29] If the defendant's renewed attack

---

[26] The Patents Act 1977, s. 61(1)(e) allows proceedings for a declaration that a patent is valid and has been infringed. However, s. 74(2) provides that proceedings cannot be instituted seeking only a declaration of validity or invalidity.

[27] *Coin Controls v. Suzo* [1997] F.S.R. 660 (Laddie J.) and *Fort Dodge v. Akzo Nobel* [1998] F.S.R. 222, CA.

[28] Unless, perhaps, validity was treated as a minor or incidental issue and either the English court regarded itself as bound by the decision of the originating court to that effect, or the English court was able to reach the same conclusion.

[29] Individual issues might be *res judicata* as a result of the uncontroversial exercise by the foreign court of jurisdiction over causes of action arising wholly under its own law. Aldous L.J. in *Kirin-Amgen Inc v. Boehringer Mannheim GmbH* [1997] F.S.R. 289, CA, gives some hypothetical examples.

on validity succeeded, then at that point he would be able to invoke Article 27(3) to prevent recognition of the foreign judgment in England. A foreign finding of liability for infringement is necessarily irreconcilable with a local finding of invalidity,[30] and the latter prevails even though later in time.[31]

8–122   But does it follow in any event that the finding of infringement and the granting of the injunction and damages are tainted by the assertion of jurisdiction over validity as *Coin Controls v. Suzo*[32] seems to contemplate? On their own, they are unobjectionable; and there might have been no breach of Article 16 if the originating court had confined its proceedings to the issue of infringement and had refused to investigate the validity of the patent, leaving the defendant to bring invalidity proceedings on a country-by-country basis.[33] It is implicit from Article 42 that a mixed judgment does not stand or fall as a whole. It may still be enforceable in part, either on the court's own initiative or at the request of the applicant. *Ex hypothesi* the defendant has not been prejudiced by the course actually taken and it may be unduly hard on the successful plaintiff to refuse recognition of the judgment on infringement, and with it the injunction and damages, simply because the originating court allowed validity to be investigated.

8–123   On the other hand, the originating court may have found for the defendant on either or both of the issues of validity and infringement. In that case, there will probably be no order to enforce abroad (other than as to costs) but the successful defendant has a legitimate interest in having the judgment in his favour recognised so as to give himself the benefit of *res judicata* under the Convention. If the defendant won on both issues, then it again seems harsh to deprive him of the benefit of a successful non-infringement defence because he challenged validity and won. Had he confined his defence to non-infringement and not pleaded invalidity, then Article 16 would not even arguably have precluded recognition. Supposing he won on infringement but lost on validity, then similar comments apply except that he would be entitled to re-litigate validity as in the previous example. If the defendant won on validity but lost on infringement, then the decision on validity would not be entitled to recognition and the plaintiff would be entitled to re-litigate the issue in fresh infringement proceedings. In any of these situations the question again arises, as in the previous example, of whether the finding of infringement or non-infringement as such is binding in any subsequent proceedings[34] or whether the decision of the originating court for or

[30] Compare Case 145/86 *Hoffmann v. Krieg* [1988] E.C.R. 645 (subsequent Dutch divorce irreconcilable with earlier German award of maintenance).

[31] Comparing Art. 27(3) to Art. 27(5).

[32] [1997] F.S.R. 660 (Laddie J.).

[33] This procedure might be regarded as unfairly prejudicial to the defendant, but that cannot affect the application of Art. 28. *Fort Dodge v. Akzo Nobel* [1998] F.S.R. 222, also seems to contemplate that the jurisdiction of the court hearing the infringement action as such on an extraterritorial basis is displaced once validity is put in issue in the courts of the country of registration.

[34] Independently of the common law doctrine of issue estoppel; *Kirin-Amgen Inc v. Boehringer Mannheim GmbH* [1997] F.S.R. 289, CA.

against the plaintiff is wholly debarred from recognition because of the assumption of jurisdiction over validity.

Article 28 has no application to foreign extraterritorial judgments in **8–124** so far as they purport to enforce or otherwise affect registered intellectual property rights existing under the law of a non-contracting state, since Article 16 in terms confers exclusive jurisdiction only in the case of registered intellectual property rights existing under the laws of the contracting states.[35] In the context of Article 16(1) it has even been asserted that the normal rules of the Convention apply to actions in respect of immovable property situated in a non-contracting state.[36] Even if this is wrong, jurisdiction would still be a matter for national law in actions against defendants not domiciled in a contracting state; and once the originating court has chosen to exercise jurisdiction its decision cannot be challenged on the grounds that the recognising court would have declined jurisdiction in similar circumstances. It appears to follow that if a court in a contracting state were, for instance, to purport to enjoin infringement of a United States patent then the judgment would be entitled to recognition and enforcement against the defendant's assets in the United Kingdom unless Article 27(5) or the public policy exception applied. The conclusion follows, subject to Article 59, regardless of whether the defendant was domiciled in the United Kingdom, another contracting state, or anywhere else.

The public policy exception applied to intellectual property

The only other provision which is of interest in the present context is **8–125** Article 27(1), providing that a judgment shall not be recognised if recognition is contrary to public policy in the State in which recognition is sought.[37] The test of public policy is expressly to be applied to the question of recognition, rather than to the actual judgment itself, although in practice the two may be difficult to separate. The Article has not yet been interpreted by the European Court of Justice—except to say that the public policy exception of Article 27(1) does not apply to situations covered elsewhere in Article 27[38]—and has received very little

---

[35] Art. 28 has yet to be interpreted by the European Court of Justice, but presumably is to receive a restricted interpretation as being a derogation from the general rule of Art. 26. *cf.* Case C–414/92 *Solo Kleinmotoren v. Boch* [1994] E.C.R. I–2237 confirming that Art. 27 should be construed strictly as a derogation from the principle of free movement of judgments.

[36] Cruz, Real and Jenard Report, para. 25(d). The implication that the *Mocambique* rule is wholly abrogated by the Convention in relation to non-contracting states is remarkably unattractive. One would not have thought that the contracting states, having re-enacted a very similar rule among themselves, intended to oblige one another to defy a widely recognised principle of international comity in their dealings with the rest of the world.

[37] The wording of Art. 27 appears to make non-recognition mandatory, but since public policy inevitably involves the exercise of a discretion there is no practical difference between *may* and *shall*.

[38] Case 145/86 *Hoffmann v. Krieg* [1988] E.C.R. 645; Case C–78/95 *Hendrikman v. Magenta Druck* [1996] E.C.R. I–4943; [1996] All E.R. (E.C.) 944; [1996] I.L.Pr. 752.

consideration in domestic law,[39] so any commentary has to be tentative. Subject to what follows, cases at common law presumably continue to apply since it is for each contracting state to define its own rules of public policy, within the scope implicitly permitted by Article 27(1).[40]

8–126   The Jenard Report comments:

> "Recognition may be refused if it is contrary to public policy in the State in which the recognition is sought. In the opinion of the Committee this clause ought to operate only in exceptional cases. As has already been shown in the commentary on Article 4, public policy is not to be invoked as a ground for refusing to recognize a judgment given by a court of a Contracting State which has based its jurisdiction over a defendant domiciled outside the Community on a provision of its internal law, such as the provisions listed in the second paragraph of Article 3 (Article 14 of the French Civil Code, etc.).
>
> Furthermore, it follows from the last paragraph of Article 27[41] that public policy is not to be used as a means of justifying refusal of recognition on the grounds that the foreign court applied a law other than that laid down by the rules of private international law of the court in which the recognition is sought.
>
> The wording of the public policy provision is similar to that adopted in the most recent conventions, in that it is made clear that there are grounds for refusal, not of the foreign judgment itself, but if recognition of it is contrary to public policy in the State in which the recognition is sought. It is no part of the duty of the court seised of the matter to give an opinion as to whether the foreign judgment is, or is not, compatible with the public policy of its country. Indeed, this might be taken as criticism of the judgment. Its duty is rather to verify whether recognition of the judgment would be contrary to public policy."

8–127   The Schlosser report adds that the public policy exception allows recognition to be refused to judgments obtained by fraud (notwithstanding that this was a separate ground of non-recognition at common law) with the proviso that the recognising court should take into account the possibilities for redress offered in the originating court or other courts in the same legal system.

---

[39] The only case of even marginal relevance is *Philip Alexander Securities and Futures v. Bamberger* [1997] I.L.Pr. 73, CA; strongly indicating that recognition would be refused of any foreign judgment obtained in wilful breach of an English anti-suit injunction. See para. 8–70, above.

[40] The common law rule against enforcement (as opposed to recognition) of foreign revenue, penal and certain other public laws is of little relevance, since they would not normally give rise to "civil and commercial matters" within the scope of the Convention. Foreign expropriatory legislation is denied recognition in certain circumstances, and that might be a reason for refusing to recognise judgments tainted by it.

[41] Art. 27(4), para. (5) having been added subsequently by the U.K. Accession Convention.

It is clear from the commentary in the Jenard Report that the public policy exception is not intended to be invoked unless in exceptional cases.[42] It would be a travesty of Article 27 to suggest that whole classes of judgments otherwise within the scope of the Convention are automatically disentitled to recognition on public policy grounds, especially where the Convention specifically addresses those grounds or similar ones and defines its own solution.[43] The relationship of Articles 27 and 28 supports this conclusion. In *Hendrikman v. Magenta Druck*[44] the Court observed of Article 27(1) that "Recourse to it is in any event precluded when the issue must be resolved on the basis of a specific provision such as Article 27(2)." Most importantly, the final paragraph of Article 28 makes it clear that the assumption of jurisdiction by the originating court cannot be reviewed or attacked under the head of public policy. In the context of intellectual property, the recognising court has only two options. It may either conclude that the jurisdiction of the originating court contravened Article 16, in which case it is bound to refuse recognition under Article 28; or it must accept the originating court's assumption of jurisdiction. There is no middle course of saying that the originating court complied with the letter of Article 16 but breached international comity in assuming jurisdiction.

The hypothetical situation of a foreign court ordering a life-saving **8–128** drug to be withdrawn from the United Kingdom market at a moment's notice might provide an example where recognition on public policy grounds would be refused. Before taking this drastic step, however, the English court ought to consider whether the provisions for staying recognition and enforcement pending an appeal did not provide a sufficient period to invoke the Crown user provisions of the Patents Act or to obtain a compulsory licence.

Enforcement of foreign judgments under the Convention

In the context of intellectual property, enforcement as such raises few **8–129** separate issues compared to recognition. It is also to be expected that the effect of the enforcement section of Title III will essentially be deterrent: given the near automatic enforcement of judgments in all contracting states, few defendants are likely to allow themselves to be put in a situation where the mechanisms of enforcement need to be invoked against them. What distinguishes the Brussels Convention from previous bilateral conventions is that this applies equally where a defendant might be tempted to defy a foreign injunction against infringement,[45] and whether the injunction was final or interlocutory.

---

[42] The relevant passage from the Jenard Report was approved in Case C–78/95 *Hendrikman v. Magenta Druck* [1996] E.C.R. I–4943; [1996] All E.R. (E.C.) 944; [1996] I.L.Pr. 752.

[43] In France, the *Eurosensory* case (*Cour d'Appel*, Paris, January 28, 1994) decided that enforcement of a Dutch extraterritorial injunction was not contrary to French public policy. See para. 1–45, above. France is, so to speak, the spiritual home of *ordre public*.

[44] Case C–78/95 [1996] I.L.Pr. 752.

[45] See para. 8–03, above.

8–130   The Convention applies "whatever the nature of the court or tribunal."[46] Although the point has not been decided, it is suggested that a patent office exercising a judicial function is included in the definition, so that decisions of foreign patent offices are entitled to recognition and enforcement, to the extent that the nature of the decision permits.[47] Judgments obtained *ex parte* are wholly outside the scope of the Convention and are not enforceable under the provisions of Title III.[48] Orders which are essentially procedural or for obtaining evidence are also probably outside its scope.[49] Otherwise, the Convention applies equally to final and interlocutory *inter partes* orders.[50] It applies to injunctive orders as well as to orders for the payment of money, including costs. In civil law practice the terms of a injunction generally specify a penalty for each infringement, known as an *astreinte*.[51] Article 43 provides that such an order is enforceable only once the actual amount payable has been finally determined by the originating court.

8–131   The procedure for enforcement of any order under Title III is deliberately simple. Where Title III applies, no other procedure for enforcement can be invoked and an action on the original claim is precluded.[52] The party wishing to enforce the judgment in England initially makes an *ex parte* application under section 4 of the Civil Jurisdiction and Judgments Act 1982 and RSC, Ord. 71 for the judgment to be registered. The application is made in the Queen's Bench Division.[53] The necessary documents in support are specified by Article 46 and RSC Ord. 71, r. 28 and the applicant must give an address for service within the jurisdiction. The application for registration may only be refused on one of the grounds for non-recognition specified by Articles 27 and 28 and the substance of the foreign judgment cannot be reviewed in any circumstances.[54] Assuming that an order for registration is made, then the order in entered in a Register at Central Office[55] and

---

[46] Art. 1.

[47] The exclusive jurisdiction of Art. 16(4) is as likely to be exercised by a patent office as by a court. *Aliter* if the function of the patent office is essentially administrative or a matter of public law.

[48] Case 125/79 *Denilauler v. Couchet Freres* [1980] E.C.R. 1553; [1981] 1 C.M.L.R. 62; applied in *EMI v. Modern Music* [1992] 1 Q.B. 115, a copyright case.

[49] Schlosser Report, para. 187.

[50] *ibid.*, para. 184.

[51] *ibid.* para. 213(bb).

[52] Case 42/76 *De Wolf v. Cox* [1976] E.C.R. 1759; [1977] 1 C.M.L.R. 12. This would in any event follow from the Civil Jurisdiction and Judgments Act 1982, s. 34.

[53] RSC, Ord. 71, r. 26. This applies whatever the nature of underlying foreign proceedings. RSC, Ord. 4, r. 7 would permit a Chancery or Patents Court judge to hear an appeal which would normally have gone to a Queen's Bench Judge; but, unless Art. 16(4) was in issue, familiarity with the law of the underlying dispute would not be called for since the merits of the foreign judgment cannot be reopened.

[54] Art. 34. See paras 8–107 *et seq.*, above. Other grounds for refusing registration are that the judgment is outside the scope of the Convention, that it is not yet enforceable, or that it has already been satisfied: Schlosser Report, para. 220(b).

[55] Civil Jurisdiction and Judgments Act 1982, s. 4; RSC, Ord. 71, r. 31. The judgment is then enforceable as if it were a judgment of the High Court, subject to the provisions for enforcement to be stayed.

notice of the registration of the judgment must be served on the person against whom the judgment was given.[56] Service of the notice outside the jurisdiction is possible, without leave. A party applying for recognition of a foreign judgment, as opposed to enforcement, may follow essentially the same procedure.[57]

An order for registration is challenged by way of appeal, which must **8–132** be lodged within one month of service.[58] The period is extended to two months if the party against whom enforcement is sought is domiciled in another contracting state.[59] Other persons affected by the order cannot appeal.[60] The appeal is to a judge in chambers by way of summons. This is the first opportunity such party has to oppose registration.[61] The court hearing the first appeal from the order for registration may, on the application of the appellant, stay its proceedings if an appeal has been lodged against the judgment in the originating state or if the time for lodging an appeal has not yet expired.[62] Execution on the registered judgment does not issue until the time for appealing under RSC, Ord. 71, r. 33 has expired, or until any such appeal has been determined.[63] The judgment on the appeal may only be contested by a single further appeal on a point of law.[64]

If the application for registration is refused, the applicant may appeal **8–133** to the Judge.[65] The party against whom registration is sought must be notified by summons, and may appear.[66] There is a single further appeal on a point of law.

Preliminary references to the European Court of Justice

The provisions for making a preliminary reference to the European **8–134** Court of Justice under the 1971 Protocol on Interpretation at the stage of recognition or enforcement differ substantially from those applying

[56] RSC, Ord. 71, r. 32. This is the first point at which he is informed of the proceedings.
[57] RSC, Ord. 71, r. 35, subject to Art. 26.
[58] Art. 36; RSC, Ord. 71, r. 33.
[59] Art. 36 so provides. RSC, Ord. 71, r. 33 extends the two-month period to all persons not domiciled in a contracting state. Unlike domiciliaries of contracting states, the latter may apply for a further extension of time.
[60] Case 148/84 *Deutsche Genossenschaftsbank v. Brasserie du Pecheur* [1985] E.C.R. 1981; [1986] 2 C.M.L.R 496. It seems to follow that there is no route by which interested third parties can object.
[61] Art. 34 expressly prohibits any submissions by the party against whom enforcement is sought at the stage of the *ex parte* application. Notice of the *ex parte* application is not in terms prohibited, but according to the Schlosser Report, para. 219(a) Art. 34 intends a measure of surprise, and notification of the *ex parte* application would be appropriate only in exceptional circumstances.
[62] Art. 38. The Article refers to an "ordinary appeal" in the originating state. The decision to stay or not is final and cannot be reviewed on appeal; and the court hearing the single further appeal on a point of law cannot impose or remove a stay: Case C–183/90 *Van Dalfsen v. Van Loon* [1991] E.C.R. I–4743; Case C–432/93 *SISRO v. Ampersand* [1995] E.C.R. I–2269; [1995] All E.R. (E.C.) 783.
[63] Art. 39; RSC, Ord. 71, r. 34.
[64] Art. 37(2); Civil jurisdiction and Judgments Act 1982, s. 6. The appeal will normally be to the Court of Appeal, unless it is to the House of Lords under the "leap-frog" procedure. If the appeal is to the Court of Appeal, there is no further appeal to the House of Lords.
[65] Art. 39–40; RSC, Ord. 71, r. 33.
[66] Art. 40(2); RSC, Ord. 71, r. 33.

under Title II of the Convention at the stage when jurisdiction is asserted or refused.[67] The general rule that references may only be made by appellate courts is preserved,[68] but with the important qualification that the "appeal" in question may be the first contested *inter partes* hearing and the High Court will frequently have a discretion to make a reference.

8–135   Article 2(3) of the 1971 Protocol provides that the High Court may make a reference when it is seised of an appeal against a decision to register a judgment under Article 37 of the Brussels Convention.[69] Whether the High Court can make a reference when it is seised of an appeal against a refusal to register depends on whether one applies the general rule of Article 2(2) of the Protocol, or one takes Article 2(3) of the latter as deliberately (if pointlessly) distinguishing appeals under Article 40 of the Convention from those under Article 37.[70] The Court of Appeal or the House of Lords must perhaps make a reference, subject to the doctrine of *acte clair*,[71] when either of them is seised of the single appeal on a point of law provided for by Articles 37(2) or 41. In any residual cases relating to recognition and enforcement, a first instance court cannot make a reference, any court sitting in an appellate capacity may request a reference[72] and the House of Lords must do so if the reference is necessary for it to give judgment.[73]

---

[67] In Tit. II cases the High Court may not request a reference at all (unless it is sitting in an appellate capacity) and the Court of Appeal may, but need not, request a reference.

[68] Cases 80/83 *Harbourdin v. Italocremona* [1983] E.C.R. 3639 and 56/84 *Von Gallera v. Gisele Maitre* [1984] E.C.R. 1769 and see the (separate) Jenard Report on the 1971 Protocol.

[69] The court may not request a reference when it is seised at first instance of the application to register.

[70] One may wonder why Art. 2(3) of the Protocol was necessary at all, since *ex hypothesi* the court referred to in Art. 37 will be hearing an "appeal". Perhaps the draftsman had in mind that "appeals" in Art. 40 cases are real appeals by the unsuccessful party against an actual decision, whereas "appeals" in Art. 37 cases are really the first challenge to what may have been an essentially administrative act. Despite what is said by Jenard, proceedings under Art. 37 are appeals in name but not in fact.

[71] As in Case 283/81 *CILFIT* [1982] E.C.R. 3415; [1983] 1 C.M.L.R. 472 under Art. 177 E.C. This assumes that the words "necessary to enable it to give judgment" in Art. 3(1) merely codify *CILFIT*. It is certainly arguable that the final instance court is given a wider discretion, but the Jenard Report on the Protocol is unhelpful as to how much discretion is contemplated.

[72] 1971 Protocol, Art. 2(2) and 3(2).

[73] *ibid.*, Art. 2(1) and 3(1).

TABLE OF COMMUNITY LEGISLATION

Introduction

This table presents, in four parallel columns, relevant provisions for the **A–01** Community trade mark, patent, plant variety right and design which are commented on in Chapters 4 and 5. The intention is to demonstrate the similarities—and differences—between the regimes for litigating the four Community intellectual property rights in national courts and in their respective Offices as conveniently as possible. Provisions of substantive law and Office procedure are omitted except to the extent necessary to understand *inter partes* litigation procedure.

The order follows that of the Community Trade Mark Regulation as closely as possible.[1] In the interest of clarity, it has therefore been necessary to present the provisions for the other three rights out of sequence, and in some cases to split or bring together individual Articles. Even so, precise correspondence between the four rights cannot always be achieved, and occasionally the extent to which provisions are intended to correspond is unclear. Provisions which apply only to one right and which have no counterparts for the other three have generally been omitted in the interest of simplicity, as have some other provisions of minor interest.

Whilst it is hoped that comparison between the four intellectual property rights is helpful, it should be borne in mind that interpretation of any given article takes place primarily in the context of the legal instrument or group of instruments in which it appears, including recitals and provisions of procedure or substantive law not reproduced here, and may be affected by the structure of the instrument including named titles and sections which it has not been possible to reproduce in this table. The division of the table into sections with sub-titles is for convenience only and does not correspond to any particular instrument.[2]

---

[1] Although the Community Patent Convention is the ultimate source of many of these provisions, it does not lend itself conveniently to comparative tabulation. The Community Trade Mark Regulation is preferred for this purpose because it is in force, it has a simpler and more logical structure, and it has the enormous advantage of being a single instrument rather than a collection of three (or four, including the European Patent Convention.)

[2] Full texts of the various instruments (except the Community Plant Variety Right Regulation, which was then in draft) are set out in *Sweet & Maxwell's E.C. Intellectual Property Materials.*

A. THE COMMUNITY INTELLECTUAL PROPERTY RIGHT AND ITS INSTITUTIONS

Trade Mark[3]	*Patent*[4]

A–02

[No provision corresponds.]

Common system of law for patents [Art.1 CPC]

1. A system of law, common to the Contracting States, concerning patents for invention is hereby established.

2. The common system of law shall govern the European patents granted for the Contracting States in accordance with the Convention on the Grant of European Patents, hereinafter referred to as 'the European Patent Convention', and the European patent applications in which such States are designated.

Community trade mark [Art. 1]

1. A trade mark for goods or services which is registered in accordance with the conditions contained in this Regulation and in the manner herein provided is hereinafter referred to as a 'Community trade mark'.

2. A community trade mark shall have a unitary character. It shall have equal effect throughout the Community: it shall not be registered, transferred or surrendered or be the subject of a decision revoking the rights of the proprietor or declaring it invalid, nor shall its use be prohibited, save in respect of the whole Community. This principle shall apply unless otherwise provided in this Regulation.

Community patent [Art. 2 CPC[5]]

1. European patents granted for the Contracting States shall be called Community patents.

2. Community patents shall have a unitary character. They shall have equal effect throughout the territories to which this Convention applies and may only be granted, transferred, revoked or allowed to lapse in respect of the whole of such territories. The same shall apply mutatis mutandis to applications for European patents in which the Contracting States are designated.

3. Community patents shall have an autonomous character. They shall be subject only to the provisions of this Convention and those provisions of the European Patent Convention which are binding upon every European patent and which shall consequently be deemed to be provisions of this Convention.

---

[3] All numbered Articles are of the Community Trade Mark Regulation 40/94.

[4] Numbered Articles may be of the Agreement relating to Community Patents, the Community Patent Convention, the Protocol on Litigation or the European Patent Convention, as indicated. The 1989 numbering scheme is used.

[5] Pursuant to Art. 142(1) EPC (unitary patents): any group of Contracting States, which has provided by a special agreement that a European patent granted for those States has a unitary character throughout their territories, may provide that a European patent may only be granted jointly in respect of all those States.

Plant Variety Right[6]	*Design*[7]

Community plant variety rights [Art. 1]

[No provision corresponds.]

A–02

A system of Community plant variety rights is hereby established as the sole and exclusive form of Community industrial property rights for plant varieties.

Uniform effect of Community plant variety rights [Art. 2]

Community plant variety rights shall have uniform effect within the territory of the Community and may not be granted, transferred or terminated in respect of the abovementioned territory otherwise than on a uniform basis.

Community design [Art. 1]

1. Designs which comply with the conditions contained in this Regulation, hereinafter referred to as 'Community Designs', shall be protected by a Community system of rights.

2. A design shall be protected under the terms of this Regulation:
   (a) By an 'Unregistered Community Design', without any formalities;
   (b) by a 'Registered Community Design', if registered in the manner provided for in this Regulation.

3. A Community Design shall have a unitary character. It shall have equal effect throughout the Community; it shall not be registered, transferred or surrendered or be the subject of a decision declaring it invalid, save in respect of the whole Community. This principle and its implications shall apply unless otherwise provided in this Regulation.

---

[6] All numbered Articles are of the Community Plant Variety Rights Regulation 2100/94.
[7] All numbered Articles are of the 1993 draft Community Design Regulation [1994] O.J. C29/20.

Trade Mark	Patent

A–03

Office [Art. 2]

An Office for Harmonization in the Internal Market (trade marks and designs), hereinafter referred to as 'the Office', is hereby established.

Setting up of special departments [Art. 4 CPC]

The following bodies common to the Contracting States shall implement the procedures laid down in this Convention:

(a) special departments which are set up within the European Patent Office and whose work shall be supervised by a Select Committee of the Administrative Council of the European Patent Organization;

(b) the Common Appeal Court established by the Protocol on the Settlement of Litigation concerning the Infringement and Validity of Community Patents, hereinafter referred to as 'the Protocol on Litigation'.

Complementary application of national law relating to infringement [Art. 14]

1. The effects of Community trade marks shall be governed solely by the provisions of this Regulation. In other respects, infringement of a Community trade mark shall be governed by the national law relating to infringement of a national trade mark in accordance with the provisions of Title X.

2. This Regulation shall not prevent actions concerning a Community trade mark being brought under the law of Member States relating in particular to civil liability and unfair competition.

3. The rules of procedure to be applied shall be determined in accordance with the provisions of Title X.

Complementary application of national law regarding infringement [Art. 34 CPC]

1. The effects of a Community patent shall be governed solely by the provisions of this Convention. In other respects, infringement of a Community patent shall be governed by the national law relating to infringement of a national patent, in accordance with and subject to the provisions of the Protocol on Litigation.

2. Paragraph 1 shall apply mutatis mutandis to a European patent application which may result in the grant of a Community patent.

Plant Variety Right	Design

Community Office [Art. 4]

For the purpose of the implementation of this Regulation a Community Plant Variety Office, hereinafter referred to as 'the Office', is hereby established.

Community Design Office [Art. 2]

A Community Design Office, hereinafter referred to as 'the Office' is hereby established.

A–03

Supplementary application of national law regarding infringement [Art. 97]

1. Where the party liable pursuant to Article 94 has, by virtue of the infringement, made any gain at the expense of the holder or of a person entitled to exploitation rights, the courts competent pursuant to Articles 101 or 102 shall apply their national law, including their private international law, as regards restitution.

2. Paragraph 1 shall also apply as regards other claims that may arise in respect of the performance or omission of acts pursuant to Article 95 in the time between publication of the application for grant of a Community plant variety right and the disposal of the request.

3. In all other respects the effects of Community plant variety rights shall be determined solely in accordance with this Regulation.

[No provision corresponds.]

549

B. THE COMMUNITY INTELLECTUAL PROPERTY RIGHT AS AN OBJECT OF PROPERTY; TRANSFER AND LICENSING

Trade Mark   *Patent*

A–04

Dealing with Community trade marks as national trade marks [Art. 16]

1. Unless Articles 17 to 24 provide otherwise, a Community trade mark as an object of property shall be dealt with in its entirety, and for the whole area of the Community, as a national trade mark registered in the Member State in which, according to the Register of Community trade marks,
   (a) the proprietor has his seat or his domicile on the relevant date; or
   (b) where subparagraph (a) does not apply, the proprietor has an establishment on the relevant date.

2. In cases which are not provided for by paragraph 1, the Member State referred to in that paragraph shall be the Member State in which the seat of the Office is situated.

3. If two or more persons are mentioned in the Register of Community trade marks as joint proprietors, paragraph 1 shall apply to the joint proprietor first mentioned; failing this, it shall apply to the subsequent joint proprietors in the order in which they are mentioned. Where paragraph 1 does not apply to any of the joint proprietors, paragraph 2 shall apply.

Dealing with the Community patent as a national patent [Art. 38 CPC]

1. Unless otherwise specified in this Convention, a Community patent as an object of property shall be dealt with in its entirety, and for the whole of the territories in which it is effective, as a national patent of the Contracting State in which, according to the Register of European Patents provided for in the European Patent Convention:
   (a) the applicant for the patent had his residence or principal place of business on the date of filing of the European patent application;
   (b) where subparagraph (a) does not apply, the applicant had a place of business on that date; or
   (c) where neither subparagraph (a) nor subparagraph (b) applies, the applicant's representative whose name is entered first in the Register of European Patents has his place of business on the date of that entry.

2. Where subparagraphs (a), (b) and (c) of paragraph 1 do not apply, the Contracting State referred to in that paragraph shall be the Federal Republic of Germany.

3. If two or more persons are mentioned in the Register of European Patents as joint applicants, paragraph 1 shall apply to the joint applicant first mentioned; if this is not possible, it shall apply to the joint applicant next mentioned in respect of whom it is applicable. Where paragraph 1 does not apply to any of the joint applicants, paragraph 2 shall apply.

4. If in a Contracting State as determined by the preceding paragraphs a right in respect of a national patent is effective only after entry in the national patent register, such a right in respect of a Community patent shall be effective only after entry in the Register of Community Patents.

550

Plant Variety Right | *Design*

Assimilation with national laws [Art. 22]

1. Save where otherwise provided in Articles 23 to 29, a Community plant variety right as an object of property shall be regarded in all respects, and for the entire territory of the Community, as a corresponding property right in the Member State in which:

   (a) according to the entry in the Register of Community Plant Variety Rights, the holder was domiciled or had his seat or an establishment on the relevant date; or

   (b) if the conditions laid down in subparagraph (a) are not fulfilled, the first-mentioned procedural representative of the holder, as indicated in the said Register, was domiciled or had his seat or an establishment on the date of registration.

2. Where the conditions laid down in paragraph 1 are not fulfilled, the Member State referred to in paragraph 1 shall be the Member State in which the seat of the Office is located.

3. Where domiciles, seats or establishments in two or more Member States are entered in respect of the holder or the procedural representatives in the Register referred to in paragraph 1, the first-mentioned domicile or seat shall apply for the purposes of paragraph 1.

4. Where two or more persons are entered in the Register referred to in paragraph 1 as joint holders, the relevant holder for the purposes of applying paragraph 1(a) shall be the first joint holder taken in order of entry in the Register who fulfils the conditions. Where none of the joint holders fulfils the conditions laid down in paragraph 1(a), paragraph 2 shall be applicable.

Dealing with Community designs as national design rights [Art. 29]   **A–04**

1. Save where Articles 30 to 34 provide otherwise, a Community Design as an object of property shall be dealt with in its entirety, and for the whole area of the Community, as a national design right of the Member State in which:
   (a) the holder has his seat or his domicile on the relevant date; or
   (b) where subparagraph (a) does not apply, the holder has an establishment on the relevant date.

2. In the case of a Registered Community Design, paragraph (1) shall apply according to the entries in the Register.

3. In the case of joint holders, if two or more of them fulfil the condition under paragraph (1)(a) or, where that provision does not apply, the condition under paragraph (1)(b), the Member State referred to in paragraph (1) shall be determined:
   (a) in the case of an Unregistered Community Design, by reference to the relevant joint holder designated by them by common agreement;
   (b) in the case of a Registered Community Design, by reference to the first of the relevant joint holders in the order in which they are mentioned in the Register.

4. Where paragraphs (1), (2) and (3) do not apply, the Member State referred to in paragraph (1) shall be the Member State in which the Office is situated.

Trade Mark   *Patent*

A–05   **Transfer [Art. 17]**

1. A Community trade mark may be transferred, separately from any transfer of the undertaking, in respect of some or all of the goods or services for which it is registered.

2. A transfer of the whole of the undertaking shall include the transfer of the Community trade mark except where, in accordance with the law governing the transfer, there is agreement to the contrary or circumstances clearly dictate otherwise. This provision shall apply to the contractual obligation to transfer the undertaking.

3. Without prejudice to paragraph 2, an assignment of the Community trade mark shall be made in writing and shall require the signature of the parties to the contract, except when it is a result of a judgment; otherwise it shall be void.

4. Where it is clear from the transfer documents that because of the transfer the Community trade mark is likely to mislead the public concerning the nature, quality or geographical origin of the goods or services in respect of which it is registered, the Office shall not register the transfer unless the successor agrees to limit registration of the Community trade mark to goods or services in respect of which it is not likely to mislead.

5. On request of one of the parties a transfer shall be entered in the Register and published.

6. As long as the transfer has not been entered in the Register, the successor in title may not invoke the rights arising from the registration of the Community trade mark.

7. Where there are time limits to be observed vis-à-vis the Office, the successor in title may make the corresponding statements to the Office once the request for registration of the transfer has been received by the Office.

8. All documents which require notification to the proprietor of the Community trade mark in accordance with Article 77 shall be addressed to the person registered as proprietor.

Transfer [Art. 39 CPC]

1. An assignment of a Community patent shall be made in writing and shall require the signature of the parties to the contract, except when it is a result of a judgment.

2. Subject to Article 24(1) a transfer shall not affect rights acquired by third parties before the date of transfer.

3. A transfer shall, to the extent to which it is verified by the papers referred to in the Implementing Regulations, only have effect via-à-vis third parties after entry in the Register of Community Patents. Nevertheless, a transfer, before it is so entered, shall have effect via-à-vis third parties who have acquired rights after the date of the transfer but who knew of the transfer at the date on which the rights were acquired.

Plant Variety Right   *Design*

Transfer [Art. 23]

1. A Community plant variety right may be the object of a transfer to one or more successors in title.

2. Transfer of a Community plant variety right by assignment can be made only to succesors who comply with the conditions laid down in Article 12 and 82. it shall be made in writing and shall require the signature of the parties to the contract, except when it is a result of a judgement or of any other acts terminating court proceedings. Otherwise it shall be void.

3. Save as otherwise provided in Article 100, a transfer shall have no bearing on the rights acquired by third parties before the date of transfer.

4. A transfer shall not take effect for the Office and may not be cited vis-à-vis third parties unless documentary evidence thereof as provided for in the implementing rules is provided and until it has been entered in the Register of Community Plant Variety Rights. A transfer that has not yet been entered in the Register may, however, be cited vis-à-vis third parties who have acquired rights after the date of transfer but who knew of the transfer at the date on which they acquired those rights.

Transfer [Art. 30]   **A–05**

1. A Community Design may be transferred.

2. The transfer of a Registered Community Design shall be subject to the following provisions:
   (a) At the request of one of the parties, a transfer shall be entered in the Register and published.
   (b) Until such time as the transfer has been entered in the Register, the successor in title may not invoke the rights arising from the Registered Community design.
   (c) Where there are time limits to be observed in dealings with the Office, the successor in title may make the corresponding statements to the Office once the request for registration of the transfer has been received by the Office.
   (d) All documents which require notification to the holder of the Registered Community Design shall be addressed to the person registered as holder or his representative, if one has been appointed.

Trade Mark	*Patent*

A–06 **Rights *in rem* [Art. 19]**

1. A Community trade mark may, independently of the undertaking, be given as security or be the subject of rights in rem.

[No provision corresponds]

2. On request of one of the parties, rights mentioned in paragraph 1 shall be entered in the Register and published.

Levy of execution [Art. 20]

1. A Community trade mark may be levied in execution.

2. As regards the procedure for levy of execution in respect of a Community trade mark, the courts and authorities of the Member States determined in accordance with Article 16 shall have exclusive jurisdiction.

3. On request of one the parties, levy of execution shall be entered in the Register and published.

Enforcement proceedings [Art. 40]

The courts and other authorities of the Contracting State determined in accordance with Article 38 shall have exclusive jurisdiction in respect of proceedings relating to judgments or other official acts in so far as they are being enforced against Community patents.

Bankruptcy or like proceedings [Art. 21]

1. Until such time as common rules for the Member States in this field enter into force, the only Member State in which a Community trade mark may be involved in bankruptcy or like proceedings shall be that in which such proceedings are first brought within the meaning of national law or of conventions applicable in this field.

2. Where a Community trade mark is involved in bankruptcy or like proceedings, on request of the competent national authority an entry to this effect shall be made in the Register and published.

Bankruptcy or like proceedings [Art. 41 CPC]

1. Until such time as common rules for the Contracting States in this field enter into force, the only Contracting State in which a Community patent may be involved in bankruptcy or like proceedings shall be that in which such proceedings are opened first.

2. Paragraph 1 shall apply mutatis mutandis in the case of joint proprietorship of a Community patent to the share of the joint proprietor.

Plant Variety Right	*Design*

Rights *in rem* on a Registered Community Design [Art. 31]   **A–06**

[No provision corresponds]

1. A Registered Community Design may be given as security or be the subject of rights in rem.

2. At the request of one of the parties, rights mentioned in paragraph (1) shall be entered in the Register and published.

Levy of execution [Art. 24]

Levy of execution on a Registered Community Design [Art. 32]

A Community plant variety right may be levied in execution and be the subject of provisional, including protective, measures within the meaning of Article 24 of the Convention on Jurisdiction and the Enforcement of Judgments in Civil and Commercial Matters, signed in Lugano on 16 September 1988, hereinafter referred to as the 'Lugano Convention'.

1. A Registered Community Design may be levied in execution.

2. As regards the procedure for levy of execution in respect of a Registered Community Design, the courts and authorities of the Member State determined in accordance with Article 29 shall have exclusive jurisdiction.

3. On request of one of the parties, levy of execution shall be entered in the Register and published.

Bankruptcy or like proceedings [Art. 25]

Bankruptcy or like proceedings [Art. 33]

1. Until such time as common rules for the Member States in this field enter into force, the only Member State in which a Community plant variety right may be involved in bankruptcy or like proceedings shall be that in which such proceedings are first brought within the meaning of national law or of conventions applicable in this field.

1. Until such time as common rules for the Member States in this field enter into force, the only Member State in which a Community Design may be involved in bankruptcy or like proceedings shall be that in which such proceedings are first brought under national law or conventions applicable in this field.

2. Where a Registered Community Design is involved in bankruptcy or like proceedings, an entry to that effect shall be made in the Register at the request of the competent national authority and shall be published.

Trade Mark	*Patent*

A–07 **Licensing [Art. 22]**

1. A Community trade mark may be licensed for some or all of the goods or services for which it is registered and for the whole or part of the Community. A licence may be exclusive or non-exclusive.

2. The proprietor of a Community trade mark may invoke the rights conferred by that trade mark against a licensee who contravenes any provision in his licensing contract with regard to its duration, the form covered by the registration in which the trade mark may be used, the scope of the goods or services for which the licence is granted, the territory in which the trade mark may be affixed, or the quality of the goods manufactured or of the services provided by the licensee.

3. Without prejudice to the provisions of the licensing contract, the licensee may bring proceedings for infringement of a Community trade mark only if its proprietor consents thereto. However, the holder of an exclusive licence may bring such proceedings if the proprietor of the trade mark, after formal notice, does not himself bring infringement proceedings within an appropriate period.

4. A licensee shall, for the purpose of obtaining compensation for damage suffered by him, be entitled to intervene in infringement proceedings brought by the proprietor of the Community trade mark.

5. On request of one of the parties the grant or transfer of a licence in respect of a Community trade mark shall be entered in the Register and published.

Contractual licensing [Art. 42]

1. A Community patent may be licensed in whole or in part for the whole or part of the territories in which it is effective. A licence may be exclusive or non-exclusive.

2. The rights conferred by the Community patent may be invoked against a licensee who contravenes any restriction in his licence which is covered by paragraph 1.

3. Article 39(2) and (3) shall apply mutatis mutandis to the grant or transfer of a licence in respect of a Community patent.

Plant Variety Right   *Design*

Contractual exploitation rights [Art. 27]

1. Community plant variety rights may form in full or in part the subject of contractually granted exploitation rights. Exploitation rights may be exclusive or non-exclusive.

2. The holder may invoke the rights conferred by the Community plant variety rights against a person enjoying the right of exploitation who contravenes any of the conditions or limitations attached to his exploitation right pursuant to paragraph 1.

Licensing [Art. 34]   **A–07**

1. A Community Design may be licensed for the whole or part of the Community. A licence may be exclusive or non-exclusive.

2. Without prejudice to the provisions of the licensing contract, the licence may bring proceedings for infringement of a Community Design only if the right holder consents thereto. However, the holder of an exclusive licence may bring such proceedings if the right holder in the Community Design, having been given notice to do so, does not himself bring infringement proceedings within an appropriate period.

3. A licensee shall, for the purpose of obtaining compensation for damage suffered by him, be entitled to intervene in an infringement action brought by the right holder in a Community Design.

4. In the case of a Registered Community Design, the grant or transfer of a licence in respect of such right shall, at the request of one of the parties, be entered in the Register and published.

Entitlement to bring an action for infringement [Art. 104]

1. Actions for infringement may be brought by the hiolder. Persons enjoying exploitation rights may bring such actions unless that has been expressly excluded by agreement with the holder in the case of an exclusive exploitation right or by the Office pursuant to Articles 29 or 100(2).

2. Any person enjoying exploitation rights shall, for the purpose of obtaining compensation for damage suffered by him, be entitled to intervene in an infringement action brought by the holder.

| *Trade Mark* | *Patent* |

A–08   **Effects vis-à-vis third parties [Art. 23]**

1. Legal acts referred to in Article 17, 19 and 22 concerning a Community trade mark shall only have effects vis-à-vis third parties in all the Member States after entry in the Register. Nevertheless, such an act, before it is so entered, shall have effect vis-à-vis third parties who have acquired rights in the trade mark after the date of that act but who knew of the act at the date on which the rights were acquired.

2. Paragraph 1 shall not apply in the case of a person who acquires the Community trade mark or a right concerning the Community trade mark by way of transfer of the whole of the undertaking or by any other universal succession.

3. The effects vis-à-vis third parties of the legal acts referred to in Article 20 shall be governed by the law of the Member State determined in accordance with Article 16.

4. Until such time as common rules for the Member States in the field of bankruptcy enter into force, the effects vis-à-vis third parties of bankruptcy or like proceedings shall be governed by the law of the Member State in which such proceedings are first brought within the meaning of national law or of conventions applicable in this field.

[See Art. 39(3) and Art. 42(3) CPC.]

The application for a Community trade mark as an object of property [Art. 24]

Articles 16 to 23 shall apply to applications for Community trade marks.

The European patent application as an object of property [Art. 44 CPC]

1. Articles 38 to 42 shall apply mutatis mutandis to a European patent application in which the Contracting States are designated, the reference to the Register of Community Patents being understood as referring to the Register of European Patents provided for in the European Patent Convention.

2. The rights acquired by third parties in respect of a European patent application referred to in paragraph 1 shall continue to be effective with regard to the Community patent granted upon that application.

Plant Variety Right	Design

Effects vis-à-vis third parties [Art. 35] **A–08**

[See Art. 23(4).]

1. The effects vis-à-vis third parties of the legal acts referred to in Articles 30, 31, 32 and 34 shall be governed by the law of the Member State determined in accordance with Article 29.

2. However, as regards Registered Community Designs, legal acts referred to in Articles 30, 31 and 34 shall have effect only vis-à-vis third parties in all the Member States after entry in the Register. Nevertheless such an act, before it is so entered, shall have effect vis-à-vis third parties who have acquired rights in the Registered Community Design after the date of that act but who knew of the act at the date on which the rights were acquired.

3. Paragraph (2) shall not apply to a person who acquires the Registered Community Design or a right relating to it by way of transfer of the whole of the undertaking or by any other universal succession.

4. Until such time as common rules for the Member States in the field of bankruptcy enter into force, the effects vis-à-vis third parties of bankruptcy or like proceedings shall be governed by the law of the Member State in which such proceedings are first brought under national law or the conventions applicable in this field.

The application for a Community plant variety right as an object of property [Art. 26]

Articles 22 to 25 shall apply to applications for Community plant variety rights. Concerning such applications, the references made in those Articles to the Register of Community Plant Variety Rights shall be regarded as references to the Register of Applications for Community Plant Variety Rights.

The application for a Registered Community Design as an object of property [Art. 36]

1. An application for a Registered Community Design as an object of property shall be dealt with in its entirety, and for the whole area of the Community, as a national design right of the Member State determined in accordance with Article 29.

2. Articles 30 to 35 shall apply mutatis mutandis to applications for Registered Community Designs. Where the effect of one of those provisions is conditional upon an entry in the Register, that formality shall have to be performed upon registration of the resulting Registered Community Design.

C. INVALIDITY

Trade Mark   *Patent*

A–09 **Grounds for revocation [Art. 50]**

1. The rights of the proprietor of the Community trade mark shall be declared to be revoked on application to the Office or on the basis of a counterclaim in infringement proceedings:

(a) if, within a continuous period of five years, the trade mark has not been put to genuine use in the Community in connection with the goods or services in respect of which it is registered, and there are no proper reasons for non-use; however, no person may claim that the proprietor's rights in a Community trade mark should be revoked where, during the interval between expiry of the five-year period and filing of the application or counterclaim, genuine use of the trade mark has been started or resumed; the commencement or resumption of use within a period of three months preceding the filing of the application or counterclaim which began at the earliest on expiry of the continuous period of five years of non-use shall, however, be disregarded where preparations for the commencement or resumption occur only after the proprietor becomes aware that the application or counterclaim may be filed;

(b) if, in consequence of acts or inactivity of the proprietor, the trade mark has become the common name in the trade for a product or service in respect of which it is registered;

(c) if, in consequence of the use made of it by the proprietor of the trade mark or with his consent in respect of the goods or services for which it is registered, the trade mark is liable to mislead the public, particularly as to the nature, quality or geographical origin of those goods or services;

(d) if the proprietor of the trade mark no longer satisfies the conditions laid down by Article 5.

Grounds for revocation [Art. 56 CPC]

1. An application for revocation of a Community patent may be filed only on the grounds that:

(a) the subject-matter of the patent is not patentable within the terms of Articles 52 to 57 of the European Patent Convention;

(b) the patent does not disclose the invention in a manner sufficiently clear and complete for it to be carried out by a person skilled in the art;

(c) the subject-matter of the patent extends beyond the content of the European patent application as filed, or, if the patent was granted on a European divisional application or on a new European application filed in accordance with Article 61 of the European Patent Convention, beyond the content of the earlier application as filed;

(d) the protection conferred by the patent has been extended;

(e) the proprietor of the patent is not, having regard to a decision which has to be recognized in all the Contracting States, entitled under Article 60(1) of the European Patent Convention;

(f) the subject-matter of the patent is not patentable within the terms of Article 36(1).

2. If the grounds for revocation affect the patent only partially, revocation shall be pronounced in the form of a corresponding limitation of the patent. The limitation may be effected in the form of an amendment to the claims, the description or the drawings.

3. In the case specified in paragraph 1(f), revocation shall be pronounced only in respect of the Contracting State in which the national patent application or national patent has been made public.

[*cont. on p. 562*]

Plant Variety Right   *Design*

Nullity of Community plant variety rights [Art. 20]

Grounds for invalidity [Art. 27]   **A–09**

1. The Office shall declare the Community plant variety right null and void if it is established:
   (a) that the conditions laid down in Articles 7 or 10 were not complied with at the time of the Community plant variety right; or
   (b) that where the grant of the Community plant variety right has been essentially based upon information and documents furnished by the applicant, the conditions laid down in Articles 8 and 9 were not complied with at the time of the grant of the right; or
   (c) that the right has been granted to a person who is not entitled to it, unless it is transferred to the person who is so entitled.

2. Where the Community plant variety right is declared null and void, it shall be deemed not to have had, as from the outset, the effects specified in this Regulation.

Cancellation of Community plant variety rights [Art. 21]

1. The Office shall cancel the Community plant variety right with effect in futurum if it is established that the conditions laid down in Article 8 or 9 are no longer complied with. If it is established that these conditions were already no longer complied with from a point in time prior to cancellation, cancellation may be made effective as from that juncture.

2. The Office may cancel a Community plant variety right with effect in futurum if the holder, after being requested to do so, and within a time limit specified by the Office:

1. A Community Design may be declared invalid only in the following cases:
   (a) if the design protected does not fulfil the requirements under Article 4; or
   (b) to the extent that its specific technical and/or interconnecting features are not eligible for protection under Article 9(1) or 92); or
   (c) to the extent that its exploitation or publication is contrary to public policy or to accepted principles of morality; or
   (d) if the right holder in the Community Design is, by virtue of a court decision, not entitled under Articles 14 and 15.

2. A Community Design may also be declared invalid if a conflicting design which has been made available to the public after the date of reference within the meaning of Article 7(a) or (b), as the case may be, is protected from a date prior to the said date of reference by a Registered Community Design or a registered design right of one or more Member States, or an application for such a right.

3. By derogation from Article 1(3):
   (a) in the case specified in paragraph (1)(c), invalidity shall be declared only in respect of the Member State or States where the ground for in validation obtains;
   (b) in the case specified in paragraph (2), to the extent that the rights in question, or applications for such rights, have effect only in respect of a Member State or States, invalidity shall be declared only in respect of such a Member State or States.

[*cont. on p. 563*]

Trade Mark   *Patent*

A–09   **Grounds for revocation [Art. 50]** (*cont.*)

2. Where the grounds for revocation of rights exist in respect of only some of the goods or services for which the Community trade mark is registered, the rights of the proprietor shall be declared to be revoked in respect of those goods or services only.

Cancellation of Community plant variety rights [Art. 21] (*cont.*)

   (a) has not fulfilled an obligation pursuant to Article 63(3); or

   (b) in the case referred to in Article 66, does not propose another suitable variety demonination; or

   (c) fails to pay such fees as may be payable to keep the Community plant variety right in force; or

   (d) either as the initial holder or as a successor in title as a result of a transfer pursuant to Article 23, no longer satisfies the conditions laid down in Articles 12 and 82.

A–09

Trade Mark	*Patent*

A–10

Consequences of revocation and invalidity [Art. 54]

1. The Community trade mark shall be deemed not to have had, as from the date of the application for revocation or of the counterclaim, the effects specified in this Regulation, to the extent that the rights of the proprietor have been revoked. An earlier date, on which one of the grounds for revocation occurred, may be fixed in the decision at the request of one of the parties.

2. The Community trade mark shall be deemed not to have had, as from the outset, the effects specified in this Regulation, to the extent that the trade mark has been declared invalid.

3. Subject to the national provisions relating either to claims for compensation for damage caused by negligence or lack of good faith on the part of the proprietor of the trade mark, or to unjust enrichment, the retroactive effect of revocation or invalidity of the trade mark shall not affect:
  (a) any decision on infringement which has acquired the authority of a final decision and been enforced prior to the revocation or invalidity decision;
  (b) any contract concluded prior to the revocation or invalidity decision, in so far as it has been performed before that decision; however, repayment, to an extent justified by the circumstances, of sums paid under the relevant contract, may be claimed on grounds of equity.

Effect of revocation of the Community patent [Art. 33 CPC]

1. A European patent application in which the Contracting States are designated and the resulting Community patent shall be deemed not to have had, as from the outset, the effects specified in this Chapter, to the extent that the patent has been revoked.

2. Subject to the national provisions relating either to claims for compensation for damage caused by negligence or lack of good faith on the part of the proprietor of the patent, or to unjust enrichment, the retroactive effect of the revocation of the patent as a result of opposition or revocation proceedings shall not effect:
  (a) any decision on infringement which has acquired the authority of a final decision and been enforced prior to the revocation decision;
  (b) any contract concluded prior to the revocation decision, in so far as it has been performed before that decision; however, repayment, to an extent justified by the circumstances, of sums paid under the relevant contract, may be claimed on grounds of equity.

Effect of judgments on validity [Art. 20 POL]

When it has become final, a judgment of a Community patent court of first instance revoking or amending a Community patent shall have, subject to Article 56(3) of the Community Patent Convention, in all Contracting States the effects specified in Article 33 of that Convention.

Effects of invalidity [Art. 34]   **A–10**

[See Arts 20 and 21, above.]

1. A Community Design which has been declared invalid shall be deemed not to have had, from the outset, the effects specified in this Regulation.

2. Subject to the national provisions relating either to claims for compensation for damage caused by negligence or lack of good faith on the part of the holder of the Community Design, or to unjust enrichment, the retroactive effect of invalidity of the Community Design shall not affect:

(a) any decision on infringement which has acquired the authority of a final decision and been enforced prior to the invalidity decision;

(b) any contract concluded prior to the invalidity decision, in so far as it has been performed before the decision; however, repayment, to an extent justified by the circumstances, of sums paid under the relevant contract, may be claimed on grounds of equity.

Declaration of invalidity [Art. 26]

1. A Community Design may only be declared invalid by a Community Design Court.

A Registered Community Design may also be declared invalid by the Office in accordance with the procedure in Title VII.

2. An application for a declaration of invalidity may be submitted even after the Community Design has lapsed or has been surrendered.

D. APPLICATIONS TO THE OFFICE FOR REVOCATION, ETC.

Trade Mark | *Patent*

A–11

Application for revocation or for a declaration of invalidity [Art. 55]

1. An application for revocation of the rights of the proprietor of a Community trade mark or for a declaration that the trade mark is invalid may be submitted to the Office:
   (a) where Articles 50 and 51 apply, by any natural or legal person and any group or body set up for the purpose of representing the interests of manufacturers, producers, suppliers of services, traders or consumers, which under the terms of the law governing it has the capacity in its own name to sue and be sued;
   (b) where Article 52(1) applies, by the persons referred to in Article 41(1);
   (c) where Article 52(2) applies, by the owners of the earlier rights referred to in that provision or by the persons who are entitled under the law of the Member State concerned to exercise the rights in question.

2. The application shall be filed in a written reasoned statement. It shall not be deemed to have been filed until the fee has been paid.

3. An application for revocation or for a declaration of invalidity shall be inadmissible if an application relating to the same subject matter and cause of action, and involving the same parties, has been adjudicated on by a court in a Member State and has acquired the authority of a final decision.

Application for revocation [Art. 55 CPC]

1. Any person may file with the European Patent Office an application for revocation of a Community patent; however, in the case specified in Article 56(1)(e) the application may be filed only by a person entitled to be entered in the Register of Community Patents as the sole proprietor of the patent or by all the persons entitled to be entered as joint proprietors of it in accordance with Article 23 acting jointly.

2. The application may not be filed in the cases specified in Article 56(1) (a) to (d) during the period within which an opposition may be filed or while opposition proceedings are pending.

3. An application may be filed even if the Community patent has lapsed.

4. The application shall be filed in a written reasoned statement. It shall not be deemed to have been filed until the revocation fee has been paid.

5. Applicants shall be parties to the revocation proceedings as well as the proprietor of the patent.

6. If the applicant has neither his residence nor his principal place of business within the territory of one of the Contracting States, he shall, at the request of the proprietor of the patent, furnish security for the costs of the proceedings. The Revocation Division shall fix at a reasonable figure the amount of the security and the period within which it must be deposited. If the security is not deposited within the period specified, the application shall be deemed to be withdrawn.

Plant Variety Right	Design

Application for a declaration of invalidity   **A–11**
[Art. 56]

[See Arts 20 and 21, above.]

1. The Commission, Member States and any other natural or legal person may submit to the Office an application for a declaration of invalidity of a Registered Community Design; however, in the case envisaged in Article 27(1)(d), the application may be filed only by the person or persons entitled and, in the case envisaged in Article 27(2), only by the right holder of the earlier right.

2. The application shall be filed in a written reasoned statement. it shall not [be] deem[ed] to have been filed until the fee has been paid.

3. The application for a declaration of invalidity shall not be admissible if an application relating to the same subject matter and cause of action, and involving the same parties, has been adjudicated on by a Community Design Court and has acquired the authority of a final decision.

Trade Mark	*Patent*

A–12

Examination of the application [Art. 56]

1. In the examination of the application for revocation of rights or for a declaration of invalidity, the Office shall invite the parties, as often as necessary, to file observations, within a period to be fixed by the Office, on communications from the other parties or issued by ifself.

(. . .)

Examination of the application [Art. 57 CPC]

1. If the application for revocation of the Community patent is admissible, the Revocation Division shall examine whether the grounds for revocation mentioned in Article 56 prejudice the maintenance of the patent.

2. In the examination of the application, which shall be conducted in accordance with the Implementing Regulations, the Revocation Division shall invite the parties, as often as necessary, to file observations, within a period to be fixed by the Revocation Division, on communications from another party or issued by itself.

Plant Variety Right	*Design*

Examination of the application [Art. 57] A–12

[No provision corresponds.]

1. If the application for a declaration of invalidity is admissible, the Office shall examine whether the grounds for invalidity referred to in Article 27 prejudice the maintenance of the Registered Community Design.

2. In the examination of the application, which shall be conducted in accordance with the Implementing Regulation, the Office shall invite the parties, as often as necessary, to file observations, within a period to be fixed by the Office, on communications by the other parties or those issued by itself.

3. The decision declaring the Registered Community Design invalid shall be entered in the Register upon becoming final.

4. The Office may, if it thinks fit, invite the parties to make a friendly settlement.

5. If the examination of the application for revocation of rights or for a declaration of invalidity reveals that the trade mark should not have been registered in respect of some or all of the goods or services for which it is registered, the rights of the proprietor of the Community trade mark shall be revoked or it shall be declared invalid in respect of those goods or services. Otherwise the application for revocation of rights or for a declaration of invalidity shall be rejected.

6. The decision revoking the rights of the proprietor of the Community trade mark or declaring it invalid shall be entered in the Register upon becoming final.

E. APPEALS IN OFFICE PROCEEDINGS

Trade Mark	*Patent*

A–13

Decisions subject to appeal [Art. 57]

1. An appeal shall lie from decisions of the examiners, Opposition Divisions, Administration of Trade Marks and Legal Division and Cancellation Divisions. it shall have suspensive effect.

2. A decision which does not terminate proceedings as regards one of the parties can only be appealed together with the final decision, unless the decision allows separate appeal.

Appeal [Art. 61 CPC][8]

1. An appeal shall lie from decisions of the Revocation Division and the Patent Administration Division.

2. Articles 106 to 109 of the European Patent Convention shall apply mutatis mutandis to this appeals procedure in so far as the Rules of Procedure of the Common Appeal Court or the Rules relating to Fees do not provide otherwise.

Decisions subject to appeal [Art. 106 EPC]

1. An appeal shall lie from decisions of the Receiving Section, Examining Divisions, Opposition Divisions, and the Legal Division. it shall have suspensive effect.

2. An appeal may be filed against the decisions of the Opposition Division even if the European patent has been surrendered or has lapsed for all the designated States.

3. A decision which does not terminate proceedings as regards one of the parties can only be appealed together with the final decision, unless the decision allows separate appeal.

4. The apportionment of costs of opposition proceedings cannot be the sole subject of an appeal.

5. A decision fixing the amount of costs of opposition proceedings cannot be appealed unless the amount is in excess of that laid down in the Rules relating to Fees.

[8] See also Art. 28 POL.

Plant Variety Right	Design

Decisions subject to appeal [Art. 67]

1. An appeal shall lie from decisions of the Office which have been taken pursuant to Articles 20, 21, 59, 61, 62, 63 and 66, as well as on decisions related to fees pursuant to Article 83, to costs pursuant to Article 85, to the entering or deletion of information in the Register pursuant to Article 87 and to the public inspection pursuant to Article 88.

2. An appeal lodged pursuant to paragraph 1 shall have suspensory effect. The Office may, however, if it considers that circumstances so require, order that the contested decisions not be suspended.

3. An appeal may lie from decisions of the Office pursuant to Articles 29 and 100(2), unless a direct appeal is lodged pursuant to Article 74. The appeal shall not have suspensory effect.

4. An appeal against a decision which does not terminate proceedings as regards one of the parties may only be made in conjunction with an appeal against the final decision, unless the decision provides for separate appeal.

Decisions subject to appeal [Art. 59]   **A–13**

1. An appeal shall lie from decisions of the Formalities Examination Divisions, Design Administation and Legal Division and Invalidity Divisions. It shall have suspensive effect.

2. A decision which does not terminate proceedings as regards one of the parties can only be appealed against if joined with the final decision, unless the decision allows separate appeal.

Trade Mark	*Patent*

A–14

Persons entitled to appeal and to be parties to appeal proceedings [Art. 58]

Any party to proceedings adversely affected by a decision may appeal. Any other parties to the proceedings shall be parties to the appeal proceedings as of right.

Persons entitled to appeal and to be parties to appeal proceedings [Art. 106 EPC]

Any party to proceedings adversely affected by a decision may appeal. Any other parties to the proceedings shall be parties to the appeal proceedings as of right.

Time limit and form of appeal [Art. 59]

Notice of appeal must be filed in writing at the Office within two months after the date of notification of the decision appealed from. The notice shall be deemed to have been filed only when the fee for appeal has been paid. Within four months after the date of notification of the decision, a written statement setting out the grounds of appeal must be filed.

Time limit and form of appeal [Art. 108 EPC]

Notice of appeal must be filed in writing at the European Patent Office within two months after the date of notification of the decision appealed from. The notice shall not be deemed to have been filed until after the fee for appeal has been paid. Within four months after the date of notification of the decision, a written statement setting out the grounds of appeal must be filed.

Interlocutory revision [Art. 60]

1. If the departmnet whose decision is contested considers the appeal to be admissible and well founded, it shall rectify its decision. This shall not apply where the appellant is opposed by another party to the proceedings.

2. If the decision is not rectified within one month after receipt of the statement of grounds, the appeal shall be remitted to the Board of Appeal without delay, and without comment as to its merit.

Interlocutory revision [Art. 109 EPC]

1. If the department whose decision is contested considers the appeal to be admissible and well founded, it shall rectify its decision. This shall not apply where the appellant is opposed by another party to the proceedings.

2. If the appeal is not allowed within one month after receipt of the statement of grounds, it shall be remitted to the Board of Appeal without delay, and without comment as to its merit.

Plant Variety Right   *Design*

Persons entitled to appeal and to be parties to appeal proceedings [Art. 68]

Any natural or legal person may appeal, subject to Article 82, against a decision, addressed to that person, or against a decision which, although in the form of a decision addressed to another person, is of direct and individual concern to the former. The parties to proceedings may, and the Office shall, be party to the appeal proceedings.

Persons entitled to appeal and to be parties to appeal proceedings [Art. 60]   **A–14**

Any party to proceedings adversely affected by a decision may appeal. Any other parties to the proceedings shall be parties to the appeal proceedings as of right.

Time limit and form [Art. 69]

Notice of appeal shall be filed in writing at the Office within two months of the service of the decision where addressed to the appealing person, or, in the absence thereof, within two months of the publication of the decision, and a written statement setting out the grounds of appeal shall be filed within four months after the aforesaid service or publication.

Time limit and form of appeal [Art. 61]

Notice of appeal must be filed in writing at the Office within two months after the date of notification of the decision appealed from. The notice shall not be deemed to have been filed until after the appeal fee has been paid. Within four months after the date of notification of the decision, a written statement setting out the grounds of appeal must be filed.

Interlocutory revision [Art. 70]

1. If the body of the Office which has prepared the decision considers the appeal to be admissible and well founded, the Office shall rectify the decision. This shall not apply where the appellant is opposed by another party to the appeal proceedings.

2. If the decision is not rectified within one month after receipt of the statement of grounds, for the appeal, the Office shall forthwith:
   – decide whether it will take an action pursuant to Article 67(2), second sentence, and
   – remit the appeal to the Board of Appeal.

Interlocutory revision [Art. 62]

1. If the department whose decision is contested considers the appeal to be admissible and well founded, it shall amend its decision. This shall not apply where the appellant is opposed by another party to the proceedings.

2. If the decision is not amended within one month after receipt of the statement of grounds, the appeal shall be remitted to the Board of Appeal without delay and without comment as to its merits.

Trade Mark	*Patent*

A–15

Examination of appeals [Art. 61]

1. If the appeal is admissible, the Board of Appeal shall examine whether the appeal is allowable.

2. In the examination of the appeal, the Board of Appeal shall invite the parties, as often as necessary, to file observations, within a period to be fixed by the Board of Appeal, on communications from the other parties or issued by itself.

[See Protocol on the Statute of the Common Appeal Court.][9]

Decisions in respect of appeals [Art. 62]

1. Following the examination as to the allowability of the appeal, the Board of Appeal shall decide on the appeal. The Board of Appeal may either exercise any power within the competence of the department which was responsible for the decision appealed or remit the case to that department for further prosecution.

2. If the Board of Appeal remits the case for further prosecution to the department whose decision was appealed, that department shall be bound by the ratio decidendi of the Board of Appeal, in so far as the facts are the same.

3. The decisions of the Boards of Appeal shall take effect only as from the date of expiration of the period referred to in Article 63(5) or, if an action has been brought before the Court of Justice within that period, as from the date of rejection of such action.

Supplementary jurisdiction of the Common Appeal Court [Art. 28 POL][10]

1. The Common Appeal Court shall decide on appeals from decisions of the Revocation Divisions and the Patent Administration Division of the European Patent Office.

2. If proceedings in respect of a Community patent are pending before it, the Common Appeal Court shall, if necessary, decide on the lapse of that patent.

3. Where the Common Appeal Court has given a judgment pursuant to paragraph 1 or 2 it shall send a copy of the judgment to the European Patent Office. Any party may request information about such transmission.

[9] Not reproduced here.

[10] See also the Protocol on the Statute of the Common Appeal Court, not reproduced here.

Plant Variety Right   *Design*   **A–15**

Examination of appeals [Art. 71]

1. If the appeal is admissible, the Board of Appeal shall examine whether the appeal is well-founded.

2. When examining the appeal, the Board of Appeal shall as often as necessay invite the parties to the appeal proceedings to file observations on notifications issued by itself or on communications from the other parties to the appeal proceedings within specified time limits. Parties to the appeal proceedings shall be entitled to make oral represenations.

Decision on appeal [Art. 72]

The Board of Appeal shall decide on the appeal on the basis of the examination carried out pursuant to Article 71. The Board of Appeal may exercise any power which lies within the competence of the Office, or it may remit the case to the competent body of the Office for further action. The latter one shall, in so far as the facts are the same, be bound by the ratio decidendi of the Board of Appeal.

Examination of appeals [Art. 63]

1. If the appeal is admissible, the Board of Appeal shall examine whether the appeal is to be allowed.

2. In the examination of the appeal, the Board of Appeal shall invite the parties, as often as necessary, to file observations, within a period to be fixed by the Board of Appeal, on communications from the other parties or those issued by itself.

Decisions in respect of appeals [Art. 64]

1. Following the examination as to the merits of the appeal, the Board of Appeal shall decide on the appeal. The Board of Apeal may either exercise any power within the competence of the department which was responsible for the decision appealed against or remit the case to that departments for further action.

2. If the Board of Appeal remits the case for further action to the department whose decision was appealed against, that department shall be bound by the ratio decidendi fo the Board of Appeal, in so far as the facts are the same.

3. The decisions of the Boards of Appeal shall take effect only as from the date of expiration of the period referred to in Article 65(5) or, if an action has been brought before the Court of Justice within that period, as from the date of dismissal of such action.

Trade Mark	*Patent*

A–16

Actions before the Court of Justice [Art. 63]

1. Actions may be brought before the Court of Justice against decisions of the Boards of Appeal on appeals.

2. The action may be brought on grounds of lack of competence, infringement of an essential procedural requirement, infringement of the Treaty, of this Regulation or of any rule of law relating to their application or misuse of power.

3. The Court of Justice has jurisdiction to annul or to alter the contested decision.

4. The action shall be open to any party to proceedings before the Board of Appeal adversely affected by its decision.

5. The action shall be brought before the Court of Justice within two months of the date of notification of the decision of the Board of Appeal.

6. The Office shall be required to take the necessary measures to comply with the judgment of the Court of Justice.

Relationship with the Community legal order [Art. 2 ACP]

(. . .)

2. In order to ensure the uniformity of the Community legal order, the Common Appeal Court established by the Protocol on Litigation shall request the Court of Justice of the European Communities to give a preliminary ruling in accordance with Article 177 of the Treaty establishing the European Economic Community whenever there is a risk of an interpretation of this Agreement being inconsistent with that Treaty.

3. Where a Member State or the Commission of the European Communities considers that a decision of the Common Appeal Court which closes the procedure before it does not comply with the principle stated in the foregoing paragraphs, it may request the Court of Justice of the European Communities to give a ruling. The ruling given by the Court of Justice in response to such request shall not affect the decision by the Common Appeal Court which gave rise to the request. The Registrar of the Court of Justice shall give notice of the request to the Member States, to the Council and, if the request is made by a Member State, the Commission of the European Communities; they shall then be entitled within two months of the notification to submit statements of case or written observations to the Court. No fees shall be levied or any costs or expenses awarded in respect of the proceedings provided for in this paragraph.

Plant Variety Right | *Design*

Further appeal [Art. 73]

1. A further appeal to the Court of Justice of the European Communities shall lie from decisions of the Board of Appeal.

2. The further appeal may be lodged on grounds of lack of competence, infringement of an essential procedural requirement, infringement of the Treaty, of this Regulation, or of any rule of law relating to their application or misuse of power.

3. The further appeal may be made by any party to the appeal proceedings who is adversely affected by its decision, or by the Commission or the Office.

4. The further appeal shall be lodged with the Court of Justice within two months of service of the decision of the Board of Appeal.

5. If the Court of Justice remits the case for further action to the Board of Appeal, the Board shall, in so far as the facts are the same, be bound by the ratio decidendi of the Court of Justice.

Direct appeal [Art. 74]

1. A direct appeal to the Court of Justice of the European Communities may lie from decisions of the Office pursuant to Article 29 and 100(2).

2. The provisions laid down in Article 73 shall apply mutatis mutandis.

Actions before the Court of Justice [Art. 65] **A–16**

1. Actions may be brought before the Court of Justice against decisions of the Office taken by the Boards of Appeal on appeals.

2. The action may be brought on grounds of lack of competence, infringement of an essential procedural requirement, infringement of the Treaty, of this Regulation or of any rule of law relating to their application or misuse of power.

3. The Court of Justice has jurisdiction to annul or alter the contested decision.

4. The action shall be open to any party to proceedings before the Board of Appeal adversely affected by its decision.

5. The action shall be brought before the Court of Justice within two months of the date of notification of the decision of the Board of Appeal.

6. The Office shall be required to take the necessary measures to comply with the judgment of the Court of Justice.

F. JURISDICTION, PROCEDURE AND REMEDIES IN INFRINGEMENT PROCEEDINGS

Trade Mark   *Patent*

A–17 **Application of the Convention on Jurisdiction and Enforcement [Art. 90]**

1. Unless otherwise specified in this Regulation, the Convention on Jurisdiction and the Enforcement of Judgments in Civil and Commercial Matters, signed in Brussels on 27 September 1968, as amended by the Conventions on the Accession to that Convention of the States acceding to the European Communities, the whole of which Convention and of which Conventions of Accession are hereinafter referred to as the 'Convention on Jurisdiction and Enforcement', shall apply to proceedings relating to Community trade marks and applications for Community trade marks, as well as to proceedings relating to simultaneous and successive actions on the basis of Community trade marks and national trade marks.

2. In the case of proceedings in respect of the actions and claims referred to in Article 92:

   (a) Articles 2, 4, 5(1), (3), (4) and (5) and Article 24 of the Convention on Jurisdiction and Enforcement shall not apply;

   (b) Articles 17 and 18 of that Convention shall apply subject to the limitations in Article 93(4) of this Regulation;

   (c) the provisions of Title II of the Convention which are applicable to persons domiciled in a Member State shall also be applicable to persons who do not have a domicile in any Member State but have an establishment therein.

Application of the Convention on Jurisdiction and Enforcement [Art. 13 POL][11]

1. Unless otherwise specified in this Protocol, the Convention on Jurisdiction and the Enforcement of Judgments in Civil and Commercial Matters, signed in Brussels on 27 September 1968, as amended by the Conventions on the Accession to that Convention of the States acceding to the European Communities, the whole of which Convention and of which Conventions of Accession are hereinafter referred to as 'the Convention on Jurisdiction and Enforcement', shall apply to proceedings governed by this Protocol.

2. Articles 2, 4, 5(1), (3), (4), (5) and 24 of the Convention on Jurisdiction and Enforcement shall not apply to proceedings governed by this Protocol. Articles 17 and 18 of that Convention shall apply subject to the limitations in Article 14(4) of this Protocol.

3. For the purpose of applying the Convention on Jurisdiction and Enforcement to proceedings governed by this Protocol, the provisions of Title II of that Convention which are applicable to persons domiciled in a Contracting State shall also be applicable to persons who do not have a domicile in any Contracting State but have an establishment therein.

---

[11] See also Art. 66 CPC (not reproduced here) in relation to actions other than those to which the POL applies.

Plant Variety Right	*Design*

Jurisdiction and procedure in legal actions relating to civil law claims [Art. 101]

1. The Lugano Convention as well as the complementary provisions of this Article and of Articles 102 to 106 of this Regulation shall apply to proceedings relating to actions in respect of the claims referred to in Articles 94 to 100.

(. . .)

Application of the Convention on Jurisdiction and Enforcement [Art. 83]   A–17

1. Unless otherwise specified in this Regulation, the Convention on Jurisdiction and the Enforcement of Judgments in Civil and Commercial Matters, signed in Brussels on 27 September 1968, as amended by the Convention on the Accession to that Convention of the States acceding to the European Communities, the whole of which Convention and of which Conventions of Accession are hereinafter referred to as the 'Convention on Jurisdiction and Enforcement', shall apply to proceedings relating to Community Designs and applications for Registered Community Designs, as well as to proceedings relating to actions on the basis of Community Designs and national design rights enjoying simultaneous protection.

2. In the event of proceedings in respect of the actions and claims referred to in Article 85:
   (a) Article 2, Article 4, Article 5 No. 1, 3, 4 and 5 and Article 24 of the Convention on Jurisdiction and Enforcement shall not apply;
   (b) Articles 17 and 18 of that Convention shall apply subject to the limitations in Article 86(4) of this Regulation;
   (c) the provisions of Title II of that Convention which are applicable to persons domiciled in a Member State shall also be applicahle to persons who do not have a domicile in any Member State but have an establishment therein.

3. Article 16 No 3 of the Convention on Jurisdiction and Enforcement shall be complied with by bringing proceedings in respect of an action or claim referred to in Article 85(c) and (d) before any Community Design Court having jurisdiction under Article 86.

Trade Mark   *Patent*

A–18   **Community trade mark courts [Art. 91]**   **Community patent courts [Art. 1 POL]**

1. The Member States shall designate in their territories as limited a number as possible of national courts and tribunals of first and second instance, hereinafter referred to as 'Community trade mark courts', which shall perform the functions assigned to them by this Regulation.

2. Each Member State shall communicate to the Commission within three years of the entry into force of this Regulation a list of Community trade mark courts indicating their names and their territorial jurisdiction.

3. Any change made after communication of the list referred to in paragraph 2 in the number, names or territorial jurisdiction of the courts shall be notified without delay by the Member State concerned to the Commission.

4. The information referred to in paragraph 2 and 3 shall be notified by the Commission to the Member States and published in the Official Journal of the European Communities.

5. As long as a Member State has not communicated the list as stipulated in paragraph 2, jurisdiction for any proceedings resulting from an action or application covered by Article 92, and for which the courts of that State have jurisdiction under Article 93, shall lie with that court of the State in question which would have jurisdiction ratione loci and ratione materiae in the case of proceedings relating to a national trade mark registered in that State.

1. The Contracting States shall designate in their territories as limited a number of possible of national courts and tribunals of first and second instance, hereinafter referred to as 'Community patent courts', which shall perform the functions assigned to them by this Protocol.

2. The names of the Community patent courts and their territorial jurisdiction are specified in the Annex to this Protocol. However, as regards the Kingdom of Spain and the Portuguese Republic, the names of these courts and their territorial jurisdiction shall be notified to the Secretary-General of the Council of the European Communities at the latest at the time of ratification of the Agreement relating to Community Patents.

3. Any change in the number, the names or territorial jurisdiction of the courts shall be notified by the Contracting State concerned to the Secretary-General of the Council of the European Communities.

Plant Variety Right	*Design*

Community Design Courts [Art. 84] A–18

[No provision corresponds, see Art. 101(4).]

1. The Member States shall designate in their territories as limited a number as possible of national courts and tribunals of first and second instance (Community Design Courts), which shall perform the functions assigned to them by this Regulation.

2. Each Member State shall communicate to the Commission within three years of the entry into force of this Regulation a list of Community Design Courts, indicating their names and their territorial jurisdiction.

3. Any change made after communication of the list referred to in paragraph (2) in the number, the names of territorial jurisdiction of the Community Design Courts shall be notified without delay by the Member State concerned to the Commission.

4. The information referred to in paragraphs (2) and (3) shall be notified by the Commission to the Member States and published in the Official Journal of the European Communities.

5. As long as a Member State has not communicated the list as stipulated in paragraph (2), jurisdiction for any proceedings resulting from an action covered by Article 85 for which the courts of that State have jurisdiction under Article 86, shall lie with that court of the State in question which would have jurisdiction ratione loci and raione materiae in the case of proceedings relating to a national design right of that State.

Trade Mark	*Patent*

A–19   **Jurisdiction over infringement and validity [Art. 92]**

Jurisdiction over infringement and validity [Art. 92]	**Jurisdiction over infringement and validity [Art. 15 POL]**
The Community trade mark courts shall have exclusive jurisdiction: (a) for all infringement actions and—if they are permitted under national law—actions in respect of threatened infringement releating to Community trade marks; (b) for actions for declaration of non-infringement, if they are permitted under national law; (c) for all actions brought as a result of acts referred to in Article 9(3), second sentence; (d) for counterclaims for revocation or for a declaration of invalidity of the Community trade mark pursuant to Article 96.	1. The Community patent courts of first instance shall have exclusive jurisdiction: (a) for all infringement actions and—if they are permitted under national law—actions in respect of threatened infringement relating to Community patents; (b) for actions for a declaration of non-infringement, if they are permitted under national law; (c) for all actions in respect of the use made of the invention during the period specified in Article 32(1) of the Community Patent Convention; (d) for counterclaims for revocation of the Community patent pursuant to paragraph 2.

(. . .)

Plant Variety Right   *Design*

Jurisdiction over infringement and validity **A–19**
[Art. 85]

[No provision corresponds, see Art. 101(1) and (4) and Arts 94 to 100.]

The Community Design Courts shall have exclusive jurisdiction:

   (a) for infringement actions and—if they are permitted under national law—actions in respect of threatened infringement of Community Designs;
   (b) for actions for declaration of non-infringement of Community Designs, if they are permitted under national law;
   (c) for actions for a declaration of invalidity of an Unregistered Community Design;
   (d) for counterclaims for a declaration of invalidity of a Community Design raised in connection with actions under (a).

Trade Mark | Patent

A–20

International jurisdiction [Art. 93] | **Jurisdiction [Art. 14 POL]**

1. Subject to the provisions of this Regulation as well as to any provisions of the Convention on Jurisdiction and Enforcement applicable by virtue of Article 90, proceedings in respect of the actions and claims referred to in Article 92 shall be brought in the courts of the Member State in which the defendant is domiciled or, if he is not domiciled in any of tbe Member States, in which he has an establishment.

1. Subject to the provisions of this Protocol as well as to any provisions of the Convention on Jurisdiction and Enforcement applicable by virtue of Article 13, proceedings governed by this Protocol shall be brought in the courts of the Contracting State in which the defendant is domiciled or, if he is not domiciled in any of the Contracting States, in which he has an establishment.

2. If the defendant is neither domiciled nor has an establishment in any of the Member States, such proceedings shall be brought in the courts of the Member State in which the plaintiff is domiciled or, if he is not domiciled in any of the Member States, in which he has an establishment.

2. If the defendant nether is domiciled nor has an establishment in any of the Contracting States, such proceedings shall be brought in the courts of the Contracting State in which the plaintiff is domiciled or, if he is not domiciled in any of the Contracting States, in which he has an establishment.

3. If neither the defendant nor the plaintiff is so domiciled or has such an establishment, such proceedings shall be brought in the courts of the Member State where the Office has its seat.

3. If neither the defendant nor the plaintiff is so domiciled or has such an establishment, such proceedings shall be brought in the courts of the Contracting State where the Common Appeal Court has its seat.

4. Notwithstanding the provisions of paragraphs 1, 2 and 3:
(a) Article 17 of the Convention on Jurisdiction and Enforcement shall apply if the parties agree that a different Community trade mark court shall have jurisdiction;
(b) Article 18 of that Convention shall apply if the defendant enters an appearance before a different Community trade mark court.

4. Notwithstanding the provisions of paragraphs 1 to 3 above:
(a) Article 17 of the Convention on Jurisdiction and Enforcement shall apply if the parties agree that a different Community patent court shall have jurisdiction;
(b) Article 18 of that Convention shall apply if the defendant enters an appearance before a different Community patent court.

5. Proceedings in respect of the actions and claims referred to in Article 92, with the exception of actions for a declaration of non-infringement of a Community trade mark, may also be brought in the courts of the Member State in which the act of infringement has been committed or threatened, or in which an act within the meaning of Article 9(3), second sentence, has been committed.

5. The proceedings governed by this Protocol, with the exception of actions for a declaration of non-infringement of a Community patent, may also be brought in the courts of the Contracting State in which the act of infringement has been committed or threatened, or in which an act within the meaning of Article 15(1)(c) has been committed.

584

Plant Variety Right | *Design*

Jurisdiction and procedure in legal actions relating to civil law claims *(cont.)* **[Art. 101]**

(. . .)

2. Proceedings of the type referred to in paragraph 1 shall be brought in the courts:
   (a) of the Member State or another Contracting Party to the Lugano Convention in which the defendant is domiciled or has his seat or, in the absence of such, has an establishment; or
   (b) if this condition is not met in any of the Member States or Contracting Parties, of the Member State in which the plaintiff is domiciled or has his seat or, in the absence of such, has an establishment; or
   (c) if this condition is also not met in any of the Member States, of the Member States in which the seat of the Office is located.
The competent courts shall have jurisdiction in respect of infringements alleged to have been committed in any of the Member States.

3. Proceedings relating to actions in respect of claims for infringement may also be brought in the courts for the place where the harmful event occurred. In such case, the court shall have jurisdiction only in respect of infringements alleged to have been committed in the territory of the Member State to which it belongs.

4. The legal processes and the competent courts shall be those that operate under the laws of the State determined pursuant to paragraph 2 or 3.

International jurisdiction [Art. 86] **A–20**

1. Subject to the provisions of this Regulation and to any provisions of the Convention on Jurisdiction and Enforcement applicable by virtue of Article 83, proceedings in respect of the actions and claims referred to in Article 85 shall be brought in the courts of the Member State in which the defendant is domiciled or, if he is not domiciled in any of the Member States, in which he has an establishment.

2. If the defendant is neither domiciled nor has an establishment in any of the Member States, such proceedings shall be brought in the courts of the Member State in which the plaintiff is domiciled or, if he is not domiciled in any of the Member States, in which he has an establishment.

3. If nether the defendant nor the plaintiff is so domiciled or has such an establishment, such proceedings shall be brought in the courts of the Member State where the Office is situated.

4. Notwithstanding the provisions of paragraphs (1), (2) and (3) above:
   (a) Article 17 of the Convention on Jurisdiction and Enforcement shall apply if the parties agree that a different Community Design Court shall have jurisdiction;
   (b) Article 18 of that Convention shall apply if the defendant enters an appearance before a different Community Design Court.

5. Proceedings in respect of the actions and claims referred to in Article 85(a) and (d) may also be brought in the courts of the Member State in which the act of infringement has been committed or threatened.

Trade Mark	*Patent*

A–21

Extent of jurisdiction [Art. 94]

1. A Community trade mark court whose jurisdiction is based on Article 93(1) to (4) shall have jurisdiction in respect of:
- acts of infringement committed or threatened within the territory of any of the Member States,
- acts within the meaning of Article 9(3), second sentence, committed within the territory of any of the Member States.

2. A Community trade mark court whose jurisdiction is based on Article 93(5) shall have jurisdiction only in respect of acts committed or threatened within the territory of the Member State in which that court is situated.

Presumption of validity—Defence as to the merits [Act. 95]

1. The Community trade mark courts shall treat the Community trade mark as valid unless its validity is put in issue by the defendant with a counterclaim for revocation or for a declaration of invalidity.

2. The validity of a Community trade mark may not be put in issue in an action for a declaration of non-infringement.

3. In the actions referred to in Article 92 (a) and (c) a plea relating to revocation or invalidity of the Community trade mark submitted otherwise than by way of a counterclaim shall be admissible in so far as the defendant claims that the rights of the proprietor of the Community trade mark could be revoked for lack of use or that Community trade mark could be declared invalid on account of an earlier right of the defendant.

Territorial jurisdiction [Art. 17 POL]

1. A Community patent court of first instance whose jurisdiction is based on Article 14(1) to (4) shall have jurisdiction in respect of:
- acts of infringement committed or threatened within the territory of any of the Contracting States,
- acts within the meaning of Article 15(1)(c) committed within the territory of any of the Contracting States.

2. A Community patent court of first instance whose jurisdiction is based on Articoe 15 (5) shall have jurisdiction only in respect of acts committed or threatened within the territory of the State in which that court is situated.

Jurisdiction over infringement and validity (*cont.*) [Art. 15 POL]

(. . .)

2. The Community patent courts of first instance shall treat the Community patent as valid unless its validity is put in issue by the defendant with a counterclaim for revocation of the Community patent. The counterclaim may only be based on the grounds for revocation mentioned in Article 56(1) of the Community Patent Convention. The second phrase of Article 55(1) and Article 55(2), (3) and (6) of the Community Patent Convention shall apply.

3. If the counterclaim is brought in a legal action to which the proprietor of the patent is not already a party, he shall be informed thereof and may be joined as a party to the action in accordance with the conditions set out in national law.

4. The validity of a Community patent may not be put in issue in an action for a declaration of non-infringement.

Plant Variety Right   *Design*

Extent of jurisdiction on infringement **A–21**
[Art. 87]

[See Art. 101(2) and (3), above.]

1. A Community Design Court whose jurisdiction is based on Article 86(1), (2), (3) or (4) shall have jurisdiction in respect of acts of infringement committed or threatened within the territory of any of the Member States.

2. A Community Design Court whose jurisdiction is based on Article 86(5) shall have jurisdiction only in respect of acts of infringement committed or threatened within the territory of the Member State in which that court is situated.

Obligation of national courts or other bodies [Art. 105]

A national court or other body hearing an action relating to a Community plant variety right shall treat the Community plant variety right as valid.

Presumption of validity—defence as to the merits [Art. 89]

1. In proceedings in respect of an infringement action or an action for threatened infringement, the Community Design court shall treat the Community Design as valid unless its validity is put in issue by the defendant with a counterclaim for a declaration of invalidity.

2. In proceedings in respect of an infringement action or an action for threatened infringement, the Community Design Court shall, when the right holder presents evidence to sustain his claim that the design has an individual character, treat the design as new within the meaning of Article 5 unless in any counterclaim for a declaration of invalidity proof is presented to the contrary by the defendant in the main action.

3. In proceedings referred to in paragraph (1), a plea relating to the invalidity of a Community Design submitted otherwise than by way of counterclaim shall be admissible in so far as the defendant claims that the Community Design should be declared invalid on account of a national design right within the meaning of Article 27(2) belonging to him.

Trade Mark	Patent

A–22 **Counterclaims [Art. 96]**

1. A counterclaim for revocation or for a declaration of invalidity may only be based on the grounds for revocation or invalidity mentioned in this Regulation.

2. A Community trade mark court shall reject a counterclaim for revocation or for a declaration of invalidity if a decision taken by the Office relating to the same subject matter and cause of action and involving the same parties has already become final.

3. If the counterclaim is brought in a legal action to which the proprietor of the trade mark is not already a party, he shall be informed thereof and may be joined as a party to the action in accordance with the conditons set out in national law.

4. The Community trade mark court with which a counterclaim for revocation or for a declaration of invalidity of the Community trade mark has been filed shall inform the Office of the date on which the counterclaim was filed. The latter shall record this fact in the Register of Community trade marks.

5. Article 56(3), (4), (5) and (6) shall apply.

6. Where a Community trade mark court has given a judgment which has become final on a counterclaim for revocation or for invalidity of a Community trade mark, a copy of the judgment shall be sent to the Office. Any party may request information about such transmission. The Office shall mention the judgment in the Register of Community trade marks in accordance with the provisions of the Implementing Regulation.

Judgments on validity [Art. 19 POL]

1. Where, in a proceeding before the Community patent courts of first instance, the validity of a Community patent has been put in issue,

(a) if any of the grounds for revocation mentioned in Article 56(1) of the Community Patent Convention are found to prejudice the maintenance of the Community patent, the court shall order the revocation of the patent;

(b) if none of the grounds for revocation mentioned in Article 56(1) of the Community Patent Convention is found to prejudice the maintenance of the Community patent, the court shall reject the application for revocation;

(c) if, taking into consideration the amendments made by the proprietor of the patent during the course of the action, none of the grounds for revocation mentioned in Article 56 (1) of the Community Patent Convention is found to prejudice the maintenance of the Community patent, the court shall order the patent to be maintained as amended.

2. Where a Community patent court of first instance has given a judgment which has become final on a counterclaim for revocation of the Community patent, it shall send a copy of the judgment to the European Patent Office. Any party may request information about such transmission.

[*cont. on p. 590*]

Plant Variety Right	*Design*

Action or counterclaim for a declaration of invalidity of a Community Design [Art. 88] **A–22**

[No provision corresponds, national courts have no jurisdiction over validity.]

1. An action or a counterclaim for a declaration of invalidity of a Community Design may only be based on the grounds for invalidity mentioned in Article 27.

2. In the case specified in Article 27(1)(d), the action or the counterclaim may be brought only by the person or persons entitled to the Community Design and, in the case specified in Article 27(2), only by the right holder of the earlier right.

3. If the counterclaim is brought in a legal action to which the rightholder in the Community Design is not already a party, he shall be informed thereof and may be joined as a party to the action in accordance with the conditions set out in the law of the Member State where the court is situated.

4. The validity of a Community Design may not be put in issue in an action for a declaration of non-infringement.

Judgments on validity [Act. 90]

1. Where in a proceeding before a Community Design Court the Community Design has been put in issue by way of a counterclaim for a declaration of invalidity:
(a) if any of the grounds mentioned in Article 27 are found to prejuduce the maintenance of the Community Design, the Court shall declare the Community Design invalid;
(b) if none of the grounds mentioned in Article 27 is found to prejudice the maintenance of the Community Design, the Court shall reject the counterclaim.

[*cont. p. 591*]

589

Trade Mark | *Patent*

A–22 **Counterclaims [Art. 96]** *(cont.)*

7. The Community trade mark court hearing a counterclaim for revocation or for a declaration of invalidity may stay the proceedings on application by the proprietor of the Community trade mark and after hearing the other parties and may request the defendant to submit in application for revocation or for a declaration of invalidity to the Office within a time limit which it shall determine. If the application is not made within the time limit, the proceedings shall continue; the counterclaim shall be deemed withdrawn. Article 100(3) shall apply.

Judgments on validity [Art. 19 POL] *(cont.)*

3. Where a Community patent court of first instance, by a judgment which has become final, has decided to maintain the Community patent as amended, it shall send a copy of the judgment to the European Patent Office with the text of the patent as amended as a result of the proceedings. Any party may request information about such transmission. The European Patent Office shall publish the text provided that:

(a) a translation of all amendments to the patent specification in one of the official languages of each of the Contracting States which does not have as an official language the language of proceedings of the court is filed within a time limit identical to that referred to in Article 58(3)(b) of the Community Patent Convention;

(b) the fee for the printing of a new specification is paid within a time limit identical to that referred to in Article 58(3)(c) of the Community Patent Convention.

4. If a translation is not filed in due time or if the fee for the printing of a new specification is not paid in due time, the European Patent Office shall, notwithstanding the decision of the Community patent court, revoke the Community patent unless these acts are done and the additional fee is paid within a further period identical to that referred to in Article 58(4) of the Community Patent Convention.

Judgments on validity [Art. 90] *(cont.)*   **A–07**

2. The Community Design Court with which a counterclaim for a declaration of invalidity of a Registered Community Design has been filed shall inform the Office of the date on which the counterclaim was filed. The latter shall record this fact in the Register.

3. The Community Design Court hearing a counterclaim for a declaration of invalidity of a Registered Community Design may, on application by the right holder in the Registered Community Design and after hearing the other parties, stay the proceedings and request the defendant to submit an application for a declaration of invalidity to the Office within a time limit which it shall determine. If the application is not made within the time limit, the proceedings shall continue; the counterclaim shall be deemed withdrawn. Article 95(3) shall apply.

4. Where a Community Design Court has given a judgment which has become final on a counterclaim for a declaration of invalidity of a Registered Community Design, a copy of the judgment shall be sent to the Office. Any party may request information about such transmission. The Office shall mention the judgment in the Register in accordance with the provisions of the Implementing Regulation.

5. No counterclaim for a declaration of invalidity of a Registered Community Design may be made if an application relating to the same subject-matter and cause of action, and involving the same parties, has already been determined by the Office in a decision which has become final.

Effects of the judgment on validity

When it has become final, a judgment of a Community Design Court declaring a Community Design invalid shall have, subject to Article 27(3), in all the Member States the effects specified in Article 28.

Trade Mark	*Patent*

A–23

Applicable law [Art. 97][12]

1. The Community trade mark courts shall apply the provisions of this Regulation.

2. On all matters not covered by this Regulation a Community trade mark court shall apply its national law, including its private international law.

3. Unless otherwise provided in this Regulation, a Community trade mark court shall apply the rules of procedure governing the same type of action relating to a national trade mark in the Member State where it has its seat.

Applicable law [Art. 32 POL]

1. The Community patent courts shall apply the provisions of the Agreement relating to Community Patents.

2. On all matters not covered by the Agreement relating to Community Patents a Community patent court shall apply its national law, including its private international law.

Procedure [Act. 33 POL]

1. Unless otherwise specified in the Agreement relating to Community Patents, a Community patent court shall apply the rules of procedure governing the same type of action relating to a national patent in the Contracting State where is has its seat.

2. Paragraph 1 shall apply mutatis mutandis in the case of a European patent application which may result in the grant of a Community patent.

3. The Community patent court shall record in writing at least the essentials of the oral proceedings, including the testimony given and the summary examination of the items produced in evidence; it shall attach the procedural acts and written statements.

[12] See also Art. 14.

Plant Variety Right	*Design*	

Application of national law [Art. 93][13]

Claims under Community plant variety rights shall be subject to limitations imposed by the law of the Member States only as expressly referred to in this Regulation.

Applicable law [Art. 92]

1. The Community Design Courts shall apply the provisions of this Regulation.

2. On all matters not covered by this Regulation, a Community Design Court shall apply its national law, including its private international law.

3. Unless otherwise provided in this Regulation, a Community Design Court shall apply the rules of procedure governing the same type of action relating to a national design right in the Member State where it is situated.

A–23

---

[13] See also Art. 101(4) for application of national procedural law.

Trade Mark	*Patent*

A–24

Sanctions [Art. 98]

1. Where a Community trade mark court finds that the defendant has infringed or threatened to infringe a Community trade mark, it shall, unless there are special reasons for not doing so, issue an order prohibiting the defendant from proceeding with the acts which infringed or would infringe the Community trade mark. It shall also take such measures in accordance with its national law as are aimed at ensuring that this prohibition is complied with.

2. In all other respects the Community trade mark court shall apply the law of the Member State to which the acts of infringement or threatened infringement were committed, including the private international law.

Sanctions [Art. 35 POL]

1. Where a Community patent court finds that the defendant has infringed or threatened to infringe a Community patent, it shall, unless there are special reasons for not doing so, issue an order prohibiting the defendant from proceeding with the acts which infringed or would infringe the Community patent. It shall also take such measures in accordance with its national law as are aimed at ensuring that this prohibition is compied with.

2. In all other respects the Community patent court shall apply the law of the Contracting State in which the acts of infringement or threatened infringement were committed.

Plant Variety Right   *Design*

[No provision corresponds, see Art. 97(1).][14]

1. Where in an action for infringement or for threatened infringement a Community Design Court finds that the defendant has infringed or threatened to infringe a Community Design, it shall, unless there are special reasons for not doing so, issue an order prohibiting the defendant from proceeding with the acts which have infringed or would infringe the Community Design.

2. Where in an action for infringement a Community Design Court finds that the defendant has infringed a Community Design, the Court shall, unless there are special reasons for not doing so:

(a) enjoin the infringer to provide forthwith information concerning the origin of the infringing product and the channels through which they are commercialized;

(b) issue an order to seize the infringing products.

3. The Community Design Court shall take such measures in accordance with its national law as are aimed at ensuring the orders referred to in paragraphs (1) and (2) are complied with.

4. In all other respects the Community Design Court shall apply the law of the Member State in which the acts of infringement or threatened infringement were committed, including its private international law.

[14] It is assumed that Art. 107 corresponds to Art. 74 CPC rather than Art. 35 POL.

Trade Mark	*Patent*

A–25

Provisional and protective measures [Art. 99]

1. Application may be made to the courts of a Member State, including Community trade mark courts, for such provisional, including protective, measures in respect of a Community trade mark or Community trade mark application as may be available under the law of that State in respect of a national trade mark, even if, under this Regulation, a Community trade mark court of another Member State has jurisdiction as to the substance of the matter.

2. A Community trade mark court whose jurisdiction is based on Article 93 (1), (2), (3) or (4) shall have jurisdiction to grant provisional and protective measures which, subject to any necessary procedure for recognition and enforcement pursuant to Title III of the Convention on Jurisdiction and Enforcement, are applicable in the territory of any Member State. No other court shall have such jurisdiction.

Provisional, including protective measures [Art. 36 POL]

1. Application may be made to the courts of a Contracting State, including Community patent courts, for such provisional, including protective, measures in respect of a Community patent as may be available under the law of that State in respect of a national patent, even if, under this Protocol, a Community patent court of another Contracting State has jurisdiction as to the substance of the matter.

2. A Community patent court whose jurisdiction is based on Article 14(1), (2), (3) or (4) shall have jurisdiction to grant provisional, including protective, measures which, subject to any necessary procedure for recognition and enforcement pursuant to Title III of the Convention on Jurisdiction and Enforcement, are applicable in the territory of any Contracting State. No other court shall have such jurisdiction.

3. The Common Appeal Court shall not be competent to order provisional, including protective, measures and no appeal may be made to the Common Appeal Court against a judgment ordering such measures.

Plant Variety Right	*Design*

Provisional measures, including protective measures [Art. 94] A–25

[No provision corresponds][15]

1. Application may be made to the courts of a Member State, including Community Design Courts, for such provisional measures, including protective measures, in respect of a Community Design as may be available under the law of that State on national design rights, or those which follow from the application of the provision in Article 93(2)(a), even if, under this Regulation, a Community Design Court of another Member State has jurisdiction as to the substance of the matter.

2. In proceedings relating to provisional measures, including protective measures, a plea otherwise than by way of counterclaim relating to the invalidity of a Community Design submitted by the defendant shall be admissible. Article 88(2) shall, however, apply mutatis mutandis.

3. A Community Design Court whose jurisdiction is based on Article 86(1), (2), (3) or (4) shall have jurisdiction to grant provisional measures, including protective measures, which, subject to any necessary procedure for recognition and enforcement pursuant to Title III of the Convention on Jurisdiction and Enforcement, are applicable in the territory of any Member State. No other court shall have such jurisdiction.

[15] Art. 24 provides that the Community plant variety right may be the *subject* of provisional including protective measures.

Trade Mark	*Patent*

A–26

Specific rules on related actions [Art. 100]

1. A Community trade mark court hearing an action referred to in Article 92, other than an action for a declaration of non-infringement shall, unless there are special grounds for continuing the hearing, of its own motion after hearing the parties or at the request of one of the parties and after hearing the other parties, stay the proceedings where the validity of the Community trade mark is already in issue before another Community trade mark court on account of a counterclaim or where an application for revocation or for a declaration of invalidity has already been filed at the Office.

2. The Office, when hearing an application for revocation or for a declaration of invalidity shall, unless there are special grounds for continuing the hearing, of its own motion after hearing the parties or at the request of one of the parties and after hearing the other parties, stay the proceedings where the validity of the Community trade mark is already in issue on account of a counterclaim before a Community trade mark court. However, if one of the parties to the proceedings before the Community trade mark court so requests, the court may, after hearing the other parties to these proceedings, stay the proceedings. The Office shall in this instance continue the proceedings pending before it.

3. Where the Community trade mark court stays the proceedings it may order provisional and protective measures for the duration of the stay.

Stay of proceedings [Art. 18 POL]

If the judgment in an action before a Community patent court of first instance relating to a European patent application which may result in the grant of a Community patent depends upon the patentability of the invention, that judgment may be given only after the European Patent Office has granted a Community patent or refused the European patent application.

Specific rules on related actions [Art. 34 POL]

1. A Community patent court hearing an action referred to in Article 15(1), other than an action for a declaration of non-infringement, shall, unless there are special grounds for continuing the hearing, at the request of one of the parties and after hearing the other parties, stay the proceedings where the validity of the Community patent is already in issue before another Community patent court or before the Common Appeal Court, or where opposition to the Community patent has already been lodged or an application for revocation or a request for limitation of the Community patent has been filed at the European Patent Office.

2. The European Patent Office, when hearing an application for revocation or a request for limitation of a community patent shall, unless there are special grounds for continuing the hearing, at the request of one of the parties and after hearing the other parties, stay the proceedings where the validity of the Community patent is already in issue before a Community patent court of before the Common Appeal Court.

Plant Variety Right	*Design*	

Stay of proceedings [Art. 106]

1. Where an action relates to claims pursuant to Article 98(4) and the decision depends upon the protectability of the variety pursuant to Article 6, this decision may not be given before the Office has decided on the application for a Community plant variety right.

2. Where an action relates to a Community plant variety right that has been granted and in respect of which proceedings for revocation or cancellation pursuant to Articles 20 or 21 have been initiated, the proceedings may be stayed in so far as the decision depends upon the validity of the Community plant variety right.

Specific rules on related actions [Art. 95] **A–26**

1. A Community Design Court hearing an action referred to in Article 85, other than an action for a declaration of non-infringement, shall unless there are special grounds for continuing the hearing, of its own motion after hearing the parties, or at the request of one of the parties and after hearing the other parties, stay the proceedings where the validity of the Community Design is already in issue before another Community Design Court on account of a counterclaim or, in the case of a Registered Community Design, where an application for a declaration of invalidity has already been filed at the Office.

2. The Office, when hearing an application for a declaration of invalidity of a Registered Community Design, shall, unless there are special grounds for continuing the hearing, of its own motion after hearing the parties, or at the request of one of the parties and after hearing the other parties, stay the proceedings where the validity of the Registered Community Design is already in issue on account of a counterclaim before a Community Design Court. However, if one of the parties to the proceedings before the Community Design Court so requests, the court may, after hearing the other parties to these proceedings, stay the proceedings. The Office shall in this instance continue the proceedings pending before it.

3. Where the Community Design Court stays the proceedings it may order provisional measures, including protective measures, for the duration of the stay.

Trade Mark	*Patent*

A–27

Jurisdiction of Community trade mark courts of second instance—Further appeal [Art. 101]

1. An appeal to the Community trade mark courts of second instance shall lie from judgments of the Community trade mark courts of first instance in respect of proceedings arising from the actions and claims referred to in Article 92.

2. The conditions under which an appeal may be lodged with a Community trade mark court of second instance shall be determined by the national law of the Member State in which that court is located.

3. The national rules concerning further appeal shall be applicable in respect of judgments of Community trade mark courts of second instance.

Jurisdiction of the Community patent courts of second instance [Art. 21 POL]

1. An appeal to the Community patent courts of second instance shall lie from judgments of the Community patent courts of first instance in respect of proceedings referred to in Artice 15(1).

2. The conditions under which an appeal may be lodged with a Community patent court of second instance shall be determined by the national law of the Contracting State in which that court is located.

Plant Variety Right	*Design*

Jurisdiction of Community Design Courts of second instance—further appeal [Art. 96]   A–27

[No provision corresponds.]

1. An appeal to the Community Design Courts of second instance shall lie from judgments of the Community Design Courts of first instance in respect of proceedings arising from the actions and claims referred to in Article 85.

2. The conditions under which an appeal may be lodged with a Community Design Court of second instance shall be determined by the national law of the Member State in which that court is located.

3. The national rules concerning further appeal shall be applicable in respect of judgments of Community Design Courts of second instance.

G.   ADMINISTRATIVE PROVISIONS

Trade Mark	*Patent*

A–28   **Competence [Art. 125]**

The departments charged with the procedure [Art. 15 EPC]

For taking decisions in connection with the procedures laid down in this Regulation, the following shall be competent:
  (a) Examiners;
  (b) Opposition Divisions;
  (c) an Administration of Trade Marks and Legal Division;
  (d) Cancellation Divisions;
  (e) Boards of Appeal.

For implementing the procedures laid down in this Convention, there shall be set up within the European Patent Office:
  (a) a Receiving Section;
  (b) Search Divisions;
  (c) Examining Divisions;
  (d) Opposition Divisions;
  (e) A Legal Division;
  (f) Boards of Appeal;
  (g) an Enlarged Board of Appeal.

The special departments [Art. 6 CPC, pursuant to Art. 143 EPC]

The special departments shall be as follows:
  (a) a Patent Administration Divison;
  (b) one or more Revocation Divisions.

Opposition Divisions [Art. 127]

Opposition Divisions [Art. 19 EPC]

1. An Opposition Division shall be responsible for taking decisions on an opposition to an application to register a Community trade mark.

2. An Opposition Division shall consist of three members. At least one of the members must be legally qualified.

1. An Opposition Divison shall be responsible for the examination of oppositions against any European patent.

2. An Opposition Division shall consist of three technical examiners, at least two of whom shall not have taken part in the proceedings for grant of the patent to which the opposition relates. An examiner who has taken part in the proceedings for the grant of the European patent shall not be the Chairman. Prior to the taking of a final decision on the opposition, the Opposition Division may entrust the examination of the opposition to one of its members. Oral Proceedings shall be before the Opposition Division itself. If the Opposition Division considers that the nature of the decision so requires, it shall be enlarged by the addition of a legally qualified examiner who shall not have taken part in the proceedings for grant of the patent. In the event of parity of votes the vote of the Chairman of the Division shall be decisive.

Plant Variety Right	Design

Establishment and powers [Art. 45]

1. There shall be established within the Office one or more Boards of Appeal.

(. . .)

Competence [Art. 113]

The following departments of the Office shall be competent for taking decisions in connection with procedures laid down in this Regulation:
  (a) Formalities Examining Divisons;
  (b) a Design Administration and Legal Division;
  (c) Invalidity Divisions;
  (d) Boards of Appeal.

A–28

Invalidity Divisions [Art. 116}

1. An Invalidity Division shall be responsible for taking decisions in relation to an application for a declaration of invalidity of a Registered Community Design.

[No provision corresponds.]

2. An Invalidity Division shall consist of three members. At least two of these members must be legally qualified.

603

Trade Mark	*Patent*

A–29   **Cancellation Divisions [Art. 129]**

1. A Cancellation Division shall be responsible for taking decisions in relation to an application for the revocation or declaration of invalidity of a Community trade mark.

2. A Cancellation Division shall consist of three members. At least one of the members must be legally qualified.

Boards of Appeal [Art. 130]

1. The Boards of Appeal shall be responsible for deciding on appeals from decisions of the examiners, Opposition Divisions, Administration of Trade Marks and Legal Division and Cancellation Divisions.

2. A Board of Appeal shall consist of three members. At least two of the members must be legally qualified.

Revocation Divisions [Art. 8 CPC]

1. The Revocation Divisions shall be responsible for the examination of requests for the limitation of and applications for the revocation of Community patents, and for determining compensation under Article 43(5).

2. A Revocation Division shall consist of one legally qualified member who shall be the Chairman, and two technically qualified members. Prior to the taking of a final decision on the request or application, the Revocation Division may entrust the examination of the request or application to one of its members. Oral proceedings shall be before the Revocation Division itself.

Boards of Appeal [Art. 21 EPC]

1. The Boards of Appeal shall be responsible for the examination of appeals from the decisions of the Receiving Section, Examining Divisions, Opposition Divisions and of the Legal Division.

(. . .)

4. For appeals from a decision of an Opposition Division a Board of Appeal shall consist of:
(a) two technically qualified members and one legally qualified member, when the decision was taken by an Opposition Division consisting of three members;
(b) three technically qualified members and two legally qualified members, when the decision was taken by an Opposition Division consisting of four members or when the Board of Appeal considers that the nature of the appeal so requires.

604

[No provision corresponds.]

[No provision corresponds, the Invalidity Divisions serve the same function.]

Establishment and powers [Art. 45]

(. . .)

2. The Board or Boards of Appeal shall be responsible for deciding on appeals from the decisions referred to in Article 67.

3. The Board of Boards of Appeal shall be convened as necessary. The number of Boards of Appeal and the work allocation shall be determined in the implementing rules pursuant to Article 114.

Composition of the Boards of Appeal [Art. 46]

1. A Board of Appeal shall consist of a Chairman and two other members.

2. The Chairman shall select for each case the other members and their respective alternates from the list of qualified members established pursuant to Article 47(2).

3. Where the Board of Appeal considers that the nature of the appeal so requires, it may call up to two further members from the aforesaid list for that case.

4. The qualifications required for the members of each Board of Appeal, the powers of individual members in the preparatory phase of the decisions and the voting conditions shall be determined in the implementing rules pursuant to Article 114.

Boards of Appeal [Art. 117]

1. A Board of Appeal shall be responsible for deciding on appeals from decisions of the Formalities Examining Divisions, Design Administration and Legal Division and Invalidity Divisions.

2. A Board of Appeal shall consist of three members. At least two of these members must be legally qualified.

INDEX

Justiciability, 6–48—6–71
  basic rule, 6–48
  Brussels Convention and,
    6–63—6–68
  concept of, 6–48—6–50
  double actionability
    distinguished, 6–93—6–95
  local and transitory actions
    distinguished, 6–52. *See
    also Mocambique* rule
  meaning, 6–01, 6–48—6–50
  Mocambique rule. *See
    Mocambique* rule
  scope of rule, 6–50—6–55
  territoriality distinguished,
    6–93—6–95
  trespass to, foreign land, 6–48
  Tyburn v. Conan Doyle,
    6–50—6–55

Kort geding,
  actual practice in, 1–35,
    1–36—1–39
  appeals, 1–31
  availability of remedies, 1–32
  balance of convenience test,
    1–32, 3–23
  basic rule, 1–30
  commencement of procedure,
    1–31
  complex multinational cases,
    1–39
  conduct of proceedings, 1–30
  conflict of laws, 1–33
  consistency, 1–30
  delegation, 1–30
  development, 1–29
  effect of findings, 1–32
  European Patent Convention,
    1–33
  evidence, 1–33
  examples of practice,
    1–36—1–39
  exchange of written arguments,
    1–31
  existence, 1–29

Kort geding—cont.
  extraterritorial relief claimed,
    1–33
  finality of order, 3–23
  identification,
    customers, 1–30
    suppliers, 1–30
  interim damages, 1–30
  interlocutory decisions. 1–32
  interlocutory relief, 1–33, 3–23
  issues litigated in, 1–32
  judgment,
    appealing, 1–31
    publication, 1–30
  jurisdiction, 1–34, 1–35
  justification for granting
    pan-European injunctions,
    3–24
  lex loci delicti commissi, 1–33
  litigated issues, 1–32
  mandatory injunctions, 1–30
  meaning, 1–30
  multiple defendants, 1–32n
  nature of proceedings, 1–31
  oral hearing, 1–31
  ordinary proceedings
    commenced after, 1–31
  outline of procedure, 1–31
  piracy, 1–30n
  prohibitory injunction, 1–30
  pronunciation, 1–30n
  provisional measures and, 3–23
  publication of judgment, 1–30
  purpose of procedure, 1–29
  recall of infringing products,
    1–30
  recognition of term, 1–30
  relief sought, 1–30
  status under Brussels
    Convention, 1–34, 1–35
  summary relief, 1–33
  summons, 1–31
  theoretical basis, 1–34
  trade marks, 1–36, 1–37
  translation, 1–30
  understanding, 1–29
  unsuitable uses, 1–39